TULSIAN'S

QUICK REVISION *for* ACCOUNTANCY

CA-IPC (Group-II)

[SUPPLEMENT TO THE MAIN TEXTBOOK TULSIAN'S ACCOUNTANCY FOR CA-IPC]

TULSIAN'S

QUICK REVISION for ACCOUNTANCY

CA-IPC (Group-II)

[SUPPLEMENT TO THE MAIN TEXTBOOK TULSIAN'S ACCOUNTANCY FOR CA-IPC]

CA (Dr.) P.C. TULSIAN

M.Com., Ph.D., FCA, PGDFM

Additional Director (Former)
Board of Studies
The Institute of Chartered Accountants of India, New Delhi
Head
Department of Commerce
Ramjas College
University of Delhi
DELHI

Recipient of an Award for 'Exemplary Services contributed to the cause of Profession' by The Institute of Chartered Accountants of India, New Delhi

CA BHARAT TULSIAN

Chartered Accountant

Assistant Manager, KPMG
Alumnus of Sri Ram College of Commerce (SRCC), University of Delhi, DELHI
Recipient of An Award for the ***'Best Article on Foreign Exchange'*** *in All India by The Institute of Chartered Accountants of India, New Delhi*

S. CHAND
PUBLISHING
empowering minds

S. CHAND & COMPANY PVT. LTD.

(AN ISO 9001 : 2008 COMPANY)

RAM NAGAR, NEW DELHI - 110 055

S. CHAND & COMPANY PVT. LTD.

S.CHAND PUBLISHING empowering minds

(An ISO 9001 : 2008 Company)

Head Office: 7361, RAM NAGAR, NEW DELHI - 110 055
Phone: 23672080-81-82, 9899107446, 9911310888
Fax: 91-11-23677446
Shop at: **schandgroup.com**; e-mail: **info@schandgroup.com**

Branches :

AHMEDABAD : 1st Floor, Heritage, Near Gujarat Vidhyapeeth, Ashram Road, **Ahmedabad** - 380 014, Ph: 27541965, 27542369, ahmedabad@schandgroup.com

BENGALURU : No. 6, Ahuja Chambers, 1st Cross, Kumara Krupa Road, **Bengaluru** - 560 001, Ph: 22268048, 22354008, bangalore@schandgroup.com

BHOPAL : Bajaj Tower, Plot No. 2&3, Lala Lajpat Rai Colony, Raisen Road, **Bhopal** - 462 011, Ph: 4274723, 4209587. bhopal@schandgroup.com

CHANDIGARH : S.C.O. 2419-20, First Floor, Sector - 22-C (Near Aroma Hotel), **Chandigarh** -160 022, Ph: 2725443, 2725446, chandigarh@schandgroup.com

CHENNAI : No.1, Whites Road, Opposite Express Avenue, Royapettah, **Chennai** - 600014 Ph. 28410027, 28410058, chennai@schandgroup.com

COIMBATORE : 1790, Trichy Road, LGB Colony, Ramanathapuram, **Coimbatore**- 6410045, Ph: 2323620, 4217136 coimbatore@schandgroup.com **(Marketing Office)**

CUTTACK : 1st Floor, Bhartia Tower, Badambadi, **Cuttack** - 753 009, Ph: 2332580; 2332581, cuttack@schandgroup.com

DEHRADUN : 1st Floor, 20, New Road, Near Dwarka Store, **Dehradun** - 248 001, Ph: 2711101, 2710861, dehradun@schandgroup.com

GUWAHATI : Dilip Commercial (Ist floor), M.N. Road, Pan Bazar, **Guwahati** - 781 001, Ph: 2738811, 2735640 guwahati@schandgroup.com

HALDWANI : Bhatt Colony, Talli Bamori, Mukhani, **Haldwani** -263139 **(Marketing Office)** Mob. 09452294584

HYDERABAD : Padma Plaza, H.No. 3-4-630, Opp. Ratna College, Narayanaguda, **Hyderabad** - 500 029, Ph: 27550194, 27550195, hyderabad@schandgroup.com

JAIPUR : 1st Floor, Nand Plaza, Hawa Sadak, Ajmer Road, **Jaipur** - 302 006, Ph: 2219175, 2219176, jaipur@schandgroup.com

JALANDHAR : Mai Hiran Gate, **Jalandhar** - 144 008, Ph: 2401630, 5000630, jalandhar@schandgroup.com

KOCHI : Kachapilly Square, Mullassery Canal Road, Ernakulam, **Kochi** - 682 011, Ph: 2378740, 2378207-08, cochin@schandgroup.com

KOLKATA : 285/J, Bipin Bihari Ganguli Street, **Kolkata** - 700 012, Ph: 22367459, 22373914, kolkata@schandgroup.com

LUCKNOW : 1st Floor, Arya Pratinidhi Sabha, 5-Mirabai Marg, Near Narhi Sabzi Mandi, Hazratganj, **Lucknow** - 226 001, Ph: 4065646, 4026791, 4027188, 4022948 lucknow@schandgroup.com

MUMBAI : Blackie House, IInd Floor, 103/5, Walchand Hirachand Marg, Opp. G.P.O., **Mumbai** - 400 001, Ph: 22690881, 22610885, mumbai@schandgroup.com

NAGPUR : Karnal Bagh, Near Model Mill Chowk, **Nagpur** - 440 032, Ph: 2720523, 2777666 nagpur@schandgroup.com

PATNA : 104, Citicentre Ashok, Mahima Palace , Govind Mitra Road, **Patna** - 800 004, Ph: 2300489, 2302100, patna@schandgroup.com

PUNE : Sadguru Enclave, Ground floor, Survey No. 114/3, Plot no. 8 Alandi Road , Vishrantwadi **Pune** – 411015 Ph: 64017298 pune@schandgroup.com

RAIPUR : Kailash Residency, Plot No. 4B, Bottle House Road, Shankar Nagar, **Raipur** - 492 007, Ph: 2443142, Mb. : 09981200834, raipur@schandgroup.com **(Marketing Office)**

RANCHI : Shanti Deep Tower, Opp.Hotel Maharaja, Radium Road, **Ranchi**-834001 Mob. 09430246440 ranchi@schandgroup.com

SILIGURI : 122, Raja Ram Mohan Roy Road, East Vivekanandapally, P.O., Siliguri, **Siliguri**-734001, Dist., Jalpaiguri, (W.B.) Ph. 0353-2520750 **(Marketing Office)** siliguri@schandgroup.com

VISAKHAPATNAM : No. 49-54-15/53/8, Plot No. 7, 1st Floor, Opp. Radhakrishna Towers, Seethammadhara North Extn., **Visakhapatnam** - 530 013, Ph-2782609 (M) 09440100555, visakhapatnam@schandgroup.com **(Marketing Office)**

First Edition 2009; Second Edition 2010, Revised Edition 2011 (Twice), 2012, 2013 (Twice), Revised Edition 2014

Revised Edition 2015

ISBN: 978-81-219-3105-2 **Code** : 1007H 477

PRINTED IN INDIA

By Nirja Publishers & Printers Pvt. Ltd., 54/3/2, Jindal Paddy Compound, Kashipur Road, Rudrapur-263153, Uttarakhand and published by S. Chand & Company Pvt. Ltd., 7361, Ram Nagar, New Delhi -110 055.

PREFACE TO NINTH REVISED EDITION

We are thankful to the Readers and Teachers for their response and encouragement given to the Eighth Edition. This edition is thoroughly revised and substantially expanded; all chapters havc been updated and expanded.

Two important Questions which usually arise in the mind of every student are:

1. What Minimum to Revise to Maximise the Marks?

2. What to Revise One Day Before Examination?

Tulsian's Quick Revision Provides Answers to above Two Questions by Providing the following Contents:

SECTION 1 : FULLY SOLVED SCANNER CHAPTER-WISE

(C.A. Professional Examination Problems with Authentic Solutions)

SECTION 2 : REVISION ONE DAY BEFORE EXAMINATION

Important Short Answer Theory Questions for Revision

SECTION 3 : TULSIAN'S MODEL TEST PAPERS FOR REVISION

SECTION 4 : IPC EXAMINATION PAPERS

IMPORTANT NOTES FOR STUDENTS

1. **Tulsian's Quick Revision is a Supplement BUT not a Substitute to the main Text Book 'Tulsian's Accountancy'.**
2. **A Good Text Book has no other alternative. AVOID SHORT-CUTS.**
3. **An Opportunity Cost of not using A Good Text Book is very high.**
4. **"DO NOT IGNORE THEORY" and "Accounting Standards"**
5. **Important Topics for Examinations** – All Topics which you think **UNIMPORTANT.**

Special word of thanks is also due to our favourite students **Vishal, Prarthana, Piyush, Pranav, Pallavi, Arushi and Antima** who provided incisive comment and useful feedback.

We are confident that these features would make this book an invaluable asset to students who can brush up their knowledge quickly.

Any criticisms or suggestions for further improvement of the book will be gratefully acknowledged and appreciated.

CA (Dr.) P.C. Tulsian
pctulsian@gmail.com

CA Bharat Tulsian
bharattulsian88@gmail.com

Tulsian's Quick Revision for Accountancy for CA-IPC (Group-II)

SECTION 1

FULLY SOLVED SCANNER CHAPTER-WISE

(CA PROFESSIONAL EXAMINATION PROBLEMS WITH AUTHENTIC SOLUTIONS)

SCANNER FOR CA EXAMINATION PROBLEMS SHORT ANSWER CARRYING 4-6 MARKS & LONG ANSWER CARRYING 8-16 MARKS

SCANNER FOR ACCOUNTING STANDARDS CA EXAMINATION PROBLEMS CARRYING 4-6 MARKS

SECTION 2

REVISION ONE DAY BEFORE EXAMINATION

SECTION 3

TULSIAN'S MODEL TEST PAPERS WITH ANSWERS

SECTION 4

IPC EXAMINATION PAPERS

SECTION 1

PAPER 5: ADVANCED ACCOUNTING [GROUP-II]

FULLY SOLVED SCANNER CHAPTER-WISE

(CA PROFESSIONAL EXAMINATION PROBLEMS WITH AUTHENTIC SOLUTIONS)

1. Scanner for Short Answer Practical CA Examination Problems Carrying 4-6 Marks and Long Answer Practical CA Examination Problems Carrying 8-16 Marks
2. Scanner for Accounting Standards CA Examination Problems Carrying 4-6 Marks

1 Dissolution of a Firm

PROBLEM 1

P, Q and *R* are partners sharing profits and losses as to 2:2:1. Their Balance Sheet as on 31st March, 2015 is as follows:

Liabilities	₹	*Assets*	₹
Capital Accounts:		Plant and Machinery	1,08,000
P	1,20,000	Fixtures	24,000
Q	48,000	Stock	60,000
R	24,000	Sundry Debtors	48,000
Reserve Fund	60,000	Cash	60,000
Creditors	48,000		
	3,00,000		3,00,000

They decided to dissolve the business. The following are the amounts realized:

	₹
Plant and Machinery	₹ 1,02,000
Fixtures	₹ 18,000
Stock	₹ 84,000
Sundry Debtors	₹ 44,400

Creditors allowed a discount of 5% and realization expenses amounted to ₹ 1,500. There was an unrecorded asset of ₹ 6,000 which was taken over by Q at ₹ 4,800. A bill for ₹ 4,200 due for sales tax was received during the course of realization and this was also paid.

You are required to prepare:

(i) Realisation Account. (ii) Partners'Capital Accounts. (iii) Cash Account.

Solution

Dr. **REALISATION ACCOUNT** *Cr.*

Particulars		₹	*Particulars*		₹
To Debtors		48,000	By Creditors		48,000
To stock		60,000	By Cash A/c (Assets realized):		
To Fixtures		24,000	Plant and Machinery	1,02,000	
To Plant and Machinery		1,08,000	Fixtures	18,000	
To Cash A/c (Creditors)		45,600	Stock	84,000	
To Cash A/c (Sales tax)		4,200	Sundry Debtors	44,400	2,48,400
To Cash A/c (Realisation Expenses)		1,500	By Q (Unrecorded Asset)*		4,800
To Profit on Realisation t/f to:					
P	3,960				
Q	3,960				
R	1,980	9,900			
		3,01,200			3,01,200

Dr. **PARTNERS' CAPITAL ACCOUNTS** Cr.

Particulars	P ₹	Q ₹	R ₹	Particulars	P ₹	Q ₹	R ₹
To Realisation A/c (unrecorded asset)	—	4,800	—	By Balance b/d	1,20,000	48,000	24,000
To Cash (Bal. Fig.)	1,47,960	71,160	37,980	By Fund	24,000	24,000	12,000
				By Realisation A/c (Profit)	3,960	3,960	1,980
	1,47,960	75,960	37,980		1,47,960	75,960	37,980

Dr. **CASH ACCOUNT** Cr.

Particulars	₹	Particulars	₹
To Balance b/d	60,000	By Realisation A/c (Creditors)	45,600
To Realisation A/c (Assets)	2,48,400	By Realisation A/c (Expenses)	1,500
		By Realisation A/c (Sales Tax)	4,200
		By P's Capital A/c	1,47,960
		By Q's Capital A/c	71,160
		By R's Capital A/c	37,980
	3,08,400		3,08,400

Note: *An unrecorded asset is in the nature of gain hence realization account is credited. Since this asset has been taken over by Q, therefore, his account has been debited.*

PROBLEM 2

Read, Write and add give you the following Balance Sheet as on 31st March, 2015:

Liabilities		₹	Assets		₹
Read's Loan		15,000	Plant and Machinery		30,000
Capital Accounts:			Fixture and Fittings		2,000
Read	30,000		Stock		10,400
Write	10,000		Debtors	18,400	
Add	2,000	42,000	*Less:* Provision	400	18,000
Sundry Creditors		17,800	Joint Life Policy		15,000
Loan on Hypothecation of Stock		6,200	Patents and Trademarks		10,000
Joint Life Policy Reserve		12,400	Cash at Bank		8,000
		93,400			93,400

The partners shared profits and losses in the ratio of read 4/9, Write 2/9 and Add 1/3. The Firm was dissolved on the same date and you are given the following information:

(a) Add had taken a loan from insurers for ₹ 5,000 on the security of Joint Life Policy. The policy was surrendered and Insurers paid a sum of ₹ 10,200 after deducting ₹ 5,000 for Add's loan and ₹ 300 as interest thereon.

(b) One of the creditors took some of the patents whose book value was ₹ 6,000 at a valuation of ₹ 4,500. The balance to that creditors was paid in cash.

(c) The firm had previously purchased some shares in a joint stock company and had written them off on finding them useless. The shares were now found to be worth ₹ 3,000 and the loan creditors agreed to accept the shares at this value.

(d) The remaining assets realized the following amount;

Plant and Machinery	17,000
Fixtures and Fittings	1,000
Stock	9,000
Debtors	16,500
Patents 50% of their book value.	

(e) The liabilities were paid and a total discount of ₹ 500 was allowed by the creditors.

(f) The expenses of realization amounted to ₹ 2,300.

Required: Prepare the Realisation Account, Bank Account and Partners Capital Accounts in Columnar from. ***[PCC (May 2012)]***

Solution

Dr. **REALISATION ACCOUNT** *Cr.*

Particulars	₹	*Particulars*		₹
To Plant and machinery	30,000	By Provision for doubtful debts		400
To Fixtures and fittings	2,000	By Loan on hypothecation of stock		
6,200				
To Stock	10,400	By Creditors		17,800
To Debtors	18,400	By Joint Life Policy Reserve A/c		12,400
To Patents and Trademarks	10,000	By Bank A/c		
To Bank A/c (Expenses)	2,300	Plant and machinery	17,000	
To Joint Life Policy A/c	15,000	Fixtures and fittings	1,000	
To Bank A/c (Creditors)	12,800	Stock	9,000	
(17,800 – 4,500 – 500)		Debtors	16,500	
To Bank A/c (Loan)	3,200	Patents and Trademarks	2,000	45,500
[6,200 – 3,000 (Shares)]		By Bank A/c (JLP)		10,200
		By Add's Capital A/c		5,300
		By Loss on Realisation t/f to:		
		Read's Capital Account	2,800	
		Write's Capital Account	1,400	
		Add's Capital Account	2,100	6,300
	1,04,100			1,04,100

Dr. **BANK ACCOUNT** *Cr.*

Particulars	₹	*Particulars*	₹
To Balance c/d	8,000	By Realisation A/c (Loan)	3,200
To Realisation A/c (JLP)	10,200	By Realisation A/c (Creditors)	12,800
To Realisation A/c (Assets)	45,500	By Creditors	12,800
To Add's Capital A/c	5,400	By Realisation A/c (expenses)	2,300
		By Read's Loan A/c	15,000
		By Read's Capital A/c	27,200
		By Write's Capital A/c	8,600
	69,100		69,100

Dr. **PARTNERS' CAPITAL ACCOUNTS** Cr.

Particulars	Read ₹	Write ₹	Add ₹	Particulars	Read ₹	Write ₹	Add ₹
To Realisation A/c			5,300	By Balance b/d	30,000	10,000	2,000
To Realisation A/c	2,800	1,400	2,100	By Bank A/c (b.f.)			5,400
To Bank (Bal. Fig.)	27,200	8,600					
	30,000	10,000	7,400		30,000	10,000	7,400

Working Notes:

Dr. **(I) READ'S LOAN ACCOUNT** Cr

Particulars	₹	Particulars	₹
To Bank A/c	15,000	By Balance b/d	15,000
	15,000		15,000

2 Partnership—Insolvency, Piecemeal Distribution and Sale

INSOLVENCY OF A PARTNER

PROBLEM 1

The firm of Kapil and Dev has four partners and as on 31st March, 2013, its Balance Sheet stood as follows:

Liabilities	₹	*Assets*	₹
Capital Accounts:		Land	50,000
F. Kapil	2,00,000	Building	2,50,000
S. Kapil	2,00,000	Office Equipment	1,25,000
R. Dev	1,00,000	Computers	70,000
Current Accounts:		Debtors	4,00,000
F. Kapil	50,000	Stock	3,00,000
S. Kapil	1,50,000	Cash at Bank	75,000
R. Dev	1,10,000	Other Current Assets	22,600
Loan from NBFC	5,00,000	*Current A/c:*	
Current Liabilities	70,000	B. Dev	87,400
	13,80,000		13,80,000

The partners have been sharing profits and losses in the ratio of 4 : 4 : 1 : 1. It has been agreed to dissolve the firm on the basis of the following understanding:

(a) The following assets are to be adjusted to the extent indicated with respect to the book values: Land 200%, Building 120%, Computers 70%, Debtors 95%, Stocks, 90%.

(b) In the case of the loan, the lenders are to be paid at their insistence a prepayment premium of 1%.

(c) B. Dev is insolvent and no amount is recoverable from him. His father, R. Dev, however, agrees to bear 50% of his deficiency. The balance of the deficiency is agreed to be apportioned according to law

Required: Prepare Bank Account, Realisation Account and the Partners' Capital Accounts.

Solution

Dr. **BANK ACCOUNT** *Cr.*

Particulars	₹	*Particulars*	₹
To Balance b/d	75,000	By Realisation A/c—	
To Realisation A/c		(payment of sundry liabilities)	5,75,000
(Realisation of Sundry assets)	12,46,600	By F. Kapil's Capital A/c	2,42,600
		By S. Kapil's Capital A/c	3,42,600
		By R. Dev's Capital A/c	1,61,400
	13,21,600		13,21,600

Dr. **REALISATION ACCOUNT** Cr.

Particulars		₹	Particulars		₹
To Land		50,000	By Current Liabilities		70,000
To Building		2,50,000	By Loan from NBFC		5,00,000
To Office Equipments		1,25,000	By Bank A/c:		
To Computers		70,000	Land	1,00,000	
To Debtors		4,00,000	Building	3,00,000	
To Stock		3,00,000	Office Equipment	1,25,000	
To Other Current Assets		22,600	Computers	49,000	
To Bank A/c:			Debtors	3,80,000	
Current liabilities	70,000		Stock	2,70,000	
Loan from NBFC	5,05,000	5,75,000	Current Assets	22,600	12,46,600
To Profit on Realisation t/f to Partner's Current A/cs:					
F. Kapil	9,600				
S. Kapil	9,600				
R. Dev	2,400				
B. Dev	2,400	24,000			
		18,16,600			18,16,600

Dr. **PARTNERS' CAPITAL ACCOUNTS** Cr.

Particulars	F. Kapil ₹	S. Kapil ₹	R. Dev ₹	B. Dev ₹	Particulars	F. Kapil ₹	S. Kapil ₹	R. Dev ₹	B. Dev ₹
To Partners's Current A/cs	—	—	—	85,000	By Balance b/d	2,00,000	2,00,000	1,00,000	—
To B. Dev A/c	—	—	42,500	—	By Partners' Current A/c	59,600	1,59,600	1,12,400	—
To B. Dev A/c	17,000	17,000	8,500	—	By R. Dev A/c	—	—	—	42,500
To Bank A/c	2,42,600	3,42,600	1,61,400	—	By F. Kapil A/c	—	—	—	17,000
					By S. Kapil A/c	—	—	—	17,000
					By R. Dev A/c (as per contra)	—	—	—	8,500
	2,59,600	3,59,600	2,12,400	85,000		2,59,600	3,59,600	2,12,400	85,000

Dr. **PARTNERS' CURRENT ACCOUNTS** Cr.

Particulars	F. Kapil ₹	S. Kapil ₹	R. Dev ₹	B. Dev ₹	Particulars	F. Kapil ₹	S. Kapil ₹	R. Dev ₹	B. Dev ₹
To Bal. b/d	—	—	—	87,400	By Bal. b/d	50,000	1,50,000	1,10,000	—
To Partners's Capital A/c (transfer)	59,600	1,59,600	1,12,400	—	By Real. A/c	9,600	9,600	2,400	2,400
					By Partners's Capital A/c (transfer)	—	—	—	85,000
	59,600	1,59,600	1,12,400	87,400		59,600	1,59,600	1,12,400	87,400

***Note:** In the absence of specific information, it is assumed that the assets are realised at the agreed values.*

PROBLEM 2

Ajay, Vijay, Ram and Shyam are partners in a firm sharing profits and losses in the ratio of 4 : 1. 2 : 3. The following is their Balance Sheet as at 31st March, 2013:

Liabilities	₹	*Assets*		₹
Sundry Creditors	3,00,000	Sundry Debtors	3,50,000	
Capital Accounts:		*Less:* Doubtful Debts	50,000	3,00,000
Ajay	7,00,000	Cash in hand		1,40,000
Shyam	3,00,000	Stock		2,00,000
		Other Assets		3,10,000
		Capital Accounts:		
		Vijay		2,00,000
		Ram		1,50,000
	13,00,000			13,00,000

On the same date, the firm is dissolved and the following points are agreed upon:

—Ajay is to take over sundry debtors at 80% of book value
—Shyam is to take over the stocks at 95% of the value and
—Ram is to discharge sundry creditors.

Others assets realise ₹ 3,00,000 and the expenses of realisation come to ₹ 30,000.
Vijay is found insolvent and ₹ 21,900 is relaised from his estate.

Required: Prepare Realisation Account, Capiital Accounts of the Partners and Cash A/c. The loss arising out of capital deficiency may be distributed following the decision in Garner *vs* Murray.

[CA (Nov) 1996]

Solution

Dr. **REALISATION ACCOUNT** *Cr.*

Particulars	₹	*Particulars*	₹
To Sundry Debtors	3,50,000	By Sundry Creditors	3,00,000
To Stock	2,00,000	By Provision for Doubtful Debts	50,000
To Other assets	3,10,000	By Ajay's Capital A/c (Debtors)	2,80,000
To Ram's Capital A/c (Creditors)	3,00,000	By Shayam's Capital A/c (Stock	1,90,000
To Cash A/c (Expenses on realisation)	30,000	By Cash A/c (Other assets)	3,00,000
		By Loss of Realisation t/f to:	
		Ajay's Capital A/c	28,000
		Vijay's Capital A/c	7,000
		Ram's Capital A/c	14,000
		Shyam's Capital A/c	21,000
	11,90,000		11,90,000

Dr. **CAPITAL ACCOUNTS OF PARTNERS** *Cr.*

Particulars	*Ajay* ₹	*Vijay* ₹	*Ram* ₹	*Shyam* ₹	*Particulars*	*Ajay* ₹	*Vijay* ₹	*Ram* ₹	*Shyam* ₹
To Balance b/f	—	2,00,000	1,50,000	—	By Balance b/f	7,00,000	—	—	3,00,000
To Realisation (Debtors)	2,80,000	—	—	—	By Realisation (Creditors	—	—	3,00,000	—
To Realisation (Stock)	—	—	—	1,90,000	By Cash	28,000	—	14,000	21,000
To Realisation(loss)	28,000	7,000	14,000	21,000	By Balance c/d	—	2,07,000	—	—
To Balance c/d	4,20,000	—	1,50,000	1,10,000					
	7,28,000	2,07,000	3,14,000	3,21,000		7,28,000	2,07,000	3,14,000	3,21,000

Particulars	Ajay ₹	Vijay ₹	Ram ₹	Shyam ₹	Particulars	Ajay ₹	Vijay ₹	Ram ₹	Shyam ₹
To Balance b/d	—	2,07,000	—	—	By Balance b/d	4,20,000	—	1,50,000	1,10,000
To Vijay's A/c	1,29,570	—	—	55,530	By Cash	—	21,900	—	—
To Cash	2,90,430	—	1,50,000	54,470	By Ajay	—	1,29,570	—	—
					By Shyam	—	55,530	—	—
	4,20,000	2,07,000	1,50,000	1,10,000		4,20,000	2,07,000	1,50,000	1,10,000

Dr. **CASH ACCOUNT** Cr.

Particulars	₹	Particulars	₹
To Balance b/f	1,40,000	By Realisation A/c (expenses)	30,000
To Realisation A/c	3,00,000	By Ajay's Capital A/c	2,90,430
To Vijay's Capital A/c	21,900	By Ram's Capital A/c	1,50,000
To Ajay's Capital A/c	28,000	By Shyam's Capital A/c	54,470
To Ram's Capital A/c	14,000		
To Shyam's Capital A/c	21,000		
	5,24,900		5,24,900

: *(i) Since creditors are taken over by Ram as per Balance Sheet figures, a direct entry for the same in Ram's Capital A/c is also correct.*

(ii) Ajay takes over Debtors at 80% of ₹ 3,50,000 i.e. ₹ 2,80,000.

(iii) Vijay's deficiency will be borne by Ajay and Shyam in the ratio of 7 : 3 i.e. on opening Capitals of ₹ 7,00,000 and ₹ 3,00,000. Ram will not bear any portion of the loss since at the time of dissolution he had a debit balance in his capital account.

PROBLEM 3

Neptune, Jupiter, Venus and Pluto had been carrying on business in partnership sharing profits and losses in the ratio of 3 : 2 : 1 :1. They decide to dissolve the partnership on the basis of the following Balance Sheet as on 31st March, 2013:

Liabilities		₹	Assets		₹
Capital Accounts:			Premises		1,20,000
Neptune	1,00,000		Furniture		40,000
Jupiter	60,000	1,60,000	Stock		1,00,000
General Reserve		56,000	Debtors		40,000
Capital Reserve		14,000	Cash		8,000
Sundry Creditors		20,000	Capital Overdrawn:		
Mortgage Loan		80,000	Venus	10,000	
			Pluto	12,000	22,000
		3,30,000			3,30,000

(i) The assets were realised as under:
Debtors ₹ 24,000, Stock ₹ 60,000, Furniture ₹ 16,000, Premises ₹ 90,000

(ii) Expenses of dissolution amounted to ₹ 4,000.

(iii) Further Creditors of ₹ 12,000 had to be met.

(iv) General Reserve unlike Capital Reserve was built up by appropriation of profits.

Required: Prepare the Realisation Account, Partners' Capital Accounts and the Cash Account assuming that Venus becomes insolvent and nothing was realised from his private estate. Apply the principles laid down in Garner vs Murray. ***[CA PE II Nov. 2003]***

Solution

Dr. **REALISATION ACCOUNT** Cr.

Particulars		₹	Particulars		₹
To Sundry Assets A/c (transfer):			By Sundry creditors A/c		20,000
Premises		1,20,000	By Mortgage Loan A/c		80,000
Furniture		40,000	By Cash A/c (assets realised):		
Stock		1,00,000	Premises	90,000	
Sundry Debtors		40,000	Furniture	16,000	
To Cash A/c (Mortgage Loan)		80,000	Stock	60,000	
To Cash A/c (creditors paid)		32,000	Debtors	24,000	1,90,000
To Cash A/c (expenses)		4,000	By Loss transferred to Capital Accounts:		
			Neptune	54,000	
			Jupiter	36,000	
			Venus	18,000	
			Pluto	18,000	1,26,000
		4,16,000			4,16,000

Dr. **CASH ACCOUNT** Cr.

Particulars		₹	Particulars	₹
To Balance b/d		8,000	By Realisation A/c (creditors)	32,000
To Realisation A/c (assets realised)		1,90,000	By Realisation A/c (expenses)	4,000
To Capital A/c (realisation loss made good):			By Realisation A/c (Mortgage Loan)	80,000
Neptune	54,000		By Neptune's Capital A/c	1,18,857
Jupiter	36,000		By Jupiter's Capital A/c	73,143
Pluto	18,000	1,08,000		
To Pluto's Capital A/c		2,000		
		3,08,000		3,08,000

Dr. **PARTNERS' CAPITAL ACCOUNTS** Cr.

Particulars	Neptune ₹	Jupiter ₹	Venus ₹	Pluto ₹	Particulars	Neptune ₹	Jupiter ₹	Venus ₹	Pluto ₹
To Balance b/d	—	—	10,000	12,000	By Balance b/d	1,00,000	60,000	—	—
To Realisation A/c (loss)	54,000	36,000	18,000	18,000	By General Reserve A/c (3 : 2 : 1 : 1)	24,000	16,000	8,000	8,000
To Venus's Capital A/c (loss)	11,143	6,857	—	—	By Capital Reserve A/c (3 : 2 : 1 : 1)	6,000	4,000	2,000	2,000
To Cash A/c	1,18,857	73,143	—	—	By Cash A/c (loss on realization)	54,000	36,000	—	18,000
					By Neptune's Capital A/c	—	—	11,143	—
					By Jupiter's Capital A/c	—	—	6,857	—
					By Cash A/c				2,000
	1,84,000	1,16,000	28,000	30,000		1,84,000	1,16,000	28,000	30,000

Note: *Venus's deficiency has been borne by Neptune and Jupiter in the proportion of 130 : 80 or 13 : 8, i.e. in the ratio of capital before dissolution but after transfer of all reserves.*

PROBLEM 4

Ram, Rahim and Robert are partners of the firm 'RR Traders' for the past 5 years. The partners decided to dissolve the firm consequent to insolvency of partner Robert in March 2013. The Balance Sheet of the firm as on 31st March 2013 is furnished below: They share profits and losses equally:

Liabilities	₹	*Assets*	₹
Capital Accounts:		Land and Building	5,00,000
Ram	4,50,000	Plant and Machinery	2,00,000
Rahim	4,50,000	Furniture and Fittings	50,000
Robert	2,00,000	Stock in Trade	3,00,000
General Reserve	2,10,000	Debtors	5,00,000
Creditors	2,90,000	Cash at Hand/Bank	50,000
	16,00,000		16,00,000

The partners Ram and Rahim decided to form a new firm 'RR Enterprises' and takeover all the assets and liabilities of the firm at values given below:

Land and Building	₹ 3,50,000
Plant and Machinery	₹ 1,50,000
Furniture and Fittings	₹ 20,000
Stock in trade	₹ 2,00,000

Debtors include ₹ 3,00,000 due from SK & Co. owned by Robert. (Nothing is recoverable from the said concern). Other debtors can be recovered fully.

Required: Prepare Realisation account, Partners' Capital accounts and the Balance Sheet of RR Enterprises (immediately after commencement). ***[CA PE II May 2003]***

Solution

Dr. **(I) REALISATION ACCOUNT** *Cr.*

Particulars	₹	*Particulars*		₹
To Sundry assets:		By Creditors		2,90,000
Land and Building	5,00,000	By RR Enterprises		9,70,000
Plant and Machinery	2,00,000	By Loss Transferred to		
Furniture and Fitting	50,000	Partners' Capital Accounts:		
Stock	3,00,000	Ram	1,10,000	
Debtors	2,00,000	Rahim	1,10,000	
Cash at Hand/Bank	50,000	Robert	1,10,000	3,30,000
To RR Enterprises (liability taken over)	2,90,000			
	15,90,000			15,90,000

Dr. **PARTNERS' CAPITAL ACCOUNTS** *Cr.*

Particulars	*Ram* ₹	*Rahim* ₹	*Robert* ₹	*Particulars*	*Ram* ₹	*Rahim* ₹	*Robert* ₹
To Sundry Debtors			3,00,000	By Balance b/d	4,50,000	4,50,000	2,00,000
To Realisation A/c	1,10,000	1,10,000	1,10,000	By General Reserve	70,000	70,000	70,000
To Robert's A/c (deficiency borne by Solvent Partners)	70,000	70,000	—	By Cash A/c	1,10,000	1,10,000	
To Balance c/d Solvent	4,50,000	4,50,000	—	By Ram and Rahim (deficiency borne by Solvent Partners)	—	—	1,40,000
	6,30,000	6,30,000	4,10,000		6,30,000	6,30,000	4,10,000

(II) BALANCE SHEET OF RR ENTERPRISES AS AT 31.03.2013 (IMMEDIATELY AFTER COMMENCEMENT)

Liabilities	₹	*Assets*	₹
Capital Accounts:		Land and building	3,50,000
Ram	4,50,000	Plant and machinery	1,50,000
Rahim	4,50,000	Furnite and fittings	20,000
Creditors	2,90,000	Stock in trade	2,00,000
		Debtors	2,00,000
		Cash at hand/bank	2,70,000
	11,90,000		11,90,000

Working Notes:

(i) *Agreed value of assets taken over by RR Enterprises*

	₹
Land and building	3,50,000
Plant and machinery	1,50,000
Furniture and fittings	20,000
Stock in trade	2,00,000
Debtors (5,00,000 – 3,00,000)	2,00,000
Cash at hand/bank	50,000
	9,70,000

(ii) *Cash in hand/bank balance of RR Enterprises*

	₹
Opening Balance	50,000
Add: Ram's and Rahim's contribution (₹ 1,10,000 + ₹ 1,00,000)	2,20,000
	2,70,000

PROBLEM 5

A, B, C and D are sharing profits and losses in the ratio 5 : 5 : 4 : 2. Frauds committed by C during the year were found out and it was decided to dissolve the partnership on 31^{si} March, 2013 when their Balance Sheet was as under:

Liabilities	₹	*Assets*	₹
Capitals:		Building	1,20,000
A	90,000	Stock	85,500
B	90,000	Investments	29,000
C	—	Debtors	42,000
D	35,000	Cash	14,500
General reserve	24,000	C's Current A/c	15,000
Trade creditors	47,000		
Bills payable	20,000		
	3,06,000		**3,06,000**

Following information is given to you:

(a) A cheque for ₹ 4,300 received from debtor was not recorded in the books and was misappropriated by C.

(b) Investments costing ₹ 5,400 were sold by C at ₹ 7,900 and the funds transferred to his personal account. This sale was omitted from the firm's books.

(c) A creditor agreed to take over investments of the book value of ₹ 5,400 at ₹ 8,400. The rest of the creditors were paid off at a discount of 2%.

(d) The other assets realized as follows:

Building	*105% of book value*
Stock	*₹ 78,000*
Investments	*The rest of investments were sold at a profit of ₹ 4,800*
Debtors	*The rest of the debtors were realized at a discount of 12%*

(e) The bills payable were settled at a discount of ₹ 400.

(f) The expenses of dissolution amounted to ₹ 4,900

(g) It was found out that realization from C's private assets would only be ₹ 4,000.

Prepare the necessary Ledger Accounts. ***[CA (IPCC) Nov. 2010]***

Solution

Dr. **REALISATION ACCOUNT** *Cr.*

Particulars	₹	*Particulars*	₹
To Building	1,20,000	By Trade Creditors	47,000
To Stock	85,500	By Bills Payable	20,000
To Investment	29,000	By Cash:	
To Debtors	42,000	Building 1,26,000	
To Cash (creditors paid)	37,828	Stock 78,000	
[98% (47,000 – 8,400)]		Investments 23,000	
To Cash (expenses)	4,900	Debtors 33,176	2,60,176
To Cash (bills payable)	19,600	[88% (42,000 – 4,300)]	
(20,000 – 400)		By C's Capital A/c	
To Profit on Realisation t/f to		[Debtors (unrecorded)]	4,300
Partners' Capital A/cs:		By C's Capital A/c	
A	171	[Investments (unrecorded)]	7,900
B	171		
C	137		
D	69		
	3,39,376		**3,39,376**

Dr. **CASH ACCOUNT** *Cr.*

Particulars		₹	*Particulars*	₹
To Balance b/d		14,500	By Realisation (creditors paid)	37,828
To Realisation (assets) realised			By Realisation (Bills Payable)	19,600
Building	1,26,000		By Realisation (expenses)	4,900
Stock	78,000		By A's Capital A/c	90,528
Investments	23,000		By B's Capital A/c	90,528
Debtors	33,176	2,60,176	By D's Capital A/c	35,292
To C's capital A/c.		4,000		
		2,78,676		**2,78,676**

Dr. **PARTNERS' CAPITAL ACCOUNTS** Cr.

Particulars	A ₹	B ₹	C ₹	D ₹	Particulars	A ₹	B ₹	C ₹	D ₹
To Balance b/d	—	—	15,000	—	By Balance b/d	90,000	90,000	-	35,000
To Realisation A/c (Debtors)	—	—	4,300	—	By General Reserve	7,500	7,500	6,000	3,000
To Realisation A/c (Investment)	—	—	7,900	—	By Realisation A/c (Profit)	171	171	137	69
To C's capital A/c	7,143	7,143	—	2,777	By Cash A/c	—	—	4,000	—
To Cash A/c	90,528	90,528	—	35,292	By A's capital A/c	—	—	7,143	—
					By B's capital A/c	—	—	7,143	—
					By D's capital A/c	—	—	2,777	—
	97,671	**97,671**	**27,200**	**38,069**		**97,671**	**97,671**	**27,200**	**38,069**

Working Notes:

(i) *Amount received from sale of investments*

Book value	29,000
Less: Misappropriated by C	(5,400)
	23,600
Less: Taken over by a creditor	(5,400)
	18,200
Add: Profit on sale of investments	4,800
	23,000

(ii) *Deficiency of C*

Balance of Capital	15,000
Debtors-misappropriation	4,300
Investment-misappropriation	7,900
	27,200
Less: Realisation Profit	(137)
General Reserve	(6,000)
Contribution from private assets	(4.000)
Net Deficiency of Capital	**17,063**

This deficiency of ₹ 17,063 in C's capital account will be shared by other partners A, B and D in their capital ratio of 90: 90 : 35

Accordingly,

A's Share of Deficiency = [17,063 x (90/215)] = ₹ 7,143

B's Share of Deficiency = [17,063 × (90/215)] = ₹ 7,143

D's Share of Deficiency = [17,063 x (35/215)] = ₹ 2,777

PROBLEM 6

P, Q, R and S had been carrying on business in partnership sharing profits & losses in the ratio of 4 : 3 : 2 : 1.They decided to dissolve the partnership on the basis of following Balance Sheet as on 30th April, 2013:

Liabilities	₹	Assets	₹
Capital Accounts:		Land & building	2,46,000
P	1,68,000	Furniture & fixtures	65,000
Q	1,08,000	Stock	1,00,000
General reserve	95,000	Debtors	72,500
Capital reserve	25,000	Cash in hand	15,500
Sundry creditors	36,000	Capital overdrawn:	
Mortgage loan	1,10,000	R	25,000
		S	18,000
	5,42,000		5,42,000

(a) The assets were realized: Land & Building ₹ 2,30,000, Furniture & Fixtures ₹ 42, 000, Stock ₹ 72,000, Debtors ₹ 65,000

(b) Expenses of dissolution amounted to ₹ 7,800.

(c) Further creditors of ₹ 18,000 had to be met.

(d) R became insolvent and nothing was realized from his private estate.

Required: Applying the principles laid down in Garner Vs. Murray, prepare the Realisation Account, Partners' Capital Accounts and Cash Account. ***[CA (IPCC) Nov., 2011]***

Solution

Dr. **REALISATION ACCOUNT** *Cr.*

Particulars	₹	Particulars	₹
To Land and building	2,46,000	By Sundry Creditors	36,000
To Furniture and fixtures	65,000	By Mortgage Loan	1,10,000
To Stock	1,00,000	By Cash A/c:	
To Debtors	72,500	Land and building	2,30,000
To Cash A/c (Expenses)	7,800	Furniture & fixtures	42,000
To Cash A/c (Creditors)	54,000	Stock	72,000
(₹ 36,000 + ₹ 18,000)		Debtors	65,000
To Cash A/c (Mortgage loan)	1,10,000	By Loss on Realisation t/f to:	
		P's Capital A/c	40,120
		Q's Capital A/c	30,090
		R's Capital A/c	20,060
		S's Capital A/c	10,030
	6,55,300		6,55,300

Dr. **PARTNERS' CAPITAL ACCOUNTS** *Cr.*

Particulars	P ₹	Q ₹	R ₹	S ₹	Particulars	P ₹	Q ₹	R ₹	S ₹
To Balance b/d	—	—	25,000	18,000	By Balance b/d	1,68,000	1,06,000		
To Realization A/c (Loss)	40,120	30,090	20,060	10,030	By General Reserve	38,000	28,500	19,000	9,500
To ₹ Capital A/c (Deficiency)	12,636	8,424	—	—	By Capital Reserve	10,000	7,500	5,000	2,500
To Cash A/c	2,03,364	1,35,576	—	—	By Cash A/c (realization loss)	40,120	30,090	—	10,030
					By P's Capital A/c			12,636	
					By Q's Capital A/c			8,424	
					By Cash A/c				6,000
	2,56,120	1,74,090	45,060	28,030		2,56,120	1,74,090	45,060	28,030

Note: P, Q and S brought cash to make good, their share of the loss on realization. However, in actual practice they will not be bringing any cash, only a notional entry will be made as per Rule in *Garner vs. Murray*.

Dr. **CASH ACCOUNT** *Cr.*

Particulars	₹	*Particulars*	₹
To Balance b/d	15,500	By Realization A/c:	
To Realization A/c:		Expenses on dissolution	7,800
Land and building	2,30,000	Creditors (36,000 + 18,000)	54,000
Furnitures fixtures	42,000	Mortgage loan	1,10,000
Stock	72,000	By P's capital A/c	2,03,364
Debtors	65,000	By Q's capital A/c	1,35,576
To P, Q, S's capital A/cs (40,120 + 30,090 + 10,030)	80,240		
To S's capital A/c	6,000		
	5,10,740		5,10,740

Working Note:

CALCULATION OF CAPITAL RATIO OF SOLVENT PARTNERS

Particulars	*P* ₹	*Q* ₹	*S* ₹
Opening Capital	1,68,000	1,08,000	(18,000)
Add: General reserve	38,000	28,500	9,500
Capital reserve	10,000	7,500	2,500
	2,16,000	1,44,000	(6.000)

Though S is a solvent partner yet he cannot be called upon to bear loss on account of insolvency of R because his capital account has a debit balance.

Therefore, capital ratio of P & Q = 216 : 144 = 3 : 2

Deficiency of R = ₹ {(25,000 + 20,060) – (19,000 + 5,000)} = ₹ 45,060 – ₹ 24,000 = ₹ 21,060.

Deficiency of R will be shared by P & Q in the capital ratio of 3 : 2 i.e.

P = ₹ 21,060 × 3/5 = ₹ 12,636

Q = ₹ 21,060 × 2/5 = ₹ 8,424

PIECEMEAL DISTRIBUTION

PROBLEM 7

The firm of CANJE was dissolved on 31.3.2013, at which date its Balance Sheet stood as follows:

Liabilities	₹	*Assets*	₹
Creditors	2,00,000	Fixed Assets	45,00,000
Bank Loan	5,00,000	Cash and Bank	2,00,000
L's Loan	10,00,000		
Capitals:			
L	15,00,000		
M	10,00,000		
S	5,00,000		
	47,00,000		47,00,000

Partners share profits equally. A firm of Chartered Accounts is retained to realise the assets and distribute the cash after discharge of liabilities. Their fees which are to include all expenses is fixed at ₹ 1,00,000. No loss is expected on realisation since fixed assets include valuable land and building.

Realisations are: 1st ₹ 5,00,000, 2nd ₹ 15,00,000, 3rd ₹ 15,00,000, 4th ₹ 30,00,000, 5th ₹ 30,00,000.

The Chartered Accountant firm decided to pay off the partners in 'Higher Relative Capital Method'.

Required: Prepare a statement showing distribution of cash.

Solution

STATEMENT SHOWING THE DISTRIBUTION TOWARDS FIRM'S OUTSIDE DEBTS' AND PARTNER'S LOAN

Particulars	*Ratio* ₹	*Total* ₹	*Creditors* ₹	*Bank Loan* ₹	*L's Loan*
A Balance Due		17,00,000	2,00,000	5,00,000	10,00,000
B *Less:* Amount paid out of its instalment	2 : 5	6,00,000	1,71,429	4,28,571	—
C Balance Due (A – B)		11,000,000	28,571	71,429	10,00,000
D *Less:* Amount paid out of 2nd installment					
First ₹ 1,00,000	2 : 5	1,00,000	28,571	71,429	—
Next ₹ 10,00,000	0 : 0 : 1	10,00,000	—	—	10,00,000
E Balance Due (C – D)		Nil	Nil	Nil	Nil

STATEMENT SHOWING THE DISTRIBUTION OF CASH AMONG PARTNERS (ACCORDING TO PROPORTIONATE CAPITAL METHOD)

Particulars	*Ratio*	*Total* ₹	*L* ₹	*M* ₹	*S* ₹
A Balance Due		30,00,000	15,00,000	10,00,000	5,00,000
B *Less:* Amount paid out of 2nd instalment	1 : 0 : 0	4,00,000	4,00,000	—	—
C Balance Due (A – B)		26,00,000	11,00,000	10,00,000	5,00,000
D *Less:* Amount paid out of 3rd					

Instalment					
First ₹ 1,00,000		1,00,000	1,00,000	—	—
Next ₹ 10,00,000	1 : 1 : 0	10,00,000	5,00,000	5,00,000	—
Balance ₹ 4,00,000	1 : 1 : 1	4,00,000	1,33,334	1,33,333	1,33,333
		15,00,000	7,33,334	6,33,333	1,33,333
E Balance Due (C – D)		11,00,000	3,66,666	3,66,667	3,66,667
F *Add:* Realisation Profit credited (₹ 30,000,000 – ₹ 11,00,000)	1 : 1 : 1	19,00,000	6,33,334	6,33,333	6,33,333
G Balance Due (after taking into Realisation Profit (E + F)		30,00,000	10,00,000	10,00,000	10,00,000
H *Less:* Amount paid out of 4th Instalment	1 : 1 : 1	30,00,000	10,00,000	10,00,000	10,00,000
I Balance Due (G – H)		Nil	Nil	Nil	Nil
J *Add:* Realisation Profit credited	1 : 1 : 1	30,00,000	10,00,000	10,00,000	10,00,000
K Balance due (after taking into Realisation profit) (I + J)		30,00,000	10,00,000	10,00,000	10,00,000
L *Less:* Amount paid out of 5th Instalment	1 : 1 : 1	30,00,000	10,00,000	10,00,000	10,00,000
M Balance Due (K – L)		Nil	Nil	Nil	Nil

Working Notes:

(I) STATEMENT SHOWING THE COMPUTATION OF HIGHEST RELATIVE CAPITAL

Particulars	*L*	*M*	*S*
A Actual Capitals	15,00,000	10,00,000	5,00,000
B Profit Sharing Ratio	1	1	1
C Actual Capitals × Profit Sharing Ratio	15,00,000	10,00,000	5,00,000
D Proportionate Capital taking *S*'s Capital as Base Capital	5,00,000	5,00,000	5,00,000
E Surplus Capital (A – D)	10,00,000	5,00,000	—
F Profit Sharing Ratio	1	1	—
G Surplus Capital × Profit Sharing Ratio	10,00,000	5,00,000	—
H Revised Proportional Capital taking *M*'s Capital as Base Capital	5,00,000	5,00,000	—
I Revised Surplus Capital (E – G)	5,00,000	—	—

(ii) *Scheme of Distribution:* First ₹ 5,00,000 will be paid to *L*, next ₹ 10,00,000 will be distributed between *L* and *M* in their profit sharing ratio (i.e. 1 : 1) and the balance will be distributed among *L*, *M* and *S* in their profit sharing ratio (i.e. 1 : 1 : 1).

(iii) It has been assumed that the amounts of realisation given in the question pertain to realisation of fixed assets.

(iv) *Calculation of amount available for distribution at the time of first realisation of fixed asset*
= Cash & Bank Balance + 1st Realisation – Liquidator's remuneration
= ₹ 2,00,000 + ₹ 5,00,000 – ₹ 1,00,000 = ₹ 6,00,000.

PROBLEM 8

A, B and C are partners sharing profits and losses in the ratio of 5:3:2. Their capitals were ₹ 9,600, ₹ 6,000 and ₹ 8,400 respectively. After paying creditors, the liabilities and assets of the firm were:

Liabilities	₹	*Assets*	₹
Liability for interest on loans from:		Investments	1,000
Spouses of partners	2,000	Furniture	2,000
Partners	1,000	Machinery	1,200
		Stock	4,000

The assets realised in full in the order in which they are listed above. B is insolvent.

Required: Prepare a statement showing the distribution of cash as and when available, applying maximum possible loss procedure. ***[CA (November, 1999)]***

Solution

STATEMENT OF DISTRIBUTION OF CASH

Particulars	*Realisation* ₹	*Interest on loans from partners' spouses* ₹	*Interest on loans from partners* ₹	*Partners' Capitals* A ₹	B ₹	C ₹	*Total* ₹
Balances due		2,000	1,000	9,600	6,000	8,400	24,000
(i) Sale of investments	1,000	(1,000)					
		1,000					
(ii) Sale of furniture	2,000	(1,000)	(1,000)				
		—	—				
(iii) Sale of Machinery	1,200						
Maximum possible loss ₹ 22,800 (total of capitals ₹.24,000 less cash available ₹.1,200) allocated to partners in the profit sharing ratio i.e. 5 : 3 : 2				(11,400)	(6,840)	(4,560)	(22,800)
Amounts at credit				(1,800)	(840)	3,840	1,200
Deficiency of A and B written off against C				1,800	840	(2,640)	—
Amount paid				—	—	1,200	1,200
Balances in capital accounts				9,600	6,000	7,200	22,800
(iv) Sale of stock	4,000						
Maximum possible loss ₹.18,800 (₹.22,800 – ₹.4,000) Allocated to partners in the ratio 5 : 3 : 2				(9,400)	(5,640)	(3,760)	(18,800)
Amounts at credit and cash paid				200	360	3,400	(4,000)
Balances in capital accounts left unpaid–Loss				9,400	5,640	3,760	18,800

PROBLEM 9

Amar, Akbar and Antony are in partnership. The following is their Balance Sheet as at March 31, 2013 on which date they dissolved their partnership. They shared profit in the ratio of 5:3:2.

Liabilities	₹	*Assets*	₹
Creditors	80,000	Plant and Machinery	60,000
Loan A/c: Amar	20,000	Premises	80,000
Capital A/cs: Amar	1,00,000	Stock	60,000
Akbar	30,000	Debtors	1,20,000
Antony	90,000		
	3,20,000		3,20,000

It was agreed to repay the amounts due to the partners as and when the assets were realised, viz. April 15, ₹.60,000, May 1, ₹ 1,46,000, May 31, ₹ 94,000,

Required: Prepare a statement showing how the distribution should be made under maximum loss method and write up the cash account and partners' capital accounts. ***[CA (PCC) May 2010]***

Solution

STATEMENT SHOWING DISTRIBUTION OF CASH BY 'MAXIMUM LOSS METHOD'

Particulars	*Creditors* ₹	*Amar's loan* ₹	*Amar* ₹	*Akbar* ₹	*Antony* ₹
Balance due	80,000	20,000	1,00,000	30,000	90,000
On 15* April realised ₹.60,000 Paid to creditors	(60.000)	—	—	—	—
Balance due	20,000	20,000	1,00,000	30,000	90,000
On 1st May, realised ₹.1 ,46,000 Paid to Creditors (₹.20,000)	(20,000)	—	—	—	—
Paid Amar's ioan (₹.20,000)		(20,000)	—	—	—
Balance due (1)	Nil	Nil	1,00,000	30,000	90,000
Balance ₹ 1,06,000 Maximum loss (1,00,000 + 30,000 + 90,000 – 1,06,000) = ₹.1,14,000 shared in Profit & Loss ratio 5:3:2			(57,000)	(34,200)	(22,800)
			43,000	(4,200)	67,200
Akbar's deficiency shared by Amar & Antony in capital ratio 100:90			(2,210)	4,200	(1,990)
Cash paid			40,790	—	65,210
Balance due (3) [1 – 2]			59,210	30,000	65,210
On 31st May, realised ₹ 94,000 Maximum Loss [59, 210 + 30,000 + 24,790 – 94,000]= ₹ 20,000 shared in 5 : 3 : 2			(10,000)	(6,000)	(4,000)
Cash paid (4)			49,210	24,000	20,790
Loss on realisation* (3 – 4)			10,000	6,000	4,000

* It is assumed that realisation from assets on 31st May, is the final realisation and no further cash expected to be received.

Dr. **CASH ACCOUNT** Cr.

Particulars	₹	Particulars	₹
To Realization A/c	60,000	By Creditors A/c	60,000
To Realization A/c	1,46,000	By Creditors A/c	20,000
To Realization A/c	94,000	By Amar's Loan A/c	20,000
		By Amar's Capital A/c	40,790
		By Antony's Capital A/c	65,210
		By Amar's Capital A/c	49,210
		By Akbar's Capital A/c	24,000
		By Antony's Capital A/c	20,790
	3,00,000		3,00,000

Dr. **PARTNERS' CAPITAL ACCOUNTS** Cr.

Particulars	Amar ₹	Akber ₹	Antony ₹	Particulars	Amar ₹	Akber ₹	Antony ₹
To Cash	40,790	—	65,210	By Balance b/d	1,00,000	30,000	90,000
To Cash	49,210	24,000	20,790				
To Realization A/c (loss)	10,000	6,000	4,000		—	—	—
	1,00,000	30,000	90,000		1.00.000	30.000	90.000

PROBLEM 10

Ajay Enterprises, a Partnership firm in which A, B and C are three partners sharing profits and losses in the ratio of 4 : 3 : 3, the balance sheet of the firm as on 31st March, 2013 is as below:

Liabilities	₹	Assets	₹
A's Capital	15,000	Factory Building	24,160
B's Capital	7,500	Plant & Machinery	16,275
C's Capital	15,000	Debtors	5,400
B's Loan A/c	4,500	Stock	12,390
Sundry creditors	16,500	Cash at Bank	275
	58,500		58,500

On balance sheet data all the three partners have decided to dissolve their partnership. Since the realization of assets was protracted, they decide to distribute amounts as and when feasible and for this purpose they appoint C who was to get as his remunerations 1% of the value of the assets realized other than cash at Bank and 10% of the amount distributed to the partners.

Assets were realized price-meal as under:

Particulars	₹
First instalment	18,650
Second instalment	17,320
Third instalment	10,000
Last instalment	7,000
Dissolution expenses were provided for estimated amount of	3,000
The creditors were settled finally for	15,900

Required: Prepare a statement showing distribution of cash amongst the partners by 'Highest Relative capital method'.

Solution

STATEMENT SHOWING DISTRIBUTION OF CASH AMONGST THE PARTNERS BY HIGHEST RELATIVE CAPITAL METHOD (HRCM)

Particulars		*Creditors*	*B's Loan*	*Capitals*		
	(₹)	*(₹)*	*(₹)*	*A(₹)*	*B(₹)*	*C(₹)*
Balance due		16,500	4,500	15,000	7,500	15,000
On receipt of 1st instalment amount	18,650					
Add: Cash at bank	275					
	18,925					
Less: Dissolution expenses provided for	(3,000)					
	15,925					
Less: C's remuneration of 1% on assets realized (₹ 18,650 × 1%)	(187)					
	15,738					
Less: Payment made to creditors	(15,738)	(15,738)				
Balance due	Nil	762				
On realization of 2nd instalment	17,320					
Less: C's remuneration of 1% on assets realized (₹ 17,320 × 1%)	(173)					
	17,147					
Less: Payment made to creditors (settled for the total ₹ 15,900)	(162)	(162)				
Transferred to P&L A/c		600				
	16,985	Nil				
Less: Payment for B's loan A/c	(4,500)		(4,500)			
Amount available for distribution to partners	12,485		nil			
Less: C's remuneration of 10% of the amount distributed to partners (₹ 12,485 × 10/110)	(1,135)					
Balance distributed to partners on the basis of HRCM	11,350					
Less: Paid to C(See W.N.)	(3,750)					(3,750)
	7,600					11,250
Less: Paid to A and C in 4 : 3 in (See W.N.)	(7,600)			(4,343)	—	(3,257)
Balance due	nil			10,657	7,500	7,993
On C's remuneration of 1% on assets realized (₹ 10,000 × 1%)	(100)					
	9,900					
Less: C's remuneration realized (₹ 10,000 × 1%)	(100)					
	9,900					
Less: C's remuneration of 10% of the amount distributed to partners (₹ 9,900 × 10/110)	(900)					
	9,000					

Particulars		Creditors	B's Loan	Capitals		
	(₹)	(₹)	(₹)	A(₹)	B(₹)	C(₹)
Less: Paid to A and C in 4 : 3 upto ₹ 8,750 (i.e. ₹ 7,600 paid on receipt of second instalment and balance of ₹ 1,150 to be paid now) (See W.N.)	(1,150)			(657)		(493)
	7,850			10,000	7,500	7,500
Less: Now, Paid to A, B and C in 4 : 3 : 3	(7,850)			(3,140)	(2,355)	(2,355)
Balance due	nil			6,800	5,145	5,145
On realization of 4th and last instalment	7,000					
Less: C's remuneration of 1% on assets realized (₹ 7,000 × 1%)	(70)					
	6,930					
Less: C's remuneration of 10% of the amount distributed to partners (₹ 6,930 × 10/110)	(630)					
	6,300					
Less: Paid to A, B and C in 4 : 3 : 3	(6,300)			(2,250)	(1,890)	(1,890)
Loss suffered by partners				4,340	3,255	3,255

Working Note:

CALCULATION OF AMOUNT PAID TO PARTNERS ON THE BASIS OF HIGHEST RELATIVE CAPITAL METHOD

Particulars	A ₹	B ₹	C ₹
Balance of Capital Accounts (A)	15,000	7,500	15,000
Profit Sharing ratio	4	3	3
Capital/Profit sharing ratio	3,750	2,500	5,000
Proportionate Capitals taking B's Capital as base	10,000	7,500	7,500
Surplus Capitals	5,000	nil	7,500
Profit Sharing Ratio	4		3
Surplus Capitals/Profit Sharing Ratio	1,250		2,500
Revised Proportionate Capitals taking A's Capital as base	5,000		3,750
Revised Surplus Capital to be paid first	nil		3,750

Scheme of Distribution: First ₹ 3,750 will be paid to C. Then A and C will receive in proportion of 4 : 3 upto ₹ 8,750 to bring the capital of all partners A, B and C in proportion to their profit sharing ratio. Thereafter, balance available will be paid to all partners viz A, B and C in their profit sharing ratio of 4 : 3 : 3.

PROBLEM 10A

The partners P, Q & R have called you to assist them in winding up the affairs of their partnership on 31.12.2013. Their balance sheet as on that date is given below:

Liabilities	₹	*Assets*	₹
Capital Accounts:		Land & Building	50,000
P	65,000	Plant & Machinery	46,000
Q	50,500	Furniture & Fixture	10,000
R	32,000	Stock	14,500
Sundry Creditors	16,000	Debtors	14,000
		Cash at Bank	9,000
		Loan P	13,000
		Loan Q	7,000
	1,63,500		1,63,500

(a) The partners share profit and losses in the ratio of 4:3:2.

(b) Cash is distributed to the partners at the end of each month.

(c) A summary of liquidatioin transactions are as follows:

January 2014

- ₹ 9,000 - collected from debtors; balance is uncollectable.
- ₹ 8,000 - received from the sale of entire furniture
- ₹ 1,000 - Liquidation expenses paid.
- ₹ 6,000 - Cash retained in the business at the end of montjh

February 2014

- ₹ 1,000 - Liquidation expenses paid.
- As part payment of his capital, R accepted a machinery for ₹ 9,000 (book value ₹ 3,500)
- ₹ 2,000 - Cash retained in the business at the end of month

March 2014

- ₹ 38,000 - received on the sale of remaining plant and machinery.
- ₹ 10,000 - received from the sale of entire stock.
- ₹ 1,700 - Liquidation expenses paid.
- ₹ 41,000 - Received on sale of land & building.
- No Cash is retained in the business.

You are required to prepare a schedule of cash payments amongst the partners by "Higher Relative Capital Method". *[May 2014]*

Solution

Particulars	*Cash* ₹	*Creditors* ₹	*Capitals* P (₹)	Q (₹)	R (₹)
Balance due after loan		16,000	52,000	43,500	32,000
January					
Balance available	9,000				
Realization less expenses and cash retained	10,000				
Amount available and paid	19,000	(16,000)	–	–	3,000

Balance due	–	–	52,000	43,500	29,000
February					
Opening Balance	6,000				
Expenses paid and cash carried forward	3,000				
Available for distribution	3,000				
Cash paid to Q and Machinery given to R			–	3,000	9,000
Balance due	–		52,000	40,500	20,000
March					
Opening Balance	2,000				
Amount realized less expenses	87,300				
Amount paid to partners	89,300		41,689	32,767	14,844
Loss			10,311	7,733	5,156

Working Note:

(i) Highest Relative Capital Basis

Particulars	*P (₹)*	*Q (₹)*	*R (₹)*
Scheme of payment for January			
Balance of Capital Accounts	65,000	50,500	32,000
Less: Loans	(13,000)	(7,000)	
A. Net Actual Capital	52,000	43,5000	32,000
B. Profit Sharing Ratio	4	3	2
C. Capital/Profit sharing Ratio [A/B]	13,000	14,500	16,000
D. Capital in profit sharing ratio, taking P's capital as base capital	52,000	39,000	26,000
E. Surplus Capital [A – D]		4,500	6,000
F. Profit Sharing Ratio		3	2
G. Surplus Capital/Profit sharing Ratio [E/F]		1,500	3,000
H. Capital in profit sharing ratio, taking Q's capital as base capital		4,500	3,000
I. Revised Surplus Capital [E – G]			3,000

(ii) Scheme of distributiion of available cash for March:

Particulars	*P (₹)*	*Q (₹)*	*R (₹)*
A. Balance of Capital Accounts end of February	52,000	40,5000	20,000
B. Profit Sharing Ratio	4	3	2
C. Capital/Profit sharing Ratio [A/B]	13,000	13,500	10,000
D. Capital in profit sharing ratio, taking R's capital as base capital	40,000	30,000	20,000
E. Surplus Capital [A – D]	12,000	10,500	
F. Profit Sharing Ratio	4	3	
G. Surplus Capital/Profit sharing Ratio [E/F]	3,000	3,500	
H. Capital in profit sharing ratio taking P's capital as base	12,000	9,000	
I. Surplus Capital [E – H]	-	1,500	
J. Payment ₹ 1500		(1,500)	
K. Balance of Surplus Capital [H – J]	12,000	9,000	
L. Payment ₹ 21000	(12,000)	(9,000)	
M. Balance due [A – J – L]	40,000	30,000	20,000
N. Balance Cash Payment [₹ 89,300 – ₹ 22,500]	(29,689)	(22,267)	(14,844)
O. Total Cash Payment (₹ 89,000)	41,689	32,767	14,844
P. Loss [A – O]	10,311	7,733	5,156

SALE TO A COMPANY

PROBLEM 11

Riu, Inu and Sinu were running Partnership business sharing Profits and Losses in 2 : 2: 1 ratio. Their Balance Sheet as on 31st March, 2013 stood as follows:

(Figure in ₹ '000)

Liabilities		₹	*Assets*		₹
Fixed Capitals:			Fixed Assets		400.00
Riu	300.00		Investments		50.00
Inu	200.00		Current Assets:		
Sinu	100.00	600.00	Stock	100.00	
Current Accounts:			Debtors	275.00	
Riu	60.00		Cash at Bank	125.00	500.00
Sinu	40.00	100.00			
Unsecured Loans		100.00			
Current Liabilities		150.00			
		950.00			950.00

On 01.04.2013, they agreed to form a new company RIS (P) Ltd. with Inu and Sinu each taking up 200 shares of ₹ 10 each, which shall take over the firm as a going concern including Goodwill, but excluding Cash and Bank Balances. The following are also agreed upon:

(a) Goodwill will be valued at 3 year's purchase of share profits.
(b) The actual profit for the purpose of Goodwill valuation will be ₹ 2,00,000.
(c) The normal rate of return will be 18% per annum on Fixed Capital.
(d) All other Assets and Liabilities will be taken over at Book values.
(e) The Purchase consideration will be payment partly in shares of ₹ 10 each and partly in cash. Payment in cash being to meet the requirement to discharge Riu, who has agreed to retire.
(f) Inu and Sinu are to acquire interest in the new company at the ratio 3 : 2.
(g) Realisation expenses amounted to ₹ 51,000

Required: Prepare Realisation Account, Cash and Bank Account, RIS (P) Limited Account and Capital Account of Partners. **[*CA PE II May 2004*]**

Solution

Dr. **REALISATION ACCOUNT** *Cr.*

Particulars		₹	*Particulars*	₹
To Sundry Assets:			By Unsecured Loans	1,00,000
Fixed Assets	4,00,000		By Current Liabilities	1,50,000
Investments	50,000		By RIS(P) Ltd.	8,51,000
Stock	1,00,000			
Debtors	2,75,000	8,25,000		
To Bank A/c (Realisation Expenses)		51,000		
To Profit on Realisation t/f to:				
Riu's Capital A/c		90,000		
Inu's Capital A/c		90,000		
Sinu's Capital A/c		45,000		
		11,01,000		11,01,000

Dr. **CASH AND BANK ACCOUNT** Cr.

Particulars	₹	Particulars	₹
To Balance b/d	1,25,000	By Realisation A/c (Expenses)	51,000
To RIS (P) Ltd. (b.f.)	3,76,000	By Riu's Capital A/c	4,50,000
	5,01,000		5,01,000

Dr. **RIS(P) LTD.** Cr.

Particulars	₹	Particulars	₹
To Realisation A/c	8,51,000	By Cash A/c	3,76,000
		By Equity Shares in RIS (P) Ltd. A/c (b.f.)	4,75,000
	8,51,000		8,51,000

Dr. **PARTNERS' CAPITAL ACCOUNTS** Cr.

Particulars	Riu ₹	Inu ₹	Sinu ₹	Particulars	Riu ₹	Inu ₹	Sinu ₹
To Cash A/c	4,50,000	—	—	By Balance b/d	3,00,000	2,00,000	1,00,000
To Sinu's A/c (Capital Adjustment)	—	5,000	—	By Current A/c	60,000	—	40,000
To Equity Shares in RIS(P) Ltd.	—	2,85,000	1,90,000	By Realisation A/c	90,000	90,000	45,000
				By Inu's A/c (Capital Adjustment)	—	—	5,000
	4,50,000	2,90,000	1,90,000		4,50,000	2,90,000	1,90,000

Working Notes:

(i) *Calculation of Goodwill*

	₹
A. Actual profits	2,00,000
B. *Less:* Normal Rate of Return @ 18% on ₹ 6,00,000	1,08,000
C. Super Profits [A – B]	92,000
D. Goodwill valued at 3 years' purchase [₹ 92,000 × 3]	2,76,000

(ii) *Calculation of Purchase Consideration*

	₹
A. Total value of assets as per Balance Sheet	9,50,000
B. *Less:* Cash and Bank Balance	1,25,000
C. *Add:* Goodwill	2,76,000
D. Total Assets taken over	11,01,000
E. *Less:* Liabilities taken over [₹ 1,00,000 + ₹ 1,50,000]	2,50,000
F. Purchase Consideration	8,51,000

(iii) Shares in New Company received as Purchase Consideration have been divided between Inu and Sinu in the ratio 3 : 2.

PROBLEM 12

X and Y carrying on business in partnership sharing Profit and Losses equally, wished to dissolve the firm and sell the business to 'X' Limited Company on 31.3.2013, when the firm's position was as follows:

Liabilities	₹	*Assets*	₹
X's Capital	1,50,000	Land and Building	1,00,000
Y's Capital	1,00,000	Furniture	40,0n00
Sundry Creditors	60,000	Stock	1,00,000
		Debtors	66,000
		Cash	4,000
	3,10,000		3,10,000

The arrangement with X Limited Company was as follows:

(a) Land and Building was purchased at 20% more than the book value.

(b) Fumiture and stock were purchased at book values *less* 15%,

(c) The goodwill of the firm was valued at ₹ 40,000.

(d) The firm's debtors, cash and creditors were not to be taken over, but the company agreed to collect the book debts of the firm and discharge the creditors of the firm as an agent, for which services, the company was to be paid 5% on all collections from the firm's debtors and 3% on cash paid to firm's creditors.

(e) The purchase price was to be discharged by the company in fully paid equity shares of ₹ 10 each at a premium of ₹ 2 per share.

The company collected all the amounts from debtors. The creditors were paid off less by ₹.1,000 allowed by them as discount. The company paid the balance due to the vendors in cash.

Required: Prepare the Realisation Account, the Capital Accounts of the Partners and the Cash account in the books of partnership firm. ***[CA (PE II) Nov. 2006]***

Solution

Dr. **REALISATION ACCOUNT** *Cr.*

Particulars	₹	*Particulars*		₹
To Land & Building	1,00,000	By Sundry Creditors		60,000
To Furniture	40,000	By X Ltd. Co. (Purchase Consideration)		2,79,000
To Stock	1,00,000	By X Ltd. Company		
To Debtors	66,000	Sundry Debtors	66,000	
To X Ltd. Co. (Sundry Creditors)	59,000	*Less:* Commission @ 5% on	3,300	62,700
To X Ltd. Co. (Comm. @ 3% on ₹ 59,000)	1,770			
To Profits transferred to:				
A's Capital A/c	17,465			
B's Capital A/c	17,465			
	4,01,700			4,01,700

Dr. **CAPITAL ACCOUNTS OF PARTNERS** *Cr.*

Particulars	₹	₹	*Particulars*	₹	₹
To Shares in X Ltd. Co.	1,63,980	1,15,020	By Balance b/d	1,50,000	1,00,000
To Cash (Final Payment)	3,485	2,445	By Realisation A/c (Profit)	17,465	17,465
	1,67,465	1,17,465		1,67,465	1,17,465

Dr. **CASH ACCOUNT** Cr.

Particulars	₹	Particulars	₹
To Balance b/d	4,000	By A's Capital A/c (Final Payment)	3,485
To X Ltd. Co. (Amount realized from Debtors less amount paid to creditors)	1,930	By B's Capital A/c (Final Payment)	2,445
	5,930		5,930

Working Notes:

(i) *Calculation of Purchase consideration:*

	₹
Land & Building	1,20,000
Furniture	34,000
Stock	85,000
Goodwill	40,000
	2,79,000

(ii) *The shares received from the company have been distributed between the two partners A & B in the ratio of their final claims i.e., 1,67,465: 1,17,465*.*

No. of shares received from the company = 2,79,000/12 = 23,250

A gets $\frac{23,250 \text{ " } 1,67,465}{2,84,930}$ = 13,665 shares valued at 13,665 x 12 = ₹.1,63,980.

B gets the 2,84,930 remaining 9,585 shares, valued at ₹.1,15,020 (9,585 x 12)

(iii) *Calculation of net amount received from X Ltd on account of amount realized from debtors less amount paid to creditors.*

		₹
A.	Amount realized from Debtors	66,000
B.	*Less:* Commission for realization from debtors (5% on 66,000)	3,300
C.	*Less:* Amount paid to creditors	59,000
D.	*Less:* Commission for cash paid to creditors (3% on 59,000)	1,770
E.	Net amount received	1,930

(iv) In the above situation, shares received from X Ltd. Company have been distributed between two partners A and B in the ratio of their final claims. Alternatively, shares received from X Ltd, can be distributed among the partners in their profit sharing ratio i.e. ₹ 2,79,000 x 1/2 = ₹ 1,39,500 each. In that case, firm will pay cash amounting ₹ 27,965 to A and will receive cash ₹.22,035 from B.

PROBLEM 13

S and T were carrying on business as equal partners. Their Balance Sheet as at 31st March, 2013 stood as follows:

Liabilities	₹	*Assets*	₹
Capital Accounts:		Stock	2,70,000
S	6,40,000	Debtors	3,65,000
T	6,60,000	Furniture	75,000
Creditors	3,27,500	Joint life policy	47,500
Bank Overdraft	1,50,000	Plant	1,72,500
Bills Payable	62,500	Building	9,10,000
	18,40,000		18,40,000

The operations of the business were carried on till 30th September, 2013. S and T both withdrew in, equal amounts half the amount of profits made during the current period of 6 months after 10% p.a.. had been written off on Building and Plant and 5% p.a. written off on furniture. During the current period of 6 months, creditors were reduced by ₹ 50,000, Bills payables by ₹ 11,500 and Bank Overdraft by ₹ 75,000. The Joint life policy was surrendered for ₹ 47,500 on 30th September, 2013. Stock was valued at ₹ 3,17,000 and debtors at ₹ 3,25,000 on 30th September, 2013. The other items remained the same as they were on 31st March, 2013.

On 30th September, 2013 the firm sold its business to ST Ltd. The goodwill was estimated at ₹ 5,40,000 and the remaining assets were valued on the basis of the Balance Sheet as on 30th September, 2013. The ST Ltd. paid the purchase consideration in equity shares of ₹ 10 each.

Required: Prepare Realisation account and Capital accounts of the partners.

[CA (PE II) May 2008, Nov. 2008]

Solution

Dr. **(I) REALISATION ACCOUNT** *Cr.*

Particulars	₹	*Particulars*	₹
To Sundry Assets:		By Creditors	2,77,500
Stock	3,17,000	By Bills Payables	51,000
Debtors	3,25,000	By Bank Overdraft	75,000
Plant	1,63,875	By Shares in ST Ltd.	18,80,000
Building	8,64,500		
Furniture	73,125		
To Profit on Realisation t/f to:			
S's Capital A/c	2,70,000		
T's Capital A/c	2,70,000		
	22,83,500		22,83,500

Dr. **(I) PARTNERS' CAPITAL ACCOUNTS** *Cr.*

Particulars	S ₹	T ₹	*Particulars*	S ₹	T ₹
To Cash	20,000	20,000	By Balance b/d	6,40,000	6,60,000
To Shares in ST Ltd.	9,30,000	9,50,000	By Profit	40,000	40,000
			By Realisation A/c (Profit)	2,70,000	2,70,000
	9,50,000	9,70,000		9,50,000	9,70,000

Working Notes:

(I) BALANCE SHEET AS AT 30.9.2013

Liabilities	₹	*Assets*		₹
Sundry Creditors	2,77,500	Stock		3,17,000
Bills Payable	51,000	Debtors		3,25,000
Bank Overdraft	75,000	Plant	1,72,500	
Total Capital (bal. fig.)	13,40,000	*Less*: Depreciation	8,625	1,63,875
		Furniture	75,000	
		Less: Depreciation	1,875	73,125
		Building	9,10,000	
		Less: Depreciation	45,500	8,64,500
	17,43,500			17,43,500

(ii) *Profit earned during six months to 30.9.2013*

	₹
Total Capital on 30th Sept.	13,40,000
Total Capital on 1st April (₹ 6,40,000 + ₹ 6,60,000)	13,00,000
Net Increases (after drawings)	40,000

Since drawings are half of profits therefore, profit earned = ₹ 40,000 × 2 = ₹ 80,000

(ii) *Purchase Consideration:*

Total Assets excluding Goodwill	17,43,500
Add: Goodwill	5,40,000
Less: Liabilities	4,03,500
Purchase Consideration	18,80,000

(iv) *Alternatively, it may be assumed that the figure of bank overdraft is given before taking into consideration the realisation of Joint Life Policy.*

PROBLEM 14

XYZ & Co. is a partnership firm consisting of Mr. *X*, Mr. *Y* and Mr. *Z* who share profits and losses in the ratio of 2:2:1 and *ABC* Ltd. is a company doing similar business.

Following is the Balance Sheet of the firm and that of the company as at 31.3.2013:

Liabilities	*XYZ & Co.* ₹	*ABC Ltd.* ₹	*Assets*	*XYZ & Co.* ₹	*ABC Ltd.* ₹
Equity Shares of ₹ 10 each		20,00,000	Plant & Machinery	5,00,000	16,00,000
			Furniture & Fixture	50,000	2,25,000
Partners Capitals:			Stock in trade	2,00,000	8,50,000
X	2,00,000		Sundry Debtors	2,00,000	8,25,000
			Cash at bank	10,000	4,00,000
Y	3,00,000		Cash in hand	40,000	1,00,000
Z	1,00,000				
General Reserve	1,00,000	7,00,000			
Sundry Creditors	3,00,000	13,00,000			
	10,00,000	40,00,000		10,00,000	40,00,000

It was decided that the firm *XYZ* & Co. be dissolved and all the assets (except cash in hand and cash at bank) and all the liabilities of the firm be taken over by *ABC* Ltd. by issuing 50,000 shares of ₹ 10 each at a premium of ₹ 2 per share.

Partners of *XYZ* & Co. agreed to divide the shares issued by *ABC* Ltd. in the profit sharing ratio and bring necessary cash for settlement of their capital.

The creditors of *XYZ* & Co. includes ₹ 1,00,000 payable to *ABC* Ltd. An unrecorded liability of ₹ 25,000 of *XYZ* & Co. must also be taken over by *ABC* Ltd.

Required: Prepare

(i) Realisation Account, Partners' Capital Accounts and Cash in hand/Bank account in the books of *XYZ* & Co and

(ii) Pass Journal Entries in the books of *ABC* Ltd. for acquisition of *XYZ* & Co. and draw the Balance Sheet after the takeover. **[CA (PCC) Nov. 2009]**

Solution

REALISATION ACCOUNT OF XYZ & CO.

Dr. Cr.

Particulars	₹	Particulars	₹
To Plant & Machinery	5,00,000	By Sundry Creditors	3,00,000
To Furniture & Fixture	50,000	By ABC Ltd.	6,00,000
To Stock in trade	2,00,000	By Partners' Capital Accounts (loss):	
To Sundry Debtors	2,00,000	X's Capital A/c	20,000
		Y's Capital A/c	20,000
		Z's Capital A/c	10,000
	9,50,000		9,50,000

PARTNERS' CAPITAL ACCOUNTS

Dr. Cr.

Particulars	X ₹	Y ₹	Z ₹	Particulars	X ₹	Y ₹	Z ₹
To Realisation A/c	20,000	20,000	10,000	By Balance b/d	2,00,000	3,00,000	1,00,000
To Shares in *ABC* Ltd.	2,40,000	2,40,000	1,20,000	By General Reserve	40,000	40,000	20,000
To Cash A/c	—	80,000	—	By Cash A/c	20,000	—	10,000
	2,60,000	3,40,000	1,30,000		2,60,000	3,40,000	1,30,000

CASH AND BANK ACCOUNT

Dr. Cr.

Particulars	₹	₹	Particulars	₹	₹
To Balance b/d	40,000	10,000	By Cash A/c (Contra)*	—	10,000
To Bank A/c (Contra)*	10,000		By Y	80,000	—
To X	20,000				
To Z	10,000				
	80,000	10,000		80,000	10,000

JOURNAL OF ABC LTD.

Date	Particulars		L.F.	Dr. (₹)	Cr. (₹)
1.	Business Purchase A/c	Dr.		6,00,000	
	To *XYZ* & Co.				6,00,000
	(Being business of *XYZ* & Co. purchased and payment due)				
2.	Plant and Machinery A/c	Dr.		5,00,000	
	Furniture and Fixture A/c	Dr.		50,000	
	Stock in Trade A/c	Dr.		2,00,000	
	Sundry Debtors A/c	Dr.		2,00,000	
	To Sundry Creditors A/c				3,00,000
	To Unrecorded Liability A/c				25,000
	To Business Purchase A/c				6,00,000
	To Capital Reserve A/c (*Bal. Fig.*)				25,000
	(Being take over of all assets and liabilities)				
3.	XYZ & Co.	Dr.		6,00,000	
	To Equity Share Capital A/c				5,00,000
	To Securities Premium A/c				1,00,000
	(Being purchase consideration discharged in the form of shares of ₹, 10 each issued at a premium of ₹, 2 each)				

Date	Particulars	L.F.	Dr. (₹)	Cr. (₹)
4.	Sundry Creditors A/c Dr. To Sundry Debtors A/c (Being mutual owings eliminated)		1,00,000	1,00,000

BALANCE SHEET OF ABC LTD. AS AT 31.3.2013

Particulars	Note No	₹
I. Equity and Liabilities		
(1) Shareholders' Funds		
(a) Share Capital	1	25,00,000
(b) Reserves and Surplus	2	8,25,000
(2) Non-Current Liabilities		
(3) Current Liabilities		
(a) Trade Payables [Creditors] [3,00,000 + 13,00,000 – 1,00,000]		15,00,000
(b) Short-term Provisions [Unrecorded Liability]		25,000
Total		48,50,000
II. Assets		
(1) Non-Current Assets		
(a) Fixed Assets		
Tangible Assets	3	23,75,000
(2) Current Assets		
(a) Inventories [2,00,000 + 8,50,000]		10,50,000
(b) Trade Receivables [2,00,000 + 8,25,000 – 1,00,000]		9,25,000
(b) Cash and Cash Equivalents [4,00,000 + 1,00,000]		5,00,000
Total		48,50,000

Notes To Accounts:

Particulars	₹
1. Share Capital	
2,50,000 Equity Shares of ₹ 10 each	25,00,000
(Of the above 50,000 Shares were issued for consideration otherwise than cash)	
2. Reserves and Surplus	
General Reserve	7,00,000
Capital Reserve	25,000
Securities Premium	1,00,000
Total	8,25,000
3. Tangible Assets	
Plant & Machinery [5,00,000 + 16,00,000]	21,00,000
Furniture & Fixtures [50,000 + 2,25,000]	2,75,000
Total	23,75,000

Working Note:

(i) **Purchase Consideration** = 5000 × ₹ 12 = ₹ 6,00,000

Equity shares distributed among partners:

Partner *X*	=	20,000 shares @ ₹ 12	= ₹ 2,40,000
Partner *Y*	=	20,000 shares @ ₹ 12	= ₹ 2,40,000
Partner *Z*	=	10,000 shares @ ₹ 12	= ₹ 1,20,000
			₹ 6,00,000

(ii) It is assumed that cash at bank has been withdrawn to pay ₹.80,000 to partner *Y*. However payment to *Y* of ₹ 80,000 can also be made by cash ₹ 70,000 & by cheque ₹ 10,000.

PROBLEM 15

XYZ Limited was incorporated for taking over the business of Y from 1st April, 2010. The following is the Balance Sheet of Y on 31st March, 2013:

Liabilities	₹	*Assets*	₹
Capital	10,08,000	Land and Building	16,00,000
Loans	12,00,000	Plant and Machinery	2,80,000
Creditors	7,12,000	Furniture	2,00,000
		Sundry Debtors	8,40,000
	29,20,000		29,20,000

The company takes over the business with fixed assets and loans on the following terms:

(a) The fixed assets should be depreciated @ 10%.

(b) The value of Goodwill is estimated at ₹ 8,00,000.

The company realized ₹ 8,00,000 from Sundry debtors as the agent of the vendor in full settlement and discharged all the trade creditors by paying ₹ 6,80,000 for a commission of 3% on the amount collected and 2% on the amount paid.

(Commission is treated as pre-incorporation profit)

The lenders accepted 10% preference shares of ₹ 100 each in discharge of their loan. After realization of debts and discharge of the liabilities, the total amount due to the vendor was settled by payment of ₹ 54,400 in cash and the balance in shares of fully paid equity shares of ₹ 10 each.

You are required to:

(i) Compute Purchase Consideration.

(ii) Pass Journal Entries in the books of XYZ Limited after taking over the business of Y.

(iii) Prepare the Balance Sheet of the company as on 1st April, 2013. ***[CA (IPCC May 2011)]***

Solution

(I) COMPUTATION OF PURCHASE CONSIDERATION

Particulars	(₹)
Assets taken over by Y	
Land and Building	16,00,000
Plant and Machinery	2,80,000
Furniture	2,00,000
	20,80,000
Less: Depreciation @ 10%	(2,08,000)
	18,72,000
Add: Goodwill	8,00,000
	26,72,000
Less: Loan	(12,00,000)
Purchase consideration	14,72,000

(II) JOURNAL OF XYZ LIMITED

Date	Particulars		Dr. (₹)	Cr. (₹)
1.4.13	Business Purchase A/c	Dr.	14,72,000	
	ToY			14,72,000
	(Being purchase consideration due for taking over the business of Y)			
	Land and Building A/c (16,00,000 – 1,60,000)	Dr.	14,40,000	
	Plant and Machinery A/c (2,80,000 – 28,000)	Dr.	2,52,000	
	Furniture A/c (2,00,000 – 20,000)	Dr.	1,80,000	
	Goodwill A/c	Dr.	8,00,000	
	To Loans A/c			12,00,000
	To Business Purchase A/c			14,72,000
	(Being assets and liabilities taken over)			
	Vendor's Debtors	Dr.	8,40,000	
	To Vendor's Suspense A/c			8,40,000
	(Being Vendor's debtors to be collected on behalf of Y)			
	Vendor's Suspense A/c	Dr.	7,12,000	
	To Vendor's Creditors			7,12,000
	(Being Vendor's creditors to be paid off on behalf of Y)			
	Bank A/c	Dr.	8,00,000	
	Vendor's Suspense A/c	Dr.	40,000	
	To Vendor's Debtors A/c			8,40,000
	(Being Vendor's debtors collected at loss)			
	Vendor's Creditors A/c	Dr.	7,12,000	
	To Bank A/c			6,80,000
	To Vendor's Suspense A/c			32,000
	(Being profit on payment to Vendor's creditors)			
	Vendor's Suspense A/c	Dr.	37,600	
	To Commission A/c			37,600
	(Being the commission @ 3% on Vendor's Debtors collected and 2% on payment to Vendor's Creditors)			
	Vendor's Suspense A/c	Dr.	82,400	
	To Y			82,400
	(Being transfer of the net balance of vendor's suspense account after realization of debtors and payment to creditors, to Y)			
	Y	Dr.	15,54,400	
	To Equity share capital A/c			15,00,000
	To Bank A/c			54,400
	(Being allotment of 1,50,000 equity shares of ₹ 10 each as fully paid up and payment of cash as agreed in discharge of total amount due to Y)			
	Loan A/c	Dr.	12,00,000	
	To 10% Preference share capital A/c			12,00,000
	(Being issue of 12,000 10% preference shares for discharge of loan)			

Date	Particulars	Dr. (₹)	Cr. (₹)
	Commission A/c Dr.	37,600	
	To Capital Reserve A/c		37,600
	(Being commission earned on settlement of vendor's debtors and creditors is treated as pre-incorporation profit which is transferred to capital reserve account)		

(III) BALANCE SHEET OF XYZ LIMITED AS AT 1ST APRIL, 2013

Particulars	Note No	₹
I. Equity and Liabilities		
(1) Shareholders' Funds		
(a) Share Capital	1	27,00,000
(c) Reserves and Surplus [Capital Reserve]		37,600
(2) Non-Current Liabilities		
(a) Long-term Borrowings		
(3) Current Liabilities		
Total		27,37,600
II. Assets		
(1) Non-Current Assets		
(a) Fixed Assets		
Tangible Assets		18,72,000
Intangible Assets [Goodwill]	2	8,00,000
(2) Current Assets		
(a) Cash and Cash Equivalents		65,600
Total		27,37,600

Notes To Accounts:

Particulars	₹
1. Share Capital	
1,50,000 Equity Shares of ₹ 10 each	15,00,000
12,000, 10% Pref. Shares of ₹ 100 each	12,00,000
(Of the above all Shares were issued for consideration otherwise than cash)	27,00,000
2. Tangible Assets	
Land & Building	14,40,000
Plant & Machinery	2,52,000
Furniture	1,80,000
	18,72,000

Working Note: *Calculation of Cash balance of XYZ Ltd.*

	₹
Cash collected from vendor's debtors	8,00,000
Less: Cash paid to vendor's creditors	(6,80,000)
Less: Cash paid to Y	(54,400)
	65,600

2A Partnership—Amalgamation and Conversion

CONVERSION OF FIRM INTO A COMPANY

PROBLEM 1

Avinash, Rohit and Madwesh were carrying on business in partnership sharing Profit and Losses in the ratio of 5:4:3 respectively. The Trial Balance of the firm as on 31st March, 2013 was the following:

Particulars	*Dr. (₹)*	*Cr. (₹)*
Plant and Machinery at cost	1,05,000	—
Stock	60,200	—
Sundry Debtors	85,000	—
Sundry Creditors	—	1,05,200
Capital A/cs:		
Avinash	—	70,000
Rohit	—	50,000
Madwesh	—	30,000
Drawings A/cs:		
Avinash	30,000	—
Rohit	25,000	—
Madwesh	20,000	—
Depreciation on Plant and Machinery	—	35,000
Trading Profit for the year	—	1,29,800
Cash at Bank	94,800	—
	4,20,000	4,20,000

Additional Information:

(a) Interest on Capital Accounts at 10% on the amount standing to the credit of partners capital accounts at the beginning of the year was not provided before preparing the above Trial Balance.

(b) On 31st March, 2013 they formed a Private Ltd. Company Anagha (P) Ltd, to take over the partnership business.

(c) You are further informed as under:

(i) Plant and Machinery is to be transferred at ₹. 80,000.

(ii) Equity Shares of ₹. 10 each of the company are to be issued to the partners at par In such numbers to ensure that by reason of their share holdings alone, they will have the same rights of sharing Profits and Losses as they had in the partnership. Balance, if any in their Capital Accounts, will be settled by giving 7½% Preference Shares of ₹ 100 each at par.

(iii) Before transferring the business, the partners withdrew by cash from partnership the following amounts over and above the drawings as shown in the Trial Balance:

(a) Avinash ₹. 20,000, (b) Rohit ₹. 10,600, (c) Madwesh ₹. 14,200

(iv) All Assets and Liabilities except Plant and Machinery and the Bank Balance are to be transferred at their value in the books of the partnership as at 31st March, 2013.

Required: Prepare:

(a) Profit and Loss Adjustment Account for the year ending 31st March, 2013.

(b) Capital Accounts showing all the adjustments required to dissolve the partnership

(c) A statement showing the number of shares of each class to be issued by the company to each of the partners to settle their accounts.

(d) Prepare Balance Sheet of the company Anagha (P) Ltd. as on 31.03.2013 after take over of the business. ***[CA (PE-II-Nov. 2002]***

Solution

Dr. **PROFIT AND LOSS ADJUSTMENT ACCOUNT FOR THE YEAR ENDING 31ST MARCH, 2013** *Cr.*

Particulars	₹.	*Particulars*	₹.
To Interest on Capital Avinash:	7,000	By Balance b/d	1,29,800
Rohit	5,000	By Plant and Machinery	10,000
Madwesh	3,000		
To Profit t/f to Capital Accounts:			
Avinash	52,000		
Rohit	41,600		
Madwesh	31,200		
	1,39,800		1,39,800

Dr. **(B) PARTNERS' CAPITAL ACCOUNTS** *Cr.*

Particulars	*Avinash* ₹	*Rohit* ₹	*Madwesh* ₹	*Particulars*	*Avinash* ₹	*Rohit* ₹	*Madwesh* ₹
To Drawings as per Trial Balance	30,000	25,000	20,000	By Balance b/d	70,000	50,000	30,000
To Additional Drawings	20,000	10,600	14,200	By Profit and Loss Adjustment A/c	52,000	41,600	31,200
To Balance c/d	79,000	61,000	30,000	By Interest on Capital	7,000	5,000	3,000
	1,29,000	96,600	64,200		1,29,000	96,600	64,200
To Equity Shares	50,000	40,000	30,000	By Balance b/d	79,000	61,000	30,000
To Preference Shares	29,000	21,000	—				
	79,000	61,000	30,060		79,000	61,000	30,000

(C) STATEMENT SHOWING THE NUMBER AND CLASSES OF SHARES ISSUED TO THE PARTNERS

Particulars	*Avinash*	*Rohit*	*Madwesh*
Closing Capital Balance (After Adjustments)	79,000	61,000	30,000
Taking Madwesh's Capital as base for ensuring same rights of share holding-Equity Shares of ₹ 10 each to be issued	50,000	40,000	30,000
Balance to be settled by issue of 7%% Preference Shares for Surplus Capital	29,000	21,000	—

BALANCE SHEET ANAGHA OF LTD. AS AT 31.3.2013

Particulars	Note No	₹
I. Equity and Liabilities		
(1) Shareholders'Funds		
(a) Share Capital	1	1,70,000
(c) Reserves and Surplus		—
(2) Non-Current Liabilities		—
(3) Current Liabilities		
(a) Trade Payables [Creditors]		1,05,200
Total		2,75,200
II. Assets		
(1) Non-Current Assets		
(a) Fixed Assets		
Tangible Assets (Plant and Machinery)		80,000
(2) Current Assets		
(a) Inventories		60,200
(b) Trade Receivables [Debtors]		85,000
(b) Cash and Cash Equivalents		50,000
Total		2,75,000

Notes To Accounts:

Particulars	₹
1. Share Capital	
12,000, Equity Shares of ₹. 10 each	1,20,000
500, 7.5% Pref. Shares of ₹. 10 each	50,000
(Of the above all Shares were issued for consideration otherwise than cash)	1,70,000

PROBLEM 2

P, Q and R are partners hsaring profits and losses in the ratio 3 : 2 : 1 after allowing interest on capital @ 9% p.a. Their balance Sheet as at 31st March, 2012 is as follows:

Liabilities	(₹)	Assets	(₹)
Capital Accounts:		Plant & Machinery	1,08,000
P	50,000	Fixtures	20,000
Q	30,000	Stock	50,000
R	20,000	Sundry Debtors	30,000
Reserve Fund	60,000		
Creditors	48,000		
	2,08,000		2,08,000

The applied for conversion of the firm into a Private Limited Company named PQR Pvt. Ltd. and the certificate was received on 01-04-2012. They decided to maintain same profit sharing ratio and the preserve the priority in regard to repayment of capital as far as possible. For that purpose they decided to insert a clause of issuance of Preference shares in Memorandum of Association in addition to issuance of Equity Shares of ₹ 10 each.

On 01.04.2012, the value of goodwill is to be determined on the basis of 2 years' purchase of the average profit from the business of the last 5 years. The particulars of profits are as under:

		₹
Year ended 31.03.2008	Profit	10,000
Year ended 31.03.2009	Loss	5,000
Year ended 31.03.2010	Profit	18,000
Year ended 31.03.2011	Profit	27,000
Year ended 31.03.2012	Profit	30,000

The loss for the year ended 31-03-2009 was on account of loss by strike to the extent of ₹ 10,000.

It was agreed that rest of the assets are valued on the basis of the Balance Sheet as at 31-03-2012 except Plant & machinery which is valued at ₹ 1,02,000.

You are required to prepare (a) the Balance Sheet of the Company as at 01.04.2012, (b) Partners' Capital Accounts and (c) Statement showing the final settlement between the partners taking Q's capital as basis. ***[CA (IPCC) Nov. 2012]***

Solution

(a) BALANCE SHEET OF THE PQR PVT LTD. AS AT 1.4.2012

Particulars	*Note No.*	*(₹)*
I. EQUITY AND LIABILITIES		
(1) Shareholders' Funds		
(a) Share Capital	1	1,90,000
(2) Non-Current Liabilities		
(3) Current Liabilities		
(a) Trade Payables		48,000
Total		2,38,000
II. ASSETS		
(1) Non-Current Assets		
(a) Fixed Assets		
(i) Tangible Assets	2	1,22,000
(ii) Intangible Assets	3	36,000
(2) Current Assets		
(a) Inventories		50,000
(b) Trade Receivables		30,000
Total		2,38,000

Notes To Accounts:

1. Share Capital

	(₹)
Authorised Capital	
18,000 Equity Shares of ₹ 10 each	1,80,000
9% Pref. Shares of ₹ 100 each	10,000
	1,90,000
Issued & Subscribed Capital	
18,000 Equity Shares of ₹ 10 each	1,80,000
9% Pref. Shares of ₹ 100 each	10,000
(All the shares have been issued for consideration other than cash)	1,90,000

2. Tangible Assets	
Plant and Machinery	1,02,000
Fixtures	20,000
	1,22,000
3. Intangible Assets	
Goodwill	36,000

(b) *Dr.* **CAPITAL ACCOUNTS OF PARTNERS** *Cr.*

Particulars	*P* ₹	*Q* ₹	*R* ₹	*Particulars*	*P* ₹	*Q* ₹	*R* ₹
To P & M A/c	3,000	2,000	1,000	By Balance b/d	50,000	30,000	20,000
To 9% Preference Shares	5,000	–	5,000	By Reserve fund	30,000	20,000	10,000
To Equity Shares	90,000	60,000	30,000	By Realization A/c (Profit on Sale of Business)	18,000	12,000	6,000
	98,000	62,000	36,000		98,000	62,000	36,000

The question of preference and equity shares to be issued to *P*, *Q* and *R* can be dealt with in the following manner:

Particulars	*P* ₹	*Q* ₹	*R* ₹
A. Total amount due as capital	95,000	60,000	35,000
B. Proportionate Capitals taking *Q*'s Capital as the Base Capital (for which Equity Shares should be issued)	90,000	60,000	30,000
C. Surplus Capital (A – B) (for which 9% Non-Cum Pref. Shares should be issued)	5,000	–	5,000

The above treatment is based on the principle that the function of interest in case of partnership is to compensate those partners who contribute capital in excess of what is required as per profit sharing ratio.

Working Notes: 1. Calculation of goodwill

Particulars	*2007-08* ₹	*2008-09* ₹	*2009-10* ₹	*2010-11* ₹	*2011-12* ₹
Profits	10,000	(5,000)	18,000	27,000	30,000
Adjustment for abnormal loss in 2008-09	–	10,000	–	–	–
	10,000	5,000	18,000	27,000	30,000
					₹
Total Profit from 2007-08 to 2011-12					90,000
Average Profit (90,000/5)					18,000
Goodwill equal to 2 years' Purchase					36,000

2. Computation of Purchase consideration

	₹	₹
Assets		
Goodwill	36,000	
Plant and Machinery	1,02,000	
Fixtures	20,000	
Stock	50,000	
Sundry Debtors	30,000	2,38,000
Less: Liabilities (Creditors)		(48,000)
Purchase Consideration		1,90,000

PROBLEM 3

The following is the Balance Sheet of M/s *P* and *Q* as on 31st March, 2012:

Liabilities	₹	*Assets*	₹
P's Capital	50,000	Machinery	54,000
Q's Capital	30,000	Furniture	5,000
Q's Loan	15,000	Investments	50,000
General Reserve	20,000	Stock	20,000
Creditors	40,000	Debtors	21,000
		Cash	5,000
	1,55,000		1,55,000

It was agreed that Mr. *R* is to be admitted for a fourth share in the future profits from 1st April, 2012. He is required to contribute cash towards goodwill and ₹ 15,000 towards capital. The following further information is furnished:

(a) *P* and *Q* share the profits in the ratio of 3 : 2.

(b) Mr *P* was receiving a salary of ₹ 750 p.m from the very inception of the firm in 2005 in addition to share of profit.

(c) The future profit sharing ratio between *P*, *Q* and *R* will be 2 : 1 : 1. Mr *P* will not get any salary after the admission of Mr *R*.

(d) The goodwill of the firm shall be determined on the basis of 3 years' purchase of the average profits from business of the last 5 years. The particulars of the profits are as under:

2007-2008 Profit ₹ 25,000, 2008-2009 Profit ₹ 12,500, 2009-2010 Loss ₹ 2,500, 2010-2011 Profit ₹ 35,000, 2011-2012 Profit ₹ 30,000.

The above profits and losses are after charging the salary of Mr *P*. The profit for the year ended. 31st March 2008 included an extraneous profits of ₹ 40,000 and the loss of the year ended 31st March 2010 was on account of loss by strike to the extent of ₹ 20,000. It was agreed that the value of the goodwill of the firm shall appear in the book of the firm.

(e) The cash trading profit for the year ended 31st March, 2013 was ₹ 50,000 before depreciation.

(f) Each partner withdrew ₹ 1,000 p.m. as drawings.

(g) The value of the other assets and liabilities as on 31st March, 2013 were Machinery (before depreciation) ₹ 60,000, Furniture (before depreciation) ₹ 10,000, Investments ₹ 50,000, Stock ₹ 15,000, Debtors ₹ 30,000, Creditors ₹ 20,000.

(h) Provide depreciation @ 10% on Machinery and @ 5% on furnitures on the closing balance and interest @ 6% on *Q*'s loan. The loan along with interest would be repaid within next 12 months.

(i) Investments are held from inception of the firm and interest is received @ 10% p.a.

(j) The partners applied for conversion of the firm into a Private Limited Company. Certificate was received on 1st April, 2013. They decided to convert Capital A/cs of the partners into share capital in the ratio of 2 : 1 : 1 on the basis of total Capital as on 31st March, 2013. If necessary, partners have to subscribe to fresh capital or withdraw.

Required: Prepare the Profit and Loss Account for the year ended 31st March, 2013 and the Balance Sheet as at 1st April 2013. ***[CA (IPCC) May 2013]***

Solution

PROFIT AND LOSS ACCOUNT

for the year ending on 31st March, 2013

Dr. Cr.

Particulars		₹	Particulars	₹
To Depreciation on Machinery		6,000	By Trading Profit	50,000
To Depreciation on furniture		500	By Interest on Investment	5,000
To Interest on Q's loan		900		
To Net Profit to:				
P's Capital A/c	23,800			
Q's Capital A/c	11,900			
R's Capital A/c	11,900	47,600		
		55,000		55,000

BALANCE SHEET OF THE PQR PVT LTD. AS AT 1.4.2013

Particulars	Note No.	(₹)
I. EQUITY AND LIABILITIES		
(1) Shareholders' Funds		
(a) Share Capital		1,41,600
(2) Current Liabilities		
(a) Short Term borrowings	1	15,900
(b) Trade Payables		20,000
Total		1,77,500
II. ASSETS		
(1) Non-Current Assets		
(a) Fixed Assets		
(i) Tangible Assets	2	63,500
(ii) Non-current investments		50,000
(2) Current Assets		
(a) Inventories		15,000
(b) Trade Receivables		30,000
(c) Cash and cash equivalents		19,000
Total		2,38,000

Notes To Accounts:

		₹
1. Short term borrowings		
Loan from Q		15,900
2. Tangible assets		
Machinery	54,000	
Furniture	9,500	63,500

Working Notes: 1. Calculation of goodwill

Particulars	2007-08 ₹	2008-09 ₹	2009-10 ₹	2010-11 ₹	2011-12 ₹
Profits/(Loss)	25,000	12,500	(2,500)	35,000	30,000
Adjustment for Abnormal Profit & Loss	(40,000)	—	20,000	—	—
Add: Salary of partner (750 × 12)	9,000	9,000	9,000	9,000	9,000
Less: Interest on Non-Trading Investments	(5,000)	(5,000)	(5,000)	(5,000)	(5,000)
	(11,000)	16,500	21,500	39,000	34,000
					₹
Total Profit for five years					1,00,000
Average Profit (` 1,00,000/5)					20,000
Goodwill equal to 3 years' Purchase					60,000
New partner's share of goodwill for 1/4 share					15,000

2. Sacrificing Ratio: P's sacrifice = 3/5 – 1/2 = 1/10, Q's sacrifice = 2/5 – 1/4 = 3/20
3. As per AS 26 "Intangible Assets", only purchased goodwill should appear in the books. Therefore, goodwill though required to be shown in the books as per the requirement of the question, has been adjusted through capital accounts of the partenrs in line with the provisions of AS 26.

4. *Dr.* **CAPITAL ACCOUNTS OF PARTNERS** *Cr.*

Particulars	P ₹	Q ₹	R ₹	Particulars	P ₹	Q ₹	R ₹
To Drawings A/c	12,000	12,000	12,000	By Balance b/d	50,000	30,000	—
To P	—	—	6,000	By General Reserve	12,000	8,000	—
To Q	—	—	9,000	By R	6,000	9,000	—
To Balance c/d	79,800	46,900	14,900	By Bank A/c	—	—	30,000
				By P & L A/c	23,800	11,900	11,900
	91,800	58,900	41,900		91,800	58,900	41,900

5. **BALANCE SHEET OF M/S XYZ & CO. AS AT 31ST MARCH, 2013**

Liabilities		₹	Assets		₹
P's Capital	79,800		Machinery	60,000	
Q's Capital	46,900		*Less* : Depreciation	(6,000)	54,000
R's Capital	14,900	1,41,600	Furniture	10,000	
			Less : Depreciation	(500)	9,500
Q's Loan	15,000		Investments		50,000
Add : Interest due	900	15,900	Stock-in-trade		15,000
Creditors		20,000	Debtors		30,000
			Cash		19,000
		1,77,500			1,77,500

6. **CALCULATION OF CLOSING CASH BALANCE**

Particulars	₹
Opening cash balance	5,000
Add: Cash brought in by R	30,000
Less: Drawings (12,000 + 12,000 + 12,000)	36,000
Less: Additions to Machine (60,000 – 54,000)	6,000
Less: Addition to Furniture (10,000 – 5,000)	5,000

Cash Trading Profit	50,000
Add: Investment Interest	5,000
Add: Decrease in Stock Balance	5,000
Less: Increase in Debtors	9,000
Less: Decrease in Creditors	20,000
Closing Cash Balance	19,000

7. ADJUSTMENT OF CAPITALS

Particulars	*P*	*Q*	*R*
A. Adjusted Capitals	79,800	46,900	14,900
B. Distribution of Shares in the ratio of 2:1:1	70,800	35,400	35,400
C. Surplus to be withdrawn (Shortage to be brought in)	9,000	11,500	(20,500)

AMALGAMATION

PROBLEM 3

Firm X & Co. conlsists of partners A and B sharing Profits and Losses in the rato of 3:2. The firm Y & Co. consists of partners B and C sharing Profits and Losses in the ratio of 5:3.

On 31st March, 2013 it was decided to amalgamate both the firms and form a new firm XY & Co., wherein A, B and C would be partners sharing Profits and Losses in the ratio of 4:5:1.

BALANCE SHEET AS AT 31.3.2013

Liabilities	*X & Co.* ₹	*Y & Co.* ₹	*Assets*	*X & Co.* ₹	*Y& CO.* ₹
Capital: A	1,50,000		Cash in hand & bank	40,000	30,000
B	1,00,000	75,000	Debtors	60,000	80,000
C	—	50,000	Stock	50,000	20,000
Reserve	50,000	40,000	Vehicles	—	90,000
Creditors	1,20,000	55,000	Machinery	1,20,000	—
			Building	1,50,000	—
	4,20,000	2,20,000		4,20,000	2,20,000

The following were the terms of amalgamation:

(i) Goodwill of X & Co., was valued at ₹. 75,000. Goodwill of Y & Co. was valued at ₹. 40,000. Goodwill account not to be opened in the books of the new firm but adjusted through the Capital accounts of the partners.

(ii) Building, Machinery and Vehicles are to be taken over at ₹. 2,00,000, ₹. 1,00,000 and ₹, 74,000 respectively.

(iii) Provision for doubfful debts at ₹, 5,000 in respect of X & Co. and ₹. 4,000 in respect of Y & Co, are to be provided.

You are required to:

(i) Show, how the Goodwill value is adjusted amongst the partners.

(ii) Propare the Balance Sheet of XY & Co. as at 31.3.2013 by keeping partners' capitals in their profit sharing ratio by taking capital of B as the basis. The excess or deficiency to be kept in the respective Partners' Current accounts. *[CA (PE II) May 2006]*

Solution

ADJUSTMENT FOR RAISING AND WRITING OFF OF GOODWILL

Raised in Old Profit Sharing Ratio X & Co. (3 : 2) ₹.	Y & Co. (5 : 3) ₹.	₹.	*Total Written off in new ratio 4 : 5 : 1* ₹.	*Difference* ₹.
45,000	—	45,000 Cr.	46,000 Dr.	1,000 Dr.
30,000	25,000	55,000 Cr.	57,500 Dr.	2,500 Dr.
—	15,000	15,000 Cr.	11,500 Dr.	3,500 Cr
75,000	40,000	1,15,000	1,15,000	Nil

BALANCE SHEET OF X Y & CO. (NEW FIRM) AS AT 31.3.2013

Liabilities	₹	Assets	₹
Capital Accounts:		Vehicle	74,000
A	1,72,000	Machinery	1,00,000
B	2,15,000	Building	2,00,000
C	43,000	Stock	70,000
Current Accounts:		Debtors	1,31,000
A	22,000	Cash & Bank	70,000
C	18,000		
Creditors	1,75,000		
	6,45,000		6,45,000

Working Notes:

(i) Balance of Capital Accounts at the time of amalgamation of firms

Particulars	X & Co. (3:2)		Y & Co. (5:3)	
	A's Capital ₹	B's Capital ₹	B's Capital ₹	A's Capital ₹
Balance as per Balance Sheet	1,50,000	1,00,000	75,000	50,000
Add: Reserves	30,000	20,000	25,000	15,000
Revaluation profit (Building)	30,000	20,000	—	—
Less: Revaluation loss (Machinery)	(12,000)	(8,000)	(10,000)	(6,000)
Provision for doubtful debt.	(3,000)	(2,000)	(2,500)	(1,500)
	1,95,000	1,30,000	87,500	57,500

(ii) Balance of Capital Accounts in the Balance Sheet of the new firm as at 31.3.2013

Particulars	A ₹	B ₹	C ₹
Balance b/d: X & Co.	1,95,000	1,30,000	
Y & Co.	—	87,500	57,500
	1,95,000	2,17,500	57,500
Adjustment for goodwill	(1,000)	(2,500)	3,500
	1,94,000	2,15,000	61,000
Total Capital ₹ 4,30,000 (B's Capital i.e. ₹ 2,15,000 × 2) to be contributed in 4:5:1 ratio.	1,72,000	2,15,000	43,000
Transfer to Current Account	22,000	—	18,000

PROBLEM 4

P and Q have been carrying on same business independently. Due to competition in the market, they decided to amalgamate and form a new company called PQ Ltd.

Following is the Balance Sheet of P and Q as at 31.3.2013:

Liabilities	P ₹	Q ₹	Assets	P ₹	Q ₹
Capital	7,75,000	8,55,000	Plant & machinery	4,85,000	6,14,000
Current liabilities	6,23,500	5,57,600	Building	7,50,000	6,40,000
			Current Assets	1,63,500	1,58,600
	13,98,500	14,12,600		13,98,500	14,12,600

Following are the additional information:

(a) The authorised capital of the new company will be ₹.25,00,000 divided into 1,00,000 equity shares of ₹. 25 each.

(b) Liabilities of P includes ₹ 50 000 due to Q for the purchases made. Q made a profit of 20% on sale to P

(c) P has goods purchased from Q, cost to him ₹. 10, 000. This is included in the Current asset of P as at 31st March, 2013.

(d) The assets of P and Q are to be revalued as under:

	P	Q
Plant and Machinery	₹ 5,25,000	₹ 6,75,000
Building	₹ 7,75,000	₹ 6,48,000

(e) The purchase consideration is to be discharged as under:

(i) Issue 24,000 equity shares of ₹. 25 each fully paid up in the proportion of their profitability in the preceding 2 years. Profits for the preceding 2 years are given below:

	P ₹	Q ₹
Ist year	2,62,800	2,75,125
IInd Year	2,12,200	2,49,875
	4,75,000	5,25,000

(ii) Issue 12% preference shares of ₹. 10 each fully paid up at par to provide income equivalent to 8% return on capital employed in the business as on 31.3.2013 after revaluation of assets of P and Q respectively.

Required:

(i) Compute the amount of equity and preference shares issued to P and Q.

(ii) Prepare the Balance Sheet of P & 0 Ltd. immediately after amalgamation.

[CA (PCC) May 2007]

Solution

(i) Calculation of amount of equity shares issued to P and Q

Profit	P ₹	Q ₹
Ist year	2,62,800	2,75,125
IInd year	2,12,200	2,49,875
Total	4,75,000	5,25,000

No. of shares to be issued = 24,000 equity shares in the proportion of the preceding 2 years profitability

24000 × 475/1000	11,400 equity shares	
24000 × 525/1000		12,600 equity shares

Calculation of amount of 12% Preference shares issued to P and Q

	P	Q
Capital Employed	₹ 8,40,000	₹ 9,24,000
8% Return on Capital Employed	₹ 67,200	₹ 73,920
12% Preference shares to be issued $\left[67{,}200 \times \frac{100}{12}\right]$	₹. 5,60,000	
$\left[73{,}920 \times \frac{100}{12}\right]$		₹ 6,16,000

Total Purchase Consideration

	P	Q
Equity Shares	₹ 2,85,000	₹ 3,15,000
12% Preference Shares	₹ 5,60,000	₹ 6,16,000
Total	₹ 8,45,000	₹ 9,31,000

(II) BALANCE SHEET OF PQ LTD. AS AT 31.3.2013

Particulars	Note No	₹ (lacs)
I. Equity and Liabilities		
(1) Shareholders' Funds		
(a) Share Capital	1	17,76,000
(b) Reserves and Surplus		—
(2) Non-Current Liabilities		—
(3) Current Liabilities		11,31,100
Total		29,07,100
II. Assets		
(1) Non-Current Assets		
(a) Fixed Assets		
Tangible Assets	2	26,23,000
Intangible Assets [Goodwill]		14,000
(2) Current Assets		2,70,100
Total		29,07,100

Notes To Accounts:

Particulars	₹ (lacs)
1. Share Capital	
24,000 Equity Shares of ₹. 25 each	6,00,000
1,17,600, 12% Pref. Shares of ₹. 10 each	11,76,000
(Of the above all Shares were issued for consideration otherwise than cash)	17,76,000
2. Tangible Assets	
Land & Building	14,23,000
Plant & Machinery	26,23,000
Total	26,23,000

Working Notes:

(i) **Goodwill**

	P ₹	*Q* ₹
Plant and machinery	5,25,000	6,75,000
Building	7,75,000	6,48,000
Current assets	1,63,500	1,58,600
	14,63,500	14,81,600
Less: Current Liabilities	6,23,500	5,57,600
Net assets taken (capital employed)	8,40,000	9,24,000
Less: Purchase consideration	8,45,000	9,31,000
Goodwill	5,000	7,000
Total purchased goodwill		12,000
Add: Unrealised profitof ₹.10,000 @ 20% ₹. 2,000 is adjusted from current assets and from goodwill (since P & L A/c is not given)		2,000
Total Goodwill		14,000

(ii) Current Assets

	P ₹	Q ₹
Balances before amalgamation	1,63,500	1,58,600
Less: Liabilities of P due to Q	—	50,000
Less: Unrealised Profit on Stock (i.e. ₹ 10,000 × 20%)	2,000	—
Total	1,61,500	1,08,600
Grand Total		2,70,100

(iii) Current Liabilities

	P ₹	Q ₹
Balances before amalgamation	6,23,500	5,57,600
Less: Liabilities of P due to Q	50,000	—
Total	5,73,500	5,57,600
Grand Total		11,31,100

PROBLEM 5

P and *Q* are partners of *P* & *Co.* sharing Profit and losses in the ratio of 3 : 1 and *Q* and *R* are partners of *R* & *Co.*, sharing profits and losses in the ratio of 2 : 1. On 31st March, 2013, they decide to amalgamate and form a new firm *M/s PQR & Co.*, wherein *P, Q* and *R* would be partners sharing profits and losses in the ratio of 3 : 2 : 1. The Balance Sheets of two firms on the above date are as under:

Liabilities	*P & Co.* ₹	*R & Co.* ₹	*Assets*	*P & Co.* ₹	*R & Co.* ₹
Capitals:			*Fixed Assets:*		
P	2,40,000	----	Building	50,000	60,000
Q	1,60,000	2,00,000	Plant & machinery	1,50,000	1,60,000
R	—	1,00,000	Office Equipment	20,000	6,000
Reserves	50,000	1,50,000	*Current Assets:*		
Sundry Creditors	1,20,000	1,16,000	Stock-in-trade	1,20,000	140,000
Due to *P* & *Co.*	....	1,00,000	Sundry Debtors	1,60,000	2,00,000
Bank overdraft	80,000	----	Bank Balance	30,000	90,000
			Cash in hand	20,000	10,000
	—	—	Due from *R* & *Co.*	1,00,000	—
	6,50,000	6,66,000		6,50,000	6,66,000

The amalgamated firm took over the business on the following terms:

(a) Building of *P* & *Co.* was valued at ₹. 1, 00, 000.

(b) Plant and machinery of *P* & *Co.* was valued at ₹. 2,50,000 and that of *R* & *Co.* at ₹. 2,00,000.

(c) All stock in trade is to be appreciated by 20%.

(d) Goodwill valued of *P* & *Co.* at ₹. 1,20,000 and *R* & *Co.* at ₹. 60,000, but the same will not appear in the books of *PQR* & *Co.*

(e) Partners of new firm wiil bring the necessary cash to pay other partners to adjust their capitals according to the profit sharing ratio.

(f) Provisions for doubtful debts has to be carried forward at ₹. 12,000 in respect of debtors of *P* & *Co.* and ₹. 26,000 in respect of debtors of *R* & *Co.*

Required: Prepare the Balance Sheet of new firm and Capital Accounts of the partners in the books of old firms. ***[CA(IPCC) May 2010]***

Solution

BALANCE SHEET OF M/S PQR & CO. AS AT 31ST MARCH, 2013

Liabilities	₹	Assets		₹
Capitals:		Building		
P	5,52,000	(₹.1, 00,000 + ₹.60,000)		1,60,000
Q	3,68,000	Plant & Machinery		
R	1,84,000	(₹. 2,50,000 + ₹. 2,00,000)		4,50,000
Sundry Creditors		Office Equipment		
(₹. 1,20,000 + 1,16,000)	2,36,000	(₹. 20,000 + ₹. 6,000)		26,000
Bank overdraft	80,000	Stock-in-trade		
		(₹.1, 44 ,000 + ₹.1, 68,000)		3,12,000
		Sundry Debtors	3,60,000	
		(₹. 1, 60,000 + ₹ .2,00,000)		
		Less: Provision	(38,000)	
		(₹. 12,000 + ₹. 26,000)		3,22,000
		Bank Balance		
		(₹. 30,000 + ₹. 90,000)		1,20,000
	—	Cash in hand		30,000*
	14,20,000			14,20,000

Dr. **PARTNERS' CAPITAL ACCOUNTS IN THE BOOKS OF P & CO.** *Cr.*

Particulars	P ₹	Q ₹	Particulars	P ₹	Q ₹
To Capital A/cs – M/s PQR & Co.	4,89,000	2,43,000	By Balance b/d	2,40,000	1,60,000
			By Reserve (3 : 1)	37,500	12,500
			By Profit on Realisation A/'c	2,11,500	70,500
	4,89,000	2,43,000		4,89,000	2,43,000

Dr. **PARTNERS' CAPITAL ACCOUNTS IN THE BOOKS OF R & CO.** *Cr.*

Particulars	P ₹	Q ₹	Particulars	P ₹	Q ₹
To Capital A/cs -M/s PQR & Co	3,68,000	1,84,000	By Balance b/d	2,00,000	1,00,000
			By Reserve (2 : 1)	1,00,000	50,000
			By Profit on Realisation	68,000	34,000
	3,68,000	1,84,000		3,68,000	1,84,000

Working Notes:

(i) Computation of Purchase Consideration

Particulars	P & Co. ₹.	R & Co. ₹.
Assets:		
Goodwill	1,20,000	60,000
Building	1,00,000	60,000
Plant & machinery	2,50,000	2,00,000
Office equipment	20,000	6,000
Stock-in-trade	1,44,000	1,68,000
Sundry Debtors	1,60,000	2,00,000

Bank balance		30,000	90,000
Cash in hand		20,000	10,000
Due from R & Co.		1,00,000	—
	(A)	9,44,000	7,94,000
Less: Liabilities:			
Creditors		1,20,000	1,16,000
Provision for doubtful debts		12,000	26,000
Due to P & Co.		—	1,00,000
Bank overdraft		80,000	—
	(B)	2,12,000	2,42,000
Purchase Consideration (A – B)		7,32,000	5,52,000

(ii) Computation of Proportionate Capital

M/s *PQR* & Co. (Purchase Consideration) (₹. 7,32,000 + ₹. 5,52,000)	12,84,000
Less: Goodwill Adjustment	(1,80,000)
Total Capital of new firm (Distributed in ratio 3 : 2 : 1)	11,04,000
P's Proportionate Capital	5,52,000
Q's Proportionate Capital	3,68,000
R's proportionate capital	1,84,000

(iii) Computation of Capital Adjustments

Particulars	*P* ₹.	*Q* ₹.	*R* ₹.	*Total* ₹.
Balance transferred from P & Co.	4,89,000	2,43,000		7,32,000
Balance transferred from R & Co.	—	3,68,000	1,84,000	5,52,000
	4,89,000	6,11,000	1,84,000	12,84,000
Less: Goodwill written off in the ratio of 3 : 2 : 1	(90,000)	(60,000)	(30,000)	(1,80,000)
Existing capital	3,99,000	5,51,000	1,54,000	11,04,000
Proportionate capital	5,52,000	3,68,000	1,84,000	11,04,000
Amount to be brought in (paid off)	1,53,000	(1,83,000)	30,000	

Dr. **REALISATION ACCOUNT IN THE BOOKS OF P & CO.** *Cr.*

Particulars		₹	*Particulars*	₹
To Building		50,000	By Creditors	1,20,000
To Plant & Machinery		1,50,000	By Bank overdraft	80,000
To Office Equipment		20,000	By M/s PQR & Co. (purchase consideration)	7,32,000
To Stock-in-trade		1,20,000		
To Sundry debtors		1,60,000		
To Bank balance		30,000		
To Cash in hand		20,000		
To Due from R & Co.		1,00,000		
To Partners' Capital A/cs				
P	2,11,500			
Q	70,500	2,82,000		
		9,32,000		9,32,000

Dr. **REALISATION ACCOUNT IN THE BOOKS OF R & CO.** Cr.

Particulars		₹	Particulars	₹
To Building		60,000	By Creditors	1,16,000
To Plant & machinery		1,60,000	By Due to P & Co.	1,00,000
To Office equipment		6,000	By M/s PQR & Co.	5,52,000
To Stock-in-trade		1,40,000	(purchase consideration)	
To Sundry debtors		2,00,000		
To Bank balance		90,000		
To Cash in hand		10,000		
To Partners' Capital A/c:				
Q	68,000			
R	34,000	1,02,000		
		7,68,000		7,68,000

PROBLEM 6

A and B are partners of AB & Co. sharing profits and losses in the ratio of 2: 1 and C and D are partners of CD & Co. sharing profits and losses in the ratio of 3:2.On 1st April 2013, they decided to amalgamate and form a new firm M/S. AD & Co. wherein all the partners of both the firm would be partners sharing profits and losses in the ratio of 2:1:3:2 respectively to A, B, C and D.

Their balance sheets on that date were as under:

Liabilities	AB & Co. ₹	CD & Co. ₹	Assets	AB & Co. ₹	CD & Co. ₹
Capitals					
A	1,50,000		Building	75,000	90,000
B	1,00,000		Machinery	1,20,000	1,00,000
C		1,20,000	Furniture	15,000	12,000
D		80,000	Stock	24,000	36,000
Reserve	66,000	54,000	Debtors	65,000	78,000
Creditors	52,000	35,000	Due from CD & Co.	47,000	
Due to AB & Co.		47,000	Cash at Bank	18,000	15,000
			Cash in hand	4,000	5,000
	3,68,000	3,36,000		3,68,000	3,36,000

The amalgamated firm took over the business on the following terms:

(a) Building was taken over at ₹ 1,00,000 and ₹ 1,25,000 of AB & Co. and CD & Co. respectively. And machinery was taken over at ₹ 1,25,000 and ₹ 1,10,000 of AB & Co. and CD & Co. respectively.

(b) Goodwill of AB & Co. was worth ₹ 75,000 and that of CD & Co. was worth ₹ 50,000. Goodwill account was not to be opened in the books of the new firm, the adjustments being recorded through capital accounts of the partners.

(c) Provision for doubtful debts has to be carried forward at ₹ 5,000 in respect of debtors of AB & Co. and ₹ 8,000 in respect of CD & Co.

You are required:

(i) Compute the adjustments necessary for goodwill.

(ii) Pass the Journal Entries in the books of AD & Co. assuming that excess/deficit capital (taking D's capital as base) with reference to share in profits are to be transferred to current accounts.

[CA (IPCC) May 2011]

Solution

(I) ADJUSTMENT FOR RAISING & WRITING OFF OF GOODWILL

	Goodwill raised in old profit sharing ratio			Goodwill written off in new ratio	Difference
	AB&Co.	CD&Co.	Total	AD&Co.	
	₹	₹	₹	₹	₹
A	50,000		50,000 Cr.	31,250 Dr.	18,750 Cr.
B	25,000		25,000 Cr.	15,625 Dr.	9,375 Cr.
C		30,000	30,000 Cr.	46,875 Dr.	16,875 Dr.
D		20,000	20,000 Cr.	31,250 Dr.	11, 250 Dr.
	75,000	50,000	1,25,000	1,25,000	

(ii) In the books of AD&Co.

JOURNAL

Date	Particulars		Dr. (₹)	Cr. (₹)
01 April	Building A/c	Dr.	1,00,000	
	Machinery A/c	Dr.	1,25,000	
	Furniture A/c	Dr.	15,000	
	Stock A/c	Dr.	24,000	
	Debtors A/c	Dr.	65,000	
	CD & Co. A/c	Dr.	47,000	
	Cash at bank A/c	Dr.	18,000	
	Cash in hand A/c	Dr.	4,000	
	To Provision for doubtful debts A/c			5,000
	To Creditors A/c			52,000
	To A's capital A/c			2,10,667
	To B's capital A/c			1,30,333
	(Being the sundry assets and liabilities of AB & Co. taken over at the values stated as per the agreement)			
	Building A/c	Dr.	1,25,000	
	Machinery A/c	Dr.	1,10,000	
	Furniture A/c	Dr.	12,000	
	Stock A/c	Dr.	36,000	
	Debtors A/c	Dr.	78,000	
	Cash at bank A/c	Dr.	15,000	
	Cash in hand A/c	Dr.	5,000	
	To Provision for doubtful debts A/c			8,000
	To Creditors A/c			35,000
	To AB & Co. A/c			47,000
	To C's capital A/c			1,74,600
	To D's capital A/c			1,16,400
	(Being the sundry assets and liabilities of CD & Co. taken over at the values stated as per the agreement)			
	C's capital A/c	Dr.	16,875	
	D's capital A/c	Dr.	11,250	
	To A's capital A/c			18,750
	To B's capital A/c			9,375
	(Being adjustment in capital accounts of the partners on account of goodwill)			

Date	Particulars		Dr. (₹)	Cr. (₹)
	AB & Co. A/c	Dr.	47,000	
	To CD & Co. A/c			47,000
	(Being mutual indebtedness of AB & Co. and CD&Co. cancelled)			
	A's Capital A/c	Dr.	1,24,267	
	To A's Current A/c			1,24,267
	(Being excess amount in A's capital A/c transferred to A's current A/c)			
	B's Capital A/c	Dr.	87,133	
	To B's Current A/c			87,133
	(Being excess amount in B's capital A/c transferred to B's current A/c)			

Working Notes:

(i) Profit on Revaluation

		AB & Co. ₹	CD & Co. ₹
Building	(1,00,000 – 75,000)	25,000	
	(1,25,000 – 90,000)		35,000
Machinery	(1,25,000 – 1,20,000)	5,000	
	(1,10,000 – 1,00,000)		10,000
		30,000	45,000
Less: Provision for doubtful debts		(5,000)	(8,000)
		25,000	37,000

(ii) Balance of Capital Accounts of Partners

	A's Capital ₹	B's Capital ₹	C's Capital ₹	D's Capital ₹
Balance as per the B/S	1,50,000	1,00,000	1,20,000	80,000
Reserves	44,000	22,000	32,400	21,600
Profit on revaluation	16,667	8,333	22,200	14,800
	2,10,667	1,30,333	1,74,600	1,16,400

(iii) Calculation of Capital of each partner in the new firm

Particulars	A ₹	B ₹	C ₹	D ₹
Balance	2,10,667	1,30,333	1,74,600	1,16,400
Adjustment for goodwill	18,750	9,375	(16,875)	(11,250)
	2,29,417	1,39,708	1,57,725	1,05,150
Total Capital ₹ 4,20,600* in the new ratio of 2 : 1 : 3 : 2	(1,05,150)	(52,575)	(1,57,725)	(1,05,150)
Transfer to Current Account	1,24,267	87,133		

* Taking D's capital as the base which is 2/8th of total capital; total capital will be 1,05,150 × 8/2 i.e ₹ 4,20,600.

MISCELLENEOUS PROBLEMS

PROBLEM 7 [Final Accounts of A Firm]

Alpha Manufacturing P. Ltd. is a company manufacturing articles. Beeta Marketing P. Ltd. is a company engaged in marketing activities. The two companies enter into a partnership on the following terms:

(a) Alpha Maufacturing P. Ltd. is to supply goods on credit of two months to the partnership firm. The partnership is to discharge the dues to Alpha Manufacturing P. Ltd. along with interest at 12% per annum regularly on due dates.

(b) Beeta Marketing P. Ltd. is to sell the goods.

(c) Expenses of sales are to be met out of the partnership funds. Alpha Manufacturing P. Ltd and Beeta Marketing P. Ltd. are to introduce capital of ₹ five lakhs each for meeting the above expenses and as working capital. Interest at 15% per annum is payable on partners' capital—payment being made every month. Accordingly the capitals are introduced on 1st April. 2012.

(d) Profits and losses are to be dealt with as follows:

  (i) 10% of the profits, if any, are to be credited to reserves for strengthening the working capital base;

  (ii) balance profits are to be shared equally be credit to current accounts;

  (iii) losses, if any, are to be borne equally by debit to capital accounts.

(e) The firm name is to be AB Traders.

During the year ended 31st March, 2013 the following were the transactions:

(a) Purchases ₹ 150 lakhs of which ₹ 30 lakhs were in the first quarter; ₹ 90 lakhs were in the next six months; the balance ₹ 30 lakhs were in the last quarter. The purchases are evently spread through the respective periods.

(b) Sales were ₹ 200 lakhs.

(c) Sales expenses were ₹ 10 lakhs and were paid in full.

(d) Discount allowed to customers amounted to ₹ 4 lakhs. On 31st March, 2013 amounts due from customers were ₹ 45 lakhs and unsold inventory was worth ₹ 15 lakhs

Required: Prepare the Final Accounts of the firm. ***[CA (May 2000)]***

Solution

TRADING AND PROFIT & LOSS ACCOUNT & PROFIT & LOSS APPROPRIATION ACCOUNT

Dr. *for the year ended 31st March, 2013* *[₹ in lakh]* *Cr.*

Particulars		₹.	Particulars	₹.
To Purchases		150.00	By Sales 200.00	
To Gross Profit c/d		65.00	By Closing Stock	15.00
		215.00		215.00
To Marketing Expenses		10.00	By Gross Profit b/d	65.00
To Discount to Customers		4.00		
To Interest to Suppliers		2.80		
To Net Profit c/d		48.20		
		65.00		65.00
To Transfer to Reserve [10% of 48.20]		4.82	By Net Profit b/d	48.20
To Interest on Capital		1.50		
To Profit t/f to:				
Aplha Mfg. (P) Ltd.	20.94			
Beeta Marketing (P) Ltd	20.94	41.88		
		48.20		48.20

BALANCE SHEET AS AT 31ST MARCH 2013 *[₹ in lakh]*

Liabilities	₹.	*Assets*	₹.
Creditors for Supplies	20.00	Inventory 15.00	
Interest accrued but not due	.20	Debtors	45.00
Reserve	4.82	Bank Balance	16.90
Current Accounts:			
Alpha Mfg. (P) Ltd.	20.94		
Beeta Marketing (P) Ltd.	20.94		
Capital Accounts:			
Alpha Mfg. (P) Ltd.	5.00		
Beeta Marketing (P) Ltd.	5.00		
	76.90		76.90

Working Notes:

Dr. **(I) BANK ACCOUNT** Cr.

Particulars	₹.	*Particulars*	₹.
To Capital Accounts:		By Selling Expenses	10.00
Alpha Mfg (P) Ltd.	5.00	By Creditors for Supplies	130.00
Beeta Marketing (P) Ltd.	5.00	By Interest to Supplier	2.60
To Debtors	151.00	By Interest to Partners:	
		Alpha Mfg (P) Ltd.	.75
		Beeta Mfg (P) Ltd	.75
		By Balance c/d	16.90
	161.00		161.00

Dr. **(II) DEBTORS' ACCOUNTS** Cr.

Particulars	₹.	*Particulars*	₹.
To Sales	200.00	By Discount Allowed	4.00
		By Bank A/c (b.f.)	151.00
		By Balance c/d	45.00
	200.00		200.00

Dr. **(III) CREDITORS' FOR SUPPLIES ACCOUNT** Cr.

Particulars	₹.	*Particulars*	₹.
To Bank A/c	130.00	By Purchases	150.00
To Balance c/d	20.00		
	150.00		150.00

(iv) *Calculation of Interest to Suppliers*

(a) Interest paid on purchases from 1st April to 31st Jan. $= ₹\ 130,00,000 \times \frac{2}{12} \times \frac{12}{100}$

$= ₹\ 2,60,000$

(b) Interest accrued on purchases in the middle of Feb. $= ₹\ 10,00,000 \times \frac{1.5}{12} \times \frac{12}{100}$

$= ₹\ 15,000$

(c) Interst accrued on purchases in the middle of Mar. $= ₹\ 10,00,000 \times \frac{.5}{12} \times \frac{12}{100}$

$= ₹\ 5,000$

(d) Total Interest [(a) + (b) + (c)] $= ₹\ 2,80,000$

PROBLEM 8 [Adjusting Entries in the Books of a Firm and Partner]

X, *Y* Ltd. and *Z* Ltd. are partners of *X* & Co. The partnership deed provided that:

(a) The working partner Mr. *X* is to be remunerated at 15% of the net profits after charging his remuneration, but before charging interest on capital and provision for taxation;

(b) Interest is to be provided on capital at 15% per annum;

(c) Balance profits after making provision for taxation, is to be shared in the ratio of 1 : 2 : 2 by the three partners.

During the year ended 31st March, 2013:

(i) The net profit before tax and before making any payment to partners amounted to ₹ 6,90,000;

(ii) Interest on capitals at 15% per annum amounted to:
₹ 60,000 for *X*; 1,50,000 for *Y* Ltd. and ₹ 1,80,000 for *Z* Ltd. The capitals have remained unchanged during the year;

(iii) Provision for tax is to be at 40% of "total income" of the firm. The total income has been computed at ₹ 1,95,000.

You are asked by:

(a) The firm to pass closing entries in relation to the above;

(b) *Y* Ltd. to pass journal entries in its books pertaining to its income from the firm and show the investment in partnership account as it would appear in its ledger;

(c) *Z* Ltd. to show, how the above information will appear in its financial statements for the year;

(d) Shri *X* to show the working if any, in relation to the above. ***[CA (Nov.)]***

Solution

(a) **JOURNAL OF PARTNERSHIP FIRM OF SHRI *X*, *Y* LTD. AND *Z* LTD.**
CLOSING ENTRIES ON 31 MARCH, 2013

Particulars		*L.F.*	*Dr. (₹)*	*Cr. (₹)*
Profit and Loss A/c	Dr.		78,000	
To Provision for Taxation for A.Y. 2011-2013				78,000
(Being provision made for taxation at 40% on total income of ₹ 1,95,000)				
Profit & Loss A/c	Dr.		6,12,000	
To Profit & Loss Appropriation A/c				6,12,000
(Being the transfer of Profit to P&L Appropriation A/c)				
Remuneration to *X* A/c	Dr.		90,000	
To *X*'s Capital A/c				90,000
(Being remuneration to *X* provided)				
Interest on Capital A/c	Dr.		3,90,000	
To *X*'s Capital A/c				60,000
To *Y* Ltd.'s Capital A/c				1,50,000
To *Z* Ltd.'s Capital A/c				1,80,000
(Being the interest on Capital Provided)				
Profit and Loss Appropriation A/c	Dr.		4,80,000	
To Remuneration to *X* (the working partner)				90,000
To Interest on capitals:				
X				60,000
Y Ltd.				1,50,000
Z Ltd.				1,80,000
(Being interest on capitals provided at 15% per annum and remuneration to working partner *X* at 15% of net profit after charging his remuneration but before providing for tax and interest on capitals—now recorded)				

Particulars		L.F.	Dr. (₹)	Cr. (₹)
Profit and Loss Appropriation A/c	Dr.		1,32,000	
(₹ 6,90,000 – ₹ 78,000 – ₹ 4,80,000)				
To *X*'s Capital A/c				26,400
To *Y* Ltd.'s Capital A/c				52,800
To *Z* Ltd.'s Capital A/c				52,800
(Being balance profits credited to partners' capital accounts in the ratio of 1 : 2 : 2)				

(b) JOURNAL ENTRIES IN THE BOOKS OF *Y* LTD.

Particulars		L.F.	Dr. (₹)	Cr. (₹)
Investment in partnership with Shri *X* and *Z* Ltd.	Dr.		2,02,800	
To Interest on Capital (taxable)				1,50,000
To Share of profits (non-taxable)				52,800
(Being entry to record interest income @ 15% p.a. on capital of ₹ 10,000 and 2/5th share of profit in the firm).				
Interest on Capital	Dr.		1,50,000	
Share of profits	Dr.		52,800	
To Profit and Loss A/c				2,02,800
(Being incomes transferred to Profit and Loss Account)				

Dr. **INVESTMENTS IN PARTNERSHIP WITH SHRI *X* AND *Z* LTD. ACCOUNT** Cr.

Particulars	₹	Particulars	₹
To Balance b/f	10,00,000	By Balance c/d	12,02,800
To Interest on capital from the firm	1,50,000		
To Share of profits in the firm	52,800		
	12,02,800		12,02,800

EXTRACTS FROM THE FINANCIAL STATEMENTS OF *Z* LTD.
REVENUE STATEMENT FOR THE YEAR ENDED 31 MARCH, 2013

	₹
Operating income:	
Income from partnership:	
Interest on capital invested	1,80,000
Share of Profits	52,800
	2,32,800

PROBLEM 9 [Admission, Retirement and Conversion]

Mr. B and Mr. E are partners sharing Profits and Losses in the ratio of 3:2. On 30th September, 2012 they admit Mr. C as a partner, and the new profit ratio is 2:2:1. C brought in Fixtures ₹. 3,000 and cash ₹. 10,000, the goodwill being (i) B and E ₹.20,000 and (ii) C ₹.10,000 but neither figure is to be brought into the books.

On 31st March, 2013, the partnership is dissolved, B retires and the other two partners forming a company called BC Limited with equal capitals, taking over all remaining assets and liabilities, goodwill being agreed at ₹.40,000 and brought into books of the company. B agrees to take over the business car at ₹.3,700: Plant was sold for ₹.3,000 being in excess of requirements. The profit of the two preceding years were ₹.17,200 and ₹.19,000 respectively and it was agreed that for the half year ended 30th September, 2012 the net profit was to be taken as equal to the average of the two preceding years and the current year.

No entries have been made when C entered, except cash. No new book being opened by BC Company Ltd., B agreed to have ₹.50,000 as loan to the company, secured by 12% Debentures. The following is the Trial Balance as on 31st March, 2013.

Particulars	*(Dr.) ₹*	*(Cr.) ₹*
Capital Accounts		
B		35,000
E		20,000
C		10,000
Drawing Accounts		
B	6,000	
E	5,000	
C	2,800	
Debtors & Creditors	31,000	12,000
Plant (Book value of plant sold ₹. 4,000)	23,000	
Fixtures	7,000	
Motor Car	2,700	
Stock on 31st March, 2013	13,000	
Bank	16,300	
P&L A/c for the year		29,800
	1,06,800	1,06,800

Required: *Prepare* Goodwill Adjustment Account, Capital Accounts of Partners, Profit and Loss Appropriation Account and Balance Sheet of B Ltd. as on 31st March, 2013. ***[CA (Nov. 1994)]***

Solution

Dr. **GOODWILL ADJUSTMENT ACCOUNT** *Cr.*

Particulars	₹.	*Particulars*	₹.
30th Sept.		30th Sept.	
To Partners Capital A/c		By Partner's Capital A/c	
(Goodwill raised)		(Goodwill Written off)	
B	12,000	B	12,000
E	8,000	E	12,000
C	10,000	C	6,000
31st March		31st March	
To Partners' Capital A/cs		By Goodwill A/c	
(goodwill raised)		(Goodwill raised in the	
B	16,000	books transferred)	40,000
E	16,000		
C	8,000		
	70,000		70,000

Dr. **PARTNERS' CAPITAL ACCOUNTS** *Cr.*

Particulars	*B* ₹.	*E* ₹.	*C* ₹.	*Particulars*	*B* ₹.	*E* ₹.	*C* ₹.
To Drawings	6,000	5,000	2,800	By Balance b/d	35,000	20,000	10,000
To Motor Car	3,700	–	–	By Fixtures			
To 12% Debentures	50,000	–	–	(not recorded earlier)	–	–	3,000
To Goodwill Adjustment	12,000	12,000	6,000	By Profit upto			
To Bank A/c	7,620	–	–	30th Sept.	13,200	8,800	
To Bank A/c	–	7,580	–	By Profit for 6 months			
To Share Capital	–	31,340	31,340	ended 31st March	3,120	3,120	1,560
				By Goodwill			
				Adjustment A/c	12,000	8,000	10,000
				By Goodwill			
				Adjustment A/c	16,000	16,000	8,000
				By Bank A/c	–	–	7,580
	79,320	55,920	40,140		79,320	55,920	40,140

PROFIT & LOSS APPROPRIATION ACCOUNT

Dr. *For the year ended 31st March, 2013* Cr.

Particulars	₹.	Particulars	₹.
To Partners' Capital Account (Distribution of Profit)		By Profit & Loss A/c (Net Profit Transferred)	29,800
B	16,320		
E	11,920		
C	1,560		
	29,800		29,800

BALANCE SHEET OF BC LTD. AS AT 31.3.2013

Particulars	Note No	₹
I. Equity and Liabilities		
(1) Shareholders' Funds		
(a) Share Capital		62,680
(2) Non-Current Liabilities [Debentures]		50,000
(3) Current Liabilities		
(a) Trade Payable [Creditors]		12,000
Total		1,24,680
II. Assets		
(1) Non-Current Assets		
(a) Fixed Assets		
Tangible Assets	1	29,000
Intangible Assets [Goodwill]		40,000
(2) Current Assets		
(a) Inventories		13,000
(b) Trade Receivable [Debtors]		31,000
(c) Cash and Cash Equivalents		11,680
Total		1,24,680

Notes To Accounts:

Particulars	₹
1. Tangible Assets	
Plant	19,000
Fixtures	10,000
Total	29,000

Working Notes:

(i) ***Goodwill adjustment as on 30th September,***

	Total (₹)	B (₹)	E (₹)	C (₹)
Goodwill raised				
B and E (3:2)	20,000	12,000	8,000	–
C	10,000			10,000
	30,000			
Goodwill written off in the new profit sharing ratio (2:2:1)	30,000	12,000	12,000	6,000

(ii) ***Calculation of half yearly profit:***

	₹.
Profit of the preceding two years (₹. 17,200 + ₹.19,000)	36,200
Current year's profit	29,800
	66,000

		E	C	Total
	Profit for six months ended 30th September, (66,000 × 1/3)			22,000
	Profit for next six months ended 31st March, (₹.29,800 – ₹.22,000)			7,800
(iii)	Share Capital of BC Ltd.	E	C	Total
	Capital before conversion	38,920	23,760	62,680
	Capital After conversion (½ × ₹ 62,680)	31,340	31,340	62,680
	C should bring in cash		7,580	
	E should withdraw cash	7,580		

Dr. **(IV) BANK ACCOUNT** Cr.

Particulars	₹.	Particulars	₹.
To Balance b/d	16,300	By B's Capital A/c	7,620
To Plant A/c (Sale of Plant)	3,000	By E's Capital (Amount withdrawn)	7,580
To Cs Capital A/c (Amount brought in)	7,580	By Balance c/d	11,680
	26,880		26,880

(v) Profit and Loss on sale and takeover of assets:		₹.
Profit on Motor car taken over (₹. 3,700 – ₹.2,700)	1,000	
Loss on sale of plant (₹.4,000 – ₹.3,000)		1,000
Net Effect		Nil

PROBLEM 10 [Retirement and Conversion]

A, B and C carried on business in partnership, sharing Profits and Losses in the ratio of 1:2:3. They decided to form a private limited company, AB (P) Ltd. and C is not interested to take over the shares in AB (P) Ltd. The authorized share capital of the company is ₹ 12,00,000 divided into 12,000 ordinary shares of ₹ 100 each.

The company was incorporated and took over goodwill as valued and certain assets of the partnership firm on 31.3.2013. The Balance Sheet of the partnership firm on that date was as follows:

Liabilities		₹.	Assets	₹
Capital Accounts:			**Fixed Assets:**	
A		1,00,000	Machinery	1,20,000
B		2,00,000	Land	1,74,000
C		3,00,000	Motorcycles	30,000
Current Accounts:			Furniture & Fittings	11,000
A		39,420	**Current Assets:**	
B		60,580	Stock	2,35,000
A's Loan A/c	28,000		Debtors	43,000
(+) Interest accrued	2,000	30,000	Cash in hand	87,000
Current Liabilities:			C's Overdrawn	1,00,000
Creditors		70,000		
		8,00,000		8,00,000

C, who retired was presented by the other partners (A and B) with one motorcycle valued in the books of the firm ₹ 9,000. The remaining motorcycles were sold in the open market for ₹ 13,000. C also received certain furniture for which he was charged ₹ 2,000. The debtors which were all considered good, were taken over by C for ₹ 40,000. A and B were charged in their profit sharing ratio for the book value of Motorcycle presented by them to C.

It was agreed that C who is not willing to take the shares in AB (P) Ltd. was discharged first by providing necessary cash. A and B should bring cash, if necessary.

AB (P) Ltd. took over the remaining furniture and fittings at a price of ₹ 13,000, the machinery for ₹ 1,25,000, the stock at an agreed value of ₹ 2,00,000 and the land at its book value. The value of the goodwill of the partnership firm was agreed at ₹ 88,000. The creditors of the firm were settled by the firm for ₹ 70,000. A's loan account together with interest accrued was transferred to his capital account.

The purchase consideration was discharged by the company by the issue of equal number of fully paid up equity shares at par to A and B.

Required: Prepare Realisation A/c, Capital Acs of the partners and Cash A/c. Also draw the Balance Sheet of AB (P) Ltd. ***[CA (PE II) May 2007]***

Solution

Dr. **REALIZATION ACCOUNT** *Cr.*

Particulars	₹	*Particulars*	₹
To Machinery	1,20,000	By Creditors	70,000
To Land	1,74,000	By AB (P) Ltd.	6,00,000
To Motor Cycles	30,000	(Purchase Consideration)	
To Furniture & Fittings	11,000	By A's Capital A/c	3,000
To Stock	2,35,000	By B's Capital A/c	6,000
To Debtors	43,000	By C's Capital A/c (2,000 + 40,000)	42,000
To Cash (Payment to creditors)	70,000	By Cash A/c (Sale of Motor Cycle)	13,000
To Profit transferred to:			
A's Capital A/c	8,500		
B's Capital A/c	17,000		
C's Capital A/c	25,500		
	7,34,000		7,34,000

Dr. **PARTNERS' CAPITAL ACCOUNTS** *Cr.*

Particulars	A ₹	B ₹	C ₹	*Particulars*	A ₹	B ₹	C ₹
To Current A/c	—	—	1,00,000	By Balance b/d	1,00,000	2,00,000	3,00,000
To Realisation A/c	3,000	6,000	42,000	By Current A/c	39,420	60,580	—
(Assets taken over)				By A's Loan A/c	30,000	—	—
To Equity Shares in AB (P) Ltd.	3,00,000	3,00,000	—	By Realization A/c (Profit)	8,500	17,000	25,500
To Cash A/c	—	—	1,83,500	By Cash A/c	1,25,080	28,420	—
	3,03,000	3,06,000	3,25,500		3,03,000	3,06,000	3,25,500

Dr. **CASH ACCOUNT** *Cr.*

Particulars	₹	*Particulars*	₹
To Balance b/d	87,000	By Realisation A/c	70,000
To Realisation A/c	13,000	By C's Capital A/c	1,83,500
To A's Capital A/c	1,25,080		
To B's Capital A/c	28,420		
	2,53,500		2,53,500

BALANCE SHEET OF AB (P) LTD. AS AT 31.3.2013

Particulars	Note No	₹
I. Equity and Liabilities		
(1) Shareholders' Funds		
(a) Share Capital	1	6,00,000
(2) Non-Current Liabilities		
(3) Current Liabilities		
Total		6,00,000
II. Assets		
(1) Non-Current Assets		
(a) Fixed Assets		
Tangible Assets	2	3,12,000
Intangible Assets [Goodwill]		88,000
(2) Current Assets		
(a) Inventories		2,00,000
Total		6,00,000

Notes To Accounts:

Particulars	₹
1. Share Capital	
6,000 Equity Shares of ₹. 100 each	6,00,000
(Of the above all Shares were issued for consideration otherwise than cash)	
2. Tangible Assets	
Land & Building	1,74,000
Plant & Machinery	1,25,000
Furnitur & Fixtures [14,000 + 6,000]	13,000
Total	3,12,000

Working Note: *Calculation of Purchase Consideration:*

		₹.
A.	Assets taken over by AB (P) Ltd.	
	Machinery	1,25,000
	Furniture & Fittings	13,000
	Land	1,74,000
	Stock	2,00,000
	Goodwill	88,000
	Purchase Consideration	6,00,000
	Total no. of Shares to be issued (6,00,000/₹ 100)	6,000

PROBLEM 11 [Admission, Retirement and Conversion]

X and Y are partners sharing profits and losses in the ratio of 3:2. On 30th September, 2012 they admitted Z as a partner The new profit sharing ratio agreed was 2:2:1

At the time of admission Z brought in a fixture valued at ₹. 6,000 and a machinery worth ₹. 24, 000. No accounting entry was passed for the fixture brought in by partner Z in the books of the firm.

Also at the time of admission the valuation of goodwill was made. The value of goodwill of X and Y was decided at ₹. 40,000 and value of goodwill of partner Z was fixed at ₹. 20,000,

No effect was given to the goodwill value in the books of the firm.

On 31.3.2013 it was decided that partner X would retire and the other partners viz., Y and Z would continue the business of the firm by converting it into a company called YZ Ltd., with equal shareholding in the company.

The partners agreed as below:

(i) The goodwill of the firm shall be fixed at ₹. 80, 000. Necessary effect for goodwill value not recorded earlier shall be given. The present goodwill value being ₹.80,000 shall be reflected in the books of the company.

(ii) All the assets and liabilities of the firm shall be taken over by the company.

(iii) Partner X would take motor car of the firm at a value of ₹. 7,400.

(iv) A plant owned by the firm is sold for ₹, 6, 000.

(v) The profit of the firm upto 30.9.2012 was ₹.44,000.

(vi) Partner X agreed to leave ₹. 90, 000 as loan with the firm in return for 12% interest per annum.

Following is the Trial Balance of the firm as on 31.3.2013:

Particulars	*Dr. (₹)*	*Cr. (₹)*
Capital Accounts:		
X	—	80,000
Y	—	50,000
Z	—	24,000
Drawing Accounts:		
X	22,000	—
Y	20,000	—
Z	9,600	—
Sundry Debtors	70,000	—
Sundry Creditors	—	32,000
Plant (book value of plant sold ₹ 8,000)	46,000	—
Fixtures	14,000	—
Stock	24,000	—
Motor car	5,400	—
Cash at bank	34,600	—
Profit and Loss A/c (for the year)	—	59,600
Total	2,45,600	2,45,600

You are required to prepare:

(i) Goodwill Adjustment Account

(ii) Profit and Loss Apporiation Account

(iii) Partner's Capital Accounts

(iv) Balance Sheet of YZ Ltd. after conversion. *[CA (PCC) Nov. 2007]*

Solution

Dr. **(I) GOODWILL ADJUSTMENT ACCOUNT** Cr.

		₹			₹
30th Sept.	To Partners' Capital A/cs:		30th June	By Partners' Capital A/cs:	
	X (3/5)	24,000		X (2/5)	24,000
	Y (2/5)	16,000		Y (2/5)	24,000
	Z	20,000		Z (1/5)	12,000
30th Sept.	To Partners' Capital A/cs:		30th July	By Goodwill A/c	
	X (2/5)	32,000		Goodwill raised in the books	80,000
	Y (2/5)	32,000			
	Z (1/5)	16,000			
		1,40,000			1,40,000

Dr. **PROFIT AND LOSS APPROPRIATION ACCOUNT** Cr.

Particulars	₹	Particulars	₹
To Plant Loss on sale of plant	2,000	By Motor Car	2,000
To Partners' Capital A/cs:		By Profit and Loss A/c	59,600
X	32,640		
Y	23,840		
Z	3,120		
	61,600		61,600

Calculation of Profit Apportionment:

	Total ₹.	X ₹.	Y ₹.	Z ₹.
Upto 30th Sept (in 3:2)	44,000	26,400	17,600	NIL
From 1st oct to 31st March (in 2:2:1)	15,600	6,240	6,240	3,120
	59,600	32,640	23,840	3,120

Dr. **PARTNERS' CAPITAL ACCOUNTS** Cr.

Particulars	X ₹	Y ₹	Z ₹	Particulars	X ₹	Y ₹	Z ₹
To Goodwill Adjustment A/c	24,000	24,000	12,000	By Balance b/d	80,000	50,000	—
To Motor Car	7,400	—	—	By Plant & Machinery	—	—	24,000
To Drawings	22,000	20,000	9,600	By Fixtures	—	—	6,000
To 12% Loan	90,000	—	—	By Goodwill Adjus. A/c	24,000	16,000	20,000
To Bank A/c	25,240	—	—	By Profit upto 30th June	26,400	17,600	—
To Balance c/d	—	77,840	47,520	By Profit for 6 months ended 31st March	6,240	6,240	3,120
				By Goodwill Adjus. A/c	32,000	32,000	16,000
	1,68,640	1,21,840	69,120		1,68,640	1,21,840	69,120
To Bank A/c		15,160	—	By Balance b/d	—	77,840	47,520
To Shares of YZ Ltd		62,680	62,680	By Bank A/c		—	15,160
		77,840	62,680			77,840	62,680

BALANCE SHEET YZ LTD. AS AT 31.3.2013

Particulars	Note No	₹ (lacs)
I. Equity and Liabilities		
(1) Shareholders'Funds		
(a) Share Capital	1	1,25,360
(b) Reserves and Surplus		
(2) Non-Current Liabilities [12% Loan]		90,000
(3) Current Liabilities		
(a) Trade Payables		32,000
(b) Short-term Provisions		—
Total		2,47,360
II. Assets		
(1) Non-Current Assets		
(a) Fixed Assets		
Tangible Assets	2	58,000
Intangible Assets [Goodwill]		80,000

Particulars	Note No	₹
(2) Current Assets		
(a) Inventories		24,000
(b) Trade Receivables		70,000
(b) Cash and Cash Equivalents		15,360
Total		2,47,360

Notes To Accounts:

Particulars	₹
1. Share Capital	
12,536 Equity Shares of ₹. 10 each	1,25,360
(Of the above all Shares were issued for consideration otherwise than cash)	
2. Tangible Assets	
Land & Building	
Plant & Machinery [46,000 – 8,000]	38,000
Furnitur & Fixtures [14,000 + 6,000]	20,000
Total	58,000

Working Notes:

Dr. **(I) BANK ACCOUNT** *Cr.*

Particulars	₹	*Particulars*	₹
To Balance b/d	34,600	By X's Capital A/c	25,240
To Plant (sold) A/c	6,000	By Y's Capital A/c	15,160
To Z's Capital A/c	15,160	By Balance c/d	15,360
	55,760		55,760

(ii) Total Capial of the Firm before conversion

Y	₹ 77,840
Z	₹ 47,520
	₹ 1,25,360

As Y and Z would continue with equal shareholding, therefore, share capital of Y and Z would be ₹ 1,25,360/2 = ₹ 62,680 each.

Z should bring in cash (₹ 62,680 – ₹ 47,520) = ₹ 15,160

Y should withdraw cash (₹ 77,840 – ₹ 62,680) = ₹ 15,160

3 Accounting for Employee Stock Option Plan

SHORT ANSWER PRACTICAL QUESTIONS

PROBLEM 1

X Co Ltd has its share capital divided into equity shares of ₹ 10 each, On 1.10.2012 it granted 20,000 employees' stock option at ₹ 50 per share, when the market price was ₹ 120 per share. The options were to be exercised between 10th December, 2012 and 31th March, 2013. The employees exercised their options for 16,000 shares only and the remaining options lapsed. The company closes its books on 31st March every year.

Show Journal entries (with narration) as would appear in the books of the company upto 31th March, 2013. *[CA (PCC) Nov. 2009]*

Solution

JOURNAL

Date	Particulars	Dr. (₹)	Cr. (₹)
1.10.2012	Employee Compensation Expense A/c Dr.	14,00,000	
	To Employee Stock Option Outstanding A/c		14,00,000
	(Being the grant of 20,000 stock options to employees at ₹.50 when market price is ₹.120)		
10.12.12 to 31.3.13	Bank A/c Dr.	8,00,000	
	Employee Stock Option Outstanding A/c Dr.	11,20,000	
	To Equity Share Capital A/c		1,60,000
	To Securities Premium A/c		17,60,000
	(Being shares issued to the employees against the options vested to them in pursuance of Employee Stock Option Plan)		
31.3.13	Employee Stock Option Outstanding A/c Dr.	2,80,000	
	To Employee Compensation Expense A/c		2,80,000
	(Being reverse entry passed for lapse of 4,000 stock options)		
31.3.13	Profit and Loss A/c Dr.	11,20,000	
	To Employee Compensation Expense A/c		11,20,000
	(Being transfer of employee compensation transferred to Profit and Loss Account)		

PROBLEM 2

A Company has its share capital divided into shares of ₹ 10 each. On 1st April 2012, it granted 20,000 employees' stock options at ₹ 40, when the market price was ₹ 130. The options were to be exercised between 1st January 2013 to 15th March 2013. The employees exercised their options for 18,000 shares only; the remaining options lapsed. The company closes its books on 31st March every year. Pass Journal entries with regard to employees' stock options. *[CA (IPCC) May 2011]*

Solution

JOURNAL

Date	Particulars		Dr. (₹)	Cr. (₹)
01.04.2012	Employees compensation expense A/c	Dr.	18,00,000	
	To Employees stock option outstanding A/c			18,00,000
	(Being grant of 20,000 stock option to employees at ₹ 40 when market price is ₹ 130)			
01.01.2013	Bank A/c	Dr.	7,20,000	
15.03.2012	Employees stock option outstanding A/c	Dr.	16,20,000	
	To Equity share capital A/c			1,80,000
	To Securities premium A/c			21,60,000
	(Being allotment to employees 18,000 equity shares of ₹ 10 each at a premium of ₹ 120 per share in exercise of their stock options)			
16.03.2013	Employees stock option outstanding A/c	Dr.	1,80,000	
	To Employees compensation expense A/c			1,80,000
	(Being entry for lapse of stock options for 2,000 shares)			
31.03.2013	Profit & Loss A/c	Dr.	16,20,000	
	To Employees compensation expense A/c			16,20,000
	(Being transfer of employees compensation expense to profit & loss account)			

PROBLEM 3

A company has its share capital divided into shares of ₹ 10 each. On 1-4-2012, it granted 5,000 employees stock option at ₹ 50, when the market price was ₹ 140. The options were to be exercised between 1-12-2012 to 28-2-2013. The employees exercised their options for 4,800 shares only; remaining options lapsed. Pass the necessary journal entries for the year ended 31-3-2013, with regard to employees' stock option. *[CA (IPCC) Nov., 2011]*

Solution

JOURNAL

Date	Particulars		Dr. (₹)	Cr. (₹)
01.04.2012	Employees compensation expenses A/c [₹ 5,000 × (140 – 50)]	Dr.	4,50,000	
	To Employees Stock Option outstanding A/c			4,50,000
	(Being grant of 5,000 ESOPs to employees @ ₹ 50 when market price was ₹ 140)			
01.12.2012	Bank A/c	Dr.	2,40,000	
to	Employees Stock Option Outstanding A/c	Dr	4,32,000	
28.02.2013	To Equity share capital A/c			48,000
	To Securities premium A/c			6,24,000
	(Being allotment to employees 4,800 shares of ₹ 10 each at a premium of ₹ 130 at an exercise price of ₹ 50 each)			
31.03.2013	Employees Stock Option Outstanding A/c	Dr	18,000	
	To Employees compensation expenses A/c			18,000
	(Being reverse entry for lapse of 200 stock options)			
31.03.2013	Profit and Loss A/c	Dr.	4,32,000	
	To Employees compensation expenses A/c			4,32,000
	(Being transfer of employees compensation expenses)			

PROBLEM 4

On 1st April, 2011, a company offered 100 shares to each to its 400 employees ₹ 25 per share. The employees are given a month to accept the shares. The shares issued under the plan shall be subject to lock-in to transfer for three years from the grant data i.e., 30, April 2013. The market price of share of the company on the grant date is ₹ 30 per share. Due to post-vesting restrictions on transfer, the fair value of shares issued under the plan is estimated at ₹ 28 per share.

Up to 30th April, 2013, 50% of employees accepted the offer and paid ₹ 25 per share purchased. Normal value of each share is ₹ 10. Record the issue of shares in the books of the company under the aforesaid plan. *[May 2012]*

Solution

Fair Value of an option = ₹ 28 – ₹ 25 = ₹ 3

Number of employees accepting the offer = 400 employees × 50% = 200 employees

Number of shares issued = 200 employees × 100 shares/employee = 20,000 shares

Fair value of ESPP = 20,000 shares × ₹ 3 = ₹ 60,000

Expenses recognized in 2013-14 = ₹ 60,000

JOURNAL

Date	*Particulars*		*Dr. (₹)*	*Cr. (₹)*
30.04.2013	Bank (20,000 shares × ₹ 25)	Dr.	5,00,000	
	Employees Compensation Expense A/c	Dr.	60,000	
	To Share Capital A/c (20,000 shares × ₹ 10)			2,00,000
	To Securities Premium A/c (20,000 shares × ₹ 18)			3,60,000
	(Being the options accepted by 200 employees)			

LONG ANSWER PRACTICAL QUESTIONS

PROBLEM 5

S Ltd. grants 1,000 options to its employees on 1.4.2010 at ₹ 60. The vesting period is two and a half years. The maximum period is one year. Market price on that date is ₹ 90. All the options were exercised on 31.7.2013. Journalize, if the face value of equity share is ₹ 10 per share.

[CA (PEII) June 2009]

Solution

JOURNAL OF S LTD.

Date	Particulars		Dr. (₹)	Cr. (₹)
31.3.11	Employees Compensation Expense A/c	Dr.	12,000	
	To Employees Stock Option Outstanding A/c			12,000
	(Being compensation expense recognized in respect of 1,000 options granted to employees at discount of ₹ 30 each, amortized on straight line basis over 2½ years)			
	Profit and Loss A/c	Dr.	12,000	
	To Employees Compensation Expense A/c			12,000
	(Being employees compensation expense of the year transferred to P&L A/c)			
31.3.12	Employees Compensation Expense A/c	Dr.	12,000	
	To Employees Stock Option Outstanding A/c			12,000
	(Being compensation expense recognized in respect of 1,000 options granted to employees at discount of ₹ 30 each, amortized on straight line basis over 2½ years)			
	Profit and Loss A/c	Dr.	12,000	
	To Employees Compensation Expense Account			12,000
	(Being employees compensation expense of the year transferred to P&L A/c)			
31.3.13	Employees Compensation Expense A/c	Dr.	6,000	
	To Employees Stock Option Outstanding A/c			6,000
	(Being balance of compensation expense amortized ₹ 30,000 *less* ₹ 24,000)			
	Profit and Loss A/c	Dr.	6,000	
	To Employees Compensation Expense A/c			6,000
	(Being employees compensation expense of the year transferred to P&L A/c)			
31.7.13	Bank A/c (₹ 60 x 1,000)	Dr.	60,000	
	Employees Stock Option Outstanding A/c (₹ 30 × 1,000)	Dr.	30,000	
	To Equity Share Capital A/c			10,000
	To Securities Premium A/c			80,000
	(Being exercise of 1,000 options at an exercise price of ₹ 60 each and an accounting value of ₹.30 each)			

Working Notes:

(i) Total Employees Compensation Expense = 1,000 × (₹ 90 – ₹ 60) = ₹ 30,000

(ii) Employees Compensation Expense has been written off during 2½ years on straight line basis as under:

I year = ₹ 12,000 (for full year)

II year = ₹ 12,000 (for full year)

III year = ₹ 6,000 (for half year)

4 Accounting for Buy-Back of Shares

LONG ANSWER PRACTICAL QUESTIONS

PROBLEM 1

KG Limited furnishes the following Balance Sheet as at 31st March, 2013.

Liabilities	*(₹ in lakhs)*	*Assets*	*(₹ in lakhs)*
Equity Share Capital (fully paid up shares of ₹ 10 each)	1,200	Machinery	1,800
		Furniture	226
Securities Premium	175	Investments	74
General Reserve	265	Stock	600
Capital Redemption reserve	200	Debtors	260
Profit & Loss A/c	170	Cash at bank	740
12% Debentures	750		
Sundry Creditors	745		
Other Current Liabilities	195		
	3,700		3,700

On 1st April, 2013, the company announced the buy back of 25% of its equity shares @ ₹ 15 per share. For this purpose, it sold all of its investments for ₹ 75 lakhs. On 5th April, 2013, the company achieved the target of buy back. On 30th April, 2013 the company issued one fully paid up equity share of ₹ 10 by way of bonus for every four equity shares held by the equity shareholders.

You are required to:

1. Pass necessary journal entries for the above transactions.
2. Prepare Balance Sheet of KG Limited after bonus issue of the shares.

[CA (PCC) Nov. 2010]

Solution

JOURNAL *[₹ in lakhs]*

Date	Particulars		Dr. (₹)	Cr. (₹)
01.04.13	Bank A/c	Dr.	75	
	To Investment A/c			74
	To Profit on sale of Investment A/c			1
	(Being investment sold on profit)			
05.04.13	Equity Shares Buy back A/c	Dr.	450	
	To Bank A/c			450
	(Being the payment made on account of buy back)			
	Equity Share Capital A/c	Dr.	300	
	Premium payable on buy back A/c	Dr.	150	
	To Equity shares buy back A/c			450
	(Being the amount due to equity shareholders on buy back)			

Date	Particulars		Dr. (₹)	Cr. (₹)
05.04.13	General Reserve A/c	Dr.	265	
	Profit and Loss A/c	Dr.	35	
	To Capital Redemption Reserve A/c			300
	(Being amount equal to nominal value of buy back shares from free reserves transferred to capital re demption reserve account as per the law)			
30.04.13	Capital Redemption Reserve A/c	Dr.	225	
	To Bonus Shares A/c			225
	(Being the utilization of capital redemption reserve to issue bonus shares)			
	Bonus Shares A/c	Dr.	225	
	To Equity Share Capital A/c			225
	(Being issue of one bonus equity share for every four equity shares held)			
	Securities Premium A/c	Dr.	150	
	To Premium payable on buy back A/c			150
	(Being premium payable on buy back adjusted from securities premium account)			

BALANCE SHEET OF KG LTD. AS AT 31.3.2013

Particulars	Note No	₹ (lacs)
I. Equity and Liabilities		
(1) Shareholders' Funds		
(a) Share Capital (₹ *10 each*)		1125
(b) Reserves and Surplus	1	436
(2) Non-Current Liabilities[12 % Debentures]		750
(3) Current Liabilities		
(a) Trade Payables[Creditors]		745
(b) Other Current Liabilities		195
Total		3251
II. Assets		
(1) Non-Current Assets		
(a) Fixed Assets		
Tangible Assets	2	2026
(2) Current Assets		
(a) Inventories		600
(b) Trade Receivables [Debtors]		260
(c) Cash and Cash Equivalents		365
Total		3251

Notes To Accounts :

Particulars	₹ (lacs)
1. Reserves and Surplus	
Capital Redemption Reserve [200 + 300 – 225]	275
Profit & Loss Account [170 + 1 – 35]	136
Securities Premium [175 – 50]	25
Total	436
2. Tangible Assets	
Plant & Machinery	1800
Furniture	226
	2026

Working Notes:

(i) Amount of bonus shares = 25% of (1,200 – 300) lakhs = ₹ 225 lakhs

(ii) Cash at Bank after issue of bonus shares

(₹ in lakhs)

Cash Balance (given)	740
Add: Sale of Investments	75
	815
Less: Payment for buy back of shares	(450)
	365

PROBLEM 2

Following is the Balance Sheet of M/S competent Limited as on 31st March, 2013:

Liabilities	₹	*Assets*	₹
Equity Shares of ₹ 10 Each)	12,50,000	Fixed Assets	46,50,000
Revenue reserve	15,00,000		
Securities Premium	2,50,000		
Profit & Loss Account	1,25,000		
Secured Loans:			
12% Debentures	18,75,000		
Unsecured Loans	10,00,000		
Current Liabilities	16,50,000		
	76,50,000		76,50,000

The company wants to buy back 25,000 equity shares of ₹ 10 each, on 1st April, 2013 at ₹ 20 per share. Buy back of shares is duly authorized by its articles and necessary resolution passed by the company towards this. The payment of buy back of shares will be made by the company out of sufficient back balance available as part of Current Assets.

Comment with your calculations, whether buy back of shares by company is within the provision of the companies Act, 1956. If you pass necessary journal entries towards buy back of shares and prepare of Balance Sheet after buy back of shares. *[May 2012]*

Solution

(a) Determination of Buy back of maximum no. of shares as per the companies Act, 1956

1. Outstanding Shares Test = Max No. of shares that can be bought back
   25% of the outstanding Shares = 25% of 1,25,000 = 31,250
2. Resources Test = Max. No of shares that can be bought back
   = 25% of Shareholders' Fund/Buy back price per share
   = [25% (12.50 + 15 + 2.50 + 1.25)]/20 = 39,063
3. Debt Equity Ratio Test

Loan funds (₹) (18,75,000 + 10,00,000 + 16,50,000)	₹ 45,25,000
Minimum equity to be maintained after buy back [45,25,000/2]	₹ 22,62,500
Present Equity	₹ 31,25,000
Maximum permitted buy back of Equity (₹) [31,25,000 – 22,62,500]	8,62,500
Maximum number of shares that can be bough back [8,62,500/₹ 20]	43,125 shares

Hence, Company qualifies all test for buy-back of shares and come to the conclusion that it can buy maximum 31,250 shares (being the least in 3 Tests) as per Sec. 77A.

However, company wants to buy-back only 25,000 equity shares @₹ 20. Therefore buy-back of 25,000 shares, as desired by the company is within the provisions of the Companies Act, 1956.

JOURNAL

Date	Particulars		Dr. (₹)	Cr. (₹)
(a)	Equity Shares buy-back A/c	Dr.	5,00,000	
	To Bank A/c			5,00,000
	(Being buy back of 25,000 equity shares of ₹ 10 each @ ₹ 20 per share)			
(b)	Equity Share Capital A/c	Dr.	2,50,000	
	Securities Premium A/c	Dr.	2,50,000	
	To Equity Shares buy-back A/c			5,00,000
	(Being cancellation of shares bought back)			
(c)	Revenue Reserve A/c	Dr.	2,50,000	
	To Capital Redemption Reserve A/c			2,50,000
	(Being transfer of free reserves to capital redemption reserve to the extent of nominal value of capital bought back through free reserves)			

BALANCE SHEET OF M/S COMPETENT LTD. AS AT 31.3.2013

Particulars	Note No	₹ (lacs)
I. Equity and Liabilities		
(1) Shareholders' Funds		
(a) Share Capital (*₹ 10 each*)		10.00
(b) Reserves and Surplus	1	16.25
(2) Non-Current Liabilities		
(a) Long-term Borrowings	2	28.75
(3) Current Liabilities		16.50
Total		71.50
II. Assets		
(1) Non-Current Assets		
(a) Fixed Assets		46.50
(2) Current Assets [30 – 5]		25.00
Total		71.50

Notes To Accounts:

Particulars	₹
1. Reserves and Surplus	
Revenue Reserves	12.50
Capital Redemption Reserve	2.50
Profit & Loss Account	1.25
Total	16.25
2. Long-term Borrowings	
12% Debentures [Secured]	18.75
Unsecured Loan	10.00
	28.75

Note: Revaluation reserve account, Securities premium account and Profit and Loss account are considered as free reserves in total.

PROBLEM 3

Dee Limited furnishes the following Balance Sheet as at 31st March, 2013.

	₹ '000	₹ '000
Liabilities		
Share Capital:		
Authorised Capital		30,00
Issued and subscribed Capital:		
2,50,000 Equity Shares of ₹.10 each fully paid up	25,00	
2,000, 10% Preference Shares of ₹ 100 each (Issued two months back for the purpose of buy back)	2.00	27,00
Reserves and Surplus:		
Capital Reserve	10,00	
Revenue Reserve	30,00	
Securities premium	22,00	
Profit and loss account	35,00	97,00
Current liabilities and provisions:		14,00
		1,38,00
Assets		
Fixed assets		93,00
Investments		30,00
Current assets, Loans and Advances (including Cash and Bank Balance)		15,00
		1,38,00

The company passed a resolution to buy back 20% of its equity capital @ ₹ 50 per share. For this purpose, it sold all of its investments for ₹ 22,00,000. You are required to pass necessary journal entries and prepare the Balance Sheet. *[CA (IPCC) Nov. 2009]*

Solution

JOURNAL OF DEE LIMITED

(₹ in '000)

Date	Particulars		Dr.	Cr.
(i)	Bank A/c	Dr.	22,00	
	Profit & Loss A/c	Dr.	8,00	
	To Investment A/c			30,00
	(Being the investments sold at loss for the purpose of buy back)			
(ii)	Equity Share Capital A/c	Dr.	5,00	
	Premium payable on buy back A/c	Dr.	20,00	
	To Equity Shares Buy Back A/c			25,00
	(Being the amount due on buy back)			
(iii)	Securities Premium A/c	Dr.	20,00	
	To Premium payable on buy back A/c			20,00
	(Being the premium payable on buy back adjusted against securities premium account)			
(iv)	Revenue Reserve A/c	Dr.	3,00	
	To Capital Redemption Reserve A/c			3,00
	(Being the amount equal to nominal value of equity share bought back out of free reserves transferred to Capital Redemption Reserve Account)			
(v)	Equity Shares buy-back A/c	Dr.	25,00	
	To Bank A/c			25,00
	(Being the payment made on buy back)			

Note: *Alternatively, 'Securities Premium' account may also be used for transfer to 'Capital Redemption Reserve Account.'

BALANCE SHEET OF DEE LTD. AS AT 31.3.2013

Particulars	Note No	₹ '000
I. Equity and Liabilities		
(1) Shareholders' Funds		
(a) Share Capital	1	22,00
(b) Reserves and Surplus	2	69,00
(2) Non-Current Liabilities		
(3) Current Liabilities		14,00
Total		105,00
II. Assets		
(1) Non-Current Assets		
(a) Fixed Assets		
Tangible Assets		93,00
(2) Current Assets [15,00 + 22,00 − 25,00]		12,00
Total		105,00

Notes To Accounts :

Particulars	₹ '000
1. Share Capital	
200000 Equity Shares of ₹ 10 each	20,00
2000, 10% Pref. Shares of ₹ 100 each	2,00
	22,00
2. Reserves and Surplus	
Revenue Reserve	29,00
Capital Reserve	10,00
Capital Redemption Reserve	3,00
Profit & Loss Account [35,00 – 8,00]	27,00
Total	69,00

5 Underwriting of Shares and Debentures

PROBLEM 1

Noman Ltd. issued 80,000 Equity Shares which were underwritten as follows:
A 48,000 Equity Shares, *B* 20,000 Equity Shares, *C* 12,000 Equity Shares

The above mentioned underwriters made applications for 'firm' underwritings as follows:
A 6,400 Equity Shares, *B* 8,000 Equity Shares, *C* 2,400 Equity Shares

The total applications excluding 'firm' underwriting, but including marked applications were for 40,000 Equity Shares.
The Marked Applications were as under:
A 8,000 Equity Shares, *B* 10,000 Equity Shares, *C* 4,000 Equity Shares

(The underwriting contracts provide that underwriters be given credit for 'firm' applications and that credit for unmarked applications be given in proportion to the shares underwritten)
You are required to show the allocation of liability. ***[CA, (Nov. 1997)]***

Solution

STATEMENT SHOWING THE LIABILITY OF UNDERWRITERS

Particulars	*A*	*B*	*C*	*Total*
Gross Liability (No. of Shares)	48,000	20,000	12,000	80,000
Unmarked Applications* (Ratio 48 : 20 : 12)	(10,800)	(4,500)	(2,700)	(18,000)
	37,200	15,500	9,300	62,000
Less: Marked Applications	(8,000)	(10,000)	(4,000)	(22,000)
	29,200	5,500	5,300	40,000
Less: Firm Underwriting	(6,400)	(8,000)	(2,400)	(16,800)
Balance to be taken under the contract	22,800	(2,500)	2,900	23,200
Credit for excess of B & Co. (ratio 48 : 12)	(2,000)	2,500	(500)	—
Net Liability	20,800	—	2,400	23,200
Add: Firm Underwriting	6,400	8,000	2,400	16,800
Total Liability	27,200	8,000	4,800	40,000

Working Note:
Unmarked applications = Total Applications – Marked Applications = 40,000 – 22,000 = 18,000

PROBLEM 2

CAMJA Ltd resolved to issue 10 lakh equity shares of ₹ 10 each at a premium of Re 1 per share. One lakh of these shares were taken up by the directors of the company, their relatives, associates and friends, the entire amount being received forthwith. The remaining shares were offered to the public, the entire amount being asked for with applications.

The issue was underwritten by *X*, *Y* and *Z* for a commission @2% of the issue price, 65% of the issue was underwritten by *X*, while *Y*'s and *Z*'s shares were 25% and 10% respectively. Their firm underwriting was as follows:

X 30,000 shares, *Y* 20,000 shares and *Z* 10,000 shares. The underwriters were to submit unmarked applications for shares underwritten firm with full application money along with members of the general public.

marked applications were as follows:

X 1,19,500 shares, *Y* 57,500 shares and *Z* 10,500 shares.

Unmarked applications totalled 7,00,000 shares.

Accounts with the underwriters were promptly settled.

You are required to:

(i) Prepare a statement calculating underwriters' liability for shares other than shares underwriten firm.

(ii) Pass journal entries for all the transactions including cash transactions.

[CA (May 2001)]

Solution

(I) STATEMENT SHOWING UNDERWRITERS' LIABILITY FOR SHARES OTHER THAN SHARES UNDERWRITTEN FIRM

Particulars	*X*	*Y*	*Z*	*Total*
Gross liability (9,00,000 shares in the ratio of 65 : 25 : 10)	5,85,000	2,25,000	90,000	9,00,000
Less: Marked applications	(1,19,500)	(57,500)	(10,500)	(1,87,500)
Balance	4,65,500	1,67,500	79,500	7,12,500
Less: Allocation of unmarked applications (including firm underwriting i.e. 7,00,000) in the ratio 65 : 25 : 10	(4,55,000)	(1,75,000)	(70,000)	(7,00,000)
Balance	10,500	(7,500)	9,500	12,500
Surplus of *Y* allocated to *X* and *Z* in the ratio 65 : 10	(6,500)	7,500	(1,000)	—
Balance	4,000	—	8,500	12,500
	₹	₹	₹	
Liability amount @ ₹ 11	44,000		93,500	
Underwriting commission payable (Gross liability × ₹ 11 × 2%)	1,28,700	49,500	19,800	
Net Amount payable	84,700	49,500		
Net Amount receivable			73,700	

JOURNAL

Date	*Particulars*	*L.F.*	*Dr. (₹)*	*Cr. (₹)*
	Bank A/c Dr.		11,00,000	
	To Equity Share Application A/c			11,00,000
	(Being application money received on 1 lakh equity shares @ ₹ 11 per share)			
	Bank A/c Dr		97,62,500	
	To Equity Share Application A/c			97,62,500
	(Application money received on 8,87,500 equity shares @ ₹ 11 per share from general public and underwriters for shares underwritten firm)			

Date	Particulars		L.F.	Dr. (₹)	Cr. (₹)
	Equity Share Application A/c	Dr.		1,08,62,500	
	X's A/c	Dr.		44,000	
	Z's A/c	Dr.		93,500	
	To Equity Share Capital A/c				1,00,00,000
	To Securities Premium A/c				10,00,000
	(Allotment of 10 lakh equity shares of ₹ 10 each at a premium of Re 1 per share)				
	Underwritting Commission A/c	Dr.		1,98,000	
	To X's A/c				1,28,700
	To Y's A/c				49,500
	To Z's A/c				19,800
	(Amount of underwriting commission payable to X, Y and Z @ 2% on the amount of shares underwritten)				
	Bank A/c	Dr.		73,700	
	To Z's A/c				73,700
	(Amount received from Z in final settlement)				
	X's A/c	Dr.		84,700	
	Y's A/c	Dr.		49,500	
	To Bank A/c				1,34,200
	(Amount paid to X and Y in final settlement)				

PROBLEM 3

Scorpio Ltd. came out with an issue of 45,00,000 equity shares of ₹ 10 each at a premium of ₹ 2 per share. The promoters took 20% of the issue and the balance was offered to the public. The issue was equally underwritten by A & Co; B & Co. and C & Co. Each underwriter took firm underwriting of 1,00,000 shares each. Subscriptions for 31,00,000 equity shares were received with marked forms for the underwriters as given below:

A & Co.		7,25,000	shares
B & Co.		8,40,000	shares
C & Co.		13,10,000	shares
	Total	28,75,000	shares

The underwriters are eligible for a commission of 5% on face value of shares. The entire amount towards shares subscription has to be paid alongwith application. You are required to:

(a) Compute the underwriters liability (number of shares)

(b) Compute the amount payable or due to underwriters; and

(c) Pass necessary journal entries in the books of Scorpio Ltd. relating to underwriting.

[CA(PE-II) Nov. 2005]

Solution

(a) COMPUTATION OF UNDERWRITERS' LIABILITY OF (NUMBER OF SHARES)

Particulars	A & Co.	B & Co.	C & Co.
A Gross Liability	12,00,000	12,00,000	12,00,000
B *Less:* Marked applications	(7,25,000)	(8,40,000)	(13,10,000)
C *Less:* Unmarked applications distributed to A & Co. and B & Co. in equal ratio	(1,12,500)	(1,12,500)	Nil
D *Less:* Firm Underwriting	(1,00,000)	(1,00,000)	(1,00,000)

Particulars	A & Co.	B & Co.	C & Co.
E Balance	2,62,500	1,47,500	(2,10,000)
F *Less:* Surplus of C & Co. distributed to A & Co. and B & Co. in equal ratio	(1,05,000)	(1,05,000)	2,10,000
G Net Liability (excluding firm underwriting)	1,57,500	42,500	Nil
H *Add:* Firm Underwriting	1,00,000	1,00,000	1,00,000
I Total Liability (number of shares)	2,57,500	1,42,500	1,00,000

(B) COMPUTATION OF AMOUNTS PAYABLE BY UNDERWRITERS

Particulars	₹	₹	₹
Liability towards shares to be subscribed @ 12 per share	30,90,000	17,10,000	12,00,000
Less: Commission (5% on 12 lakhs shares @ 10 each)	(6,00,000)	(6,00,000)	(6,00,000)
Net Amount to be paid by underwriters	24,90,000	11,10,000	6,00,000

(C) JOURNAL OF SCORPIO LTD.

Date	Particulars		L.F.	Dr. (₹)	Cr. (₹)
	Underwriting commission A/c	Dr.		18,00,000	
	To A & Co. A/c				6,00,000
	To B & Co. A/c				6,00,000
	To C & Co. A/c				6,00,000
	(Being underwriting commission on the shares underwritten)				
	A & Co. A/c	Dr.		30,90,000	
	B & Co. A/c	Dr.		17,10,000	
	C & Co. A/c	Dr.		12,00,000	
	To Equity Share Capital A/c				50,00,000
	To Securities Premium A/c				10,00,000
	(Being shares including firm underwritten shares allotted to underwriters)				
	Bank A/c	Dr.		42,00,000	
	To A & Co. A/c				24,90,000
	To B & Co. A/c				11,10,000
	To C & Co. A/c				6,00,000
	(Being the amount received towards shares allotted to underwrittens less underwriting commission due to them)				

PROBLEM 4

Albert Ltd. issued 50,00,000 Equity shares of ₹.10 each. The whole issue was underwritten by A, B and C as below:

A 15,00,000 shares; *B* 25,00,000 shares; *C* 10,00,000 shares

Applications were received for 48,50,000 shares of which the marked applications were as follows:

A 12,00,000 shares, *B* 25,00,000 shares, *C* 8,50,000 shares

Calculate the number of shares to be taken up by the underwriters. **[CA (PCE) May 2008]**

Solution

NUMBER OF SHARES TO BE TAKEN UP BY UNDERWRITERS

	A	*B*	*C*
Gross Liability (3:5:2)	15,00,000	25,00,000	10,00,000
Less: Marked applications	12,00,000	25,00,000	8,50,000
	3,00,000	Nil	1,50,000
Less: Unmarked applications. in 3:5:2 ratio	90,000	1,50,000	60,000
	2,10,000	(1,50,000)	90,000
Less: Surplus of B allocated to A & C in 3:2 ratio	90,000	1,50,000	60,000
Number of shares to be taken up by the underwriters	1,20,000	Nil	30,000

PROBLEM 5

Consider the following data pertaining to three underwriters, Ajay, Samay and Vijay:

Particulars	*Ajay*	*Samay*	*Vijay*
Shares underwritten	8,000	16,000	24,000
Marked application	6,000	8,000	11,000

If total applications received are for 44,800 shares, compute the final liability of Vijay.

[CA (PCE) Nov 2008]

Solution

NUMBER OF SHARES TO BE TAKEN UP BY UNDERWRITERS

Particulars	*Ajay*	*Samay*	*Vijay*	*Total*
Shares underwritten	8,000	16,000	24,000	48,000
Less: 19,800. Unmarked applications (in the ratio 1:2:3)	3,300	6,600	9,900	19,800
	4,700	9,400	14,100	28,200
Less: Marked applications	6,000	8,000	11,000	25,000
	(1,300)	1,400	3,100	3,200
Less: Surplus of Ajay's share (in the ratio 2:3)	1,300	520	780	Nil
Final liability	Nil	880	2,320	3,200

PROBLEM 6

'*X*' Ltd., issued 1,00,000 equality shares of ₹ 10 each at par. The entire issue was underwritten as follows:

A – 60,000 shares (Firm underwriting 8,000 shares)

B – 30,000 shares (Firm underwriting 10,000 shares)

C – 10,000 shares (Firm underwriting 2,000 shares)

The total applications including firm underwriting were for 80,000 shares.

The marked applications were as follows:

A- 20,000 shares; B- 14,000 shares: C- 6,000 shares.

The underwriting contract provides that credit for unmarked applications be qiven to the underwriters in proportion to the shares underwritten. Determine the liability of each underwriter.

[*CA (PE-II) Nov. 2009*]

Soltuion

STATEMENT SHOWING LIABILITY OF UNDERWRITERS

Particulars	No. of shares			
	A	*B*	*C*	*Total*
Gross Liability	60,000	30,000	10,000	1,00,000
Less: Firm Underwriting	(8,000)	(10,000)	(2,000)	(20,000)
Less: Marked Applications	(20,000)	(14,000)	(6,000)	(40,000)
	32,000	6,000	2,000	40,000
Less: Unmarked applications (total application *less* firm underwriting *less* marked applications) in gross liability ratio (i.e. 80,000 – 20,000 – 40,000)	(12,000)	(6,000)	(2,000)	(20,000)
Net Liability	20,000	—	—	20,000
Add: Firm Underwriting	8,000	10,000	2,000	20,000
Total Liability of Underwriters	28,000	10,000	2,000	40,000

Note: *The solution is given on the basis that 'the benefit of firm underwriting is given to individual underwriters.'*

PROBLEM 7

Chaitanya Limited issues 40,000 shares. Issue is underwritten by *A*, *B* and *C* in the ratio of 5 : 3 : 2 respectively. Unmarked applications totalled 2,000 whereas marked applications are as follows:

Underwriters	*Application (Number of Shares)*
A	16,000
B	5,700
C	8,300

Calculate the net liability of each one of the underwriters. **[*CA (IPCC) May 2010*]**

Solution

SATEMENT SHOWING THE LIABILITY OF UNDERWIRTERS

Particulars	*A*	*B*	*C*	*Total*
Gross Liability	20,000	12,000	8,000	40,000
Less: Unmarked application in the ratio of 5:3:2	(1,000)	(600)	(400)	(2,000)
	19,000	11,400	7,600	38,000
Less: Marked Applications	(16,000)	(5,700)	(8,300)	(30,000)

Particulars	A	B	C	Total
	3,000	5,700	(700)	8,000
Credit of *C*'s surplus to *A* and *B* in the ratio of 5:3	(438)	(262)	700	—
Net Liability	2,562	5,438	—	8,000

PROBLEM 8

Rising Sun Limited came up with an issue of 25,00,000 Equity shares of ₹ 10 each at par. 4,00,000 shares were issued to the promoters and balance offered to the public. Issue was underwritten by three underwriters A & Co., B & Co., and C & Co., equally, with firm underwriting of 1,00,000 shares each. Subscription totalled 17,26,000 shares, including the marked forms which were as under:

A&Co. 5,1 8,000 Shares
B&Co. 5,50,000 Shares
C&Co. 4,72,000 Shares

The underwriters had applied for the number of shares covered by firm underwriting. The amount payable on application and allotment were ₹ 3 & ₹ 2 respectively. The agreed commission is 3%.

You are required to calculate:

(i) The liability of each underwriter.

(ii) The amount payable and/or receivable by the underwriter. *[CA (PCC) May 2011]*

Solution

(I) CALCULATION OF LIABILITY OF UNDERWRITERS (IN SHARES)

	A&Co.	B&Co.	C& Co.	Total
Gross Liability	7,00,000	7,00,000	7,00,000	21,00,000
Less: Firm Underwriting	(1,00,000)	(1,00,000)	(1,00,000)	(3,00,000)
	6,00,000	6,00,000	6,00,000	18,00,000
Less: Marked applications	(5,18,000)	(5,50,000)	(4,72,000)	(15,40,000)
	82,000	50,000	1,28,000	2,60,000
Less: Unmarked applications 1/3 of (17,26,000 – 15,40,000)	(62,000)	(62,000)	(62,000)	(1,86,000)
	20,000	(12,000)	66,000	74,000
Adjustment of B & Co.'s Surplus in 1:1	(6,000)	12,000	(6,000)	—
Liability excluding the firm underwriting	14,000	—	60,000	74,000
Add: Firm Underwriting	1,00,000	1,00,000	1,00,000	3,00,000
Total liability	1,14,000	1,00,000	1,60,000	3,74,000

(II) CALCULATION OF AMOUNT PAYABLE/RECEIVABLE BY THE UNDERWRITERS

Total liability (No. of shares)	*1,14,000* ₹	*1,00,000* ₹	*1,60,000* ₹
Amount payable @ ₹ 5 (i.e. 3 + 2) per share	5,70,000	5,00,000	8,00,000
Less: Amount paid on firm application @ ₹ 3 per share	(3,00,000)	(3,00,000)	(3,00,000)
Balance payable	2,70,000	2,00,000	5,00,000
Underwriting Commission receivable (7,00,000x10x3%)	(2,10,000)	(2,10,000)	(2,10,000)
Amount payable/(receivable)	60,000	(10,000)	2,90,000

PROBLEM 9

Delta Ltd. issued 25,00,000 equity shares of ₹ 10 each at par. 7,00,000 shares were issued to the promoters and the balance offered to the public was underwritten by three underwriters P, Q & R in the ratio of 2 : 3 : 4 with firm underwriting of 50,000, 60,000 and 70,000 shares each respectively. Total subscription received for 3,88,000 shares including marked application and excluding firm underwriting. Marked applications were as follows:

P	3,00,000
Q	3,50,000
R	4,50,000

Unmarked and surplus applications to be distributed in gross liability ratio.

Required: Ascertain the liability of each underwriter. *[CA (IPCC) May 2011]*

Solution

CALCULATION OF LIABILITY OF UNDERWRITERS (IN SHARES)

Particulars	*P*	*Q*	*R*	*Total*
Gross liability	4,00,000	6,00,000	8,00,000	18,00,000
Less: Firm underwriting	(50,000)	(60,000)	(70,000)	(1,80,000)
	3,50,000	5,40,000	7,30,000	16,20,000
Less: Marked applications received	(3,00,000)	(3,50,000)	(4,50,000)	(11,00,000)
	50,000	1,90,000	2,80,000	5,20,000
Less: Unmarked applications (In gross liability ratio 4 : 6 : 8)	(64,000)	(96,000)	(1,28,000)	(2,88,000)
Balance	(14,000)	94,000	1,52,000	2,32,000
Excess of P distributed to Q & R in ratio (3 : 4)	14,000	(6,000)	(8,000)	—
Net liability (other than firm underwriting)	—	88,000	1,44,000	2,32,000
Add: Firm underwriting	50,000	60,000	70,000	1,80,000
Total liability of underwriters including firm underwriting	50,000	1,48,000	2,14,000	4,12,000
Total liability in amount @ ₹ 10 each	₹ 5,00,000	₹ 14,80,000	₹ 21,40,000	₹ 41,20,000

PROBLEM 10

ABC Ltd. came up with public issue of 3,00,000 Equity Shares of ₹ 10 each ₹ 15 per share. P, Q and R took underwriting of the issue in ratio of 3 : 2 : 1 with the provisions of firm underwriting of 20,000, 14,000 and 10,000 shares respectively.

Applications were received for 2,40,000 shares excluding firm underwriting. The marked applications from public were received as under:

P - 60,000; Q-50,000; R-60,000

Compute the liability of each underwriter as regards the number of shares to be taken up assuming that the benefit of firm underwriting is not given to individual underwriters.

[CA (IPCC) Nov. 2012]

Solution

CALCULATION OF LIABILITY OF EACH UNDERWRITER (IN NO. OF SHARES) ASSUMING THAT THE BENEFIT OF FIRM UNDERWRITING IS NOT GIVEN TO INDIVIDUAL UNDERWRITERS

Particulars	*P*	*Q*	*R*	*Total*
Gross Liability	1,50,000	1,00,000	50,000	3,00,000
Less: Marked Applications (excluding firm underwriting)	(60,000)	(50,000)	(60,000)	(1,70,000)
Balance	90,000	50,000	(10,000)	1,30,000
Less: Surplus of R allocated to P and Q in the ratio of 3.2	(6,000)	(4,000)	10,000	
Balance	84,000	46,000	–	1,30,000
Less: Unmarked applications including firm underwriting (Refer W.N.)	(57,000)	(38,000)	(19,000)	(1,14,000)
Net Liability	27,000	8,000	(19,000)	16,000
Less: Surplus of R allocated to P and Q in the ratio of 3 : 2	(11,400)	(7,600)	19,000	
	15,600	400	–	16,000
Add: Firm underwriting	20,000	14,000	10,000	44,000
Total Liability	35,600	14,400	10,000	60,000

Working Note:

A. Applications received from public	2,40,000
B. *Add:* Shares underwritten firm (20,000 + 14,000 + 10,000)	44,000
C. Total Applciations [A + B]	2,84,000
D. *Less:* Marked applications (60,000 + 50,000 + 60,000)	(1,70,000)
E. Unmarked applications including firm underwriting [C – D]	1,14,000

PROBLEM 11

A company issued 1,50,000 shares of ₹ 10 each at a premium of ₹ 10. The entire issue was underwritten as follows:

X – 90,000 shares (Firm underwriting 12,000 shares)
Y – 37,500 shares (Firm underwriting 4,500 shares)
Z – 22,500 shares (Firm underwriting 15,000 shares)

Total applications received by the company (excluding firm underwriting and marked applications) were 22,500 shares.

The marked applications (excluding firm underwriting) were as follows:
X- 15,000 shares; Y- 30,000 shares: Z- 7,500 shares.

Commission payable to underwriters is at 5% of the issue price. The underwriting contract provides that credit for unmarked applications be given to the underwriters in proportion to the shares underwritten and benefit of firm underwiriting is to be given to individual underwriters.

(i) Determine the liability of each underwriter (number of shares)
(ii) Compute the amount payable or due to underwriters; and
(iii) Pass necessary journal entries in the books of co. relating to underwriting.

[CA (IPCC) May 2013]

Solution

COMPUTATION OF UNDERWRITERS' LIABILITY (NUMBER OF SHARES)

Particulars	X	Y	Z
A Gross Liability	90,000	37,500	22,500
B *Less:* Marked applications	(15,000)	(30,000)	(7,500)
C *Less:* Unmarked applications in ratio of 12:5:3	(13,500)	(5,625)	3,375
D *Less:* Firm Underwriting	(12,000)	(4,500)	(15,000)
E Balance	49,500	(2,625)	(3,375)
F *Less:* Surplus of Y & Z distributed to X	(6,000)	2,625	3,375
G Net Liability (excluding firm underwriting)	43,500	Nil	Nil
H *Add:* Firm Underwriting	12,000	4,500	15,000
I Total Liability (number of shares)	55,500	4,500	15,000

(b) COMPUTATION OF AMOUNTS PAYABLE BY UNDERWRITERS

Particulars	₹	₹	₹
Liability towards shares to be subscribed @ 20 per share	11,10,000	90,000	3,00,000
Less: Commission @ 5% on 1,50,000 shares @ ₹ 20	(90,000)	(37,500)	(22,500)
Net Amount to be paid by Underwriters	10,20,000	52,500	2,77,500

(c) JOURNAL OF THE COMPANY

Date	Particulars	L.F.	Dr. (₹)	Cr. (₹)
	X Dr.		11,10,000	
	Y Dr.		90,000	
	Z Dr.		3,00,000	
	To Share Capital A/c			7,50,000
	To Securities Premium A/c			7,50,000
	(Being shares including firm underwritten shares allotted to underwriters)			
	Underwriting Commission A/c Dr.		1,50,000	
	To X			90,000
	To Y			37,500
	To Z			22,500
	(Being underwriting commission on the shares underwritten)			
	Bank A/c Dr.		13,50,000	
	To X			10,20,000
	To Y			52,500
	To Z			2,77,500
	(Being the amount received towards shares allotted to underwrittens less underwriting commission due to them)			

6 Redemption of Debentures

SHORT ANSWER PRACTICAL PROBLEMS

REDEMPTION BY CONVERSION

PROBLEM 1

A Company had issued 20,000, 13% Convertible debentures of ₹ 100 each on 1st April, 2011. The debentures are due for redemption on 1st July, 2013. The terms of issue of debentures provided that they were redeemable at a premium of 5% and also conferred option to the debentureholders to convert 20% of their holding into equity shares (Nominal value ₹ 10) at a price of ₹ 15 per share. Debentureholders holding 2,500 debentures did not exercise the option. Calculate the number of equity shares to be allotted to the Debentureholders exercising the option to the maximum.

[CA (IPCC) May 2010]

Solution

Calculation of Number of Equity Shares to be allotted

Total number of debentures	20,000
Less: Debenture holders not opted for conversion	(2,500)
Debenture holders opted for conversion	17,500
Option for conversion	20%
Number of debentures to be converted (20% of 17,500)	3,500
Redemption value of 3,500 debentures at a premium of 5% [3, 500 × (100 + 5)]	₹ 3,67,500
Equity shares of ₹.10 each issued on conversion [₹ 3,67,500/ ₹.15]	24,500 shares

PROBLEM 2

A Company had issued 30,000, 15% Convertible debentures of ₹ 100 each on 1st April, 2010. The debentures are due for redemption on 1st March, 2013. The terms of issue of debentures provided that they were redeemable at a premium of 5% and also conferred option to the debentureholders to convert 20% of their holding into equity shares (Nominal value ₹ 10) at a price of ₹ 15 per share. Debentureholders holding 2,500 debentures did not exercise the option. Calculate the number of equity shares to be allotted to the Debentureholders exercising the option to the maximum.

[CA (IPCC) May 2011]

Solution

Calculation of Number of Equity Shares to be allotted

Total number of debentures	30,000
Less: Debenture holders not opted for conversion	(2,500)
Debenture holders opted for conversion	27,500
Option for conversion	20%
Number of debentures to be converted (20% of 27,500)	5,500
Redemption value of 5,500 debentures at a premium of 5% [5,500 × (100 + 5)]	₹ 5,77,500
Equity Shares of ₹.10 each issued on conversion [₹ 5,77,500/ ₹.15]	38,500 shares

SINKING FUND METHOD

PROBLEM 3

.A company had 16,000, 12% debentures of 100 each outstanding as on 1st April, 2012, redeemable on 31st March, 2013. On that day, Sinking fund was ₹ 14,98,000 represented by 2,000 own debentures purchased at the average price of ₹ 99 and 9% stocks face value of ₹ 13,20,000. The annual instalment was ₹ 56,800.

On 31st March, 2013 the investments were realized at ₹ 98 and the debentures were redeemed. You are required to write up the following accounts for the year ending 31si March 2013:

(a) 12% Debentures Account

(b) Debenture Redemption Sinking Fund Account. *[CA (PCC) Nov. 2010]*

Solution

Dr. **(I) 12% DEBENTURES ACCOUNT** Cr.

Particulars	₹	Particulars	₹
To Own Debentures A/c	2,00,000	By Balance b/d	16,00,000
To Bank A/c	14,00,000		
	16,00,000		**16,00,000**

Dr. **(II) DEBENTURE REDEMPTION SINKING FUND ACCOUNT** Cr.

Particulars	₹	Particulars	₹
To 9% Stock A/c (loss)	6,400	By Balance b/d	14,98,000
To General Reserve A/c (b.f.)	16,93,200	By Profit and loss A/c	56,800
		By Interest on Sinking Fund A/c	1,42,800
		By Own Debentures A/c	2,000
	16,99,600		**16,99,600**

Working Notes:

(i) Amount of 9% Stock as on 1st April, 2012

Sinking Fund Balance as on 1st April, 2012	₹ 14,98,000
Less: Own debentures	₹ (1,98,000)
	₹ 13,00,000

(ii) Sales Value of 9% Stock = (₹ 13,20,000/ ₹ 100) × ₹ 98 = ₹ 12, 93,600

(iii) Interest credited to Sinking Fund = (₹ 13,20,000 × 9%) + (₹ 2,00,000 × 12%)= ₹ 1,42,800

Dr. **(IV) OWN DEBENTURES ACCOUNT** Cr.

Particulars	₹	Particulars	₹
To Balance b/d	1,98,000	By 12% Debentures A/c	2,00,000
To Sinking Fund A/c	2,000		
	2,00,000		**2,00,000**

Dr. **(V) 9% STOCK ACCOUNT** Cr.

Particulars	₹	Particulars	₹
To Balance (Face value 13,20,000)	13,00,000	By Bank A/c	12,93,600
		By Sinking Fund A/c (loss on sales)	6,400
	13,00,000		**13,00,000**

PROBLEM 4

The following balances appeared in the books of Paradise Ltd on 1-4-2012:

(i) 12% Debentures ₹ 7,50,000
(ii) Balance of Sinking Fund ₹ 6,00,000
(iii) Sinking Fund investment ₹ 6,00,000 represented by 10% ₹ 6,50,000 secured bonds of government of India.

Annual contribution to the Sinking funds was ₹ 1,20,000 made on 31st March each year. On 31-03-2013, balance at bank was ₹ 3,00,000 before receipt of interest. The company sold the investment at 90% for redemption of debentures at a premium of 10% on the above date.

You are required to prepare the following accounts for the year ended 31st March, 2013.

(1) Debentures Account
(2) Sinking Fund Account
(3) Sinking Fund Investment Account
(4) Bank Account
(5) Debenture Holders Account

[May 2012]

Solution

Dr. **1. 12% DEBENTURES ACCOUNT** Cr.

Data	Particulars	₹	Date	Particulars	₹
31.3.13	To Debentures holders A/c	7,50,000	1.4.12	By Balance b/d	7,50,000
		7,50,000			7,50,000

Dr. **2. SINKING FUND ACCOUNT** Cr.

Data	Particulars	₹	Date	Particulars	₹
31.3.13	To 10% Sec. Bond A/c (loss)	15,000	1.4.12	By Balance b/d	6,00,000
31.3.13	To General reserve A/c (Bal. fig.)	7,70,000	31.3.13	By Profit and loss A/c	1,20,000
				By Interest on Sinking Fund A/c (interest on 10% Govt. bond (₹ 6,50,000 × 10%))	65,000
		7,85,000			7,85,000

Dr. **3. SINKING FUND INVESTMENT ACCOUNT (10% SECURED BONDS OF GOVT.)** Cr.

Data	Particulars	₹	Date	Particulars	₹
1.4.12	To Balance b/d	6,00,000	31.3.13	By Bank A/c (6,50,000 × 90% = 5,85,000)	5,85,000
			31.3.13	By Sinking Fund A/c	15,000
		6,00,000			6,00,000

Dr. **4. BANK ACCOUNT** Cr.

Data	Particulars	₹	Date	Particulars	₹
31.3.13	To Balance b/d	3,00,000	31.3.13	By 12% Debentures	8,25,000
	To Sinking Fund A/c Interest)	65,000		By Balance c/d	1,25,000
	To Sinking fund Investment A/c	5,85,000			
		9,50,000			9,50,000

Dr. **5. DEBENTURE HOLDERS ACCOUNT** Cr.

Data	Particulars	₹	Date	Particulars	₹
31.3.13	To Bank A/c	8,25,000	31.3.13	By 12% Debentures	7,50,000
			31.3.13	By Premium on redemption of debentures	75,000
		8,25,000			8,25,000

REDEMPTION BY PURCHASE IN THE OPEN MARKET

PROBLEM 5

Mr. *X* purchased 1,000, 6% Government Bonds of ₹ 100 each on 31st January, 2013 at ₹ 95 each. Interest is payable on 30th June and 31th December. The price quoted is cum interest. Journalise the transaction. *[CA (IPCC) May 2010]*

Solution

JOURNAL

Date	Particulars		Dr. (₹)	Cr. (₹)
31.1.13	Investment A/c	Dr.	94,500	
	Interest A/c [₹ 1,00,000 × 6% × 1/12]	Dr.	500	
	To Bank A/c			95,000
	(Being the purchase of 1,000, 6% Government bonds of ₹.100 each at ₹ 95 each cum interest)			

PROBLEM 6

A company purchased its own 11% debentures in the open market for ₹.50,00,000 (cum-interest). The interest amount included in the purchase price is ₹.1,50,000. The face value of the debentures purchased is ₹.52,00,000. The company cancelled the debentures so purchased.
Pass Journal Entries in the books of the company for purchase and immediate cancellation of debentures. *[CA (PCC) Nov. 2007]*

Solution

JOURNAL

Date	Particulars		Dr. (₹)	Cr. (₹)
	11% Own Debentures A/c	Dr.	48,50,000	
	Debenture Interest A/c	Dr.	1,50,000	
	To Bank A/c			50,00,000
	(Being the purchase of cum-interest own debentures from the market)			
	11% Debentures A/c	Dr.	52,00,000	
	To 11% Own Debentures A/c			48,50,000
	To Capital Reserve A/c			3,50,000
	(Being the profit on cancellation of own debentures transferred to Capital Reserve Account)			

PROBLEM 7

Arjun Ltd. issued 10,000 (Nos.) of 12% Debentures or ₹.100 each in April, 2011. Interest is payable on 30th September and 31st March every year. The company purchased 2,000 Debentures at ₹ 104 per debenture on cum-interest basis on 1.7.2012. The own debentures were cancelled on 30.9.2013. Show Journal entries that are required to be passed for purchase of own debentures, interest on own debentures and for cancellation of those debentures. *[CA (PCC) Nov. 2009]*

Solution

JOURNAL

Date	Particulars		Dr. (₹)	Cr. (₹)
1.7.2012	12% Own Debentures A/c	Dr.	2,02,000	
	Interest on Own Debentures A/c	Dr.	6,000	
	To Bank A/c			2,08,000
	(Being purchase of 12% own debenture on cum interest basis)			
30.9.2012	12% Debenture Interest A/c	Dr.	60,000	
	To Bank A/c			48,000
	To Interest on Own Debentures A/c			12,000
	(Being interest on Debentures including own debentures for 6 months)			
31.3.2013	12% Debenture Interest A/c	Dr.	60,000	
	To Bank A/c			48,000
	To Interest on Own Debentures A/c			12,000
	(Being the Interest on Debentures including own debentures for 6 months)			
30.9.2013	12% Debenture Interest A/c	Dr.	60,000	
	To Bank A/c			48,000
	To Interest on Own Debentures A/c			12,000
	(Being the Interest interest on Debentures including own debentures for 6 months)			
30.9.2013	12% Debentures A/c	Dr.	2,00,000	
	Loss on cancellation of 12% Debentures A/c	Dr.	2,000	
	To 12% Own Debentures A/c			2,02,000
	(Being the cancellation of 2,000 own debentures)			
30.9.2013	Profit and Loss A/c	Dr.	2,000	
	To Loss on cancellation of 12% Debentures A/c			2,000
	(Being the loss on cancellation transferred)			

PROBLEM 8

Rama Limited issued 8% Debentures of ₹ 3,00,000 in earlier year on which interest is payable half yearly on 31st March and 30th September. The company has power to purchase its own debentures in the open market for cancellation there of. The following purchases were made during the financial year 2012-13 and cancellation made on 31st March, 2013:

(a) On 1st April, ₹ 50,000 nominal value debentures purchased for ₹ 49,450, ex-interest.

(*b*) On 1st September, ₹ 30,000 nominal value debentures purchased for ₹ 30,250 cum interest.

Show the Journal Entries (without narrations) for the transactions held in the year 2012-13.

[CA (IPCC) Nov. 2010]

Solution

JOURNAL OF RAMA LIMITED

Date	Particulars		Dr. (₹)	Cr. (₹)
01.04.12	Own Debentures A/c	Dr.	49,450	
	To Bank A/c			49,450

01.04.12	Own Debentures A/c	Dr.	29,250	
	Interest on Own Debentures A/c	Dr.	1,000	
	[30,000 × 8% × 5/12]			
	To Bank A/c			30,250
30.09.12	Interest on Debentures A/c	Dr.	12,000	
	To Bank A/c			8,800
	To Interest on Own Debentures A/c			3,200
31.09.12	Interest on Debentures A/c	Dr.	12,000	
	To Bank A/c			8,800
	To Interest on own debentures A/c			3,200
31.03.13	8% Debentures A/c	Dr.	80,000	
	To Own Debentures A/c			78,700
	To Profit on cancellation of Debentures A/c			1,300
	Interest on Own Debentures A/c	Dr.	5,400	
	To Profit and Loss A/c			5,400
	(3,200 + 3,200 – 1,000)			
	Profit and Loss A/c (1,000+12,000)	Dr.	24,000	
	To Interest on Debentures A/c			24,000
	Profit on cancellation of Debentures A/c	Dr.	1,300	
	To Capital Reserve A/c			1,300

PROBLEM 9

On 1st April, 2012, A Ltd. had outstanding in its books 1,00,000 Debentures of ₹ 700 each, interest @ 12% per annum. The interest on debentures was paid half-yearly on 30th September and 31st March of every year. On 31st May, 2012 the company purchased 30,000 Debentures of its own @ ₹ 98 (ex-interest) per debenture. The company cancelled the debentures so purchased on 31st March, 2013.

Required: Pass the necessary Journal Entries to record the above transactions for the year ended 31st March, 2013. ***[CA (IPCC) Nov., 2011]***

Solution

JOURNAL OF 'A' LIMITED

Date	*Particulars*		*Dr. (₹)*	*Cr. (₹)*
31.05.2012	Investment in own debentures A/c	Dr.	29,40,000	
	Debenture interest A/c	Dr.	60,000	
	To Bank A/c			30,00,000
	(Being the purchase of own 30,000 debentures @ ? 98 ex-interest)			
30.09.2012	Debenture interest A/c	Dr.	5,40,000	
	To Bank A/c			4,20,000
	To Interest on own debentures A/c			1,20,000
	(Being interest @ 12% paid on 70,000 debentures & adjustment of interest on 30,000 own debentures for4 months)			

31.03.2013	Debenture interest A/c Dr. To Bank A/c To Interest on own debentures A/c (Being interest @ 12% paid on 70,000 debentures & adjustment of interest on 30,000 own debentures for 6 months)	6,00,000	 4,20,000 1,80,000
	12% Debentures A/c Dr. To Investment in own debentures A/c To Capital reserve A/c (Being cancellation of 30,000, 12% own debentures)	30,00,000	 29,40,000 60,000
	Profit and Loss A/c Dr. To Debenture interest A/c (Being total interest transferred to Profit & Loss account)	12,00,000	 12,00,000
	Interest on own debentures A/c Dr. To Profit & Loss A/c (Being total interest on own debentures credited to Profit & Loss account)	3,00,000	 3,00,000

PROBLEM 10

Himalayas Ltd. had ₹ 10,00,000, 8% Debentures of ₹ 100 each as on 31st March, 2012. The company purchased in the open market following debentures for immediate cancellation:

On 01-07-2012-1,000 Debentures @ ₹ 97 (cum interest)

On 29-02-2013-1,800 Debentures @ ₹ 99 (ex interest)

Debenture interest due date is 30th September and 31st March.

Give Journal Entries in the books of the company for the year ended 31st March, 2013.

[CA (IPCC) Nov., 2012]

Solution

Journal

Date	*Particulars*	*Dr. (₹)*	*Cr. (₹)*
01.07.12	Own Debentures A/c Dr. Debenture Interest A/c Dr. [1,000 × 100 × 8% × (3/12)] To Bank A/c (Being 1,000 Debentures purchased @ ₹ 97 cum interest for immediate cancellation)	95,000 2,000	 97,000
01.07.12	8% Debentures A/c Dr. To Own Debentures A/c To Capital Reserve A/c (Being profit on cancellation of own Debentures t/f)	1,00,000	 95,000 5,000
30.09.12	Debenture Interest A/c Dr. [9,000 × 100 × 8% × (1/2)] To Debenture holders A/c (Being interest accrued on 9,000 Debentures)	36,000	 36,000
	Debentureholders A/c Dr. To Bank A/c (Being interest amount paid)	36,000	 36,000

29.02.13	Own Debentures A/c Debenture Interest Account A/c [1,800 × 100 × 8% × (5/12)] To Bank A/c (Being the Purchase of 1,800 Debentures @ ₹ 99 ex interest for immediate cancellation)	Dr. Dr.	1,78,200 6,000	 1,84,200
29.02.13	8% Debentures A/c To Own Debentures A/c To Capital Reserve A/c (Being the Profit on cancellation of own Debentures t/f)	Dr.	1,80,000	 1,78,200 1,800
31.03.13	Debentures Interest A/c [7,200 × 100 × 8% × (1/2)] To Debentureholders A/c (Being interest accrued on 7,200 Debentures)	Dr.	28,800	 28,800
31.3.13	Profit and Loss A/c To Debentures Interest A/c (Being interest on debentures for the year transferred)	Dr.	72,800	 72,800

LONG ANSWER PRACTICAL QUESTIONS

PROBLEM 11

Libra Limited recently made a public issue in respect of which the following information is available:

(a) No. of partly convertible debentures issued 2,00,000; face value and issue price ₹ 100 per debenture.
(b) Convertible portion per debenture 60%, date of conversion on expiry of 6 months from the date of closing of issue.
(c) Date of closure of subscription lists 1.5.2012, date of allotment 1.6.2012, rate of interest on debenture 15% payable from the date of allotment, value of equity share for the purpose of conversion ₹ 60 (Face Value ₹ 10).
(d) Underwritting Commission 2%.
(e) No. of debentures applied for 1,50,000.
(f) Interest payable on debentures half-yearly on 30th September and 31st March.

Required: Write relevant journal entries for all transactions arising out of the above during the year ended 31st March, 2013 (including cash and bank entries). ***[CA (May 1995)]***

JOURNAL

Date	Particulars		L.F.	Dr. (₹)	Cr. (₹)
2012					
May 01	Bank A/c	Dr.		150,00,000	
	To Debenture Application A/c				150,00,000
	(Being the Application money received on 1,50,000 debentures @ ₹ 100 each)				
June 01	Debenture Application A/c	Dr.		150,00,000	
	Underwriters A/c	Dr.		50,00,000	
	To 15% Debentures A/c				200,00,000
	(Being the Allotment of 1,50,000 debentures to applicants and 50,000 debentures to underwriters)				
	Underwriting Commission A/c	Dr.		4,00,000	
	To Underwriters' A/c				4,00,000
	(Being the Commission payable to underwriters @ 2% on ₹ 200,00,000)				
	Bank A/c	Dr.		46,00,000	
	To Underwriters A/c				46,00,000
	(Being the Amount received from underwriters in settlement of account)				
Sept. 30	Debenture Interest A/c	Dr.		10,00,000	
	To Bank A/c				10,00,000
	(Being the Interest paid on debentures for 4 months @ 15% on ₹ 200,00,000)				
Oct. 31	15% Debentures A/c	Dr.		120,00,000	
	To Equity Share Capital A/c				20,00,000
	To Securities Premium A/c				100,00,000
	(Being the Conversion of 60% of debentures into shares of ₹ 60 each with a face value of ₹ 10)				
2013					
Mar. 31	Debenture Interest A/c	Dr.		7,50,000	
	To Bank A/c				7,50,000
	(Being the Interest paid on debentures for the half year)				

***Working Notes:** Calculation of Debenture Interest for the half year ended 31st March, 2013*

On ₹ 80,00,000 for 6 months @ 15% = ₹ 6,00,000
On ₹ 120,00,000 for 1 month @ 15% = ₹ 1,50,000 = ₹ 7,50,000

PROBLEM 12

CANIH Ltd. issued ₹ 10,00,000, 6% Debenture Stock at par on 21.1.2010. Interest was payable on 30th June and 31st December, in each year.

Under the terms of the Debentures Trust the owned stock is redeemable at par. The trust deed obliges the Company to pay to the trustees on 31st December, 2011 and annually thereafter the sum of ₹ 1,00,000 to be utilised for the redemption and cancellation of an equivalent amount of stock, which is to be selected by drawing lots.

Alternatively, the Company is empowered as from 1st January, 2011 to purchase its own debentures on the open market. These Debentures must be surrendered to the Trustees for cancellation and any adjustments of accrued interest recorded in the books of account. If in any year the nominal amount of the stock surrendered under this alternative does not amount to ₹ 1,00,000 then the shortfall is to be paid by the Company to the Trustees in cash on 31st December. The following purchases of stock were made by the Company:

	Nominal value of stock purchased ₹	*Purchase price per ₹ 100 of stock* ₹
(1) 30th September, 2011	1,20,000	98
(2) 31st May, 2012	75,000	95 (Ex-interest)
(3) 31st July, 2013	1,15,000	92

The Company fulfilled all its obligations under the trust deed.

Required: Prepare the following Ledger Accounts: (a) Debenture Stock A/c, (b) Debenture Redemption A/c, (c) Debenture Interest A/c.

Note: *Ignore costs and taxation.* **[*CA (Nov. 1998)*]**

Solution

CANIH LTD.
6% DEBENTURE STOCK ACCOUNT

Dr. *Cr.*

Date	*Particulars*	₹	*Date*	*Particulars*	₹
2011			2011		
Sept. 30	To Debenture Redemption A/c	1,20,000	Jan. 01	By Balance b/d	10,00,000
Dec. 31	To Balance c/d	8,80,000			
		10,00,000			10,00,000
2012			2012		
May 31	To Debenture Redemption A/c	75,000	Jan. 01	By Balance b/d	8,80,000
Dec, 31	To Debenture Redemption A/c	25,000			
	To Balance c/d	7,80,000			
		8,80,000			8,80,000
2013			2013		
July, 31	To Debenture Redemption A/c	1,15,000	Jan. 01	By Balance b/d	7,80,000
Dec. 31	To Balance c/d	6,65,000			
		7,80,000			7,80,000

Dr. **6% DEBENTURE REDEMPTION ACCOUNT** Cr.

Date	Particulars	₹	Date	Particulars	₹
2011			2011		
Sept. 30	To Bank A/c	1,15,800	Sept. 30	By Debenture Stock A/c	1,20,000
	To Capital Reserve A/c	4,200			
		1,20,000			1,20,000
2012			2012		
May, 31	To Bank A/c	71,250	May, 31	By 6% Debenture Stock	75,000
Dec. 31	To Bank A/c		Dec. 31	By 6% Debenture Stock	25,000
	(shortfall made good)	25,000			
	To Capital Reserve	3,750			
		1,00,000			1,00,000
2013			2013		
July 31	To Bank A/c	1,05,225	July 31	By 6% Debenture Stock	1,15,000
	To Capital Reserve A/c	9,775			
		1,15,000			1,15,000

It is assumed that debentures are cancelled on the date of purchase.

Dr. **DEBENTURE INTEREST ACCOUNT** Cr.

Date	Particulars	₹	Date	Particulars	₹
2011			2011		
June 30	To Bank A/c	30,000	Dec. 31	By Profit & Loss A/c	58,200
Sept. 30	To Bank A/c	1,800			
Dec. 31	To Bank A/c	26,400			
		58,200			58,200
2012			2012		
May, 31	To Bank A/c	1,875	Dec. 31	Profit & Loss A/c	50,175
June, 30	To Bank A/c	24,150			
Dec. 31	To Bank A/c	24,150			
		50,175			50,175
2013			2013		
June 30	To Bank A/c	23,400	Dec. 31	By Profit & Loss A/c	43,925
July, 31	To Bank A/c	575			
Dec. 31	To Bank A/c	19,950			
		43,925			43,925

Note: *Alternatively, the students may assume that debentures purchased are cancelled at year-end i.e. on 31st December. In such a case, the interest on debentures purchased will be charged for full six months period, and the interest for the period for which debentures were held by the company before cancellation will be take as income.*

PROBLEM 13

The summarised Balance Sheet of CANHE Limited, as on 30th June 2013, stood as follows:

Liabilities:	₹
Share Capital: 5,00,000 equity shares of ₹ 10 each full paid	50,00,000
General Reserve	75,00,000
Debenture Redemption Reserve	50,00,000
13.5% Convertible Debentures of ₹ 100 each	1,00,00,000
Other loans	50,00,000
Current Liabilities and Provisions	1,25,00,000
	4,50,00,000

Assets:

Fixed Assets (at cost *less* depreciation)	1,60,00,000
Debenture Redemption Fund investments	40,00,000
Cash and Bank Balances	50,00,000
Other Current Assets	2,00,00,000
	4,50,00,000

The debentures are due for redemption on 1st July, 2013. The terms of issue of debentures provided they were redeemable at a premium of 5% and also conferred option to the debenture-holders to convert 20% of their holding into equity shares at a predetermined price of ₹ 15.75 per share and the payment in cash.

Assuming that:-

(i) except for 100 debenture holders holding totally 25,000 debentures, the rest of them exercised the option for maximum conversion;

(ii) the investments realise ₹ 44 lakhs on sale; and

(iii) all the transactions are put through, without any lag, on 1st July 2013.

Required: Redraft the Balance Sheet of the company as on 1st July, 2013 after giving effect to the redemption. Show your calculations in respect of the number of equity shares to be allotted and the cash payment necessary. ***[CA]***

Solution

BALANCE SHEET OF CANHE LTD. AS AT 31.3.2013

Particulars	*Note No*	*₹ (lacs)*
I. Equity and Liabilities		
(1) Shareholders' Funds		
(a) Share Capital (*₹ 10 each)*		60.00
(b) Reserves and Surplus	1	129.75
(2) Non-Current Liabilities[Loans]		50.00
(3) Current Liabilities		125.00
Total		364.75
II. Assets		
(1) Non-Current Assets		
(a) Fixed Assets		
Tangible Assets		160.00
(2) Current Assets		
(a) Cash and Cash Equivalents		4.75
(b) Other Current Assets		200.00
Total		364.75

Notes To Accounts:

Particulars	*₹ (lacs)*
1. Reserves and Surplus	
General Reserve	75.00
Debentures Redemption Reserve	49.00
Securities Premium	5.75
Total	129.75

Working Notes:

(i) *Calculation of number of shares to be allotted:*

A	Total number of debentures	1,00,000
B	*Less:* number not opting for conversion	25,000
		75,000
C	20% of 75,000	15,000
D	Redemption value of 15,000 debentures	15,75,000
E	Redemption value per Debenture	15.75
F	Number of Equity Shares to be allotted [15,75,000/15.75]	1,00,000

(ii) *Calculation of Cash to be paid:*

A	Number of debentures	1,00,000
B	*Less:* number of debentures to be converted into Equity Shares	15,000
		85,000
C	Redemption value for Debenture	₹ 105
D	Redemption value of 85,000 debentures [85,000 × ₹ 105]	89,25,000

(iii) *Cash and Bank Balance:*

		₹
A	Balance before redemption	50,00,000
B	*Add:* proceeds of investments sold	44,00,000
C	*Less:* Cash paid to debenture-holders	89,25,000
D	Balance [A + B − C]	4,75,000

(iv) *Calculation of Transfer to Debenture Redemption Reserve*

A	Debenture Redemption Fund	50,00,000
B	*Add:* Profit on Sale of Investments	4,00,000
C	*Less:* Premium on Redemption of Debentures	5,00,000
		49,00,000

Note: *(i) The premium on redemption of debentures may also be adjusted against Securities Premium Account.*

(ii) As per SEBI Guidelines, Debenture Redemption Reserve A/c must have a credit balance at least equal to 50%.

PROBLEM 14

On 1st January, 2008 CAMIB Limited issued 10,000 fifteen years debentures of ₹ 100 each bearing interest at 10% p.a. One of the conditions of issue was that the company could redeem the debentures by giving six month's notice at any time after 5 years, at a premium of 4%, either by payment in cash or by allotment of preference shares and/or other debentures at the option of the debenture holders.

On 1st April 2013 the Company gave notice to the debenture holders of its intention to redeem the debentures on 1st October, 2013 either by payment in cash or by allotment of 11% preference shares of ₹ 100 each at ₹ 130 per share or 11% Second Debentures of ₹ 100 at ₹ 96 per debenture.

Holders of 4,000 debentures accepted the offer of the preference shares; holders of 4,800 debentures accepted the offer of the 11% second debentures and the rest demanded cash on 1st, October 2013.

Required: Give the journal entries to give effect to the above as of 1st October, 2013. Suggest how discount on issue of debentures can be dealt in the accounts. Ignore Interest. ***[CA]***

Solution

JOURNAL

Date	Particulars		L.F.	Dr. (₹)	Cr. (₹)
2013	10% Debentures A/c	Dr.		10,00,000	
Oct.01	Premium on Redemption of Debentures A/c	Dr.		40,000	
	To Debenture holders A/c				10,40,000
	(Being transfer of amount due on redemption of 10% debentures—nominal value ₹ 10,00,000 *plus* premium (₹ 40,000)				
	Debenture-holders A/c	Dr.		4,16,000	
	To 11% Preference Share Capital A/c				3,20,000
	To Securities Premium A/c				96,000
	(Being issue of 3200 preference shares of ₹ 100 each at a premium of ₹ 30 each in exchange of 4000 debentures)				
Oct.01	Debenture holders' A/c	Dr.		4,99,200	
	Discount on Issue of 11% Second Debentures A/c	Dr.		20,800	
	To 11% Second Debentures A/c				5,20,000
	(Issue of 5,200 11% Second Debentures of ₹ 100 each at a discount or ₹ 4 in exchange of 4800 Debentures)				
	Debenture holders' A/c	Dr.		1,24,800	
	To Bank A/c				1,24,800
	(Being the redemption of 1,200 debentures by cash)				
	Profit & Loss Appropriation A/c	Dr.		60,000	
	To Debenture Redemption Reserve A/c				60,000
	[Being the transfer of profits to DRR as per sec 117(c)]				

Working Notes:

(i) *Redemption of debentures by issuing preference shares:*

A	Claim of the holders of 4,000 debentures @ ₹ 104	₹	4,16,000
B	Issue Price of a Preference Share	₹	130
C	Number of preference shares to be issued [₹ 4,16,000/130]	₹	3,200
D	Face value of preference shares @ ₹ 100 each [3,200 × ₹ 100]	₹	3,20,000
E	Premium of preference shares @ ₹ 30 each [₹ 3,200 × ₹ 30]	₹	96,000

(ii) *Redemption of debentures by issuing 11% Second Debentures:*

A	Claim of the holders of 4,800 debentures @ ₹ 104	₹	4,99,200
B	Issue Price of a Preference Share	₹	96
C	Number of 11% Second Debentures to be issued [₹ 4,99,200/96]	₹	5,200
D	Face value of 11% Second Debentures @ ₹ 100 each [5,200 × 100]	₹	5,20,000
E	Discount on issue of debentures @ ₹ 4 each [5,200 × 4]	₹	20,800

(iii) *Redemption of debentures in cash:*

Claim of the holders of 1,200 debentures @ ₹ 104
(10,000 — 4,000 — 4,800 = 1,200) 1,24,800

Treatment of discount on issue of debentures in accounts:

Discount on issue of debentures is usually written off against the profit and loss account as early as possible. However, when the debentures are redeemed after a certain period of time, the discount on issue of such debentures may be written off at the ratio of amount outstanding at the end of each year. Under Section 78 of the Companies Act, balance of securities premium account can also be used to write off the discount on issue of debentures.

PROBLEM 15

CANIC Limited, a trading company decided that the value of its building could be used to provide additional working capital. The Balance Sheet of the Company as on 31st March 2013 was as under:

Liabilities	₹	*Assets*		₹
Paid up Capital:		**Fixed Assets:**		
10,000 Equity Shares of ₹ 10 each	1,00,000	Building at cost	2,00,000	
5,000 12% Redeemable		*Less:* Depreciation	40,000	1,60,000
Preference Shares of ₹ 10 each	50,000	Furniture at cost	90,000	
Reserves & Provisions:		*Less:* Depreciation	30,000	60,000
Securities Premium	5,000	**Current Assets, Loans and Advances:**		
Profit & Loss Account	1,30,000			
Secured Loans:		Stock		58,000
12% Debentures	70,000	Debtors		52,000
Unsecured Loans:	Nil			
Current Liabilities & Provisions:		Bank		65,000
Creditors	40,000			
	3,95,000			3,95,000

Depreciation on building has been provided @ 2% per annum on cost. The following action was taken:

(a) The building was sold for ₹ 2,20,000 to another company, who leased it back to CANIC Limited for 21 years at annual rent of ₹ 16,000.

(b) 12% Debentures were discharged at a premium of 10%.

(c) Preference shares were redeemed at a premium of 10%.

The directors expect that the profit of the company will further increased by ₹ 20,000 for the coming year due to change in working capital.

Required: (i) Draft the journal entries necessary to record the above transactions.

(ii) Calculate the effect of future annual profits (before taxation) available for distribution to equity shareholders. Calculate the additional pre-tax increase in earnings per share. ***[CA]***

Solution

(i) Journal

Date	*Particulars*	*L.F.*	*Dr. (₹)*	*Cr. (₹)*
	Bank A/c Dr.		2,20,000	
	To Building A/c			1,60,000
	To Capital Reserve A/c			60,000
	(Sale proceeds of building received and profit on sale credited to Capital Reserve)			

Date	Particulars		L.F.	Dr. (₹)	Cr. (₹)
	P & L Appropriation A/c	Dr.		70,000	
	To Deb. Red. Reserve A/c				70,000
	(Being the transfer of profits to DRR)				
	12% Debentures A/c	Dr.		70,000	
	Premium on Redemption of Debentures A/c	Dr.		7,000	
	To Debenture holders A/c				77,000
	(Amount payable to debenture-holders on redemption at a premium of 10% vide Board's Resolutions on...dated...)				
	Debenture holders' A/c	Dr.		77,000	
	To Bank A/c				77,000
	(Amount paid to debenture holders on redemption)				
	12% Redeemable Preference Share Capital A/c	Dr.		50,000	
	Premium on Redemption of Preference Shares A/c	Dr.		5,000	
	To Preference Shareholders A/c				55,000
	(Amount payable to preference shareholders on redemption at a premium of 10% vide Board's Resolution no......dated....)				
	Preference Shareholders' A/c	Dr.		55,000	
	To Bank A/c				55,000
	(Amount paid to preference shareholders on redemption)				
	Profit and Loss A/c	Dr.		50,000	
	To Capital Redemption Reserve A/c				50,000
	(Amount transferred to Capital Redemption Reserve on redemption of preference shares out of profit vide Board's Resolution no....dated....)				
	Profit and Loss A/c	Dr.		7,000	
	To Premium on Redemption of Debentures A/c				7,000
	(Premium on redemption of debentures charged to P & L A/c)				
	Securities Premium A/c	Dr.		5,000	
	To Premium on Redemption of Preference Shares A/c				5,000
	(Premium on redemption of preference shares charged to Securities Premium Account)				

(ii) (a) *Calculation of the effect on the future annual profit (before taxation):*

	₹
Increase in profit	
Depreciation no longer chargeable	4,000
Debenture interest no longer payable	8,400
Preference divided no longer payable	6,000
Effects on profit due to change in working capital	20,000
	38,400
Less: Decrease in profit:	
Annual rent payable	16,000
	22,400

(ii) (b) Additional pre-tax increase in earning per equity share $\frac{\text{Rs. } 22,400}{10,000} = \text{Rs. } 2.24.$

PROBLEM 16

The summarised Balance Sheet of CAMID Ltd. as at 30th September, 2013 was:

Liabilities	₹	*Assets*	₹
Share Capital:		**Fixed Assets:**	15,00,000
Issued and fully paid 5000 equity shares of ₹ 100 each fully paid	5,00,000	**Investments:** (Own 10% Debentures of Nominal value of ₹ 1,00,000)	95,000
6% Redeemable preference share of ₹ 100 each (*less* calls in arrears on 200 shares)	4,95,000	Other Securities	1,00,000
		Current Assets:	
		Stock	2,00,000
Reserves and surplus:		Debtors	1,00,000
Securities Premium	1,00,000	Cash at Bank	6,00,000
Capital Reserve	1,00,000		
General Reserve	2,00,000		
Profit & Loss Account	3,00,000		
Secured Loans:			
10% Debentures	2,00,000		
Current Liabilities:			
Creditors	7,00,000		
	25,95,000		25,95,000

On 30th September, 2013 the following were due for redemption:

(i) 5,000 6% Redeemable Preference Shares at a premium of ₹ 25 per share.

(ii) 2,000 10% Redeemable Debentures at a premium of 10%

The Redemption was made on that date or subsequently thus:

(a) For the half year ending 30th September 2013, the debenture interest and Preference dividend were paid out of the profits of the Company.

(b) On an offer made to the 10% Debenture holders, the outsiders agreed to take new 12% Debentures at par in exchange of old debentures; the company also decided to assume the new debentures.

(c) A fresh issue of 1,000 equity shares of ₹ 100 each were made at a premium of ₹ 50 per share and subscribed in full. All moneys due were received forthwith.

(d) Redemption of all preference shares were made on 10th October, 2013.

Required: Show all journal entries for the above transactions and give the company's opening Balance Sheet after giving effect to them. ***[CA]***

Solution

JOURNAL

Date	*Particulars*	*L.F.*	*Dr. (₹)*	*Cr. (₹)*
	Profit and Loss A/c Dr.		24,850	
	To Interest on Debentures A/c			10,000
	To Preference Dividend A/c			14,850
	(Interest on debentures @ 10% for 6 months and dividend on paid up value of preference share capital @ 6% for 6 months)			

Date	Particulars	L.F.	Dr. (₹)	Cr. (₹)
	Interest on Debentures A/c Dr.		10,000	
	To Interest on own Debentures A/c			5,000
	To Bank A/c			5,000
	(Adjustment for interest on investment in own debentures and payment of interest to the outside debenture holders)			
	Preference Dividend A/c Dr.		14,850	
	To Bank A/c			14,850
	(Payment of preference dividend)			
	Bank A/c	Dr.	5,000	
	To Calls in Arrears A/c			5,000
	(Calls in arrear on 200 preference shares received)			
	10% Debentures A/c Dr.		2,00,000	
	Premium on redemption of debentures A/c Dr.		20,000	
	To Debenture holders' A/c			2,20,000
	(Redemption of 10% debenture at a premium of 10%)			
	Debenture holders' A/c Dr	.	2,20,000	
	To 12% Debentures A/c			`2,20,000
	(Issue of new 12% debentures to the debenture-holders)			
	Investment in Own 12% Debentures A/c Dr.		1,10,000	
	To Investment A/c			95,000
	To Profit and Loss A/c			15,000
	(Exchange of own 10% debentures by own 12% debentures, surplus being transferred to Profit and Loss A/c)			
	Bank A/c	Dr.	1,50,000	
	To Equity Share Capital A/c			1,00,000
	To Securities Premium A/c			50,000
	(Fresh issue of equity shares of ₹ 100 each at a premium of ₹ 50 per share made for the purpose of redemption of preference Shares)			
	General Reserve A/c Dr	.	2,00,000	
	Profit and Loss A/c Dr.		2,00,000	
	To Capital Redemption Reserve A/c			4,00,000
	(Transfer out of reserves and surplus an amount equal to nominal value of preference shares redeemable otherwise then out of the proceeds of fresh issue)			
	6% Redeemable Preference Share Capital A/c Dr		5,00,000	
	Premium on redemption of preference shares A/c Dr.		1,25,000	
	To Preference shareholders A/c			6,25,000
	(Redemption of 6% redeemable preference share of ₹ 100 each at a premium of ₹ 25 per share)			
	Preference shareholders' A/c Dr.		6,25,000	
	To Bank A/c			6,25,000
	(Amount paid to Preference shareholders on redemption)			

Date	Particulars	L.F.	Dr. (₹)	Cr. (₹)
	Interest on own Debentures A/c Dr.		5,000	
	To Profit and Loss A/c			5,000
	(Transfer of interest on own debentures)			
	Securities Premium A/c Dr.		1,45,000	
	To Premium on Redemption of Debentures A/c			20,000
	To Premium on Redemption of Preference Shares A/c			1,25,000
	(Premium on redemption of debentures and preference sharers provided for out of securities premium)			

BALANCE SHEET OF CAMFD LTD. AS AT 10.10.2013

Particulars	Note No	₹
I. Equity and Liabilities		
(1) Shareholders' Funds		
(a) Share Capital (*₹ 100 each)*		6,00,000
(b) Reserves and Surplus	1	6,00,150
(2) Non-Current Liabilities [12 % Debentures]		2,20,000
(3) Current Liabilities		
(a) Trade Payables[Creditors]		7,00,000
Total		21,20,150
II. Assets		
(1) Non-Current Assets		
(a) Fixed Assets		
Tangible Assets		15,00,000
(b) Non-Current Investments [Own Deb. + Securities] [1,10,000 + 1,00,000]		2,10,000
(2) Current Assets		
(a) Inventories		2,00,000
(b) Trade Receivables		1,00,000
(c) Cash and Cash Equivalents		1,10,150
Total		21,20,150

Notes To Accounts:

Particulars	₹
1. Reserves and Surplus	
Capital Reserve	1,00,000
Capital Redemption Reserve	4,00,000
Profit & Loss Account	95,150
Securities Premium	5,000
Total	6,00,150

Working Notes:

(i) *Dr.* **CASH AT BANK ACCOUNT** *Cr.*

Particulars	₹	Particulars	₹
To Balance b/d	6,00,000	By Pref. Dividend	14,850
To Calls-in-arrears	5,000	By Deb. Interest	5,000
To Equity Share Capital A/c	1,00,000	By Pref. Shareholders' A/c	6,25,000
To Secutities Premium A/c	50,000	By Balance c/d	1,10,150
	7,55,000		7,55,000

(ii) *Dr.* **PROFIT & LOSS ACCOUNT** *Cr.*

Particulars	₹	Particulars	₹
To Capital Redemption Reserve	2,00,000	By Balance b/d	3,00,000
To Pref. Dividend	14,850	By Interest on Own Deb.	5,000
To Interest on Debentures	10,000	By Profit on Conversion of	
To Balance c/d	95,150	Investments	15,000
	3,20,000		3,20,000

(iii) Preference dividend is in proportion to the amount paid up on preference shares in pursuance of Section 93 of the Companies Act, 1956. In the absence of information, it is assumed that the articles of association of the company authorise such payment.

PROBLEM 17

Balance Sheet of Dee Limited on 31st March, 2013 was as follows:

Liabilities	₹	*Assets*	₹
Share Capital:		Fixed Assets (at cost *less* depreciation)	8,00,000
Authorised Capital 50,000, Equity Shares of ₹ 10 each	5,00,000	Debenture Redemption Fund Investment	2,00,000
Issued and Subscribed Capital 25,000 Equity shares of ₹ 10 each fully paid up	2,50,000	Cash balance	2,50,000
Reserves and Surplus:		Other Current Assets	10,00,000
General Reserve	2,75,000		
Profit and Loss A/c	1,00,000		
Debenture Redemption Reserve	2,50,000		
Secured Loans:			
12% Convertible Debentures (5,000 Debentures of ₹.100 each)	5,00,000		
Other Secured loans	2,50,000		
Current Liabilities and	6,00,000		
Provisions:			
Proposed Dividend	25,000		
	22,50,000		22,50,000

At the General Meeting it was resolved to:

1. Pay proposed dividend of 10% in cash.
2. Give existing shareholders the option to purchase one share of ₹.10 each at ₹.15 for every five shares held. This option was taken up by all the shareholders.
3. Redeem the debentures at a premium of 5% and also confer option to the debentureholders to convert 50% of their holding into equity shares at a predetermined price of ₹ 15 per share and balance payment to be made in cash.

Holders of 3,000 debentures opted to get their debentures redeemed in cash only while the rest opted for getting the same converted into equity shares as per the terms of issue. Debenture Redemption Fund Investments realized ₹ 1,80,000 on sales.

Required: Redraft the Balance Sheet after giving effects to the right issue and redemption of debentures. Also show the calculations in respect of number of equity shares issued and cash payment. *[CA (IPCC) Nov. 2009]*

Solution

BALANCE SHEET OF DEE LTD. AS AT 31.3.2013

Particulars	*Note No*	₹
I. Equity and Liabilities		
(1) Shareholders' Funds		
(a) Share Capital (*₹ 10 each)*		3,70,000
(b) Reserves and Surplus	1	6,40,000
(2) Non-Current Liabilities [Secured Loans]		2,50,000
(3) Current Liabilities		6,00,000
Total		18,60,000
II. Assets		
(1) Non-Current Assets		
(a) Fixed Assets		
Tangible Assets		8,00,000
(2) Current Assets		
(a) Cash and Cash Equivalents		60,000
(b) Other Current Assets		10,00,000
Total		18,60,000

Notes To Accounts:

Particulars	₹
1. Reserves and Surplus	
General Reserve	4,80,000
Profit & Loss Account	1,00,000
Securities Premium	60,000
Total	6,40,000

CALCULATION OF NUMBER OF EQUITY SHARES ISSUED

I.	Number of equity shares issued as right issue (25,000 Shares/5)	5,000 shares
II.	Debentureholders who opted for the scheme of conversion into equity shares	
	2,000 debentureholders opted for the scheme	
	Total value (2,000 debentures × ₹.100)	₹ 2,00,000
	Premium on redemption @ 5%	₹ 10,000
		2,10,000
	50% of their holding converted into equity shares	₹ 1,05,000
	Number of equity shares to be issued to debentureholders = (₹ 1,05,000/₹ 15)	7,000 shares
	Total number of equity shares issued = (5,000 + 7,000) shares	12,000 shares

CASH PAYMENT TO DEBENTUREHOLDERS

	Particulars		₹
I.	3,000 Debentureholders preferred cash		
	Total cash paid to them	3,00,000	
	Premium on redemption @ 5%	15,000	3,15,000
II.	2,000 Debentureholders opted for the scheme		
	Total Value	2,00,000	
	Add: Premium on redemption @ 5%	10,000	
		2,10,000	
	50% of their value converted into equity shares	1,05,000	
	Balance paid to debentureholders in cash		1,05,000
	Total cash paid to debentureholders		4,20,000

Working Notes:

Dr. **(I) DEBENTURE REDEMPTION RESERVE ACCOUNT** *Cr.*

Particulars	₹	Particulars	₹
To Premium on redemption of debentures (15,000 + 10,000)	25,000	By Balance b/d	2,50,000
To Loss on sale of Debenture Redemption Reserve Investment	20,000		
To General Reserve	2,05,000		
	2,50,000		2,50,000

Dr. **(II) GENERAL RESERVE ACCOUNT** *Cr.*

Particulars	₹	Particulars	₹
To Balance c/d	4,80,000	By Balance b/d	2,75,000
		By Debenture Redemption Reserve	2,05,000
	4,80,000		4,80,000

(iii) Total of Securities Premium = 12000 shares × ₹ 5 = ₹ 60,000

Dr. **(IV) CASH ACCOUNT** *Cr.*

Particulars	₹	*Particulars*	₹
To Balance b/d	2,50,000	By Proposed Dividend	25,000
To Equity Shareholders (5,000 × 15)	75,000	By Debentureholders (₹ 1,05,000 + ₹ 3,15,000)	4,20,000
To Sale of Debenture Redemption Reserve Investment	1,80,000	By Balance c/d	60,000
	5,05,000		5,05,000

PROBLEM 18

Extra Ltd. furnishes you with the following Balance Sheet as on 31st March, 2013: *[₹ in lakhs]*

Liabilities	₹	*Assets*	₹
Share Capital		*Fixed Assets Less* depreciation	50
Equity shares of ₹ 10 each fully paid	100	Investments at cost	120
9% Redeemable Preference Shares of ₹ 100 each fully paid	20	Current Assets	142
Capital Reserves	8		
Revenue Reserves	50		
Securities Premium	60		
10% Debentures	4		
Current liabilities	70		
	312		312

(a) The company redeemed the preference shares at a premium of 10% on 1st April, 2013.

(b) It also bought back 3 lakhs equity shares of ₹ 10 each at ₹ 30 per share.

The payment for the above were made out of huge bank balances, which appeared as a part of the current assets.

(c) Included in its investment were "investments in own debentures" costing ₹ 2 lakhs (face value ₹ 2.20 lakhs). These debentures were cancelled on 1st April, 2013.

(d) The company had 1,00,000 equity stock options outstanding on the above mentioned date, to the employees at ₹ 20 when the market price was ₹ 30. (This was included under current liabilities). On 01.04.2013 employees exercised their options for 50,000 shares.

Pass the journal entries to record the above & Prepare Balance Sheet as at 01.04.2013.

[CA (IPCC) Nov. 2010]

Solution

JOURNAL

(₹ in lakhs)

Date	Particulars		L.F	Dr. (₹)	Cr. (₹)
01.04.2013	9% Redeemable Preference Share Capital A/c	Dr.		20.00	
	Premium on redemption of Preference Shares A/c	Dr.		2.00	
	To Preference Sheraholders A/c				22.00
	(Being preference Share Capital Transferred to shareholders account)				
01.04.2013	Preference Shareholders A/c	Dr.		22.00	
	To Bank A/c				22.00
	(Being payment made to shareholders)				
01.04.2013	Equity Shares Buy Back A/c	Dr.		90.00	
	To Bank A/c				90.00
	(Being 3 lakhs equity shares of 10 each bought back @ 30 per share)				
01.04.2013	Equity Share Capital A/c	Dr.		30.00	
	Securities Premium A/c	Dr.		60.00	
	To Equity Shares buy back A/c				90.00
	(Being cancellation of shares bought back)				
01.04.2013	Revenue Reserve A/c (20 + 30)	Dr.		50.00	
	To Capital Redemption Reserve A/c				50.00
	(Being creation of capital redemption reserve account to the extent of the face value of preference shares redeemed and equity shares bought back as per the law)				
01.04.2013	10% Debentures A/c	Dr.		2.20	
	To Investments (Own Debentures) A/c				2.00
	To Capital Reserve A/c				0.20
	(Being cancellation of own debentures and the Profit on cancellation of debentures t/f to Capital Reserve)				
01.04.2013	Bank A/c	Dr.		10.00	
	Employees Stock Option Outstanding (Current liabilities) A/c	Dr.		5.00	
	To Equity Share Capital A/c				5.00
	To Securities Premium A/c				10.00
	(Being the allotment to employees, of 50,000 shares of ₹ 10 each at a premium of ₹ 20 per share in exercise of stock options by employees)				
01.04.2013	Securities Premium A/c	Dr.		2.00	
	To Premium on Redemption of Preference Shares A/c				2.00
	(Being premium on redemption of preference shares adjusted through securities premium)				

BALANCE SHEET OF EXTRA LTD. AS AT 01.04.2013

Particulars	Note No	₹ (lacs)
I. Equity and Liabilities		
(1) Shareholders' Funds		
(a) Share Capital (*₹ 10 each)[100+5-30]*		75.00
(b) Reserves and Surplus	1	66.20
(2) Non-Current Liabilities [10% Debentures] [4.00 – 2.20]		1.80
(3) Current Liabilities [70 – 5]		65.00
Total		208.00
II. Assets		
(1) Non-Current Assets		
(a) Fixed Assets		
Tangible Assets		50.00
(b) Non-Current Investments [120 – 2]		118.00
(2) Current Assets [142 + 10 – 22 – 90]		40.00
Total		208.00

Notes To Accounts:

Particulars	₹ (lacs)
1. Reserves and Surplus	
Revenue Reserve [50 – 50]	0
Capital Reserve [8.00 + 0.20]	8.20
Capital Redemption Reserve	50.00
Securities Premium [60 + 10 – 60 – 2]	8.00
Total	66.20

PROBLEM 19

M Ltd. furnishes the followinh summarized Balance Sheet as at 31st March, 2013:

Equity & Liabilities	*Rs' 000*	*Assets*	*Rs' 000*
Share Capital:		Fixed Assets (at cost *less* depreciation)	2,750
Authorised *Issued and Subscribed*		Non-Current Investments	5,000
3,00,000, Equity Shares of ₹ 10 each	3,000	Current Assets	4,000
20,000, 9% Preference Shares of ₹ 100 each fully paid up Issued two months back for buy back purposes)	2,000		
Reserves and Surplus:			
Capital Reserve	10		
Revenue Reserve	4,000		
Securities Premium	500		
Profit and Loss A/c	1,800		
Non-Current Liabilities:			
10% Convertible Debentures	400		
Current Liabilities	40		
	11,750		11,750

(1) The company passed a resolution to buy back 20% of its equity capital @ ₹ 15 per share. For this purpose, it sold its investments of ₹ 30 lakhs for ₹ 25 lakhs.

(2) The company redeemed the preference shares at a premium of 10% on 1st April, 2013.

(3) Included in its investments were 'Investments in own debentures' costing ₹ 3 lakhs (face value ₹ 3.30 lakhs). These debentures were cancelled on 1st April, 2013.

You are required to pass necessary Journal entries and prepare the Balance Sheet on 01.04.2013 **[CA (IPCC) Nov. 2012]**

Solution

JOURNAL

(₹ in '000)

Date	Particulars		L.F	Dr. (₹)	Cr. (₹)
	Bank A/c	Dr.		2,500	
	Profit and Loss A/c	Dr.		500	
	To Investments A/c	Dr.			3,000
	(Being the investments sold for Buy back)				
	9% Redeemable Preference Share Capital A/c	Dr.		2,000	
	Premium on redemption of Preference Shares A/c	Dr.		200	
	To Preference Sheraholders A/c				2,200
	(Being the amount due to Preference Shareholders)				
	Preference Shareholders A/c	Dr.		2,200	
	To Bank A/c				2,200
	(Being the payment made to Preference Shareholders)				
	Revenue Reserve A/c	Dr.		2,000	
	To Capital Redemption Reserve A/c				2,000
	(Being the creation of Capital Redemption Reserve to the extent of the face value of preference shares redeemed and equity shares bought back as per the law)				
	Equity Share Capital A/c	Dr.		600	
	Securities Premium A/c	Dr.		300	
	To Equity Shares buy back A/c				900
	(Being cancellation of shares bought back)				
	Equity Shares Buy Back A/c	Dr.		90.00	
	To Bank A/c				90.00
	(Being the payment made for shares bought back)				
	10% Debentures A/c	Dr.		330	
	To Investments (Own Debentures) A/c				300
	To Capital Reserve A/c				30
	(Being cancellation of own debentures and T/F of profit on cancellation of debentures)				
	Securities Premium A/c	Dr.		200	
	To Premium on Redemption of Preference Shares A/c				200
	(Being premium on redemption of preference shares adjusted through securities premium)				

Balance Sheet of M Ltd. as at 01.04.2013

Particulars	Note No	₹ ('000)
I. Equity and Liabilities		
(1) Shareholders' Funds		
(a) Share Capital	1	2,400
(b) Reserves and Surplus	2	5,340
(2) Non-Current Liabilities [10% Debentures] [400 – 330]		70
(3) Current Liabilities [70 – 5]		40
Total		7,850
II. Assets		
(1) Non-Current Assets		
(a) Fixed Assets		2,750
(b) Non-Current Investments [5,000 – 3,000 – 300]		1,700
(2) Current Assets [4,000 + 2,500 – 2,200 – 900]		3,400
Total		7,850

Notes To Accounts:

Particulars	₹ ('000)
1. Share Capital	
Authorised Capital	
2,40,000 Equity Shares of ₹ 10 each	2,400
Issued & Subscribed Capital	
2,40,000 Equity Shares of ₹ 10 each (60,000 Equity Shares bought back)	2,400
2. Reserves and Surplus	
Revenue Reserve [4,000 – 2,000]	2,000
Capital Reserve [10 + 30]	40
Capital Redemption Reserve	2,000
Securities Premium [500 – 200 – 300]	0
Surplus (P & L A/c) [1800 – 500]	1,300
Total	5,340

7 Amalgamation of Companies

SHORT ANSWER PRACTICAL QUESTIONS

PROBLEM 1

A and B decide to amalgamate themselves into Sharp Limited. The following are their Balance Sheets as on 31st March, 2013.

Liabilities	*A Ltd.* ₹	*B Ltd.* ₹	*Assets Investments*	*A Ltd.* ₹	*B Ltd.* ₹
Investments:					
Share Capital	5,00,000	4,00,000	1,000 Shares in B Ltd.	1,30,000	
(₹ 100 each)			2,000 shares in A Ltd.	—	2,10,000
General Reserves	2,00,000	1,00,000	Sundry Assets	7,70,000	4,40,000
10% Debentures	2,00,000	1,50,000			
	9,00,000	**6,50,000**		**9,00,000**	**6,50,000**

Required: Compute the amount of purchase consideration for each of these companies under purchase method as per AS 14. ***[CA (IPCC) Nov. 2010]***

Solution

(c) Let the net assets of A Ltd. be x and net assets of B Ltd. be y.

Then $x = 7,70,000 - 2,00,000 + \frac{1}{4}y$

$x = 5,70,000 + \frac{1}{4}y$

$4x - y = 22,80,000$ (i)

Similarly $y = 4,40,000 - 1,50,000 + 2/5\,x$

$y = 2,90,000 + 2/5\,x$

$-2x + 5y = 14,50,000$ (ii)

By multiplying equation (ii) by 2, we get

$-4x + 10y = 29,00,000$ (iii)

By adding equation (i) with equation (iii), we get

$4x - y = 22,80,000$

$-4x + 10y = 29,00,000$

$9y = 51,80,000$ i.e. $y = \frac{51,80,000}{9}$ = ₹ 5,75,556

Putting the value of y in equation (i) we get

$4x - 5,75,556 = 22,80,000$

$4x = 22,80,000 + 5,75,556$

$x = 28,55,556/4 = 7,13,889$

	A Ltd. ₹	B Ltd. ₹
Total Value of net assets	7,13,889	5,75,556
Less: 1/4 for shares held by A Ltd.	–	1,43,889
Less: 2/5 for shares held by B Ltd.	2,85,556	–
Purchase Consideration	**4,28,333**	**4,31,667**

Presuming that the shares in Sharp Ltd. consist of ₹ 100 each, Sharp Ltd. may satisfy the purchase consideration as follows:

	A Ltd. ₹	B Ltd. ₹
Shares in Sharp Ltd. (₹ 100)	4,28,300	4,31,600
Cash	33	67
	4,28,333	**4,31,667**

LONG ANSWER PRACTICAL QUESTIONS

PROBLEM 2

1. *Following is the Balance Sheet of Y Ltd., as at 31sl March, 2013:*

Liabilities	₹	Assets	₹
Share Capital:		***Fixed Assets***	
Issued & Paid up:		Goodwill	8,00,000
2,50,000 Equity Shares of ₹ 10		Building	7,00,000
each, ₹ 8 per share paid up	20,00,000	Plant and machinery	13,00,000
1,00,000 (10 %) Preference	10,00,000	**Current Assets:**	
shares of ₹ 10 each fully paid up		Stock	7,00,000
Reserves & Surplus:		Sundry Debtors	9,00,000
General reserve	6,00,000	Bank Balance	6,60,000
Profit & Loss A/c	8,00,000	**Miscellaneous Expenditure:**	
Current Liabilities:		Preliminary Expenses	40,000
Creditors	4,00,000		
Workmen's Profit Sharing Fund	3,00,000		
	51,00,000		**51,00,000**

X Ltd. decided to absorb the business of Y Ltd., at the respective book value of assets and trade liabilities except building which was valued at ₹ 12,00,000 and Plant & Machinery at ₹ 10,00,000.

The purchase consideration was payable as follows:

(i) Payment of liquidation expenses ₹ 5,000 and workmen's profit sharing fund at 10% premium;

(ii) Issue of equity share of ₹ 10 each fully paid at ₹ 11 per share for every preference share and every equity share of Y Ltd., and a payment of 4 per equity share in cash.

Calculate the purchase consideration, show the necessary ledger accounts in the books of Y Ltd., and opening journal entries in the books of X Ltd. ***[CA (IPCC) Nov. 2010]***

Solution

(i) Calculation of Purchase Consideration

	₹ in lakhs	₹ in lakhs
Cash payment for:		
Liquidation Expenses	5,000	
Workmen's Profit Sharing fund	3,30,000	
Cash to Equity Shareholders (2,50,000 × 4)	10,00,000	13,35,000
Payment by Equity Shares to		
Preference Shareholders (1,00,000 × 11)	11,00,000	
Equity Shareholders (2,50,000 × 11)	27,50,000	38,50,000
Purchase Consideration		**51,85,000**

Dr. **(II) REALISATION ACCOUNT** Cr.

Particulars	₹	Particulars	₹
To Goodwill	8,00,000	By Creditors	4,00,000
To Building	7,00,000	By X Ltd.	51,85,000
To Plant & Machinery	13,00,000		
To Stock	7,00,000		
To Sundry Debtors	9,00,000		
To Bank	6,60,000		
To Workmen's Profit Sharing Fund	30,000		
To Preference shareholders	1,00,000		
To Bank (Expenses)	5,000		
To Profit	3,90,000		
	55,85,000		**55,85,000**

Dr. **X LTD. ACCOUNT** Cr.

Particulars	₹	Particulars	₹
To Realisation A/c	51,85,000	By Bank	13,35,000
		By Equity shares in X Ltd.	38,50,000
	51,85,000		**51,85,000**

Dr. **BANK ACCOUNT** Cr.

Particulars	₹	Particulars	₹
To X Ltd.	13,35,000	By Realisation (Expenses)	5,000
		By Workmen's Profit Sharing Fund	3,30,000
		By Equity Shareholders A/c	10,00,000
	13,35,000		**13,35,000**

Dr. **PREFERENCE SHAREHOLDERS ACCOUNT** Cr.

Particulars	₹	Particulars	₹
To Equity Shares in X Ltd.	11,00,000	By Preference Shares CapitalA/c	10,00,000
		By Realisation A/c (Bal. fig.)	1,00,000
	11,00,000		**11,00,000**

Dr. **EQUITY SHAREHOLDERS ACCOUNT** Cr.

Particulars	₹	Particulars	₹
To Preliminary Expenses	40,000	By Equity Share Capital	20,00,000
To Bank A/c	10,00,000	By General Reserve	6,00,000
To Equity shares in Y Ltd.	27,50,000	By Profit & Loss A/c	8,00,000
		By Profit on realisation (Bal. fig.)	3,90,000
	37,90,000		**37,90,000**

Dr. **EQUITY SHARES IN X LTD. ACCOUNT** Cr.

Particulars	₹	Particulars	₹
To X Ltd.	38,50,000	By Preference A/c Shareholders	11,00,000
		By Equity shareholders A/c	27,50,000
	38,50,000		**38,50,000**

Dr. **WORKMEN'S PROFIT SHARING FUND ACCOUNT** Cr.

Particulars	₹	Particulars	₹
To Bank	3,30,000	By Balance b/d	3,00,000
		By Realisation A/c *(Bal. Fig.)*	30,000
	3,30,000		**3,30,000**

(III) JOURNAL OF X LTD.

Date	Particulars		Dr. (₹)	Cr. (₹)
1.	Business Purchase A/c	Dr.	51,85,000	
	To Liquidators of Y Ltd.			51,85,000
	(Being business purchased of Y Ltd.)			
2.	Building A/c	Dr.	12,00,000	
	Plant & Machinery A/c	Dr.	10,00,000	
	Stock A/c	Dr.	7,00,000	
	Debtors A/c	Dr.	9,00,000	
	Bank A/c	Dr.	6,60,000	
	Goodwill A/c (Bal. fig.)	Dr.	**11,25,000**	
	To Creditors			4,00,000
	To Business purchase A/c			51,85,000
	(Being assets and liabilities taken over and purchase consideration due)			
3.	Liquidators of Y Ltd.	Dr.	51,85,000	
	To Bank A/c			13,35,000
	To Equity Share Capital A/c			35,00,000
	To Securities Premium A/c			3,50,000
	(Being payment of purchase consideration)			

PROBLEM 3

X Ltd. and Y Ltd. were carrying on same business independently. The companies agreed to amalgamate on and from 1-4-2012 and formed a new company Z Ltd. to take over the assets and liabilities of the existing companies. The Balance Sheets of two companies as on 31-3-2013 are as follows:

Liabilities	*X Ltd.* ₹	*Y Ltd.* ₹	*Assets*	*X Ltd.* ₹	*Y Ltd.* ₹
Share capital: Equity			Land & building	27,00,000	13,50,000
shares of ₹ 10 each			Plant & machinery	15,00,000	11,40,000
(fully paid up)	30,00,000	18,00,000	Investments		
Securities premium	6,00,000	—	(15,000 shares		
General reserve	9,00,000	7,50,000	of Y Ltd.)	2,40,000	—
Profit & loss account	5,40,000	4,80,000	Stock	15,60,000	10,50,000
10% Debentures	15,00,000	—	Debtors	12,30,000	7,80,000
Secured loan	—	9,00,000	Cash at bank	90,000	1,20,000
Sundry creditors	7,80,000	5, 10,000			
	73,20,000	44,40,000		73,20,000	44,40,000

Following are the additional information:

(i) For the purpose of amalgamation, the shares of the existing companies are to be valued as under:

X Ltd. = ₹ 18 per share

Y Ltd. = ₹ 20 per share.

(ii) A contingent liability ofX Ltd. of ₹ 1,80,000 is to be treated as actual existing liability.

(iii) The shareholders ofX Ltd. and Y Ltd. are to be paid by issuing sufficient number of shares of Z Ltd. at a premium of ₹ 6 per share.

(iv) The face value of shares of Z Ltd. is to be of ₹ 10 each.

You are required to:

(i) Calculate the purchase consideration (i.e. the number of shares to be issued to X Ltd. and Y Ltd.)

(II) Prepare Realisation Account and Shareholders Account in the books of X Ltd. & Y Ltd.

(iii) Prepare the Balance Sheet of Z Ltd. after amalgamation. ***[CA (IPCC) Nov., 2011]***

Solution

(I) CALCULATION OF PURCHASE CONSIDERATION

No. of shares

Particulars	*X Ltd.*	*Y Ltd.*
Existing Number of shares	3,00,000	1,80,000
Less: Number of shares held bv X Ltd. in Y Ltd.	—	(15,000)
Net Number of Shares	3,00,000	1,65,000
Value per share	₹ 18	₹ 20
Purchase consideration	₹ 54,00,000	₹ 33,00,000
Number of shares of Z Ltd. @? 16 per share	3,37,500 shares	2,06,250 shares

DISCHARGE OF PURCHASE CONSIDERATION

Particulars	X Ltd.	Y Ltd.
Face Value of Share Capital		
X Ltd. = 3,37,500 shares × ₹ 10 each	33,75,000	
Y Ltd. = 2,06,250 shares × ₹ 10 each		20,62,500
Securities premium		
X Ltd. = 3,37,500 shares × ₹ 6 each	20,25,000	
Y Ltd. = 2,06,250 shares × ₹ 6 each		12,37,500
	54,00,000	33,00,000

(ii)

IN THE BOOKS OF X LTD.
REALIZATION ACCOUNT

Dr. Cr.

Particulars	₹	Particulars	₹
To Sundry Assets:		By 10%Debentures	15,00,000
Land and building	27,00,000	By Sundry creditors	
Plant and machinery	15,00,000	(7,80,000+1,80,000)	9,60,000
Investments	2,40,000	By Z Ltd.	
Stock	15,60,000	(Purchase consideration)	54,00,000
Debtors	12,30,000		
Bank	90,000		
To Equity Shareholders A/c (Profit)	5,40,000		
	78,60,000		78,60,000

EQUITY SHAREHOLDER'S ACCOUNT

Dr. Cr.

Particulars	₹	Particulars	₹
To Shares in Z Ltd. A/c	54,00,000	By Share capital	30,00,000
		By Securities premium	6,00,000
		By General reserve	9,00,000
		By Profit & loss A/c	3,60,000
		(5,40,000 – 1,80,000)	
		By Realization A/c	5,40,000
	54,00,000		54,00,000

(b)

IN THE BOOKS OF Y LTD.
REALIZATION ACCOUNT

Dr. Cr.

Particulars	₹	Particulars	₹
To Sundry Assets:		By Secured loan	9,00,000
Land and building	13,50,000	By Sundry creditors	5,10,000
Plant and machinery	11,40,000	By Z Ltd.	
Stock	10,50,000	(Purchase consideration)	33,00,000
Debtors	7,80,000		
Bank	1,20,000		
To Equity Shareholders A/c (Profit)	2,70,000		
	47,10,000		47,10,000

Dr. **EQUITY SHAREHOLDERS ACCOUNT** Cr.

Particulars	₹	Particulars	₹
To Shares in Z Ltd. A/c	33,00,000	By Share capital	18,00,000
		By General reserve	7,50,000
		By Profit & loss A/c	4,80,000
		By Realization A/c	2,70,000
	33,00,000		33,00,000

BALANCE SHEET OF Z LTD. AS AT 31.3.2013

Particulars	Note No	₹
I. Equity and Liabilities		
(1) Shareholders' Funds		
(a) Share Capital (₹ 10 each)	1	54,37,500
(c) Reserves and Surplus [Securities Premium]		32,62,500
(2) Non-Current Liabilities [10% Debentures + Loan]		24,00,000
(3) Current Liabilities		
(a) Trade Payables [Creditors]		14,70,000
Total		125,70,000
II. Assets		
(1) Non-Current Assets		
(a) Fixed Assets		
Tangible Assets	2	66,90,000
Intangible Assets [Goodwill]		10,50,000
(2) Current Assets		
(a) Inventories		26,10,000
(b) Trade Receivables [Debtors]		20,10,000
(b) Cash and Cash Equivalents		2,10,000
Total		125,70,000

Notes To Accounts:

Particulars	₹
1. Share Capital	
5,43,750 Equity Shares of ₹ 10 each	54,37,500
(Of the above all Shares were issued for consideration otherwise than cash)	
2. Tangible Assets	
Land & Building	40,50,000
Plant & Machinery	26,40,000
Total	66,90,000

Working Note:

CALCULATION OF GOODWILL / (CAPITAL RESERVE)

Particulars		*X Ltd.* ₹	*Y Ltd.* ₹
Purchase consideration	(A)	54,00,000	33,00,000
Assets taken over of			
XLtd.		70,80,000	
(27,00,000 + 15,00,000 + 15,60,000 + 12,30,000 + 90,000)			
YLtd.			44,40,000
(13,50,000 + 11,40,000 + 10,50,000 + 7,80,000 + 1,20,000)			
Less: Liabilities taken over of X Ltd.			
(15,00,000 + 7,80,000 + 1,80,000)		(24,60,000)	
Liabilities taken over of Y Ltd.			
(9,00,000 + 5,10,000)			(14,10,000)
Net Assets	(B)	46,20,000	30,30,000
Goodwill (B – A)		7,80,000	2,70,000

PROBLEM 4

Given below balance sheet of Vasudha Ltd. and Vaishali Ltd. as at 31st March 2013:

Liabilities	*Vasudha Ltd.*	*Vaishali Ltd.*	*Assets*	*Vasudha Ltd*	*Vaishali Ltd*
Issued Share Capital:			Factory Building	2,10,000	1,60,000
Equity Shares of			Debtors	2,86,900	1,72,900
₹ 10 each	5,40,000	4,03,300	Stock	91,500	82,500
General Reserves	1,01,000	65,000	Goodwill	50,000	35,000
Profit & Loss A/c	66,000	43,500	Cash at Bank	98,000	1,09,590
Sundry Creditors	44,400	58,200	Preliminary Expenses	15,000	10,010
	7,51,400	5,70,000		7,51,400	5,70,000

Goodwill of the Companies Vasudha Ltd. and Vaishali Ltd. is to be valued at ₹ 75,000 and ₹ 50,000 respectively. Factory Building of Vasudha Ltd is worth ₹ 1,95,000 and Vaishali Ltd. ₹ 1,75,000. Stock of Vaishali Ltd. Has been shown at 10% above of its cost.

It is decided that Vasudha Ltd will absorb Vaishali Ltd, by taking over its entire business by issue of shares at the intrinsic Value.

Required: To draft the balance sheet of the Vasudha Ltd. after putting through the scheme.

[May 2012]

Solution

BALANCE SHEET OF VASUDHA LTD. AS AT 31.3.2013

Particulars	*Note No*	₹
I. Equity and Liabilities		
(1) Shareholders' Funds		
(a) Share Capital (₹ 10 each)	1	9,43,300
(b) Reserves and Surplus	2	2,72,990
(2) Non-Current Liabilities		
(3) Current Liabilities		
(a) Trade Payables [44,400 + 58,200]		1,02,600
Total		13,18,890

II. Assets	
(1) Non-Current Assets	
(a) Fixed Assets	
Tangible Assets [Factory Building] [2,10,000 + 1,75,000]	3,85,000
Intangible Assets [Goodwill] [50,000 + 50,000]	1,00,000
(2) Current Assets	
(a) Inventories [91,500 + 75,000]	1,66,500
(b) Trade Receivables [7,86,900 + 1,72,900]	4,59,800
(b) Cash and Cash Equivalents [98,000 + 1,09,590]	2,07,590
Total	13,18,890

Notes To Accounts:

Particulars	₹
1. Share Capital	
94,330 Equity Shares of ₹ 10 each	9,43,300
(Of the above 40,330 Shares were issued for consideration otherwise than cash)	
2. Reserves and Surplus	
Securities Premium	1,20,990
General Reserve	1,01,000
Profit & Loss Account [66,000 – *15,000] (Preliminary Exp)]	51,000
	2,72,990

*As per para 56 of As 26, Preliminary Expenses are to be written of in the year in which these are incurred.

Working Note:

(I) COMPUTATION OF SHARES ISSUED ON THE BASIS OF INTRINSIC VALUES

	Vasudha Ltd. ₹	*Vaishali Ltd.* ₹
A. Assets taken over		
Goodwill	75,000	50,000
Factory building	1,95,000	1,75,000
Debtors	2,86,900	1,72,900
Stock	91,500	(82,500/110%) = 75,000
Cash at Bank	98,000	1,09,590
	7,46,400	5,82,490
B. *Less:* Sundry Creditors takeover	(44,400)	(58,200)
C. Net Assets	7,02,000	5,24,290
D. Number of Shares	54,000	40,330
E. Intrinsic Value [C/D]	₹ 13	₹ 13

F. Exchange Ratio: Vasudha Ltd. will give its 40,330 shares of ₹ 10 each @ ₹ 13 each to Vaishali Ltd.

(ii) Discharge of Purchase consideration

Share Capital 40,330 Shares @ ₹ 10 each	4,03,330
Securities Premium 40,330 Shares @ ₹ 3 each	1,20,990

PROBLEM 5

P Ltd. and Q Ltd. were carrying on the business of manufacturing of auto components. both the companies decided to amalgamare and a new company PQ Ltd. is to be formed with an Authorized Capital of ₹ 10,00,000 divided into 1,00,000 equity shares of ₹ 10 each. The Balance Sheet of the companies as on 31.03.2014 were as under:

Balance Sheet of P Limited as at 31.03.2014

Particulars	*Amount (₹)*
I. Equity and Liabilities	
1. Shareholder's Fund	
(a) Share Capital	1,40,00
(b) Reserves & Surplus (Profit & Loss A/c)	30,000
2. Non Current Liabilities (8 % Secured Debentures)	1,10,000
3. Current Liabilities (Trade Payables)	54,000
Total	3,34,000
II. Assets	
1. Non-current Assets	
(a) Fixed Assets	
Bulding at cost less Depreciation	1,00,000
Plant & Machinery at cost *less* Depreciation	25,000
2. Current Assets	
(a) Inventories	1,35,000
(b) Trade Receivables	44,000
(c) Cash at bank	30,000
Total	3,34,000

Balance Sheet of Q Limited as at 31.03.2014

Particulars	*Amount (₹)*
I. Equity and Liabilities	
1. Shareholder's Fund	
(a) Share Capital	2,50,000
(b) Reserves & Surplus	
General Reserve	1,20,000
Profit & Loss A/c	35,000
2. Current Liabilities (Trade Payables)	1,40,000
Total	5,45,000
II. Assets	
1. Non-current assets	
(a) Fixed Assets	
Building at cost less depreciation	1,90,000
Plant & Machinery at cost less depreciation	80,000
Furniture & Fixture at cost less depreciation	25,000
2. Current Assets	
(a) Inventories	50,000
(b) Trade Receivables	1,42,000
(c) Cash at bank	58,000
Total	5,45,000

The assets and liabilities of the existing companies are to be transferred at book value with the exception of some items detailed below:

(i) Goodwill of P Ltd. was worth ₹ 50,000 and of Q Ltd. was worth ₹ 1,50,000,.

(ii) Furniture & Fixture of Q Ltd. was valued at ₹ 35,000.

(iii) The debtors of P Ltd. are realized fully and bank balance of P Ltd. are to be retained by the liquidator and the sundry creditors are to be paid of the proceeds thereof.

(iv) The debentures of P Ltd. are to be dischareged by issue of 8% debentures of PQ Ltd. at a premium of 10%.

You are required to:

(i) Compute the basis on which shares in PQ Ltd. will be issued at par to the shareholders of the existing companies.

(ii) Draw up a Balance Sheet of PQ Ltd. as at 1st April, 2014, the date of completiion of amalgamatiion.

(iii) Write up Journal entires including bank entries for closing the books of P Ltd.

[May 2014]

Solution

Calculation of Purchase Consideration

	P Ltd. (₹)	*Q Ltd. (₹)*
Assets taken over:		
Goodwill	50,000	1,50,000
Building	1,00,000	1,90,000
Plant & Machinery	25,000	80,000
Furniture & Fixtures	–	35,000
Inventories	1,35,000	50,000
Trade Receivables	–	1,42,000
Cash at Bank	–	58,000
	3,10,000	7,05,000
Less: Liabilities taken over:		
8% Debentures	(1,21,000)	–
Trade Payables	–	(1,40,000)
Net Assets taken over	1,89,000	5,65,000
To be satisfied by issue of shares of PQ Ltd. of ₹ 10 each at par	18,900	56,500

Balance Sheet of PQ Limited as at 1st April, 2014

Particulars	*Note No.*	*Amount (₹)*
I. Equity and Liabilities		
(1) Shareholder's Funds		
(a) Share Capital	1	7,54,000
(b) Reserve & Surplus	2	11,000
(2) Non-Current Liabilities		
(a) Long term borrowings	3	1,10,000
(3) Current Liabilities		
(a) Trade Payables		1,40,000
Total		10,15,000

	Note No.	₹
II. Assets		
(1) Non-Current assets		
(a) Fixed Assets		
Tangible	4	4,30,000
Intangible	5	2,00,000
(2) Current Assets		
(a) Inventories		1,85,000
(b) Trade Receivables		1,42,000
(c) Cash at Bank		58,000
Total		10,15,000

Notes to Accounts:

		₹
1. Share Capital		
Authorized		
1,00,000 shares of ₹ 10 eac		10,00,000
Issued, Subscribed and Paid up		
75,400 shares of ₹ 10 each		7,54,000
(All the above shares are allotted as fully paid up pursuant to scheme of amalgamation withut payments being received in cash)		
2. **Reserve & Surplus**		
Securities Premium Account [₹ 1,10,000 × 10%]		11,000
3. **Long term borrowings**		
8% Debentures		1,10,000
4. **Tangible Fixed Assets**		
Building		
P Ltd.	1,00,000	
Q Ltd.	1,90,000	2,90,000
Plant & Machinery		
P Ltd.	25,000	
Q Ltd.	80,000	1,05,000
Furniture & Fixture		
Q Ltd.		35,000
		4,30,000
5. **Intangible Asset**		
Goodwill		
P Ltd.	50,000	
Q. Ltd.	1,50,000	2,00,000

Journal of P Ltd.

Date	*Particulars*		*Dr. (₹)*	*Cr. (₹)*
1	Realization A/c	Dr.	3,04,000	
	To Building			1,00,000
	To Plant & Machinery			25,000
	To Inventories			1,35,000
	To Trade Receivables			44,000
	(Being all assets except cash transferred to Realization A/c)			

Date	Particulars		Dr. (₹)	Cr. (₹)
2	8% Debentures A/c	Dr.	1,10,000	
	Trade Payables	Dr.	54,000	
	To Realization A/c			1,64,000
	(Being all liabilities transferred to Realization Account)			
3	Equity Share Capital A/c	Dr.	1,40,000	
	Profit & Loss A/c	Dr.	30,000	
	To Equity Shareholder's A/c			1,70,000
	(Being Equity transferred to Equity Shareholder's Account)			
4	PQ Ltd	Dr.	1,89,000	
	To Realization A/c			1,89,000
	(Being Purchase consideration due)			
5	Bank A/c	Dr.	44,000	
	To Realization A/c			44,000
	(Being cash received from trade receivables in full)			
6	Realization A/c	Dr.	54,000	
	To Bank A/c			54,000
	(Being payment made to Trade Payables)			
7	Share in PQ Ltd.	Dr.	1,89,000	
	To PQ Ltd.			1,89,000
	(Being purchase consideration received in the form of Equity Shares of PQ Ltd.)			
8	Realization A/c (balancing figure)	Dr.	39,000	
	To Equity Shareholder's A/c			39,000
	(Being profit on realization transferred to Equity Shareholder's A/c)			
9	Equity Shareholder's A/c	Dr.	2,09,000	
	To Shares in PQ Ltd.			1,89,000
	To Bank A/c			20,000
	(Being final payment made to shareholders)			

8 Internal Reconstruction

LONG ANSWER PRACTICAL QUESTIONS

PROBLEM 1

Balance Sheet of *Y* Ltd. as at 31st March, 2013 was as follows:

	₹		₹
5,00,000 Equity Shares of ₹ 10 each fully paid	50,00,000	Goodwill	10,00,000
		Patent	5,00,000
9% 20,000 Preference Shares of ₹ 100 each fully paid	20,00,000	Land and Building	30,00,000
		Plant and Machinery	10,00,000
10% First Debentures	6,00,000	Furniture and Fixtures	2,00,000
10% Second Debentures	10,00,000	Computers	3,00,000
Debentures interest outstanding	1,60,000	Trade Investment	5,00,000
Trade Creditors	5,00,000	Debtors	5,00,000
Directors' Loan	1,00,000	Stock	10,00,000
Bank O/D	1,00,000	Discount on issue of Debentures	1,00,000
Outstanding Liabilities	40,000	Profit and Loss Account (Loss)	15,00,000
Provision for Tax	1,00,000		
	96,00,000		96,00,000

Note: *Preference Dividend is in arrears for last three years.*

A holds 10% first debentures for ₹ 4,00,000 and 10% second debentures for ₹ 6,00,000. He is also a creditor for ₹ 1,00,000. *B* holds 10% first debentures for ₹ 2,00,000 and 10% second debentures for ₹ 4,00,000 and is also a creditor for ₹ 50,000.

The following scheme of reconstruction has been agreed upon and duly approved by the court:

(a) All the equity shares be converted into fully paid equity shares of ₹ 5 each.

(b) The preference shares be reduced to ₹ 50 each and the preference shareholders agree to forego their arrears of preference dividends in consideration of which 9% preference shares are to be converted into 10% preference shares.

(c) Mr. '*A*' is to cancel ₹ 6,00,000 of his total debt including interest on debentures and to pay ₹ 1 lakh to the company and to receive new 12% debentures for the Balance Amount.

(d) Mr. '*B*' is to cancel ₹ 3,00,000 of his total debt including interest on debentures and to accept new 12% debentures for the balance amount.

(e) Trade creditors (other than *A* and *B*) agreed to forego 50% of their claim.

(f) Directors to accept settlement of their loans as to 60% thereof by allotment of equity shares and balance being waived.

(g) There were capital commitments totalling ₹ 3,00,000. These contracts are to be cancelled on payment of 5% of the contract price as a penalty.

(h) The Directors refund ₹ 1,10,000 of the fees previously received by them.

(i) Reconstruction expenses paid ₹ 10,000.

(j) The taxation liability of the company is settled at ₹ 80,000 and the same is paid immediately.

(k) The assets are revalued as under:

	₹
Land and Building	28,00,000
Plant and Machinery	4,00,000
Stock	7,00,000
Debtors	3,00,000
Computers	1,80,000
Furniture and Fixtures	1,00,000
Trade Investment	4,00,000

Required: Pass Journal entries for all the above mentioned transactions including amounts to be written off of Goodwill, Patents, Loss in Profit and Loss Account and Discount on issue of debentures. Prepare Bank Account and working of allocation of Interest on Debentures between *A* and *B*.

[CA (PE II) November 2003]

Solution

JOURNAL ENTRIES IN THE BOOKS OF *Y* LTD.

		. .	. (₹)	. (₹)
(i) Equity Share Capital (₹ 10 each) A/c	Dr.		50,00,000	
To Equity Share Capital (₹ 5 each) A/c				25,00,000
To Reconstruction A/c				25,00,000
(Being conversion of 5,00,000 equity shares of ₹ 10 each fully paid into same number of fully paid equity shares of ₹ 5 each as per scheme of reconstruction)				
(ii) 9% Preference Share Capital (₹ 100 each) A/c	Dr.		20,00,000	
To 10% Preference Share Capital (₹ 100 each) A/c			10,00,000	
To Reconstruction A/c				10,00,000
(Being conversion of 9% preference shares of 100 each into same number of 10% preference share of ₹ 50 each and claims of preference dividends settled as per scheme of reconstruction)				
(iii) 10% First Debentures A/c	Dr.		4,00,000	
10% Second Debentures A/c	Dr.		6,00,000	
Trade Creditors A/c	Dr.		1,00,000	
Interest on Debentures Outstanding A/c	Dr.		1,00,000	
Bank A/c	Dr.		1,00,000	
To 12% New Debentures A/c				7,00,000
To Reconstruction A/c				6,00,000
(Being ₹ 6,00,000 due to *A* (Including creditors) cancelled and 12% new debentures allotted for balance amount as per scheme of reconstruction)				
(iv) 10% First Debentures A/c	Dr.		2,00,000	
10% Second Debentures A/c	Dr.		4,00,000	
Trade Creditors A/c	Dr.		50,000	
Interest on Debentures Outstanding A/c	Dr.		60,000	
To 12% New Debentures A/c	Dr.			4,10,000
To Reconstruction A/c				3,00,000
(Being ₹ 3,00,000 due to *B* (including creditors) cancelled and 12% new debentures allotted for balance amount as per scheme of reconstruction)				
(v) Trade Creditors A/c	Dr.		1,75,000	
To Reconstruction A/c				1,75,000
(Being remaining creditors sacrificed 50% of their claim)				
(vi) Directors' Loan A/c	Dr.		1,00,000	
To Equity Share Capital (₹ 5) A/c				60,000
To Reconstruction A/c				40,000
(Being Directors' loan claim settled by issuing 12,000 equity shares of ₹ 5 each as per scheme of reconstruction)				

		(₹)	(₹)
(vii) Reconstruction A/c	Dr.	15,000	
To Bank A/c			15,000
(Being payment made for cancellation of capital commitments)			
(viii) Bank A/c	Dr.	1,10,000	
To Reconstruction A/c			1,10,000
(Being refund of fees by directors credited to reconstruction A/c			
(ix) Reconstruction A/c	Dr.	10,000	
To Bank A/c			10,000
(Being payment of reconstruction expenses)			
(x) Provision for Tax A/c	Dr.	1,00,000	
To Bank A/c			80,000
To Reconstruction A/c			20,000
(Being payment of tax for 80% of liability in full settlement)			
(xi) Reconstruction A/c	Dr.	47,20,000	
To Goodwill A/c			10,00,000
To Patent A/c			5,00,000
To Profit and Loss A/c			15,00,000
To Discount on issue of Debentures A/c			1,00,000
To Land and Building A/c			2,00,000
To Plant and Machinery A/c			6,00,000
To Furniture and Fixture A/c			1,00,000
To Computers Alc			1,20,000
To Trade Investment Alc			1,00,000
To Stock A/c			3,00,000
To Debtors A/c			2,00,000
(Being Writing off of losses and reduction in the value of assets as per scheme of reconstruction)			

Working Notes:

(i) *Outstanding interest on debentures have been allocated between A and B as follows:*

	A ₹	B ₹	Total
10% First Debentures	4,00,000	2,00,000	
10% Second Debentures	6,00,000	4,00,000	
	10,00,000	6,00,000	
Interest @ 10%	1,00,000	60,000	1,60,000

Dr. **(II) BANK ACCOUNT** Cr.

	₹		₹
To A (reconstruction)	1,00,000	By Balance b/d	1,00,000
To Reconstruction A/c (paid by directors)	1,10,000	By Reconstruction A/c (Capital commitment penalty paid)	15,000
		By Reconstruction A/c (reconstruction expenses paid)	10,000
		By Provision for tax A/c (tax paid)	80,000
		By Balance c/d	5,000
	2,10,000		2,10,000

(iii) *Capital Reduction or Reorganisation Account can also be used in place of Reconstruction Account.*

PROBLEM 2

The Balance Sheet of Munna Ltd. on 31st March, 2013 is as under:

	₹		₹
Equity Share Capital	20,00,000	Goodwill	2,00,000
20,000 shares of ₹ 100 each		Plant and Machinery	18,00,000
10,000, 7% preference shares of	10,00,000	Stock	3,00,000
₹ 100 each		Debtors	7,50,000
Sundry Creditors	7,00,000	Preliminary Expenses	1,00,000
Bank overdraft	3,00,000	Cash	1,50,000
		Profit & Loss Account	7,00,000
	40,00,000		40,00,000

Two years' preference dividend are in arrears. The company had been bad time during the last two years and hopes for better business in future, earning profit and paying dividend provided the capital base is reduced.

An internal reconstruction scheme as follows was agreed to by all concerned:

(a) Creditors agreed to forego 50% of the claim.

(b) Preference shareholders withdrew arrears dividend claim. They also agreed to lower their capital claim by 20% by reducing nominal value in consideration of 9% dividend effective after reorganisation in case equity shareholders' loss exceeded 50% on the application of the scheme.

(c) Bank agreed to convert overdraft into term loan to the extent required for making current ratio equal to 2 : 1.

(d) Revalued figure for plant and machinery was accepted as ₹ 15,00,000.

(e) Debtors to the extent of ₹ 4,00,000 were considered good.

(f) Equity shares shall be exchanged for the same number of equity shares at a revised denomination as required after the reorganisation.

Required:

(a) Total loss to be borne by the equity and preference shareholders for the reorganisation;

(b) Shares of loss to the individual classes of shareholders;

(c) New structure of share capital after reorganisation;

(d) Working capital of the reorganised Co.; and

(e) A proforma balance sheet after reorganisation. *[CA (PE II) May 2005]*

Solution

(a) Loss to be borne by Equity and Preference Shareholders:

	₹
Profit and Loss A/c (debit balance)	7,00,000
Preliminary Expenses	1,00,000
Goodwill	2,00,000
Plant and Machinery (₹ 18,00,000 – ₹ 15,00,000)	3,00,000
Debtors	3,50,000
Amount to be written off	16,50,000
Less: 50% of Sundry Creditors	3,50,000
Loss to be borne by equity and preference shareholders	13,00,000

Note: *Since preference dividend for 2 years which is in arrears is sacrificed by preference shareholders, the same may be ignored in the above calculation or alternatively may be included in the amount to be written off and then reduced therefrom as preference shareholders' sacrifice.*

(b) Shares of loss to preference shareholders and equity shareholders

Total loss being more than 50% of equity share capital:

Preference shareholders' share of loss = 20% of ₹ 10,00,000 =	₹ 2,00,000
Equity shareholders' share of loss (₹ 13,00,000 – ₹ 2,00,000)	₹ 11,00,000
Total	₹ 13,00,000

(c) New structure of capital

	₹
Equity Shares	
20,000 shares of ₹ 45 each fully paid	9,00,000
Preference Shares	
10,000, 9% shares of ₹ 80 each fully paid	8,00,000
	17,00,000

(d) Working Capital of the reorganised company

	₹	₹
Current Assets		
Stock		3,00,000
Debtors		4,00,000
Cash		1,50,000
		8,50,000
Less: Current Liabilities		
Creditors	3,50,000	
Bank overdraft (see Note)	75,000	4,25,000
Working Capital		4,25,000

Note: *Current ratio shall be 2: 1, i.e., total current liabilities shall be 50% of ₹ 8,50,000 = ₹ 4,25,000. Therefore, Bank overdraft = ₹ 4,25,000 – ₹ 3,50,000 = ₹ 75,000.*

BALANCE SHEET OF MUNNA LTD. (AND REDUCED) AS AT 31.3.2013

Particulars	*Note No*	₹
I. Equity and Liabilities		
(1) Shareholders' Funds		
(a) Share Capital	1	17,00,000
(b) Reserves and Surplus		
(2) Non-Current Liabilities [Term Loan with Bank]		2,25,000
(3) Current Liabilities		
(a) Short-term Borrowings[Bank O/D]		75,000
(b) Trade Payables [Creditors]		3,50,000
Total		23,50,000
II. Assets		
(1) Non-Current Assets		
(a) Fixed Assets		
Tangible Assets [18,00,000 – 3,00,000 (Amt. w/o)]		15,00,000
Intangible Assets [Goodwill] [2,00,000 – 2,00,000(Amt. w/o)]		0
(2) Current Assets		
(a) Inventories		3,00,000
(b) Trade Receivables [Debtors]		4,00,000
(c) Cash and Cash Equivalents		1,50,000
Total		23,50,000

Notes To Accounts:

Particulars	₹
1. Share Capital	
20000 Equity Shares of ₹ 45 each	9,00,000
10000,9% Pref. Shares of ₹ 80 each	8,00,000
	17,00,000

PROBLEM 3

Following is the Balance Sheet as at March 31, 2013:

(₹ '000)

Share capital:			Goodwill	20	—
Equity shares of			Other fixed assets	1,500	760
₹ 100 each	1,500	1,000	Debtors	651	440
9% Preference shares of			Stock	393	680
₹ 100 each	500	400	Cash at bank	26	130
General reserve	180	170	Own debentures		
Profit and loss account	—	15	[Nominal value		
12% Debentures of			₹ 2,00,000]	192	—
₹ 100 each	600	200	Discount on issue of		
Sundry Creditors	415	225	debentures	2	—
			Profit and loss account	411	—
	3,195	2,010		3,195	2,010

On 1.4.2013, Max Ltd. adopted the following scheme of reconstruction:

(a) Each equity share shall be sub-divided into 10 equity shares of ₹ 10 each fully paid up. 50% of the equity share capital would be surrendered to the company.

(b) Preference dividends are in arrear for 3 years. Preference shareholders agreed to waive 90% of the dividend claim and accept payment for the balance.

(c) Own debentures of ₹ 80,000 were sold at ₹ 98 own-interest and remaining own debentures were cancelled.

(d) Debentureholders of ₹ 2,80,000 agreed to accept one machinery of book value of ₹ 3,00,000 in full settlement.

(e) Creditors, debtors and stocks were valued at ₹ 3,50,000, ₹ 5,90,000 and ₹ 3,60,000 respectively. The goodwill, discount on issue of debentures and profit and loss (Dr.) are to be written off.

(f) The Company paid ₹ 15,000 as penalty to avoid capital commitments of ₹ 3,00,000.

On 2.4.2013 a scheme of absorption was adopted. Max Ltd. would take over Mini Ltd. The purchase consideration was fixed as below:

(i) Equity shareholders of Mini Ltd. will be given 50 equity shares of ₹ 10 each fully paid up, in exchange for every 5 shares held in Mini Ltd.

(ii) Issue of 9% preference shares of ₹ 100 each in the ratio of 4 preference shares of Max Ltd. for every 5 preference shares held in Mini Ltd.

(iii) Issue of one 12% debentures of ₹ 100 each of Max Ltd. for every 12% Debentures in Mini Ltd.

Required: Give journal entries in the books of Max Ltd. and draw the resultant Balance Sheet as at 2nd April, 2013. ***[CA (PE II) Nov. 2005]***

Solution

JOURNAL

Date	Particulars		L.F.	Dr. (₹)	Cr. (₹)
01 April	Equity Share Capital A/c	Dr.		15,00,000	
	To Equity Share Capital A/c				15,00,000
	(Being the sub-division of one share of ₹ 100 each into 10 shares of ₹ 10 each)				
	Equity Share Capital A/c	Dr.		7,50,000	
	To Reconstruction A/c				7,50,000
	(Being the reduction of capital by 50%)				
	Reconstruction A/c	Dr.		13,500	
	To Bank A/c				13,500
	(Being the payment in cash of 10% of arrear of preference dividend)				
	Bank A/c	Dr.		78,400	
	To Own Debentures A/c				76,800
	To Reconstruction A/c				1,600
	(Being the transfer of profit on sale of own debentures to capital reduction A/c)				
	12% Debentures A/c	Dr.		1,20,000	
	To Own debentures A/c				1,15,200
	To Reconstruction A/c				4,800
	(Being the T/f of profit on cancellation of own debentures to Capital Reduction A/c)				
	12.% Debentures A/c	Dr.		2,80,000	
	Reconstruction A/c	Dr.		20,000	
	To Machinery A/c				3,00,000
	(Being the machinery taken up by debenture-holders for ₹ 2,80,000)				
	Reconstruction A/c	Dr.		94,000	
	To Debtors A/c				61,000
	To Stock A/c				33,000
	(Being assets and liabilities revalued)				
	Creditors A/c	Dr.		65,000	
	To Reconstruction A/c				65,000
	(Being the liabilities revalued)				
	Reconstruction A/c	Dr.		4,33,000	
	To Goodwill A/c				20,000
	To Discount on debentures A/c				2,000
	To Profit and Loss A/c				4,11,000
	(Being the balance of Reconstruction account transferred to capital reserve account				
	Reconstruction A/c	Dr.		15,000	
	To Bank A/c				15,000
	(Being the penalty paid for avoidance of capital commitments)				
	Reconstruction A/c	Dr.		2,45,900	
	To Capital reserve A/c				2,45,900
	(Being the transfer of Balance to Capital Reserve)				

Date	Particulars		L.F.	Dr. (₹)	Cr. (₹)
02 April	Business Purchase A/c	Dr.		13,20,000	
	To Liquidators of Mini Ltd.				13,20,000
	(Being the purchase of business)				
	Fixed assets A/c	Dr.		7,60,000	
	Stock A/c	Dr.		6,80,000	
	Debtors A/c	Dr.		4,40,000	
	Cash at bank A/c	Dr.		1,30,000	
	To Sundry creditors A/c				2,25,000
	To 12% Debentures A/c of Mini Ltd.				2,00,000
	To Profit and loss A/c				15,000
	To General Reserve A/c ₹ (1,70,000 + 80,000*)				2,50,000
	To Business Purchase A/c				13,20,000
	(Being the recording over of all assets and liabilities taken over)				
	Liquidators of Mini Ltd. A/c	Dr.		13,20,000	
	To Equity share capital A/c				10,00,000
	To 9% Preference share capital A/c				3,20,000
	(Being the purchase consideration discharged)				
	12% Debentures of Mini Ltd. A/c	Dr.		2,00,000	
	To 12% Debentures A/c				2,00,000
	(Being the issue of 12% Debentures against Debentures of Mini Ltd.)				

**₹ 80,000 is the balancing figure adjusted to general reserve account as per AS 14 "Accounting for Amalgamation".

BALANCE SHEET OF MAX LTD. AS AT 02.04.2013

Particulars	Note No	₹
I. Equity and Liabilities		
(1) Shareholders' Funds		
(a) Share Capital	1	25,70,000
(b) Reserves and Surplus	2	6,90,900
(2) Non-Current Liabilities[12%Debentures]		4,00,000
(3) Current Liabilities		
(a) Trade Payables [Creditors]		5,75,000
Total		42,35,900
II. Assets		
(1) Non-Current Assets		
(a) Fixed Assets		
Tangible Assets		19,60,000
(2) Current Assets		
(a) Inventories		10,40,000
(b) Trade Receivables [Debtors]		10,30,000
(c) Cash and Cash Equivalents		2,05,900
Total		42,35,900

Notes To Accounts :

Particulars	₹
1. Share Capital	
175000 Equity Shares of ₹ 10 each	17,50,000
8200,9% Pref. Shares of ₹ 100 each	8,20,000
(Of the above 100000 *Equity* Shares & 3200,*9% Pref. Shares* were issued for consideration otherwise than cash)	25,70,000
2. Reserves and Surplus	
General Reserve	4,30,000
Profit & Loss Account	15,000
Capital Reserve	2,45,900
Total	6,90,900

Working Notes:

(i) *Purchase Consideration:* ₹

Equity share capital $10{,}000 \times \frac{50}{5} \times ₹\,10$ = 10,00,000

9% Preference share capital $4{,}000 \times \frac{4}{5} \times ₹\,100$ = 3,20,000

13,20,000

(ii) *General Reserve:*

	₹
Share capital of Mini Ltd. (Equity + Preference)	14,00,000
Less: Share capital issued by Max Ltd.	13,20,000
General reserve (resulted due to absorption)	80,000
Add: General reserve of Mini Ltd.	1,70,000
General reserve of max Ltd.	1,80,000
	4,30,000

PROBLEM 4

Following is the Balance Sheet of Weak Ltd. as at 31st March, 2013.

	₹		₹
Equity shares of ₹ 100 each	1,00,00,000	Fixed assets	1,25,00,000
12% Cumulative Preference Shares of ₹ 100 each	50,00,000	Investments (Market Value ₹ 9,50,000)	10,00,000
10% Debentures of ₹ 100 each	40,00,000	Current assets	1,00,00,000
Sundry Creditors	50,00,000	P & L A/c	4,00,000
Provision for taxation	1,00,000	Preliminary expenses	2,00,000
	2,41,00,000		2,41,00,000

The following scheme of reorganization is sanctioned:

(a) All the existing equity shares are reduced to ₹ 40 each.
(b) All preference shares are reduced to ₹ 60 each.
(c) The rate of interest on debentures is increased to 12%. the debentureholders surrender their existing debentures of ₹ 100 each and exchange the same for fresh debentures of ₹ 70 each for every debenture held by them.
(d) One of the creditors of the company to whom the company owes ₹ 20,00,000 decides to forgo 40% of his claim. He is allotted 30,000 equity shares of ₹ 40 each in full satisfaction of his claim.
(e) Fixed assets are to be written down by 30%.
(f) Current assets are to be revalued at ₹ 45,00,000.
(g) The taxation liability of the company is settled at ₹ 1,50,000.
(h) Investments to be brought to their market value.
(i) It is decided to write off the fictitious assets.

Required: Pass Journal entries and show the Balance Sheet of the company after giving effect to the above. ***[CA (PE II) May 2007]***

Solution

JOURNAL

Date	*Particulars*		*L.F.*	*Dr. (₹)*	*Cr. (₹)*
(i)	Equity Share Capital (₹ 100) A/c	Dr.		1,00,00,000	
	To Equity Share Capital (₹ 40) A/c				40,00,000
	To Capital Reduction A/c				60,00,000
	(Being conversion of equity share capital of ₹ 100 each into ₹ 40 each as per reconstruction scheme)				
(ii)	12% Cumulative Preference Share Capital (₹ 100) A/c	Dr.		50,00,000	
	To 12% Cumulative Preference Share Capital (₹ 60) A/c				30,00,000
	To Capital Reduction A/c				20,00,000
	(Being conversion of 12% cumulative preference share capital of ₹ 100 each into ₹ 60 each as per reconstruction scheme)				
(iii)	10% Debentures A/c	Dr.		40,00,000	
	To 12% Debentures A/c				28,00,000
	To Capital Reduction A/c				12,00,000
	(Being 12% debentures issued to 10% debentures-holders for 70% of their claims. The balance transferred to capital reduction account as per reconstruction scheme)				
(iv)	Sundry Creditors A/c	Dr.		20,00,000	
	To Equity Share Capital A/c				12,00,000
	To Capital Reduction A/c				8,00,000
	(Being a creditor of ₹ 20,00,000 agreed to surrender his claim by 40% and was allotted 30,000 equity shares of ₹ 40 each in full settlement of his dues as per reconstruction scheme)				

Date	Particulars		L.F.	Dr. (₹)	Cr. (₹)
(v)	Provision for Taxation A/c	Dr.		1,00,000	
	Capital Reduction A/c	Dr.		50,000	
	To Liability for Taxation A/c				1,50,000
	(Being conversion of the provision for taxation into liability for taxation for settlement of the amount due)				
(vi)	Capital Reduction A/c	Dr.		99,50,000	
	To P & L A/c				4,00,000
	To Preliminary Expenses A/c				2,00,000
	To Fixed Assets A/c				37,50,000
	To Current Assets A/c				55,00,000
	To Investments A/c				50,000
	To Capital Reserve A/c				50,000
	(Being amount of Capital Reduction utilized in writing off P & L A/c (Dr.) Balance, Preliminary Expenses, Fixed Assets, Current Assets, Investments and the Balance transferred to Capital Reserve)				
(vii)	Liability for Taxation A/c	Dr.		1,50,000	
	To Current Assets (Bank A/c)				1,50,000
	(Being the payment of tax liability)				

BALANCE SHEET OF WEEK LTD. (AND REDUCED) AS AT 31.03.2013

Particulars	Note No	₹ (lacs)
I. Equity and Liabilities		
(1) Shareholders'Funds		
(a) Share Capital	1	82.00
(b) Reserves and Surplus[Capital Reserve]		0.50
(2) Non-Current Liabilities [12% Debentures]		28.00
(3) Current Liabilities		
(a) Trade Payables [Creditors] [50 – 20]		30.00
Total		140.50
II. Assets		
(1) Non-Current Assets		
(a) Fixed Assets		
Tangible Assets [125 – 37.50(Amt. w/o)]		87.50
(b) Non Current Investments [10 – 0.50(Amt. w/o)]		9.50
(2) Current Assets [100 – 55 (Amt. w/o)]]		43.50
Total		140.50

Notes To Accounts:

Particulars	₹ (lacs)
1. Share Capital	
130000, Equity Shares of ₹ 40 each	52
50000, 12% Pref. Shares of ₹.60 each	30
	82

Working Note:

Dr. **CAPITAL REDUCTION ACCOUNT** *Cr.*

Liabilities	₹	*Assets*	₹
To Liability for Taxation A/c	50,000	By Equity Share capital	60,00000
To P & L A/c	4,00,000	By 12% Cumulative	
To Preliminary Expenses	2,00,000	preference share capital	20,00,000
To Fixed Assets	37,50,000	By 10% Debentures	12,00,000
To Current Assets	55,00,000	By Sundry Creditors	8,00,000
To Investment	50,000		
To Capital Reserve (*balancing figure*)	**50,000**		
	1,00,00,000		1,00,00,000

PROBLEM 5

The following is the Balance Sheet of ABC Ltd. as at 31st March, 2013:

	₹		₹
Share Capital:		Plant and machinery	9,00,000
2,00,000 Equity shares of ₹ 10		Furniture and fixtures	2,50,000
each fully paid up	20,00,000	Patents and copyrights	70,000
6,000 8% Preference shares of		Investments (at cost)	
₹ 100 each	6,00,000	(Market value ₹ 55,000)	68,000
9% Debentures	12,00,000	Stock	14,00,000
Bank overdraft	1,50,000	Sundry Debtors	14,39,000
Sundry Creditors	5,92,000	Cash and bank balance	10,000
		Profit and Loss A/c	4,05,000
	45,42,000		45,42,000

The following scheme of reconstruction was finalised:

(a) Preference shareholders would give up 30% of their capital in exchange for allotment of 11% Debentures to them.

(b) Debentureholders having charge on plant and machinery would accept plant and machinery in full settlement of their dues.

(c) Stock equal to ₹ 5,00,000 in book value will be taken over by sundry creditors in full settlement of their dues.

(d) Investment value to be reduced to market price.

(e) The company would issue 11% Debentures for ₹ 3,00,000 and augment its working capital requirement after settlement of bank overdraft.

Required: Pass necessary Journal Entries and Prepare Capital Reduction account and Balance Sheet of the company after internal reconstruction. ***[CA(PCC) Nov. 2007]***

Solution

JOURNAL

Date	Particulars		L.F.	Dr. (₹)	Cr. (₹)
	8% Preference Share Capital A/c	Dr.		6,00,000	
	To Preference Shareholders A/c				4,20,000
	To Capital Reduction A/c				1,80,000
	(Being 30% reduction in liability of preference share capital)				
	Preference Shareholders A/c	Dr.		4,20,000	
	To 11% Debentures A/c				4,20,000
	(Being the issue of debentures to preference shareholders)				
	9% Debentures A/c	Dr.		12,00,000	
	To Debenture holders A/c				12,00,000
	(Being transfer of 9% debentures to debenture holders A/c)				
	Debenture holders A/c	Dr.		12,00,000	
	To Plant & Machinery A/c				9,00,000
	To Capital Reduction A/c				3,00,000
	(Being the settlement of debenture holders by allotment of plant & machinery)				
	Sundry Creditors	Dr.		5,92,000	
	To Stock A/c				5,00,000
	To Capital Reduction A/c				92,000
	(Being the settlement of creditors by giving stocks)				
	Bank A/c	Dr.		3,00,000	
	To 11% Debentures A/c				3,00,000
	(Being the fresh issue of debentures)				
	Bank overdraft A/c	Dr.		1,50,000	
	To Bank A/c				1,50,000
	(Being the settlement of bank overdraft)				
	Capital Reduction A/c	Dr.		5,72,000	
	To Investment A/c				13,000
	To Profit and Loss A/c				4,05,000
	To Capital Reserve A/c (Bal. Fig.)				1,54,000
	(Being decrease in investment and Profit and Loss Account (Dr. Bal.); and balance of Capital Reduction Account trasnferred to Capital Reserve)				

Dr. **CAPITAL REDUCTION ACCOUNT** *Cr.*

Particulars	₹	Particulars	₹
To Investment A/c	13,000	By Preference Share Capital A/c	1,80,000
To Profit and Loss A/c	4,05,000	By 9% Debenture Holders A/c	3,00,000
To Capital Reserve A/c (Bal. Fig.)	1,54,000	By Sundry Creditors A/c	92,000
	5,72,000		5,72,000

BALANCE SHEET OF WEEK LTD. (AND REDUCED) AS AT 31.03.2013

Particulars	Note No	₹ (lacs)
I. Equity and Liabilities		
(1) Shareholders' Funds		
(a) Share Capital		20.00
(b) Reserves and Surplus [Capital Reserve]		1.54
(2) Non-Current Liabilities [11% Debentures] [4.20 + 3]		7.20
(3) Current Liabilities		
Total		28.74
II. Assets		
(1) Non-Current Assets		
(a) Fixed Assets		
Tangible Assets [125 – 37.50 (Amt. w/o)]	1	2.50
Intangible Assets [Patents & Copy Rights]		0.70
(b) Non-Current Investments[0.68 – 0.13 (Amt. w/o)]		0.55
(2) Current Assets		
(a) Inventories [14 – 5]		9.00
(b) Trade Receivables		14.39
(c) Cash and Cash Equivalents		1.60
Total		28.74

Notes To Accounts:

Particulars		₹ (lacs)
1. Tangible Assets		
Plant & Machinery	9	
Less: Amt. w/o under Reconstruction Scheme	(9)	0
Furniture & Fixtures		2.5
Total		2.5

Working Note: *Calculation of Cash at Bank*

Cash at Bank = Opening balance + 11% Debenturs issued – Bank overdraft paid
= ₹ 10,000 + ₹ 3,00,000 – ₹ 1,50,000
= ₹ 1,60,000

PROBLEM 6

The Balance Sheet of R Ltd., at 31st March, 2013 was as follows:

Liabilities	₹	Assets	₹
Share Capital *Authorised*:	14,00,000	Intangibles	68,000
Issued: 64,000, 8%		Freehold Premises at cost	1,40,000
Cumulative Preference Shares		Plant and Equipment at cost	
of ₹ 10 each, fully paid	6,40,000	*less* depreciation	2,40,000
64,000 Equity shares of ₹		Investments in shares in *Q* Ltd.	
10 each, ₹ 7.5 paid	4,80,000	(at cost)	3,24,000
Loans from directors	60,000	Stocks	2,48,000
Sundry Creditors	4,40,000	Debtors	3,20,000
Bank Overdraft	2,08,000	Deferred Revenue Expenditure	48,000
		Profit & Loss Account	4,40,000
	18,28,000		18,28,000

Note: The arrears of Preference Dividends amount to ₹ 51,200.

A scheme of reconstruction was duly approved with effect from 1st April, 2013 under the conditions stated below:

(*a*) The unpaid amount on the equity shares would be called up.

(*b*) The preference shareholders would forego their arrear dividends. In addition, they would accept a reduction of ₹ 2.5 per share. The dividend rate would be enhanced to 10%.

(*c*) The equity shareholders would accept a reduction of ₹ 7.5 per share.

(*d*) R Ltd. holds 21,600 shares in Q Ltd. This represents 15% of the share capital of that company. Q Ltd. is not a quoted company. The average net profit (after tax) of the company is ₹ 2,50,000. The shares would be valued based on 12% capitalization rate.

(*e*) A bad debt provision at 2% would be created.

(*f*) The other assets would be valued as under:
Intangibles ₹ 48,000, Plant ₹ 1,40,000, Freehold premises ₹ 3,80,000, Stocks ₹ 2,50,000

(*g*) The profit and loss account debit balance and the balance standing to the debit of the deferred revenue expenditure account would be eliminated.

(*h*) The directors would have to take equity shares at the new face value of ₹ 2.5 per share in settlement of their loan.

(*i*) The equity shareholders, including the directors, who would receive equity shares in settlement of their loans, would take up two new equity shares for every one held.

(*j*) The preference shareholders would take up one new preference share for every four held.

(*k*) The authorised share capital would be restated to ₹ 14,00,000.

(*l*) The new face values of the shares-preference and equity will be maintained at their reduced levels.

Required: Prepare the Necessary ledger accounts and the Balance Sheet of the company after reconstruction. ***[CA (PCE) Nov 2008]***

Solution

(*i*) *Dr.* **CAPIAL REDUCTION ACCOUNT** *Cr.*

Particulars	₹	*Particulars*	₹
To Intangibles (₹ 68,000 – ₹ 48,000)	20,000	By 8% Cumulative Preference Shares Capital A/c	1,60,000
To Plant and Equipment A/c (₹ 2,40,000 – ₹ 1,40,000)	1,00,000	By Equity Share Capital A/c	4,80,000
To Deferred Revenue Expenditure A/c	48,000	By Freehold Premises A/c (₹ 3,80,000 – ₹ 1,40,000)	2,40,000
To Profit and Loss A/c	4,40,000	By Stock A/c (₹ 2,50,000 – ₹ 2,48,000)	2,000
To Investment A/c	11,500		
To Provision for Doubtful Debts	6,400		
To Capital Reserve A/c (Balance Transferred)	2,56,100		
	8,82,000		8,82,000

(*i*) *Dr.* **EQUITY SHARE CAPITAL ACCOUNT** *Cr.*

Particulars	₹	*Particulars*	₹
To Capital Reduction Account	4,80,000	By Balance b/d	4,80,000
To Balance c/d	6,60,000	By Bank A/c - (final call) (64,000 × ₹.2.5)	1,60,000
		By Loan from Directors A/c	60,000
		By Bank A/c [(64,000+24,000) × 2 × ₹.2.5]	4,40,000
	11,40,000		11,40,000

Dr. **8% CUMULATIVE PREFERENCE SHARE CAPITAL ACCOUNT** Cr.

Particulars	₹	Particulars	₹
To 10% Cumulative preference Share Capital A/c	4,80,000	By Balance b/d	6,40,000
To Capital Reduction A/c	1,60,000		
	6,40,000		6,40,000

Dr. **BANK ACCOUNT** Cr.

Particulars	₹	Particulars	₹
To Equity Share Capital A/c	1,60,000	By Balance b/d (overdraft)	2,08,000
To Equity Share Capital A/c	4,40,000	By Balance c/d	5,12,000
To 10% Cumulative Preference Share Capital A/c	1,20,000		
	7,20,000		7,20,000

Dr. **10 % CUM PREF. SHARE CAPITAL ACCOUNT** Cr.

Particulars	₹	Particulars	₹
To Balance c/d	6,00,000	By 8% Cumulative Preference Share Capital A/c	4,80,000
		By Bank (16,000 × ₹ 7.5)	1,20,000
	6,00,000		6,00,000

BALANCE SHEET OF R LTD. (AND REDUCED) AS AT 31.03.2013

Particulars	Note No	₹
I. Equity and Liabilities		
(1) Shareholders' Funds		
(a) Share Capital	1	12,60,000
(b) Reserves and Surplus[Capital Reserve]		2,56,100
(2) Non-Current Liabilities		
(3) Current Liabilities		
(a) Trade Payables [Creditors]		4,40,000
Total		19,56,100
II. Assets		
(1) Non-Current Assets		
(a) Fixed Assets		
Tangible Assets	2	5,20,000
Intangible Assets [Goodwill] [[68,000 – 20,000 (Amt. w/o)]		48,000
(b) Non-Current Investments [3,24,000 – 11,500 (Amt. w/o)]		3,12,500
(2) Current Assets		
(a) Inventories		2,50,000
(b) Trade Receivables [3,20,000 – 6,400]		3,13,600
(c) Cash and Cash Equivalents		5,12,000
Total		19,56,000

Notes To Accounts:

Particulars		₹
1. Share Capital		
264000 Equity Shares of ₹ 2.50 each		6,60,000
80000,10% Pref. Shares of ₹ 7.50 each		6,00,000
		12,60,000
2. Tangible Assets		
Frehold Premises	2,40,000	
Add: Amt. increased under Reconstruction Scheme	1,40,000	3,80,000
Plant & Machinery	2,40,000	
Less: Amt. w/o under Reconstruction Scheme	1,00,000	1,40,000
Total		5,20,000

Working Notes:

(*i*) Valuation of investments in shares of *Q* Ltd.= (2,50,000/.12) × 15% = ₹ 3,12,500

(*ii*) Reduction in the value of investment in shares of *Q* Ltd.
= ₹ 3,24,000 – ₹.3,12,500 = ₹.11,500.

PROBLEMS 7

Following is the Balance Sheet of M Ltd. as at 31st March, 2013:

Liabilities	₹	*Assets*	₹
15,000, 10% Preference Shares of ₹ 100 each	15,00,000	Goodwill	3,50,000
		Land & Buildings	15,00,000
35,000 Equity Shares of		Plant & Machinery	10,00,000
₹ 100 each	35,00,000	Stock	6,00,000
Securities Premium account	1,00,000	Debtors	15,00,000
7% Debentures of ₹ 100 each	5,00,000	Cash at bank	1,00,000
Creditors	12,50,000	Preliminary Expenses	4,00,000
Loan from Director	1,50,000	Profit & Loss A/c	15,50,000
	70,00,000		70,00,000

No dividend on Preference shares has been paid for the last 5 years.

The following scheme of reorganization was duly approved by the court:

(a) Each Equity share to be reduced to ₹.25.

(b) Each existing Preference share to be reduced to ₹ 75 and then exchanged for 1 new 13% Preference share of ₹ 50 each and 1 Equity share of ₹ 25 each.

(c) Preference shareholders have forgone their right for dividend for four years. One year 's dividend at the old rate is however, payable to them in fully paid equity Shares of ₹ 25.

(d) The Debentureholders be given the option to either accept 90% of their claims in cash or to convert their claims in full into new 13% Preference shares of ₹ 50 each issued at par. One half (in value) of the debenlurehoders accepted Preference snares for their claims. The rest were paid cash.

(e) Contingent liability of ₹ 1,50,000 is payable, which has been created by wrong action of one Director. He has agreed to compensate this ioss out of the loan given by the Director to the company.

(f) Goodwill does not have any value in the present. Decrease the value of Plant and Machinery, Stock and Debtors by ₹ 4,00,000, ₹ 1,00,000 and ₹ 1,50,000 respectively. Increase the value of Land and Buildings to ₹ 18,00,000.

(g) 40,000 new Equity shares of ₹ 25 each are to be issued at par, payable in full on application. The issue was underwritten for a commission of 4%. Shares were fully taken up.

(h) The total expenses incurred by the company in connection with the scheme excluding, underwriting commission amounted to ₹ 15,000.

Required: Pass necessary Journal Entries to record the above transactions. *[CA (PEII) June 2009]*

Solution

JOURNAL OF M LTD.

Date	Particulars		Dr. (₹)	Cr. (₹)
	Equity Share Capital (₹.100) A/c	Dr.	35,00,000	
	To Equity Share Capital (₹ 25) A/c			8,75,000
	To Capital Reduction A/c			26,25,000
	(Being Equity shares of ₹ 100 each reduced to ₹ 25 each and balance transferred to Capital Reduction A/c)			
	10% Preference Share Capital (₹.100) A/c	Dr.	15,00,000	
	To 10% Preference Share Capital (₹ 75) A/c			11,25,000
	To Capital Reduction A/c			3,75,000
	(Being Preference shares of ₹ 100 each reduced to ₹ 75 each and balance transferred to Capital Reduction A/c)			
	10% Preference Share Capital (₹ 75) A/c	Dr.	11,25,000	
	To 13% Preference Share Capital (₹ 50) A/c			7,50,000
	To Equity Share Capital A/c			3,75,000
	(Being one new 13% Preference share of ₹ 50 each and one equity share of ₹ 25 each issued against 10% Preference Share of ₹ 75 each)			
	Capital Reduction A/c	Dr.	1,50,000	
	To Preference Share Dividend Payable A/c			1,50,000
	(Being arrear of Preference share dividend payable for one year)			
	Preference Share Dividend Payable A/c	Dr.	1,50,000	
	To Equity Share Capital A/c			1,50,000
	(Being Equity Shares of ₹ 25 each issued for arrears of Preference Share Dividend]			
	7% Debentures A/c	Dr.	5,00,000	
	To Debenture holders A/c			5,00,000
	(Being balance of 7% Debentures transferred to Debenture Holders A/c)			
	Debenture Holders A/c	Dr.	5,00,000	
	To 13% Preference Share Capital A/c			2,50,000
	To Bank A/c			2,25,000
	To Capital Reduction A/c			25,000
	(Being 50% of Debenture holders opted to take 13% Preference shares at par and remaining took 90% cash payment for their claims)			
	Loan from Director A/c	Dr.	1,50,000	
	To Provision for Contingent Liability A/c			1,50,000
	(Being contingent liability of ₹ 1,50,000 is payable and adjusted against Loan from director A/c)			

Date	Particulars		Dr. (₹)	Cr. (₹)
	Bank A/c To Equity Share Application & Allotment A/c (Being application money received on 40,000 Equity shares @ ₹ 25 each)	Dr.	10,00,000	 10,00,000
	Equity Share Application & Allotment A/c To Equity Share Capital A/c (Being application money transferred to capital A/c. on allotment)	Dr.	10,00,000	 10,00,000
	Underwriting Commission A/c To Bank A/c (Being underwriting commission paid)	Dr.	40,000	 40,000
	Land & Buildings A/c To Capital Reduction A/c (Being value of Land & Buildings appreciated)	Dr.	3,00,000	 3,00,000
	Expenses on Reconstruction A/c To Bank A/c (Being payment of expenses on reconstruction)	Dr.	15,000	 15,000
	Capital Reduction A/c To Goodwill A/c To Plant & Machinery A/c To Stock A/c To Debtors A/c To Preliminary Expenses A/c To Profit & Loss A/c To Expenses on Reconstruction A/c To Underwriting Copmmision A/c To Capital Reserve A/c (Being various losses written off and balance of Capital Reduction A/c transferred to Capital Reserve A/c)	Dr.	31,75,000	 3,50,000 4,00,000 1,00,000 1,50,000 4,00,000 15,50,000 15,000 40,000 1,70,000

PROBLEM 8

The Balance Sheet of Neptune Ltd as on 31.3.2013 is given below:

Liabilities	₹	₹	Assets	₹
80,000, Equity Shares of ₹ 10 each fully paid		8,00,000	Freehold property	5,00,000
			Plant & Machinery	1,80,000
5,000, 6% Cumulative Preference Shares of ₹ 100 each fully paid		5,00,000	Trade investment (at cost)	1,70,000
			Sundry Debtros	4,50,000
			Stock in trade	2,00,000
6% Debentures (secured by free hold property)	3,75,000		Deferred Advertisement Expenditure	1,50,000
			Profit and Loss A/c	3,65,000
Arrear interest	22,500	3,97,500		
Sundry Creditors		17,500		
Director's loan		3,00,000		
		20,15,000		20,15,000

The Court approved a scheme of re-organisation to take effect on 1.4.2013 and the terms are given below:

(a) Preference shares are to be written down to ₹ 75 each and equity shares to ₹ 2 each.
(b) Preference dividend in arrear for 4 years to be waived by 75% and for the balance equity shares of ₹ 2 each to be allotted.
(c) Arrear of debenture interest to be paid in cash.
(d) Debentureholders agreed to take one freehold property (Book value ₹ 3,00,000) at a valuation of ₹ 3,00,000 in part payment of their holding. Balance debentures to remain as liability of the company.
(e) Deferred advertisement expenditure to be written off.
(f) Stock value to be written off fully in the books.
(g) 50% of the Sundry Debtors to be written off as bad debt.
(h) Remaining freehold property (after take over by debentureholders) to be valued at ₹ 3,50,000.
(i) Investment sold out for ₹ 2,00,000.
(j) 80% of the Director's loan to be waived and for the balance, equity shares of ₹ 2 each to be issued,
(k) Company's contractual commitments amounting to ₹ 5,00,000 to be cancelled by paying penalty at 3% of contract value.
(l) Cost of re-construction scheme is ₹ 20,000.

Required: Show the Journal entries (with narration) to be passed for giving effect to the above transactions and draw Balance Sheet of the company after effecting the scheme.

[*CA (PCC) Nov. 2009*]

Solution

JOURNAL OF NEPTUNE LTD.

Date	Particulars		Dr. (₹)	Cr. (₹)
(i)	6% Preference Share Capital A/c (₹ 100)	Dr.	5,00,000	
	To 6% Preference Share Capital A/c (₹ 75)			3,75,000
	To Capital Reduction A/c			1,25,000
	(Being preference shares of ₹.100 each reduced to ₹ 75 each as per the scheme)			
(ii)	Equity Share Capital A/c (₹ 10)	Dr.	8,00,000	
	To Equity Share Capital A/c (₹ 2)			1,60,000
	To Capital Reduction A/c			6,40,000
	(Being equity shares of ₹ 10 each reduced to ₹ 2 each as per the scheme)			
(iii)	Capital Reduction A/c	Dr.	30,000	
	To Equity Share Capital A/c			30,000
	(Being arrears of preference share dividend of one year to be satisfied by issue of 1,500 equity shares of ₹ 2 each as per the scheme)			
(iv)	Accrued Debenture Interest A/c	Dr.	22,500	
	To Bank A/c			22,500
	(Being accrued interest on debentures paid)			
(v)	6% Debentures A/c	Dr.	3,00,000	
	To Freehold Property A/c			3,00,000
	(Being claim of debentureholders settled in part by transfer of freehold property as per the scheme)			

Date	Particulars		Dr. (₹)	Cr. (₹)
(vi)	Capital Reduction A/c	Dr.	9,40,000	
	To Profit and Loss A/c			3,65,000
	To Deferred advertising expenses A/c			1,50,000
	To Stock A/c			2,00,000
	To Sundry Debtors A/c			2,25,000
	(Being the various assets written off as per the scheme)			
(vii)	Freehold Property A/c	Dr.	1,50,000	
	To Capital Reduction A/c			1,50,000
	(Being appreciation in the value of remaining property)			
(viii)	Bank A/c	Dr.	2,00,000	
	To Trade Investment A/c			1,70,000
	To Capital Reduction A/c			30,000
	(Being trade investment sold on profit)			
(ix)	Director's Loan A/c	Dr.	3,00,000	
	To Equity Share Capital A/c			60,000
	To Capital Reduction A/c			2,40,000
	(Being Director's loan reduced by 80% and remaining balance discharged by issue of equity shares of ₹ 2 each)			
(x)	Capital Reduction A/c	Dr.	15,000	
	To Bank A/c			15,000
	(Being payment of 3% penalty on cancellation of contractual commitments)			
(xi)	Capital Reduction A/c	Dr.	20,000	
	To Bank A/c			20,000
	(Being reconstruction expenses paid)			
(xii)	Capital Reduction A/c	Dr.	1,80,000	
	To Capital Reserve A/c			1,80,000
	(Being balance of capital reduction account transferred)			

Balance Sheet of Neptune Ltd. (and reduced) as at 31.03.2013

Particulars	Note No	₹
I. Equity and Liabilities		
(1) Shareholders' Funds		
(a) Share Capital	1	6,25,000
(b) Reserves and Surplus[Capital Reserve]		1,80,000
(2) Non-Current Liabilities [8% Debentures]		
[3,75,000 – 3,00,000]		75,000
(3) Current Liabilities		
(a) Trade Payables [Creditors]		17,500
Total		8,97,500

Particulars	Note No	₹
II. Assets		
(1) Non-Current Assets		
(a) Fixed Assets		
Tangible Assets	2	6,30,000
(2) Current Assets		
(a) Trade Receivables [4,50,000 – 2,25,000]		2,25,000
(b) Cash and Cash Equivalents [2,00,000 – 22,500 – 15,000 – 20,000]		1,42,500
Total		8,97,500

Notes To Accounts:

Particulars		₹
1. Share Capital		
1250000 Equity Shares of ₹.2 each		2,50,000
5000,6% Pref. Shares of Rs75 each		3,75,000
(Of the above 45000 *Equity* Shares were issued for consideration otherwise than cash)		6,25,000
2. Tangible Assets		
Frehold Property	5,00,000	
Less: T/f to Debentureholders	(3,00,000)	
Add: Amt. increased under Reconstruction Scheme	1,50,000	3,50,000
Plant & Machinery		1,80,000
Total		6,30,000

PROBLEM 9

The Following is the Balance Sheet of *X* Ltd. as at 31st March, 2013:

Liabilities	₹	Assets	₹
12,000, 10% Preference Shares of ₹ 100 each	12,00,000	Goodwill	90,000
		Land & building	12,00,000
24,000, Equity Shares of ₹ 100 each	24,00,000	Plant & Machinery	18,00,000
		Stock	2,60,000
10% Debentures	6,00,000	Debtors	2,80,000
Bank Overdraft	6,00,000	Cash	30,000
Sundry Creditors	3,00,000	Profit & Loss Account	14,00,000
		Preliminary Expenses	40,000
	51,00,000		**51,00,000**

On the above date, the company adopted the following scheme of reconstruction:

(a) The equity shares are to be reduced to shares of ₹ 40 each fully paid and the preference shares to be reduced to fully paid shares of ₹ 75 each.

(b) The debentureholders took over stock and debtors in full satisfaction of their claims.

(c) The Land and Building to be appreciated by 30% and Plant and machinery to be depreciated by 30%.

(d) The fictitious and intangible assets are to be eliminated,

(e) Expenses of reconstruction amounted to ₹ 5,000.

Required : Pass Journal Entries and prepare the reconstructed Balance Sheet.

[CA (PE-II) Nov. 2009]

Solution

JOURNAL X LTD.

Date	Particulars		Dr. (₹)	Cr. (₹)
(i)	Equity Share Capital A/c (₹ 1 00)	Dr.	24,00,000	
	To Equity Share Capital A/c (₹ 40)			9,60,000
	To Capital Reduction A/c			14,40,000
	(Being 24,000 equity shares of ₹.100 each reduced to ₹ 40 each fully paid up)			
(ii)	10% Preference Share Capital A/c (₹.100)	Dr.	12,00,000	
	To 10% Preference Share Capital A/c (₹.75)			9,00,000
	To Capital Reduction A/c			3,00,000
	(Being 12,000 Preference shares of ₹.100 each reduced to ₹.75 each fully paid up)			
(iii)	10% Debentures A/c	Dr.	6,00,000	
	To Stock A/c			2,60,000
	To Debtors A/c			2,80,000
	To Capital Reduction A/c			60,000
	(Being Debentureholders given stock and debtors in full settlement of their claims)			
(iv)	Land & Building A/c	Dr.	3,60,000	
	To Capital Reduction A/c			3,60,000
	(Being Land & Building appreciated by 30%)			
(v)	Reconstruction Expenses A/c	Dr.	5,000	
	To Cash A/c			5,000
	(Being expenses of reconstruction paid)			
(vi)	Capital Reduction A/c	Dr.	21,60,000	
	To Goodwill A/c			90,000
	To Profit and Loss A/c			14,00,000
	To Plant & Machinery A/c			5,40,000
	To Preliminary expenses A/c			40,000
	To Reconstruction expenses A/c			5,000
	To Capital Reserve A/c (Bal. Fig.)			85,000
	(Being various losses written off, assets written down and balance in Capital Reduction A/c transferred to Capital Reserve A/c)			

BALANCE SHEET OF X LTD. AS AT 31.03.2013

Particulars	Note No	₹ (lacs)
I. Equity and Liabilities		
(1) Shareholders' Funds		
(a) Share Capital	1	18.60
(b) Reserves and Surplus [Capital Reserve]		0.85
(2) Non-Current Liabilities		
(3) Current Liabilities		
(a) Short-term Borrowings[Bank O/D]		6.00
(b) Trade Payables[Creditors]		3.00
Total		28.45

Particulars	Note No	₹ (lacs)
II. Assets		
(1) Non-Current Assets		
(a) Fixed Assets		
Tangible Assets	2	28.20
(2) Current Assets [45 – 1.50 (Amt. w/o)**]**		
(a) Inventories [2,60,000 – 2,60,000]		0
(b) Trade Receivables [2,80,000 – 2,80,000]		0
(c) Cash and Cash Equivalents[0.30 – 0.05]		0.25
Total		28.45

Notes To Accounts:

Particulars		₹ (lacs)
1. Share Capital		
24000 Equity Shares of ₹ 40 each		9.60
12000, 10% Pref. Shares of ₹ 75 each		9.00
		18.60
2. Tangible Assets		
Land & Building	12.00	
Add: Amt. increased under Reconstruction Scheme	3.60	15.60
Plant & Machinery	18.00	
Less: Amt. w/o under Reconstruction Scheme	(5.40)	12.60
Total		28.20

PROBLEM 10

Following is the Balance Sheet of *XYZ* Ltd. as at 31st March, 2013:

Liabilities	₹	Assets	₹
8,000 – 7½ Preference Shares @ ₹.100 each fully paid	8,00,000	Plant and Machinery	8,50,000
		Furniture and Fittings	1,60,000
1,80,000 Equity Shares @ ₹.10 each fully paid	18,00,000	Patents and Copyright	60,000
		Goodwill	35,000
11% Debentures	10,00,000	Investments (at cost)	65,000
Bank overdraft	1,65,000	Sundry debtors	12,00,000
Loan from director	15,000	Stock	13,00,000
Trade creditors	6,20,000	Cash in hand	12,000
		Profit & Loss A/c	7,18,000
	44,00,000		**44,00,000**

Due to heavy losses and overvaluation of assets, the following scheme of reconstruction was finalised:

(a) Preference shareholders will surrender their 20% shares and they have been allotted 9% (new) preference shares for the remaining amount.

(b) Debentureholders having charge on plant and machinery would accept plant and machinery in full settlement.

(c) Trade creditors accepted to take over the stock upto the value of ₹.6,20,000.

(d) Equity shareholders are to accept reduction of ₹.4 per share.

(e) Investment is to be valued at market price i.e., ₹.60.000.
(f) Sundry debtors and remaining stock is to be valued at 90 % of their book value.
(g) Directors have to forgo their loan in full.
(h) Patents and Copyright and Goodwill have no more value.

Required: Pass necessary journal entries in the books of *XYZ* Ltd. assuming that all the legal formalities have been completed. Prepare Capital Reduction Account and Balance Sheet of the company after reduction. *[CA (IPCC) May 2010]*

Solution

JOURNAL OF XYZ LTD.

Date	*Particulars*		*Dr.* (₹)	*Cr.* (₹)
(i)	7½% Preference Share Capital A/c	Dr.	8,00,000	
	To 9% Preference Share Capital A/c			6,40,000
	To Capital Reduction A/c			1,60,000
	(Being surrender of 20% shares by 7.5% Preference shareholders and issuance of 9% preference shares for remaining balance as per the scheme of reconstruction)			
(ii)	11% Debentures A/c	Dr.	10,00,000	
	To Debenture holders A/c			10,00,000
	(Being 11% debentures transferred to debenture holders account)			
(iii)	Debenture holders A/c	Dr.	10,00,000	
	To Plant & machinery A/c			8,50,000
	To Capital reduction A/c			1,50,000
	(Being plant and machinery given to debenture holders in full settlement as per the scheme of reconstruction)			
(iv)	Trade Creditors A/c	Dr.	6,20,000	
	To Stock A/c			6,20,000
	(Being stock given to trade creditors against their dues as per the scheme of reconstruction)			
(v)	Equity Share Capital A/c (₹.10)	Dr.	18,00,000	
	To Equity Share Capital A/c (₹ 6)			10,80,000
	To Capital Reduction A/c			7,20,000
	(Being reduction of ₹ 4 per equity share as per the scheme of reconstruction)			
(vi)	Capital Reduction A/c	Dr.	10,06,000	
	To Debtors A/c			1,20,000
	To Investment A/c			5,000
	To Stock A/c			68,000
	To Patents and Copyright A/c			60,000
	To Goodwill A/c			35,000
	To Profit and Loss A/c			7,18,000
	(Being writing off losses and reduction in the values of assets as per the scheme of reconstruction)			
(vii)	Director's loan A/c	Dr.	15,000	
	To Capital reduction A/c			15,000
	(Being loan forgo by directors as per the scheme of reconstruction)			

Date	Particulars		Dr. (₹)	Cr. (₹)
(viii)	Capital Reduction A/c	Dr.	39,000	
	To Capital Reserve A/c			39,000
	(Being balance of capital reduction account transferred to capital reserve account)			

Dr. **CAPITAL REDUCTION ACCOUNT** Cr.

Particulars	₹	Particulars	₹
To Provision for Doubtful Debts A/c	1,20,000	By 7½% Preference Share Capital A/c	1,60,000
To Investment A/c	5,000	By 11% Debentures A/c	1,50,000
To Stock A/c	68,000	By Equity Share Capital A/c	7,20,000
To Patents and Copyright A/c	60,000	By Director's loan A/c	15,000
To Goodwill A/c	35,000		
To Profit and loss A/c	7,18,000		
To Capital reserve A/c	39,000		
	10,45,000		**10,45,000**

BALANCE SHEET OF XYZ LTD. AS AT 31.03.2013

Particulars	Note No	₹ (lacs)
I. Equity and Liabilities		
(1) Shareholders' Funds		
(a) Share Capital	1	17.20
(b) Reserves and Surplus[Capital Reserve]		0.39
(2) Non-Current Liabilities		
(3) Current Liabilities		
(a) Short-term Borrowings [Bank O/D]		1.65
Total		19.24
II. Assets		
(1) Non-Current Assets		
(a) Fixed Assets		
Tangible Assets	2	1.60
Intangible Assets [Goodwill] [[60,000 – 60,000(Amt. w/o)]		0
(b) Non-Current Investments [0.65 – 0.05 (Amt. w/o)]		0.60
(2) Current Assets		
(a) Inventories [13 – 6 – 0.68]		6.12
(b) Trade Receivables [12 – 1.20]		10.80
(c) Cash and Cash Equivalents		0.12
Total		19.24

Notes To Accounts:

Particulars		₹ (lacs)
1. Share Capital		
180000 Equity Shares of ₹ 6 each		10.80
6400, 9% Pref. Shares of ₹ 100 each		6.40
		17.20
2. Tangible Assets		
Plant & Machinery	8.50	
Less: Amt. w/o under Reconstruction Scheme	(8.50)	0
Furniture & Fixtures		1.60
Total		1.60

PROBLEM 11

The Balance Sheet of X Limited as at 31st March 2013, was as follows:

Liabilities	₹	*Assets*	₹
Authorised and subscribed capital:	10,00,000	Fixed Assets:	
Equity shares of ₹ 100 each fully paid		Machineries	3,50,000
		Current Assets:	
Unsecured loans:		Stock	2,53,000
15% Debentures	3,00,000	Debtors	2,30,000
Accrued interest	45,000	Bank	20,000
Creditors	52,000	Profit & loss A/c	5,80,000
Provision for income tax	36,000		
	14,33,000		14,33,000

It was decided to reconstruct the company for which necessary resolution was passed and sanctions were obtained from the appropriate authorities. Accordingly, it was decided that:

(a) Each share be sub-divided into 10 fully paid up equity share of ₹ 10 each.

(b) After sub-division, each shareholder shall surrender to the company 50% of his holding for the purpose of reissue to debentureholders and creditors as necessary.

(c) Out of shares surrendered 10,000 shares of ₹ 10 each shall be converted into 10% Preference shares of ₹ 10 each fully paid up.

(d) The claims of the debentureholders shall be reduced by 50%. In consideration of the reduction, the debentureholder shall receive Preference Shares of ₹ 1,00,000 which are converted out of shares surrendered.

(e) Creditors claim shall be reduced by 25%.Remaining creditors are to be settled by the issue of equity shares of ₹ 10 each of out of shares surrendered.

(f) Balance of Profit and Loss account to be written off.

(g) The shares surrendered and not re-issued shall be cancelled.

Required: Pass Journal Entries giving effect to the above and the resultant Balance Sheet.

[CA (IPCC) May 2011]

Solution

JOURNAL OF X LIMITED

Date	Particulars		Dr. (₹)	Dr. (₹)
(i)	Equity Share Capital (₹ 100) A/c	Dr.	10,00,000	
	To Share Surrender A/c			5,00,000
	To Equity Share Capital (? 10) A/c			5,00,000
	(Sub-division of 10,000 equity shares of ₹ 100 each into 1,00,000 equity shares of ₹ 10 each and surrender of 50,000 of such sub-divided shares as per capital reduction scheme)			
(ii)	15% Debentures A/c	Dr.	1,50,000	
	Accrued Interest A/c	Dr.	22,500	
	To Reconstruction A/c			1,72,500
	(Transferred 50% of the claims of the debentureholders to Reconstruction A/c in consideration of which 10% Preference shares are being issued, out of share surrender A/c as per capital reduction scheme)			
(iii)	Creditors A/c	Dr.	52,000	
	To Reconstruction A/c			52,000
	(Transferred claims of the creditors to Reconstruction A/c, 25% of which is reduction and equity shares are issued in consideration of the balance amount)			
(iv)	Share Surrender A/c	Dr.	5,00,000	
	To 10% Preference Share Capital A/c			1,00,000
	To Equity Share Capital A/c			39,000
	To Reconstruction A/c			3,61,000
	(Issued preference and equity shares to discharge the claims of the debentureholders and the creditors respectively as per scheme and the balance in share surrender account is transferred to reconstruction account)			
(v)	Reconstruction A/c	Dr.	5,85,500	
	To Profit & Loss A/c			5,80,000
	To Capital Reserve A/c			5,500
	(Adjusted debit balance of profit and loss account against reconstruction account and the balance is transferred to Capital Reserve account)			

BALANCE SHEET OF X LTD. (AND REDUCED) AS AT 31.03.2013

Particulars	Note No	₹
I. Equity and Liabilities		
(1) Shareholders' Funds		
(a) Share Capital	1	6,39,000
(c) Reserves and Surplus (Capital Reserve)		5,500
(2) Non-Current Liabilities 15% (Debentures)		1,50,000
(a) Long-term Borrowings		
(3) Current Liabilities		
(a) Trade Payables		
(b) Short-term Provisions		36,000
(c) Other Current Liabilities [Accrued Interest]		22,500
Total		8,53,000

Particulars	Note No	₹
II. Assets		
(1) Non-Current Assets		
(a) Fixed Assets		
Tangible Assets (Machineries)		3,50,000
(2) Current Assets		
(a) Inventories		2,53,000
(b) Trade Receivables		2,30,000
(b) Cash and Cash Equivalents		20,000
Total		8,53,000

Notes To Accounts:

Particulars	₹
1. Share Capital	
53,900 Equity Shares of ₹ 10 each	5,39,000
10,000, 10% Pref. Shares of ₹ 10 each	1,00,000
(Of the above 10,000 Pref. Shares were issued for consideration otherwise than cash)	6,39,000

PROBLEM 12

Crystal Company Limited decided to reconstruct its business as it has accumulated huge losses. The following is the Balance Sheet of the company as on 31.03.2013 before reconstruction:

BALANCE SHEET AS ON 31.03.2013

Liabilities	₹	Assets	₹
3,00,000 Equity shares of ₹ 10 each fully paid up	30,00,000	Goodwill	5,20,000
		Patents	1,50,000
1,60,000, 6% Preference shares of f 10 each fully paid up	16,00,000	Land & building	17,00,000
		Plant & machinery	2,00,000
6% Debentures (Secured against land & building)	15,00,000	Investments (at cost)	2,20,000
		Sundry debtors	17,40,000
Bank overdraft	5,80,000	Stock	17,00,000
Sundry creditors	12,00,000	Profit & loss A/c	18,50,000
Provision for income tax	2, 00, 000		
	80,80,000		80,80,000

Following scheme of reconstruction has been approved by all interested parties and the Court:

1. All equity shares are reduced to ₹ 3 each and preference shares to ₹ 7 each.
2. Debentureholders agree to take over a part of land and building, book value of which is ₹ 7,00,000, towards their 50% claim.Rate of interest of balance 50% debentures increased to 9%.
3. Goodwill and patent will be mitten off.
4. 10% of sundry debtors to be provided for bad debts.
5. Stock to be written off by ₹ 2,60,000.
6. 50% of balance land & building sold for ₹ 6,00,000 and remaining land & building valued at ₹ 6,00,000.

7. Investments to be sold for ₹ 2,00,000.
8. There are pending contracts amounting to ₹ 70,00,000. These contracts are to be cancelled on payment of penalty @ 5% of pending contract amount.
9. The income tax liability of the company is settled at ₹ 3, 06, 000. Provision for income tax will be raised accordingly.
10. 1/3 of sundry creditors decided to forgo their claim.
11. After making all the above adjustments, balance amount available through scheme, will be utilized to write off the value of plant & machinery to that extent.

Required: Pass the journal entries and draw up Balance Sheet of the company after reconstruction.

[CA (PCC) May 2011]

Solution

JOURNAL OF CRYSTAL COMPANY LIMITED

Date	Particulars		Dr. (₹)	Cr. (₹)
1.	Equity Share Capital A/c (₹ 10)	Dr.	30,00,000	
	To Equity Share Capital A/c (₹ 3)			9,00,000
	To Reconstruction A/c			21,00,000
	(Being reduction of equity share of ₹ 10 each to shares of ₹ 3 each as perthe reconstruction scheme)			
2.	6% Preference Share Capital A/c (₹ 10)	Dr.	16,00,000	
	To 6% preference Share Capital A/c (₹ 7)			11,20,000
	To Reconstruction A/c			4,80,000
	(Being reduction of preference shares of ₹ 10 each to shares of ₹ 7 each as per the reconstruction scheme)			
3.	6% Debentures A/c	Dr.	15,00,000	
	To Land & Building A/c			7,00,000
	To 9% Debentures A/c			7,50,000
	To Reconstruction A/c			50,000
	(Being 50% claim of debentureholders discharged by transfer of a part of land & building having book value ₹ 7,00,000 and rate of interest of balance 50% debentures increased to 9% as per the reconstruction scheme)			
4.	Bank A/c	Dr.	6,00,000	
	To Land & building A/c			5,00,000
	To Reconstruction A/c			1,00,000
	(Being 50% of balance land & building having book value ₹ 5,00,000 sold for ₹ 6,00,000 as per the reconstruction scheme)			
5.	Land & building A/c	Dr.	1,00,000	
	To Reconstruction A/c			1,00,000
	(Being 50% of balance land & building having book value ₹ 5,00,000, valued at ₹ 6,00,000, as per the reconstruction scheme)			
6.	Bank A/c	Dr.	2,00,000	
	Reconstruction A/c	Dr.	20,000	
	To Investment A/c			2,20,000
	(Being all the investments sold as per the reconstruction scheme)			

Date	Particulars		Dr. (₹)	Cr. (₹)
7.	Sundry creditors A/c	Dr.	4,00,000	
	To Reconstruction A/c			4,00,000
	(Being 1/3 of sundry creditors decided to forgo their claim as perthe reconstruction scheme)			
8.	Reconstruction A/c	Dr.	32,10,000	
	To Goodwill A/c			5,20,000
	To Patents A/c			1,50,000
	To Provision of doubtful debts A/c			1,74,000
	To Stock A/c			2,60,000
	To Bank A/c			50,000
	To Provision for income tax A/c			1,06,000
	To Profit & loss A/c			18,50,000
	To Plant & machinery A/c (Bal. fig.)			1,00,000
	(Being goodwill, patent, profit and loss, part value of stock, plant and machinery, penalty paid for cancellation of contracts written off and provisions made for doubtful debts and income tax, as per the reconstruction scheme)			

BALANCE SHEET OF CRYSTAL COMPANY LTD. AS AT 31.03.2013

Particulars	Note No	₹
I. Equity and Liabilities		
(1) Shareholders' Funds		
(a) Share Capital	1	20,20,000
(b) Minority Interest		—
(c) Reserves and Surplus		7,50,000
(2) Non-Current Liabilities [9% Debentures]		
(3) Current Liabilities		
(a) Trade Payables [12,00,000 – 4,00,000]		8,00,000
(b) Short-term Provisions [Provision for Tax] [2,00,000 + 1,06,000]		3,06,000
Total		38,76,000
II. Assets		
(1) Non-Current Assets		
(a) Fixed Assets		
Tangible Assets	2	7,00,000
(2) Current Assets		
(a) Inventories [17,00,000 – 2,60,000]		14,40,000
(b) Trade Receivables [17,40,000 – 1,74,000]		15,66,000
(b) Cash and Cash Equivalents		1,70,000
Total		38,76,000

Notes To Accounts:

Particulars	₹
1. Share Capital	
3,00,000 Equity Shares of ₹ 3 each	9,00,000
1,60,000, 6% Pref. Shares of ₹ 7 each	11,20,000
	20,20,000

2. Tangible Assets

Land & Building	5,00,000	
Add: Amt. increased under Reconstruction Scheme	1,00,000	6,00,000
Plant & Machinery	2,00,000	
Less: Amt. w/o under Reconstruction Scheme	(1,00,000)	1,00,000
Total		7,00,000

Working Note:

Dr. **BANK ACCOUNT** *Cr.*

Particulars	₹	*Particulars*	₹
To Land & building A/c	5,00,000	By Balance b/d	5,80,000
To Reconstruction A/c	1,00,000	By Reconstruction A/c	50,000
To Investment A/c	2,00,000	By Balance c/d (Bal.fig.)	1,70,000
	8,00,000		8,00,000

PROBLEM 13

Following are the Balance Sheets as at March 31, 2013:

(₹ '000)

Liabilities	*K Ltd.*	*W Ltd.*	*Assets*	*K Ltd.*	*W Ltd.*
Share capital:			Goodwill	20	—
Equity Shares of			Other Fixed Assets	2,400	1,150
₹ 100 each	2,000	1,500	Debtors	625	615
9% Preference Shares of			Stock	412	680
₹ 100 each	700	400	Cash at bank	38	155
General Reserve	240	170	Own debentures		
Profit & Loss A/c	—	15	[Nominal value		
12% Debentures of			₹ 2,00,000]	192	—
₹ 100 each	600	200	Discount on issue of		
Sundry Creditors	560	315	debentures	2	—
			Profit & Loss A/c	411	—
	4,100	2,600		4,100	2,600

On 1.4.2013, K Ltd. adopted the following scheme of reconstruction:

(a) Each equity share shall be sub-divided into 10 equity shares of ₹ 10 each fully paid up. 50% of the equity share capital would be surrendered to the company.

(b) Preference dividends are in arrear for 3 years. Preference shareholders agreed to waive 80% of the dividend claim and accept payment for the balance.

(c) Own debentures of ₹ 80,000 were sold at ₹ 98 own-interest and remaining own debentures were cancelled.

(d) Debentureholders of ₹ 3,00,000 agreed to accept one machinery of book value of ₹ 3,20,000 in full settlement.

(e) Creditors, Debtors and Stocks were valued at ₹ 5,00,000 , ₹ 6,00,000 and ₹ 4,00,000 respectively. The goodwill, discount on issue of Debentures & Profit and Loss (Dr.) are to be written off.

(f) The Company paid ₹ 20,000 as penalty to avoid capital commitments of ₹ 4,00,000.

On 2.4.2013 a scheme of absorption was adopted. K Ltd. would take over W Ltd. The purchase consideration was fixed as below:

(i) Equity shareholders of W Ltd. will be given 50 equity shares of ₹ 10 each fully paid up, in exchange for every 5 shares held in W Ltd.

(ii) Issue of 10% Preference Shares of ₹ 100 each in the ratio of 4 Preference Shares of K Ltd. for every 5 Preference Shares held in W Ltd.

(iii) Issue of one 12% Debentures of ₹ 100 each of K Ltd. for every 12% Debentures in W Ltd.

Required: Give journal entries in the books of K Ltd. and draw the resultant Balance Sheet as at 2nd April, 2013. *[CA (IPCC) Nov. 2012]*

Solution

JOURNAL

Date	Particulars		L.F.	Dr. (₹)	Cr. (₹)
01.04.13	Equity Share Capital A/c	Dr.		20,00,000	
	To Equity Share Capital A/c				20,00,000
	(Being the sub-division of one share of ₹ 100 each into 10 shares of ₹ 10 each)				
	Equity Share Capital A/c	Dr.		10,00,000	
	To Reconstruction A/c				10,00,000
	(Being the reduction of capital by 50%)				
	Reconstruction A/c	Dr.		42,000	
	To Bank A/c				42,000
	(Being the payment in cash for 20% of arrears of preference dividend)				
	Bank A/c	Dr.		78,400	
	To Own Debentures A/c [(1,92,000/2,00,000) × 80,000]				76,800
	To Reconstruction A/c				1,600
	(Being the T/f of profit on sale of own Debentures)				
	12% Debentures A/c	Dr.		1,20,000	
	To Own debentures A/c [(1,92,000/2,00,000) × 1,20,000]				1,15,200
	To Reconstruction A/c				4,800
	(Being the T/f of profit on cancellation of own Debentures)				
	12.% Debentures A/c	Dr.		3,00,000	
	Reconstruction A/c	Dr.		20,000	
	To Machinery A/c				3,20,000
	(Being the machinery taken up by debentureholders)				
	Reconstruction A/c	Dr.		37,000	
	To Debtors A/c				25,000
	To Stock A/c				12,000
	(Being the Assets revalued)				
	Creditors A/c	Dr.		60,000	
	To Reconstruction A/c				60,000
	(Being the liabilities revalued)				
	Reconstruction A/c	Dr.		4,33,000	
	To Goodwill A/c				20,000
	To Discount on debentures A/c				2,000
	To Profit and Loss A/c				4,11,000
	(Being the losses w/o)				

Date	Particulars		L.F.	Dr. (₹)	Cr. (₹)
	Reconstruction A/c To Bank A/c (Being the penalty paid for avoidance of capital commitments)	Dr.		20,000	20,000
	Reconstruction A/c To Capital Reserve A/c (Being the transfer of Balance to Capital Reserve)	Dr.		5,14,400	5,14,400
02.04.13	Business Purchase A/c To Liquidators of W Ltd. (Being the purchase of business)	Dr.		18,20,000	18,20,000
	Fixed assets A/c	Dr.		11,50,000	
	Stock A/c	Dr.		6,80,000	
	Debtors A/c	Dr.		6,15,000	
	Cash at bank A/c	Dr.		1,55,000	
	To Sundry Ceditors A/c				3,15,000
	To 12% Debentures A/c of W Ltd.				2,00,000
	To Profit and loss A/c				15,000
	To General Reserve A/c ₹ (1,70,000 + 80,000*)				2,50,000
	To Business Purchase A/c (Being the recording over of all assets and liabilities taken over)				18,20,000
	Liquidators of W Ltd. A/c To Equity share capital A/c To 10% Preference share capital A/c (Being the purchase consideration discharged)	Dr.		18,20,000	15,00,000 3,20,000
	12% Debentures of W Ltd. A/c To 12% Debentures A/c (Being the issue of 12% Debentures against Debentures of W Ltd.)	Dr.		2,00,000	2,00,000

**₹ 80,000 is the balancing figure adjusted to General Reserve Account as per AS 14 "Accounting for Amalgamation".

BALANCE SHEET OF K LTD. AS AT 02.04.2013

Particulars	Note No	₹
I. Equity and Liabilities		
(1) Shareholders' Funds		
(a) Share Capital	1	35,20,000
(b) Reserves and Surplus	2	10,19,400
(2) Non-Current Liabilities [12%Debentures]	3	3,80,000
(3) Current Liabilities		
(a) Trade Payables [Creditors]	4	8,15,000
Total		57,34,400
II. Assets		
(1) Non-Current Assets		
(a) Fixed Assets		
Tangible Assets	5	32,30,000
(2) Current Assets		
(a) Inventories	6	10,80,000
(b) Trade Receivables [Debtors]	7	12,15,000
(c) Cash and Cash Equivalents	8	2,09,400
Total		57,34,400

Notes To Accounts :

Particulars	₹
1. Share Capital	
2,50,000 Equity Shares of ₹ 10 each	25,00,000
10,200,9% Pref. Shares of ₹ 100 each	10,20,000
(Of the above 1,50,000 *Equity* Shares & 3200,*9% Pref. Shares* were issued for consideration otherwise than cash)	35,20,000
2. Reserves and Surplus	
General Reserve (2,40,000 + 2,50,000)	4,90,000
Profit & Loss Account	15,000
Capital Reserve	5,14,400
Total	10,19,400
3. Long-term Borrowings	
12% Debentures	6,00,000
Less: Settled in consideration of machinery	(3,00,000)
Less: Cancelled debentures	(1,20,000)
Add: 12% Debentures issue to W Ltd.	2,00,000
Total	3,80,000
4. Trade Payables	
of K Ltd.	5,60,000
Less: Reduction due to revaluation	(60,000)
Add: Trade Payables of W Ltd.	3,15,000
Total	8,15,000
5. Tangible assets	
Balance of Other Fixed Assets	24,00,000
Less: Machinery taken up by debenture holders	(3,20,000)
Add: Other Fixed Assets of W Ltd.	11,50,000
Total	32,30,000
6. Inventories	
of K Ltd.	4,12,000
Less: Reduction due to revaluation	(12,000)
Add: Inventories of W Ltd.	6,80,000
Total	10,80,000
7. Trade Receivables	
of K Ltd.	6,25,000
Less: Reduction due to revaluation	(25,000)
Add: Trade Receivables of W Ltd.	6,15,000
Total	12,15,000
8. Cash and Cash Equivalents	
of K Ltd.	38,000
Less: Payment of Arrear of Preference dividend	(42,000)

Add: Profit on Sale of own Debentures	78,400
Less: Penalty Paid	(20,000)
Add: Cash and Cash Equivalents of W Ltd.	1,55,000
Total	2,09,400

Working Notes:

(i) *Purchase Consideration:*

	₹
Equity share capital [(15,000 × 50/5) × ₹ 10]	15,00,000
9% Preference share capital [(4,000 × 4/5) × ₹ 100]	3,20,000
	18,20,000

(ii) *General Reserve:*

	₹
Share capital of W Ltd. (Equity + Preference)	19,00,000
Less: Share capital issued by K Ltd.	18,20,000
General reserve (resulted due to absorption)	80,000

PROBLEM 14

The summarized Balance Sheet of Bad Luck Ltd. as on 31st March, 2013 was as follows:

Particulars	*Note No*	*₹ (lacs)*
I. Equity and Liabilities		
(1) Shareholders' Funds		
(a) Share Capital	1	7.50
(b) Reserves and Surplus	2	(10.00)
(2) Non-Current Liabilities (Long-term Borrowings)	3	5.00
(3) Current Liabilities		
(a) Short-term Borrowings	4	5.00
(b) Trade Payables [Creditors]		2.50
Total		10.00
II. Assets		
(1) Non-Current Assets		
(a) Fixed Assets		
Tangible Assets	5	5.50
Intangible Assets	6	1.50
(2) Current Assets		
(a) Inventories		1.50
(b) Trade Receivables		1.25
(c) Deferred revenue expenditure		0.25
Total		10.00

Notes To Accounts:

Particulars		₹ (lacs)
1. Share Capital		
5000 Equity Shares of ₹ 100 each		5.00
2500, 8% Pref. Shares of ₹ 100 each		2.50
		7.50
2. Reserves and Surplus (Profit and Loss A/c)		(10.00)
3. Long-term Borrowings (8% Debentures)		5.00
4. Short-term Borrowings		
Loan from Directors		3.00
Bank Overdraft		2.00
		5.00
5. Tangible Assets		
Freehold Property		4.00
Plant & Machinery		1.50
Total		5.50
6. Intangible Assets		
Goodwill		1.00
Trademark		0.50
		1.50

The followig scheme of internal reconstruction was framed, approved by the Court, all the concerned parties and implemented:

(i) The preference shares to be written down to ₹ 25 each and the equity shares to ₹ 20 each. Each class of shares then to be conveted into shares of ₹ 100 each.

(ii) The debenture holders to take over freehold property (book value ₹ 2,00,000) at a valuation of ₹ 2,50,000 in part repayment of their holdings. Remaining freehold property to be revalued at ₹ 6,00,000.

(iii) Loan from directors to be waived off in full.

(iv) Stock of ₹ 50,000 to be written off, ₹ 12,500 to be provided for bad debts.

(v) Profit and Loss account balance, Trademark, Goodwill and Deferred Revenue Expenditure to be written off.

Pass Journal Entries for all the above mentioned transactions. Also, Prepare Capital Reducation account and company's Balance Sheet immediately after reconstruction. *[CA (IPCC) May 2013]*

Solution

JOURNAL OF BAD LUCK LTD.

Date	Particulars		Dr. (₹)	Cr. (₹)
(i)	8% Preference Share Capital A/c (₹ 100)	Dr.	2,50,000	
	To 8% Preference Share Capital A/c (₹ 25)			62,500
	To Capital Reduction A/c			1,87,500
	(Being preference shares of ₹100 each reduced to ₹ 25 each as per the scheme)			

	Particulars		Dr. (₹)	Cr. (₹)
(ii)	Equity Share Capital A/c (₹ 100)	Dr.	5,00,000	
	To Equity Share Capital A/c (₹ 20)			1,00,000
	To Capital Reduction A/c			4,00,000
	(Being equity shares of ₹ 100 each reduced to ₹ 20 each as per the scheme)			
(iii)	8% Preference Share Capital A/c (₹ 25)	Dr.	62,500	
	To 8% Preference Share Capital A/c (₹ 100)			62,500
	(Being the conversion of 2,500 shares of ₹ 25 each into 625 shares of ₹ 100 each as per the scheme)			
(iv)	Equity Share Capital A/c (₹ 20)	Dr.	1,00,000	
	To Equity Share Capital A/c (₹ 100)			1,00,000
	(Being the conversion of 5,000 shares of ₹ 20 each in to 1,000 shares of ₹ 100 each as per the scheme)			
(v)	Freehold Property A/c	Dr.	50,000	
	To Capital Reduction A/c			50,000
	(Being appreciation in the value of property)			
(vi)	8% Debentures A/c	Dr.	2,50,000	
	To Freehold Property A/c			2,50,000
	(Being claim of debentureholders settled in part by transfer of freehold property as per the scheme)			
(vii)	Freehold Property A/c	Dr.	4,00,000	
	To Capital Reduction A/c			4,00,000
	(Being appreciation in the value of remaining property)			
(viii)	Director's Loan A/c	Dr.	3,00,000	
	To Capital Reduction A/c			3,00,000
	(Being Director's loan waived in full)			
(ix)	Capital Reduction A/c	Dr.	13,37,500	
	To Profit and Loss A/c			10,00,000
	To Deferred Revenue Expenditure A/c			25,000
	To Inventories A/c			50,000
	To Provision for Doubtful Debts A/c			12,500
	To Goodwill A/c			1,00,000
	To Trademark			50,000
	To Capital Reserve A/c			1,00,000
	(Being the various assets written off as per the scheme)			

Dr. **CAPITAL REDUCTION ACCOUNT** Cr.

Particulars	₹	Particulars	₹
To Provision for Doubtful Debts A/c	12,500	By Preference Share Capital A/c	1,87,500
To Inventories A/c	50,000	By Freehold Property A/c	4,50,000
To Trademark A/c	50,000	By Equity Share Capital A/c	4,00,000
To Deferred Revenue Exp. A/c	60,000	By Director's loan A/c	3,00,000
To Goodwill A/c	1,00,000		
To Profit and loss A/c	10,00,000		
To Capital reserve A/c	1,00,000		
	13,37,500		**13,37,500**

BALANCE SHEET OF BAD LUCK LTD. (AND REDUCED) AS AT 31.03.2013

Particulars	Note No	₹
I. Equity and Liabilities		
(1) Shareholders' Funds		
(a) Share Capital	1	1,62,500
(b) Reserves and Surplus[Capital Reserve]		1,00,000
(2) Non-Current Liabilities		
Long-term Borrowings [8% Debentures]		2,50,000
(3) Current Liabilities		
(a) Short-term Borrowings [Bank Overdraft]		2,00,000
(b) Trade Payables [Creditors]		2,50,000
Total		9,62,500
II. Assets		
(1) Non-Current Assets		
(a) Fixed Assets		
Tangible Assets	2	7,50,000
(2) Current Assets		
(a) Inventories		1,00,000
(b) Trade Receivables [1,50,000 – 12,500]		1,12,500
Total		9,62,500

Notes To Accounts:

Particulars	₹
1. Share Capital	
1,000 Equity Shares of ₹ 100 each	1,00,000
625,8% Pref. Shares of ₹ 100 each	62,500
	1,62,500
2. Tangible Assets	
Frehold Property	6,00,000
Plant & Machinery	1,50,000
Total	7,50,000

PROBLEM 15

The Balance Sheet of X Ltd, as at 31st March 2014, was as follows:

Particulars		₹
Equity and Liabilities		
1. Share Holder's Funds		
Share Capital:	(a) 40,000 Equity Shares of ₹ 100 each fully paid	40,00,000
	(b) 20,000, 10% Preference Shares of ₹ 100 each fully paid	20,00,000
Reserves & Surplus:	(a) Securities Premium Account	1,50,000
	(b) Profit & Loss Account	(23,00,000)
2. Non-Current Liabilities: Long Term borrowings –7% Debentures of ₹ 100 each		4,00,000

3. Current Liabilities: Other Current Liabilities	– Creditors		10,00,000
	– Loan from Director		2,00,000
Total Liabilities			**54,50,000**
Assets			
1. Non-Current Assets			
Fixed Assets	(a) Land & Building	20,00,000	
	(b) Plant and Machinery	12,00,000	32,00,000
Intangible Assets: Goodwill			4,00,000
2. Current Assets			
	(a) Debtors	12,00,000	
	(b) Stock	5,00,000	
	(c) Cash at Bank	1,50,000	18,50,000
Total Assets			**54,50,000**

No Dividend on Prefernce Shares has been paid for last 5 years.

The following scheme of reorganization was duly approved by the Court:

(a) Each Equity Share be reduced to ₹ 25.

(b) Each existing Preference Share to be reduced to ₹ 75, and then exchanged for one new 13% Preference Share of ₹ 50 each and one Equity Share of ₹ 25 each.

(c) Preference Shareholders have forgone their right for Dividend for four years. One year's Dividend at the old rate is however, payable to them in fully paid Equity Shares of ₹ 25.

(d) The Debenture Holders be given the option to either acdept 90% of their claims in cash or to convert their claims in full into new 13% Preference Shares of ₹ 50 each issued at par. One-fourth (in value) of the Debentrue Holders accepted Preference Shares for their claims. The rest were paid in cash.

(e) Contingent Liability of ₹ 2,00,000 is payable which has been created by wrong ac tion of one Director. He has agreed to compensate this loss out of the Loan given by the Director to the Company

(f) Goodwill does not have any value in the present. Decrease the value of Plant & Machinery, Stock and Debtors by ₹ 3,00,000, ₹ 1,00,000 and ₹ 2,00,000 respectively. Increase the value of Land & Building to ₹ 25,00,000.

(g) 50,000 new Equity Shares of ₹ 25 each are to be issued at par payable in full on application. The issue was underwritten for a Commission of 4%. Shares were fully taken up.

(h) Total Expenses incurred by the Company in connection with the Scheme excluding Underwriting Commission amounted to ₹ 20,000.

Pass necessary Journal Entries to record the above transactions.

[Nov. 2014]

Solution

Journal

Date	Particulars		Dr. (₹)	Cr. (₹)
1.	Equity Share Capital (₹ 100) A/c	Dr.	40,00,000	
	To Equity Share Capital (₹ 25) A/c			10,00,000
	To Reconstruction A/c			30,00,000
	(Being Equity Shares of ₹ 100 each reduced to 25 each, and balance transferred to Reconstruction A/c, as per approved Scheme of Reconstruction dated....)			
2.	10% Preference Share Capital (₹ 100) A/c	Dr.	20,00,000	
	To 13% Preference Share Capital (₹ 50) A/c			10,00,000
	To Equity Share Capital (₹ 25) A/c			5,00,000
	To Reconstruction A/c			5,00,000
	(Being 20,000 Preference Shares of ₹ 100 each are converted into 20,000 13% Preference Shares of ₹ 50 each & 20,000 Equity Shares of ₹ 25 each)			
3.	Reconstruction A/c	Dr.	2,00,000	
	To Equity Share capital (₹ 25) A/c			2,00,000
	(Being Equity Shares issued for arrears of Pref. Share Dividend)			
4.	7% Debentures A/c	Dr.	4,00,000	
	To 13% Preference Share Capital (₹ 50) A/c			1,00,000
	To Bank A/c			2,70,000
	To Reconstruction A/c			30,000
	(Being 3/4 of Debentureholders opting to take 13% Preference Shares at par, and remaining Debentureholders taking 90% cash payment for their Claims.)			
5.	Director's Loan A/c	Dr.	2,00,000	
	To Provision for Expenses/Contingent Liability			2,00,000
	(Being Contingent Liability provided & adjusted Interest of Loan payable to Director)			
6.	Bank A/c	Dr.	12,50,000	
	To Equity Share Application & Allotment A/c			12,50,000
	(Being application money received on the 50,000 Equity Shares at ₹ 25 each)			
7.	Equity Share Application & Allotment A/c	Dr.	12,50,000	
	To Equity Share Capital (₹ 25) A/c			12,50,000
	(Being Application Money transferred to Equity Capital A/c, on allotment)			
8.	Reconstruction A/c	Dr.	50,000	
	To Bank A/c			50,000
	(Being Underwriting Commission paid, 4% on ₹ 12,50,000)			
9.	Land and Buildings A/c	Dr.	5,00,000	
	To Reconstruction A/c			5,00,000
	(Being value of Land and Buildings appreciated as per Reconstruction Scheme)			

Date	Particulars		Dr. (₹)	Cr. (₹)
10.	Reconstruction A/c	Dr.	20,000	
	To Bank A/c			20,000
	(Being payment of expenses on reconstruction)			
11.	Reconstruction A/c	Dr.	23,00,000	
	To Profit and Loss A/c			23,00,000
	Being Profit and Loss A/c Debit balance written off using Reconstruction A/c)			
12.	Reconstruction A/c	Dr.	10,00,000	
	To Goodwill A/c			4,00,000
	To Plant and Machinery A/c			3,00,000
	To Stock A/c			1,00,000
	To Debetors A/c			2,00,000
	(Being various losses/intangible items written off using Reconstruction A/c, as per approvied Scheme of Reconstruction dated....)			
13.	Reconstruction A/c	Dr.	4,60,000	
	To Capital Reserve A/c			4,60,000
	(Being balance in Reconstruction A/c t/f to Capital Reserve)			

Working Note:

Dr. **Reconstruction Account** Cr.

Particulars	₹	Particulars	₹
To Bank A/c (Preference Dividend)	2,00,000	By Equity Share Capital (₹ 100) A/c	30,00,000
To Bank, (Expenses)	20,000	By 10% Preference Share Capital (₹ 100) A/c	5,00,000
To Goodwill A./c	4,00,000	By Debentureholders A/c	30,000
To Plant and Machinery A/c	3,00,000	By Land and Buildings A/c	5,00,000
To Stock A/c	1,00,000		
To Debtores A/c	2,00,000		
To Profit & Loss A/c	23,00,000		
To Bank A/c (Underwriting Comm.)	50,000		
To Capital Reserve A/c **(b.f)**	**4,60,000**		
	40,30,000		40,30,000

9 Liquidation of Companies

SHORT ANSWER PRACTICAL QUESTIONS

CALCULATION OF PREFERENTIAL CREDITORS

PROBLEM 1

A company went into liquidation whose creditors are ₹ 36,000 includes ₹ 6,000 on account of wages of 15 men at ₹ 100 per month for 4 months immediately before the date of winding up; ₹ 9,000 being the salaries of 5 employees at ₹ 300 per month for the previous 6 months, Rent for godown for the last six months amounting to ₹ 3,000; Income-tax deducted out of salaries of employees ₹ 1,000 and Directors fees ₹ 500; in addition it is estimated that the company would have to pay ₹ 5,000 as compensation to an employee for injuries suffered by him, which was contingent liability not accepted by the company and not included in above said creditors figure.

Find the amount of Preferential Creditors. *[CA (IPCC) Nov. 2010]*

Solution

CALCULATION OF PREFERENTIAL CREDITORS

	₹
Tax deducted at source on salaries	1,000
Wages (15 men for 4 months at ₹ 100 each)	6,000
Salaries (5 men for 4 months at ₹ 300 each)	6,000
Workmen's compensation	5,000
Total	**18,000**

Notes :

(i) Salaries payable to any employee due for the period not exceeding 4 months within the twelve months next before commencement of winding up subject to maximum 20,000 per person.

(ii) Directors fees, rent for godown are not included in preferential creditors.

CALCULATION OF LIQUIDATOR'S REMUNERATION

PROBLEM 2

The liquidator of a company is entitled to a remuneration of 2% on assets realized and 3% on the amount distributed to unsecured creditors. The assets realized ₹ 10,00,000. Amount available for distribution to unsecured creditors before paying liquidator's remuneration is ₹ 4,12,000. calculate liquidator's remuneration if the surplus is insufficient to pay off unsecured creditors, in toto.

[CA (PCC) May 2010]

Solution

Liquidator's remuneration on assets realised (₹ 10,00,000 × 2/100)	₹ 20,000
Liquidator's remuneration on payment to unsecured creditors [(₹ 4,12,000 – ₹ 20,000) × 3/103]	11,417
Total Liquidator's Remuneration	₹ 31,417

PROBLEM 3

A Liquidator is entitled to receive remuneration at 2% on the assets realized, 3% on the amount distributed to Preferential Creditors and 3% on the payment made to Unsecured Creditors. The assets were realized for ₹ 25,00,000 against which payment was made as follows:

Liquidation expenses	₹ 25,000
Secured Creditors	₹ 10,00,000
Preferential Creditors	₹ 75,000

The amount due to Unsecured Creditors was ₹ 15,00,000. You are asked to calculate the total Remuneration payable to Liquidator. Calculation shall be made to the nearest multiple of a rupee.

[PCC (May 2012)]

Solution

CALCULATION OF TOTAL REMUNERATION PAYABLE TO LIQUIDATOR

Particulars		₹
2% on Assets realised	25,00,000 × 2%	50,000
3% on payment made to Preferential creditors	75,000 × 3%	2,250
3% on payment made to Unsecured creditors (Refer W.N.)		39,255
Total Remuneration payable to Liquidator		91,505

Notes:

Remuneration on payment to unsecured creditors

= Cash available for unsecured creditors × 3/103

= (₹ 25,00,000 – ₹ 25,000 – ₹ 10,00,000 – ₹ 75,000 – ₹ 50,000 – ₹ 2,250) × 3/103

= ₹ 39,225

LIQUIDATOR'S FINAL STATEMENT OF ACCOUNT

PROBLEM 4

The position of Valueless Ltd. on its liquidation is as under:

Issued and paid up Capital:

3,000 11% Preference Shares of ₹ 100 each fully paid.
3,000 Equity Shares of ₹ 100 each fully paid.
1,000 Equity Shares of ₹ 50 each, ₹ 30 per share paid.

Calls in Arrears are ₹ 10,000 and Calls received in Advance ₹ 5,000. Preference dividends are in arrears for one year. Amount left with the liquidator after discharging all liabilities is ₹ 4,13,000. Articles of Association of the company provide for payment of preference dividend arrears in priority to return of equity capital. You are required to prepare the Liquidators Final Statement of Account.

[CA (PE-II) November 2004]

Solution

LIQUIDATOR'S FINAL STATEMENT OF ACCOUNT

Receipts	₹	Payments	₹
Cash	4,13,000	Return to Contributors:	
Realisation from:		Preference Dividend	33,000
Calls in arrears	10,000	Preference Share holders	3,00,000
Final call of ₹ 5 per Equity Share of ₹ 50 each (₹ 5 × 1,000)	5,000	Calls in Advance	5,000
		Equity Share holders of ₹ 100 each (3,000 × ₹ 30)	90,000
	4,28,000		4,28,000

Working Note:

(i) *Calculation of Deficiency*

A. Total Paid-up Share Capital	₹.3,30,000
B. *Less:* Cash Available [₹ 4,13,000 + 10,000 (Arrears)] – [(3,33,000) (Pref) + 5,000 (Adv.)]	₹ (85,000)
C. Deficiency to be borne (A–B)	2,45,000
D. Total Nominal Share Capital	3,50,000
E. Deficiency as % of Nominal Capital $\left(\frac{C}{D} \times 100\right)$	70%

(ii) *Calculation of Net Amount returnable for Shares*

Class of Shares	*A*	*B*
A. Paid-up Amount Per Share	100	30
B. *Less:* Deficiency to be borne @ 70% of Nominal value	(70)	(35)
C. Net Amount Returnable (A–B)	30	(5)

PROBLEM 5

The following particulars relate to a Limited Company which has gone into voluntary liquidation. You are required to prepare the Liquidator's Statement of Account allowing for his remuneration @2½% on all assets realized excluding call money received and 2% on the amount paid to unsecured creditors including preferential creditors.

Share capital issued:

10,000 Preference shares of ₹ 100 each fully paid up.
50,000 Equity shares of ₹ 10 each fully paid up.
30,000 Equity shares of ₹ 10 each, ₹ 8 paid up.

Assets realized ₹ 20,00,000 excluding the amount realized by sale of securities held by partly secured creditors.

	₹
Preferential creditors	50,000
Unsecured creditors	18,00,000
Partly secured creditors (Assets realized ₹ 3,20,000)	3,50,000
Debentureholders having floating charge on all assets of the company	6,00,000
Expenses of liquidation	10,000

A call of ₹ 2 per share on the partly paid equity shares was duly received except in case of one shareholder owning 1,000 shares.

Also calculate the percentage of amount paid to the unsecured creditors to the total unsecured creditors.

[*CA (PE II) Nov. 2007*]

Solution

LIQUIDATOR'S FINAL STATEMENT OF ACCOUNT

Receipts	₹	*Payments*		₹
Assets Realised	20,00,000	Liquidator's remuneration		
Receipt of call money on 29,000 equity shares @2 per share	58,000	2.5% on 23,20,000*	58,000	
		2% on 50,000	1,000	
		2% on 13,12,745	26,255	85,255
		Liquidation Expenses		10,000
		Debenture holders having a floating charge on all assets		6,00,000
		Preferential creditors		50,000
		Unsecured creditors		13,12,745
	20,58,000			20,58,000

(ii) Percentage of amount paid to unsecured creditors to total unsecured creditors

$$? \frac{13,12,745}{18,30,000} ?100 ? 71.73\%$$

Working Notes:

(i) Total assets realised = ₹ 20,00,000 + ₹ 3,20,000 = ₹ 23,20,000

(ii) Unsecured portion in partly secured creditors = ₹ 3,50,000 – ₹ 3,20,000 = ₹ 30,000

(iii) Total unsecured creditors = ₹ 18,00,000 + ₹ 30,000 = ₹ 18,30,000

(iv) Liquidator's remuneration on payment to unsecured creditors

Cash available for unsecured creditors after all payments including payment to preferential creditors & liquidator's remuneration on it = ₹ 13,39,000

$$\text{Liquidator's remuneration on unsecured creditors} = \frac{2}{102} ?13,39,000 \ ?\text{Rs. } 26,255$$

STATEMENT OF LIABILITIES OF B LIST CONTRIBUTORIES

PROBLEM 6

Pessimist Ltd. has gone into liquidation on 10th May, 2013. The details of members, who have ceased to be members, within the year ended 31st March, 2013 are given below. The debts that could not be paid out of realisation of assets and contribution from present members ('A' contributories) are also given with their date-wise break up. Shares are of ₹.10 each, ₹.6 per share paid up.

You are to determine the amount realisable from each person.

Shareholders	*No. of Shares transferred*	*Date of transfer*	*Unpaid Debts*
P	1,000	20.04.2012	3,000
Q	1,200	15.05.2012	5,000
R	1,500	18.09.2012	9,200
S	800	24.12.2012	10,500
T	500	12.03.2013	11,000

[CA (November 2000)]

Solution

STATEMENT OF LIABILITIES OF B LIST CONTRIBUTORIES

Creditors outstanding on the date of transfer (ceasing to be member)			Q 1,200 Shares	R 1,500 Shares	S 800 Shares	T 500 Shares	Amount to be paid to creditors
Date		₹	₹	₹	₹	₹	₹
15 May		5000	1500	1875	1000	625	5000
19 Sept.	9,200						
	–5,000	4,200	–	2,250	1,200	750	4,200
	10,500						
24 Dec.	–9,200	1,300	–	–	800	500	1,300
	11,000						
12 March	10,500	500	–	–	–	500	125*
Total (a)		11,000	1,500	4,125	3,000	2,375	10,625
Maximum liability on shares held (b)		4,800	6,000	3,200	2,000		
Amount paid (a) and (b) whichever is lower			1,500	4,125	3,000	2,000	

Working Notes:

(i) P will not be liable since he transferred his shares prior to one year preceding the date of winding up.

(ii) The amount of ₹.5,000 outstanding on 15th May will have to contributed by Q, R, S and T in the ratio of number of shares held by them, i.e. in the ratio of 12:15:8:5; thus Q will have to contribute ₹.1,500; R ₹.18,75; S ₹.1,000; T ₹.625.

(iii) Similarly, the further debts incurred between 15th May to 18th September viz. ₹.4,200 for which Q is not liable will be contributed by R, S and T in the ratio of 15:8:5. R will have to contribute ₹.2,250. S and T will contribute ₹.1,200 and ₹.750 respectively.

(iv) The further increase from ₹.9,200 to ₹.10,500 viz. ₹.1,300 occurring between 18th September and 24th December will be shared by S and T who will be liable for ₹.800 and ₹.500 respectively.

(v) The increase between 24th December and 12th March, is solely the responsibility of T.

PROBLEM 7

In a winding up CAMHH Ltd. which commenced on 15th September, 2013, certain creditors could not receive payments out of the realisation of assets and out of contribution from '*A*' list of contributories. Following are the details of certain share transfers that took place prior to liquidation and the amount of creditors remaining unpaid:

Shareholders	*No. of shares transferred*	*Date when ceased to be member*	*Creditors remaining unpaid and outstanding at the date of ceasing to be a member* ₹
A	2,000	31-8-2012	8,000
B	1,800	20-9-2012	12,000
C	1,200	15-11-2012	17,400
D	1,000	22-4-2013	18,600
E	500	10-7-2013	22,000

All the shares were of ₹ 10 each, on which ₹ 5 per share had been called and paid up. Ignoring expenses of liquidation, remuneration to liquidator etc., work out the amount to be realised from the above contributories.

Solution

Only a person who had transferred his shares within 12 months preceding the date of winding up is liable for contribution under List B. Hence out of the five persons, one having transferred his holdings more than 12 months prior to the date of winding up is not liable as contributory. The rest of the transferors are liable subject to the restriction that an individual not being made liable for more than unpaid value on the shares.

STATEMENT OF LIABILITY OF '*B*' LIST CONTRIBUTORIES

Creditors Outstanding on the date of ceasing to be Member ₹	*B 1,800 Shares* ₹	*C 1,200 Shares* ₹	*D 1,000 Shares* ₹	*E 500 Shares* ₹	*Amount to be paid to the creditors* ₹
(i) 12,000	4,800	3,200	2,667	1,333	12,000
(ii) 5,400 (i.e. 17,400 – 12,000)		2,400	2,000	1,000	5,400
(iii) 1,200 (i.e. 18,600 – 17,400)			800	400	500*
(iv) 3,400 (i.e. 22,000 – 18,600)				3,400	Nil
A Total	4,800	5,600	5,467	6,133	
B Maximum liability on Shares held	9,000	6,000	5,000	2,500	
C Amount paid-lower of A or B	4,800	5,600	5,000	2,500	

*From D ₹ 333 *plus* from E ₹ 167.

PROBLEM 8

Liquidation of YZ Ltd. commenced on 2nd April, 2013. Certain creditors could not receive payments out of the realisation of assets and out of the contribution from A list contributories. The following are the details of certain transfers which took place in 2012 and 2013.

Share holders	*No. of Shares Transferred*	*Date of ceasing to be a member*	*Creditors remaining unpaid and outstanding on the date of such transfer*
A	2,000	1st March, 2012	₹ 5,000
P	1,500	1st May, 2012	₹ 3,300
Q	1,000	1st October, 2012	₹ 4,300
R	500	1st November, 2012	₹ 4,600
S	300	1st February, 2013	₹ 6,000

All the shares were of ₹ 10 each, ₹ 8 per share paid up. Show the amount to be realised from the various persons listed above ignoring expenses and remuneration to liquidator etc.

[CA (PE II) November 2004]

Solution

STATEMENT OF LIABILITIES OF B LIST CONTRIBUTORIES

Share holders	No. of Shares t/f	Maximum Liability (upto ₹ 2 per share)	Division of Liability as on				Total
			1 May	1 Oct.	1 Nov.	1 Feb.	
		₹	₹	₹	₹	₹	₹
P	1,500	3,000	1,500	—	—	—	1,500
Q	1,000	2,000	1,000	555	—	—	1,555
R	500	1,000	500	278	188	—	966
S	300	600	300	167	112	21	600
	3,300	6,600	3,300	1,000	300	21	4,621

Working Notes:

Date	Cumulative Liability	Increase in Liability	Ratio of no. of shares held by the members
1 May	3,300	—	30 : 20 : 10 : 6
1 Oct.	4,300	1,000	20 : 10 : 6
1 Nov.	4,600	300	10 : 6
1 Feb.	6,000	1,400	Only S

Liability of *S* has been estricted to the maximum allowable limit of ₹ 600, therefore amount payable by S is restricted to ₹ 21 only, on 1 Feb.

(i) A will not be liable to pay to the outstanding creditors since he transferred his shares prior to one year preceding the dae of winding up.

(ii) P will not be responsible for further debts incurred after 1st May, from the date when he ceases to be member). Similarly, Q and R wil not be responsible for the debs incurred after the date of their transfer of shares.

PROBLEM 9

M/s. ABC Limited has gone into liquidation on 25th June, 2013. Certain creditors could not receive payments out of realization of assets and contributions from A list contributories. The following are the details of certain transfers which took place in the year ended 31st March, 2013:

Shareholders	No. of shares transferred	Date of ceasing to be a member	Creditors remaining unpaid and outstanding on the date of transfer (₹)
P	4,000	10-5-2012	9,000
Q	3,000	22-7-2012	12,000
R	2,400	15-9-2012	13,500
S	1,600	14-12-2012	14,000
T	1,000	09-03-2013	14,200

All the shares are of ₹ 10 each, ₹ 8 per share paid up. Show the amount to be realized from the persons listed above. Ignore remuneration to liquidator and other expenses.

[CA (IPCC) Nov., 2011]

Solution

(A) STATEMENT OF LIABILITIES OF B LIST CONTRIBUTORIES

Shareholder	*No. of shares transferred*	*Maximum liability upto ₹ 2 per share*	*Division of liability as on*				*Total*
			22 July	15 Sept.	14 Dec.	09 March	
Q	3,000	6,000	4,500	—	—	—	4,500
R	2,400	4,800	3,600	720	—	—	4,320
S	1,600	3,200	2,400	480	308	—	3,188
T	1,000	2,000	1,500	300	192	8	2,000
	8,000	1 6,000	1 2,000	1 ,500	500	8	1 4,008

Notes:

(i) 'P' transferred shares before one year preceding the date of winding up, therefore, he cannot be held liable for any liability on liquidation.

(ii) Liability of 'T' has been restricted to the maximum allowable limit of ₹ 2,000. Therefore, amount payable by T on 09 March is ₹ 8 only.

(iii) 'Q' will not be responsible for further debts incurred after 10th May (from the date when he ceases to be a member). Similarly, 'R' & 'S' will not be liable for the debts incurred after the date of their transfer of shares.

Working Note:

CALCULATION OF RATIO FOR DISCHARGE OF LIABILITIES

Date	*Cumulative liability (₹)*	*Increase in liabilities (₹)*	*Ratio of no. of shares held by Q, R, S&T*
22 July	12,000	—	30 : 24 : 16 : 10
15 Sept.	13,500	1,500	24 : 16 : 10
14 Dec.	14,000	500	16 : 10
09 March	14,200	200	Only T

LONG ANSWER PRACTICAL QUESTIONS

STATEMENT OF AFFAIRS

PROBLEM 10

'*A' Ltd* is to be liquidated. Their summarised Balance Sheet as at 30th September, 2013 appears as under:

	₹
Liabilities:	
5,00,000 equity shares of ₹ 100 each	50,00,000
Secured Debentures (on Land and Buildings)	20,00,000
Unsecured Loans	40,00,000
Trade Creditors	70,00,000
	1,80,00,000
Assets:	
Land and Buildings	10,00,000
Other Fixed Assets	40,00,000
Current Assets	90,00,000
Profit and Loss Account	40,00,000
	1,80,00,000
Contingent liabilities are:	
For bills discounted	2,00,000
For excise duty demands	3,00,000

On investigation, it is found that the contingent liabilities are certain to devolve and the the assets are likely to be realised as follows:

	₹
Land and Building	₹ 22,00,000
Other fixed assets	₹ 36,00,000
Current Assets	₹ 70,00,000

Taking the above into account, prepare the Statement of affairs. *[CA (PE-II) Nov. 2009]*

Solution

STATEMENT OF AFFAIRS OF 'A' LTD. (IN LIQUIDATION)
AS AT 30TH SEPTEMBER, 2013

Assets	*Estimated Realisable Value (₹)*
Assets not specifically pledged (as per List A):	
Other Fixed Assets	36,00,000
Current Assets	70,00,000
	1,06,00,000

Assets specifically pledged (as per List *B*):

	Estimated Realizable value	Due to secured creditors	Deficiency ranking as unsecured	Surplus carried to the last column	
	₹	₹	₹	₹	
Land and Building	22,00,000	20,00,000	–	2,00,000	2,00,000
Estimated total assets available for preferential creditors, debenture holders secured by a floating charge and unsecured creditors					1,08,00,000

Summary of Gross Assets:

Gross Realizable Value of Assets Specifically Pledged	22,00,000	
Other Assets	1,06,00,000	
Total Assets	1,28,00,000	

LIABILITIES

Gross Liabilities	*Liabilities*	
20,00,000	Secured creditors (as per List B) to the extent to which claims are estimated to be covered by assets specifically pledged	
3,00,000	Preferential creditors (as per List C) – for demand of excise duty	3,00,000
	Balance of assets available for debentureholders secured by floating charge and unsecured creditors	1,05,00,00
–	Debentureholders secured by floating charge (as per List D)	–
	Unsecured creditors (as per List E):	
40,00,000	Unsecured Loans	40,00,000
70,00,000	Trade Creditors	70,00,000
2,00,000	Liability for bills discounted (Contingent)	2,00,000
1,35,00,000	Estimated deficiency as regards creditors (difference between gross assets and gross liabilities)	7,00,000
	Issued and called up capital:	
	5,00,000 Equity Shares of ₹.10 each (as per List G)	50,00,000
	Estimated Deficiency as regards members/ contributories	57,00,000

PROBLEM 11

TM Ltd. went in for voluntary liquidation on 31st March, 2013.

The Balance Sheet of the company as at 31.3.2013 is given below:

Liabilities	₹	*Assets*	₹
Share Capital:		Freehold Property	11,85,000
1,00,000 Equity Shares of	10,00,000	Plant	6,03,000
₹ 10 each fully paid up		Motor Vehicles	1,15,000
10% Preference Shares of	12,00,000	Stock	3,72,000

₹.100 each fully paid up		Sundry Debtors	1,48,000
Securities Premium	1,00,000	Profit & Loss A/c	4,28,000
5% Debentures	2,00,000		
Interest on Debentures	5,000		
Bank overdraft	1,16,000		
Sundry Creditors	2,30,000		
	28,51,000		28,51,000

The preference dividends are in arrear for the years 2011-12 and 2012-13.

The company's Articles provide that on liquidation, out of surplus assets remaining after payment of liquidation costs and outside liabilities, it shall be applied firstly towards arrears of preference dividend, secondly to preference shareholders with a premium thereon at ₹.10 per share and finally any residue shall be paid to the equity shareholders.

The Liquidator realised the assets as below:

	₹
Freehold property	₹ 14,25,000
Plant	₹ 5,05,000
Motor Vehicles	₹ 1,18,000
Stock in trade	₹ 3,00,000
Sundry Debtors	₹ 1,20,000

Creditors were paid less discount of 5%. Debentureholders were paid alongwith accrued interest upto 30.6.2013.

Liquidators remuneration is 2% of the assets realised and cost of liquidation was ₹ 7,640.

Required: Prepare the Liquidator's Statement of Account. *[CA (PCC) Nov. 2009]*

Solution

LIQUIDATOR'S FINAL STATEMENT OF ACCOUNT

Particulars	₹	*Particulars*		₹
X Ltd.	38,50,000	Preference		11,00,000
Assets realised:		Liquidator's		49,360
Freehold Property	14,25,000	remuneration		
Plant	5,05,000	(24,68,000 × 2/100)		
Motor vehicles	1,18,000	Liquidation Cost		7,640
Stock	3,00,000	Debenture holders:		
Debtors	1,20,000	5% Debentures	2,00,000	
		Add: Debenture Interest	5,000	
		Interest for 3 months		
		upto 30.6.2009	2,500	2,07,500
		Bank overdraft		1,16,000
		Creditors	2,30,000	
		Less: 5% Discount	11,500	2,18,500

		Preference Shareholders:		
		Share Capital	12,00,000	
		Add: 10% premium	1,20,000	
		Add: O/s dividend		
		(for 2 years)	2,40,000	15,60,000
		Equity Shareholders		
		[(Bal. Fig.) at the rate of		
		₹ 3.09 per share)		3,09,000
	24,68,000			24,68,000

PROBLEM 12

From the following Trial Balance of *PQ* Ltd. on 31.12.2012, prepare liquidators' final statement of account:

	₹	₹
9% Preference Share Capital (1,250 Preference Shares @ ₹.100 each fully paid up)	—	1,25,000
Equity Share Capital:		
2,000 Equity Shares @ ₹ 100 each fully paid up	—	2,00,000
2,000 Equity Shares @ ₹ 1 00 each, ₹.50 paid up	—	1,00,000
Plant	3,00,000	
Stock-in-trade	3,60,000	
Sundry Debtors	85,000	—
Sundry Creditors	—	2,21,000
Bank balance	1,20,000	
Preliminary expenses	6,000	—
6% Mortgage loan	—	2,30,000
Outstanding liabilities for expenses	—	25,000
Profit and Loss account (Trading loss for the year 2009)	30,000	
	9,01,000	9,01,000

Following points should be kept in mind:

(i) On 21st January, 2013 the liquidator of *PQ* Ltd. sold plant for ₹ 2,95,000 and stock in trade at 10% less than the book value. He realised 80% of Sundry debtors and incurred cost of collection of ₹ 1,850 (remaining debtors are to be treated as bad).

(ii) The loan mortagage was discharged on 3st January, 2013 along with interest for 6 months. Creditors were discharged subject to 5% discount. Outstanding expenses paid at 20% less.

(iii) Preference share dividend is due for one year and paid with final payment.

(iv) Liquidation expenses incurred are ₹.1,800 and liquidators remuneration is settled at 4% on disbursement to members (excluding preference dividend), subject to minimum of ₹ 10,000.

[CA (IPCC) May 2010]

Solution

LIQUIDATOR'S FINAL STATEMENT OF ACCOUNT

Receipts	₹	Payments		₹
Assets realised:		Liquidation expenses		1,800
Bank	1,20,000	Liquidator's remuneration		12,510
Plant	2,95,000	Mortgage loan	2,30,000	
Stock	3,24,000	*Add:* Interest for 6		
Debtors		months	6,900	2,36,900
(₹ 68,000 – Rs1,850)	66,150	Unsecured creditors		2,09,950
		Outstanding liabilities		20,000
		Preference Shareholders:		
		Preference Share Capital	1,25,000	
		Arrears of Dividend	11,250	1,36,250
		Equity Shareholders		
		₹ 50 on 2,000 fully paid shares		1,00,000
		₹ 21.935 on 4,000 equity shares		87740
	8,05,150			8,05,150

Working Notes:

(i) Liquidator's Remuneration = ₹ 3,25,250 × 4/104 = ₹ 3,12,740

(ii) Disposal of amount to Members

	₹
Balance available for members	3,12,740
Less: Preference share capital	1,25,000
	1,87,740
Less: ₹ 50 on 2,000 fully paid Equity shares	1,00,000
₹ 21.935 on 4,000 Equify shares	87,740

PROBLEM 13

The summarized Balance Sheet of Full Stop Limited as on 31st March 2013, being the date of voluntary winding up is as under:

Liabilities	₹	Assets	₹
Share capital:		Land & building	5,20,000
5,000, 10% Cumulative		Plant & machinery	7,80,000
Preference shares of ₹ 700		Stock in trade	3,25,000
each fully paid up	5,00,000	Book debts	10,25,000
Equity share capital:		Profit & loss account	5,50,000
5,000 Equity shares of ₹ 100			
each ₹ 60 per share called			
and paid up	3,00,000		
5,000 Equity shares of ₹ 100			
each ₹ 50 per share called up			
and paid up	2,50,000		
Securities premium	1,50,000		
10% Debentures	2,10,000		
Preferential creditors	1,05,000		
Bank overdraft	4,85,000		
Trade creditors	6,00,000		
	32,00,000		32,00,000

Preference dividend is in arrears for three years. By 31-03-2013, the assets realized were as follows:

	₹
Land & building	6,20,000
Stock in trade	3,10,000
Plant & machinery	7,10,000
Book debts	6,60,000

Expenses of liquidation are ₹ 86,000. The remuneration of the liquidator is 2% of the realization of assets. Income tax payable on liquidation is ₹ 67,000. Assuming that the final payments were made on 31-03-2013, prepare the Liquidator's Statement of Account.

[CA (IPCC) May 2011]

Solution

(A) LIQUIDATOR'S STATEMENT OF ACCOUNT

Receipts	₹	*Payments*	₹
Land & building	6,20,000	Liquidator's remuneration	46,000
Stock in trade	3,10,000	Liquidation expenses	86,000
Plants machinery	7,10,000	10% Debentures	2,10,000
Book debts	6,60,000	Preferential creditors	1,05,000
		Income tax payable	67,000
		Bank overdraft	4,85,000
		Trade creditors	6,00,000
		Preference shareholders: Capital	5,00,000
		Arrears of preference dividend for 3 years	1,50,000
		Refund on 5,000 shares of ₹ 60 paid up@ ₹ 10.10 per share	50,500
		Refund on 5,000 shares of ₹ 50 paid up @₹ 0.10 per share	500
	23,00,000		23,00,000

Working Note: *Calculation of Refund to Equity Shareholders*

	₹
Total equity capital paid up (3,00,000 + 2,50,000)	5,50,000
Less: Balance available after payment to secured, unsecured, preferential creditors and preference shareholders (23,00,000 – 46,000 – 86,000 – 2,10,000 – 1,05,000 – 67,000 – 4,85,000 – 6,00,000 – 5,00,000 – 1,50,000)	(51,000)
Loss to be borne bv 10,000 equity shareholders	4,99,000
Loss per share	₹ 49.90
Hence, amount of refund on ₹ 50 per share paid up (₹ 50 – ₹ 49.90)	₹ 0.10
Amount of refund on ₹ 60 per share paid up (₹ 60 – ₹ 49. 90)	₹ 10.10

10 Financial Statements of Banking Companies

SHORT ANSWER PRACTICAL QUESTIONS

CALCULATION OF INTEREST ON PERFORMING ASSETS AND NON-PERFORMING ASSETS

PROBLEM 1

Following are the statements of interest on advances in respect of performing and non-performing assets of YES Bank Ltd. Find out the income to be recognised for the year ended 31st March, 2013:

(₹ in lakhs)

Assets	*Interest earned*	*Interest received*
Performing Assets		
Cash Credit and Overdrafts	1,800	1,060
Term Loan	480	320
Bills Purchased and Discounted	700	550
Non-Performing Assets		
Cash Credit and Overdrafts	450	70
Term Loan	300	40
Bills Purchased and Discounted	350	36

Solution

Interest on Performing Assets should be recognised on accrual basis, but interest on Non Performing Assets should be recognised on cash basis.

CALCULATION OF INTEREST INCOME *(₹ in lakhs)*

Interest *A*	*On Performing Assets* *B*	*On Non-Performing Assets* *C*	*Total* *D = B + C*
Interest on Cash Credit and Overdraft	1,800	70	1,870
Interest on Term Loan	480	40	520
Interest on Bills Purchased & Discounted	700	36	736
	2,980	146	3,126

PROBLEM 2

Find out the income to be recognised in the case of YES Bank Ltd. for the year ended 31st March, 2013:

(₹ in lakhs)

	Performing Assets		*Non-performing Assets*	
	Interest accrued	*Interest received*	*Interest accrued*	*Interest received*
Term Loans	240	160	150	10
Cash Credits and Overdrafts	1,500	1,240	300	24

[CA (PCC) Nov 2009]

Solution

CALCULATION OF INTEREST INCOME OF YES BANK LTD.

		(₹ in lacs)
Term Loans		
Interest accrued on Performing Assets	240	
Interest received on Non - Performing Assets	10	250
Cash credit and overdraft		
Interest accrued on Performing Assets	1,500	
Interest received on Non - Performing Assets	24	1,524
Total Interest to be recognised		1,774

PROBLEM 2A

Find out the Income to be recognized by ABC Bank Ltd, for the year ended 31st Marchd 2014, in respect of Interest on Advance [₹ in Lakhs] as detailed below:

	Performing Assets		*Non-performing Assets*	
	Interest earned	*Interest received*	*Interest earned*	*Interest received*
Term Loans	280	180	170	20
Cash Credits and Overdrafts	1,700	1,630	310	48
Bills Purchased and Discounted	400	400	180	70

[Nov. 2014]

Solution

CALCULATION OF INTEREST INCOME

Particulars	*Performing Asset (On Accrual basis)*	*Non-Performing Asset (On Receipt Basis)*	*Total Interest (in ₹ Crores)*
Interest on Term Loan	280	20	300
Interest on Cash Credit and Overdrafts	1,700	48	1,748
Interest on Bills Purchased and Discounted	40	70	470
Total Income to be recognised	**2380**	**138**	**2,518**

CALCULATION OF PROVISION ON ADVANCES 10 BE MADE IN PROFIT AND LOSS ACCOUNT

PROBLEM 3

From the following information find out the amount of provisions to be shown in the Profit and Loss Account of a Commercial Bank:

Assets	₹ (in lakhs)
Standard	4,000
Sub-standard	2,000
Doubtful upto one year	900
Doubtful upto three years	400
Doubtful more than three years	300
Loss Assets	500

[CA (PE II) Nov 2004, May 2010)

Solution

COMPUTATION OF PROVISION

Assets	*Amount*	*% of Provision (₹ in lakhs)*	*Provision (₹ in lakhs)*
Standard	4,000	0.40	16
Sub-standard	2,000	15	300
Doubtful upto one year*	900	25	225
Doubtful upto three years*	400	40	160
Doubtful more than three years*	300	100	300
Loss	500	100	500
			1501

* Dobutful assets are taken as fully secured.

PROBLEM 4

From the following information, compute the amount of provisions to be made in the Profit and Loss Account of a Commercial Bank:

Assets	*₹ in lakhs*
(i) Standard (Value of security ₹ 6,000 lakhs)	7,000
(ii) Sub-standard	3,000
(iii) Doubtful	
(a) Doubtful for less than one year (Realisable value of security ₹ 500 lakhs)	1,000
(b) Doubtful for more than one year, but less than 3 years (Realisable value of security ₹ 300 lakhs)	500
(c) Doubtful for more than 3 years (No security)	300

[CA (PE II) May 2006)

Solution

COMPUTATION OF PROVISION

(a) *Asset*	*Amount ₹ in lakhs*	*% of Provision*	*Provision ₹ in lakhs*
Standard	7,000	0.40	28
Sub-standard	3,000	15	450
Doubtful (less than one year)			
On Secured Portion	500	25	125
On Unsecured Portion	500	100	500
Doubtful (more than one year but less than			

three year)			
On Secured Portioin	300	40	120
On Unsecured Portion	200	100	200
Doubtful Unsecured (more than three years)	300	100	300
Total Provision			1,723

PROBLEM 5

From the following information of details of advances of X Bank Limited calculate the amount of provisions to be made in Profit and Loss Account:

Asset Classification	₹ in lakhs
Standard	6,000
Sub-standard	4,400
Doubtful:	
For one year	1,800
For two years	1,200
For three years	800
For more than three years	600
Loss Assets	1,600

[CA (PE II), May 2007)]

Solution

CALCULATION OF PROVISIONS ON VARIOUS ASSETS

Asset Classification	*Amount ₹ in lakhs*	*Provision %*	*Amount of Provision ₹ in lakhs*
Standard	6,000	0.40	24
Sub-standard**	4,400	15	660
Doubtful**			
one year	1,800	25	450
2 years	1,200	40	480
3 years	800	40	320
More than 3 years	600	100	600
Loss assets	1,600	100	1,600
			4,134

Note: ** Sub standard and doubtful assets have been treated as fully secured.

PROBLEM 6

From the following information of Great Bank Limited, compute the provisions to be made in the Profit and Loss account:

	₹ *in lakhs*
Assets:	
Standard	20,000
Substandard	16,000
Doubtful	
For one year (secured)	6,000
For two years and three years (secured)	4,000
For more than three years (secured by mortgage of plant and machinery ₹.600 lakhs)	2,000
Non-recoverable Assets	1,500

Non-Recoverable Assets *[CA (PCE) Nov 2008]*

Solution

CALCULATION OF AMOUNT OF PROVISION TO BE MADE IN THE P & L ACCOUNT

Classification of Assets	*Amount of advances (₹ in lakhs)*	*Amount of Provision*	*% age of Provision (₹ in lakhs)*
Standard assets	20,000	0.40	80
Sub-standard assets	16,000	15*	2,400
Doubtful assets:			
For one year (secured)	6,000	25	1,500
For two to three years (secured)	4,000	40	1,600
For more than three years (unsecured)	1,400	100	1,400
(secured)	600	100	600
Non-recoverable assets (Loss assets)	1,500	100	1,500
Total Provision required			9,080

*Sub-standards assets have been assumed as fully secured.

PROBLEM 7

From the followings information of details of advances of Zenith Bank Ltd., calculate the amount of provisions to be made in Profit and Loss Account:

	₹
Assets classification	10,000
Standard	6,400
Substandard	3,200
Doubtful:	
for one year	3,200
for two year	1,800
For three years	900
For more than three years	1,100
Loss assets	3,000

[CA (IPCC) Nov. 2010]

CALCULATION OF PROVISIONS ON VARIOUS ASSETS

Assets classification	*Amount (₹) in lakhs)*	*Provision (%)*	*Amount of provision in lakhs)*
Standard	10,000	0.40	40
Sub-standard	6,400	15	960
Doubtful:			
for one year	3,200	25	800
for two years	1,800	40	720
for three years	900	40	360
for more than 3 years	1,100	100	1,100
Loss assets	3,000	100	3,000
		Total	**6,980**

Note: It is assumed that substandard assets and all doubtful assets are fully secured.

PROBLEM 8

From the information given below, find out the amount of provision to be shown in the Profit and Loss Account of a Commercial Bank:

Assets	*(₹ in lakhs)*
Standard	4,500
Sub-standard	3,000
Doubtful for more than three years (Fully Secured)	250
Loss Assets	750

[CA (PCC) Nov. 2011]

Solution

CALCULATION OF PROVISION ON ASSETS

Assets	*Amount (₹ in lakhs)*	*% of provision***	*Provision (₹ in lakhs)*
Standard	4,500	0.40	18
Sub-standard	3,000	15	450
Doubtful for more than three years (Fully secured)	250	100	250
Loss assets	750	100	750
Total	8,500		1468

*It is assumed that sub-standard assets are fully secured.

PROBLEM 9

From the following information, compute the amount of provisions to be made in the Profit and Loss Account of A commercial Bank:

Assets (Category of Advances)	*₹ in Lakhs*
Standard Advances	7,000
Sub-standard Advances	3,500
(include secured exposures ₹ 1,000 lakhs and balances unsecured exposures ₹ 2,500 Lakhs includes ₹ 1,500 Lakhs in respect of infrastructure loan accounts where escrow accounts are available)	
Doubtful advances-unsecured portion	1,500
Doubtful advances-secured portion	
For doubtful up to 1 year	500
For doubtful more than 1 year and up to 3 years	600
Four doubtful more than 3 years	300
Loss Advances	200

[May 2012]

Solution

CALCULATION OF THE AMOUNT OF PROVISIONS ON ASSETS *[₹ in lakhs]*

Assets	*Amount*	*% of Provision*	*Provision*
Standard	7,000	0.40	28
Sub-standard:			
Secured portion	1,000	15	150
Unsecured infrastructure loan account where escrow account is available	1,500	20	300
Other unsecured	1,000	25	250
Doubtful-Secured portion:			
Upto one year	500	25	125
More than 1 year but upto 3 years	600	40	240
For more than three years	300	100	300
Doubtful-unsecured portion	1,500	100	1,500
Loss	200	100	200
Required provision			**3,093**

CALCULATION OF PROVISION ON ADVANCES GUARANTEED BY DICGC/ECGC

PROBLEM 10

Rajatapeeta Bank Ltd. had extended the following credit lines to a Small Scale Industry, which had not paid any Interest since 1st March, 2007:

	Term Loan	*Export Loan*
Balance Outstanding on 31.03.2013	₹ 35 lakhs	₹ 30 lakhs
DICGC/ECGC cover	40%	50%
Securities held	₹ 15 lakhs	₹ 10 lakhs
Realisable value of Securities	₹ 10 lakhs	₹ 8 lakhs

Required: Compute necessary provisions to be made for the year ended 31st March, 2013.

[CA (PE II) May 2004]

Solution

CALCULATION OF PROVISION

	Particulars	*Term Loan*	*Export Loan*
A.	Balance Outstanding	35.0	30.0
B.	*Less:* Realisable Value of security	(10.0)	(8.0)
		25.0	22.0
C.	*Less:* DICGC cover @ 40%	(10.0)	
	ECGC cover @ 50%		(11.0)
D.	Unsecured Amount	15.0	11.0
E.	Provision for Unsecured Portion (100%)	15.0	11.0
F.	Provision for Secured Portion (100%)	10.0	8.0
G.	Total Provision required	25.0	19.0

PROBLEM 11

In X Bank Ltd., the doubtful asset (more than 3 years) as on 31.3.2008 is ₹.1,000 lakhs. The value of security (including DICGC 100% cover of ₹.100 lakhs) is ascertained at ₹ 500 lakhs. How much provision must be made in the books of the Bank towards doubtful assets?

[CA (PCE) Nov 2008]

Solution

CALCULATION OF PROVISION

	(₹ in lakhs)
Doubtful Assets (more than 3 years)	1,000
Less: Value of security (excluding DICGC cover)	(400)
	600
Less: 100% DICGC cover of ₹.100 lakhs	100
Unsecured portion	500
Provision thereon:	
for unsecured portion @ 100%	500 lakhs
for secured portion @ 100% w.e.f 31.3.2007	400 lakhs
Total provision to be made	900 lakhs

PROBLEM 12

A loan account remains out of order as on the date of Balance Sheet of a Bank. The account has been classified as doubtful assets (upto 1 year).

Details of the accounts are:

Outstanding	₹ 6,73,000
ECGC coverage	25% (Limited to ₹ 1,00,000)
Value of security held	₹ 1,50,000

Compute the necessary provision to be made by a bank as per applicable rates.

[CA (IPCC) Nov. 2012]

Solution

COMPUTATION OF PROVISION

	₹
Doubtful Assets (upto 1 year)	6,73,000
Less: Value of security (excluding ECGC cover)	(1,50,000)
	5,23,000
Less: ECGC coverage (limited to ₹ 1,00,000)	(1,00,000)
Unsecured portion	4,23,000
Provision: for unsecured portion @ 100% on ₹ 2,23,000	4,23,000
for secured portion @ 25% on ₹ 1,50,000	37,000
Total provision to be made in the books of the bank	4,60,500

PROBLEM 13

A loan account remains out of order as on the date of Balance Sheet of a Bank. The account has been classified as doubtful assets (up to 3 years). Detail of the account is:

Outstanding	₹ 7,24,000
ECGC Cover	30% of outstanding (Subject to maximum of ₹ 1,50,000)
Value of security	
As per valuation on the date of grant of loan	2,25,000
As per realizable value as on date of Balance Sheet	1,75,000

Compute the necessary provision to be made by bank as per applicable rate.

[May 2014]

Solution

Computation of provision to be made by a Bank

	₹
Outstanding Value of Doubtful Asset (up to 3 years)	7,24,000
Less: Value of security (excluding ECGC cover)	(₹ 1,75,000)
Sub Total	₹ 5,49,000
Less: ECGC Cover (subject to ₹ 1,50,000 maximum)	(₹ 1,50,000)
Unsecured Portion	₹ 3,99,000
Provision:	
For unsecured portion @ 100% of ₹ 3,99,000	₹ 3,99,000
₹For secured portion @ 40% of ₹ 1,75,000	₹ 70,000
Total Provision	₹ 4,69,000

CALCULATION OF REBATE ON BILL DISCOUNTED

PROBLEM 14

The following particulars are extracted from the (Trial Balance) Books of the M/s Commercial Bank Ltd. for the year ending 31st March. 2013:

	₹
(i) Interest and Discounts	1,96,62,400
(ii) Rebate on Bills Discounted (balance on 1.4.2012)	65,040
(iii) Bills Discounted and Purchased	67,45,400

It is ascertained that proportionate discount not yet earned on the Bills Discounted which will mature during 2013-2014, amounted to ₹ 92,760.

Pass the necessary Journal with narration adjusting the above and show:

(a) Rebate on Bill Discounted Account; and

(b) Interest and Discount Account in the ledger of the Bank. *[CA (PE II) November 2003]*

Solution

(A) JOURNAL OF THE COMMERCIAL BANK LTD.

Date	Particulars		L.F.	Dr. (₹)	Cr. (₹)
1.4.12	Rebate on Bills Discounted A/c	Dr.		65,040	
	To Interest and Discount A/c				65,040
	(Being the amount of provision for unexpired discount brought forward from the previous year credited to Interest and Discount A/c)				
31.03.13	Interest and Discount A/c	Dr.		92,760	
	To Rebate on Bills Discounted A/c				92,760
	(Being provision for unexpired discount required at the end of the current year)				
31.03.13	Interest and Discount A/c	Dr.		1,96,34,680	
	To Profit and Loss A/c				1,96,34,680
	(Being transfer of balance to Profit & Loss A/c)				

(B) REBATE ON BILLS DISCOUNTED ACCOUNT

Dr. Cr.

Date	Particulars	₹	Date	Particulars	₹
01.04.12	To Interest and Discount A/c	65,040	01.04.12	By Balance b/d	65,040
31.03.13	To Balance c/d	92,760	31.03.13	By Interest and Discount A/c (rebate required)	92,760
		1,57,800			1,57,800

(c) Interest and Discount Account

Dr. Cr.

Date	Particulars	₹	Date	Particulars	₹
31.03.13	To Rebate on Bills Discounted A/c	92,760	01.04.12	By Rebate on Bills Discounted A/c (Opening Balance)	65,040
31.03.13	To Profit& Loss A/c (transfer)	1,96,34,680	2012-13	By Cash and Sundries	1,96,62,400
		1,97,27,440			1,97,27,440

PROBLEM 15

The following information is available in the books of X Bank Limited as on 31st March, 2013:

	₹
Bill discounted	1,37,05,000
Rebate on Bills discounted (as on 1.4.2012)	2,21,600
Discount received	10,56,650

Details of bills discounted are as follows:

Value of bill (₹)	*Due date*	*Rate of Discount*
18,25,000	5.6.2013	12%
50,00,000	12.6.2013	12%
28,20,000	25.6.2013	14%
40,60,000	6.7.2013	16%

Required: Calculate the rebate on bills discounted as on 31.3.2013 and give necessary journal entries.

[CA (PCC) Nov.2007]

Solution

STATEMENT SHOWING REBATE ON BILLS DISCOUNTED

Value of bill (₹)	*Due Date*	*Days after 31 March*	*Rate of discount*	*Discount Amount*
18,25,000	5 June	(30+31+5) = 66	12%	39,600
50,00,000	12 June	(30+31+12) = 73	12%	1,20,000
28,20,000	25 June	(30+31+25) = 86	14%	93,021
40,60,000	6. July	(30+31+30+6) = 97	16%	1,72,633
1,37,05,000		Rebate on bills discounted on 31.3.20084,25,254		

JOURNAL

Particulars		*Dr. (₹)*	*Cr. (₹)*
Rebate on Bills Discounted A/c To Discount on Bills A/c (Being the opening balance of rebate on bills discounted account transferred to discount on bills account)	Dr.	2,21,600	2,21,600
Discount on Bills A/c To Rebate on Bills Discounted A/c (Being the provision made on 31st March 2008)	Dr.	4,25,254	4,25,254
Discount on Bills A/c To Profit and Loss A/c (Being the transfer of discount on bills, of the year, to Profit and Loss Account)	Dr.	8,52,996*	8,52,966

Note: * Credit to Profit and Loss A/c = ₹.10,56,650 + ₹ 2,21,600 – ₹.4,25,254

= ₹.8,52,996

PROBLEM 16

The following facts have been taken out from the records of Dee Bank Ltd. as on 31st March, 2013:

	Dr. (₹)	Cr. (₹)
Rebate on Bills Discounted (not due on March 31st, 2012)		45,800
Discount Received		2,02,500
Bills Discounted	12,25,000	

An analysis of the bills discounted is as follows:

	Amount ₹	Due date 2013	Rate of discount
(i)	3,75,000	April 8	12%
(ii)	1,50,000	May 5	14%
(iii)	2,20,000	June 12	14%
(iv)	4,80,000	July 15	15%

You are required to:

(i) Calculate rebate on bills discounted as on 31st March, 2013.

(ii) The amount of discount to be credited to the Profit and Loss Account.

(iii) Show necessary journal entries in the books of Dee Bank Ltd. as on 31st March, 2013.

[CA (PE-II) Nov. 2009]

Solution

(I) CALCULATION OF REBATE ON BILLS DISCOUNTED

S.No.	Amount (₹)	Due date	No. of Days after 31st March	Rate of Discount	Rebate on bills Discounted (₹,)
(i)	3,75,000	April 8	8 days	12%	986
(ii)	1,50,000	May 5	35 days	14%	2,014
(iii)	2,20,000	June 12	73 days	14%	6,160
(iv)	4,80,000	July 15	106 days	15%	20,910
			Rebate on Bills Discounted30,070		

(II) AMOUNT OF DISCOUNT TO BE CREDITED TO THE PROFIT AND LOSS ACCOUNT

Particulars	₹
Opening Rebate on bills discounted	45,800
Add: Discount received during the year	2,02,500
	2,48,300
Less: Closing Rebate on bills discounted	(30,070)
Discount credited to Profit and Loss Account	2,18,230

JOURNAL OF DEE BANK LTD

Date	Particulars		Dr. (₹)	Cr. (₹)
(1)	Rebate on Bills Discounted A/c	Dr.	45,800	
	To Discount on Bills A/c			45,800
	(Being the transfer of opening balance of rebate on bills discounted account to discount on bills acount)			
(2)	Discount on Bills A/c	Dr.	30,070	
	To Rebate on Bills Discounted A/c			30,070
	(Being the unexpired portion of discount in respect of the discounted bills of exchange carried forward)			
(3)	Discount on Bills A/c	Dr.	2,18,230	
	To Profit and Loss A/c			2,18,230
	(Being the amount of income for the year transferred from Discount on bills A/c Profit and Loss A/c)			

PROBLEM 17

Given below is an extract from the trial balance of *T.K.* Bank Limited as on 31st December 2012:

Particulars	Debit ₹	Credit ₹
Bills Discounted	12,64,000	—
Rebate on Bills Discounted (Opening)	—	8,340
Discount received for the year		85,912

AN ANALYSIS OF THE BILLS DISCOUNTED IS SHOWN BELOW:

Amount ₹	Due date in 2013	Rate of discount (% p.a.)
1,40,000	March 6th	5
4,36,000	March 12th	4.5
2,82,000	March 26th	8
4,06,000	April 6th	4

Show the workings, how the relevant items will appear in the bank's Profit and Loss account as on 31st December, 2012 and in bank's Balance Sheet as on 31st December, 2012. ***[CA (IPCC) May 2010]***

Solution

AN EXTRACT OF PROFIT & LOSS ACCOUNT
for the period ending 31.12.2012

Particulars	₹
Opening 'Rebate on bills discounted'	8,340
Add: Discount for the year	85,912
Less: Closing Rebate on bills discounted	(13,274)
	80,978

AN EXTRACT OF BALANCE SHEET AS ON 31.12.2012

Liabilities	₹
Other Liabilities & Provisions:	
Rebate on bills discounted	13,274

Working Note:

STATEMENT OF REBATE ON BILLS DISCOUNTED AS ON 31.12.2012

Due date	*Amount (₹)*	*No. of days after 31 Dec.*	*Rate of discount (%)*	*Discount of the unexpired period*
March 6th	1,40,000	65	5	1,247
March 12th	4,36,000	71	4.5	3,816
March 26th	2,82,000	85	6	3,940
April 6th	4,00,000	96	4	4.271
Total Rebate on bills discounted to be carried forward				13,274

PROBLEM 18

As on 31st March 2012, Strong Bank Ltd. has a balance of ₹ 27 crores in "Rebate on Bills Discounted" Account. The bank provides you the following further information:

(1) During the financial year ending 31st March 2013, Strong Bank Ltd. discounted bills of exchange of ₹ 4,000 crores charging interest @ 15% p.a. and the average period of discount being 146 days.

(2) Bills of exchange of ₹ 600 crores were due for realization from the acceptors/customers after 31st March 2013, the average period outstanding after 31st March 2013, being 73 days.

You are required to pass necessary journal entries in the books of Strong Bank Ltd. for the above transactions. *[CA (PCC) Nov. 2010]*

Solution

JOURNAL OF STRONG BANK LTD.

[₹ in Crores]

Particulars		*Dr. (₹)*	*Cr. (₹)*
Rebate on Bills Discounted A/c	Dr.	27	
To Discount on bills A/c			27
(Being the transfer of opening balance in 'Rebate on bills discounted A/c' to 'Discount on bills A/c')			
Bills Purchased and Discounted A/c	Dr.	4,000	
To Discount on Bills A/c			240
To Clients A/c			3,760
(Being the discounting of bills of exchange during the year)			
Discount on Bills A/c	Dr.	18	
To Rebate on Bills Discounted A/c			18
(Being the unexpired portion of discount in respect of the discounted bills of exchange carried forward)			

Discount on Bills A/c	Dr.	249	
To Profit and Loss A/c			249
(Being the amount of income for the year from discounting of bills of exchange transferred to Profit and loss A/c)			

Working Notes:

(i) Discount received = ₹ 4,000 crores $\times \frac{15}{100} \times \frac{146}{365}$ = Rs. 240 crores

(ii) Rebate on bill discounted = Rs. 600 crores $\times \frac{15}{100} \times \frac{73}{365}$ = Rs. 18 crores

(it is assumed that discounting rate of 15% is used for the bill of ₹ 600 crores also)

(iii) Income from bills discounted transferred to Profit and Loss A/c would be calculated by preparing Discount on Bills A/c

₹ in crores

Date	*Particulars*	*₹*	*Date*	*Particulars*	*₹*
31.03.13	To Rebate on Bills Discounted	18	1.04.12	By Rebate on bills Discounted	27
	To Profit and Loss A/c (b.f.)	249	2012-13	By Bills Purchased and Discounted	240
		267			267

PROBLEM 19

The following particulars are extracted from the records of Mis. Engco Bank Limited for the year ended 31st March, 2013:

	Amount (₹)
Rebate on bills discounted (not due on March 31st, 2012)	60,610
Discount received	6,10,800
Bills discounted	24,42,250

An analysis of the bills discounted is a follows:

Amount (₹)	*Due Date*
3,75,000	April 15, 2013
4,90,000	May6, 2013
2,45,000	June 1,2013
3,68,000	June 20, 2013
4,85,000	July 4, 2013

The rate of discount is 12% per annum. You are required to:

(i) Calculate rebate on bills discounted as on 31st March, 2013.

(ii) Determine the amount of discount to be credited to the profit and loss account for the year ended 31st March, 2013.

(iii) Show the necessary journal entries in the books of M/s. Engco Bank Ltd. as on 31st March, 2013.

[CA (IPCC) Nov. 2011]

Solution

(I) CALCULATION OF REBATE ON BILLS DISCOUNTED AS ON 31ST MARCH, 2013

Amount (₹)	Due date	No. of days after 31st March	Product
3,75,000	April 15, 2013	15	56,25,000
4,90,000	May06, 2013	36	1,76,40,000
2,45,000	June 01, 2013	62	1,51,90,000
3,68,000	June 20, 2013	81	2,98,08,000
4,85,000	July 04, 2013	95	4,60,75,000
19,63,000			11,43,38,000

Amount of rebate on bills = ₹ 11,43,38,000 × 12% × 1/365 = ₹ 37,591 (approx.)

(II) DETERMINATION OF AMOUNT OF DISCOUNT TO BE CREDITED TO THE PROFIT AND LOSS ACCOUNT FOR THE YEAR ENDED 31ST MARCH, 2013

Particulars	₹
Opening Rebate on Bills Discounted	60,610
Add: Discount received during the year	6,10,800
	6,71,410
Less: Closing Rebate on bills discounted	(37,591)
Amount transferred to Profit and Loss Account	6,33,819

JOURNAL OF ENGCO BANK LTD.

Date	Particulars		Dr. (₹)	Cr. (₹)
(i)	Rebate on bills discounted A/c	Dr.	60,610	
	To Discount on bills A/c			60,610
	(Being transfer of Opening unexpired discoount on bills)			
(ii)	Discount on bills A/c	Dr.	37,591	
	To Rebate on bills discounted A/c			37,591
	(Being the closing unexpired discount provided)			
(iii)	Discount on bills A/c	Dr.	6,33,819	
	To Profits Loss A/c			6,33,819
	(Being the t/f of discount earned)			

PROBLEM 20

The following particulars are extracted from the Books of the Commercial Bank Ltd. for the year ending 31st March, 2012.

(i)	Interest and Discounts	1,98,64,800
(ii)	Rebated on Bills Discounted (opening balance)	70,080
(iii)	Bills discounted and purchased	77,46,400

It is ascertained that proportionate discount not yet earned on the Bills Discounted which will mature during 2012-13 amount to ₹ 96,860.

Pass the necessary Journal entries with narration adjusting the above and show:

(a) Rebate on Bills Discounted Account; and

(b) Interest and Discount Account in the ledger of the Commercial Bank Limited.

[PCC(May 2012)]

Solution

(A) JOURNAL OF THE COMMERCIAL BANK LTD.

Date	Particulars		Dr. (₹)	Cr. (₹)
March 31	Rebate on Bills Discounted A/c	Dr.	70,080	
	To Interest and Discount A/c			70,080
	(Being the amount of provision for unexpired discount brought forward from the previous year credited to interest and Discount A/c)			
March 31	Interest and Discount A/c	Dr.	96,860	
	To Rebate on Bills Discounted A/c			96,860
	(Being provision for unexpired discount required at the end of the current year)			
March 31	Interest and Discount A/c	Dr.	1,98,38,020	
	To Profit & Loss A/c			1,98,38,020
	(Being transfer of balance to Profit and Loss A/c)			

Dr. **REBATE ON BILLS DISCOUNTED ACCOUNT** Cr.

Date	Particulars	₹	Date	Particulars	₹
March 31	To Interest and Discount A/c	70,080	April 1	By Balance b/d	70,080
March 31	To Balance c/d	9,860	March 31,	By interest and Discount A/c (Rebate carried forwarded)	96,860
		1,66,940			1,66,940

(B) INTEREST AND DISCOUNT ACCOUNT

Date	Particulars	₹	Date	Particulars	₹
March 31	To Profit & Loss A/c (transfer)	1,98,38,020	April 1	By Rebate on Bills Discounted A/c (opening balance)	70,080
March 31	To Rebate on Bills Discounted A/c	96,860	March 31	By Bills Discounted & purchased	1,98,64,800
		1,99,34,880			1,99,34,880

PREPARATION OF SCHEDULE 9: ADVANCES

PROBLEM 21

How will you disclose the following Ledger balances in the Final accounts of DVD bank:

₹ *in lacs*

Current accounts	700
Saving accounts	500
Fixed deposits	700

₹ *in lacs*

Cash credits	600
Term Loans	500
Bills discounted & purchased	800

Additional information:

(i) Included in the current accounts ledger are accounts overdrawn to the extent of ₹ 250 lacs.

(ii) One of the cash credit account of ₹ 10 lacs (including interest ₹ 1 lac) is doubtful.

(iii) 60% of term loans are secured by government guarantees, 20% of cash credits are unsecured, other portion is secured by tangible assets. ***[CA (IPCC) May 2010]***

Solution

RELEVANT SCHEDULES (FORMING PART OF THE BALANCE SHEET) OF DVD BANK
SCHEDULE 3: DEPOSITS

₹ *in lacs*

A Demand Deposits (700 + 250)	950
B Saving Bank deposits	500
C Term Deposits	700
	2,150

Schedule 9: Advances

₹ *in lacs*

A. (i) Bills Discounted and Purchased	800
(ii) Cash Credits and Overdrafts (600 + 250)	850
(iii) Term Loans	500
	2.150
B. (i) Secured by tangible assets (bal. fig.)	1,730
(ii) Secured by Bank/Government Guarantees (500 × 60%)	300
(iii) Unsecured (600 × 20%)	120
	2.150

Schedule 5: Other Liabilities & Provisions

₹ *in lacs*

Others (Provision for doubtful debts)	10

Profit and Loss Account (an extract)

₹ *in lacs*

Less: Provision for doubtful debts*	10

***Note:** It is assumed that the cash credit has been in 'doubtful' category for more than three years

BILLS FOR COLLECTION ACCOUNT

PROBLEM 22

From the following details, prepare bills for collection (Asset) Account and Bills for collection (Liability) Account:

	₹
On 1.4.2012, Bills for Collection were	51,00,000
During the year 2012–13 Bills received for Collection amounted to	75,00,000
Bill collected during the year 2012–13	98,47,000
Bill dishonoured and returned during the year	27,10,000

[CA (PE II) May 2006]

Solution

(b) *Dr.* **BILLS FOR COLLECTION (ASSET) ACCOUNT** *Cr.*

Date	*Particulars*	₹	*Date*	*Particulars*	₹
1.4.2012	To Balance b/d	51,00,000	2012–13	By Bills for collection (Liability) A/c	98,47,000
2012–13	To Bills for collection	75,00,000		By Bills for collection (Liability) A/c	27,10,000
			31.3.2013	By Balance c/d	43,000
		1,26,00,000			1,26,00,000
1.4.2013	To Balance b/d	43,000			

Dr. **BILLS FOR COLLECTION (LIABILITY) ACCOUNT** *Cr.*

Date	*Particulars*	₹	*Date*	*Particulars*	₹
2012–13	To Bills for collection (Asset) A/c	98,47,000	1.4.2012	By Balance b/d	51,00,000
	To Bills for collection (Asset) A/c	27,10,000	2012–13	By Bills for collection (Asset) A/c	75,00,000
31.3.2013	To Balance c/d	43,000			
		1,26,00,000			1,26,00,000
				By Balance b/d	43,000

Note: ** Sub standard and doubtful assets have been treated as fully secured.

CALCULATION OF RISK-ADJUSTED AND RISK WEIGHTED ASSETS AND CAPITAL ADEQUACY RATIO

PROBLEM 23

A loan outstanding of ₹.50,00,000 has DICGC cover. The loan guaranteed by DICGC is assigned a risk weight of 50%. What is the value of Risk-adjusted asset?

[CA (PCE) May 2008]

Solution

Loan outstanding	₹	50,00,000
Guaranteed by DICGC – Risk weight		50%
Value of Risk Adjusted Asset = ₹.50,00,000 × 50% =	₹	25,00,000

PROBLEM 24

A commercial Bank has the following capital funds and assets. Segregate the capital founds into Tier-1 and tire-II Capitals. Found out the Risk-Adjusted and Risk Weighted Assets and Capital Adequacy Ratio:

Capital Funds:	₹
Paid up Equity Share Capital	750
Statutory Reserve	150
Securities Premium	150
Capital Reserve (of which Capital Funds ₹ 40 Crore were due to revaluation of assets and balance due to sale)	
Assets:	
Cash balance with RBI	60
Claims on Banks	170
Other investments	2,300
Loss and Advances:	
Guaranteed by Government of India/State Government	400
Granted to Staff of bank fully covered by Supper Annuation	
Benefits and mortgage of Flat/house	50
Other Loans and Advances	6,170
Premises, Furniture and Fixtures, Other Assets	3,925
Intangible Assets	15
Off-Balance Sheet Items;	
Acceptance, Endorsements and Letter of Credit, Guarantees and Other obligations.	1,550

[May 2012]

Solution

CALCULATION OF CAPITAL FUNDS

Particulars	*₹ in crores*	*₹ in crores*
(i) Capital Funds – Tier I		
Equity Share Capital		750
Statutory Reserve		150
Securities Premium		150
Capital reserve (arising out of sale of assets) (90 – 40)		50
		1,100
Less: Intangible Assets		(15)
		1,085
Capital Funds – Tier II		
Capital reserve (arising out of revaluation of assets)	40	
Less: Discount to the extent of 55%	(22)	18
		1,103

CALCULATION OF RISK ADJUSTED ASSETS

Particulars	*₹ in crores*	*% in risk weight*	*₹ in Crores*
(ii) Risk Adjusted Assets			
Funded Risk Assets			
Cash balance with RBI	60	0	0
Claims on banks	170	20	34
Other investments	2,300	100	2,300
Loans and advances:			
(i) Guaranteed by the government	400	0	0
(ii) Granted to staff of bank, fully covered by super Annuation Benefits and mortgage of Flat/House	50	20	10
(iii) Other loans and advances	6,170	100	6,170
Other assets			
Premises, furniture and fixtures and other assets	3,925	100	3,925
			12,439
Off Balance Sheet Items:			
Acceptances, endorsements and Letters of credit, Guarantees and other obligations	1,550	100	1,550
			13,989

$$\text{Capital Adequacy Ratio} = \frac{\text{Capital fund}}{\text{Risk adjusted assets}} \times 100 = \frac{\text{Rs } 1{,}103 \text{ crores}}{\text{Rs } 13{,}989 \text{ crores}} \times 100 = 7.89\%$$

PROBLEM 25

A Commercial Bank has the following capital funds and assets. Segregate the capital funds into Tier I and Tier II capitals. Find out the risk adjusted asset and risk weighted assets ratio.

	(₹ in crores)
Equity Share Capital	500.00
Statutory Reserve	270.00
Capital reserve (of which ₹ 16 crores were due to revaluation of assets and the balance due to sale of capital asset)	78.00
Assets:	
Cash balance with RBI	10.00
Balance with other banks	18.00
Other investments	36.00
Loans and advances:	
(i) Guaranteed by the Government	16.50
(ii) Others	5,675.00
Premises, furniture and fixtures	78.00
Off-Balance Sheet items:	
(i) Guarantee and other obligations	800.00
(ii) Acceptances, endorsements and letter of credit	4,800.00

[CA (IPCC) Nov. 2010]

Solution

CALCULATION OF CAPITAL FUNDS

	₹ in crores	*₹ in crores*
Capital Funds-Tier I		
Equity ShareCapital		500
Statutory Reserve		270
Capital Reserve (arising out of sale of assets) (78-16)		62
		832
Capital Funds-Tier II		
Capital reserve (arising out of revaluation of assets)	16	
Less: Discount to the extent of 55%	(8.8)	7.2
		824.8

	₹ in crores	*% of weight*	*₹ in crores*
(ii) Risk Adjusted Assets			
Funded Risk Assets			
Cash balance with RBI	10	0	0
Balance with other banks	18	20	3.60
Other investments	36	100	36
Loans and advances:			
(i) Guaranteed by the government	16.5	0	0
(ii) Others	5,675	100	5,675
Premises, furniture and fixtures	78	100	78
			5,792.60

	₹ in crores	Credit conversion factor	
Off-Balance Sheet items:			
Guarantees and other obligations	800	100	800.00
Acceptances, endorsements and letters of credit	4,800	100	4,800.00
			11,392.60

Risk Weighted Assets Ratio:

$$\frac{\text{Capital Fund}}{\text{Risk Adjusted Assets}} \times 100 = (824.88 / 11{,}392.60) \times 100 = 7.24\%$$

PROBLEM 26

A Commercial Bank has the following Capital Funds and Assets. Segregate the Capital Funds into Tier I and Tier II capitals. Find out the Risk Adjusted Asset and Risk Weighted Asset Ratio. State your observation on the Risk Weighted Asset Ratio.

Particulars	*₹ Crores*
Equity Share Capital	400.00
Statutory Reserve	250.00
Capital Reserve (of which ₹ 18 Crores were deu to Revaluation of Assets & balance due to Sale of Capital Assets)	86.00
Assets:	
Cash Balance with RBI	12.00
Balance with other Banks	20.00
Other Investments	40.000
Loans & Advances	
(a) Guaranteed by Government	14.50
(b) Others	5,465.00
Premises, Furniture & Fixtures	74.00
Off Balance Sheet Items	
(a) Guarantees and Other Obligations	700.00
(b) Acceptance, Endorsements and Letter of Credit	4,900.00

[Nov. 2014]

Solution

1. Computation of Tier I and Tier II Capital

Particulars		*₹ Crores*
Tier I – Capital:	Equity Share Capital	400.00
	Statutory Reserve	250.00
	Capital Reserve arising out of Surplus on Sale of Assets = Total 86 – Revaluation of Assets 18	68.000
	Total (A)	**718.00**

Tier II – Capital:	Revaluation Reserve		18.00
	Less: Discount at 55%		(9.90)
	Total	**(B)**	**8.10**
	Grand Total	**(A + B)**	**726.10**

2. Computation of Risk Weighted Assets

Particulars	*(%) Weight*	*₹ Crores*	*₹ Crores*
Cash Balance with RBI	0	12.00	0
Balance with Other Banks	20	20.00	4.00
Other Investments (assumed Other than Equikty Shares)	100	40.00	40.00
Loans and Advances:			
(i) Guaranteed by the Government	0	14.50	0
(ii) Others	100	5,465.00	5,465.00
Premises, Furniture and FIxtures	100	74.00	74.00
Off-Balance Sheet Items:			
(i) Guarantees and other Obligations	100	700.00	700.00
(ii) Acceptance, Endorsements and Letter of Credit	100	4,900.00	4,900.00
Total			**11,183.00**

3. Capital to Risk-Weighted Assets Ratio (CRAR)

$$= \frac{\text{Capital Funds}}{\text{Risk Adjusted Assets}} \times 100 = \frac{726.00}{11183.00} \times 100 = 6.49\%.$$

Inference: Benchmark CRAR is 9% whereas the Bank's CRAR is only **6.49%.** Higher the CRAR – better stability – less risky, and lower the CRAR – lower stability – more risky.

LONG ANSWER PRACTICAL QUESTIONS

PREPARATION OF PROFIT AND LOSS ACCOUNT

PROBLEM 27

From the following information, calculate the amount of Provisions and Contingencies and prepare Profit and Loss Account of 'Hamara Bank Limited' for the year ending 31st March, 2013:

	₹ in lakhs		*₹ in lakhs*
Interest and discount	4,430	Interest expended	1, 360
Other Income	125	Operating Expenses	1,331
Interest accrued on Investments	10		

Additional Information:

	₹
(i) Rebate on bills discounted to be provided for	15
(ii) Classifications of Advances:	
Standard Assets	2,500
Sub-Standard Assets	560
Doubtful Assets not covered by security	255
Doubtful Assets covered by security	
For 1 year	25
For 2 years	50
For 3 years	100
For 4 years	75
Loss Assets	100
(iii) Make tax provisions @ 35% of the profit.	
(iv) Profit and Loss Account (Cr.) brought forward from the previous year	40

Solution

(A) CALCULATION OF PROVISIONS AND CONTINGENCIES

(i) Provision on Non-Performing Assets*

Particulars	*Amount*	*% of Provision*	*₹ in lakhs Provision*
Standard Assets	2,500	0.4	10
Sub-standard Assets	560	15	84
Doubtful Assets not covered by security	255	100	255
Doubtful Assets covered by security:			
For 1 Year	25	25	6.25
For 2 Years	50	40	20
For 3 Years	100	40	40
For 4 Years	75	100	75
Loss Assets	100	100	100
	3,665		590.25

Note: It is assumed that all sub standards assets are fully secured.

(ii) Calculation of Provision for tax = 35% of [Total Income – Total Expenditure (excluding tax)]
= 35% of [(4,415 + 125) – (1,360 + 1,331 + 590.25)] = ₹ 440.5625 lakhs

Total Provisions and contingencies = Provisions on NPAs + Provisions for tax
= 590.25 + 440.5625 = 1030.8125 lakhs

HAMARA BANK LIMITED P & L AC FOR THE YEAR ENDED 31ST MARCH, 2013

Particulars	Schedule No.	₹ lakhs
I Income		
Interest Earned	13	4,415
OtherIncome		125
		4,540
II Expenditures		
Interest Expended		1,360
Operating Expenses		1,331
Provisions & Contingencies		1030.8125
		3721.8125
III Profit/Loss		
Net Profit/Loss for the year		818.1875
Profit/Loss brought forward		40
		858.1875
IV Appropriations		
Transfer to Statutory Reserve @25%of 818.1875		204.5469
Balance carried over to Balance Sheet		653.6406
		858.1875
Schedule 13 - Interest earned		
I Interest & Discount (4,430 – 15 (Rebate) – 10 (Accrued Interest)		4405
II Income on Investments		10
		4,415

PROBLEM 28

The following are the figures extracted from the books of New Generation Bank Limited as on 31.3.2013:

	₹
Interest and discount received	37,05,738
Interest paid on deposits	20,37,452
Issued and Subscribed capital	10,00,000
Salaries and allowances	2,00,000
Directors fee and allowances	30,000
Rent and Taxes paid	90,000
Postage and Telegrams	60,286
Statutory reserve fund	8,00,000
Commission, exchange and brokerage	1,90,000
Rent received	65,000
Profit on sale of investments	2,00,000
Depreciation on Bank's properties	30,000
Statutory expenses	40,000
Preliminary expenses	25,000
Auditor's fees	5,000

The following further information is given:

(i) A customer to whom a sum of ₹ 10 lakhs has been advanced has become insolvent and it is expected only 50% can be recovered from his estate.

(ii) There were also other debts for which a provision of ₹ 1,50,000 was found necessary by the auditors.

(iii) Rebate on Bills discounted on 31.3.2012 was ₹ 12,000 and on 31.3.2013 was ₹ 16,000.

(iv) Provide ₹ 6,50,000 for Income-tax.
(v) The Directos desire to declare 10% dividend.

Required: Prepare the Profit and Loss account of New Generation Bank Limited for the year ended 31.3.2013 and also show, how the Profit and Loss account will appear in the Balance Sheet, if the Profit and Loss account opening balance was Nil as on 31.3.2012.

[CA (PE II) May 2008]

Solution

NEW GENERATION BANK LIMITED

Profit and Loss Account for the year ended 31st March, 2013

	Particulars	*Schedule*	*Year ended 31.03.2013*
I.	**Income:**		
	Interest earned	13	3,701.74
	Other income	14	455.00
	Total		4,156.74
II.	**Expenditure**		
	Interest expended	15	2,037.45
	Operating expenses	16	480.29
	Provisions and Contingencies (₹ 5,00,000 + 1,50,000 + 6,50,000)		1,300.00
	Total		3,817.74
III.	**Profits / Losses**		
	Net Profit for the year		339.00
	Profit brought forward		NIL
			339.00
IV.	**Appropriations**		
	Transfer to Statutory Reserve (25%)		84.75
	Proposed Dividend		100.00
	Balance carried over to Balance Sheet		154.25
			339.00

The Profit & Loss Account balance of ₹ ('000) 154.25 will appear in the Balance Sheet under the head 'Reserve and Surplus' in Schedule 2.

Schedule 13 – Interest Earned

		Year ended 31.03.2013 ₹ ('000)
I.	**Income:**	
	Interest earned	3,701.74
		3,701.74

Schedule 14 – Other Income

I.	Commission, exchange and brokerage	190.00
II.	Profit on sale of investments	200.00
III.	Rent received	65.00
		455.00

Schedule 15–Interest Expended

I.	Interests on Deposits	2,037.45

Schedule 16 – Operating Expenses

I.	Payment to and provisions for employees	200.00
II.	Rent, taxes and lighting	90.00
III.	Depreciation on Bank's property	30.00
IV.	Director's fees, allowances and expenses	30.00
V.	Auditor's fees	5.00
VI.	Law (statutory) charges	40.00
VII.	Postage and telegrams	60,29
VIII.	Preliminary expenses	*25.00
		480.29

*In the absence of information, preliminary expenses have been fully written off. Students may assume vice-versa.

Working Note:

Interest/discount (net of rebate on bills discounted) (W.N. 1)	3,705.74
Add: Rebate on bills discounted on 31.3.2007	12.00
Less: Rebate on bills discounted on 31.3.2008	(16.00)
	3,701.74

PROBLEM 29

From the following information, you are required to prepare Profit and Loss Account of Zee Bank Ltd., for the year ending 31st March, 2013:

	₹		₹
Interest and Discount	44,00,000	Interest expended	13,60,000
Other Income	1,25,000	Operating expenses	13,31,000
Income on investments	5,000	Interest on balance with RBI	25,000

Additional information:

(a) Rebate on bills discounted to be provided for ₹ 15,000

(b) Classification of advances:

	₹
Standard assets	25,00,000
Sub-standard assets	5,60,000
Doubtful assets not covered by security	2,55,000
Doubtful assets covered by security	
For 1 year	25,000
For 2 years	50,000
For 3 years	1,00,000
For 4 years	75,000
Loss assets	1,00,000

(c) Make tax Provision @ 35%

(d) Profit and Loss A/c (Cr.) ₹ 40,000.

[CA (PCC) May 2010]

Solution

Form 'B'
ZEE BANK LTD.
PROFIT & LOSS ACCOUNT FOR THE YEAR ENDED 31ST MARCH, 2013

	Particulars	Schedule No.	Year ended 31st March, 2013
I.	**Income:**		
	Interest Earned	13	44,15,000
	Other Income	14	1,25,000
	Total		45,40,000
II.	**Expenditure**		
	Interest Expended	15	13,60,000
	Operating Expense	16	13,31,000
	Provisions and Contingencies		10,30,813
	Total		37,21,813
III.	**Profit/Loss**		
	Net profit for the year		8,18,187
	Profit brought forward		40,000
	Total		8,58,187
IV.	**Appropriations:**		
	Transfer to Statutory Reserve (@ 25% on ₹ 8,18,187)		2,04,547
	Balance carried forward to Balance Sheet		6,53,640
	Total		8,58,187

Schedule 13: Interest Earned

Particulars	₹
Interest and discount [44,00,000 – 15,000 (Rabate)]	43,85,000
Income on Investment	5,000
Interest on balance with RBI	25,000
Total	44,15,000

Working Notes:

(I) CALCULATION OF PROVISIONS ON ASSETS

Particulars	Amount ₹	% of Provisions	Provision ₹
Standard assets	25,00,000	0.40	10,000
Sub-standard assets (assumed all fully secured)	5,60,000	15	84,000
Doubtful assets not covered by security	2,55,000	100	2,55,000
Doubtful assets covered by security			
For 1 year	25,000	25	6,250
For 2 years	50,000	40	20,000
For 3 years	1,00,000	40	40,000
For 4 years	75,000	100	75,000
Loss assets	1,00,000	100	1,00.000
			5,90,250

(ii) Calculation of Provision for tax

Tax = 35% of [Total Income – Total Expenditure (excluding tax)].

Tax = 35% of [₹ 44,15,000 + ₹ 1,25,000 – (₹ 13,60,000 + ₹ 13,31,000 + ₹ 5,90,250)]

Tax = ₹ 4,40,563

(iii) Total Amount of Provisions and Contingencies

= Provision for non-performing assets + Provision for tax + Rebate on bills discounted

= ₹ 5,90,250 + ₹ 4,40,563 = ₹ 10,30,813

PROBLEM 30

From the following information prepare the Profit & Loss Account of Jawahar Bank Limited for the year ended 31st March, 2013. Also give necessary Schedules.

	Figures are in ₹ thousands
Interest earned on term loans	17.26
Interest earned on term loans classified as NPA	4.52
Interest received on term loans classified as NPA	2. 04
Interest on cash credits and overdrafts	38.54
Interest earned but not received on cash credit and overdraft treated as NPA	8.39
Interest on deposits	27.20
Commission	1.97
Profit on sale of investments	11.76
Profit on revaluation of investments	2. 76
Income from investments	15.53
Salaries, bonus and allowances	18. 75
Rent, taxes and lighting	1. 70
Printing and stationary	0. 75
Director's fees, allowances expenses	1.33
Law charges	0.22
Repairs and maintenance	0. 18
Insurance	0.30
Other information:	
Make necessary provision on risk assets:	
(i) Sub-standard	15.00
(ii) Doubtful for one year	7.00
(iii) Doubtful for two years	2.40
(iv) Loss assets	0.65
Investments	3700

Bank should not keep more than 25% of its investments as 'held-for-maturity' investment. The market value of its best 75% investments is ₹ 9,00,000 as on 31st March, 2013.

[CA (IPCC) May 2011]

Solution

JAWAHAR BANK LIMITED
PROFIT & LOSS ACCOUNT FOR THE YEAR ENDED 31ST MARCH, 2013

Particulars	Schedule	₹ '000s
I. Income		
Interest earned	13	60.46
Other income	14	16.49
Total		76.95
II. Expenditure		
Interest expended	15	27.20
Operating expenses	16	23.23
Provisions & Contingencies (Refer W.N.)		1880.61
Total		1931.04
III. Profit/Loss		(1854.09)
IV. Appropriations		Nil

Schedule 13 - Interest Earned

	Rs'000s
Interest/discount on advances bills	
Interest on term loans [17.26 – (4.52 – 2.04)]	14.78
Interest on cash credits and overdrafts (38.54 – 8.39)	30.15
Income on investments	15.53
	60.46

Note: Interest on non-performing assets is recognized on receipt basis.

Schedule 14 - Other Income

	Rs'000s
Commission, exchange and brokerage	1.97
Profit on sale of investments	11.76
Profit on revaluation of investments	2.76
	16.49

Schedule 15 - Interest Expended

	Rs'000s
Interest on deposits	27.20

Schedule 16 - Operating Expenses

	Rs'000s
Payments to and provision for employees - salaries, bonus and allowances	18.75
Rent, taxes and lighting	1.70
Printing & stationery	0.75
Director's fee, allowances and expenses	1.33
Law charges	0.22
Repairs & maintenance	0.18
Insurance	0.30
	23.23

Working Note:

Provisions & Contingencies		₹ '000s
Provision for non-performing assets*		
Sub-standard (15 × 15%)		2.25
Doubtful for one year (7 × 25%)		1.75
Doubtful for two years (2. 40 x 40%)		0.96
Loss Assets (0.65 × 100%)		0.65
		5.61
Diminution in the value of current Investments:		
Cost 75% of ₹ 3,700 thousands**	27,75	
Less: Market value	(900)	1875.00
		1880.61

Note: It is assumed that all sub-standard and doubtful assets are fully secured.

**25% of investments classified as 'held for maturity' need not be marked to market as per RBI Guidelines. However, the remaining 75% investments have been marked to market according to RBI Guidelines.

PROBLEM 31

The following are the figures extracted from the books of KLM Bank Limited as on 31.3.2013:

	₹
Interest and discount received	38,00,160
Interest paid on deposits	22,95,360
Issued and Subscribed capital	10,00,000
Salaries and allowances	2,50,000
Directors fee and allowances	35,000
Rent and Taxes paid	1,00,000
Postage and Telegrams	65,340
Statutory Reserve Fund	8,00,000
Commission, Exchange and Brokerage	1,90,000
Rent received	72,000
Profit on sale of Investments	2,25,800
Depreciation on Bank's properties	40,000
Statutory Expenses	38,000
Preliminary Expenses	30,000
Auditor's Fees	12,000

The following further information is given:

(i) A customer to whom a sum of ₹ 10 lakhs has been advanced has become insolvent and it is expected only 55% can be recovered from his estate.

(ii) There were also other debts for which a provision of ₹ 2,00,000 was found necessary by the auditors.

(iii) Rebate on Bills discounted on 31.3.2012 was ₹ 15,000 and on 31.3.2013 was ₹ 20,000.

(iv) Provide ₹ 2,00,000 for Income-tax.

(v) The Directos desire to declare 5% dividend.

Required: Prepare the Profit and Loss account of KLM Bank Limited for the year ended 31.3.2013 and also show, how the Profit and Loss account will appear in the Balance Sheet, if the Profit and Loss account opening balance was Nil as on 31.3.2012.

[CA (IPCC) Nov. 2012]

Solution

KLM BANK LIMITED

PROFIT AND LOSS ACCOUNT FOR THE YEAR ENDED 31ST MARCH, 2013

	Particulars	*Schedule*	*Year ended 31.03.2013*
I.	**Income:**		
	Interest earned	13	37,95,160
	Other income	14	4,87,800
	Total		42,82,960
II.	**Expenditure**		
	Interest expended	15	22,95,360
	Operating expenses	16	5,70,340
	Provisions and Contingencies (₹ 4,50,000 + 2,00,000 + 2,00,000)		8,50,000
	Total		37,15,700
III.	**Profits / Losses**		
	Net Profit for the year		5,67,260
	Profit brought forward		NIL
			5,67,260
IV.	**Appropriations**		
	Transfer to Statutory Reserve (25%)		1,41,815
	Proposed Dividend		50,000
	Balance carried over to Balance Sheet		3,75,445
			5,67,260

The Profit & Loss Account balance of ₹ 3,75,445 will appear in the Balance Sheet under the head 'Reserve and Surplus' in Schedule 2.

Schedule 13 – Interest Earned

		Year ended 31.03.2013 ₹
I.	**Income:**	
	Interest earned	37,95,160

Schedule 14 – Other Income

I.	Commission, exchange and brokerage	1,90,000
II.	Profit on sale of investments	2,25,800
III.	Rent received	72,000
		4,87,800

Schedule 15–Interest Expended

I.	Interests on Deposits	22,95,360

Schedule 16 – Operating Expenses

I.	Payment to and provisions for employees	2,50,000
II.	Rent, taxes and lighting	1,00,000
III.	Depreciation on Bank's property	40,000
IV.	Director's fees, allowances and expenses	35,000
V.	Auditor's fees	12,000
VI.	Law (statutory) charges	38,000
VII.	Postage and telegrams	65,340
VIII.	Preliminary expenses*	30,000
		5,70,340

*As per AS 26 Preliminary Expenses have been fully written off.

Working Note:

Interest/discount (net of rebate on bills discounted) (W.N. 1)	38,00,160
Add: Opening Rebate on bills discounted	15,000
Less: Closing Rebate on bills discounted	(20,000)
	37,95,160

PREPARATION OF BALANCE SHEET

PROBLEM 32

From the following information, prepare a Balance Sheet of CANID Bank Ltd. as on 31st March, 2013 giving the relevant schedules and also specify at least four important Principal Accounting Policies:

(₹ in lakhs)

Particulars	*Dr. (₹)*	*Cr. (₹)*
Share Capital		198.00
19,80,000 Shares of ₹ 10 each		
Statutory Reserve		231.00
Net Profit Before Appropriation		150.00
Profit and Loss Account		412.00
Fixed Deposit Account		517.00
Savings Deposit Account		450.00
Current Accounts	28.00	520.12
Bills Payable		0.10
Cash Credits	812.10	
Borrowing from other Banks		110.00
Cash on Hand	160.15	
Cash with RBI	37.88	
Cash with other Banks	155.87	
Money at Call	210.12	
Gold	55.23	
Government Securities	110.17	
Premises	155.70	
Furniture	70.12	
Term Loan	792.88	
	2,588.22	2,588.22

Additional Information:

Bills for collection		18,10,000
Acceptances and endorsements		14,12,000
Claims against the Bank not acknowledged as debt		55,000
Depreciation charge—	Premises	1,10,000
	Furniture	78,000

50% of the Term Loans are secured by Government guarantees. 10% of cash credit is unsecured. Also calculate cash reserves required and statutory liquid reserves required.

Note: *Cash reserve required 3% of demand and time liabilities; liquid reserves required 25% of demand and time liabilities.* **[CA (Nov. 1994) (Modified)]**

Solution

BALANCE SHEET OF CANID BANK LTD. AS ON 31ST MARCH, 2013

(₹ in lakhs)

Particulars	*Schedule No.*	*As on 31st March 2013 (₹ '000)*	*As on 31st March 2012 (₹ '000)*
Capital and Liabilities:			
Share Capital	1	1,98.00	
Reserves and Surplus	2	7,93.00	
Deposits	3	14,87.12	
Borrowings	4	1,10.00	
Other liabilities and provisions	5	0.10	
		25,88.22	

Assets:			
Cash and balances with RBI	6	2,04.76	
Balances with banks and money at call and short notice	7	3,59.26	
Investments	8	1,65.40	
Advances	9	16,32.98	
Fixed Assets	10	2,25.82	
Other Assets	11	—	
		25,88.22	
Contingent Liabilities	12	14.67	
Bills for Collection		18.10	

Schedule 1—Capital

Particulars	*As on 31st March, 2013 (₹ '000)*	*As on 31st March, 2012 (₹ '000)*
Authorized Capital		
Issued, Subscribed and Paid up Capital	19,800	
19,80,000 shares of ₹ 10 each	19,800	

Schedule 2—Reserves and Surplus

Particulars	*As on 31st March, 2013 (₹ '000)*	*As on 31st March, 2012 (₹ '000)*
(1) Statutory Reserve-Opening balance	2,31.00	
Additions during the year	37.50	
	268.50	
(2) Balance in Profit & Loss Account [Refer to Working Note (i)]	524.50	
	7,93.00	

Schedule 3—Deposits

Particulars	*As on 31st March, 2013 (₹ '000)*	*As on 31st March, 2012 (₹ '000)*
(i) Demand deposits from others	5,20.12	
(ii) Saving bank deposits	4,50.00	
(iii) Fixed Deposits	5,17.00	
	14,87.12	

Schedule 4—Borrowing

Particulars	*As on 31st March, 2013 (₹ '000)*	*As on 31st March, 2012 (₹ '000)*
Borrowing in India-Other banks	1,10.00	

Schedule 5—Other Liabilities and Provisions

Particulars	*As on 31st March, 2013 (₹ '000)*	*As on 31st March, 2012 (₹ '000)*
Other liabilities and provisions	0.10	

Schedule 6—Cash and balance with RBI

Particulars	*As on 31st March, 2013 (₹ '000)*	*As on 31st March, 2012 (₹ '000)*
(i) Cash in hand	1,60.15	
(ii) Balances with RBI-		
In current account [Refer to Working Note (ii)]	44.61	
	2,04.76	

Schedule 7—Balance with Banks and money at call and short notice

Particulars	*As on 31st March, 2013 (₹ '000)*	*As on 31st March, 2012 (₹ '000)*
I. In India		
(i) Balances with Banks		
(a) in current accounts		
[Refer to Working Note (iii)]	1,49.14	
(ii) Money at call and short notice	2,10.12	
	3,59.26	

Schedule 8—Investments

Particulars	*As on 31st March, 2013 (₹ '000)*	*As on 31st March, 2012 (₹ '000)*
(1) Investments in India in		
(i) Government securities	1,10.17	
(ii) Others—Gold	55.23	
	1,65.40	

Schedule 9—Advances

Particulars	*As on 31st March, 2013 (₹ '000)*	*As on 31st March, 2012 (₹ '000)*
A.(i) Cash credits, overdrafts	8,40.10	
(ii) Term Loans	7,92.88	
	16,32.98	
B.(i) Secured by tangible assets	11,52.53	
(ii) Secured by bank/govt. guarantees	3,96.44	
(iii) Unsecured	84.01	
	16,32.98	

Schedule 10—Fixed Assets

Particulars	As on 31st March, 2013 (₹ '000)	As on 31st March, 2012 (₹ '000)
1. Premises		
At cost on 31st March, 2012	156.80	
Depreciation to date	1.10	
	155.70	
2. Other Fixed Assets		
Furniture at cost on 31st March, 2012	70.90	
Depreciation to date	0.78	
	70.12	
Total (1 + 2)	2,25.82	

Schedule 11—Other Assets

Nil

Schedule 12—Contingent Liabilities

Particulars	As on 31st March, 2013 (₹ '000)	As on 31st March, 2012 (₹ '000)
(i) Claims against bank not acknowledged as debts	0.55	
(ii) Acceptances, endorsements	14.12	
	14.67	

Calculation of cash reserves and statutory liquid reserves

Total of demand & time liabilities (₹ 5,17.00 + ₹ 4,50.00 + ₹ 5,20.12)	14,87.12
Cash reserves (3% of above)	44.61
Statutory liquid reserves (25% of demand and time liabilities)	371.78

Working Notes:

(i) *Balance in Profit & Loss Account:*

Net Profit before appropriation	1,50.00
Add: Profit for the year	4,12.00
	5,62.00
Less: Transfer of Statutory Reserve (25% of 1,50.00)	37.50
	5,24.50

(ii) *Transfer from Cash with other banks to Cash with RBI*

Cash reserve required	44.61
Cash with RBI	37.88
Transfer needed to maintain cash reserve	6.73

(iii) *Liquid Assets:*

Cash on hand	1,60.15
Cash with other Banks (155.87 – 6.73)	1,49.14
Money at call and short notice	2,10.12
Gold	55.23
Government securities	1,10.17
	6,84.81
Excess Liquidity (6,84.81 – 371.78)	313.03

Principal Accounting Policies:

(a) *Foreign Exchange Transactions*

(i) Monetary assets and liabilities have been translated at the exchange rate prevailing at the close of the year. Non-monetary assets have been carried in the books at the historical cost.

(ii) Income and Expenditure in respect of Indian branches have been translated at the exchange rates on the date of transactions and in respect of foreign branches at the exchange rates prevailing at the close of the year.

(iii) Profit or Loss on foreign currency position including pending forward exchange contracts have been accounted for all the exchange rates prevailing at the close of the year.

(b) *Investments:*

Permanent category investments are valued at cost. Valuation of investment in current category depends on the nature of securities. While valuation of government securities held as current investments have been made on yield to maturity basis, the investments in shares of companies are valued on the basis of book value.

(c) *Advances:*

Advances due from sick nationalized units under nursing programmes and in respect of various sticky, suit filed and decreed accounts have been considered good on the basis of....

(i) Available estimated value of existing and prospective primary and collateral securities including personal worth of the borrowers and guarantors.

(ii) The proposed/on going revival/rehabilitation programmes.

(iii) The claim lodged/to be lodged under various credit guarantee schemes.

(iv) Pending settlement of claims by Govt.

Provisions to the satisfaction of auditors have been made and deducted from advances. Tax relief available when the advance is written off will be accounted for in the year of write-off.

(d) *Fixed Assets:*

The premises and other fixed assets except for foreign branches are accounted for at their historical cost. Depreciation has been provided on written down value method at the rates specified in the Income Tax Rules, 1962. Depreciation in respect of assets of foreign branches has been provided as per the local laws.

11 Financial Statements of Life Insurance Companies

SHORT ANSWER PRACTICAL QUESTIONS

PROBLEM 1

From the following figures of CAMJB Life Assurance Co. Ltd. prepare a Valuation Balance Sheet and Profit Distribution Statement for the year ended 31st March, 2013, also pass necessary Journal Entries to record the above transactions with narration.

(₹ in lacs)

Balance of Life Assurance Fund as on 1.4.2012	167.15
Interim Bonus paid for the valuation period	25.00
Balance of Revenue Account for the year ended 31.3.2013	240.00
Net Liability as per Valuer's certificate as on 31.3.2013	165.00

The company declared a reversionary bonus of ₹ 185 per ₹ 1,000 and gave the policyholders an option to take bonus in cash ₹ 105 per ₹ 1,000. Total business conducted by the company was ₹ 600 lacs. The company issued with profit policy only. 3/5 of the policy holders in value opted for cash bonus. **[*CA*]**

Solution

CAMJB LIFE ASSURANCE COMPANY LTD.
Valuation Balance Sheet as at 31st March, 2013

Particulars	₹ *(in Lakhs)*	*Particulars*	₹ *(in Lakhs)*
Net Liability Profit	165.00 75.00	Life Assurance Fund as on 31.3.2013	240.00
	240.00		240.00

Distribution Statement (₹ in lakhs)

Profit as per Valuation Balance Sheet	75.00	
Add: Interim Bonus Paid	25.00	100.00
Policy holders Share (95%)	95.00	
Less: Interim Bonus paid	(25.00)	70.00

JOURNAL (₹ in lakhs)

Particulars		*L.F.*	*Dr. (₹)*	*Cr. (₹)*
Life Assurance Fund A/c	Dr.		75.00	
To Profit and Loss A/c				75.00
(Being profit transferred as per Valuation Balance Sheet)				

Profit and Loss A/c Dr. To Bonus Payable in Cash A/c (Being Cash bonus payable @ 105 per thousand on 3/5 of 600 lakh)		37.80	37.80
Profit and Loss A/c Dr. To Life Assurance Fund A/c (Being Bonus @ ₹ 185 per thousand on 2/5 of 600 lakhs transferred to Life Assurance Fund for reversionary Bonus)		44.40	44.40

PROBLEM 2

The Life Assurance Fund of an Insurance Company was on 31.3.2013, ₹ 60 lakhs before providing for dividend of ₹ 20,000 for the year 2012-2013. While ascertaining the above fund figure, the following items were omitted:

(i) Interest received on investments ₹ 63,000 after deduction of tax at source 10%.
(ii) Bonus utilized for reduction of premium ₹ 14,000.
(iii) Death claim intimated, but not yet admitted ₹ 36,000.
(iv) Death claim covered under re-insurance ₹ 12,000.
(v) Consideration for annuities granted ₹ 9,000.

Interim bonus for the valuation period paid was ₹ 80,000.

Net liabilities as per valuation was ₹ 50 lakhs. It is now proposed to carry forward ₹ 2,70,000. The company declared a reversionary bonus of ₹ 12 per ₹ 1,000 and gave the policyholders an option to get the bonus in cash for ₹ 5 per ₹ 1,000. Total business of the company is ₹ 15 crores, 40% of the policyholders decided to get bonus in cash.

Prepare:

(i) Valuation Balance Sheet as at 31.3.2013.
(ii) Distribution Statement showing the amount due to the policyholders.

Also give journal Enries relating to reversionary bonus. *[CA (November) 2004]*

Solution

VALUATION BALANCE SHEET AS AT 31.3.2013

Particulars	₹	*Particulars*	₹
Net Liability Net Profit	50,00,000 10,34,000	Life Insurance Fund (adjused) (W.N. 1)	60,34,000
	60,34,000		60,34,000

Distribution Statement

	₹
Net Profit as per Valuation Balance Sheet	10,34,000
Add: Interim bonus paid	80,000
	11,14,000
Less: Dividend provided	20,000
	10,94,000
Less: Carried forward	2,70,000
True Surplus	8,24,000
Share of Policy holders [₹ 8,24,000 × 95%]	7,82,800
Less: Interim bonus paid	80,000
Amount due to policy holders	7,02,800

JOURNAL

Particulars		L.F.	Dr. (₹)	Cr. (₹)
Profit and Loss A/c	Dr.		3,00,000	
To Bonus payable in cash A/c				3,00,000
(Being the bonus payable in cash)				
Profit and Loss A/c	Dr.		10,80,000*	
To Life Insurance Fund A/c				10,80,000
(Being transfer to Life Insurance Fund for nw liability)				

Working Notes:

(i) *Calculation of Adjusted Life Insurance Fund as on 31.3.2013*

			₹
Life Insurance Fund before adjustments			60,00,000
Add: Interest on investment (gross) $\frac{63,000 \times 100}{(100-10)}$	70,000		
Less: Tax deduced at source	7,000	63,000	
Consideration for annuities granted		9,000	72,000
			60,72,000
Less: Death claim intimated	36,000		
Add: Death claim covered under reinsurance	12,000	(24,000)	
Less: Bonus utilised in reduction of premium		(14,000)	38,000
Adjusted Life Insurance Fund			60,34,000

(ii) **Bonus**

₹ 15 crores × 4/10 × 5/1,000 = ₹ 3,00,000 payable in cash

₹ 15 crores × 6/10 × 12/1,000 = ₹ 10,80,000 transfer to fund

(iii) In the present case, the total of bonus payable in cash amounting ₹ 3,00,000 and the bonus by transfer to life insurance fund amounting 10,80,000 comes to ₹ 13,80,000 and the amount due to policyholders is ₹ 7,02,800.

The above solution has been worked out on the basis that the company has sufficient balance in Profit and Loss account for declaration of bonus.

PROBLEM 3

The Life Fund of Well-life Assurance Co. was ₹.90,00,000 as on 31st March 2013. The interim bonus paid during the valuation period was ₹.1,50,000. The periodical actuarial valuation determined the net liability at ₹.75,00,000. Surplus brought forward from the previous valuation was ₹.9,00,000. The directors of the company proposed to carry forward ₹.10,00,000 and to divide the balance between the shareholders and the policy holders. You are required to show:

(i) The Valuation Balance Sheet.

(ii) The Net Profit for the valuation period.

(iii) The Distribution of the Surplus. [CA (PE-II) November, 2006]

Solution

WELL LIFE ASSURANCE CO. LTD.
Valuation Balance Sheet as at March 31, 2013

Particulars	₹	*Particulars*	₹
Net Liability as per actuarial valuation	75,00,000	Life Fund as per Balance Sheet	90,00,000
Surplus (Bal. Fig.)	15,00,000		
	90,00,000		90,00,000

Net Profit for valuation period:

	₹
A. Surplus as per valuation balance sheet	15,00,000
B. *Add:* Interim Bonus distributed	1,50,000
C. *Less:* Surplus in the beginning	(9,00,000)
D. Net Profit for the valuation period	7,50,000

Distribution of Surplus

	₹
A. Total Surplus	16,50,000
B. *Less:* Surplus to be carried forward	10,00,000
	6,50,000
C. Shareholders (5% of ₹.6,50,000)	32,500
D. Policy holders (95% of ₹.6,50,000)	6,17,500
E. *Less:* Interim bonus already distributed	1,50,000
F. Bonus still due to Policy holders	4,67,500

PROBLEM 4

The life fund of a life assurance company was ₹ 8,64,80,000 as on 31.3.2010. The interim bonus paid during the intervaluation period was ₹ 14,80,000. The periodical actuarial valuation determined the net liability at ₹ 7,42,50,000. Surplus brought forward from the previous valuation was ₹ 85,00,000. Calculate the net profit for the valuation period. ***[CA (PCC) May 2010]***

Solution

VALUATION BALANCE SHEET AS AT 31.3.2010

Particulars	₹	*Particulars*	₹
To Net Liability as per Actuarial Valuation	7,42,50,000	By Life Fund as per Balance Sheet	8,64,80,000
To Surplus (Bal. fig.)	1,22,30,000		
	8,64,80,000		8,64,80,000

CALCULATION OF NET PROFIT FOR THE VALUATION PERIOD

Particulars	₹
Surplus as per the Valuation Balance Sheet	1,22,30,000
Add: Interim bonus distributed	14,80,000
	1,37,10,000
Less: Surplus at the beginning of the period	(85,00,000)
Net Profit for the valuation period	52,10,000

PROBLEM 5

Domestic Assurance Co. Ltd. received ₹.5,90,000 as premium on new policies and ₹.1,20,000 as renewal premium. The company received ₹.90,000 towards reinsurance accepted and paid ₹.70,000 towards reinsurance ceded. How much will be credited to Revenue Account towards premium? *[CA (PCE May 2008]*

Solution

	₹
Premium received in respect of new policies	5,90,000
Add: Renewal premium	1,20,000
	7,10,000
Add: Re-insurance premium accepted	90,000
	8,00,000
Less: Re-insurance ceded	70,000
Premium amount to be credited to Revenue A/c	7,30,000

12 Financial Statements of General Insurance Companies

SHORT ANSWER PRACTICAL QUESTIONS

CALCULATION OF NET CLAIM

PROBLEM 1

From the following figures appearing in the books of Fire Insurance division of a General insurance Company, show the amount of claim as it would appear in the Revenue Account for the period ended 31st March 2013.

Particulars	Direct Business	Re-insurance
	₹	₹
Claim paid during the year	46,70,000	7,00,000
Claim Payable— 1st April, 2012	7,63,000	87,000
31st March, 2013	8,12,000	53,000
Claims received	—	
Claims receivable—1st April,2012	—	2,30,000
31st March, 2013	—	65,000
Expenses of Management (include ₹.35,000 Surveyor's Fee and ₹.45,000 Legal Expenses for settlement of claims	2,30,000	—

[*CA (Nov) 1999*]

Solution

AN EXTRACT OF FIRE REVENUE ACCOUNT for the year ended on 31st March, 2013

Particulars	*Schedule No.*	*Current Year (₹ '000)*	*Previous Year (₹ '000)*
Claim Incurred (Net)	2	5187	

Schedule 2 Claim incured (Net)

Particulars	*Current Year (₹ '000)*	*Previous Year (₹ '000)*
Claims paid on direct business	4799	
Less: Claims received on re-insurance ceded	(278)	
Add: Claim paid on re-insurance accepted	666	
Net Claim paid	5187	

Working Notes:

CLAIMS INCURRED

Particulars	*Direct Business (₹ '000)*	*Re-insurance Accepted (₹ '000)*	*Re-Insurance Ceded ₹ '000*
A. Paid / Received	4670	700	230
B. *Add:* Outstanding at end	812	53	113
C. *Add:* Exp. in connection with settlement of claim [35,000+45,000]	80		
D. *Less:* Outstanding at beginning	(763)	(87)	(65)
	4799	666	278

PROBLEM 2

Modern Insurance Company's Fire Insurance division provide the following information, show the amount of claim as it would appear in the Revenue Account for the year ended 31st March, 2013.

	Direct Business ₹	*Re-insurance* ₹
Claim paid during the year	35,30,000	8,20,000
Claim received		3,20,000
Claim payable		
1st April, 2012	8,23,000	58,000
31st March, 2013	8,75,000	87,000
Claim receivable:		
1st April, 2012	—	85,000
31st March, 2013	—	1,42,000
Expenses of management (Includes ₹ 38,000 Surveyor's fee and ₹ 42,000 Legal expenses for settlement of claims)	3,45,000	

[CA (IPCC) May 2011]

Solution

CALCULATION OF NET CLAIMS INCURRED

Particulars		₹
Claims paid on direct business (35,30,000 + 38,000 + 42,000)		36,10,000
Add: Re-insurance	8,20,000	
Add: Outstanding at the end	87,000	
Less: Outstanding in the beg.	(58,000)	8,49,000
		44,59,000
Less: Claims received from re-insurance	3,20,000	
Add: Outstanding at the end	1,42,000	
Less: Outstanding in the beg.	(85,000)	(3,77,000)
		40,82,000
Add: Outstanding Direct Claims at the end of the year		8,75,000
Less: Outstanding Claims at the beginning of the year		(8,23,000)
Net Claims incurred		41,34,000

PROBLEM 3

From the following figures of Fire Insurance division of a General Insurance Company, show the amount of claim as it would appear in the Revenue Account for the year ended 31st March, 2013:

	Direct Business ₹	*Re-Insurance* ₹
Claims paid during the year	70,05,000	10,50,000
Claims payable		
1st April, 2012	11,44,500	1,30,500
31 March, 2013	12,18,000	79,500
Claims received	—	3,45,000
Claims receivable		
1st April, 2012	—	97,500
31st March, 2013	—	1,69,500
Expenses of management (includes ₹ 52,500 surveyor's fee and ₹ 67,500 legal expenses for settlement of claims)	3,45,000	

[CA (PCC) Nov. 2011]

Solution

STATEMENT SHOWING THE AMOUNT OF CLAIMS FOR THE YEAR ENDED 31ST MARCH, 2013

Particulars	*(₹)*	*(₹)*
Claim paid on		
Claims paid on direct business (70,05,000 + 52,500 + 67,500)		71,25,000
Add: Re-insurance	10,50,000	
Add: Outstanding at the end	79,500	
Less: Outstanding in the beg.	(1,30,500)	9,99,000
		81,24,000
Less: Claims received from Re-insurance	3,45,000	
Add: Outstanding at the end	1,69,500	
Less: Outstanding in the beg.	(97,500)	(4,17,000)
		77,07,000
Add: Outstanding Direct Claims at the end		12,18,000
Less: Outstanding Direct Claims in the beg.		(11,44,500)
Net Claims incurred		77,80,500

CALCULATION OF NET PREMIUMS AND NET CLAIMS

PROBLEM 4

From the following information of Reliable of Marine Insurance Ltd. for the year ending 31st March, 2013 find out the

(*i*) Net Premiums earned
(*ii*) Net Claims incurred

	(₹) Direct Business	(₹) Re-insurance
Premium:		
Received	88,00,000	7,52,000
Receivable – 01.04.2012	4,39,000	36,000
Receivable – 31.03.2013	3,77,000	32,000
Paid	6,09,000	
Payable – 01.04.2012		27,000
Payable – 31.03.2013		18,000
Claims:		
Paid	69,00,000	5,54,000
Payable – 01.04.2012	89,000	15,000
Payable – 31.03.2013	95,000	12,000
Received		2,01,000
Receivable – 01.04.2012		40,000
Receivable – 31.03.2013		38,000

[CA (IPCC) Nov. 2010]

Solution

(i) Net Premiums earned

	(₹)	(₹)
Premium from direct business received	88,00,000	
Add : Receivable at the end	3,77,000	
Less: Receivable at the begnning	(4,39,000)	87,38,000
Add: Premium on Re-insurance accepted	7,52,000	
Add: Receivable at the end	32,000	
Less: Receivable at the begnning	(36,000)	7,48,000
		94,86,000
Less: Premium on Re-insurance ceded	6,09,000	
Add: Payable at the end	18,000	
Less: Payable at the begnning	(27,000)	(6,00,000)
Net Premium earned		**88,86,000**

(ii) Net Claims incurred

	(₹) Direct Business	(₹) Re-insurance
Claims paid on direct business		69,00,000
Add: Re-insurance	5,54,000	
Add: Outstanding at the end	12,000	
Less: Outstanding at the begnning	(15,000)	5.51,000
		74,51,000

Less: Claims received from Re-insurance	2,01,000	
Add: Outstanding at the end	38,000	
Less: Outstanding at the begnning	(40,000)	(1,99,000)
		72,52,000
Add: Outstanding direct claims at the end of the year		95,000
		73,47,000
Less: Outstanding claims at the beginning of the year		(89,000)
Net Claims incurred		72,58,000

UNEXPIRED RISK RESERVE ACCOUNT

PROBLEM 5

From the following information furnished to you by Ayushman Insurance Co. Ltd., you are required to pass Journal entires relating to unexpired risk reserve and show in columnar form "Unexpired Risks Reserve Account" for 2013.

(a) On 31.12.2012, it had reserve for unexpired risks amounting to ₹ 40 crores. It comprised of ₹.15 crores in respect of marine insurance business, ₹ 20 crores in respect of fire insurance business and ₹ 5 crores in respect of miscellaneous insurance business.

(b) Ayushman Insurance Co. Ltd. creates reserves at 100% of net premium income in respect of marine insurance policies and at 50% of net premium income in respect of fire and miscellaneous income policies.

(c) During 2013, the following business was conducted:

	(Amount in crores)		
	Marine	*Fire*	*Miscellaneous*
Premium collected from:			
(a) Insured in respect of policies issued	18.00	43.00	12.00
(b) Other insurance companies in respect of risks undertaken	7.00	5.00	4.00
Premium paid/payable to other insurance companies on business ceded	6.70	4.30	7.00

[CA (IPCC) May 2010]

Solution

JOURNAL OF AYUSHMAN INSURANCE CO. LTD.

(₹ in crores)

Date	*Particulars*		*Dr.*	*Cr.*
1.1.2013	Unexpired Risk Reserve (Fire) A/c	Dr.	20.00	
	Unexpired Risk Reserve (Marine) A/c	Dr.	15.00	
	Unexpired Risk Reserve (Miscellaneous) A/c	Dr.	5.00	
	To Fire Revenue A/c			20.00
	To Marine Revenue A/c			15.00
	To Miscellaneous Revenue A/c			5.00

	(Being unexpired risk reserve brought forward from last year)		
31.12.2013	Marine Revenue A/c Dr.	18.30	
	To Unexpired Risk Reserve A/c		18.30
	(Being Closing reserve for unexpired risk created at 100% of net premium income amounting to ₹.18.3 crores i.e. 18 + 7- 6.70)		
	Fire Revenue A/c Dr.	21.85	
	To Unexpired Risk Reserve A/c		21.85
	(Being closing reserve for unexpired risk created at 50% of net premium income of ₹ 43.7 crores i.e. 43 + 5-4,30)		
	Miscellaneous Revenue A/c Dr.	4.50	
	To Unexpired Risk Reserve A/c		4.50
	(Being closing reserve for unexpired risk created at 50% net premium income of ₹ 9 crores i.e. 12+4-7)		

Dr. **UNEXPIRED RISK RESERVE ACCOUNT** Cr.

Date	Particulars	Marine (₹)	Fire (₹)	Misc. (₹)	Date	Particulars	Marine (₹)	Fire (₹)	Misc. (₹)
1.1.2013	To Revenue A/c	15.00	20.00	5.00	1.1.2013	By Balance b/d	15.00	20.00	500
31.12.2013	To Balance c/d	18.30	21.85	4.50	31.12.2013	By Revenue A/c	18.30	21.85	4.50
		33.30	41.85	9.50			33.30	41.85	9.50

PREPARATION OF FIRE INSURANCE REVENUE ACCOUNT

PROBLEM 6

Prepare the Fire Insurance Revenue A/c as per IRDA regulations for the year ended 31st March, 2013 from the following details:

	₹
Claims paid	4,90,000
Legal expenses regarding claims	10,000
Premiums received	13,00,000
Re-insurance premium paid	1,00,000
Commission	3,00,000
Expenses of Management	2,00,000
Provision against unexpired risk on 1st April, 2012	5,50,000
Claims unpaid on 1st April, 2012	50,000
Claims unpaid on 31st March, 2013	80,000

[CA (PE II) May, 2008]

Solution

Since Rule 6 E of Income Tax Rules permits the insurance companies to claim a deduction of 50% of net premium income in respect of Fire and Miscellaneous Business. In view of this reserve has been created at the rates allowed under Income Tax act.

FORM B - RA

Name of the Insurer :
Registration No. and Date of Registration with the IRDA

FIRE INSURANCE REVENUE ACCOUNT
For the year ended 31st March, 2013

	Particulars	Schedule	Amount
1.	Premium earned	1	11,50,000
2.	Other income		—
3.	Interest, dividend and rent		—
	Total (A)		11,50,000
4.	Claims incurred	2	5,30,000
5.	Commission	3	3,00,000
6.	Operating expenses related to Insurance business	4	2,00,000
	Total (B)		10,30,000
	Operating Profit (A) – (B)		1,20,000

Schedule 1: Premium earned

	₹
Premium received	13,00,000
Less: Re-insurance Premium	(1,00,000)
	12,00,000
Less: Change in provision for unexpired risk (Refer W.N.)	(50,000)
	11,50,000

Schedule 2: Claims Incurred

Claims paid including legal expenses (4,90,000 + 10,000)	5,00,000
Add: Claims outstanding at the end of the year	80,000
Less: Claims outstanding at the beginnging of the year	(50,000)
Total claims incurred	5,30,000

Schedule 3: Commission

Commission paid	3,00,000

Schedule 4: Operating Expenses

Expenses of Management	2,00,000

Working Note: **Change in the provision for un-expired risk**

	₹
Unexpired Risk Reserve on 31st March, 2008 = 50% of Net Premium i.e. 50% of ₹ 12,00,000 =	6,00,000
Unexpired Risk Reserve on 1st April 2007	5,50,000
	50,000

Note: Alternatively, Reserve for unexpired risk may be taken @ 40% of net premium as per the provisions of the Insurance Act, 1938.

PROBLEM 7

Sunlife General Insurance Company submits the following information for the year ended 31st March 2013:

Particulars		Direct Business (₹)	Re-insurance (₹)
Premium received		65,75,000	9,50,000
Premium paid		—	4,75,000
Claims paid during the year		42,50,000	5,00,000
Claims payable	1st April, 2012	6,25,000	87,000
	31st March, 2013	7,18,000	60,0001
Claims received		—	3,25,000
Claims receivable	1st April, 2012		65,000
	31st March, 2013		1,10,000
Expenses of management		2,30,000	
Commission:			
On insurance accepted		1,50,000	11,000
On insurance ceded			14,000

The following additional information is also available:

(1) Expenses of management include ₹, 35,000 surveyor's fee and ₹ 45,000 legal expenses for settlement of claims.

(2) Reserve for unexpired risk is to be maintained @ 40% The balance of reserve for unexpired risk as on 1.4.2012 was ₹, 24,50,000.

You are required to prepare the Revenue Account for the year ended 31st March, 2013.

Solution

FORM B-RA (PRESCRIBED BY IRDA)
SUNLIFE GENERAL INSURANCE COMPANY
REVENUE ACCOUNT FOR THE YEAR ENDED 31ST MARCH, 2013

Particulars	Schedule	₹
Premium Earned (net)	1	66,80,000
Interest, Dividend and Rent		—
Other income		—
Total A)		66,80,000
Claims incurred (Net)	2	45,26,000
Commission	3	1,47,000
Operating Expenses related to insurance business	4	50,000
Bad Debts	—	
Total (B)		48,23,000
Operating Profit from insurance business (A – B)		18,57,000

Schedules forming part of revenue account

Schedule 1 : Premium Earned (Net)

Particulars	₹
Premium from direct business	65,75,000
Add: Premium on reinsurance accepted	9,50,000
Less: Premium on reinsurance ceded	(4,75,000)
Net Premium	70,50,000
Adjustment for change in reserve for unexpired risks	(3,70,000)
Total Premium earned (net)	66,80,000

Schedule 2 : Claims Incurred (Net)

Particulars	₹
Claims paid on direct business (W.N.1)	43,30,000
Add: Reinsurance accepted (W.N.1)	4,73,000
Less: Reinsurance ceded (W.N.1)	(3,70,000)
Net Claims paid	44,33,000
Add: Claims outstanding at the end of the year	7,18,000
Less: Claims outstanding at the beginning of the year	(6,25,000)
Total claims incurred	45,26,000

Schedule 3 : Commission

Particulars	₹
Commission paid on direct business	1,50,000
Add: Commission on reinsurance accepted	11,000
Less: Commission on reinsurance ceded	(14,000)
	1,47,000

Schedule 4 : Operating Expenses related to Insurance Business

Particulars	₹
Expenses of Management (2,30,000 – 35,000 – 45,000)	1,50,000
	1,50,000

Working Notes:

(i) Claims Incurred

Particulars	*Direct Business (₹)*	*Reinsurance Accepted (₹)*	*Reinsurance Ceded (₹)*
Paid/received	42,50,000	5,00,000	3,25,000
Add: Outstanding at the end of the year		60,000	1,10,000
Expenses in connection with settlement of claim (35,000 + 45,000)	80,000		
Less: Outstanding at the beginning of the year	(87,000)	(65,000)	
	43,30,000	4,73,000	3,70,000

(ii) Change in Reserve for Unexpired Risk

	₹
Opening Reserve	24,50,000
Less: Closing Reserve (₹ 70,50,000 × 40%)	28,20,000
Change in Reserve for Unexpired Risk	**3,70,000**

PROBLEM 8

From the following information of M/s. Bigfish Marine Insurance Co. Ltd., prepare the Revenue Account as per regulations of IRDA for theyear ended 31S* March, 2013:

Particulars		*Amount (₹)*
Premium received		18,75,000
Premium outstanding on March 31,2013		1,25,000
Premium paid on reinsurance ceded		2,28,000
Claimspaid		10,54,000
Estimated liability in respect of outstanding claims:	On April 1,2012	1,89,000
	On March 31,2013	2,25,000
Expenses of management (includes ₹ 45, 000 surveyor's fee and ₹ 65,000 legal expenses paid for settlement of claims)		4,85,000
Interest and dividend (Gross)		1, 65,250
Income tax on the above		49,575
Profit on sale of investments		46,000
Commission paid		1,94,000

Balance of fund on 1st April, 2012 was ₹ 18,50,000 including additional reserve of ₹ 1,80,000. Additional reserve has to be maintained at 10% of Net Premium for the year.

[CA (IPCC) Nov., 2011]

Solution

FORM B-RA NAME OF THE INSURER: M/S BIGFISH MARINE INSURANCE CO. LTD.
REVENUE ACCOUNT FOR THE YEAR ENDED 31ST MARCH, 2013

Particulars	*Schedule*	₹
Premium earned (Net)	1	16,72,800
Profit on sale of investment		46,000
Interest, dividend and rent (Gross)		1 ,65,250
Total (A)		18,84,050
Claims incurred (Net)	2	12,00,000
Commission	3	1,94,000
Operatinq expenses related to insurance business	4	3,75,000
Total (B)		17,69,000
Profit for Marine Insurance Business (A-B)		1,15,050

Schedule -1

Premium Earned (Net)	₹
Premium received	18,75,000
Add: Outstanding Premium at the end	1,25,000
Less: Premium on reinsurance ceded	(2,28,000)
Less: Adjustment for change in reserve for Unexpired Risk	(99,200)
Net premium earned	16,72,800

Schedule-2

Claim Incurred (Net)	₹
Claim paid	10,54,000
Add: Surveyor's fee & legal expenses paid for settlement of claim (₹ 45,000 + ₹ 65,000)	1,10,000
Add: Outstanding claims at the end	2,25,000
Less: Outstanding claims in the beg.	(1,89,000)
Claim incurred (Net)	12,00,000

Schedule-3

Commission	₹
Commission paid	1,94,000

Schedule-4

Operating expenses related to insurance business	₹
Expenses of Management	4,85,000
Less: Surveyor's fee & legal expenses	(1,10,000)
	3,75,000

Working Notes:

(I) CALCULATION FOR CHANGE IN RESERVE FOR UNEXPIRED RISK

		₹
Unexpired risk reserve at the beginning (including additional reserve)		18,50,000
Less: Reserve for unexpired risk as at the end (100% of ₹ 17,72,000)	17,72,000	
Additional reserve at the end (10% of ₹ 17,72,000)	1,77,200	(19,49,200)
Change in Provision for Unexpired Risk		99,200

(ii) Income tax on interest and dividend ₹ 49,575 is part of Profit & Loss Account, therefore, not given effect to in the Revenue Account.

PROBLEM 9

Prepare the Fire Insurance Revenue A/c as per IRDA regulations for the year ended 31st March, 2013 from the following details:

	₹
Claims paid	5,00,000
Legal expenses regarding claims	10,000
Premiums received	12,50,000
Re-insurance premium paid	50,000
Commission	3,00,000
Expenses of Management	2,00,000
Provision against unexpired risk on 1st April, 2012	5,75,000
Claims unpaid on 1st April, 2012	50,000
Claims unpaid on 31st March, 2013	80,000

Provision against unexpired risk @ 50% **less** Re-insurance *[CA (IPCC) Nov., 2012]*

Solution

FORM B - RA

Name of the Insurer : Jasmine Fire Insurance Co. Ltd.

Registration No. and Date of Registration with the IRDA: ....

Fire Insurance Revenue Account
For the year ended 31st March, 2013

	Particulars	*Schedule*	*Amount*
1.	Premium earned	1	11,75,000
2.	Other income		—
3.	Interest, dividend and rent		—
	Total (A)		11,75,000
4.	Claims incurred	2	5,40,000
5.	Commission	3	3,00,000
6.	Operating expenses related to Insurance business	4	2,00,000
	Total (B)		10,40,000
	Operating Profit (A) – (B)		1,35,000

Schedule 1: Premium earned

	₹
Premium received	12,50,000
Less: Re-insurance Premium	(50,000)
	12,00,000
Less: Adjustment for Change in provision for un-expired risk (Refer W.N.)	25,000
	11,75,000

Schedule 2: Claims Incurred

Claims paid including legal expenses (5,10,000 + 10,000)	5,10,000
Add: Claims outstanding at the end of the year	80,000
Less: Claims outstanding at the beginnging of the year	(50,000)
Total claims incurred	5,40,000

Schedule 3: Commission

Commission paid	3,00,000

Schedule 4: Operating Expenses

Expenses of Management	2,00,000

Working Note:

Change in the Provision for Unexpired Risk

Closing Unexpired Risk Reserve [50% of ₹ 12,00,000]	₹6,00,000
Opening Unexpired Risk Reserve	₹(5,75,000)
	₹25,000

PROBLEM 10

From the following information of M/s. Bachao Insurance Co. Ltd., engaged in fire insurance business, prepare the Revenue Account reserving 40% of the net premiums for unexpired risks and an additional reserve of ₹ 3,50,000:

Particulars		*Amount (₹)*
Reserve for unexpired risk (opening)		7,50,000
Additional Reserve (opening)		1,50,000
Premium received		16,80,000
Re-insurance premium		1,12,500
Re-insurance recoveries		30,000
Claims paid		9,60,000
Estimated liability in respect of outstanding claims:	On April 1,2012	97,500
	On March 31,2013	1,35,000
Expenses of management (includes ₹ 45, 000 in connection with claims)		4,20,000
Interest and dividend		75,000
Profit on sale of investments		15,000
Commission		1,75,000

[CA (IPCC) May 2013]

Solution

FORM B-RA NAME OF THE INSURER: M/S BACHAO INSURANCE CO. LTD.
REVENUE ACCOUNT FOR THE YEAR ENDED 31ST MARCH, 2013

Particulars	*Schedule*	₹
Premium earned (Net)	1	14,90,500
Profit on sale of investment		15,000
Interest, dividend and rent (Gross)		75,000
Total (A)		15,80,500
Claims incurred (Net)	2	10,12,500
Commission	3	1,75,000
Operatinq expenses related to insurance business	4	3,75,000
Total (B)		15,62,500
Operating Profit for Fire Insurance Business (A-B)		18,000

SCHEDULE -1

Premium Earned (Net)	₹
Premium received	16,80,000
Less: Premium on reinsurance ceded	(1,12,500)
Less: Adjustment for change in reserve for Unexpired Risk	(77,000)
Net premium earned	14,90,500

SCHEDULE-2

Claim Incurred (Net)	₹
Claim paid	9,60,000
Add: Surveyor's fee & legal expenses paid for settlement of claim	45,000
Add: Outstanding claims at the end	1,35,000
Less: Outstanding claims in the beg.	(97,500)
Claim incurred (Net)	10,12,500

SCHEDULE-3

Commission	₹
Commission paid	1,75,000

SCHEDULE-4

Operating expenses related to insurance business	₹
Expenses of Management	4,20,000
Less: Surveyor's fee & legal expenses	(45,000)
	3,75,000

Working Note:

CALCULATION FOR CHANGE IN RESERVE FOR UNEXPIRED RISK

		₹
Unexpired risk reserve at the beginning (including additional reserve)		9,00,000
Less: Reserve for unexpired risk as at the end		
(40% of ₹ 15,67,500)	6,27,000	
Additional reserve at the end	3,50,000	(9,77,000)
Change in Provision for Unexpired Risk		77,000

LONG ANSWER PRACTICAL QUESTIONS

PROBLEM 10

Prepare Revenue Account in proper form for the year ended 31st March, 2013, from the following particulars related to Krishna General Insurance Co. for the year ended 2012 – 2013:

	Related to Direct business (₹)	*Related to Reinsurance (₹)*
Premiums:		
Amount received	30,00,000	2,40,000
Receivable at the beginning	1,80,000	24,000
Receivable at the end	2,40,000	36,000
Amount paid	–	3,60,000
Payable at the beginning	–	30,000
Payable at the end	–	42,000
Claims:		
Amount paid	18,00,000	1,80,000
Payable at the beginning	60,000	12,000
Payable at the end	1,20,000	18,000
Amount recovered	–	1,20,000
Receivable at the beginning	–	18,000
Receivable at the end	–	12,000
***Commission*:**		
Amount paid	72,000	10,800
Amount received	–	14,400

Additional information:

(*i*) Interest, dividend and rent received — 30,000

Income-tax in respect of above — 6,000

(*ii*) Management expenses including ₹ 12,000 related to legal expenses regarding claims 1,32,000

(*iii*) Provision for income tax existing at the beginning of the year was ₹ 1,95,000, the income-tax actually paid during the year ₹ 1,68,000 and the provision necessary at the year end ₹ 2,07,000.

(*iv*) The net premium income of the company during the previous year was ₹ 24,00,000 on which reserve for unexpired risk @ 50% and additional reserve @ 7 ½% was created. This year, the balance to be carried forward is 50% of net premium on reserve for unexpired risk and 5% on additional reserve. ***[CA (PCE) Nov 2008]***

Solution

FORM B – RA

NAME OF THE INSURER : KRISHNA GENERAL INSURANCE COMPANY

REGISTRATION NO. AND DATE OF REGISTRATION WITH IRDA : ....

Revenue Account for the year ended 31.3.2013

Particulars	*Schedule*	₹
1. Premium earned (Net)	1	27,03,000
2. Profit/Loss on sales/Redemption of investment	–	–
3. Other	–	–
4. Interest, dividend & rent (Gross)	–	30,000
Total (A)		27,33,000
1. Claims incurred (Net)	2	19,44,000
2. Commission	3	68,400
3. Operating expenses related to insurance business	4	1,20,000
Total (B)		21,32,400
Operating profit/Loss from insurance business (C) = (A – B)		6,00,600

Schedule – 1 Premium Earned (Net)

Particulars	₹
Premium received from direct business	30,60,000
Add: Premium on reinsurance accepted (2,40,000 + 36,000 – 24,000)	2,52,000
	33,12,000
Less: Premium on reinsurance ceded (3,60,000 + 42,000 – 30,000)	3,72,000
Net Premium	29,40,000
Adjustment for change in reserve for unexpired risk	2,37,000
Total premium earned (Net)	27,03,000

Schedule – 2 Claims Incurred (Net)

Particulars	₹
Claims paid (Direct)	18,00,000
Add: Legal expenses regarding claims	12,000
	18,12,000
Add: Reinsurance Accepted	1,80,000
	19,92,000
Less: Reinsurance ceded (1,20,000 + 12,000 –18,000)	1,14,000
	18,78,000
Add: Claims outstanding at the end (1,20,000 + 18,000)	1,38,000
	20,16,000
Less: Claims outstanding at the beginning (60,000 + 12,000)	72,000
Total Claim incurred	19,44,000

Schedule –3 Commission

Particulars	₹
Commission paid Direct	72,000
Add: Re-insurance accepted	10,800
	82,800
Less: Re-insurance ceded	14,400
Net Commission	68,400

Schedule – 4 Operating Expenses related to Insurance Business

Particulars	₹
Expenses of management (1,32,000 – 12,000)	1,20,000
	1,20,000

Working Notes :

(i) Calculation of premium received from direct business	₹
Premium on direct business	30,00,000
Add: Premium outstanding at the end	2,40,000
Less: Premium outstanding at the beginning	1,80,000
	30,60,000
(ii) Computation of change in reserve for unexpired risk	
Closing Reserve for unexpired risk (29,40,000 × 50%)	14,70,000
Add: Closing Additional reserve for unexpired risk (29,40,000 × 5%)	1,47,000
Less: Opening Reserve for unexpired risk (24,00,000 × 50%)	12,00,000
Opening Additional reserve for unexpired risk (24,00,000 × 7.5%)	1,80,000
	2,37,000

PROBLEM 11

On 31st March, 2013 the books ot Zee insurance company umuea, following particulars in respect of fire insurance:

Particulars	*Amount (₹)*
Reserve for unexpired risks on March 31, 2012	5,00,000
Additional reserve for unexpired risks on March 31, 2012	1,00,000
Premiums	11,20,000
Claims paid	6,40,000
Estimated liability in respect of outstanding claims:	
On March 31, 2012	65,000
On March 31, 2013	90,000
Expenses of management (including ₹.30,000 legal expenses paid in connection with the claims)	2,80,000
Interest and dividend	64,250
Income tax on the above	6,520
Profit on sale of investment	11,000
Commission paid	1,52,000

On 31st March, 2013 provide ₹ 5,60,000 as unexpired risk reserve and ₹ 75,000 as Additional reserve.

You are required to prepare the Fire Insurance Revenue account as per the regulations of IRDA, for the year ended 31st March, 2013. *[CA (PE-II) Nov. 2009]*

Solution

FORM B- RA

Name of the Insurer: Zee Insurance Company Limited

Registration No. and Date of registration with IRDA:.........................

REVENUE ACCOUNT FOR THE YEAR ENDED 31ST MARCH, 2013

Particulars	*Schedule*	*Amount (₹)*
Premium earned (net)	1	10,85,000
Profit or loss on Sale/Redemption of Investments		11,000
Others	–	
Interest, Dividend & Rent (gross)		64,250
Total (A)		11,60,250
Claims incurred (Net)	2	6,95,000
Commission	3	1,52,000
Operating expenses related to insurance	4	2,50,000
Total (B)		10,97,000
Operating Profit/loss from insurance business (B) – (A)		63,250

Schedule -1 Premium earned (net)

Particulars	₹
Premium received	11,20,000
Less: Adjustment for change in Reserve for Unexpired risk (as per W.N.)	35,000
Total premium earned	10,85,000

Schedule -2 Claims incurred (net)

Particulars	₹
Claims paid	6,40,000
Add: Legal expenses regarding claims	30,000
	6,70,000
Add: Claims outstanding at the end	90,000
	7,60,000
Less: Claims outstanding at the beginning	65,000
Particulars	6,95,000

Schedule -3 Commission

Particulars	₹
Commission paid	1,52,000
Schedule-4 Operating Expenses related to Insurance Business	
Expenses of management (₹.2,80,000 – ₹.30,000)	2,50,000

Working Note:

CALCULATION FOR CHANGE IN RESERVE FOR UNEXPIRED RISK

Particulars		₹
Opening Reserve for Unexpired Risk	5,60,000	
Opening Additional Reserve	75,000	6,35,000
Less: Closing Reserve for Unexpired Risk	5,00,000	
Closing Additional Reserve	1,00,000	(6,00,000)
		35,000

Note: *Interest and dividends are shown at gross value in Revenue account. Income tax on it will not be included in the Revenue account as it is the part of Profit and Loss account of an insurance company.*

13 Financial Statements of Electricity Companies

No Question has been asked so far on the basis of The Electricity Act, 2003 and Regulations 2009.

14 Accounting for Departments

SHORT ANSWER PRACTICAL QUESTIONS

PROBLEM 1

Goods are transfered from Department *P* to Department *Q* at a price 50% above cost. If closing stock of Department *Q* is ₹ 27,000, compute the amount of Stock Reserve. *[CA (IPC) Nov. 2009]*

Solution

Stock Reserve = ₹ 27,000 × 50/150 = ₹ 9,000

PROBLEM 2

Z Ltd. has three departments and submits the following information for the year ending on 31st March, 2013:

	A	*B*	*C*	*Total (₹)*
Purchases (units)	6,000	12,000	14,400	
Purchases (Amount)				6,00,000
Sales (Units)	6,120	11,520	14,976	
Selling Price (per unit) ₹	40	45	50	
Closing Stock (Units)	600	960	36	

You are required to prepare departmental trading account of Z Ltd., assuming that the rate of profit on sales is uniform in each case. *[CA (PE – II JUNE 2009)]*

Solution

Dr. **DEPARTMENTAL TRADING ACCOUNT** *Cr.*

Particulars	*A* ₹	*B* ₹	*C* ₹	*Particulars*	*A* ₹	*B* ₹	*C* ₹
To Opening Stock	11,520	8,640	12,240	By Sales	2,44,800	5,18,400	7,48,800
To Purchases	96,000	2,16,000	2,88,000	By Closing Stock	9,600	17,280	720
To Gross Profit	1,46,880	3,11,040	4,49,280				
	2,54,400	5,35,680	7,49,520		2,54,400	5,35,680	7,49,520

Working Notes:

(i) *Profit Margin Ratio*

	₹
Selling price of unit purchased:	
Department A (6,000 x 40)	2,40,000
Department B (12,000 x 45)	5,40,000
Department C (14,400 x 50)	7,20,000
Total Selling Price	15,00,000
Less Purchase (Cost) Value	6,00,000
Gross Profit	9,00,000

Profit Margin Ratio = (90,00,000/15,00,000) × 100 = 60%

(II) STATEMENT SHOWING DEPARTMENT-WISE PER UNIT COST AND PURCHASE COST

	A	B	C
Selling Price (Per unit) (₹)	40	45	50
Less: Profit Margin @ 60% (₹)	(24)	(27)	(30)
Purchase Price per unit (₹)	16	18	20
Number of units purchased	6,000	12,000	14,400
(Purchased cost per unit X Units purchased)	96,000	2,16,000	2,88,000

(III) STATEMENT SHOWING CALCULATION OF DEPARTMENT-WISE OPENING STOCK (IN UNITS)

	A	B	C
Selling (Units)	6,120	11,520	14,976
Add: Closing Stock (Units)	600	960	36
Less: Purchases (Units)	(6,000)	(12,000)	(14,400)
Opening Stock (Units)	720	480	612

(IV) STATEMENT SHOWING DEPARTMENT-WISE COST OF OPENING STOCK & CLOSING STOCK

	A	B	C
Cost of Opening Stock	₹ 11,520 (₹ 720 x 16)	₹ 8,640 (₹ 480 x 18)	₹ 12,240 (₹ 612 x 20)
Cost of Closing Stock	₹ 9,600 (₹ 600 x 16)	17,280 (₹ 960 x 18)	720 (₹ 36 x 20)

PROBLEM 3

Brahma Limited has three departments and submits the following information for the year ending on 31st March, 2013:

Particulars	A	B	C	*Total (₹)*
Purchases (units)	5,000	10,000	15,000	
Purchases (Amount)				8,40,000
Sales (units)	5,200	9,800	15,300	
Selling price (₹ per unit)	40	45	50	
Closing Stock (Units)	400	600	700	

Required: Prepare departmental trading account of Brahma Limited assuming that the rate of profit on sales is uniform in each case. ***[CA (IPCC) May 2011]***

Solution

Dr. **DEPARTMENTAL TRADING ACCOUNT FOR THE YEAR ENDED 31ST MARCH, 2013** *Cr.*

Particulars	*A* ₹	*B* ₹	*C* ₹	*Particulars*	*A* ₹	*B* ₹	*C* ₹
To Opening Stock	14,400	10,800	30,000	By Sales	2,08,000	4,41,000	7,65,000
To Purchases	1,20,000	2,70,000	4,50,000	By Closing stock	9,600		21,000
To Gross profit	83,200	1,76,400	3,06,000				
	2,17,600	4,57,200	7,86,000		2,17,600	4,57,200	7,86,000

Working Notes:

(I) GROSS PROFIT RATIO

Selling price of units purchased:		₹
Department A	(5,000 units × ₹ 40)	2,00,000
Department B	(10,000 units × ₹ 45)	4,50,000
Department C	(15,000 units × ₹ 50)	7,50,000
Total selling price of purchased units		14,00,000
Less: Purchases		(8,40,000)
Gross profit		5,60,000

$$\text{Gross Profit Ratio} = \frac{\text{Gross profit}}{\text{Selling price}} \times 100 = \frac{5,60,000}{14,00,000} \times 100 = 40\%$$

(II) STATEMENT SHOWING DEPARTMENT-WISE PER UNIT COST & PURCHASE COST

Particulars	*A*	*B*	*C*
Selling price per unit (₹)	40	45	50
Less: Profit margin @ 40% (₹)	(16)	(18)	(20)
Purchase price per unit (₹)	24	27	30
No. of units purchased	5,000	10,000	15,000
Purchases (purchase cost per unit × units purchased)	1,20,000	2,70,000	4,50,000

(III) STATEMENT SHOWING CALCULATION OF DEPARTMENT-WISE OPENING STOCK (IN UNITS)

Particulars	*A*	*B*	*C*
Sales (Units)	5,200	9,800	15,300
Add: Closing Stock (Units)	400	600	700
	5,600	10,400	16,000
Less: Purchases (Units)	(5,000)	(10,000)	(15,000)
Opening Stock (Units)	600	400	1,000

(VI) STATEMENT SHOWING DEPARTMENT-WISE COST OF OPENING AND CLOSING STOCK

Particulars	*A*	*B*	*C*
Cost of Opening Stock (₹)	600 × 24	400 × 27	1,000 × 30
	14,400	10,800	30,000
Cost of Closing Stock (₹)	400 × 24	600 × 27	700 × 30
	9,600	16,200	21,000

PROBLEM 4

X Ltd. has three departments A, B and C. From the particulars given below compute:

(a) the values of stock as on 31st March 2013 and

(b) the departmental results

(i)

	A ₹	*B* ₹	*C* ₹
Opening Stock	24,000	36,000	12,000
Purchases	1,46,000	1,24,000	48,000
Actual Sales	1,72,500	1,59,400	74,600
Gross Profit on normal selling price	20%	25%	33.1/3%

(ii) During the year certain items were sold at discount and these discounts were reflected in the value of sales shown above. The items sold at discount were:

	A ₹	B ₹	C ₹
Sales at normal price	10,000	3,000	1,000
Sales at actual price	7,500	2,400	600

[PCC (May 2012)]

Solution

1. CALCULATION OF DEPARTMENTAL RESULTS (ACTUAL GROSS PROFIT)

Particulars	*A (₹)*	*B (₹)*	*C (₹)*
Actual Sales	1,72,500	1,59,400	74,600
Add back: Discount	2,500	600	400
Normal Sale	1,75,000	1,60,000	75,000
Gross Profit % on normal Sales	20%	25%	33.33%
Normal Gross Profit	35,000	40,000	25,000
Less: Discount	(2,500)	(600)	(400)
Actual Gross Profit	32,500	39,400	24,600

2. COMPUTATION OF VALUE OF STOCK AS ON 31ST MARCH, 2013

Particulars	*A (₹)*	*B (₹)*	*C (₹)*
Opening Stock	24,000	36,000	12,000
Add: Purchases	1,46,000	1,24,000	48,000
	1,70,000	1,60,000	60,000
Add: Actual Gross Profit	32,500	39,400	24,600
	2,02,500	1,99,400	84,600
Less: Actual Sales	(1,72,500)	(1,59,400)	(74,600)
Closing Stock as on 31.12.2011 (bal Fig.)	30,000	40,000	10,000

Working Note:

COMPUTATION OF DISCOUNT ON SALES

Particulars	*A (₹)*	*B (₹)*	*C (₹)*
Sales at normal price	10,000	3,000	1,000
Less: Sales at actual price	(7,500)	(2,400)	(600)
	2,500	600	400

LONG ANSWER PRACTICAL QUESTIONS

PROBLEM 5

Siva Ltd. has two departments *X* and *Y*. From the following particulars prepare departmental trading accounts and General Profit and Loss Account for the year ending 31st March. 2013:

	Department *X* ₹	Department *Y* ₹
Opening Stock (at cost)	80,000	48,000
Purchases	3,68,000	2,72,000
Carriage inward	8,000	8,000
Wages	48,000	32,000
Sales	5,60,000	4,48,000
Purchased good transferred		
By department *Y* to *X*	40,000	-
By department *X* to *Y*	–	32,000
Finished goods transferred		
By department *Y* to *X*	1,40,000	–
By department *X* to *Y*	–	1,60,000
Return of finished goods		
By department *Y* to *X*	40,000	–
By department *X* to *Y*	–	28,000
Closing stock		
Purchased goods	18,000	24,000
Finished goods	96,000	56,000

Purchased goods have been transferred mutually at their respective departmental purchase cost and finished goods at departmental market price and that 25% of the closing finished stock with each department represents finished goods received from the other department. *[CA (PCC) May 2010]*

Solution

DEPARTMENTAL TRADING ACCOUNT OF SIVA LTD.

for the year ended 31st March 2013

Dr. *Cr.*

Particulars	*Department X* ₹	*Department Y* ₹	*Particulars*	*Department X* ₹	*Department Y* ₹
To Opening Stock	80,000	48,000	By Sales	5,60,000	4,48,000
To Purchases	3,68,000	2,72,000	By Transfers:		
To Carriage inward	8,000	8,000	Purchased goods	32,000	40,000
To Wages	48,000	32,000	Finished goods	1,20,000*	1,12,000*
To Transfers:			By Closing Stock:		
Purchased goods	40,000	32,000	Purchased goods	18,000	24,000
Finished goods	1,12,000	1,20,000	Finished goods	96,000	56,000
To Gross Profit c/d	1,70,000	1,68,000			
	8,26,000	6,80,000		8,26,000	6,80,000

*Net transfers of finished goods by

Department *X* to *Y* = ₹.1,60,000 – ₹ 40,000 = ₹ 1,20,000

Department *Y* to *X* = ₹ 1,40,000 – ₹ 28,000 = ₹ 1,12,000

PROFIT AND LOSS ACCOUNT

Dr. ***for the year ended 31st March, 2013*** Cr.

Particulars	₹	*Particulars*	₹
To Provision for unrealized profit included in Closing Stock:		By Gross Profit b/d:	
Department X	1,70,000	Department X	7,200
Department Y	1,68,000	Department Y	3,500
To Net Profit	3,27,300		
	3,38,000		3,38,000

Working Notes:

(i) *Calculation of Rates of Gross Profit Margin on Sales*

	Department X ₹	*Department Y* ₹
Sales	5,60,000	4,48,000
Add: Transfer of finished goods	1,60,000	1,40,000
	7,20,000	5,88,000
Less: Return of finished goods	(40,000)	(28,000)
	6,80,000	5,60,000
Gross Profit	1,70,000	1,68,000
Gross Profit Margin =	$\frac{1,70,000}{6,80,000}\times 100 = 25\%$	$\frac{1,68,000}{5,60,000}\times 100 = 30\%$

(ii) *Finished goods from other department included in the Closing Stock*

	Department X ₹	*Department Y* ₹
Stock of Finished goods	96,000	56,000
Stock related to other department (25% of finished goods)	24,000	14,000

(iii) Unrealized profit included in the closing stock

Department X = 30% of ₹ 24,000 = ₹ 7,200

Department Y = 25% of ₹ 14,000 = ₹ 3,500

PROBLEM 6

Mis. AM Enterprise had two departments, Cloth and Readymade Clothes. The readymade clothes were made by the firm itself out of the cloth supplied by the Cloth Department at its usual selling price. From the following figures, prepare Departmental Trading and Profit & Loss Account for the year ended 31st March, 2013:

	Cloth Department ₹	Readymade Clothes Department ₹
Opening Stock on 1st April, 2012	31,50,000	5,32,000
Purchases	2,10,00,000	1,68,000
Sales	2,31,00,000	47,25,000
Transfer to Readymade Clothes Department	31,50,000	—
Manufacturing expenses	—	6,30,000
Selling expenses	2, 10,000	73,500
Rent & warehousing	8,40,000	5,60,000
Stockon 31st March, 2013	21,00,000	6,72,000

In addition to the above, the following information is made available for necessary consideration:

The stock in the Readymade Clothes Department may be considered as consisting of 75% cloth and 25% other expenses. The Cloth Department earned a gross profit at the rate of 15% in 2011-12. General expenses of the business as a whole amount to ₹ 10,85,000. *[CA (IPCC) Nov., 2011]*

Solution

(a) **DEPARTMENTAL TRADING AND PROFIT AND LOSS ACCOUNT**

Dr. *for the year ended 31st March, 2013* **Cr.**

Particulars	Cloth (₹)	Ready-made Clothes (₹)	Total (₹)	Particulars	Cloth (₹)	Ready-made Clothes (₹)	Total (₹)
To Opening stock	31,50,000	5,32,000	36,82,000	By Sales	2,31,00,000	47,25,000	2,78,25,000
To Purchases	2,10,00,000	1,68,000	2,11,68,000	By Transferto Ready-made Clothes Deptt.	31,50,000	—	31,50,000
To Transfer from Cloth Department	—	31,50,000	31,50,000	By Closing from Cloth Stock	21,00,000	6,72,000	27,72,000
To Manufacturing expenses	—	6,30,000	6,30,000				
To Gross profit c/d	42,00,000	9,17,000	51,17,000				
	2,83,50,000	53,97,000	3,37,47,000		2.83.50.000	53.97.000	3.37.47.000
To Sellingexpenses	2,10,000	73,500	2,83,500	By Gross profit b/d	42,00,000	9,17,000	51,17,000
To Rent & warehousing	8,40,000	5,60,000	14,00,000				
To Net profit	31,50,000	2,83,500	34,33,500				
	42,00,000	9,17,000	51,17,000		42,00,000	9,17,000	51,17,000

Dr. **GENERAL PROFIT AND LOSS ACCOUNT** *Cr.*

Particulars	₹	Particulars	₹
To General Expenses	10,85,000	By Net Profit	34,33,500
To Stock Reserve on Closing Stock	80,640	By Stock Reserve on Opening Stock (No longer required)	59,850
To General Net Profit (Bal. fig.)	23,27,710		
	34,93,350		34,93,350

Working Note: **Calculation of Stock Reserve**

$$\text{Gross Profit Ratio of Cloth Department} = \frac{\text{Gross Proflt}}{\text{Total Sales}} \times 100$$

$$= \frac{\text{Rs } 42,00,000}{\text{Rs } (2,31,000 + 31,50,000)} \times 100 = 16\%$$

Stock Reserve on Closing Stock = ₹ 6,72,000 × 75% × 16% = ₹ 80,640

Stock reserve on opening stock = (₹ 5,32,000 × 75% × 15%) = ₹ 59,850

PROBLEM 7

Department R sells goods to Department S at a profit of 25% on cost and Department T at 10% profit on cost. Department S sells goods to R and T at a profit of 15% and 20% on sales respectively. Department T charges 20% and 25% profit on cost to Department R and S respectively.

Department managers are entitled to 10% commission on net profit subject to unrealized profit on departmental sales being eliminated. Departmental profits after charging manager's commission, but before adjustment of unrealized profit are as under.

		₹
Department	*R*	54,000
Department	*S*	40,500
Department	*T*	27,000

STOCK LYING AT DIFFERENT DEPARTMENTS AT THE END OF THE YEAR ARE AS UNDER:

	Deptt. R ₹	*Deptt. S* ₹	*Deptt. T* ₹
Transfer from Department R	–	22,500	16,500
Transfer from Department S	21,000	–	18,000
Transfer from Department T	9,000	7,500	–

[CA (IPCC) Nov. 2010]

Find out the correct departmental profits after charging manager's commission.

Solution

CALCULATION OF CORRECT DEPARTMENTAL PROFITS AFTER CHARGING DEPARTMENTAL MANAGER'S COMMISSION

Particulars	*Departments* R ₹	S ₹	T ₹
Profit	54,000	40,500	27,000
Add: Managerial commission (1/9)	6,000	4,500	3,000
	60,000	45,000	30,000
Less: Unrealised profit on stock	(6,000)	(6,750)	(3,000)
	54,000	38,250	27,000
Less: Managers'Commission @ 10%	5,400	3,825	2,700
	48,600	34,425	24,300

***Working Notes:* Amount of Unrealised Profit**

Transfer by Department R to

S department (22,500 × 25/125)	= 4,500
T department 16,500 × 10/110)	= 1,500
	6,000

Transfer by department S to

R department (21,000 x 15/100)	= 3,150
T department (18,000 x 20/100)	= 3,600
	6,750

Transfer by department T to

R department (9,000 x 20/120)	= 1,500
S department (7,500 × 25/125)	= 1,500
	3,000

PROBLEM 8

Department *X* sells goods to Department *Y* at a profit of 20% on cost and to Department *Z* at 15% profit on cost. Department *Y* sells goods to *X* and *Z* at a profit of 10% and 20% on sales, respectively. Department *Z* charges 15% and 10% profit on cost to Department *X* and *Y*, respectively.

Department Managers are entitled to 10% commission on net profit after eliminating unrealised profit on departmental sales being eliminated. Departmental profits after charging Managers' commission, but before adjustment of unrealised profit are as under:

	₹
Department *X*	36,000
Department *Y*	27,000
Department *Z*	18,000

Stocks lying at different departments at the end of the year are as under:

	Dept. X ₹	*Dept. Y* ₹	*Dept. Z* ₹
Transfer from Department *X*	—	7,200	5,750
Transfer from Department *Y*	19,000	—	15,000
Transfer from Department *Z*	4,600	3,300	—

Required: Find out the correct departmental Profits after charging Managers' commission. ***[CA (IPCC) Nov. 2013]***

Solution

CALCULATION OF CORRECT DEPARTMENTAL PROFITS AFTER CHARGING DEPARTMENTAL MANAGER'S COMMISSION

Particulars	*Deptt. X* (₹)	*Deptt. Y* (₹)	*Deptt. Z* (₹)
Profit after charging managers' commission	36,000	27,000	18,000
Add: Managers' commission (1/9)	4,000	3,000	2,000
Profit before commission & unrealised profit	40,000	30,000	20,000
Less: Unrealised profit on stock	(1,950)	(4,900)	(900)
Profit before Manager's Commission	38,050	25,100	19,100
Less: Commission of Departmental Managers @10%	(3,805)	(2,510)	(1,910)
Correct Departmental Profits	34,245	22,590	17,190

Working Note:

UNREALISED PROFIT ON STOCK

Particulars	*Department X* ₹	*Department Y* ₹	*Department Z* ₹	*Total* ₹
Unrealised Profit of Department *X*	—	1/6 of 7,200 = 1,200	15/115 of 5,750 = 750	1,950
Unrealised Profit of Department *Y*	10% of 19,000 = 1,900	—	20% of 15,000 = 3,000	4,900
Unrealised Profit of Department *Z*	15/115 of 4,600 = 600	1/11 of 3,300 = 300	—	900

15 Accounting for Branches

DEPENDENT BRANCH—DEBTORS METHOD

PROBLEM 1

Widespread Ltd. invoices goods to its branch at cost *plus* 20%. The branch sells goods for cash as well as on credit. The branch meets its expenses out of cash collected from its debtors and cash sales and remits the balance of cash to head office after withholding ₹ 10,000 necessary for meeting immediate requirements of cash. On 31st March, 2012 the assets at the branch were as follows:

	₹('000)
Cash in Hand	10
Trade Debtors	384
Stock, at Invoice Price	1,080
Furniture and Fittings	500

During the accounting year ended 31st March, 2013 the invoice price of goods dispatched by the head office to the branch amounted to ₹ 1 crore 32 lakhs. Out of the goods received by it, the branch sent back to head office invoiced at ₹ 72,000. Other transactions at the branch during the year were as follows:

	₹('000)
Cash Sales	9,700
Credit Sales	3,140
Cash collected by Branch from Credit Customers	2,842
Cash Discount allowed to Debtors	58
Returns by Customers	102
Bad Debts written off	37
Expenses paid by Branch	842

On 1st January, 2013 the branch purchased new furniture for ₹ 1 lakh for which payment was made by head office through a cheque.

On 31st March, 2013 branch expenses amounting to ₹ 6,000 were outstanding and cash in hand was again ₹ 10,000. Furniture is subject to depreciation @ 16% per annum on diminishing balance method.

Required: Prepare Branch Account in the books of head office for the year ended 31st March, 2013. ***[CA (May 2001)]***

Solution

BRANCH ACCOUNT IN THE HEAD OFFICE BOOKS

Dr. *for the year ended 31st March, 2013* *Cr.*

Particulars	₹'000	Particulars	₹'000
To Balance b/d:		By Balance b/d	
Cash in Hand	10	Stock Reserve (₹ 1,080 × 20/120)	180

Trade Debtors	384	By Goods sent to branch A/c	72
Stock	1,080	(Returns to H.O.)	
Furniture and Fittings	500	By Goods sent to branch A/c	2,188
To Goods sent to branch A/c	13,200	(Loading on net goods sent	
To Bank A/c (Payment for Furniture)	100	(₹ 13,128 x 20/120)	
To Balance c/d		By Bank A/c	
Stock Reserve (₹.1,470 x 20/120)	245	(Remittance from branch to H.O.)	11,700
Outstanding Expenses	6	By Balance c/d:	
To Profit and Loss A/c (Net Profit)	1,096	Cash in hand	10
		Trade debtors	485
		Stock	1,470
		Furniture and fittings	516
	16,621		16,621

Working Notes:

Dr. **(I) BRANCH STOCK ACCOUNT** Cr.

Particulars	₹ ('000)	Particulars	₹ ('000)
To Balance b/d	1,080	By Goods sent to branch	72
To Goods sent to branch	13,200	By Branch Cash	9,700
To Branch debtors	102	By Branch Debtors	3,140
		By Balance c/d (b.f.)	1,470
	14,382		14,382

Dr. **(II) BRANCH DEBTORS ACCOUNT** Cr.

Particulars	₹ ('000)	Particulars	₹ ('000)
To Balance b/d	384	By Balance Branch	2,842
To Branch Stock	3,140	By Branch Expenses Discount	58
		By Branch Stock (Returns)	102
		By Branch Expenses (Bad Debts)	37
		By Balance c/d (b.f.)	485
	3,524		3,524

Dr. **(III) BRANCH FURNITURE AND FITTINGS ACCOUNT** Cr.

Particulars	₹ ('000)	Particulars	₹ ('000)
To Balance b/d	500	By Depreciation (80 + 4)	84
To Bank	100	By Balance c/d (b.f.)	516
	600		600

Dr. **(IV) BRANCH CASH ACCOUNT** Cr.

Particulars	₹ ('000)	Particulars	₹ ('000)
To Balance b/d	10	By Branch Expenses	842
To Branch Stock	9,700	By Remittances to H.O.	11,700
To Branch Debtors	2,842	By Balance c/d	10
	12,552		12,552

PROBLEM 2

Pawan & Co. of Delhi has a branch at Jaipur. Goods are invoiced to the branch at cost *plus* 25%. The branch is instructed to deposit the receipts everyday in the head office account with the bank. All the expenses are paid through cheque by the head office except petty cash expenses which are paid by the Branch. From the following information, you are required to prepare Branch Account in the books of Head office for the year ending 31st March, 2013:

	₹
Opening Stock at invoice price	1,64,000
Closing Stock at invoice price	1,92,000
Opening Debtors	63,400
Closing Debtors	84,300
Opening Furniture & fixtures	46,800
Cash sales	8,02,600
Credit sales	7,44,200
Goods invoiced to branch by head office	12,56,000
Expenses paid by h ead office	2,64,000
Petty expenses paid by the branch	20,900
Furniture acquired by the branch on 1.10.12 (payment was made by the branch from cash sales and collection from debtors)	5,000

Depreciation to be provided on branch furniture & fixtures @ 10% p.a. on WDV basis.

[CA (PCC) Nov. 2009]

Solution

Dr. **JAIPUR BRANCH ACCOUNT** *Cr.*

Particulars	₹	*Particulars*	₹
To Opening Balances:		By Branch stock reserve	32,800
Branch Stock A/c	1,64,000	By Bank A/c	15,00,000
Branch Debtors A/c	63,400	By Goods Sent to branch A/c	2,51,200
Branch Furniture A/c	46,800	(Loading)	
To Goods sent to branch	12,56,000	By Closing Balances:	
To Bank A/c (branch expenses)	2,64,000	Branch Stock A/c	1,92,000
To Branch Stock Reserve A/c	38,400	Branch Debtors A/c	84,000
To Profit and Loss A/c (Bal. Fig.)	2,74,570	Branch Furniture A/c	46,870
	21,07,170		21,07,170

Working Notes:

(i) Depreciation on Furniture = (₹ 46,800 × 10/100) + (5,000 × 10/100 × 6/12) = ₹ 4,930

Dr. **(ii) BRANCH FURNITURE ACCOUNT** *Cr.*

Particulars	₹	*Particulars*	₹
To Balance b/d	46,800	By Depreciation A/c	4,930
To Bank A/c (Purchases)	5,000	BY balance c/d	46,870
	51,800		51,800

Dr. **(iii) BRANCH BEBTORS ACCOUNT** Cr.

Particulars	₹	Particulars	₹
To Balance b/d	63,400	By Bank A/c (Bal. Fig.)	7,23,300
To Sales	7,44,200	By Balance c/d	84,300
	8,07,600		8,07,600

(iv) Cash remitted by the branch to head office

Cash sales + Collection from debtors – Petty expenses – Furniture acquired by branch

= ₹ 8,02,600 + ₹ 7,23,300 – ₹ 20,900 – ₹ 5,000 = ₹.15,00,000

PROBLEM 3

XYZ Company is having its Branch at Kolkata. Goods are invoiced to the branch at 20% profit on sale. Branch has been instructed to send all cash daily to head office. All expenses are paid by head office except petty expenses which are met by the Branch Manager. From the following particulars prepare Branch Account in the books of Head Office.

Liabilities	₹	Assets	₹
Opening Stock (invoice price)	30,000	Discount allowed to debtors	160
Opening Sundry Debtors	18,000	Expenses paid by head office:	
Opening Cash in hand	800	Rent	1,800
Opening Office Furniture	3,000	Salary	3,200
Goods invoiced from the head office (invoice price)	1,60,000	Stationery & Printing	800
		Petty expenses paid by the branch	600
Goods return to Head Office	2,000	Depreciation to be provided	
Goods return by debtors	960	on branch furniture at 10% p.a.	
Cash received from debtors	60,000	Closing Stock (at invoice price)	28,000
Cash Sales	1,00,000	Credit sales	60,000

[CA (IPCC) May 2011]

Solution

Dr. **KOLKATA BRANCH ACCOUNT IN THE BOOKS OF HEAD OFFICE** Cr.

Particulars		₹	Particulars		₹
To Balance b/d:			By Stock Reserve (opening)		6,000
Stock		30,000	By Remittances:		
Debtors		18,000	Cash Sales	1,00,000	
Cash in hand		800	Cash from Debtors	60,000	1,60,000
Furniture		3,000	By Goods sent to branch (loading)		32,000
To Goods sent to branch A/c		1,60,000	By Goods returned by		
To Goods returned by branch (loading)		400	branch (Return to H.O.)		2,000
To Bank (expenses paid by H.O.)			By Balance c/d:		
Rent	1,800		Stock		28,000
Salary	3,200		Debtors		16,880
			Cash (800 – 600)		200
Stationary & Printing	800	5,800	Furniture (3,000 – 300)		2,700
To Stock Reserve (closing)		5,600			
To Profit transferred to General Profits Loss A/c		24,180			
		2,47,780			2,47,780

Working Note:

Dr. **DEBTORS ACCOUNT** *Cr.*

Particulars	₹	*Particulars*	₹
To Balance b/d	18,000	By Cash A/c	60,000
To Sales A/c (credit)	60,000	By Sales Return A/c	960
		By Discount allowed A/c	160
		By Balance c/d	16,880
	78,000		78,000

Note: It is assumed that goods returned by branch are at invoice price.

PROBLEM 4

CAMIB Ltd. had three branches at Coimbatore, Trivandrum and Bangalore. The Head Office at Madras purchases goods and sends them to branches, to be sold at a uniform percentage of profit on cost. The following particulars are made available to you to prepare a Combined Trading Account for the year ending on 31st March, 2013:

Particulars	*Madras (₹)*	*Coimbatore (₹)*	*Trivandrum (₹)*	*Banglore (₹)*
Opening Stock	54,000	16,000	12,500	10,000
Purchases in the year	2,74,000	—	—	—
Sales	—	1,80,000	1,20,000	1,00,000
Closing Stock	28,000	6,000	5,000	2,500
Branch Accounts on 1st April,				
Coimbatore	15,000			
Triovandrum	32,000			
Bangalore	4,000			
Remittances from Branches	3,20,000	1,50,000	1,00,000	70,000

Madras Office invoices goods to the branches at fixed sales prices but maintains branch accounts in its ledgers at cost price. Show Branch Accounts in Madras Head Office Books.

Solution

COMBINED TRADING ACCOUNT OF MADRAS OFFICE AND ITS BRANCHES

Dr. *for the year ending on 31st March, 2013* *Cr.*

Particulars	*Madras H.O.* ₹	*Coim-batore* ₹	*Trivan-drum* ₹	*Bangalore* ₹	*Total* ₹
To Opening Stock at cost [See Working Note (iv)]	54,000	12,800	10,000	8,000	84,800
To Purchases	2,74,000	—	—	—	2,74,000
To Goods received from H.O. at cost (balancing figure)	—	1,36,000	90,000	74,000	3,00,000
To Gross Profit @ 20% on sales [See Working Note (i), (ii), (iii)]	—	36,000	24,000	20,000	80,000
	3,28,000	1,84,800	1,24,000	1,02,000	7,38,800
By Sales	—	1,80,000	1,20,000	1,00,000	4,00,000
By Goods sent to branch at cost	3,00,000	—	—	—	3,00,000
By Closing stock-at cost [See Working Note (iv)]	28,000	4,800	4,000	2,000	38,800
	3,28,000	1,84,800	1,24,000	1,02,000	7,38,800

Dr. **BRANCH ACCOUNT** Cr.

Particulars	Coimbatore ₹	Trivandrum ₹	Bangalore ₹	Particulars	Coimbatore ₹	Trivandrum ₹	Bangalore ₹
To Balance b/d	15,000	32,000	4,000	By Bank A/c	1,50,000	1,00,000	70,000
To Goods sent to branches —at cost	1,36,000	90,000	74,000	By Balance c/d (b.f)	37,000	46,000	28,000
To Combined Trading A/c— Gross profit	36,000	24,000	20,000				
	1,87,000	1,46,000	98,000		1,87,000	1,46,000	98,000

Working Notes:

(i) Dr. **STOCK ACCOUNT** Cr.

Particulars	₹	Particulars	₹
To Balance b/d	54,000	By Goods sent to Branches-at cost (balancing figure)	3,00,000
To Purchases	2,74,000	By Balance c/d	28,000
	3,28,000		3,28,000

(ii) *Computation of the amount of goods sent to branches at invoice price.*

Dr. **CONSOLIDATED BRANCH TRADING ACCOUNT** Cr.

Particulars	₹	Particulars	₹
To Opening Stock at branches (at invoice price)	38,500	By Sales	4,00,000
To Goods from H.O. (at invoice price) (b.f.)	3,75,000	By Closing Stock (at invoice price)	13,500
	4,13,500		4,13,500

(iii) *Computation of rate of profit added to the cost of goods sent to the branches:*

	₹
Goods sent to branches at invoice price	3,75,000
Less: Goods sent to branches at cost	(3,00,000)
Profit	75,000

Rate of profit at invoice price = (₹ 75,000/₹ 3,75,000) × 100 = 20%

(iv) *Valuation of Stock at cost*

	Opening Stock	*Closing Stock*
Coimbatore	[16,000 × 80/100] = ₹ 12,800	[6,000 × 80/100] = ₹ 4,800
Trivandrum	[12,500 × 80/100] = ₹ 10,000	[5,000 × 80/100] = ₹ 4,000
Bangalore	[10,000 × 80/100] = ₹ 8,000	[2,500 × 80/100] = ₹ 2,000

PROBLEM 5

LMN is having branch at Mumbai. Goods are invoiced to the Branch at 25% Profit on Sale. Branch has been instructed to send all cash daily to Head Office. All expenses are paid by Head Office except Petty Expenses, which are met by the Branch. From the following particulars, prepare Branch Account in the Books of Head Office:

Particulars	₹	Particulars	₹
Opening Stock (Invoice Price)	40,000	Credit Sales	70,000
Opening Sundry Debtors	25,000	Discount Allowed to Debetors	300
Opening Cash in Hand	1,000	Expenses Paid by Head Office:	
Opening Office Furntirue	4,000	Salary	4,000
Goods Invoiced from Head Office (Invoice Price)	1,80,000	Staff Welfare	750
Goods Return to Head Office	6,000	Telephone Expense	1,200
Goods Return by Debtors	1,250	Other Misc. Expenses paid by Branch	700
Cash Received from Debtors	65,000	Closing Stock (at Invoice Price)	35,000
Cash Sales	1,20,000	Depreciation to be provided on Branch Furniture	10%

[Nov. 2014]

Solution

Dr. **Branch Account in the books of Head Office** Cr.

Particulars		₹	Particulars		₹
To Balance b/d:			By Stock Reserve on Op Stock (₹ 40,000 × 25%)		10,000
– Stock	40,000		By Stock Reserve (₹ 1,80,000 × 25%)		45,000
– Debtors	25,000				
– Furniture	4,000		By Goods Sent to Branch A/c (Returns)		6,000
– Cash	1,000	70,000	By H.O Cash (65,000 + 1,20,000)		1,85,000
To Goods sent to Branch A/c		1,80,000			
To Stock Reserve (₹ 6,000 × 25%)		1,500	By balance c/d:		
To Bank A/c:			– Stock	35,000	
– Staff Welfare	750		– Debetors	28,450	
– Salary	4,000		– Cash (1,000 – 700)	300	
– Telephone	1,200	5,950	– Furniture (4,000 – 10%)	3,600	67,350
To Stock Reserve on Cl Stock (35,000 × 25%)		8,750			
To P & L A/c –		47,150			
		3,13,350			**3,13,350**

Working Notes:

1. BRANCH DEBETORS ACCOUNT (TO ASCERTAIN CLOSING DEBTORS)

Particulars	₹	Particulars	₹
To balance b/d	25,000	By Cash (Collections)	65,000
To Credit Sales	70,000	By Sales Returns	1,250
		By Discount Allowed	300
		By balance c/d **(balancing figure)**	**28,450**
	95,000		**95,000**

2. Depreciation on Furniture is not debited as a separate item in the Branch Account since the Furniture (Closing Balance) at the end is shown at the Depreciated Value.
3. Sales Returns and Discount are accounted for automatically since opening and Closing baliances of Debetors are state in the Branch Account.

DEPENDENT BRANCH—STOCK & DEBTORS METHOD

PROBLEM 6

Concept & Co., with its Head Office at Mumbai has a branch at Nagpur. Goods are invoiced to the Branch at cost *plus* 33-1/3%. The following information is given in respect of the branch for the year ended 31st March, 2013:

	₹
Goods sent to Branch (invoice price)	4,80,000
Opening Stock at Branch (invoice price)	24,000
Cash Sales	1,80,000
Return of goods by customers to the Branch	6,000
Branch expenses (paid in cash)	53,500
Opening Branch Debtors	30,000
Discount allowed	1,000
Bad debts	1,500
Collection from Debtors	2,70,000
Branch debtors cheques returned dishonoured	5,000
Closing Stock at Branch (invoice price)	48,000
Closing Branch Debtors	36,500

Prepare, under the Stock and Debtors system, the following Ledger Accounts in the books of the Head Office:

(i) Nagpur Branch Stock Account.

(ii) Nagpur Branch Debtors Account.

(iii) Nagpur Branch Adjustment Account.

[CA (PE-II) May 2006]

Solution

Dr. **NAGPUR BRANCH STOCK ACCOUNT** *Cr.*

Particulars	₹	*Particulars*		₹
To Balance b/d	24,000	By Bank A/c (Cash Sales)		1,80,000
To Goods Sent to Branch A/c	4,80,000	By Branch Debtors (Credit Sales)		2,80,000
To Branch Debtors	6,000	By Stock Shortage:		
		Branch P&L A/c	1,500	
		Branch Adjustment A/c (Loading)	500	2,000
		By Balance c/d		48,000
	5,10,000			5,10,000

Dr. **NAGPUR BRANCH DEBTORS ACCOUNT** *Cr.*

Particulars	₹	*Particulars*	₹
To Balance b/d	30,000	By Bank A/c (Collection)	2,70,000
To Bank A/c (Dishonour of cheques)	5,000	By Branch Stock A/c	6,000
To Branch Stock A/c (b.f.)	2,80,000	By Bad Debts	1,500
		By Discount allowed	1,000
		By Balance c/d	36,500
	3,15,000		3,15,000

Dr. **NAGPUR BRANCH ADJUSTMENT ACCOUNT** Cr.

Particulars	₹	Particulars	₹
To Branch Stock A/c (Loading of Loss)	500	By Stock Reserve A/c [₹ 24,000 × 25%]	6,000
To Stock Reserve [₹ 48,000 × 25%]	12,000	By Goods Sent to Branch A/c [₹ 4,80,000 × 25%]	1,20,000
To Gross Profit c/d	1,13,500		
	1,26,000		1,26,000
To Branch Stock A/c (Cost of Loss)	1,500	By Gross Profit b/d	1,13,500
To Branch Expenses [₹.53,500 + ₹.1,500 + ₹.1,000]	56,000		
To Net Profit t/f to General P&L A/c	56,000		
	1,13,500		1,13,500

PROBLEM 7

Ram Limited of Chennai has a branch at Nagpur to which office, goods are invoiced at cost *plus* 25%. The branch makes sales both for cash and on credit. Branch expenses are paid direct from Head Office and the branch has to remit all cash received into the Head Office Bank Account at Nagpur.

From the following details, relating to the year 2012-13, prepare the accounts in Head Office Ledger and ascertain Branch Profit as per stock and debtors method. Branch does not maintain any books of accounts, but sends weekly returns to head office:

	₹
Goods received from head office at invoice price	1,20,000
Returns to head office at invoice price	2,400
Opening Stock at Nagpur branch at invoice price	12,000
Sales during the year – Cash	40,000
Credit	72,000
Opening Debtors at Nagpur branch	14,400
Cash received from debtors	64,000
Discounts allowed to debtors	1,200
Bad debts during the year	800
Sales returns at Nagpur branch	1,600
Salaries and wages at branch	12,000
Rent, rates and faxes at branch	3,600
Office expenses at Nagpur branch	1,200
Closing Stock at branch at invoice price	24,000

[CA (IPCC) May 2010]

Solution

Dr. **NAGPUR BRANCH STOCK ACCOUNT** Cr.

Particulars	₹	Particulars	₹
To Balance b/d	12,000	By Goods sent to branch A/c (Returns)	2,400
To Goods sent to Branch A/c	1,20,000	By Bank A/c (Cash sales)	40,000
To Branch Bebtors A/c (Returns)	1,600	By Branch debtors A/c	72,000

To Branch Adjustment A/c (Surplus over Invoice Price)	4,800	(credit sales) By Balance c/d	24,000
	1,38,400		1,38,400

Dr. **NAGPUR BRANCH ADJUSTMENT ACCOUNT** Cr.

Particulars	₹	Particulars	₹
To Stock Reserve [₹ 24,000 × 20/100]	4,800	By Stock Reserve [₹ 12,000 × 20/120]	2,400
To Branch Profit & Loss A/c (Gross profit)	25,920	By Goods sent to branch A/c [₹ 1,17,600 × 20.120]	23,520
		By Branch Stock A/c	4,800
	30,720		30,720

Dr. **BRANCH PROFIT & LOSS ACCOUNT** Cr.

Particulars	₹	Particulars	₹
To Branch Expenses A/c	16,800	By Branch Adjustment A/c (Gross Profit)	25,920
To Branch Debtors A/c (Discount)	1,200		
To Branch Debtors A/c (Bad Debts)	800		
To Net Profit (transferred to Profit & Loss A/c)	7,120		
	25,920		25,920

Dr. **BRANCH EXPENSES ACCOUNT** Cr.

Particulars	₹	Particulars	₹
To Bank A/c (Rent, rates & taxes)	3,600	By Branch Profit and Loss A/c (Transfer)	16,800
To Bank A/c (Salaries & Wages)	12,000		
To Bank A/c (Office Expenses)	1,200		
	16,800		16,800

Dr. **BRANCH DEBTORS ACCOUNT** Cr.

Particulars	₹	Particulars	₹
To Balance b/d	14,400	By Bank A/c	64,000
To Branch Stock A/c	72,000	By Branch Profit and Loss A/c (Bad debts and discount)	2,000
		By Branch Stock A/c (Sales Returns)	1,600
		By Balance c/d (bal.fig.)	18,800
	86,400		86,400

Dr. **GOODS SENT TO BRANCH ACCOUNT** Cr.

Particulars	₹	Particulars	₹
To Branch Stock A/c	2,400	By Branch stock A/c	1,20,000
To Branch Adjustment A/c	23,520		
To Purchases A/c	94,080		
	1,20,000		1,20,000

PROBLEM 8

Neo Ltd., with headquarters at Mumbai, maintains a branch at Goa . Goods are invoiced at cost *plus* 25%. In respect of Goa branch, the following information pertaining to the year 'ended 31st March, 2013 are made available to you:

	₹
Goods sent to Branch (at Invoice price)	6,75,000
Goods returned by branch during the year (at Invoice price)	24,000
Cash sales effected by branch	1,85,000
Discount allowed to customers	2,500
Amount received from branch debtors	3,25,000
Cheques of customers which got dishonoured	8,000
Branch expenses met in cash	72,500
Sales return at Goa branch	10,000
Bad debts	5,500

	Closing	Opening
Branch debtors	1,05,000	50,000
Stock at branch (at Invoice price)	2,36,000	1,50,000

Adopting the Stock and debtors system, you are required to prepare the following Ledger accounts, as appearing in the books of the Head Office:

(i) Goa Branch Debtors Account;

(ii) Goa Branch Adjustment Account;

(iii) Goa Branch Profit and Loss Account. *[CA (PE-II) Nov. 2009]*

Solution

Dr. **GOA BRANCH DEBTORS ACCOUNT** Cr.

Particulars	₹	Particulars	₹
To Balance b/d	50,000	By Bank (Collection from debtors)	3,25,000
To Bank A/c (Dishonour of cheques)	8,000	By Branch Stock (Goods returned by customers)	10,000
To Branch Stock A/c (Credit sales)	3,90,000	By Bad debts	5,500
		By Discount allowed	2,500
		By Balance c/d	1,05,000
	4,48,000		4,48,000

Dr. **GOA BRANCH ADJUSTMENT ACCOUNT** Cr.

Particulars	₹	Particulars	₹
To Goods sent to Goa Branch A/c (goods returns to H.O.)	4,800	By Balance b/d (Opening stock reserve)	30,000
To Branch P & L A/c (Profit on sale at invoice price) (Bal. Fig.)	1,13,000	By Goods sent to Goa Branch A/c (Loading)	1,35,000
To Balance c/d (Closing Stock Reserve)	47,200		
	1,65,000		1,65,000

Dr. **GOA BRANCH PROFIT AND LOSS ACCOUNT FOR THE YEAR ENDING 31ST MARCH, 2013** Cr.

Particulars	₹	Particulars	₹
To Branch Expenses A/c	72,500	By Branch Adjustment A/c	1,13,000
To Branch Debtors - Discount	2,500		
Bad debts	5,500		
To Net Profit (Transferred to General Profit & Loss A/c)	32,500		
	1,13,000		1,13,000

Working Note :

Dr. **GOA BRANCH STOCK ACCOUNT** Cr.

Date	Particulars	₹	Date	Particulars	₹
	To Balance b/d	1,50,000		By Bank (Cash sales)	1,85,000
	To Goods sent to Goa Branch	6,75,000		By Branch Debtors (Credit sales)	3,90,000
	To Branch Debtors (Goods Returned)	10,000		By Goods sent to Goa Branch (Goods returned to H.O.)	24,000
	By Balance c/d	2,36,000			
		8,35,000			8,35,000

DEPENDENT BRANCH—WHOESALE BRANCH METHOD

PROBLEM 9

Rahul Limited operates a number of retail outlets to which goods are invoiced at wholesale price which is cost *plus* 25%. These outlets sell the goods at the retail price which is wholesale price *plus* 20%.

Following is the information regarding one of the outlets for the year ended 31.3.2013:

	₹
Opening Stock at the outlet	30,000
Goods invoiced to the outlet during the year	3,24,000
Gross profit made by the outlet	60,000
Goods lost by fire	?
Expenses of the outlet for the year	20,000
Closing Stock at the outlet	36,000

Required: Prepare the following accounts in the books of Rahul Limited for the year ended 31.3.2013:

(a) Outlet Stock Account.

(b) Outlet Profit & Loss Account.

(c) Stock Reserve Account. ***[CA (May 1997)]***

Solution

Dr. **Outlet Stock Account** *Cr.*

Particulars	₹	*Particulars*	₹
To Balance b/d	30,000	By Sales [₹ 60,000 × 150/25]	3,60,000
To Goods sent to outlet A/c	3,24,000	By Goods Lost by fire [b.f]	18,000
To Gross Profit c/d	60,000	By Balance c/d	36,000
	4,14,000		4,14,000

Dr. **Outlet Profit & Loss Account** *Cr.*

Particulars	₹	*Particulars*	₹
To Expenses	20,000	By Gross Profit b/d	60,000
To Goods lost by fire	18,000		
To Profit Transferred	22,000		
	60,000		60,000

Dr. **Stock Reserve Account** *Cr.*

Particulars	₹	*Particulars*	₹
To HO P&L A/c (Transfer)	6,000	By Balance b/d [₹ 30,000 × 25/125]	6,000
To Balance c/d	7,200	By HO P&L A/c [₹ 36,000 × 25/125]	7,200
	13,200		13,200

Working Note: Cost-Price Relationship

	₹
A. Cost	100
B. *Add:* Wholesale Profit	25
C. Wholesale Price [A + B]	125
D. *Add:* Retail Profit + [20% of 125]	25
E. Retail Price	150

PROBLEM 10

Following is the information of the Jammu branch of Best Ltd., New Delhi for the year ending 31st March, 2013 from the following:

(1) Goods are invoiced to the branch at cost *plus* 20%

(2) The sale price is cost *plus* 50%.

(3) Other informations:

Opening Stock	₹ 2,20,000
Goods sent during the year	₹ 11,00,000
Sales during the year	₹ 2,00,000
Expenses incurred at the branch	₹ 45,000

Ascertain:

(i) the profit earned by the branch during the year

(ii) branch stock reserve in respect of unrealized profit.

[CA (IPCC) Nov. 2010]

Solution

(a) (i) Calculation of Profit earned by the branch

Dr. **Jammu Branch Trading Account** *Cr.*

Particulars	₹	*Particulars*	₹
To Opening Stock	2,20,000	By Sales	12,00,000
To Goods received by Head office	11,00,000	By Closing stock	3,60,000
To Expenses	45,000		
To Gross Profit	1,95,000		
	15,60,000		**15,60,000**

(ii) Stock reserve in respect of unrealised profit = ₹ 3,60,000 × (20/120) = 60,000

(iii) Calculation of Closing Stock at Invoice Price

Opening Stock at invoice price	2,20,000	
Goods received during the year at invoice price	11,00,000	
	13,20,000	
Less: Cost of goods sold at invoice price	(9,60,000)	[12,00,000 x (120/150)]
Closing Stock	**3,60,000**	

Note : It is assumed that all figures given in the questions is at invoice price.

PROBLEM 11

A Limited has retail branch at Noida. Goods are sold to customers at cost plus 100%. The wholesale price is cost plus 80%. Goods are invoiced to Noida at wholesale price. From the following particulars, find out the profit made by the Head Office and Noida Branch for the year ended 31st March, 2013 using invoice method.

	Head Office ₹	Noida ₹
Opening Stock	50,000	—
Purchases	3,00,000	—
Goods sent to branch (at invoice value)	1,08,000	—
Sales	3,06,000	1,00,000
Expenses	90,000	4,000

Sales at Head Office are made only on wholesale basis and sales at branch are made only to customers. Stock at branch is valued at invoice price. ***[CA (PCC) May 2011]***

Solution

TRADING ACCOUNT FOR THE YEAR ENDED 31ST MARCH, 2013

Dr. *Cr.*

Particulars	*HO* ₹	*Branch* ₹	*Particulars*	*HO* ₹	*Branch* ₹
To Opening Stock	50,000	—	By Sales	3,06,000	1,00,000
To Purchases	3,00,000	—	By Goods sent to Branch	1,08,000	—
To Goods received from Head Office	—	1,08,000	By Closing Stock	1,20,000	18,000
To Gross Profit	1,84,000	10,000			
	5,34,000	1,18,000		5,34,000	1,18,000

PROFIT AND LOSS A/C FOR THE YEAR ENDED 31ST MARCH, 2013

Dr. *Cr.*

Particulars	₹	₹	*Particulars*	₹	₹
To Expenses	90,000	4,000	By Gross Profit	1,84,000	10,000
To Stock Reserve against Branch $\left(18,000 \times \frac{80}{180}\right)$	8 000	—			
To Net Profit	86,000	6,000			
	184,000	10,000		184,000	10,000

***Working Note:* Calculation of Closing Stock**

Particulars	Head Office ₹	Noida Branch ₹
Opening Stock	50,000	—
Goods purchased or Received from Head Office	3,00,000	1,08,000
Less: Cost of Goods sold or sent to Branch:		
Head Office [3,06,000 + 1,08,000) x 100/180]	(2,30,000)	
Branch 1,00,000 × 180/200]		(90,000)
Value of Closing Stock	1,20,000	18,000

PROBLEM 12

Beta Ltd. having head office at Mumbai has a branch at Nagpur. The head office does wholesale trade only at cost *plus* 80%. The goods are sent to branch at the wholesale price viz., cost *plus* 80%. The branch at Nagpur is wholly engaged in retail trade and the goods are sold at cost to H.O. *plus* 100%.

Following details are furnished for the year ended 31st March, 2013:

	Head Office ₹	*Branch* ₹
Opening Stock	2,25,000	—
Purchases	25,50,000	—
Goods sent to branch (Cost to H.O. plus 80%)	9,54,000	—
Sales	27,81,000	9,50,000
Office Expenses	90,000	8,500
Selling Expenses	72,000	6,300
Staff Salary	65,000	12,000

Required: Prepare Trading and Profit and Loss Account of the head office and branch for the year ended 31st March, 2013. ***[CA (PCC) Nov. 2007]***

Solution

TRADING AND PROFIT AND LOSS A/C OF BETA LTD.

Dr. *for the year ended 31st March 2013* *Cr.*

Particulars	*Head Office* ₹	*Branch* ₹	*Particulars*	*Head Office* ₹	*Branch* ₹
To Opening Stock	2,25,000	—	By Sales	27,81,000	9,50,000
To Purchases	25,50,000	—	By Goods sent to branch	9,54,000	—
To Goods received from head office	—	9,54,000	By Closing Stock	7,00,000	99,000
To Gross Profit c/d	16,60,000	95,000			
	44,35,000	10,49,000		44,35,000	10,49,000
To Office Expenses	90,000	8,500	By Gross Profit b/d	16,60,000	95,000
To Selling Expenses	72,000	6,300			
To Staff Salaries	65,000	12,000			
To Branch Stock Reserve	44,000	—			
To Net Profit	13,89,000	68,200			
	16,60,000	95,000		16,60,000	95,000

Working Notes:

(i) Closing Stock of head office = ₹ 2,25,000 + ₹ 25,50,000 – (37,35,000 × 100/180) = ₹ 7,00,000

(ii) Closing stock of branch = ₹ 9,54,000 – (9,50,000 × 180/200) = ₹ 99,000

(iii) Unrealised Profit in branch stock = ₹ 99,000 × 80/180 = ₹ 44,000

INDEPENDENT BRANCH—SHORT ANSWER QUESTIONS

PROBLEM 13

Head Office passes adjustment entry at the end of each month to adjust the position arising out of inter-branch transactions during the month. From the following inter-branch transactions in January, 2013 make the entry in the books of Head Office:

(a) Bombay Branch

(1) Received Goods: ₹ 6,000 from Calcutta Branch, ₹ 4,000 from Patna Branch.

(2) Sent Goods to: ₹ 10,000 to Patna, ₹ 8,000 to Calcutta.

(3) Received B/R: ₹ 6,000 from Patna.

(4) Sent Acceptance: ₹ 4,000 to Calcutta, ₹ 2,000 to Patna.

(b) Madras Branch (*Apart from the above*)

(5) Received Goods: ₹ 10,000 from Calcutta, ₹ 4,000 from Bombay.

(6) Cash Sent: ₹ 2,000 to Calcutta, ₹ 6,000 to Bombay.

(c) Calcutta Branch (*Apart from the above*)

(7) Sent Goods to Patna: ₹ 6,000.

(8) Paid B/P: ₹ 4,000 to Patna, ₹ 4,000 cash to Patna. ***[CA (May 1996)]***

Solution

In the Books of Head Office
Journal

Date	Particulars		L.F.	Dr. (₹)	Cr. (₹)
2013 Jan. 31	Madras Branch A/c	Dr.		6,000	
	Patna Branch A/c	Dr.		16,000	
	To Bombay Branch A/c				6,000
	To Calcutta Branch A/c				16,000
	(Being adjustment entry passed by head office in respect of inter-branch transactions during the month.)				

Working Note:

Particulars	Inter-branch transactions			
	Bombay ₹	Madras ₹	Calcutta ₹	Patna ₹
(a) *Bombay Branch*				
(1) Received Goods	10,000 (Dr.)		6,000 (Cr.)	4,000 (Cr.)
(2) Sent Goods	18,000 (Cr.)		8,000 (Dr.)	10,000 (Dr.)
(3) Received B/R	6,000 (Dr.)			6,000 (Cr.)
(4) Sent Acceptance	6,000 (Cr.)		4,000 (Dr.)	2,000 (Dr.)
(b) *Madras Branch*				
(5) Received Goods	4,000 (Cr.)	14,000 (Dr.)	10,000 (Cr.)	
(6) Cash Sent	6,000 (Dr.)	8,000 (Cr.)	2,000 (Dr.)	
(c) *Calcutta Branch*				
(7) Sent Goods			6,000 (Cr.)	6,000 (Dr.)
(8) Paid B/P and Cash			8,000 (Cr.)	8,000 (Dr.)
	6,000 (Cr.)	6,000 (Dr.)	16,000 (Cr.)	16,000 (Dr.)

PROBLEM 14

Show adjustment Journal entry in the books of Head Office at the end of April, 2013 for incorporation of inter-branch transactions assuming that only Head Office maintains different branch accounts in its books.

A. Delhi Branch:
1. Received goods from Mumbai – ₹ 35,000 and 15,000 from Kolkata.
2. Sent goods to Chennai – ₹ 25,000, Kolkata – ₹ 20,000.
3. Bill Receivable received – ₹ 20,000 from Chennai.
4. Acceptances sent to Mumbai – ₹ 25,000, Kolkata – ₹ 10,000.

B. Mumbai Branch (apart from the above):
5. Received goods from Kolkata – ₹ 15,000 , Delhi – ₹ 20,000.
6. Cash sent too Delhi – ₹ 15,000, Kolkata – ₹ 7,000.

C. Chennai Branch (apart from the above):
7. Received goods from Kolkata – ₹ 30,000.
8. Acceptances and cash sent to Kolkata – ₹ 20,000 and ₹ 10,000 respectively.

D. Kolkata Branch (apart from the above):
9. Sent goods to Chennai – ₹ 35,000.
10. Paid cash to Chennai – ₹ 15,000.
11. Acceptances sent to Chennai – ₹ 15,000

All working should form part of the answer. *[CA PE II May 2003]*

Solution

Journal Entry in the Books of Head Office

Date	Particulars		Dr. (₹)	Cr. (₹)
30.4.13	Mumbai Branch A/c	Dr.	3,000	
	Chennai Branch A/c	Dr.	70,000	
	To Delhi Branch A/c			15,000
	To Kolkata Branch A/c			58,000
	(Being adjustment entry passed by head office in respect of inter-branch transactions for the month of April, 2003.			

Working Note: **INTER-BRANCH TRANSACTIONS**

Particulars	Delhi ₹	Mumbai ₹	Chennai ₹	Kolkata ₹
A. Delhi Branch				
1. Received goods	50,000 (Dr.)	35,000 (Cr.)		15,000 (Cr.)
2. Sent goods	45,000 (Cr.)		25,000 (Dr.)	20,000 (Dr.)
3. Received B/R	20,000 (Dr.)		20,000 (Cr.)	
4. Sent acceptance	35,000 (Cr.)	25,000 (Dr.)		10,000 (Dr.)
B. Mumbai Branch				
5. Received goods	20,000 (Cr.)	35,000 (Dr.)		15,000 (Cr.)
6. Sent cash	15,000 (Dr.)	22,000 (Cr.)		7,000 (Dr.)
C. Chennai Branch				
7. Received goods			30,000 (Dr.)	30,000 (Cr.)
8. Sent cash and acceptances			30,000 (Cr.)	30,000 (Dr.)
D. Kolkata Branch				
9. Sent goods			35,000 (Dr.)	35,000 (Cr.)
10. Sent cash			15,000 (Dr.)	15,000 (Cr.)
11. Sent acceptances			15,000 (Dr.)	15,000 (Cr.)
	15,000 (Cr.)	3,000 (Dr.)	70,000 (Dr.)	58,000 (Cr.)

PROBLEM 15

Alphs & Co., having head office in Mumbai has a branch in Nagpur. The branch at Nagpur is an independent branch maintinaing separate books of account. On 31.3.2013, it was found that the goods dispatched by head office for ₹ 2,00,000 was received by the branch only to the extent of ₹ 1,50,000. The balance goods are in transit. What is the accounting entery to be passed by the branch for recording the goods in transit, in its books? ***[CA (PCC) May 2007]***

Solution

Nagpur Branch must include the inventory in its books as goods in transit

Goods in transit A/c	Dr.	₹ 50,000	
To Head office A/c			₹ 50,000
(Being Goods sent by Heat office is still in transit on the closing date)			

PROBLEM 16

Give Journal Entries in the books of Branch A to rectify or adjust the following:

(i) Head Office exp. ₹ 1,35,000 allocated to the Branch, but not recorded in Branch Books.

(ii) Depreciation of branch assests, whose accounts are kept by the Head Office not provided earlier for ₹ 1,15,000.

(iii) Branch paid ₹ 1,40,000 as salary to a H.O. Inspector, but the amount paid has been debited by the Branch to Salaries account.

(iv) H.O. collected ₹ 1,30,000 directly from a customer on behalf of the Branch, but no intimation to this effect has been received by the Branch.

(v) A remittance of ₹ 1,50,000 sent by the Branch has not yet been received by Head Office.

(vi) Branch A incurred advertisement expenses of ₹ 30,000 on behalf of Branch of B.

[CA (IPCC) Nov. 2011]

Solution

Journal of Branch A

Particulars		*L.F.*	*Dr. (₹)*	*Cr. (₹)*
(i) H.O. Expenses A/c	Dr.		1,35,000	
To Head Office A/c				1,35,000
(Being the allocated expenditure by the head office recorded in branch books)				
(ii) Depreciation A/c	Dr.		1,15,000	
To Head Office A/c				1,15,000
(Being the depreciation provided)				
(iii) Head Office A/c	Dr.		1,40,000	
To Salaries A/c				1,40,000
(Being the rectification of salary paid on behalf of H.O.)				
(iv) Head Office A/c	Dr.		1,30,000	
To Debtors A/c				1,30,000
(Being the adjustment of collection from branch debtors)				
(v) No entry in branch books but Cash-in-transit will be shown in H.O. Books				
(vi) Head Office A/c	Dr.		30,000	
To Cash A/c				30,000
(Being the expenditure on account of Branch B, recorded in books)				

PROBLEM 17

Give Journal entires in the books of Head Office to rectify or adjust the following:

(i) Goods set to Branch ₹ 12,000 stolen during transit. Branch manager refused to accept any liability.

(ii) Branch paid ₹ 15,000 as salary to the office of Head Office on his visit to the branch.

(iii) On 28th March the H.O. dispatched goods to the Branch invoiced at ₹ 25,000 which was not received by Branch till 31st March.

(iv) A remittance of ₹ 10,000 sent by the branch on 30th March, 2012, received by the Head Office on 1st April.

(v) Head Office made payment of ₹ 25,000 for purchase of goods by Branch and wrongly debited its own purchase account. **[CA (IPCC) Nov. 2012]**

Solution

Journal of Head Office

Date	Particulars		L.F	Dr. (₹)	Cr. (₹)
(i)	Loss in transit A/c	Dr.		12,000	
	To Purchases A/c				12,000
	(Being the Goods lost on account of theft during transit)				
(ii)	Salaries A/c	Dr.		15,000	
	To Branch A/c				15,000
	(Being salary paid by the branch for H.P. employee)				
(iii)	No entry in the books of head office for goods sent to branch not received by branch till 31st March				
(iv)	Cash in transit A/c	Dr.		10,000	
	To Branch A/c				10,000
	(Being remittance by branch not received by 31st March)				
(v)	Branch A/c	Dr.		25,000	
	To Purchases A/c				25,000
	(Being rectification of entry for payment for goods purchased by branch wrongly debited to Purchase A/c)				

Note: In entry (i), it is assumed that refusal of branch manager (to accept liability of stolen goods) is accepted by the Head Office. Alternatively, Branch account will be credited on the basis of assumption that refusal of branch manager is not accepted by the Head Office.

PROBLEM 18

Pass necessary Journal entries in the books of an independent Brach of a Company, wherever required, to rectify or adjust the following:

(i) Income of ₹ 2,800 allocated to the Branch by Head Office but not recorded in the Branch books.

(ii) Provision for doubtful debts, whose accounts are kept by the Head Office, not provided earlier for ₹ 1,000.

(iii) Branch paid ₹ 3,000 as salary to a Head Office Manager, but the amount paid has been debited by the Branch to Salaries Account.

(iv) Branch incurred travelling expenses of ₹ 5,000 on behalf of other Branches, but not recorded in the books of Branch.

(v) A remittance of ₹ 1,50,000 sent by the Branch has not received by Head Office on the date of reconcillation of Accounts.

(vi) Head Office allocates ₹ 75,000 to the Branch as Head Office expenses, which has not yet been recorded by the Branch.

(vii) Head Office collected ₹ 30,000 directly from a branch Customer. The intimation of the fact has been received by the Branch only now.

(viii) Goods dispatched by the Head office amounting to ₹ 10,000, but not received by the Branch till date of reconcillation. The Goods have been received subsequently. **[May 2014]**

Solution

Journal of Branch

Date	Particulars	Dr. (₹)	Cr. (₹)
(i)	Head Office A/c Dr. To Income A/c (Being the income allocated by the Head office not recorded earlier, now recorded)	2,800	2,800
(ii)	Provision for Doubtful Debts A/c Dr. To Head Office A/c (Being the provision for doubtful debts not provided earlier, now provided for)	1,000	1,000
(iii)	Head Office A/c Dr. To Salaries A/c (Being rectification of salary paid on behalf of Head Office)	3,000	3,000
(iv)	Head Office A/c Dr. To Cash A/c (Being expenditure incurred on account of other branch, now recorded in books)	5,000	5,000
(v)	No entry in Branch Books is required.		
(vi)	Expenses A/c Dr. To Head Office A/c (Being allocated expenses of Head Office recorded)	75,000	75,000
(vii)	Head Office A/c Dr. To Debtors A/c (Being adjustment entry for collection from Branch Debtrors directly by Head Office)	30,000	30,000
(viii)	Good-in-transit A/c Dr. To Head Office Account (Being goods sent by Head Office still in-transit)	10,000	10,000

INDEPENDENT BRANCH—LONG ANSWER QUESTIONS

PROBLEM 19

The following Trial Balance is extracted from the Books of the Nagpur Branch of CANGE Ltd as on 31st March, 2013:

Particulars	Dr. (₹)	Cr. (₹)
Opening Stock at Invoice price	25,000	
Branch Debtors	10,000	
Cash in hand	500	
Branch Creditors		3,000
Goods received from Head Office	80,000	
Branch Expenses	9,000	
Branch Sales		1,80,000
Current Account with Head Office	58,500	
	1,83,000	1,83,000

As on that date, Closing Stock with branch at invoice price were valued at ₹ 30,000. There was an amount of ₹ 18,500 remitted by the branch on 31st March, which had not been received by the head office on that date. The head office had sent goods, costing ₹ 20,000, to the branch on 29th March. These had not been received by the branch till the closing date.

The head office enters in its books all goods sent to the branch at cost. The branch enters these, in its books, at invoice price but sells them at an even higher one. At the end of each year, the difference is adjusted by being debited to the Branch and credited to the Profit and Loss Account in the books of the Head Office. The proportional difference, between cost and invoice price, was the same at all relevant times. The credit balance as on 31st March, 2013 of the Branch Account in the Head Office books, was ₹ 60,000 before making any of the above adjustment (though the above mentioned despatch of goods of ₹ 20,000, on 29th March, had of course, been duly debited to the Branch account).

Required: Prepare the Branch Profit and Loss Account and Head Office Profit and Loss Account (relevant protions only) for the year ending on 31st March, 2013. **[CA]**

Solution

It will be first appropriate to reconcile balance in H.O. Current Account as per Branch Books and balance in Branch Current Account as per H.O. Books:

Dr. **ADJUSTED BRANCH CURRENT ACCOUNT (IN H.O. BOOKS)** Cr.

Particulars	₹	Particulars	₹
To Profit and Loss A/c **(balancing figure)** (Loading on goods invoiced to branch)	**40,000**	By Balance b/d	60,000
		By Cash-in-transit	18,500
To Balance c/d	58,500	By Goods sent to Branch A/c (Reversal of entry as goods were not received by the branch till 31st March)	20,000
	98,500		98,500

Dr. **(MEMORANDUM) BRANCH PROFIT AND LOSS ACCOUNT** Cr.

Particulars	₹	Particulars	₹
To Opening Stock	25,000	By Branch Sales	1,80,000
To Goods received from H.O.	80,000	By Closing Stock	30,000
To Branch Expenses	9,000		
To Net Profit c/d	96,000		
	2,10,000		2,10,000

AN EXTRACT OF H.O. PROFIT AND LOSS ACCOUNT

for the year ending on 31st March, 2013

Dr. *Cr.*

Particulars	₹	Particulars	₹
To Stock Reserve (on Closing Stock)	15,000	By Branch A/c (Profit)	96,000
To Net Profit c/d	1,33,500	By Profit on goods sent to Branch	40,000
		By Stock Reserve (on Opening Stock)	12,500
	1,48,500		1,48,500

Working Notes:

(i) The Stock Reserve for unrealised profit on opening and closing stock is @ 50% of the respective stock at invoice price. This can be made out from the fact that goods sent to branch of ₹ 80,000, includes a loading of ₹ 40,000, as can be seen from the Adjusted Branch Current Account.

(ii) The Branch Profit and Loss A/c has been prepared at invoice price.

PROBLEM 20

CANGH Ltd commenced business on 1.4.2012 with the head office at Calicut and branch at Tiruchur. All goods were purchased by head office and normally packed immediately, but on 31.03.2013, goods costing ₹ 5,000 remained unpacked. Only the packed goods were sent to the branch which was charged at selling price *less* 10%. The following information is furnished to you as on 31st March 2013, from the Head Office and Branch Office books:

Particulars	H.O. ₹	Branch ₹
Capital Account	40,000	—
Drawing by Proprietor	10,000	—
Purchases	4,00,000	—
Packing materials bought	6,000	—
Sales	3,20,000	1,00,000
Despatch of goods to Branch	1,13,400	—
Selling expenses	16,000	800
Clerk's salary, wages, etc.	20,000	3,000
Sundry Debtors	28,000	4,200
Sundry Creditors	26,600	5,000
Head Office Current A/c	—	12,000
Branch Office Current A/c	19,000	—
Bank Balances	2,000	—
Goods received from Head office	—	1,08,000

Information:

(a) Sales by head office were a uniform gross profit, after charging packing materials, of 20% on the fixed selling price;

(b) Sales at Branch were at fixed selling price;

(c) Goods invoiced and despatched by head office to branch in March for ₹ 5,400 were received in the Branch only on 10th April.

(d) Stock of packing materials on hand as on 31st March was valued at ₹ 1,000.

(e) Remittance of ₹ 1,600 from the branch to the Head Office was in transit on 31st March.

(f) ₹ 2,000 worth of stock at selling price was damaged at the branch. For valuing stock, this was reduced by ₹ 1,090 below the invoice cost to the branch. It was decided that the Head office and branch would share equally the loss occasioned by this and also the deficit in stock, ascertained on actual stock taking at the Branch of goods at selling price of ₹ 500.

Required: Prepare the Profit and Loss Account of the Tiruchur and Calicut Office and also a Balance Sheet as at 31.03.2013 of the business. **[CA]**

Solution

TRADING AND PROFIT AND LOSS ACCOUNT

for the year ending on 31st March, 2013

Dr. *Cr.*

Particulars	H.O. ₹	Branch ₹	Particulars	H.O ₹	Branch ₹
To Purchases (*less* unpacked goods)	3,95,000	—	By Sales	3,20,000	1,00,000
To Packing material consumed	5,000	—	By Goods sent to Branch A/c (in transit ₹ 5,400)	1,13,400	—
To Goods from H.O. (including in transit)	—	1,13,400	By Stock damaged and shortage	—	1,540
To Gross Profit c/d [Working Notes (i) & (ii)]	76,600	10,000	By Closing Stock (balancing figure)	43,200	21,860
	4,76,600	1,23,400		4,76,600	1,23,400
To Salaries and Wages	20,000	3,000	By Gross Profit b/d	76,600	10,000
To Selling Expenses	16,000	800			
To Stock Reserve (Unrealised Profit)	2,350	—			
To Stock damaged and shortage	770	770			
To Net Profit t/f to Captial A/c	37,480	5,430			
	76,600	10,000		76,600	10,000

BALANCE SHEET AS AT 31ST MARCH, 2013

Liabilities		₹	Assets		₹
Capital	40,000		Stock-in-trade:		
Add: Net Profit	42,910		H.O.: Packed	43,200	
	82,910		Unpacked	5,000	
Less: Drawings	10,000	72,910	Packing Material	1,000	49,200
Sundry Creditors:			Branch: In hand	16,460	
H.O.	26,600		In transit	5,400	
Branch	5,000	31,600		21,860	
			Less: Unrealised Profit	2,350	19,510
			Sundry Debtors: H.O	28,000	
			Branch	4,200	32,200
			Cash at Bank		2,000
			Cash-in-transit		1,600
		1,04,510			1,04,510

Working Notes:

	₹
(i) Gross Profit made by Head Office (20% of Sales of ₹ 3,20,000)	64,000
10/90 of Goods sent to Branch (Since Invoice Price is 90% of normal selling price) [₹ 1,13,400× 100/90 × 10%]	12,600
	76,600

(ii)	The Gross Profit made by branch is 10% of sales (10% of ₹ 1,00,000)		10,000
(iii)	The amount to be written off at invoice value at branch is:		
	Amount written off on damaged goods	1,090	
	Invoice price of deficit in stock (₹ 500 × 90/100)	450	1,540
(iv)	*Value of damaged goods included in Closing Stock*		
	A Selling Price of Goods Damaged		2,000
	B Invoice Price of Goods Damaged (₹ 2,000 × 90/100)		1,800
	C Amount already written off		1,090
	D Amount still included in Closing Stock (B – C)		710
(v)	*Calculation of Stock Reserve Required*		
	A Stock (including Goods-in-transit)		21,860
	B *Less*: Value of damaged goods included		(710)
	C Value of Total Goods (A – B)		21,150
	D Stock Reserve required (₹ 21,150 × 10/90)		2,350

PROBLEM 21

CAS Ltd manufactures a range of goods which it sells to wholesale customers only from its head office. In addition, the H.O. transfers goods to a newly opened branch at factory cost *plus* 15%. The branch then sells these goods to the general public on cash basis. The selling price to wholesale customers is designed to give the factory profit which amounts to 30% of the sale value. The selling price to the general public is designed to give a gross margin (i.e., selling price *less* cost of goods from H.O.) of 30% of the sales value. The company operates from rented premises and leases all other types of fixed assets. The rent and hire charges for these are included in the overhead costs shown in the trial balances.

From the information given below, you are required to prepare for the year ending on 31st March 2013 in columnar form.

(a) A Profit and Loss Account for (i) H.O. (ii) the branch (iii) the entire business.

(b) A Balance Sheet as on 31st March 2013 for the entire business.

Particulars	*H.O.*		*Branch*	
	Dr. (₹)	*Cr. (₹)*	*Dr. (₹)*	*Cr. (₹)*
Raw materials purchased	35,000			
Direct Wages	1,08,500			
Factory overheads	39,000			
Opening Stock:				
Raw materials	1,800			
Finished goods	13,000		9,200	
Debtors	37,000			
Cash	22,000		1,000	
Administrative Salaries	13,900		4,000	
Salesmen's Salaries	22,500		6,200	
Other Administrative & Selling overheads	12,500		2,300	
Inter unit accounts	5,000			2,000
Capital		50,000		
Sundry Creditors		13,000		
Provision for unrealised profit in stock		1,200		
Sales		2,00,000		65,200
Goods sent to Branch		46,000		
Goods received from H.O.			44,500	
	3,10,200	3,10,200	67,200	67,200

Information:

(i) On 28th March the branch remitted ₹ 1,500 to the H.O. and this has not yet been recorded in the H.O. books. Also on the same date, the H.O. despatched goods to the branch invoiced at ₹ 1,500 and these too have not yet been entered into branch books, it is the company's policy to adjust items in transit in the books of the receipient.

(ii) The stock of raw materials held at the H.O. on 31st March was valued at ₹ 2,300.

(iii) You are advised that:

(a) no stock losses were incurred at the H.O. or at the branch;

(b) it is the company's practice to value finished goods stock at the H.O. at factory cost.

(c) there were no opening or closing stock of work-in progress.

(iv) Branch employees are entitled to bonus of ₹ 156 under a bilateral agreement. **[CA]**

Solution

TRADING AND PROFIT AND LOSS ACCOUNT

for the year ending on 31st March, 2013

Dr. Cr.

Particulars	H.O ₹	Branch ₹	Total ₹	Particulars	H.O. ₹	Branch ₹	Total ₹
*To Material consumed	34,500			By Sales	2,00,000	65,200	2,65,200
To Wages	1,08,500			By Goods sent to Branch	46,000	—	—
To Factory Overheads	39,000			By Closing Stock	15,000	9,560	24,560
Factory cost	1,82,000		1,82,000				
Add: Opening Stock	13,000	9,200	22,200				
	1,95,000						
To Goods from H.O.	—	46,000	—				
To Gross Profit	66,000	19,560	85,560				
	2,61,000	74,760	2,89,760		2,61,000	74,760	2,89,760
To Adm. Salaries	13,900	4,000	17,900	By Gross Profit	66,000	19,560	85,560
To Salesman Salaries	22,500	6,200	28,700	By Stock Reserve	1,200	—	1,200
To Other Adm. and Overheads	12,500	2,300	14,800				
To Stock Reserve	1,247	—	1,247				
To Bonus to Staff	—	156	156				
To Net Profit	17,053	6,904	23,957				
	67,200	19,560	86,760		67,200	19,560	86,760

BALANCE SHEET AS AT 31ST MARCH, 2013

Liabilities	*H.O* ₹	*Branch* ₹	*Total* ₹	*Assets*	*H.O.* ₹	*Branch* ₹	*Total* ₹
Capital	50,000	—	50,000	Fixed Assets	Nil	Nil	Nil
Profit-H.O.	17,053			Current Assets			
-Branch	6,904		23,957	Raw material	2,300	—	2,300
Trade Creditors	13,000		13,000	Finished Goods	15,000	9,560	**23,313
Bonus Payable		156	156	(*Less* Stock Reserve)			
H.O. Account		10,404					
Stock Reserve	1,247			Debtors	37,000		37,000
				Cash	23,500	1,000	24,500
				Branch A/c	10,404		
	88,204	10,560	87,113		88,204	10,560	87,113

*Material Consumed = ₹ 1,800 + ₹ 35,000 – ₹ 2,300 = ₹ 34,500

**Closing Stock = ₹ 15,000 + ₹ 9,560 – ₹ 1,247 = ₹ 23,313

PROBLEM 22

CAMHA Ltd. commenced business on 1st April, 2012 with a head office and a branch. Purchases were made exclusively by the head office where the goods were processed before sale. There was no loss or wastage. Only processed goods received from the head office were handled by the branch, and these were charged to the branch at processed cost *plus* 10 per cent. All sales, whether by head office or the branch, were at uniform gross profit of 25 per cent on their respective cost. The following Trial Balance as on 31st March, 2013 was extracted from the books.

Particulars	*H.O.*		*Branch*	
	Dr. (₹)	*Cr. (₹)*	*Dr. (₹)*	*Cr. (₹)*
Capital		2,20,000		
Drawings	25,000			
Purchases	19,93,350			
Cost of Processing	34,650			
Sales		14,20,000		6,40,000
Goods sent to Branch/Received by Branch		6,51,200	6,40,200	
Selling & General Expenses	2,24,000		27,000	
Debtors/Creditors	2,30,000	5,83,350	92,000	2,400
Branch/H.O. Current A/c	2,05,550			1,50,800
Balance at Bank	1,62,000		34,000	
Total	28,74,550	28,74,550	7,93,200	7,93,200

Information:

(i) Goods charged by head office to branch in March at ₹ 11,000, were not received by the branch until April. A remittance of Rs 43,750 from the branch to head office in March is still in transit.

(ii) Stock-taking at Branch disclosed shortage of ₹ 5,000 (at selling price).

(iii) Cost of unprocessed goods at head office as on 31st March, 2013 was ₹ 1,80,000.

Required: Prepare in columnar from Profit and Loss Account and Balance Sheet of the Head Office, branch and the business as a whole. ***[CA]***

Solution

Dr. **PROFIT AND LOSS ACCOUNT FOR THE YEAR ENDING ON 31ST MARCH, 2013** Cr.

Particulars	*H.O* ₹	*Branch* ₹	*Total* ₹	*Particulars*	*H.O.* ₹	*Branch* ₹	*Total* ₹
Purchases	19,93,350	—	19,93,350	Sales	14,20,000	6,40,000	20,60,000
Cost of processing	34,650	—	34,650	Goods sent to Branch	6,51,200	—	—
				Shortage		4,000	4,000
Goods Received from H.O.	—	6,51,200	—	Closing Stock	—	—	11,000
				Unprocessed	1,80,000	—	1,80,000
Gross Profit c/d	3,43,200	1,28,000	4,71,200	Processed	1,20,000	1,24,200	2,44,200
	23,71,200	7,79,200	24,99,200		23,71,200	7,68,200	24,99,200
Selling Exp.	2,24,000	27,000	2,51,000	Gross Profit b/d	3,43,200	1,28,000	4,71,200
Provision for unrealised profit on:							
Branch Stock	11,291	—	11,291				
Goods in transit	1,000	—	1,000				
Shortage	—	4,000	4,000				
Net Profit	1,06,909	97,000	2,03,909				
	3,43,200	1,28,000	4,71,200		3,43,200	1,28,000	4,71,200

BALANCE SHEET AS AT 31ST MARCH, 2013

Liabilities	*H.O* ₹	*Branch* ₹	*Total* ₹	*Assets*	*H.O.* ₹	*Branch* ₹	*Total* ₹
Capital	2,20,000			Sundry Debtors	2,30,000	92,000	3,22,000
Add: Profit	2,03,909			Stocks:			
	4,23,909			Unprocessed	1,80,000	—	1,80,000
Less: Drawings	25,000			Processed	1,20,000	1,24,200	2,44,200
	3,98,909		3,98,909	(*Less*: Reserve)			(11,291)
				In transit	—	11,000	11,000
				(Less: Reserve)			(1,000)
Sundry Creditors	5,83,350	2,400	5,85,750	Balance at Bank	1,62,000	34,000	1,96,000
H.O. Current A/c		2,58,800		Remittance in transit	43,750	—	43,750
Provision for unrealised profit on Stock (₹ 11,291 + ₹ 1,000)	12,291	—	—	Branch Current A/c	2,58,800	—	—
	9,94,550	2,61,200	9,84,659		9,94,550	2,61,200	9,84,659

Working Notes:

(i) *Calculation of Head Office Stock*

	₹
A. Purchases	19,93,350
B. *Less*: Stock of unprocessed goods	1,80,000
C. Cost of Goods consumed before processing (A – B)	18,13,350
D. *Add*: Cost of Processing	34,650

E. Cost of Processed goods (C + D)		18,48,000
F. *Less*: (a) Cost of goods sent to Branch (₹ 6,51,200 × 100/110)	5,92,000	
(b) Cost of goods sold by H.O. (₹ 14,20,000 × 80/100)	11,36,000	17,28,000
G. Closing Stock at head office (E – F)		1,20,000

(ii) *Calculation of Branch Stock*

A. Received from the H.O.		6,40,200
B. *Less*: (a) Invoice Price of Goods Sold (₹ 6,40,000 × 80/100)	5,12,000	
(b) Invoice Price of Shortage (₹ 5,000 × 80/100)	4,000	5,16,000
C. Stock at Branch, at Invoice Price (A – B)		1,24,200
D. Unrealised Profit included (₹ 1,24,200 × 10/110)		11,291

(ii) *Dr.* **BRANCH CURRENT ACCOUNT** *Cr.*

Particulars	₹	*Particulars*	₹
To Balance b/d	2,05,550	By Cash in transit	43,750
To Net Profit	97,000	By Balance c/d	2,58,800
	3,02,550		3,02,550

(IV) *DR.* **CAPITAL ACCOUNT OF H.O.** *CR.*

Particulars	₹	*Particulars*	₹
To Drawings	25,000	By Balance b/d	2,20,000
To Balance c/d	3,98,909	By Profit and Loss A/c (Profit)	2,03,909
	4,23,909		4,23,909

PROBLEM 23

COJIH Ltd. operates a branch as well as a head office. The following Trial Balance has been extracted from the books of the concern as on 31st March, 2013:

Particulars	*H.O.*		*Branch*	
	Dr. (₹)	*Cr. (₹)*	*Dr. (₹)*	*Cr. (₹)*
Capital account	—	4,71,000	—	—
Drawings	84,000	—	—	—
Plant at cost	2,40,000	—	1,20,000	—
Accumulated depreciation on plant	—	1,20,000	—	60,000
Goods to branch/from head office	—	7,92,000	7,20,000	—
Head Office Current Account	—	—	—	1,56,000
Branch Current Account	2,58,000	—	—	—
Branch Stock Provisions (Opening)	—	6,000	—	—
Operating expenses	30,000	—	15,000	—
Purchases	22,92,000	—	—	—
Rent and rates	45,000	—	18,000	—
Sales	—	21,00,000	—	9,00,000
Opening Stock	1,80,000	—	36,000	—
Debtors	90,000	—	75,000	—
Creditors	—	1,35,000	—	—
Salaries and wages	3,60,000	—	1,20,000	—
Cash and bank	45,000	—	12,000	—
	36,24,000	36,24,000	11,16,000	11,16,000

Additional information:

(a) All goods are purchased by the head office. The goods required by the branch are invoiced by the head office to the branch at cost *plus* 20%. On 31st March, 2013, the head office held stocks which had cost it ₹ 2,40,000. On the same date the branch held stocks which had been invoiced to it at ₹ 54,000.

(b) Fixed assets are to be depreciated at the rate of 50% per annum based on the reducing balance method. There had been no purchase or sale of fixed assets during the year.

(c) At 31st March, 2013, cash ₹ 30,000 was in transit from the branch to the head office.

(d) The following expenses were outstanding on 31st March, 2013.

	Head Office	*Branch*
	₹	₹
Salaries	2,000	1,000
Rent	1,000	2,000

Required: Prepare, in columnar form, for (i) the head office, (ii) the branch, and (iii) the business as a whole, the Trading and Profit & Loss Accounts for the year ended 31st March, 2013. Also, prepare a combined Balance Sheet as on that date. **[CA]**

Solution

TRADING AND PROFIT AND LOSS ACCOUNT

for the year ended 31st March, 2013

Dr. *Cr.*

Particulars	*H.O* ₹	*Branch* ₹	*Total* ₹	*Particulars*	*H.O.* ₹	*Branch* ₹	*Total* ₹
To Op. Stock	1,80,000	36,000	2,16,000	By Sales	21,00,000	9,00,000	30,00,000
To Purchases	22,92,000	—	22,92,000	By Branch transfer	7,92,000	—	—
To Head Office-transfer	—	7,92,000	—	By Clo. Stock	2,40,000	54,000	2,94,000
				By Stock *less* Provisions	—	—	3,45,000
To Gross Profit c/d.	6,60,000	1,98,000	8,58,000	By Goods-in-transit		72,000	72,000
	31,32,000	10,26,000	33,66,000		31,32,000	10,26,000	33,66,000
To Salaries & Wages	3,62,000	1,21,000	4,83,000	By Gross Profit b/d	6,60,000	1,98,000	8,58,000
To Rent & Rates	46,000	20,000	66,000	By Stock Reserve (36,000 × 20/120)	6,000		6,000
To Operating exp.	30,000	15,000	45,000				
To Depreciation	60,000	30,000	90,000				
To Stock Reserve	21,000		21,000				
To Net Profit c/d	1,47,000	12,000	1,59,000				
	6,66,000	1,98,000	8,64,000		6,66,000	1,98,000	8,64,000

BALANCE SHEET AS AT 31ST MARCH, 2013

Liabilities		₹	*Assets*		₹
Capital:			Plant at cost	3,60,000	
Opening balance	4,71,000		*Less:* Depreciation	2,70,000	90,000
Add: Profit	1,59,000		Stock		
	6,30,000		H.O.	2,40,000	
Less: Drawings	(84,000)	5,46,000	Branch	54,000	
Creditors		1,35,000	Goods-in-Transit	72,000	
Outstanding expenses		6,000		3,66,000	
			Less: Reserve	21,000	3,45,000
			Debtors		1,65,000
			Cash & Bank		57,000
			Cash in transit		30,000
		6,87,000			6,87,000

Working Note: *Adjustment for Cash in transit:*

Cash in transit A/c. Dr.	₹ 30,000	
To Branch Current A/c		₹ 30,000

PROBLEM 24

On 31st March, 2013 Kanpur Branch submits the following Trial Balance to its Head Office at Lucknow:

Debit Balances:	*₹ in lacs*
Furniture and Equipment	18
Depreciation on Furniture	2
Salaries	25
Rent	10
Advertising	6
Telephone, Postage and Stationery	3
Sundry Office Expenses	1
Opening Stock	60
Goods Received from Head Office	288
Debtors	20
Cash at Bank and in hand	8
Carriage Inwards	7
	448
Credit Balances:	
Outstanding Expenses	3
Goods Returned to Head Office	5
Sales	360
Head Office	80
	448

Additional Information:

Closing Stock was valued at ₹ 62 lacs. On 29th March the Head Office despatched goods costing ₹ 10 lacs to its branch. Branch did not receive these goods before 1st April. Hence, the figure of goods received from Head Office does not include these goods. Also the head office has charged the branch ₹ 1 lac for centralised services for which the branch has not passed the entry.

You are required to:

(i) Pass Journal Entries in the books of the Branch to make the necessary adjustments

(ii) Prepare Final Accounts of the Branch including Balance Sheet, and

(iii) Pass Journal Entries in the books of the Head Office to incorporate the whole of the Branch Trial Balance. **[CA (May 2002)]**

Solution

JOURNAL OF BRANCH

[₹ in lacs]

Particulars		*L.F.*	*Dr. (₹)*	*Cr. (₹)*
Goods in Transit A/c	Dr.		10	
To Head Office A/c				10
(Being the goods despatched by head office but not received by branch before 1st April)				
Expenses A/c	Dr.		1	
To Head Office A/c				1
(Being the amount charged by head office for centralised services)				

(III) TRADING AND PROFIT & LOSS ACCOUNT OF THE BRANCH

for the year ended 31st March, 2013

Dr. Cr.

Particulars		*₹ (in lacs)*	*Particulars*	*₹ in (lacs)*
To Opening Stock		60	By Sales	360
To Goods received from			By Closing Stock	62
Head Office	288			
Less: Returns	5	283		
To Carriage Inwards		7		
To Gross Profit c/d		72		
		422		422
To Salaries		25	By Gross Profit b/d	72
To Depreciation on Furniture		2		
To Rent		10		
To Advertising		6		
To Telephone, Postage & Stationery		3		
To Sundry Office Expenses		1		
To Head Office Expenses		1		
To Net Profit Transferred to Head Office A/c		24		
		72		72

BALANCE SHEET AS AT 31ST MARCH, 2013

Liabilites		₹ (in lacs)	Assets		₹ in (lacs)
Head Office	80		Furniture & Equipment	20	
Add: Goods in transit	10		*Less:* Depreciation	2	18
Head Office Expenses	1		Stock in hand		62
Net Profit	24	115	Goods in Transit		10
Outstanding Expenses		3	Debtors		20
			Cash at bank and in hand		8
		118			118

JOURNAL OF HEAD OFFICE *[₹]*

Particulars		L.F.	Dr. (₹)	Cr. (₹)
Branch Trading A/c	Dr.		355	
To Branch A/c				355
(Being the Opening Stock, Goods received, Carriage Inwards debited to Branch Trading Account)				
Branch A/c	Dr.		427	
To Branch Trading A/c				427
((Being the Total sales, closing stock and goods returned to Head Office credited to Branch Trading Account)				
Branch Trading A/c	Dr.		72	
To Branch Profit and Loss A/c				72
(Being the gross profit earned by branch credited to Branch P& L A/c				
Branch Profit and Loss A/c	Dr.		48	
To Branch A/c				48
(Being the total of the Branch Expenses debited to Branch P& L A/c)				
Branch Profit & Loss A/c	Dr.		24	
To Profit and Loss A/c				24
(Net Profit at branch credited to (general) Profit & Loss A/c)				
Branch Furniture & Equipment	Dr.		18	
Branch Stock	Dr.		62	
Branch Debtors	Dr.		20	
Branch Cash at Bank and in Hand	Dr.		8	
Goods in Transit	Dr.		10	
To Branch A/c				118
(Being the incorporation of different assets at the branch in H.O. books)				
Branch A/c	Dr.		3	
To Branch Outstanding Expenses A/c				3
(Being the Incorporation of Branch Outstanding expenses in H.O. books)				

PROBLEM 25

M/s Shah & Co. commenced business on 01.04.2012 with Head Office at Mumbai and a Branch at Chennai. Purchases were made exclusively by the Head Office, where the goods were processed before sale. There was no loss or wastage in processing.

Only the processed goods received from Head Office were handled by the Branch. The goods were sent to branch at processed cost *plus* 10%.

All sales, whether by Head Office or by the Branch, were at uniform gross profit of 25% on their respective cost.

Following is the Trial Balance as on 31.03.2013:

Particulars	Head Office Dr. (₹)	Head Office Cr. (₹)	Branch Dr. (₹)	Branch Cr. (₹)
Capital	–	3,10,000	–	–
Drawings	55,000			
Purchases	19,69,500			
Cost of Processing	50,500			
Sales	–	12,80,000	–	8,20,000
Goods sent to Branch	–	9,24,000	–	–
Administrative expenses	1,39,000	–	15,000	–
Selling Expenses	50,000	–	6,200	–
Debtors	3,09,600	–	1,13,600	–
Branch Current Account	3,89,800	–	–	–
Creditors	–	6,01,400	–	10,800
Bank Balance	1,52,000	–	77,500	–
Head Office Current Account	–	–	–	2,61,500
Goods received from H.O.	–	–	8,80,000	–
	31,15,400	31,15,400	10,92,300	10,92,300

Following further information is provided:

(i) Goods sent by Head Office to the Branch in March of ₹.44,000 were not received by the Branch till 2nd April.

(ii) A remittance of ₹.84,300 sent by the Branch to Head Office was also similarly not received upto 31st March.

(iii) Stock taking at the Branch disclosed a shortage of ₹.20,000 (at selling price to the branch).

(iv) Cost of unprocessed goods at Head Office on 31.03.2013 was ₹.1,00,000.

Prepare Trading and Profit and Loss Account in columnar form and Balance Sheet of the business as a whole as at 31.03.2013. ***[Nov. 2005]***

Solution

Dr. **TRADING AND PROFIT AND LOSS ACCOUNT** Cr.

Particulars	H.O. ₹	Branch ₹	Total ₹	Particulars	H.O. ₹	Branch ₹	Total ₹
To Purchases	19,69,500	–	19,69,500	By Sales	12,80,000	8,20,000	21,00,000
To Cost of processing	50,500	–	50,500	By Goods sent to BR. (incl. GIT)	9,24,000	–	–
To Goods rec. from H.O. (Incl. GIT)	–	9,24,000	–	By Stock Shortage	–	16,000	16,000
To Gross Profit c/d	3,40,000	1,64,000	5,04,000	By Goods in transit	–	44,000	44,000
				By Closing Stock:			
				Processed goods	56,000	2,08,000	2,64,000
				Unprocessed goods	1,00,000	–	1,00,000
	23,60,000	10,88,000	25,24,000		23,60,000	10,88,000	25,24,000
To Admn. expenses	1,39,000	15,000	1,54,000	By Gross profit b/d	3,40,000	1,64,000	5,04,000
To Selling expenses	50,000	6,200	56,200				
To Stock shortage	–	16,000	16,000				
To Stock reserve	22,909	–	22,909				
To Net Profit	1,28,091	1,26,800	2,54,891				
	3,40,000	1,64,000	5,04,000		3,40,000	1,64,000	5,04,000

BALANCE SHEET AS AT 31ST MARCH, 2013

Liabilities		₹	Assets		₹
Capital	3,10,000		Debtors		
Add: Net Profit	2,54,891		H.O.	3,09,600	
	5,64,891		Branch	1,13,600	4,23,200
Less: Drawings	55,000	5,09,891	Closing Stock:		
Creditors			Processed Goods		
H.O.	6,01,400		H.O.	56,000	
Branch	10,800	6,12,200	Branch	2,08,000	
				2,64,000	
			Less: Stock Reserve	18,909	2,45,091
			Unprocessed goods		1,00,000
			Bank Balance		
			H.O.	1,52,000	
			Branch	77,500	2,29,500
			Goods in transit	44,000	
			Less: Stock reserve	4,000	40,000
			Cash in transit		84,300
		11,22,091			11,22,091

Working Notes:

(i) Stock at Head Office:

		₹
Cost of goods processed ₹(19,69,500 + 50,500 – 1,00,000)		19,20,000
Less: Cost of goods sent to Branch (₹.9,24,000 × 100/110)	8,40,000	
Cost of goods sold (₹.12,80,000 × 100/125)	10,24,000	18,64,000
Stock of processed goods with H.O.		56,000

(ii) Stock at Branch:

		₹
Goods received from H.O. (at invoice price)		8,80,000
Less: Invoice value of goods sold ₹.8,20,000 × 100/125)	6,56,000	
Invoice value of stock shortage (₹.20,000 × 100/125)	16,000	6,72,000
Stock at Branch at invoice price		2,08,000
Less: Stock Reserve (2,08,000 × 10/110)		18,909
Stock of processed goods with Branch (at cost)		1,89,091

(iii) Stock Reserve

Unrealised profit on Branch Stock (₹ 2,08,000 × 10/110)	18,909
Unrealised profit on goods in transit (₹ 44,000 × 10/110)	4,000
	22,909

15A Accounting for Foreign Branches

LONG ANSWER PRACTICAL QUESTIONS

PROBLEM 1

The Washington branch of XYZ Limited, Mumbai sent the following trial balance as on 31st December, 2013:

	$	$
Head Office A/c	—	22,800
Sales —	—	84,000
Debtors and Creditors	4,800	3,400
Machinery	24,000	—
Cash at Bank	1,200	—
Opening Stock	11,200	—
Goods from H.O.	64,000	—
Expenses	5,000	—
	1,10,200	1,10,200

In the books of head office, the Branch a/c stood as follows:

WASHINGTON BRANCH ACCOUNT

Dr. *Cr.*

Particulars	₹	*Particulars*	₹
To Balance b/d	8,10,000	By Cash	28,76,000
To Goods sent to branch	29,26,000	By Balance c/d	8,60,000
	37,36,000		37,36,000

Goods are sent to the branch at cost *plus* 10% and the branch sells goods at Inovice price *plus* 25%. Machinery was acquired on 1st January, 2012, when \$ 1.00 = ₹ 48.

Rates of Exchange were:

1st January, 2013	\$ 1.00 = ₹ 46
31st December, 2013	\$ 1.00 = ₹ 48
Average	\$ 1.00 = ₹ 47

Machinery is depreciated @ 10% and the Branch Manager is entitled to a commission of 5% on the profit of the branch.

You are required to:

(i) Prepare the Branch Trading & Profit & Loss A/c in dollars.

(ii) Convert the Trial Balance of branch into Indian currency and prepare Branch Trading & Profit and Loss A/c and the Branch A/c in the books of head office.

[CA (PE II) May 2008]

Solution

Dr. **(i) TRADING AND PROFIT & LOSS A/C (IN DOLLARS)** Cr.

Particulars	₹	Particulars	₹
To Opening Stock	11,200	By Sales	84,000
To Goods from H.O.	64,000	By Closing Stock	8,000
To Gross Profit c/d	16,800		
	92,000		92,000
To Expenses	5,000	By Gross Profit b/d	16,800
To Depreciation	2,400		
To Manager's Commission	448		
To Net Profit c/d	8,952		
	16,800		16,800

(II) (A) CONVERTED TRIAL BALANCE

Particulars	Rate per Re.	Dr. (₹)	Cr. (₹)
Machinery	48	11,52,000	
Opening Stock	46	5,15,200	
Goods from H.O.	—	29,26,000	
Sales	47	—	39,48,000
Expenses	47	2,35,000	—
Debtors & Creditors	48	2,30,400	1,63,200
H.O. A/c	—	—	8,60,000
Cash at Bank	—	57,600	—
Difference of Exchange	—	—	1,45,000
	—	51,16,200	51,16,200
Closing Stock $ 8,000 (W.N.2)	48		₹ 3,84,000

Dr. **(B) TRADING AND PROFIT & LOSS ACCOUNT** Cr.

Particulars	₹	Particulars	₹
To Opening Stock	5,15,200	By Sales	39,48,000
To Goods from H.O.	29,26,000	By Closing Stock	3,84,000
To Gross Profit c/d	8,90,800		
	43,32,000		43,32,000
To Expenses	2,35,000	By Gross Profit b/d	8,90,000
To Depreciation @ 10% on ₹ 11,52,000	1,15,200	By Exchange difference	1,45,000
To Manager's Commisson (W.N.1)	21,504		
To Net Profit c/d	6,63,296		
	10,35,000		10,35,000

Working Notes:

(i) Manager's Commission = 5/105 of [16,800 – (5,000 + 2,400] = $ 448 (approx)
Manager's commission in Rupees = $ 448 × 48 = ₹ 21,504

(ii) *Calculation of Closing Stock*

Opening Stock	11,200
Add: Goods from H.O.	64,000
Less: Cost of Goods Sold (at invoice price) [100/125 × 84,000]	(67,200)
Closing Stock	8,000

(iii) Alternatively, Manager's Commission may be calculated on Profit before charging Commission.

PROBLEM 2

DM Ltd., Delhi has a branch in London. London branch is an integral foreign operation of *DM* Ltd. At the end of the year 31st March, 2013, the branch furnishes the following trial balance in U.K. Pound:

Particulars	£ *Dr.*	£ *Cr.*
Fixed Assets (acquired on 1st April, 2009)	24,000	
Opening Stock	11,200	
Goods from head office	64,000	
Expenses	4,800	
Debtors	4,800	
Creditors		3,200
Cash at bank	1,200	
Head office account		22,800
Purchases	12,000	
Sales		96,000
	1,22,000	1,22,000

In head office books, the branch account stood as shown below:

LONDON BRANCH ACCOUNT

Dr. *Cr.*

Particulars	₹	*Particulars*	₹
To Balance b/d	20,10,000	By Bank A/c	52,16,000
To Goods sent to branch A/c	49,26,000	By Balance c/d	17,20,000
	69,36,000		69,36,000

The following further information are given:

(a) Fixed assets are to be depreciated @ 10% p.a on straight line basis.

(b) On 31st March, 2013:

Expenses outstanding	-	£400
Prepaid expenses	-	£200
Closing stock	-	£8,000

(c) Rate of Exchange:

1st April, 2009	-	₹ 70 to £ 1
1st April, 2012	-	₹ 76 to £ 1

31st March, 2013	-	₹ 77 to £ 1
Average	-	₹ 75 to £ 1

You are required to prepare:

(i) Trial balance, incorporating adjustments of outstanding and prepaid expenses, converting U.K. pound into Indian rupees.

(ii) Trading and profit and loss account for the year ended 31st March, 2013 and the Balance Sheet as on that date of London branch as would appear in the books of Delhi head office of *DM* Ltd.

[CA (IPCC) Nov. 2009]

Solution

(I) TRIAL BALANCE OF LONDON BRANCH AS ON 31ST MARCH, 2013

Particulars	*U.K. Pound*	*Rate per U.K. Pound*	*Dr. (₹)*	*Cr. (₹)*
Fixed assets	24,000	70	16,80,000	
Opening Stock	11,200	76	8,51,200	
Goods from head office	64,000	–	49,26,000	–
Sales	96,000	75	–	72,00,000
Purchases	12,000	75	9,00,000	–
Expenses (4,800 + 400 – 200)	5,000	75	3,75,000	–
Debtors	4,800	77	3,69,600	–
Creditors	3,200	77	–	2,46,400
Outstanding expenses	400	77	–	30,800
Prepaid expenses	200	77	15,400	–
Cash at bank	1,200	77	92,400	–
Head office account		–		17,20,000
Difference in foreign exchange translation				– 12,400
			92,09,600	92,09,600

Closing Stock will be (£ 8,000 × ₹ 77) = ₹.6,16,000

(II) TRADING AND PROFIT & LOSS ACCOUNT FOR THE YEAR ENDED 31ST MARCH, 2013

Particulars	₹	*Particulars*	₹
To Opening stock	8,51,200	By Sales	72,00,000
To Purchases	9,00,000	By Closing stock	6,16,000
To Goods from head office	49,26,000		
To Gross Profit	11,38,800		
	78,16,000		78,16,000
To Expenses	3,75,000	By Gross Profit	11,38,000
To Depreciation	1,68,000	By Profit due to foreign exchange difference	1,20,400
To Net Profit	6,08,200		
	11,51,200		11,51,200

(III) BALANCE SHEET AS AT 31ST MARCH, 2013

Liabilities	₹	₹	Assets	₹	₹
Head Office			Fixed Assets	16,80,000	
Balance	17,20,000		*Less*: Depreciation	(1,68,000)	15,12,000
Add: Net Profit	6,08,200	23,28,200	Debtors		3,69,600
Outstanding expenses		30,800	Prepaid expenses		15,400
Creditors		2,46,400	Closing stock		6,16,000
			Cash at bank		92,400
		26,05,400			26,05,400

PROBLEM 3

An Indian company Moon Star Limited has a branch at Verginia (USA). The Branch is a non-integral foreign operation of the Indian Company. The trial balance of the Branch as at 31st March, 2013 is as follows:

Particulars	*US $* Dr.	Cr.
Office equipments	48,000	
Furniture	32,00	
Opening Stock	22,400	
Purchases	96,000	
Sales	—	1,66,400
Goods Sent from HO	32,000	
Salaries	3,200	
Carriage inward	400	
Rent, Rate & Taxes	800	
Insurance	400	
Trade Expenses	400	
Head Office Account	—	45,600
Sundry Debtors	9,600	
Sundry Creditors	—	6,800
Cash at Bank	2,000	
Cash in Hand	400	
	2,18,800	2,18,800

The following further information's are given:

(1) Salaries outstanding $400.
(2) Depreciate Office Equipment and Furniture @ 10% p.a. at written down value.
(3) The Head Office sent goods to Branch for ₹ 15,80,000
(4) The head Office shown an amount of ₹ 20,50,000 due from Branch.
(5) Closing Stock $21,500.
(6) There were no transit items either at the start or at the end of the year.
(7) On April 1,2011 when the fixed assets were purchased the rate of exchange was ₹ 43 to one $. On April, 1, 2012, the rate was ₹ 47 per $. On March 31, 2013 the rate was ₹ 50 per $. Average Rate during the year was ₹ 45 to one $.

Prepare:

(a) Trial Balance incorporating adjustment given converting dollars into rupees.
(b) Trading Profit and Loss Account for the year ended 31st March, 2013 and Balance Sheet as on

date depicting the profitability and net position of the Branch as would appear in the books of Indian company for the purpose of incorporating in the main Balance Sheet.

[May 2012]

Solution

(A) IN THE BOOKS OF MOON STAR LTD. – AN INDIAN COMPANY TRIAL BALANCE (IN RUPEES) OF VERGINIA (USA) BRANCH AS ON 31ST MARCH, 2013

Dr. *Cr.*

Particulars	*Dr. US $*	*Cr. US $*	*Conversion rate*	*Dr. US $*	*Cr. US $*
Office Equipment	43,200		50	21,60,000	
Depreciation on Office Equipment	4,800		50	2,40,000	
Furniture and Fixtures	2,880		50	1,44,000	
Depreciation of furniture and fixtures	320		50	16,000	
Opening Stock	22,400		47	10,52,800	
Purchase	96,000		45	43,20,000	
Sales		1,66,400	45		74,88,000
Goods sent from H.O.	32,000			15,80,000	
Carriage inward	400		45	18,000	
Salaries (3,200 + 400)	3,600		45	1,62,000	
Outstanding salaries		400	50		20,000
Rent, rates and taxes	800		45	36,000	
Insurance	400		45	18,000	
Trade expenses	400		45	18,000	
Head Office A/c		45,600			20,50,000
Trade debtors	9,600		50	4,80,000	
Trade creditors		6,800	50		3,40,000
Cash at bank	2,000		50	1,00,000	
Cash in hand	400		50	20,000	
Exchange gain (bal. fig.)					4,66,800
	2,19,200	2,19,200		1,03,64,800	1,03,64,800

TRADING AND PROFIT AND LOSS ACCOUNT OF VERGINIA BRANCH

for the year ended 31st March, 2013

Dr. *Cr.*

Particulars	₹	*Conversion*	₹
To Opening stock	10,52,800	By Sales	74,88,000
To Purchases	43,20,000	By Closing Stock	
To Goods from Head Office	15,80,000	(21,500 US $ × 50)	10,75,000
To Carriage inward	18,000		
To Gross profit c/d	15,92,200		
	85,63,000		85,63,000
To Salaries	1,62,000	By Gross profit b/d	15,92,200
To Rent, rates and taxes	36,000		
To Insurance	18,000		
To Trade expenses	18,000		
To Depreciation on office equipment	2,40,000		
To Depreciation on Furniture	16,000		
To Net Profit c/d	11,02,200		
	15,92,200		15,92,200

BALANCE SHEET OF VERGINIA BRANCH AS ON 31ST MARCH, 2013

Liabilities	₹	₹	*Particulars*	₹	₹
Head Office A/c	20,50,000		Office Equipment	24,00,000	
Add: Net Profit	11,02,200	31,52,000	*Less:* Depreciation	2,40,000	21,60,000
Foreign Currency			Furniture and fixtures	1,60,000	
Translation Reserve		4,66,800	*Less:* Depreciation	16,000	1,44,000
Trade creditors		3,40,000	Closing Stock		10,75,000
Outstanding salaries		20,000	Trade Debtors		4,80,000
			Cash in hand		20,000
			Cash at bank		1,00,000
		39,79,000			39,79,000

PROBLEM 4

ABCD Ltd., Delhi, has a branch in New York, USA which is an integral foreign operation of the Company. At the end of 31st March, 2013, the following ledger balances have been extracted from the books of the Delhi Office and the New York office.

Particulars	*Delhi (₹ thousands)*		*New York ($ thousands)*	
	Debit	*Credit*	*Debit*	*Credit*
Share Capital	—	1,250	—	—
Reserve & Surplus	—	940	—	—
Land	475	—	—	—
Buildings (Cost)	1,000	—	—	—
Buildings Depreciation Reserve	—	200	—	—
Plant & Machinery (Cost)	2,000	—	100	—
Plant & Machinery Depreciation Reserve	—	500	—	20
Trade Receivables/ Payables	500	270	60	20
Opening Stock	250	—	25	—
Branch Stock Reserve	—	65	—	—
Cash & Bank Balances	125	—	4	—
Purchases/Sales	275	600	25	125
Goods sent to Branch	—	1500	30	—
Managing Director's salary	50	—	—	—
Wages & Salaries	100	—	18	—
Rent	—	—	6	—
Office Expenses	25	—	12	—
Commission Receipts	—	275	—	100
Branch/H.O. Current A/c	800	—	—	15
	5,600	5,600	280	280

Additional Information

(i) Closing Stock: Delhi ₹ 2,00,000, New York $ 10 (ii) Head Office always sent goods to the Branch at cost *plus* 25%, (iii) Provision is to be made for doubtful debts at 5%, (iv) Depreciation is to be provided on buildings at 10% and on plant and machinery at 20% on written down values,

You are required:

(a) to convert the Branch Trial balance into rupees; (use the following rates of exchange) Opening rate 1 $ = ₹ 50, Closing rate 1 $ = ₹ 55, Average rate 1 $ = ₹ 52, For Fixed Assets 1 $ = ₹ 45

(b) to prepare the Trading and Profit & Loss Account for the year ending on 31st March, 2013, showing to the extent possible, H.O. results and Branch results separately. ***[CA (IPCC) May 2013]***

Solution

ABCD LTD.

(a) NEW YORK BRANCH TRIAL BALANCE (IN RUPEES) AS ON 31ST MARCH, 2013

Particulars	*Conversion rate per A $*	*(₹ '000) Dr.*	*(₹ '000) Cr.*
Plant & Machinery (cost)	₹ 45	45,00	
Plant & Machinery Depreciation Reserve	₹ 45		9,00
Trade Receivables/Trade Payables	₹ 55	33,00	11,00
Opening Stock	₹ 50	12,50	
Cash & Bank Balances	₹ 55	2,20	
Purchases/Sales	₹ 52	13,00	65,00
Goods received from H.O.	Actual	15,00	
Wages & Salaries	₹ 52	9,36	
Rent	₹ 52	3,12	
Office expenses	₹ 52	6,24	
Commission Receipts	₹ 52		52,00
H.O. Current Account	Actual		8,00
		139,42	145,00
Exchange loss (*balancing figure*)		5,58	—
		145,00	145,00

(b) TRADING AND PROFIT & LOSS ACCOUNT

for the year ending on 31st March, 2013

Dr. *Cr.*

(₹ '000)

Particulars	*H.O.* ₹	*Branch* ₹	*Total* ₹	*Particulars* ₹	*H.O.* ₹	*Branch* ₹	*Total*
To Opening Stock	250	1250	1500	By Sales	600	6500	7100
To Purchases	275	1300	1575	By Goods sent to Branch	1500	—	1500
To Goods received	—	1500	1500				
To Wages & Salaries	100	936	1036				
To Gross Profit	1675	1514.55	3189.55	By Closing Stock	200	0.55	200.55
	2300	6500.55	8800.55		2300	6500.55	8800.55
				By Gross Profit b/d	1675	1514.55	3189.55
To Rent	—	312	312	By Commission receipts	275	5200	5475
To Office expenses	25	624	649				
To Provision for doubtful debts @ 5%	25	165	190				
To Depreciation	380	720	1100				
To Balance c/d	1520	4893.55	6413.55				
	1950	6714.55	8664.55		1950	6714.55	8664.55
To Exchange loss			558	By Balance b/d			6413.55
To MD Salary			50	By Branch Stock Reserve			64.89
To Balance c/d			5870.44				
			6478.44				6478.44

Working Notes:

(i) *Calculation of Depreciation*

			(₹ '000)
		H.O.	*Branch*
A	Building-Cost	1000	—
B	*Less* : Depreciation Reserve	200	—
C	Building at WDV	800	
D	Depreciation on Building @ 10%	80	
E	Plant & Machinery Cost	2000	4500
F	*Less*: Depreciation Reserve	(500)	(900)
G	Plant & Machinery at WDV	1500	3600
H	Depreciation on Plant & Machinery @ 20%	300	720
I	Total Depreciation (D + H)	380	720

(ii) *Calculation of Branch Stock Reserve* (₹ '000)

A	Reserve on closing stock (0.55 × 1/5)	0.11
B	*Less* : Opening Branch Stock Reserve	(65)
C	Reversal of Reserve required	(64.89)

Scanner for Accounting Standards CA Examination Problems

CONCEPTUAL FRAMEWORK FOR PREPARATION AND PRESENTATION OF FINANCIAL STATEMENTS

PROBLEM 1

Give the four qualitative characteristics which the financial statements should observe.

[CA (PCC) Nov 2008]

Solution

The financial statements should observe the following qualitative characteristics:

(*a*) Understandability
(*b*) Relevance
(*c*) Reliability
(*d*) Comparability.

PROBLEM 2

What are the qualitative characteristics of the financial statements which improve the usefulness of the information furnished therein? ***[CA (IPCC) Nov. 2011]***

Solution

The qualitative characteristics are attributes that improve the usefulness of information provided in financial statements. The framework suggests that the financial statements should observe and maintain the following qualitative characteristics as far as possible within limits of reasonable cost benefit.

1. Under-standability	The financial statements should present information in a manner as to be readily understandable by the users with reasonable knowledge of business and economic activities. It is not right to think that more disclosures are always better. A mass of irrelevant information creates confusion and can be even more harmful than non-disclosure. No relevant information can be however withheld on the grounds of complexity.
2. Relevance	The financial statements should contain relevant information only. Information, which is likely to influence the economic decisions by the users, is said to be relevant. Such information may help the users to evaluate past, present or future events or may help in confirming or correcting past evaluations. The relevance of a piece of information should be judged by its materiality. A piece of information is said to be material if its omission or misstatement can influence economic decisions of a user.

3. **Reliability**	To be useful, the information must be reliable; that is to say they must be free from material error and bias. The information provided are not likely to be reliable unless: (*a*) Transactions and events reported are faithfully represented. (*b*) Transactions and events are reported in terms of their substance and economic reality not merely on the basis of their legal form. This principle is called the principle of 'substance over form'. (*c*) The reporting of transactions and events are neutral, i.e. free from bias. (*d*) Prudence is exercised in reporting uncertain outcome of transactions or events.
4. **Comparability**	Comparison of financial statements is one of the most frequently used and most effective tools of financial analysis. The financial statements should permit both inter-firm and intra-firm comparison. One essential requirement of comparability is disclosure of financial effect of change in accounting policies.
5. **True and Fair View**	Financial statements are required to show a true and fair view of the performance, financial position and cash flows of an enterprises. The conceptual framework does not deal directly with this concept of true and fair view, yet the application of the principal qualitative characteristics and of appropriate accounting standards normally results in financial statements portraying true and fair view of information about an enterprise.

PROBLEM 3

"One of the characteristics of financial statements is neutrality"- Do you agree with this statement?

[CA (PCC) May 2008]

Solution

Yes, one of the characteristics of financial statements is neutrality. To be reliable, the information contained in financial statement must be neutral, that is free from bias. Financial Statements are not neutral if by the selection or presentation of information, they influence the making of a decision or judgement in order to achieve a predetermined result or outcome. Financial statements are said to depict the true and fair view of the business of the organization by virtue of neutrality.

PROBLEM 4

Discuss the concept of Cost v/s Fair value with reference to Indian Accounting Standards.

Solution

Cost Basis: The term Cost refers to cost of purchase, costs of conversion on other costs incurred in bringing the goods to its present condition and location. Assets are recorded at the amount of cash or cash equivalents paid or the fair value of the other consideration given to acquire them at the time of their acquisition. Liabilities are recorded at the amount of proceeds received in exchange for the obligation, or in some circumstances (*for example*, income taxes), at the amounts of cash or cash equivalents expected to be paid to satisfy the liability in the normal course of business.

Fair Value: Fair Value of an asset is the amount at which an enterprise expects to exchange an asset between knowledgeable and willing parties in an arm's length transaction.

Indian Accounting Standards are generally based on historical cost with a very few exceptions:

AS 2 "Valuation of Inventories"	Inventories are valued at net realizable value (NRV) if cost of inventories is more than NRV.
AS 10 "Accounting for Fixed Assets"	Items of fixed assets that have been retired from active use and are held for disposal are stated at net realizable value if their net book value is more than NRV.
AS 13 "Accounting for Investments"	Current investments are carried at lower of cost and fair value. The carrying amount of long term investments is reduced to recognise the permanent decline in value.
AS 15 "Employee Benefits"	The provision for defined benefits is made at fair value of the obligations.
AS 26 "Intangible Assets"	If an intangible asset is acquired in exchange for shares or other securities of the reporting enterprise, the asset is recorded at its fair value, or the fair value of the securities issued, whichever is more clearly evident.
AS 28 "Impairment of Assets"	Provision is made for impairment of assets.

On the other hand IFRS and US GAAPs are more towards fair value. Fair value concept requires a lot of estimation and to the extent, it is subjective in nature.

AS-4

PROBLEM 4.1

A major fire has damaged the assets in a factory of a Limited Company on 5th April – five days after the year end and closure of accounts. The loss is estimated at ₹.10 crores out of which ₹.7 crores will be recoverable from the insurers. Explain briefly how the loss should be treated in the final accounts for the previous year. ***[CA (PE – II JUNE 2009)]***

Solution

The loss due to break out of fire is an example of event occurring after the balance sheet date. The event does not relate to conditions existing at the balance sheet date. It has not affected the financial position as on the date of balance sheet and therefore requires no specific adjustments in the financial statements. However, paragraph 8.6 of AS 4 states that disclosure is generally made of events occurring after balance sheet date i.e.in subsequent periods that represent unusual changes affecting the existence or substratum of the enterprise after the balance sheet date. In the given case, the amount of loss of assets in a factory is material and may be considered as an event affecting the substratum of the enterprise. Hence, as recommended in paragraph 15 of AS 4, disclosure of the event should be made in the report of the approving authority.

PROBLEM 4.2

In Raj Co. Ltd., theft of cash of ₹ 2 lakhs by the cashier in January, 2010 was detected in May, 2011. The accounts of the company were not yet approved by the Board of Directors of the company.

Whether the theft of cash has to be adjusted in the accounts of the company for the year ended 31.3.2011. Decide. ***[CA (PCC) May, 2007, 2010]***

Solution

AS-4	As per AS 4(revised), assets and liabilities should be adjusted for events occurring after the balance sheet date that provide additional evidence to assist the estimation of amounts relating to conditions existing at the balance sheet date.
Advice	Since the theft of cash is an additional information materially affecting the determination of the cash amount relating to conditions existing at the balance sheet date, it is necessary to adjust theft of cash in the financial statements of the company for the year ended 31st March, 2011.

PROBLEM 4.3

A Company follows April to March as its financial year. The Company recognizes cheques dated 31st March or before, received from customers after balance sheet date, but before approval of financial statement by debiting 'Cheques in hand account' and crediting 'Debtors account'. The 'cheques in hand' is shown in the Balance Sheet as an item of cash and cash equivalents. All cheques in hand are presented to bank in the month of April and are also realised in the same month in normal course after deposit in the bank. State with reasons, whether the collection of cheques bearing date 31st March or before, but received after Balance Sheet date is an adjusting event and how this fact is to be disclosed by the company?

[CA (IPCC) May, 2010, 2012]

Solution

AS-4	(a) Since the cheques bearing the date 31st March or before, and received after 31st March do not represent any **condition existing on the balance sheet** date i.e. 31st March. The collection of cheques after balance sheet date is not an adjusting event. Cheques that are received after the Balance Sheet Date should be accounted for in the period in which they are received.
Advice	(b) Since the collection of cheques after balance sheet date does not represent any **material change affecting financial position of the enterprise,** no disclosure in the Director's Report is **necessary**.

PROBLEM 4.4

An earthquake destroyed a major warehouse of ACO Ltd. on 20.5.2011. The accounting year of the company ended on 31.3.2011. The accounts were approved on 30.6.2011. The loss from earthquake is estimated at ₹ 30 lakhs. State with reasons, whether the loss due to earthquake is an adjusting or non-adjusting event and how the fact of loss is to be disclosed by the company?

[CA (PCC) Nov. 2009]

Solution

AS-4	As per AS 4 adjustments to assets and liabilities are not appropriate for events occurring after the balance sheet date, if such events do not relate to conditions existing at the balance sheet date.
Advice	(i) The destruction of warehouse due to earthquake did not exist on the balance sheet date i.e. 31.3.2011. Therefore, loss occurred due to earthquake is not to be recognised in the financial year 2010-11. (ii) Since the earthquake has caused major destruction; fundamental accounting assumption of going concern is called upon. Hence, the fact of earthquake together with an estimated loss of ₹ 30 lakhs should be disclosed in the Report of the Directors for the financial year 2010-11.

PROBLEM 4.5

A company entered into an agreement to sell its immovable property to another company for 35 lakhs. The property was shown in the Balance Sheet at ₹ 7 lakhs. The agreement to sell was concluded on 15th February, 2011 and sale deed was registered on 30th April, 2011. The financial statements for the year 2010-11 were approved by the Board on 12th May, 2011.

You are required to state, how this transaction would be dealt with in the financial statements for the year ended 31st March, 2011. ***[CA (IPCC) Nov. 2009]***

Solution

AS-4	As per AS 4 assets and liabilities should be adjusted for events occurring after the balance sheet date that provide additional evidence to assist the estimation of amounts relating to conditions existing at the balance sheet date.
Advice	Since agreement to sell before the balance sheet date and Registration of the sale deed after the balance sheet date provides additional information relating to the conditions existing at the balance sheet date, adjustment to assets for sale of immovable property is necessary in the financial statements for the year ended 31st March, 2011.

PROBLEM 4.6

While preparing its final accounts for the year ended 31st March 2012, a company made a provision for bad debts @25% of its total debtors (as per trend follows from the previous years). In the first week of March 2011, a debtor for ₹ 8,00,000 had suffered heavy loss due to an earthquake; the loss was not covered by any insurance policy. In April, 2012 the debtor became a bankrupt. Can the company provide for the full loss arising out of insolvency of the debtor in the final accounts for the year ended 31st March, 2012. ***[CA (IPCC) Nov. 2010]***

Solution

AS-4	As per AS 4 adjustment to assets and liabilities are required for events occuring after the balance sheet date that provide additional information materially affecting the determination of the amounts relating to conditions existing at the Balance Sheet date.
Advice	A debtor for ₹ 8,00,000 suffered heavy loss due to earthquake in the first week of March, 2012 and he became bankrupt in April, 2012 (after the balance sheet date). The loss was also not covered by any insurance policy. Accordingly, full provision for bad debts amounting ₹ 8,00,000 should be made, to cover the loss arising due to the insolvency of a debtor, in the final accounts for the year ended 31st March 2012.

PROBLEM 4.7

(i) The Company's sales tax assessment for assessment year 2008-09 has been completed on 14th February, 2011 with a demand of ₹ 2.76 crore. The company paid the entire due under protest without prejudice to its right of appeal. The Company files its appeal before the appellate authority wherein the grounds of appeal cover tax on additions made in the assessment order for a sum of 2.10 crore. Advise.

(ii) The Company has entered into a wage agreement in May, 2011 whereby the labour union has accepted a revision in wage from June, 2010. The agreement provided that the hike till May, 2011 will not be paid to the employees but will be settled to them at the time of retirement. The company agrees to deposit the arrears in Government Bonds by September, 2011. ***[CA (June 2009)]***

Solution

(i) Since the company is not appealing against the addition of ₹ 0.66 crore, the same should be provided for, in its accounts for the year ended on 31st March, 2011. The amount paid under protest can be kept under the heading 'Loans & Advances' and disclosed along with the contingent liability of ₹ 2.10 crore.

(ii) The arrears for the period from June, 2007 to March, 2011 are required to be provided for in the accounts of the company for the year ended on 31st March, 2011:

PROBLEM 4.8

AS-4 prescribes that adjustments to assets and liabilities are required for events occurring after the Balance Sheet date that provide additional information materially affecting the determination of the amount relating to conditions existing at the Balance sheet date-generally called adjusting events. "Proposed Dividend" is shown and adjusted in the Balance Sheet even if it is not an adjusting event as per AS-4 because it is proposed by the Board of Directors of the company after the Balance sheet date.

Keeping this in view, is it not violation of AS-4 to show proposed dividends as current liabilities and provisions? Comment ***[CA (Nov. 2010)]***

Solution

AS 4	As per para 8 of AS 4 "Contingencies arid Events occurring after the Balance sheet Date", adjustments to assets and liabilities are required for events occurring after the balance sheet date that provide additional information materially affecting the determination of the amounts relating to conditions existing at the balance sheet date. Accordingly, proposed dividend is not an adjusting event. However, para 14 of the Standard states that dividends stated to be in respect of the period covered by the financial statements, which are proposed or declared by the enterprise after the balance sheet date but before approval of the Financial statements, should be adjusted in the financial statements. Revised Schedule VI of the Companies Act 1956 prescribes that proposed dividend should be in the Notes to Accounts.
Advice	Proposed Dividends under the head **'Current Liabilities'** and Subhead, **'Short-term Provisions'** by adjusting it in the Balance Sheet is not in violation of AS 4.

PROBLEM 4.9

The Company invested ₹ 50 lakhs in April, 2012 in the acquisition of another company doing similar business, the negotiations for which had started during the current financial year. How will you deal with the financial statements for the year ended 31st March 2012?

Solution

AS 4	As per AS 4 no adjustment to assets and liabilities is required if the event does not affect the determination and the condition of the amounts stated in the financial statements for the year ended 31st March, 2012: Disclosure should be made in the report of the approving authority of those events occurring after the balance sheet date that represent material changes and commitments affecting the financial position of the enterprise.
Advice	The investment in April, 2012 in the acquisition of another company should be disclosed in the report of the Board of Directors to enable users of financial statements to make proper evaluations and decisions.

PROBLEM 4.10

Cashier of A-One Limited embezzled cash amounting to ₹ 6,00,000 during March, 2012. However same comes to the notice of Company management during April, 2012 only. financial statements of the company are not approved by the Board of Directors of the company.

(a) With the help of provisions of AS 4 "contingencies and Event Occurring after the Balance Sheet Date" decide, whether the embezzlement of cash should be adjusted in the books of accounts for the ending March, 2012?

(b) What will be your replay, if embezzlement of cash comes to the notice of company management only after approval of financial statements by the Board Directors of the company?

[May 2012]

Solution

AS 4	As per AS 4, assets and Liabilities should be adjusted for events occurring after the balance sheet date that provide additional evidence to assist the estimation of amounts relating to conditions existing at the balance sheet date.
Advice	(a) Though the theft, by the cashier ₹ 6,00,000 was detected after the balance sheet date (before approval of financial statements) but it is an additional information materially affecting the determination of the cash amount relating to conditions existing at the balance sheet date. Therefore, it is necessary to make the necessary adjustments in the financial statements of the company for the ended 31st March, 2012 for recognition of the loss amounting ₹ 6,00,000. (b) If embezzlement of cash comes to the notice of company management only after approval of financial statements by board of directors of the company, then the treatment will be done as per the provisions of AS 5. This being extra ordinary item should be disclosed in the Statement of Profit and Loss as a part of loss for the year ending March, 2013. The nature and the amount of prior period item should be separately disclosed on the Statement of Profit and Loss in a manner that its impact on current profit on loss can be perceived.

PROBLEM 4.11

Neel Limited has its corporate office in Mumbai and sells its products to stockists all over India. On 31st March, 2013, the company wants to recognize receipt of cheques bearing date 31st March, 2013 or before, as "Cheques in Hand" by reducing "Trade Receivables". The "Cheques in Hand" is shown in the Balance Sheet as an item of cash and cash equivalents. All cheques are presented to the bank in the month of April 2013 and are also realized in the same month in normal course after deposit in the bank. State with reasons, whether each of the following is an adjusting event and how this fact is to be disclosed by the company, with reference to the relevant accounting standard.

(i) Cheques collected by the marketing personnel of the company from the stockists on or before 31st March, 2013.

(ii) Cheques sent by the stockists through courier on or before 31st March, 2013. *[May 2013]*

Solution

(i) 1. Collection of cheques by the marketing personnel is an adjusting event as per AS 4 'Contingencies and Events Occurring after the Balance Sheet Date'.

2. **Reason:** Handing over of cheques by the stockist to the marketing employees discharges the liability of the stockist. Therefore, cheques collected by the marketing personnel of the company on or before 31-3-2013 require adjustment from the Stockists' Accounts i.e. from 'Trade Receivables A/c' even though these cheques (dated on or before 31-3-2013) are presented in the bank in the month of April, 2013 in the normal course.

3. **Disclosure:** Such 'cheques in hand' will be shown in the Balance Sheet as 'Cash and Cash equivalents' with a disclosure in the Notes to accounts about the accounting policy followed by the company from such cheques.

(ii) **1.** The collection of cheques after balance sheet date is not an adjusting event since Collection of cheques after 31-3-2013 does not represent any condition existing on the Balance Sheet date i.e. 31st March.

2. Cheques that are received after the balance sheet date should be accounted for in the period in which they are received even though the same may be dated 31st March or before as per AS 4.

3. The collection of cheques after Balance Sheet date does not represent any material change affecting financial position of the enterprise, hence no disclosure in the Director's Report is necessary.

AS-5

PROBLEM 5.1

What is meant by Accounting Estimate? Give two examples for accounting estimate.

[CA (PCC) Nov. 2007]

Solution

As a result of the uncertainties in business activities, many financial statement items cannot be measured with precision but can only be estimated. This is called accounting estimates. On account of such uncertainties, management makes various estimates and assumptions of assets, liabilities, income and expenses as on the date of preparation of financial statements. This process of estimation involves judgments, which is based on the latest information available.

Examples of estimation in *some* fields are:

(i) Estimation of useful life of depreciable assets.

(ii) Estimation of provision to be made for bad and doubtful debts.

PROBLEM 5.2

When can an item qualify to be a prior period item as per AS 5? ***[CA (PCC) May 2008]***

Solution

According to para 16 of AS 5 on 'Net Profit or Loss for the Period, Prior Period Items and Changes in Accounting Policies', prior period items refers to those income or expenses, which arise in the current period as a result of errors or omissions in the preparation of financial statements of one or more prior periods. The term does not include other adjustments necessitated by circumstances, which though related to prior periods, are determined in the current period e.g., arrears payable to workers in current period as a result of revision of wages with retrospective effect.

PROBLEM 5.3

Explain the provisions of AS -5 regarding accounting treatment of prior period items.

[CA (PCC JUNE 2009)]

Solution

As per AS 5, prior period items are income or expenses, which arise, in the current period as a result of errors or omission in the preparation of financial statements of one or more prior periods. The term does not include other adjustments necessitated by circumstances, which though related to prior periods, are determined in the current period. *Example*: arrears payable to workers in current period as a result of retrospective revision of wages.

The nature and amount of prior period items should be separately disclosed in the statement of profit and loss in manner that their impact on current profit or loss can be perceived.

As per para 19 of AS 5, prior period items are normally included in determination of net profit or loss for the current profit, they can be added (or deducted as the case may be) from the current profit. An alternative approach is to show such items in the statement of profit or loss after determination of current net profit or loss. In either case, the objective is to indicate the effect of such items on the current profit or loss.

PROBLEM 5.4

The company finds that the stock sheets of 31.3.2010 did not include two pages containing details of inventory worth ₹ 20 lakhs. State, how will you deal with this matter in the accounts of A Ltd. for the year ended 31st March, 2011 with reference to AS 5. ***[CA (PCC) Nov 2008]***

Solution

As per para 16 of AS 5 on 'Net Profit or Loss for the Period, Prior Period Items and Changes in Accounting Policies', omission of two pages containing details of inventory worth ₹ 20 lakhs in 31.3.2010 is a prior period item. As per para 19 of the standard, prior period items are normally included in the determination of net profit or loss for the current period. Accordingly, ₹ 20 lakhs must be added to opening stock of 1.4.2010. An alternative approach is to show such items in the statement of profit and loss after determination of current net profit or loss. In either case, the objective is to indicate the effect of such items on the current profit or loss.

PROBLEM 5.5

A company created a provision of ₹ 75,000 for staff welfare while preparing the financial statements for the year 2010-11. On 31st March, in a meeting with staff welfare association, it was decided to increase the amount of provision for staff welfare to ₹ 1,00,000. The accounts were approved by Board of Directors on 15th April, 2011.

Explain the treatment of such revision in financial statements for the year ended 31st March, 2011. ***[CA (IPCC) Nov. 2009]***

Solution

AS-5	As per AS 5 normally, all items of income and expense which are recognised in a period are included in the determination of the net profit or loss for the period. This includes extraordinary items and the effects of changes in accounting estimates. However, the effect of such change in accounting estimate should be classified using the same classification in the statement of profit and loss, as was used previously, for the estimate.
Advice	As per AS 5 in the change in amount of staff welfare provision amounting ₹ 25,000 is neither a prior period item nor an extraordinary item. It is a change in estimate, which has occurred in the year 2010-11.

PROBLEM 5.6

Closing stock for the year ending on 31.3.2013 is ₹ 1,50,000 which includes stock damaged in a fire in 2011-12. On 31.3.2012, the estimated net realisable value of the damaged stock was ₹ 12,000. The revised estimate of net realisable value of damaged goods amounting ₹ 4,000 has been included in closing stock as on 31.3.2013.

Find the value of closing stock to be shown in Profit and Loss account for the year 2012-13. ***[CA (IPCC) May, 2010,2013]***

Solution

AS-5	As per AS 5 the effect of a change in accounting estimate should be classified using the same classification in the statement of profit and loss as was used previously for the estimate.
Advice	The fall in estimated net realisable value of damaged stock ₹ 8,000 is the effect of change in accounting estimate. Thus, the value of closing stock for the year 2012-13 will be as follows:

	₹
Closing Stock (including damaged goods)	1,50,000
Less: Revised value of damaged goods	(4,000)
Closing stock (excluding damaged goods)	1,46,000

PROBLEM 5.7

Goods of ₹ 5,00,000 were destroyed due to flood in September, 2008. A claim was lodged with insurance company, but no entry was passed in the books for insurance claim.

In March, 2011, the claim was passed and the company received a payment of ₹ 3,50,000 against the claim. Explain the treatment of such receipt in final accounts for the year ended 31st March, 2011. ***[CA (IPCC) Nov. 2009]***

Solution

AS-5	As per the provisions of AS 5 prior period items are income or expenses, which arise, in the current period as a result of error or omissions in the preparation of financial statements of one or more prior periods. Further, the nature and amount of prior period items should be separately disclosed in the statement of profit and loss in a manner that their impact on current profit or loss can be perceived.
Advice	It is clearly a case of error in preparation of financial statements for the year 2008-09. Hence, claim received in the financial year 2010-11 is a prior period item and should be separately disclosed in the Statement of Profit and Loss.

PROBLEM 5.8

XY Ltd. was making provisions for non-moving stocks based on no issues for the last 12 months upto 31.03.10. Based on technical evaluation the company wants to make provisions during the year 31.03.11

Total value of stock — ₹ 150 lakhs.

Provisions required based on 12 months issue ₹ 4.0 lakhs.

Provisions required based on technical evaluation ₹ 3.20 lakhs.

Does this amount to change in accounting policy? Can the company change the method of provision? ***[CA (Nov. 2009)]***

Solution

AS 5	1. As per AS 5. The method of estimating the amount of provision may be changed, in case, a more prudent estimate can be made by adopting the changed method. 2. The decision of making provision for non-moving stocks on the basis of technical evaluation does not amount to change in accounting policy as per AS 5.
Advice	Considering the total value of stocks, the change in the amount of required provision of non-moving stocks from ₹ 4.0 lakhs to ₹ 3.20 lakhs is also not material. The disclosure can be made for such change by way of notes to the accounts in the financial statements of XY Ltd. for the year ending on 31.03.11, in the following manner: "*The company has provided for non-moving stocks on the basis of technical evaluation unlike preceding years. Had the same method been followed as in the previous year, the profit for the year and the corresponding effect on the year end, the net assets would have been higher by ₹ 0.80 lakhs*".

PROBLEM 5.9

There was a major theft of stores valued at ₹ 46 lakhs in the preceding year detected only during the current financial year. ***[CA (Nov. 2009)]***

Solution

AS 5	As per AS 5. The adjustments are required o be made in the current year as 'Prior Period Items'.
Advice	Due to major theft of stores in the preceding year which was detected only during the current financial year there was overstatement of closing stock of stores in the preceding year. This must have also resulted in the overstatement of profits of previous year, brought forward to the current year; Accordingly, the adjustments relating to both opening stock of the current year and profit brought forward from the previous year should be separately disclosed in the Statement of Profit and Loss together with their nature and amount in a manner that their Impact on the current profit or loss can be perceived. The disclosure as to the theft and the resulting loss is required in the notes to the accounts for the current year.

PROBLEM 5.10

M/s Dinesh & Company signed an agreement with workers tor increase in wages with retrospective effect. The out-flow on account of arrears was for 2007–08—₹ 10.00 lakhs, for 2008–09 ₹ 12.00 lakhs and for 2009-10 ₹ 12.00 lakhs. This amount is payable in September, 2010. The accountant wants to charge ₹ 22.00 lakhs as prior period charges in financial statement for 2010-11. Discuss. ***[CA (Nov. 2008, May 2011)]***

Solution

AS 5	As per AS 5 the term prior period item refers only to income or expenses which arise in the current period as a result of errors or omission in the preparation of the financial statements of one or more prior periods. The term does not include other adjustments necessitated by circumstances, which though related to prior periods are determined in the current period.
Advice	1. The full amount of wage arrears paid to workers will be treated as an expense of current year and it will be charged to profit and loss account as current expenses and not as prior period expenses. 2. Additional wages is an expense arising from the ordinary activities of the company. Although abnormal in amount, such an expense does not qualify as an extraordinary item. However, as per Para 12 of AS 5 (Revised), when items of income and expense within profit or loss from ordinary activities are of such size, nature or incidence that their disclosure is relevant to explain the performance of the enterprise for the period, the nature and amount of such items should be disclosed separately.

PROBLEM 5.11

A Limited company created a provision for bad and doubtful debts at 5% on debtors in preparing the financial statements for the year 2011-12. Subsequently on a review of the credit period allowed and financial capacity of the customers, the company decided to increase the provision to 10% on debtors as on 31-03-2012. The accounts are not approved by the Board of Directors till the date of decision. While applying the relevant accounting standard, can this revision be considered as an extraordinary item or prior period item? ***[CA (PCC) May 2011]***

Solution

AS 5	As per AS 5 'Net Profit or Loss for the Period, Prior Period Items and Changes in Accounting Policies', the preparation of financial statements involve making estimates which are based on the circumstances existing at the time when the financial statements are prepared. It may be necessary to revise an estimate in a subsequent period if there is a change in the circumstances on which the estimate was based. Revision of an estimate, by its nature, does not bring the adjustment within the definitions of a prior period item or an extra ordinary item.
Advice	The change in estimated provision for doubtful debts is neither a prior period item nor an extra ordinary item. However, as per para 27 of the standard, a change in accounting estimate which has material effect in the current period should be disclosed and quantified. Any change in the accounting estimate which is expected to have a material effect in later periods should also be disclosed and quantified.

PROBLEM 5.12

X Co. Ltd. signed an agreement with its employees union for revision of wages in June, 2011. The wage revision is with retrospective effect from 1.4.2007. The arrear wages upto 31.3.2011 amounts to ₹ 80 lakhs. Arrear wages for the period from 1.4.2011 to 30.6.2011 (being the date of agreement) amounts to ₹ 7 lakhs.

Decide whether a separate disclosure of arrear wages is required. *[May 2012]*

Solution

AS 5	As per AS 5, when items of income and expense within profit or loss from ordinary activities are of such size, nature or incidence that their disclosure is relevant to explain the performance of the enterprise for the period, the **nature and amount of such items should be disclosed separately.**
Advice	It is given that revision of wages took place in June, 2011 with retrospective effect from 1.4.2007. The arrear wages payable for the period from 1.4.2007 to 30.6.2011 cannot be taken as an error or omission in the preparation of financial statements and hence this expenditure **cannot be taken as a prior period item.** Additional liability on account of wages amounting ₹ 87 lakhs (from 1.4.2007 to 30.6.2011) should be included in current year's wages. It may be mentioned that additional wages is an expense arising from the ordinary activities of the company. Although abnormal in amount, such an expense does not qualify as an extraordinary item. However, wages payable for the current year (from 1.4.2011 to 30.6.2011) amounting ₹ 7 lakhs is not a prior period item hence need not be disclosed separately. This may be shown as current year wages.

PROBLEM 5.13

Give two examples on each of the following items:

(i) Change in Accounting Policy

(ii) Change in Accounting Estimate

(iii) Extra Ordinary Items

(iv) Prior Period Items. *[Nov. 2012]*

Solution

(i) Examples of Changes in Accounting Policy:

a. Change of Depreciation method from WDV to SLM and vice-versa.

b. Change in Cost formula in measuring the cost of inventories.

(ii) Examples of Changes in Accounting Estimates:

a. Change in estimate of provision for doubtful debts on sundry debtors.

b. Change in estimate of useful life of fixed assets.

(iii) Examples of Extraordinary items:

a. Loss due to earthquakes/fire/strike

b. Attachment of property of the enterprise by government

(iv) Examples of Prior period items:

a. Applying incorrect Rate of Depreciation in one or more prior periods.

b. Omission to account for Income or Expenditure in one or more prior periods.

AS-11

PROBLEM 11.1

Goods purchased on 1.1.2010 of US $ 10,000 — ₹.45 per US$
Exchange rate on 31.3.2010 — ₹.44 per US$
Date of actual payment 7.7.2010 — ₹.43 per US$

Ascertain the loss/gain for financial years 2009-10 and 2010-11, also give their treatment as per AS 11. *[CA (PCC) Nov 2008]*

Solution

Treatment at Date of Transaction	As per AS 11 'The Effects of Changes in Foreign Exchange Rates', all foreign currency transactions should be recorded by applying the exchange rate on the date of transactions. Accordingly, Goods purchased on 1.1.2010 and corresponding creditor would be recorded at ₹ 4,50,000 (i.e. $10,000 × ₹ 45). At the balance sheet date all monetary transactions should be reported using the closing rate.
Treatment at Reporting Date	As per AS 11 Creditor of US $10,000 on 31.3.2010 should be reported at ₹.4,40,000 (i.e. $10,000 × ₹.44) and exchange profit of ₹.10,000 (i.e. 4,50,000 – 4,40,000) should be credited to Profit and Loss account in the year 2009-10.
Treatment at Settlement Date	As per AS 11, exchange difference on settlement of the account should also be transferred to Profit and Loss account. Therefore, ₹.10,000 (i.e. 4,40,000 – 4,30,000) will be credited to Profit and Loss account in the year 2010-11.

PROBLEM 11.2

Goods purchased on 24.2.2010 of US $ 1,000 — ₹.46.60 per US$
Exchange rate on 31.3.2010 — ₹.47.00 per US $
Date of actual payment 05.06.2010 — ₹.47.50 per US $

Calculate the loss/gain for the financial year 2009-2011 and 2010-2011 as per AS 11. *[CA (PE – II JUNE 2009)]*

Solution

Treatment at Date of Transcaction	As per para 9 of AS 11 on 'The Effects of Changes in Foreign Exchange Rates', a foreign currency transaction should be recorded, on initial recognition in the reporting currency, by applying to the foreign currency amount the exchange rate between the reporting currency and the foreign currency at the date of the transaction. Accordingly, goods purchased on 24.02.2010 and corresponding creditors would be recorded at ₹ 46.60 = 1 US $ i.e. 1,000 × 46.60 = ₹ 46,600.
Treatment at Reporting Date	As per para 11 of AS 11, at balance sheet date all monetary items should be reported using the closing rate, therefore creditors of US$ 1,000 outstanding on 31.03.2010 will be reported. i.e. 1,000 × 47.00 = ₹.47,000. Exchange Loss (47,000 – 46,600) = ₹.400 should be debited in Profit and loss Account for the year 2009-2010.
Treatment on Settle-ment Date	Exchange differences on settlement of monetary items should be transferred to Profit and loss Account as gain or loss, therefore 1,000 x 47.50 = 47,500 – 47,000 = ₹ 500 will be debited to Profit and loss Account for the year 2010-2011.

PROBLEM 11.3

A Ltd. purchased fixed assets costing ₹ 6,000 lakhs on 1.4.2010. This was financed by foreign currency loan (U.S. Dollars) payable in three annual equal instalments. Exchange rates were 1 Dollar = ₹ 40 and ₹ 45 as on 1.4.2010 and 31.3.2011 respectively. First instalment was paid on 31.3.2011. A Ltd. provides depreciation on Fixed Assets @20% on WDV basis.

You are required to state, how these transactions would be accounted for?

[CA (PCC) May, 2010]

Solution

AS-11	As per AS 11 (Revised) exchange differences arising on the settlement of monetary items or on reporting an enterprise's monetary items at rates different from those at which they were initially recorded during the period, or reported in previous financial statements, should be recognized as income or as an expense in the period in which they arise. Thus, exchange differences arising on repayment of liabilities incurred for the purpose of acquiring fixed assets are recognized as income or expenses.
Exchange	Foreign Exchange Loan = $\frac{\text{Rs. } 6,000}{\text{Rs. } 40}$ = US \$150 lakhs. Exchange Difference = US \$150 lakhs × (45 – 40) = ₹ 750 lakhs.
Treatment	Loss due to exchange difference amounting ₹ 750 lakhs should be charged to Profit and Loss Account for the year ended 31st March 2011, Depreciation of ₹ 1200 lakhs (i.e. 20% of ₹ 6000 lakhs) should be provided in the financial Statements for the year ended 31st March 2011.

PROBLEM 11.4

On 31st March, 2011, the following ledger balances have been extracted from the books of Washington branch office:

Ledger Accounts	*$*
Building	180
Stock as on 1. 4. 2010	26
Cash and Bank Balances	57
Purchases	96
Sales	110
Commission receipts	28
Debtors	46
Creditors	65

You are required to convert above Ledger balances into Indian Rupees.

Use the following rates of exchange:

	₹ per $
Opening rate	46
Closing rate	50
Average rate	48
For fixed assets	42

[CA (IPCC) May, 2010]

Solution

Conversion of ledger balances (in Dollars) into Rupees

	$	*Rate per $*	*Amount in Rupees*
Building	180	42	7,560
Stock as on 01.04.2010	26	46	1,196
Cash and bank balances	57	50	2,850
Purchases	96	48	4,608
Sales	110	48	5,280
Commission receipts	28	48	1,344
Debtors	46	50	2,300
Creditors	65	50	3,250

PROBLEM 11.5

Sterling Ltd. purchased a plant for US $20,000 on 31st December, 2010 payable after 4 months. The company entered into a forward contract for 4 months @ ₹ 48.85 per dollar. On 31st December, 2010, the exchange rate was ₹ 47.50 per dollar.

How will you recognize the profit or loss on forward contract in the books of Sterling Limited for the year ended 31st March, 2011. ***[CA (IPCC) Nov. 2009]***

Solution

Calculation of profit or loss to be recognized in the books of Sterling Limited

Particulars	₹
Forward contract rate	48.85
Less: Spot rate	47.50
Loss	1.35
Forward Contract Amount	$20,000
Total loss on entering into forward contract = ($20,000 × ₹ 1.35)	₹ 27,000
Contract period	4 months
Loss for the period 1st January, 2011 to 31st March, 2011 i.e. 3 months falling in the year 2010-11 will be ₹ 27,000 × $\frac{3}{4}$ =	20,250

Balance loss of ₹ 6,750 (i.e. ₹ 27,000 – ₹ 20,250) for the month of April, 2011 will be recognised in the financial year 2011-2012.

PROBLEM 11.6

Mr. A bought a forward contract for three months of US $ 1,00,000 on 1st December at 1 US $ = ₹ 47.10 when exchange rate was US $ 1 = ₹ 47.02, On 31st December when he closed his books, exchange rate was US $ 1 = ₹ 47.15. On 31st January, he decided to sell the contract at ₹ 47.18 per dollar. Show how the profits from contract will be recognised in the books.

[CA (May, 2010)]

Solution

AS 11	It is apparent from the facts given in the question that Mr. A entered into forward exchange contract for speculation purpose. Gain or loss on forward exchange contracts intended for trading or speculation purpose should be computed by multiplying the foreign currency amount of the forward exchange contract by the **difference between the forward rate available at the reporting date for the remaining maturity of the contract and the contracted forward rate** (or the forward rate last used to measure a gain or loss on that contract for an earlier period). The gain or loss so computed should be recognised in the Statement of Profit and Loss for the period and the premium or discount on the forward exchange contract is ignored and not recognised separately. In recording such contract, at each balance sheet date, the value of the contract is marked to its current market value and the gain or loss on the contract is recognised.
Advice	The premium on contract i.e., the difference between the contract rate and the spot rate amounting ₹ 8,000 [US$ 1,00,000 × (₹.47.10 – ₹.47.02)] will be ignored and not be recorded in the books. However, the profit on contract i.e. the difference between the sale rate and contract rate amounting ₹ 8,000 [US$ 1,00,000 × 0.08* (₹ 47.18 – ₹ 47.10)] will be recognized in the books of Mr. A on 31st January. **Note**: The answer has been given on the basis thai Mr. A is a small and mediumsized entity and AS 30 "Financial Instruments: Recognition and Measurement" is not applicable to him.

PROBLEM 11.7

Mr. Y bought a forward contract for three months of US $ 2,00,000 on 7st December 2010 at 1 US $ = ₹ 44.70 when the exchange rate was 1 US $ = ₹ 45.90. On 31-12-2010, when he closed his books, exchange rate was 1 US $ = ₹ 44.20. On 31st January, 2011 he decided to sell the contract at ₹ 44.30 per Dollar. Show how the profits from the contract will be recognized in the books of Mr. Y. *[CA (PCC) Nov. 2011]*

Solution

AS 11	As per AS 11 'Effect of Changes in Foreign Exchange Rates', in recording a forward exchange contract intended for trading or speculation purpose, the premium or discount on the contract is ignored and at each balance sheet date, the value of contract is marked to its current market value and the gain or loss on the contract is recognised.	
Advice	Since the forward contract was for speculation purposes the premium on forward contract i.e. the difference between the spot rate and the forward contract rate will not be recorded in the books. Only when the forward contract is sold the difference between the forward contract rate and sale rate will be recorded in the Profit & Loss Account.	
	Sale rate	₹ 44.30
	Less: Contract rate	(₹ 44.10)
	Profit on sale of contract per US$	₹ 00.20
	Contract Amount	US $ 2,00,000
	Total profit (2,00,000 x 0.20)	₹ 40,000
	Disclosure:	
	An enterprise should disclosure the following:	

	(i) The amount of exchange differences included in the net profit or loss for the period. (ii) Net exchange differences accumulated in foreign currency translation reserve as a separate component of shareholder's funds, and a reconciliation of the amount of such exchange differences at the beginning and end of the period.

PROBLEM 11.8

Sunshine Company Limited imported raw materials worth US Dollars 9,000 on 25th February, 2011, when the exchange rate was ₹ 44 per US Dollar. The transaction was recorded in the books at the above mentioned rate. The payment for the transaction was made on 10th April, 2011, when the exchange rate was ₹ 48 per US Dollar. At the year end 31st March, 2011, the rate of exchange was ₹ 49 per US Dollar.

The Chief Accountant of the company passed an entry on 31st March, 2011 adjusting the cost of raw material consumed for the difference between ₹ 48 and ₹ 44 per US Dollar. Discuss whether this treatment is justified as per the provisions of AS-11 (Revised).

[CA (IPCC) Nov., 2011]

Solution

AS 11	As per AS 11, 'The Effects of Changes in Foreign Exchange Rates', initial recognition of a foreign currency transaction is done in the reporting currency by applying the exchange rate at the date of the transaction.
Advice	1. On 25th February 2011, the raw material purchased and its creditors will be recorded at US dollar 9,000 × ₹ 44 = ₹ 3,96,000. 2. On Balance Sheet date such transaction is reported at closing rate of exchange, hence it will be valued at the closing rate i.e. ₹ 49 per US dollar (USD 9,000 × ₹ 49 = ₹ 4,41,000) at 31st March, 2011, irrespective of the payment made for the same subsequently at lower rate in the next financial year. 3. The difference of ₹ 5 (i.e., 49 – 44) per US dollar i.e. ₹ 45,000 (USD 9,000 × ₹ 5) will be shown as an exchange loss in the profit and loss account for the year ended 31st March, 2011 and will not be adjusted against the cost of raw materials. 4. In the subsequent year on settlement date, the company would recognize or provide in the Profit and Loss account an exchange gain of ₹ 1 per US dollar, i.e. the difference from balance sheet date to the date of settlement between ₹ 49 and ₹ 48 per US dollar i.e. ₹ 9,000. 5. Hence, the accounting treatment adopted by the Chief Accountant of the company is incorrect i.e. it is not as per AS 11.

PROBLEM 11.9

RAJASTHALI & CO.. purchased fixed assets costing ₹ 3,000 lakhs on 1.4.2011 and the same was fully financed by foreign currency loan (U.S. Dollars) payable in three annual equal instalments. Exchange rates were 1 Dollar = ₹ 40.00 and ₹ 42.50 as on 1.4.2011 and 31.03.2012 respectively. First instalment was paid on 31.03.2012 As per AS 11 (Revised 2003). State the treatment of Exchange Difference.

Solution

Foreign Currency Loan = ₹ 3,000 lakhs/₹ 40 =₹ 75 lakhs
Exchange difference = 75 lakhs US Dollars × (42.50 – 40.00) = ₹ 187.50 lakhs
(including exchange loss on payment of first instalment)

- Therefore, entire loss due to exchange differences amounting ₹ 187.50 lakhs should be charged to Profit and Loss Account for the year.

PROBLEM 11.10

Explain "monetary item" as per Accounting Standard 11. How are foreign currency monetary items to be recognized at each Balance Sheet date? Classify the following as monetary or non-monetary item:

(i) Share Capital
(ii) Trade Receivables
(iii) Investments
(iv) Fixed Assets

[CA (PCC) May 2013]

Solution

1. As per AS 11 'The Effects of Changes in Foreign Exchange Rates', Monetary items are money held and assets and liabilities to be received or paid in fixed or determinable amounts of money.
2. Foreign currency monetary items should be reported using the closing rate at each balance sheet date. However, in certain circumstances, the closing rate may not reflect with reasonable accuracy the amount in reporting currency that is likely to be realised from, or required to disburse, a foreign currency monetary item at the balance sheet date. In such circumstances, the relevant monetary item should be reported in the reporting currency at the amount which is likely to be realised from or required to disburse, such item at the balance sheet date.

Share capital	Non-monetary
Trade receivables	Monetary
Investments	Non-monetary
Fixed assets	Non-monetary

AS-12

PROBLEM 12.1

How Government grant relating to specific fixed asset is treated in the books as per AS-12. *[CA (PCC) Nov. 2007]*

Solution

Refer to AS-12 from Chapter 16 on Accounting Standards

PROBLEM 12.2

How would you record a non-monetary grant received from the Government as per AS 12? *[CA (PCC) May 2008]*

Solution

According to para 7.1 of AS 12 'Accounting for Government Grants', Government grants may take the form of non-monetary assets such as land or other resources, given at concessional rates. In these circumstances, it is usual to account for such assets at their acquisition cost. Non-monetary grants given free of cost are recorded at a nominal value.

PROBLEM 12.3

A company purchased on April 1, 2010 a special purpose machinery for ₹ 1 crore, and received Central Government subsidy for 25% of the price. Effective life of the machinery is 8 years. Explain the accounting treatment and quote the relevant AS. *[CA (Nov. 2010)]*

Solution

AS 12	As per AS 12, two methods of presentation in financial statements of grants related to specific fixed assets are regarded as acceptable alternatives. (a) **Capital Receipt Alternative**—The grant is shown as a deduction from the gross value of the asset concerned in arriving at its book value. The grant is thus recognised in the profit and loss statement over the useful life of a depreciable asset by way of a reduced depreciation charge. (b) **Deferred Income Alternative**—Grants related to depreciabfe assets are treated as deferred income which is recognised in the profit and loss statement on a systematic and rational basis over the useful life of the asset. Such allocation to income is usually made over the periods and in the proportions in which depreciation on related assets is charged.
Advice	(a) **Under Capital Receipt Alternative**—The cost of special purpose machinery will be recorded in trie books after reducing it by the amount of government subsidy of ₹ 25 lakhs. Thus the depreciable value of the machinery recorded in the books will be ₹ 75 lakhs (i.e. ₹ 1 crore – ₹ 25 lakhs). Depreciation of ₹ 9.375 lakhs (i.e. ₹ 75 lakhs/8 years) will be charged on it every year on straight line method. (b) **Under Deferred Income Alternative**—Machinery will be recorded in the books at ₹ 1 crore and depreciation will be charged on it for ₹ 12.5 lakhs (i.e. ₹ 1 crore/8 years) per year on straight line method. Government subsidy of ₹ 25 lakhs will be treated as deferred income and ₹ 13.125 iakhs (i.e. ₹ 25 iakhs / 8 years) will be recognized as income in the Statement of Profit and Loss every year.

PROBLEM 12.4

X Ltd. acquired a fixed asset for ₹ 50,00,000. The estimated useful life of the asset is 5 years. The salvage value after useful life was estimated at ₹ 5,00,000. The State Givernment gave a grant of 20% to encourage the asset acquisition. At the end of the second year, the subsidy of the State Government became refundable. What is the fixed asset value after refund of grant/subsidy to the State Government but before amortising the asset value at the end of the second year? ***[CA (PCC) Nov. 2007]***

Solution

Statement showing the calculation of Fixed Assets at the end of the second year

Particulars	₹
Original Cost of Fixed Assets	50,00,000
Less: State Government grant received	(10,00,000)
Less: Amount to be written off in the first year [(40,00,000 – 5,00,000)/5 years]	(7,00,000)
	33,00,000
Add: Refund of State Government grant	10,00,000
Value of fixed assets, at the end of the second year, after refund of grant but before depreciation	43,00,000

PROBLEM 12.5

Weak Ltd. acquired the fixed assets of ₹ 100 lakhs on which it received the grant of ₹ 10 lakhs. What will be the cost of the fixed assets as per AS 12 and how it will be disclosed in the financial statements? ***[CA (IPCC) May, 2010]***

Solution

AS-12	As per AS 12 the there are two different methods for recognition of a government grant. In the first method, Government grants related to specific fixed assets should e presented in the balance sheet by showing the grant as a deduction from the gross value of the assets concerned in arriving at their book value. Under the second method, government grants related to depreciable fixed assets may be treated as deferred income which should be recognised in the profit and loss statement on a systematic and rational basis over the useful life of the asset, i.e., such grants should be allocated to income over the periods and in the proportions in which depreciation on those assets is charged.
Advice	As per first method, fixed assets should be presented at ₹ 90 lakhs (₹ 100 lakhs less ₹ 10 lakhs) in the Balance Sheet. As per second method fixed assets will be shown at ₹ 100 lakhs in the balance sheet and the corresponding grant amounting ₹ 10 lakhs will be treated as deferred income to be recognized over useful life of the fixed asset.

PROBLEM 12.6

Santosh Ltd. has received a grant of ₹ 8 crores from the Government for setting up a factory in a backward area. Out of this grant, the company distributed ₹ 2 crores as divided. Also, Santosh Ltd. received land free of cost from the State Government but it has not recorded it at all in the books as no money has been spent. In the light of AS 12 examine, whether the treatment of both the grants is correct. ***[CA (IPCC) May, 2010]***

Solution

As per AS 12, when government grant is received for a specific purpose, it should be utilized for the same. So the grant received for setting up a factory is not available for distribution of dividend.

In the second case, even if the company has not spent money for the acquisition of land, land should be recorded in the books of accounts at a nominal value. The treatment of both the grants is incorrect as per AS 12.

PROBLEM 12.7

A Ltd. purchased a machinery for ₹ 40 lakhs. (Useful life 4 years and residual value ₹ 8 lakhs) Government grant received is ₹ 16 lakhs.

Show the Journal Entry to be passed at the time of refund of grant in the begning of 3rd year and the value of the fixed assets, if:

1. **the grant is credited to fixed assets.**
2. **the grant is credited to Deffered Grant Account.** ***[CA (PCC) Nov. 2010]***

Solution

Journal of A Ltd. (at the time of refund of grant)

If the grant is credited to fixed assets:

			Dr.	Cr.
I	Fixed Assets A/c	Dr.	₹ 16 lakhs	
	To Bank A/c			₹ 16 lakhs

II The balance of fixed assets after two years depreciation will be ₹ 16 lakhs and now it will become (₹ 16 lakhs + ₹ 16 lakhs) = ₹ 32 lakhs on which depreciation will be charged for remaining two years. Depreciation = (32 – 8)/2 = ₹ 12 lakhs p.a. will be charged for next two years.

If the grant is credited to Deferred Grant Account:

As per para 14 of AS 12 income from Deffered Grant Account is allocated to Profit and Loss account usually over the periods and in the proportions in which depreciation on related assets is charged. Accordingly, in the first two years (₹ 16 lakhs/4 years) = ₹ 4 lakhs × 2 = ₹ 8 lakhs were credited to Profit and Loss Account and ₹ 8 lakhs was the balance of Deferred Grant Account after two years.

Therefore, on refund in the 3rd year, following entry will be passed:

			Dr.	Cr.
I	Deferred Grant A/c	Dr.	₹ 8 lakhs	
	Profit & Loss A/c	Dr.	₹ 8 lakhs	
	To Bank A/c			₹ 16 lakhs
	(Being Government grant refunded)			

II Deferred grant account will become Nil. The fixed assets will continue to be shown in the books at ₹ 24 lakhs and depreciation will continue to be charged at 8 lakhs per annum.

Working Notes:

(i) Balance of Fixed Assets after two years but before refund (under first alternative) = (₹ 40 lakhs – ₹ 16 lakhs) – (₹ 4 lakhs × 2) = ₹ 16 lakhs

(ii) Balance of Fixed Assets after two years but before refund (under second alternative) = ₹ 40 lakhs – (₹ 8 lakhs × 2) = ₹ 24 lakhs

Note: It is assumed that value of fixed assets is to be given after refund of government grant.

PROBLEM 12.8

X Ltd. received a revenue grant of ₹ 15 crores during 2009-10 from Government for welfare activities to be carried on by the company for its employees. The grant prescribed the conditions for utilization.

However during the year 2011-12, it was found that the prescribed conditions were not fulfilled and the grant should be refunded to the Government.

State how this matter will have to be dealt with in the financial statements of X Ltd. for the year ended 2011-12. ***[CA (IPCC) Nov. 2009, May 2011]***

Solution

AS-12	As per AS 12, a grant that became refundable should be treated as an extra-ordinary item as per AS-5. The amount refundable in respect of a government grant related to revenue, is applied first against any unamortised deferred credit remaining in respect of the grant. To the extent that the amount refundable exceeds any such deferred credit, or where no deferred credit exists, the amount is charged immediately to Profit and Loss Statement.
Advice	Refund of grant of ₹ 15 crores should be charged to the Profit and Loss Account of the company as an extra-ordinary item during the financial year 2011-12.

PROBLEM 12.9

Explain the treatment of refund of Government Grants as per Accounting Standard 12.

[CA (IPCC) Nov. 2011]

Solution

HOW TO ACCOUNT FOR GRANT THAT BECOME REFUNDABLE

Case	Treatment
(i) The amount refundable in respect of a grant related to revenue.	Reduce the balance of unamortized deferred credit and charge excess refund to Profit and Loss Statement. **Journal Entry:** Grant A/c Dr. [with Unamortized Cr. Balance] P&L A.c Dr. [With Excess of Refund over Unamortized Cr. Balance] To Bank A/c [with Refund]
(ii) The amount refundable in respect of a grant related to a specific fixed asset.	Increase the book value of the asset & provide depreciation on the revised book value prospectively over the residual useful life of the asset. **Journal Entry:** Fixed Asset A/c Dr. To Grant A/c *or* Reduce the Capital Reserve or the deferred income balance, as appropriate, by the amount refundable. **Journal Entry:** Capital Reserve A/c Dr. To Grant A/c
(iii) The amount refundable in respect of a Government grants in the nature of promoters' contribution.	Reduce from the Capital Reserve. **Journal Entry:** Capital Reserve A/c Dr. To Grant A/c

PROBLEM 12.10

Z Ltd. Purchased a fixed assets for ₹ 75 lakhs, which has the estimated useful life of 5 years with the salvage value of ₹ 7,50,000. On purchase of the assets, government granted it a grant of ₹ 15 lakhs. Pass the necessary journal entries in the books of the company for first two years. ***[PCC (May) 2012]***

Solution

AS 12 states two method of presentation of grants, related to fixed assets, in the financial statements. Under first method, the grant is shown as a deduction from the gross value of the asset concerned in arriving at its books value as follows:

Journal of Z Ltd.

Year	*Particulars*	*Dr. (₹)*	*Cr. (₹)*
1st	Fixed Asset A/c Dr. To Bank A/c (Being Fixed Asset purchased)	75,00,000	 75,00,000
	Bank A/c Dr. To Fixed Asset A/c (Being grant received from the government)	15,00,000	 15,00,000
	Depreciation A/c ₹(60,00,000 – 7,50,000)/5 Dr. To Fixed Asset A/c (Being Depreciation charged on Straight line method)	10,50,000	 10,50,000
	Profit & Loss A/c Dr. To Depreciation A/c (Being depreciation transferred to Profit & Loss A/c)	10,50,000	 10,50,000
2nd	Depreciation A/c Dr. To Fixed Asset A/c (Being Depreciation charged on Straight line method)	10,50,000	 10,50,000
	Profit & Loss A/c Dr. To Depreciation A/c (Being depreciation transferred to Profit & Loss A/c)	10,50,000	 10,50,000

Note: Alternatively the question may be solved on the basis of the second method as stated in AS 12 where grants related to depreciable assets are treated as deferred income and is recognised in the profit and loss statement over the useful life of the asset.

PROBLEM 12.11

ABC Limited purchased a machinery for ₹ 25,00,000 which has estimated useful life of 10 years with the salvage value of ₹ 5,00,000. On purchase of the assets Central Government pays a grant for ₹ 5,00,000. Pass the journal entries with narration in the *books of the company for the first year, treating Grant as deferred income.* ***[May 2012]***

Solution

Journal of ABC Ltd.

Year	Particulars	Dr. (₹)	Cr. (₹)
1st	Machinery A/c Dr. To Bank A/c (Being machinery purchased)	25,00,000	25,00,000
	Bank A/c Dr. To Deferred Government Grant A/c (Being grant received from the government treated as deferred income)	5,00,000	5,00,000
	Depreciation A/c (25,00,000 – 5,00,000)/10 Dr. To Machinery A/c (Being depreciation charge on straight line method)	2,00,000	2,00,000
	Profit & Loss A/c Dr. To Depreciation A/c (Being depreciation transferred to P/L Account)	2,00,000	2,00,000
	Deferred Government Grant A/c (5,00,000)/10 Dr. To Profit & Loss A/c (Being proportionate government grant taken to P/L Account)	50,000	50,000

AS-16

PROBLEM 16.1

Briefly indicate the items which are included in the expressions "Borrowing Cost" as per AS 16.

Solution

Borrowing costs are interest and other costs incurred by any enterprise in connection with the borrowing of funds. Borrowing cost may include:

(a) Interest and commitment charges on bank borrowings and other short term and long term borrowings.
(b) Amortisation of discounts or premiums relating to borrowings.
(c) Amortisation of ancillary costs incurred in connection with the arrangement of borrowings.
(d) Finance charges in respect of assets required under finance leases or under other similar arrangements; and
(e) Exchange differences arising from foreign currency borrowings to the extent that they are regarded as an adjustment to interest costs.

PROBLEM 16.2

Enumerate two points which the financial statements should disclose in respect of Borrowing Costs as per AS 16. ***[CA (PCC JUNE 2009)]***

Solution

As per AS 16, the Financial Statements should disclose the following:

(a) The accounting policy adopted for borrowing costs and
(b) The amount of borrowing costs capitalized during the period

PROBLEM 16.3

An industry borrowed ₹ 40,00,000 for purchase of machinery on 1.6.2010. Interest on loan is 9% per annum. The machinery was put to use from 1.1.2011. Pass journal entries for the year ended 31.3.2011 to record the borrowing cost of loan as per AS 16. ***[CA (PCC) May 2008]***

Solution

	₹
Interest upto 31.3.2008 (40,00,000 × 9% × 10/12 months)	3,00,000
Less: Interest relating to pre-operative period [3,00,000 × 7/10]	2,10,000
Amount to be charged to P & L A/c	90,000
Pre-operative interest to be capitalized	2,10,000

Journal

Date	*Particulars*	*Dr. (₹)*	*Cr. (₹)*
1.6.10	Machinery A/c Dr. To Loan A/c (*Being interest on loan for pre-operative period capitalized*)	2,10,000	2,10,000
31.3.11	Interest on loan A/c Dr. To Loan A/c (*Being the interest on loan for the post-operative period*)	90,000	90,000

Date	Particulars		Dr. (₹)	Cr. (₹)
31.3.11	Profit and Loss A/c	Dr.	90,000	
	To Interest on loan A/c			90,000
	(Being interest on loan transferred to P&L A/c)			

PROBLEM 16.4

Axe Limited began construction of a new plant on 1st April, 2010 and obtained a special loan of ₹ 4,00,000 to finance the construction of the plant. The rate of interest on loan was 10%.

The expenditure that were made on the project of plant were as follows:

	₹
1st April, 2010	**5,00,000**
1st August, 2010	**12,00,000**
1st January, 2011	**2,00,000**

The company's other outstanding non-specific loan was ₹ 23,00,000 at an interest rate of 12%.

The construction of the plant completed on 31st March, 2011. You are required to:

(a) Calculate the amount of interest to be capitalized as per the provisions of AS 16 "Borrowing Cost".

(b) Pass a journal entry for capitalizing the cost and the borrowing cost in respect of the plant.

[CA (IPCC) Nov. 2009]

Solution

Total Expenses to be capitalized for borrowings as per AS 16 "Borrowing Costs".

	₹
Cost of Plant (5,00,000 + 12,00,000 + 2,00,000)	19,00,000
Add: Amount of interest to be capitalised	1,54,000
	20,54,000

Journal

Date	Particulars		Dr. (₹)	Cr. (₹)
31.03.11	Plant A/c	Dr.	20,54,000	
	To Bank A/c			20,54,000
	[Being amount of cost of plant and borrowing cost thereon capitalized]			

Working Notes:

(i) *Computation of average Accumulated Expenses*

		₹
1st April, 2010	Rs. 5,00,000 × 12 / 12	5,00,000
1st August, 2010	Rs. 12,00,000 × 8 / 12	8,00,000
1st January, 2011	Rs. 2,00,000 × 3 / 12	50,000
		13,50,000

(ii) *Amount of interest capitalised*

Particulars	₹
On specific borrowing (₹ 4,00,000 × 10%)	40,000
On non-specific borrowings (₹ 13,50,000 – ₹ 4,00,000) × 12%	1,14,000
Amount of interest to be capitalised	1,54,000

PROBLEM 16.5

Rohini Limited has obtained loan from an Institution for ₹ 500 lakhs for modernization and renovation of its plant and machinery. The installation of plant and machinery was completed on 31.3.2011 amounting to ₹ 320 lakhs and ₹ 50 lakhs was advanced to suppliers of additional assets and the balance of ₹ 130 lakhs has been utilized for working capital requirements. Total interest paid for the above loan amounted to ₹ 65 lakhs during 2010-11. You are required to state how the interest on institutional loan is to be accounted for in the year 2010-11.

[CA (IPCC) May, 2010]

Solution

AS-16

As per AS 16 borrowing costs that are directly attributable to the acquisition, construction or production of qualifying assets should be capitalized as part of the cost of that asset. Other borrowing costs are recognized as expense in the period in which they are incurred. A qualifying asset is an asset that necessarily takes substantial period of time to get ready for its intended use or sale.

Advice

Purpose	*Nature*	*Interest to be capitalized (₹ in lakhs)*	*Interest to be charged to Profit and Loss A/c (₹ in lakhs)*
Installation of Plant and Machinery	Qualifying Asset	$320 \times \frac{65}{500} =$ 41.60	— —
Advance to suppliers for additional assets	Qualifying Asset	$50 \times \frac{65}{500}$ 6.50	
Working Capital	Not a qualifying asset		$130 \times \frac{65}{500} =$ 16.90
		48.10	16.90

Problem 16.6

On 1st April, 2010, Amazing Construction Ltd. obtained a loan of ₹ 32 crores to be utilized as under.

(i) Construction of sealink across two cities: (work was held up totally for a month during the year due to high water levels) : ₹ 25 crores

(ii) Purchase of equipments and machineries : ₹ 3 crores

(iii) Working capital : ₹ 2 crores
(iv) Purchase of Vehicles : ₹ 50,00,000
(v) Advance for tools/cranes etc. : ₹ 50,00,000
(vi) Purchase of technical know-how : ₹ 1 crores
(vii) Total interest charged by the bank for the year ending 31st March, 2011 : ₹ 80,00,000

Show the treatment of interest by Amazing Construction Ltd. ***[CA (IPCC) Nov. 2010]***

Solution

AS-16	As per AS 16 qualifying asset is an asset that necessarily takes substantial period of time to get ready for its intended use. As per para 6 of the standard, borrowing costs that are directly attributable to the acquisition, construction or production of a qualifying asset should be capitalised as part of the cost of that asset. Other borrowing costs should be recognised as an expense in the period in which they are incurred.
Advice	

	Whether Qualifying Asset	*Interest to be capitalized*	*Interest to be charged to Profit & Loss A/c*	*Interest Computation*
Construction of sea-link	Yes	62,50,000	—	(80,00,000*(25/32))
Purchase of equipments and machineries	No		7,50,000	(80,00,000*(3/32))
Working capital	No		5,00,000	(80,00,000*(2/32))
Purchase of vehicles	No		1,25,000	(80,00,000*(5/32))
Advance for tools, cranes etc.	No		1,25,000	(80,00,000*(5/32))
Purchase of technical know-how	No		2,50,000	(80,00,000*(1/32))
Total		62,50,000	17,50,000	

PROBLEM 16.7

Rainbow Limited borrowed an amount of ₹ 150 crores on 1.4.2010 for construction of boiler plant @ 11% p.a. The plant is expected to be completed in 4 years. The weighted average cost of capital is 13% p.a. The accountant of Rainbow Ltd. capitalised interest of ₹.19.50 crores for the accounting period ending on 31.3.2011. Due to surplus fund out of ₹ 150 crores, an income of ₹.3.50 crores was earned and credited to profit and loss account. Comment on the above treatment of accountant with reference to relevant accounting standard.

Solution

AS-16	As per AS 16 'Borrowing Cost' states, To the extent that funds are borrowed specifically for the purpose of obtaining a qualifying asset, the amount of borrowing costs eligible for capitalisation on that asset should be determined as the actual borrowing costs incurred on that borrowing during the period less any income on the temporary investment of those borrowings". The capitalisation rate should be the weighted average

	of the borrowing costs applicable to the borrowings of the enterpnse that are outstanding during the period, other than borrowings made specifically for the purpose of obtaining a qualifying asset.
Advice	The amount of ₹ 150 crores was specifically borrowed for construction of boiler plant. Therefore, treatment of accountant of Rainbow Ltd. is not correct and the amount of borrowing costs to be capitalised for the financial year 2010-11 should be calculated as follows:

	₹ (in crores)
Interest paid for 2010-11 (11% on ₹ 150 crores)	16.50
Less: Income on temporary investment from specific borrowings	3.50
Borrowing costs to be capitalised during 2010-11	13.00

PROBLEM 16.8

Southern Tower Ltd. purchased a plant from M/s. Tatamaco Ltd. on 30.09.2010 with a quoted price ₹ 180 lakhs. Tatamaco offer 3 months credit with a condition that discount of 1.25% will be allowed if the payment were made within one month. VAT is 12.5% on the quoted price. Company incurred 2% on transportation costs and 3% on erection costs of the quoted price, Preoperative cost amount ₹ 1.50 lakhs. To Finance the purchase of the machinery, company took a term bank loan of ₹ 125 lakhs at an interest rate of 14.50% per annum. The machine was ready for use on 31.12.2010; however, it was put to use only on 01-04-2011:

(i) Find out the original cost.

(ii) Suggest the accounting treatment for the cost incurred during the period between the date the machine was ready for use and the actual date the machine was put to use.

Solution

(i) Original Cost of the Machine

Particulars	*In lakhs*	*In lakhs*
Quoted price	180.00	
Less: Discount @ 1.25%	2.25	177.75
Add: VAT @ 12.5%		22.50
Transportation @ 2%		3.60
Erection Cost @ 3%		5.40
Pre-operative Cost		1.50
Finance Cost (14.5% on ₹ 125 lakhs for the period 01.10.10 to 31.12.10)		4.53
Total		215.28

(ii) Cost incurred during the period between the date the machine was ready for use and the actual date the machine was put to use

Finance cost amounting to ₹ 4.53 lakhs (14.50% on ₹ 125 lakhs for the period 01.01.2011 to 31.03.2011) will be charged to Profit and Loss Account as per AS 16 "Borrowing Costs".

PROBLEM 16.9

The borrowings profile of Santra Pharmaceutical Ltd. set up for the manufacture of antibiotics at Navi Mumbai is as under:

Date	*Nature of borrowings*	*Amount borrowed ₹*	*Purpose of borrowings*	*Incidental expenses*
1.1.2010	15% Demand loan	60 lakhs	Acquisition of Fixed Assets	8.33%
1.7.2010	14.5% Term Loan	40 lakhs	Acquisition of plant and Machinery	5%
1.10.2010	14% Bonds	50 lakhs	Acquisition of Fixed Assets	8%

The incidental expenses consist of commission and service charges for arranging the loans and are paid after founding off to the nearest lakh.

Fixed assets considered as qualifying assets are as under: ₹

Sterile Manufacturing shed	**10,00,000**
Plant and machinery (total)	**90,00,000**
Other fixed assets	**10,00,000**

The Project is completed on 1st January, 2011 and is ready for commercial production. Show the capitalization of the borrowing costs.

Solution

(a) Specific Borrowings

14.5% Term Loan for acquisition of Plant & Machinery	₹
Interest from 1.7.2010 to 31.12.2010 [₹ 40,00,000 × 14.5% × 6/12]	2,90,000
Incidental Expenses	2,00,000
Total	4,90,000

General Borrowings

15% Demand Loan

Interest from 1.1.2010 to 31.12.2010 [₹ 60,00,000 × 15%]	9,00,000
Incidental Expenses	5,00,000
Sub Total (A)	14,00.000

14% Bonds

Interest from 1.10.2010 to 31.12.2010 [₹ 50,00,000 × 14% × 3/12]	1,75,000
Incidental Expenses	4,00,000
Sub Total (B)	5,75,000
Total General Borrowing Cost (A + B)	19,75,000
Total Average Outstanding Borrowings = [(60,00,000 × 12 + 50,00,000 × 3)/12]	72,50,000

$$\text{Weighted Average Borrowing Cost} = \frac{\text{Total Borrowing Cost}}{\text{Total Average Outstanding}} \times \frac{19{,}50{,}000 \times 100}{72{,}50{,}000} = 27.24\%$$

Allocation of General Borrowing Fund

Item	*Cost*	*Specific Borrowing*	*Net of specific borrowing*
Sterile Manufacturing Shed	10,00,000	Nil	10,00,000
Plant & Machinery	90,00,000	40,00,000	50,00,000
Other Fixed Assets	10,00,000	Nil	10,00,000

Item	*Expenditure on qualifying asset out of general borrowing fund*	*Capitalization Rate*	*Cost eligible for capitalization*
Sterile Manufacturing Shed	10,00,000	27.24	2,72,400
Plant & Machinery	50,00,000	27.24	13,62,000
Other Fixed Assets	10,00,000	27.24	2,72,400

Borrowing Costs to be Capitalized

Asset	*Specific Borrowing Cost*	*General Borrowing Cost*	*Total*
Sterile Manufacturing shed	Nil	2,72,400	2,72,400
Plant & Machinery	4,90,000	13,62,000	18,52,000
Other Fixed Assets	Nil	2,72,400	2,72,400
Total	4,90,000	19,06,800*	23,96,800

PROBLEM 16.10

GHI Limited obtained a loan for ₹ 70 lakhs on 15th April, 2011 from JKL Bank, to be utilized as under:

	₹ in lakhs
Construction of Factory shed	25
Purchase of Machinery	20
Working capital	15
Advance for purchase of Truck	10

In March 2012, construction of the factory shed was completed and machinery, which was ready for its intended use, was installed. Delivery of Truck was received in the next financial year. Total interest of ₹ 9,70,000 was charged by the bank for the financial year ending 31-03-2012.

Show the treatment of interest under AS 16 and also explain the nature of Assets.

[CA (PCC) May 2011]

Solution

Treatment of Interest (Borrowing cost) as per AS 16 'Borrowing Costs'

S. No.	Particulars	Nature	Interest to be capitalized ₹	interest to be charged to P &LA/c ₹
(i)	Construction of Factory Shed (Refer Note 1)	Qualifying Asset	$9,10,000 \times \frac{25}{70}$ = Rs 3,25,000	
(ii)	Purchase of Machinery (Refer Note 2)	Not a Qualifying Asset		$9,10,000 \times \frac{20}{70}$ = Rs 2,60,000
(iii)	Working Capital	Not a Qualifying Asset		$9,10,000 \times \frac{15}{70}$ = Rs 1,95,000
(iv)	Advance for Purchase of Truck	Not a Qualifying Asset		$9,10,000 \times \frac{10}{70}$ = Rs 1,30,000
	Total		₹ 3.25.000	₹ 5.85.000

Notes:

1. It is assumed that construction of a factory shed was completed on 31st March, 2012.
2. It is assumed that the machinery was ready for its intended use at the time of its acquisition. As per AS 16, assets have been defined as 'qualifying asset' and 'non-qualifying asset'.
   (i) **Qualifying asset** is an asset that necessarily takes a substantial period of time to get ready for its intended use or sale; whereas,
   (ii) **Non-qualifying asset** is an asset which is ready for its intended use or sale at the time of its acquisition.

PROBLEM 16.11

On 25th April, 2011, Neel Limited obtained a loan from the bank for ₹ 70 lakhs to be utilized as under:

	₹ in lakhs
Construction of factory shed	28
Purchase of machinery	21
Working capital	14
Advance for purchase of truck	7

In March, 2012, construction of shed was completed and machinery installed. Delivery of truck was not received. Total interest charged by the bank for the year ending 31st March, 2012 was ₹ 12 lakhs. Show the treatment of interest under Accounting Standard 16.

[CA (IPCC) Nov. 2011]

Solution

Treatment of Interest as per AS 16

S. No.	Particulars	Nature	Interest amount to be capitalized	Interest amount to be charged to Profit & Loss account
1	Construction of Factory Shed	Qualifying asset	₹ 12 lakhs × $\frac{\text{Rs 28 lakhs}}{\text{Rs 70 lakhs}}$ = ₹ 4.80 lakhs	
2	Purchase of Machinery	Not a Qualifying Asset		₹ 12 lakhs × $\frac{\text{Rs 21 lakhs}}{\text{Rs 70 lakhs}}$ = ₹ 3.60 lakhs
3	Working Capital	Not a Qualifying Asset		₹ 12 lakhs × $\frac{\text{Rs 14 lakhs}}{\text{Rs 70 lakhs}}$ = ₹ 2.40 lakhs
4	Advance for purchase of truck	Not a Qualifying Asset		₹ 12 lakhs × $\frac{\text{Rs 7 lakhs}}{\text{Rs 70 lakhs}}$ = ₹ 1.20 lakhs
	Total		₹ 4.80 lakhs	₹ 7.20 lakhs

Notes:

(i) It is assumed that construction of factory shed was completed at the end of March, 2012. Accordingly, interest for the full year has been capitalized.

(ii) It is assumed that machinery was ready to use at the time of purchase only and on this basis it has been treated as non-qualifying asset.

PROBLEM 16.12

BHARAT & TUSHAR LTD. obtained a loan from a bank for ₹ 120 lakhs on 30-04-2011. It was utilized as follows:

Particulars	Amount (₹ in lakhs)
Construction of a shed	50
Purchase of a machinery	40
Working Capital	20
Advance for purchase of truck	10

Construction of shed was completed in March 2012. The machinery was installed on the same date. Delivery truck was not received. Total interest charged by the bank for the year ending 31-03-2012 was ₹ 18 lakhs. Calculate the Interest to be debited to Profit & Loss Account.

Solution

Qualifying Asset as per AS-16 = ₹ 50 lakhs (construction of a shed)

Borrowing cost to be capitalized = 18 × 50/120 = ₹ 7.5 lakhs

Interest to be debited to Profit or Loss account = ₹ (18 – 7.5) lakhs = ₹ 10.5 lakhs

PROBLEM 16.13

X Ltd. began construction of a new building on 1st April, 2011. It obtained Rs1 lakh special loan to finance the construction of the building on 1st 1st April, 2011 at an interest rate of 10%. The company's other outstanding two non-specific loans were:

Loans	*Rate of Interest*
₹ 5,00,000	11%
₹ 9,00,000	13%

The expenditure that were made on the building project were as follows:

	₹
1st April 2011	2,00,000
1st July 2011	2,50,000
1st Oct 2011	4,50,000
1st March 2011	1,20,000

Building was completed by 31st March, 2012 Following the principles prescribed in AS-16'Borrowing Cost,' calculate the amount of interest to be capitalized and pass one Journal Entry for capitalizing the cost and borrowing cost in respect of the building. ***[CA (May, 2008)]***

Solution

(i) Computation of Average Accumulated Expenses

	₹
₹ 2,00,000 × 12/12	= 2,00,000
₹ 2,50,000 × 9/12	= 1,87,500
₹ 4,50,000 × 6/12	= 2,25,000
₹ 1,20,000 × 1/12	= 10,000
	6,22,500

(ii) Calculation of Average Interest rate other than for Specific Borrowings

Amount of loan (in ₹)	*Rate of interest*	*Ampount of interest (in ₹)*
5,00,000	11%	= 55,000
9,00,000	13%	= 1,17,000
14,00,000		1,72,000
Weighted average rate of interest	$\left(\frac{1,72,000}{1,40,000} \times 100\right)$	= 12.285% (approx)

(iii) Interest on Average Accumulated Expenses

Specific borrowings (₹ 1,00,000 × 10%)	= 10,000
Non-specific borrowings (₹ 5,22,500 × 12.285%)	= 64,189
Amount of interest to be capitalized	= 74,189

(iv) Total Expenses to be capitalized for building

	₹
Cost of building ₹(2,00,000 + 2,50,000 + 4,50,000 + 1,20,000)	10,20,000
Add: Amount of interest to be capitalised	74,189
	10,94,189

(v) Journal Entry

Date	*Particulars*	*Dr. (₹)*	*Cr. (₹)*
31.03.2012	Building account Dr. To Bank account (Being amount of cost of building and borrowing cost thereon capitalized)	10,94,189	10,94,189

PROBLEM 16.14

Suhana Ltd. issued 12% secured debentures of ₹ 100 Lakhs on 01.05.2013, to be utilized as under:

Particulars	*Amount (₹ in lakhs)*
Construction of factory building	40
Purchase of Machinery	35
Working Capital	25

In March 2014, construction of the factory building was completed and machinery was installed and ready for it's intended use. Total interest on debentures for the financial year ended 31.03.2014 was ₹ 11,00,000. During the year 2013-14, the company had invested idle fund out of money raised from debentures in banks' fixed deposit and had earned an interest of ₹ 2,00,000.

Show the treatment of interest under Accounting Standard 16 and also explain nature of assets. ***[May, 2014]***

Solution

AS 16: According to para 6 of AS 16 "Borrowing Costs", borrowing costs that are directly attributable to the acquisition, construction or proiduction of a qualifying asset should be capitalised as part of the cost of that asset. The amount of borrowing costs eligible for capitalisation should be determined in accordance with this Standard. Other borrowing costs should be recognised as an expense in the period in which they are incurred.

Also para 10 of AS 16 "Borrowing Costs" states that to the extent that funds are borrowed specifically for the purpose of obtaining a qualifying asset, the amoubnt of borrowing costs eligible for capiotalisation on that asset should be determined as the actual borrowing costs incurred on that borrowing during the period less any income on the temporary investment of those borrowings.

Decision: Eligible borrowing cost = ₹ 11,00,000 – ₹ 2,00,000 = ₹ 9,00,000

Sr. No.	*Particulars*	*Nature of assets*	*Interest to be Capitalized (₹)*	*Interest to be charged to Profit & Loss Account (₹)*
i.	Construction of factory building	Qualifying Asset	9,00,000 × 40/100 = ₹ 3,60,000	NIL
ii.	Purchase of Machinery	Not a Qualitfying Asset	NIL	9,00,000 × 35/100 = ₹ 3,15,000
iii.	Working Capital	Not a Qualifying Asset	NIL	9,00,000 × 25/100 = ₹ 2,25,000
	Total		₹ 3,60,000	₹ 5,40,000

AS-19

PROBLEM 19.1

Explain the types of leases as per AS 19. *[CA (PCC) June, 2009]*

Solution

For the purpose of accounting AS 19 'Leases' classify the lease into two categories as follows:

Finance Lease	It is a lease, which transfers substantially all the risks and rewards incidental to ownership of an asset to the lessee by the lessor but not the legal ownership. As per para 8 of the standard, in following situations, the lease transactions are called Finance lease: 1. The lessee will get the ownership of leased asset at the end of the lease term. 2. The lessee has an option to buy the leased asset at the end of the lease term at price, which is lower than is its expected fair value at the date on which option will be exercised. 3. The lease term covers the major part of the life of asset even if title is not transferred. 4. At the beginning of lease term, present value of minimum lease rental covers the initial fair value. 5. The asset given on lease to lessee is of specialized nature and can only be used by the lessee without major modification.
Operating Lease	It is lease, which does not transfer all the risks and rewards incidental to ownership.

PROBLEM 19.2

Suraj Limited wishes to obtain a machine costing ₹ 30 lakhs by way of lease. The effective life of the machine is 14 years, but the company requires it only for the first 5 years. It enters into an agreement with Ashok Ltd., for a lease rental for ₹ 3 lakhs p.a. payable in arrears and the implicit rate of interest is 15%. The chief accountant of Suraj Limited is not sure about the treatment of these lease rentals and seeks your advise. *[CA (June, 09)]*

Solution

AS 19	As per AS 19, "Leases', a lease will be classified as finance lease if at the inception of the lease, the present value of minimum lease payments amounts to at least substantially equal to the fair value of leased asset.
Advice	1. The given lease agreement is an **operating lease** since: (a) the present value of minimum lease payment amounts [₹ 10.08 lakhs (i.e.₹ 3 lakhs × 3.36)] is substantially less than the fair value of leased asset(i.e ₹ 30 lakhs.) (b) the lease term (5 years) is substantially less than economic life of the asset (15 years) 2. Therefore, Lease payments under an **operating lease** should be recognized as an **expense** in the statement of profit and loss on a straight line basis over the lease term unless another systematic basis is more representative of the time pattern of the user's benefit.

PROBLEM 19.3

B&P Ltd. availed a lease from N&L Ltd. The conditions of the lease terms are as under:

(i) Lease period is 3 years, in the beginning of the year 2011, for equipment costing ₹ 10,00,000 and has an expected useful life of 5 years.

(ii) The Fair market value is also ₹ 10,00,000.

(iii) The property reverts back to the lessor on termination of the lease.

(iv) The unguaranteed residual value is estimated at ₹ 1,00,000 at the end of the year 2013.

(v) 3 equal annual payments are made at the end of each year.
Consider IRR = 10%.
The present value of Re. 1 due at the end of 3rd year at 10% rate of interest is Re. 0.7513.
The present value of annuity of Re. 1 due at the end of 3rd year at 10% IRR is ₹ 2.4868.
State whether the lease constitute finance lease and also calculate unearned Finance income.

[CA (IPCC) May, 2010]

Solution

(i) Computation of annual lease payment to the lessor

Particualrs	₹
Cost of equipment	10,00,000
Unguaranteed residual value	1,00,000
Present value of residual value after third year @ 10% (₹ 1,00,000 × 0.7513)	75,130
Fair value to be recovered from lease payments (₹ 10,00,000 – ₹ 75,130)	9,24,870
Present value of annuity for three years is 2.4868	
Annual lease payment = ₹ 9,24,870/2.4868	3,71,911.70

The present value of lease payment i.e., ₹ 9,24,870 equals 92.48% of the fair market value i.e., 10,00,000. As the present value of minimum lease payments substantially covers the initial fair value of the leased asset and lease term (i.e. 3 years) covers the major part of the life of asset (i.e. 5 years). Therefore, it constitutes a finance lease.

(ii) Computation of Unearned Finance Income

Particulars	₹
Total lease payments (₹ 3,71,911.70 × 3)	11,15,735
Add: Unguaranteed residual value	1,00,000
Gross investment in the lease	1,215,735
Less: Present value of investment (lease payments and residual value) (₹ 75,130 + ₹ 9,24,870)	(10,00,000)
Unearned finance income	2,15,735

PROBLEM 19.4

S. Square Private Limited has taken machinery on lease from S.K. Ltd. The information is as under:

Lease term = 4 years
Fair value at inception of lease = ₹ 20,00,000
Lease rent = ₹ 6,25,000 p.a. at the end of year
Guaranteed Residual Value = ₹ 1,25,000

Expected Residual Value = ₹ 3,75,000
Implicit interest rate = 15%
Discounted rates for 1st year, 2nd year, 3rd year and 4th year are 0.8696, 0.7561, 0.6575 and 0.5718 respectively.
Calculate the value of the lease liability as per AS-19, ***[CA (Nov. 2010)]***

Solution

AS — As per AS 19 "Leases", the lessee should recognise the lease as an asset and a liability at an amount equal to the fair value of the leased asset at the inception of the finance lease. However, if the fair value of the leased asset exceeds the present value of the minimum lease payments from the standpoint of the lessee, the amount recorded as an asset and a liability should be the present value of the minimum lease payments from the standpoint of the lessee. In calculating the present value of the minimum lease payments the discount rate is the interest rate implicit in the lease.

PV of MLP — Present value of minimum lease payments will be calculated as follows:

Year	*Minimum Lease Payment ₹*	*Internal rate of return (Discount/ate @5%)*	*Present value ₹*
1	6,25,000	0.8696	5,43,500
2	6,25,000	0.7561	4,72,563
3	6,25,000	0.6575	4,10,937
4	7,50,000*	0.5718	4,28,850
Total	26,25,000		18,55,850

Present value of minimum lease payments ₹ 18,55,850 is less than fair value at the inception of lease i.e. ₹ 20,00,000, therefore, the lease liability should be recognized at ₹ 18,55,850 as per AS 19.

PROBLEM 19.5

Lessee Ltd. took a machine on lease from Lessor Ltd., the fair value being ₹ 7,00,000. The economic life of machine as well as the lease term is 3 years. At the end of each year Lessee Ltd. pays ₹ 3,00,000. The Lessee has guaranteed a residual value of ₹ 22,000 on expiry of the lease to the Lessor. However Lessor Ltd., estimates that the residual value of the machinery will be only ₹ 15,000.The implicit rate of return is 15% p.a. and present value factors at 15% are 0.869, 0.756 and 0.657 at the end of first, second and third years respectively.

Calculate the value of machinery to be considered by Lessee Ltd. and the finance charges in each year. ***[CA (IPCC) May 2011]***

Solution

As per para 11 of AS 19 "Leases", the lessee should recognize the lease as an asset and a liability at the inception of a finance lease. Such recognision should be at an amount equal to the fair value of the leased asset at the inception of lease. However, if the fair value of the leased asset exceeds the present value of minimum lease payment from the standpoint of the lessee, the amount recorded as an asset and liability should be the present value of minimum lease payments from the standpoint of the lessee.

Value of machinery

In the given case, fair value of the machinery is ₹ 7,00,000 and the net present value of minimum lease payments is ₹ 6,99,054*. As the present value of the machine is less than the fair value of the machine, the machine will be recorded at value of ₹ 6,99,054.

Calculation of Finance Charges for each year

Year	Finance charge ₹	Payment ₹	Reduction in outstanding liability ₹	Outstanding liability ₹
1st year beginning	—	—	—	6,99,054
End of 1st year	1,04,858	3,00,000	1,95,142	5,03,912
End of 2nd year	75,587	3,00,000	2,24,413	2,79,499
End of 3rd year	41,925	3,00,000	2,58,075	21,424**

*Present value of minimum lease payments:

Annual lease rental × PV factor + Present value of guaranteed residual value

= ₹ 3,00,000 × (0.869 + 0.756 + 0.657) + ₹ 22,000 × (0.657)

= ₹ 6,84,600 + ₹ 14,454 = ₹ 6,99,054.

**The difference between this figure and guaranteed residual value (₹ 22,000) is due to approximation in computing the interest rate implicit in the lease.

PROBLEM 19.6

An equipment having expected useful life of 5 years, is leased for 3 years. Both the cost and the fair value of the equipment are ₹ 6,00,000. The amount will be paid in 3 equal instalments and at the termination of lease, lessor will get back the equipment. The unguaranteed residual value at the end of 3rd year is ₹ 60,000. The IRR of the investment is 10%. The present value of annuity factor of ₹ 1 due at the end of 3rd year at 10% IRR is 2.4868. The present value of ₹ 1 due at the end of 3rd year at 10% rate of interest is 0.7513. State with reason whether the lease constitutes finance lease and also compute the unearned finance income.

[CA (IPCC) Nov. 2011]

Solution

(i) Determination of Nature of Lease

It is assumed that the fair value of the leased equipments is equal to the present value of minimum lease payments.

Present Value of Residual Value at the end of 3rd year = ₹ 60,000 × 0.7513
= ₹ 45,078

Present Value of Lease Payments = ₹ 6,00,000 − ₹ 45,078
= ₹ 5,54,922

The percentage of present value of lease payments to fair value of the equipment is (₹ 5,54,922/₹ 6,00,000) × 100 = 92.487%.

Since, it substantially covers the major portion of the lease payments, the lease constitutes a finance lease.

(ii) Calculation of Unearned Finance Income

Annual Lease Payment = ₹ 5,54,922/2.4868 = ₹ 2,23,147 (approx)

Gross Investment in the lease = Total Minimum Lease Payment + unguaranteed residual value

= (₹ 2,23,147 × 3) + ₹ 60,000

= ₹ 6,69,441 + ₹ 60,000 = ₹ 7,29,441

Unearned Finance Income = Gross Investment – Present Value of Minimum Lease Payments and unguaranteed residual value

= ₹ 7,29,441 – ₹ 6,00,000 = ₹ 1,29,441

PROBLEM 19.7

X Ltd. sold JCB Machine having WDV of ₹ 50 Lakhs to Y Ltd. for ₹ 60 Lakhs and the same JCB was leased back of Y Ltd to X Ltd. The lease is operating lease.

Comment according to relevant Accounting Standard if

(i) Sale price of ₹ 60 Lakhs is equal to fair value

(ii) Fair Value is ₹ 50 Lakhs and sale price is ₹ 45 Lakhs.

(iii) Fair value is ₹ 55 Lakhs and sale price is ₹ 62 Lakhs

(iv) Fair value is ₹ 45 Lakhs and sale price is ₹ 48 Lakhs *[May 2012]*

Solution

According to AS 19, follows will be the treatment in the given situations:

(i) X Ltd. should immediately recognized the profit of ₹ 10 lakhs (i.e. 60 – 50) in its books.

(ii) The loss of ₹ 5 lakhs (50 – 45) to be immediately recognized by X Ltd. in its books provided loss is not compensated by future lease payments.

(iii) Profit of ₹ 5 lakhs (55 – 50) to be immediately recognized by X Ltd. in its books and balance profit of ₹ 7 lakhs (62-55) is to be amortised/deferred over lease period.

(iv) The loss of ₹ 5 lakhs (50 – 45) to be immediately recognized by X Ltd. in its books and profit of ₹ 3 lakhs (48 – 45) should be amortised/deferred over lease period.

PROBLEM 19.8

Annual lease rent = ₹ 40,000 at the end of each year

Lease period = 5 years

Guaranteed Residual Value = ₹ 14,000

Five value at the inception (beginning) of lease = ₹ 1,50,000

Interest rate implict on lease is 12.6%. The present value factors at 12.6% are 0.89, 0.79, 0.7, 0.622, 0.552 at the end of first, second, third, fourth and fifth year respectively.

Show the Journal entry to record the asset taken on finance lease in the books of the lessee.

[Nov. 2012]

Solution

Journal of Lessee

Date	*Particulars*	*L.F.*	*Dr. (₹)*	*Cr. (₹)*
	Asset A/c Dr. To Lessor (Being recognition of finance lease as an asset and a liability)		1,49,888	1,49,888

Working Note:

Year	Lease Payments ₹	Discounting Factor (12.6%)	Present Value ₹
1	40,000	0.89	35,600
2	40,000	0.79	31,600
3	40,000	0.70	28,000
4	40,000	0.622	24,880
5	40,000	0.552	22,080
5	14,000 (GRV)	0.552	7,728
			1,49,888

PROBLEM 19.9

What do you uinderstand by the term "Interest rate implicit on lease"? Calculate the interest rate implicit on lease from the following details:

Annual Lease Rent	**₹ 80,000 at the end of each year**
Lease Period	**5 Years**
Guaranteed Residual Value	**₹ 40,000**
Unguaranteed Residual Value	**₹ 24,000**
Fair Value at the inception of the lease	**₹ 3,20,000**

Discounted rates for the first 5 years are as below:

At 10% 0.909, 0.826, 0.751, 0.683, 0621

At 14% 0.877, 0.769, 0.675, 0.592, 0.519 ***[May 2014]***

Solution

AS 19: As per para 3 of AS 19 'Leases' the interest rate implicit in the lease is the discount rate that, at the inception of the lease, causes the aggregate present value of

(a) the minimum lease payments under a finance lease from the standpoint of the lessor; and

(b) any unguaranteed residual value accruing to the lessor, to be equal to the fair value of the leased asset.

Calculation of Interest rate Implicit on Lease

Present value at discount rate of 10%

Year	Liease Payments (₹)	Disc. Factor (10%)	Present Value (₹)
1	80,000	0.909	72,720
2	80,000	0.826	66,080
3	80,000	0.751	60,080
4	80,000	0.683	54,640
5	80,000	0.621	49,680
5	40,000	0.621	24,840
5	24,000	0.621	14,904
	Total		3,42,944

Present value at a discount rate of 14%

Year	Liease Payments (₹)	Disc. Factor (10%)	Present Value (₹)
1	80,000	0.877	70,160
2	80,000	0.769	61,520
3	80,000	0.675	54,000
4	80,000	0.592	47,360
5	80,000	0.519	41,520
5	40,000	0.519	20,760
5	24,000	0.519	12,456
	Total		3,07,776

$$\text{Interest Rate Implicit on Lease} = 10\% + \frac{14\% - 10\%}{3,42,944 - 3,07,776} \times (3,42,944 - 3,20,000)$$

$$= 10\% + 2.609\% = 12.609\% \text{ or say } 12.61\%$$

AS-20

PROBLEM 20.1

From the following information relating to Y Ltd. Calculate Earnings Per Share (EPS):

	₹ in crores
Profit before V.R.S. payments but after depreciation	75.00
Depreciation	10.00
VRS payments	32.10
Provision for taxation	10.00
Fringe benefit tax	5.00
Paid up share capital (shares of ₹ 10 each fully paid)	93.00

[CA (PCC) Nov. 2007]

Solution

Statement showing the calculation of Earnings for share of Y Ltd.

Particualrs		₹ in crores
Profit after depreciation but before VRS payment		75.00
Less: Depreciation	No adjustment required	
VRS payments	32.10	
Provision for taxation	10.10	
Fringe benefit tax	5.00	47.10
Net Earnings	27.90	
Number of Shares	9.30 crores shares	
Earnings Per Share = $\frac{\text{Net Earnings}}{\text{Number of shares}} = \frac{27.90 \text{ crores}}{9.30 \text{ crores}}$ = ₹ 3 per share.		

PROBLEM 20.2

Compute Basic Earnings per share from the following information:

Date	Particulars	No. of shares
1st April, 2010	Balance at the beginning of the year	1,500
1st August, 2010	Issue of shares for cash	600
31st March, 2011	Buy back of shares	500

Net profit for the year ended 31st March, 2011 was ₹ 2,75,000. *[CA (PCC) Nov. 2009]*

Solution

Computation of Weighted Average Number of Shares Outstanding

Date	No. of equity Share O/s	Period	Weights (Months)	Weighted Average No. of shares
(1)	(2)	(3)	(4)	(5) = (2) × (4)
01.04.10	1,500 (Opening)	12 months	12/12	1,500
01.08.10	600 (Additional)	8 months	8/12	400
31.03.11	500 (Buy back)	0 months	0/12	—
Total				1,900

Basic Earning Per Share

$$= \frac{\text{Net Profit or Loss for the period attributable to Equity Shareholders}}{\text{Weighted Average Number of Equity Shares outstanding during the period}}$$

$$= \frac{\text{Rs. 2,75,000}}{\text{1,900 shares}} = \text{Rs. 144.74}$$

PROBLEM 20.3

Goverdhan Ltd. has equity capital of ₹ 20,00,000 consisting of fully paid equity shares of ₹ 10 each. The net profit for the year 2010-11 was ₹ 30,00,000. It has also issued 18,000, 10% convertible debentures of ₹ 50 each. Each debenture is convertible into five equity shares. The tax rate applicable is 30%. Compute the diluted earnings. ***[CA (PCC) May, 2010]***

Solution

Calculation of Diluted Earnings

Particulars	₹
Interest on Debentures @ 10% for the year	
(18,000 Debentures × ₹ 50 × 10%)	90,000
Less: Tax on Interest @ 30%	(27,000)
	63,000
Add: Net Profit for the year 2010-2011	30,00,000
Diluted Earnings	30,63,000

PROBLEM 20.4

Ram Ltd. had 12,00,000 equity shares on April 1, 2010. The company earned a profit of ₹ 30,00,000 during the year 2010-11. The average fair value per share during 2010-11 was ₹ 25. The company has given share option to its employees of 2,00,000 equity shares at option price of ₹ 15. Calculate basic E.P.S. and diluted E.P.S.

Solution

Computation of Earnings Per Share

Particulars	*Earnings* ₹	*Shares*	*Earnings per Share*
Net Profit for the year 2009-10	30,00,000		
Weighted Average Number of shares outstanding during the year 2010-11		12,00,000	
Basic Earning Per Share (30,00,000/12,00,000)			2.50
Number of shares under option		2,00,000	
Number of shares that would have been issued at fair value (As indicated in Working Note) (2,00,000 × 15/25)		(1,20,000)	
Diluted Earnings Per Share [30,00,000/12,80,000]	30,00,000	12,80,000	2.34

Working Note:

The earnings have not been increased as the total number of shares has been increased only by the number of shares (80,000) deemed for the purpose of the computation to have been issued for no consideration.

PROBLEM 20.5

"While calculating diluted earning per share, effect is given to all dilutive potential equity shares that were outstanding during that period." Explain. Also calculate the diluted earnings per share from the following information:

Net Profit for the current year	**85,50,000**
No. of equity shares outstanding	**20,00,000**
No. of 8% convertible debentures of 100 each	**1,00,000**
Each debenture is convertible into 10 equity shares	
Interest expenses for the current year	**6,00,000**
Tax relating to interest expenses	**30%**

[CA (PCC) Nov. 2010]

Solution

(a) "In calculating diluted earnings per share, effect is given to all dilutive potential equity shares that were outstanding during the period." As per para 26 of AS 20 'Earnings per Share', the net profit or loss for the period attributable to equity shareholders and the weighted average number of shares outstanding* during the period should be adjusted for the effects of all dilutive potential equity shares for the purpose of calculation of diluted earnings per share.

$$\text{Diluted EPS} = \frac{\text{Adjusted Net Profit for the current year}}{\text{Weighted Average Number of Equity Shares}}$$

Adjusted Net Profit for the current year

Particulars	₹
Net Profit for the current year (assumed to be after tax)	85,50,000
Add: Interest expense for the current year	6,00,000
Less: Tax relating to interest expense (30% of ₹ 6,00,000)	(1,80,000)
Adjusted net profit for the current year	89,70,000

Weighted Average Number of Equity Shares

Number of equity shares resulting from conversion of debentures

$$= \frac{1{,}00{,}000 \times 100}{10} = 10{,}00{,}000 \text{ Equity shares}$$

Weighted Average Number of Equity Shares used to compute diluted earnings per share = [(20,00,000 × 12) + (10,00,000 × 9**)]/12 = 27,50,000 shares

Diluted earnings per share $= \dfrac{89{,}70{,}000}{27{,}50{,}000 \text{ shares}}$ = Rs. 3.26 per share

Note: Interest on debentures for full year amounts to ₹ 8,00,000 (i.e. 8% of ₹ 1,00,00,000). However, interest expense amounting ₹ 6,00,000 has been given in the question. It may be concluded that debentures have been issued during the year and interest has been provided for 9 months.

PROBLEM 20.6

From the following information compute diluted earnings per share.

Net Profit for the year	₹ 12,00,000
Weighted average number of equity shares outstanding	5,00,000 shares
Average fair value of one equity share	₹ 20
Weighted average number of shares under option	1,00,000 shares
Exercise price per share under option	₹ 15

[CA (Nov. 2009, May 2013)]

Solution

COMPUTATION OF DILUTED EARNINGS PER SHARE

Particulars	*Earnings* (₹)	*Shares*	*Earning per share* (₹)
Net Profit for the year	12,00,000		
Weighted average number of equity shares outstanding		5,00,000	
Basic earnings per share (12,00,0000/5,00,000)			2.40
Weighted average number of shares under option		1,00,000	
Number of shares that would have been issued at fair value (1,00,000 ×15.00)/20.00)	——	(75,000)	——
Diluted earnings per share (12,00,0000/5,25,000)	12,00,000	5,25,000	2.29

*The earnings have not been increased as the total number of shares has been increased only by the number of shares (25,000) deemed for the purpose of computation to have been issued for no consideration.

PROBLEM 20.7

From the following information of Beta Ltd. calculate Earning Per Share (EPS) in accordance with AS-20:

	Year 31.3.11	(₹) Year 31.3.10
1. Net Profit before tax	3,00,000	1,00,000
2. Current tax	40,000	30,000
Tax relating to earlier years	24,000	(13,000)
Deferred tax	30,000	10,000
3. Profit after tax	2,06,000	73,000

4. **Other information:**
   (a) **Profit includes compensation from Central Government towards loss on account of 1,00,000 NIL earthquake in 2008 (non-taxable)**
   (b) **Outstanding convertible 6% Preference shares 1,000 issued and paid on. 30.9.2009. Face value ₹ 100, Conversion ratio 15 equity shares for every 7 preference share.**
   (c) **15% convertible debentures of ₹ 1,000 each total face value ₹ 1,00,000 to be converted into 10 Equity shares per debenture issued and paid on 30.6.2009.**
   (d) **Total no. of Equity shares outstanding as on 31.3.2011, 20,000 including 10,000 bonus shares issued on 1.1.11 face value ₹ 100.**

Solution

Calculation of Earning Per Share (EPS) of Beta Ltd.

	Particulars	₹ Year ended 31.3.11	₹ Year ended 31.3.10
1. A.	Earning after extra ordinary items (2,06,000 – 6,000) (73,000 – 3,000)	2,00,000	70,000
B.	No. of Equity Shares	20,000	20,000
C.	Basic Earnings Per share [A/B]	10.00	3.50
A.	Earning before extra ordinary items	1,00,000	70,000
B.	No. of Equity Shares	20,000	20,000*
C.	Basic Earnings Per share [A/B]	5.00	3.50
2.	Tax Rate applicable		
	40,000 + 30,000/2,00,000	35%	
	30,000 + 10,000/1,00,000		40%
3. A.	Dividend on Weighted Average Preference Shares	6,000	3,000
B.	Incremental shares	15,000	7,500
C.	EPS on Incremental Shares [A/B]	0.40 (dilutive)	0.40 (dilutive)
4.	Convertible Debentures		
A.	Increase in earnings $\left(1{,}00{,}000 \times \frac{15}{100} \times 0.65\right)$	9,750	
	$1{,}00{,}000 \times \frac{15}{100} \times 0.60 \times \frac{9}{12}$		6,750
B.	Increase in shares	1,000	750
C.	Increase in EPS [A/B]	9.75 (Anti dilutive)	9.00 (Anti dilutive)

* Since the bonus issue is without consideration, the issue is treated as if it had occurred prior to the beginning of the year 2010

It is anti-dilutive as it increases the EPS from continuing ordinary operations (Para 39, AS 20)

	Calculation of Diluted EPS	Year ended 31.3.11 ₹	Year ended 31.3.10 ₹
A.	Profit from continuing ordinary activities before Preference Dividend	1,06,000	73,000
	No. of ordinary equity shares	20,000	20,000
	Adjustment for dilutive potential of 6% convertible pref. shares	15,000	7,500
B.	Total no. of shares	35,000	27,500
C.	Diluted EPS from continuing ordinary operations [A/B]	3.02	2.65
D.	Profit including extra ordinary items	2,06,000	73,000
E.	Adjusted No. of shares	35,000	27,500
F.	Diluted EPS including extra ordinary items [D/E]	5.88	2.65

Disclosure of EPS in accordance with AS 20 in the Profit and Loss Account

Earning per share (Face value ₹.100)	*31.3.11 (₹)*	*31.3.10 (₹)*
Basic EPS from continuing ordinary operations	5.00	3.50
Diluted EPS from continuing ordinary operations	3.02	2.65

PROBLEM 20.8

In April, 2010, A Limited issued 18,00,000 Equity shares of ₹ 10 each, ₹ 5 per share was called up on that date which was paid by all the shareholders. The remaining ₹ 5 was called up on 1-9-2010. All the Shareholders (except one having 3,60,000 shares) paid the sum in September 2010. The net profit for the year ended 31-3-2011 is ₹ 33 lakhs after dividend on preference shares and dividend distribution tax of ₹ 6. 60 lakhs.

Compute the basic EPS for the year ended 31st March, 2011 as per AS 20.

[CA (PCC) May 2011]

Solution

Basic Earnings per share (EPS)

$$= \frac{\text{Net profit attributable to equity shareholders}}{\text{Weighted average number of equity shares outstanding during the year}}$$

$$= \frac{33,00,000}{13,20,000 \text{ Shares (as per working note)}} = ₹\ 2.5 \text{ per share}$$

Net profit attributable to equity shareholders Weighted average number of equity shares outstanding during the year

Working Note: Calculation of Weighted Average Number of equity shares

As per para 19 of AS 20 'Earnings Per Share', partly paid equity shares are treated as a fraction of equity share to the extent that they were entitled to participate in dividend relative to a fully paid equity share during the reporting period. Assuming that the partly paid shares are entitled to participate in the dividend to the extent of amount paid, weighted average number of shares will be calculated as follows:

Date	*No. of Equity Shares*	*Amount paid per share ₹*	*Weighted Average no. of Equity Shares ₹*
1.4.2010	18,00,000	5	18,00,000 × 5/10 × 5/12 = 3,75,000
1.9.2010	14,40,000	10	14,40,000 × 7/12 = 8,40,000
1.9.2010	3,60,000	5	3,60,000 × 5/10 × 7/12 = 1,05,000
Total shares			13,20,000

PROBLEM 20.9

The following information is available for Raja Ltd. for the accounting year 2009-10 and 2010-11:

Net profit for	₹
Year 2009-10	25,00,000
Year 2010-11	40,00,000

No. of shares outstanding prior to right issue 12, 00,000 shares.

Right issue : One new share for each three outstanding i.e. 4,00,000 shares
: Right issue price ₹ 22
: Last date to exercise rights 30-6-2010

Fair value of one equity share immediately prior to exercise of rights on 30-6-2010 = ₹ 28.

Required:* You are required to compute the basic earnings per share for the years 2009-10 and 2010-11. ***[CA (IPCC) May 2011]***

Solution

Computation of basic earnings per share (EPS)

	Year 2009-10	*Year 2010-11*
EPS for the year 2009-10 as originally reported $= \frac{\text{Net profit of the year attributable to equity shareholders}}{\text{Weighted average number of equity shares outstanding during the year}}$ $= \frac{\text{Rs } 25,00,000}{12,00,000 \text{ shares}}$	2.08	
EPS for the year 2009-10 restated for rights issue $= \frac{\text{Rs } 25,00,000}{(12,00,000 \text{ shares} \times 1.06)}$	1.97 (approx.)	
EPS for the year 20 10- 11 including effects of right issue $= \frac{40,00,000}{\left(12,00,000 \times 1.06 \times \frac{3}{12}\right) + \left(16,00,000 \times \frac{9}{12}\right)}$		2.64 (approx.)

*The number of equity shares to be used in calculating basic earnings per share for periods prior to the rights issue is the number of equity shares outstanding prior to the issue, multiplied by the adjustment factor. The adjustment factor has been calculated in Working Note (ii).

Working Notes:

(i) Computation of theoretical ex-rights fair value per share

$$\frac{\text{Fair value of all outstanding shares immediately prior to exercise of rights + total amount received from exercise}}{\text{Number of shares outstanding prior to exercise + number of shares issued in the exercise}}$$

$$= \frac{(\text{Rs } 28 \times 12,00,000 \text{ shares}) + (\text{Rs } 22 \times 4,00,000 \text{ shares})}{12,00,000 \text{ shares} + 4,00,000 \text{ shares}} = ₹\ 26.50$$

(ii) Computation of adjustment factor

$$= \frac{\text{Fairvalue pershare priorto exercise of rights}}{\text{Theoretical ex-right value per share}}$$

$$= \frac{\text{Rs } 28}{\text{Rs } 26.5} = 1.06 \text{ (approx.)}$$

PROBLEM 20.10

S.S.SECURITIES LTD. provides the following information:

Net Profit for the current year	**₹ 1,00,00,000**
No. of equity shares outstanding	**50,00,000**
No. of 12% convertible debentures of ₹ 100 each	**1,00,000**
Each debenture is convertible into 10 equity shares	
Interest expense for the current year	**₹ 12,00,000**
Tax relating to interest expense	**30%**

Calculate Diluted Earnings Per Share as per AS 20. ***[PCC (May 2012)]***

Solution

Adjusted net profit for the current year (1,00,00,000 + 12,00,000 – 3,60,000) = ₹ 1,08,40,000
No. of equity shares resulting from conversion of Debentures = 10,00,000 × 10 Shares
No. of equity shares used to compute diluted EPS: (50,00,000 + 10,00,000) = 60,00,000 Shares
Diluted Earnings per Share: (1,08,40,000/60,00,000) = ₹ 1.81

PROBLEM 20.11

Explain the concept of 'Weighted average number of equity shares outstanding during the period".

State how would you compute, based on AS-20 the weighted average number of equity shares in the following cases:

		No. of Shares
1st April, 2011	Balance of Equity Shares	4,80,000
31st August, 2011	Equity shares issued for cash	3,60,000
1st February, 2012	Equity shares bought back	1,80,000
31st March, 2012	Balance of equity shares	6,60,000

Solution

(a) As per para no. 16 of AS 20, the weighted average number of equity shares outstanding during the period reflected the fact that the amount of shareholder's capital may have varied during the period as a result of a larger or lesser number of shares outstanding at any time. Therefore, For the purpose of calculating basic or diluted earnings per share, the number of equity shares should be the weighted average number of equity shares outstanding during the period.

(b) **Weighted average number of equity shares**

Period		*Weighted shares*
1st April, 2011 to 31st August, 2011	4,80,000 shares × 5/12	2,00,000 shares
1st September, 2011 to 31st January, 2012	8,40,000 shares × 5/12	3,50,000 shares
1st February, 2012 to 31st March, 2012	6,60,000 shares × 2/12	1,10,000 shares
		6,60,000 shares

PROBLEM 20.12

Compute adjust earning per share and basic earning per share based on the following information:

Net Profit 2010-11	₹ 11,40,000
Net Profit 2011-12	₹ 22,50,000
No of Equity Shares outstanding	5,00,000

Unit 31st December, 2011

Bonus issue on 1st January, 2012: 1 Equity Share for each equity share outstanding as at 31st December, 2011 ***[May 2012]***

Solution

(a) Earning per share

Basic EPS 2010-11 = ₹ 11,40,000/5,00,000 shares = ₹ 2.28

Basic EPS 2011-12 = ₹ 22,50,000/10,00,000 shares = ₹ 2.25

Adjusted EPS 2010-11 = ₹ 11,40,000/10,00,000 shares = ₹ 1.14

Since the bonus issue is an issue without consideration, the issue is treated as if it has occurred prior to the beginning of the year 2010-11, the earliest period reported.

PROBLEM 20.13

The following informatiion is available for AB Ltd. for the accounting year 2012-13 and 2013-14:

Net profit for	**₹**
Year 2012-13	**22,00,000**
Year 2013-14	**30,00,000**

No of shares outstanding prior to right issue 10,00,000 shares.

Right issue: One new share for each five shares outstanding i.e. 2,00,000 *shares.*

Right issue: Right Issue price ₹ 25

Right issue: Last date to exercise right 31st July, 2013

Fair value of one equity share immediately prior to exercise of rights on 31.07.2013 is ₹ 32.

You are required to compute:

(i) Basic earnings per share for the year 2012-13.

(ii) Restated basic earnings per share for the year 2012-13 for right issue.

(iii) Basic earnings per share for the year 2013-14. ***[May, 2014]***

Solution

Computation of Basic Earnings per Share

	Particulars	*Previous (₹)*	*Current (₹)*
(i)	EPS for the previous year as originally reported = Net profit for the year attributable to equity share holder/weighted average number of equity shares outstanding during the year [₹ 22,00,000/10,00,000]	2.20	

	Particulars	Previous (₹)	Current (₹)
(ii)	EPS for previous year restated for the right issue [₹ 22,00,000/10,00,000 shares × 1.04]	2.12	
(iii)	EPS for the current year (including effect of right issue) $\frac{₹\ 30,00,000}{(10,00,000 \times 1.04 \times 4/) + (12,00,000 \times 8/12)}$		2.62

Working Notes: 1. Computation of theoretical ex-rights fair value per share =

$$\frac{\text{Fair value of all oustanding shares immediately prior to exercise of rights+total amount received from exercise}}{\text{Number of shares outstanding prior to exercise + number of shares issued in the exercise}}$$

$$\frac{(₹\ 32 \times 10,00,000) + (₹\ 25 \times 2,00,000)}{10,00,000 + 2,00,000} = ₹\ 30.83$$

2. Computation of adjustment factor =

$$\frac{\text{Fair value per share prior to exercise of rights}}{\text{Theoretical ex-rights value per share}} = ₹\ 32/₹\ 30.83 = 1.04 \text{ (approx.)}$$

AS-26

PROBLEM 26.1

ABC Ltd. developed a know-how by incurring expenditure of ₹ 20 lakhs. The know-how was used by the company from 1.4.2004. The useful life of the asset is 10 years from the year of commencement of its use. The company has not amortised the asset till 31.3.2011. Pass Journal entry to give effect to the value of know-how as per Accounting Standard-26 for the year ended 31.3.2011. *[CA (PCC) Nov. 2009]*

Solution

Journal Entry

Particulars		*Dr. (₹)*	*Cr. (₹)*
Profit and Loss A/c (Prior period item)	Dr.	12,00,000	
Depreciation A/c	Dr.	2,00,000	
To Know-how A/c			14,00,000
[Being depreciation of 7 years (out of which of 6 years charged as prior period item)]			

PROBLEM 26.2

SAD Enterprises, a partnership firm, had purchased business of SWAD enterprises on 01.04.2010 and paid ₹ 50,000 towards goodwill. On 01.04.2011, SAD enterprises decided to admit W as partner and the goodwill was valued at ₹ 1,00,000 for the purpose.
Please explain with reasons, at what price goodwill can be shown in the books of account. *[CA (IPCC) Nov. 2009]*

Solution

AS-26	As per AS 16 goodwill can be recorded in the books only when some consideration in money or moeny's worth has been paid for it. Therefore, only purchased goodwill should be recorded in the books.
Advice	Payment of ₹ 50,000 was made towards purchase of goodwill, hence to this extent goodwill can be recorded in the books. Additional goodwill of ₹ 50,000 is self generated goodwill, which should not be recorded. On admission, death or retirement of a partner, goodwill adjustmens can be carried can be carried out through capital accounts.

PROBLEM 26.3

P, N and T are equal partners. The decided to change their profit sharing ratio into 5:4:3. They raised the goodwill in the books to the extent of ₹ 2,40,000 and it is to be written off immediately. Show Journal entries with narration to be passed for raising the goodwill and for its subsequent write off. *[CA (PCC) Nov. 2009]*

Solution

Journal

Particulars		Dr. (₹)	Cr. (₹)
Goodwill A/c	Dr.	2,40,000	
To A's Capital A/c			80,000
To B's Capital A/c			80,000
To C's Capital A/c			
(Being the value of goodwill raised in the books, in old profit sharing ratio)			
A's Capital A/c	Dr.	1,00,000	
B's Capital A/c	Dr.	80,000	
C's Capital A/c	Dr.	60,000	
To Goodwill A/c			2,40,000
(Being the value of goodwill written off from the books of the firm, in new profit sharing ratio)			

Note: As per AS 20 goodwill should be recorded in the books only when some consideration in money's worth has been paid for it. Therefore, the goodwill valued at the time of change in profit and loss sharing ratio is to be adjusted through capital accounts of the partners directly. The journal entries for raising goodwill and then writing it off is not in accordance with the said standard but have been given due to the requirement of the question.

Alternatively, Capital accounts of partner A and partner C may be adjusted to give net effect to the above entries by passing an adjusting Journal Entry.

Adjusting Journal Entry

Particulars		Dr. (₹)	Cr. (₹)
A's Capital A/c	Dr.	20,000	
To C's Capital A/c			20,000
(Being adjusting entry passed for goodwill, due to change in Profit and Loss sharing ratio)			

PROBLEM 26.4

M Ltd. launched a project for producing product A in Nov. 2009. The company incurred ₹ 30 lakhs towards Research and Development expenses upto 31st March, 2011. Due to unfavourable market conditions the management feels that it is not possible to manufacture and sold the product in the market for next so many years.

The management hence wants to defer the expenditure write off to future years.

Advise the company as per the applicable Accounting Standard. *[CA (IPCC) Nov. 2010]*

Solution

AS-26	As per AS 26 expenditure on research should be recognised as an expense when it is incurred. An intangible asset arising from development (or from the development phase of an internal project) should be recognized if and only if, an enterprise can demonstrate all of the conditions specified in para 44 of the standard. An intangible asset (arrising from development) should be derecognised when no future economic benefits are expected from its use.
Advice	The management can not defer the expenditure write off to future years and the company is required to expense the entire amount of ₹ 30 lakhs in the Profit and Loss account of the year ended 31st March, 2011.

PROBLEM 26.5

NDA Corporation is engaged in research on a new process design for its product. It had incurred an expenditure of ₹ 530 lakhs on research upto 31st March, 2010.

The development of the process began on 1st April, 2010 and Development phase expendture was ₹ 360 lakhs upto 31st March, 2011 which meets assets recognition criteria.

From 1st April, 2011, the company will implement the new process design which will result in after tax saving of ₹ 80 lakhs per annum for the next five years.

The cost of capital of company is 10%

Explain:

(i) Accounting treatment for research expenses.

(ii) The cost of internally generated intangible asset as per AS 26.

(iii) The amout of amortization of the assets. (The present value of annuity factor of ₹ 1 for 5 years @ 10% = 3.7908) ***[CA (IPCC) Nov. 2010]***

Solution

(i) **Reasearch Expenditure**—As per AS 26 the expenditure on research of new process design for its product 530 lakhs should be charged to Profit and Loss Account in the year in which it is incurred. It is presumed that the entire expenditure is incurred in the financial year 2008-09. Hence, it should be written off as an expense in that year itself.

(ii) **Cost of internally generated intangible asset**—The question states that the development phase expenditure amounting ₹ 360 lakhs incurred upto 31st March, 2011 meets asset recognization criteria. As per AS 26 for measurement of such internally generated intangible asset, fair value can be estimated by discounting estimated future net cash flows.

	₹
Savings (after tax) from implementation of new design for next 5 years	80 lakhs p.a
Company's cost of capital	10%
Annuity factor@ 10% for 5 years	3.7908
Present value of net cash flows (₹ 80 lakhs × 3.7908)	303.26 lakhs

The cost of an internally generated intangible asset would be lower of cost value 360 lakhs or present value of future net cash flows ₹ 303.26 lakhs.

Hence, cost of an internally generated intangible asset will be ₹ 303.26 lakhs.

The difference of ₹ 56.74 lakhs (i.e. ₹ 360 lakhs – ₹ 303.26 lakhs) will be amortized by the enterprise for the financial year 2009-10.

(iii) **Amortization**—The company can amortise ₹ 303.26 lakhs over a period of five years by charging ₹ 60.65 lakhs per annum from the financial year 2011-12 onwards.

PROBLEM 26.6

An intangible item is appearing in the Balance Sheet of A Ltd. ₹ 15 lakhs on 1-4-2010. The item was acquired for ₹ 25 lakhs on 1-4-2009. The enterprise has been following a policy of amortizing the intangible item over a period of 5 years on straight line basis. Applying paragraph 63 of AS 26 the enterprise determines the amortization period to be 8 years, being the best estimate of its useful life, from the date when the item was amiable for use i.e., April 1, 2009. Comment.

[CA (Nov. 2010)]

Solution

AS	As per AS 26 the intangible asset was Acquired i.e. 1st April 2009, the revision of amortization period from 5 years to 8 years is a change in Accounting estimate and accordingly, para 78 of AS 26 would apply in this case. As per AS 26 if the expected useful life of the asset is significantly different from previous estimates, the amortisation period should be changed accordingly. AS 5 provides that in case of change in estimate, the effect should be given prospectively over the remaining useful life of the intangible asset i.e. 6 years. **Note:** It is assumed that since the date of purchase of intangible item, the enterprise has been following a policy of amortizing the intangible asset over a period of 5 years on straight line basis by applying paragraph 63 of AS 26 i.e. being the best estimate of its useful life. On 1.4.2011, the company again reviewed the useful life of the intangible asset.

PROBLEM 26.7

Refiners and Projects Limited is a company in the oil and gas sector, it undertakes extensive research and development work as part of its operations. It has till the end of the financial year 31 March, 2009 spent ₹ 592,23 crores on research expenses.

The development of a new process was completed in the accounting year 2009-10 after incurring an expenditure of ₹ 322.26 crores. In the accounting year 2010-2011 the company implemented the new process resulting in a post tax saving of ₹ 100 crores in the first year of operation and savings of ₹ 80 crores per annum thereafter for the next four years.

The cost of capital to the company is 12 per cent

Kindly indicate how you will, in the background of accounting standards prescribed, proceed to record the transactions in the books of accounts of the company.

You are given to understand that the research expenses shown above do not include any general or selling and administrative expenses.

The present value discounted at 12 per cent of a Rupee can be adopted at .893, .797, .712, .636 and .567 for the purposes of calculation. ***[CA (May, 2010)]***

Solution

Accounting Treatment

Item	Provision of AS 26	Accounting Treatment
Reserach Expenses	As per AS 26 no intangible asset arising from research (or from the research phase of an internal project) should be recognised. Expenditure on research (or on the research phase of an internal project) should be recognised as an expense when it is incurred.	₹ 592.23 crores incurred on research till the end of financial year ended 31st March, 2009 cannot be capitalised and hence has to expensed in the year in which it is incrred. In case the same is still unexpensed it will have to be written off under 'Prior period Expenditure'.
Developement Expenditure	As per para 44 of the standard, an intangible asset arising from development (or from the development phase of an internal project) should be recognised if, and only if, an enterprise can demonstrate all of the conditions specified in the standard.	Development cost of ₹ 322.26 crores is eligible for capitalization assuming that the enterprise can demonstrate all the specified conditions.

Item	Provision of AS 26	Accounting Treatment
Carrying Amount	As per AS 26, after initial recognition, an intangible asset should be carried at its cost less any accumulated amortization and any accumulated impairment losses.	Present value of future cash flows amounting ₹ 306.26 crores [(₹ 100 crores × 0.893) + (₹ 80 crores × 0.797) + (₹ 80 crores × 0.712) + (₹ 80 crores × 0.636) + (₹ 80 crores × 0.567)] is less than the cost incurred, it is prudent to carry the intangible asset at the discounted value of future cash flows (₹ 306.26 crores). The excess of cost incurred over present values amounting ₹ 16 crores (322.26 – 306.26) has to be recognised as an impairment loss in the year 2009-10.
Depreciation Amount	As per AS 26 depreciable amount of an intangible asset should be allocated on a systematic basis over the best estimate of its useful life. There is a rebuttable presumption that the useful life of an intangible asset will not exceed 10 years from the date when the asset is available for use. Amortization should commence when the asset is available for use.	The value of intangible asset should be amortized over a period of 5 years by following the straight line method. Therefore, an annual depreciatoon of ₹ 61.25 crores ₹ 306.26 (₹ 306.26 crores/5) should be charged for each year beginning with 2010-11.

PROBLEM 26.8

Base Ltd. is showing an intangible Asset at ₹ 85 lakhs as on 01.04.2012 and that item was required for ₹ 112 lakhs on 01.04.2008 and that item was available for use from that date. Himalayas Ltd. has been following the policy of amortisation of the intangible asset over a period of 12 years on straight line basis. Comment on the accounting treatment of the above with reference to relevant accounting standard. ***[CA (May 2011)]***

Solution

AS	As per AS 26, the depreciable amount of an intangible asset should be allocated on a systematic basis over the best estimate of its useful life. There is a rebuttable presumption that the useful life of an intangible asset will not exceed 10 years from the date when the asset is available for use. Amortisation should commence when the asset is available for use.
Advice	The Company has been following the policy of amortisation of the intangible asset over a period of 12 years on straight line basis. The period of 12 years is more than the maximum period of 10 years specified under AS 26. Accordingly, the Company would be required to restate the carrying amount of intangible asset as on 1.4.2012 at ₹ 112 lakhs *less* ₹ 33.6 lakhs (₹ 11.2 lakhs × 3 years) = ₹ 78.4 lakhs. If amortisation had been as per AS 26, the carrying amount would have been ₹ 78.4 lakhs. The difference of ₹ 6.6 lakhs i.e. (₹ 85 lakhs – 78.4 lakhs) would be required to be adjusted against the opening balance of revenue reserves. The carrying amount of ₹ 78.4 lakhs would be amortised over 7 (10 less 3) years in future by ₹ 11.2 lakhs per year.

PROBLEM 26.9

An engineering goods compnay provides after sales warranty for 2 years to its customers. Based on past experience, the company has the following policy for making provision for warranties on the invoice amount, on the remaining balnce warranty period:

Less than 1 year: 2% provision

More than 1 year: 3% provision

The company has raised invoices as under:

Invoice Date	Amount ₹
19th January, 2011	40,000
29th January, 2012	25,000
15th October, 2012	90,000

Calculate the provision to be made for warranty under Accounting Standard 29 as at 31st March, 2012 and 31st March, 2013. Also compute amount to be debited to Profit and Loss Account for the year ended 31st March, 2013. ***[CA (May 2013)]***

Solution

A. Provision as at 31-3-2013 = ₹ 25,000 × 0.2 + ₹ 90,000 × .03 = ₹ 3,200

B. *Less:* Provision as at 31-3-2012 = ₹ 40,000 × 0.2 + ₹ 25,000 × .03 = ₹ 1,550

C. Amount debited to Profit and Loss Account (A – B) = ₹ 1,650

Note: *No provision is to be made on 31-3-2013 in respect of sales amounting to ₹ 40,000 made on 19-01-2011 because the warranty period of 2 years has already expired.*

AS-28

PROBLEM 28.1

Carrying amount of a machine is ₹ 1,00,000 (Historical cost less depreciation). The machine is expected to generate ₹ 25,000 net cash flow for 5 years. The net realizable value (or net selling price) of the machine on current date is ₹ 85,000. The enterprises required rate of earning is 10% p.a. State the value at which the enterprise should carry its machine. The present value factors at 10% are 0.909, 0.826, 0.751, 0.683 and 0.621 at the end of first, second, third, fourth and fifth year respectively. ***[CA (IPCC) May 2011]***

Solution

A. Value in use* = ₹ 25,000 × (0.909 + 0.826 + 0.751 + 0.683 + 0.621) = ₹ 94,750

B. Net Selling Price = ₹ 85,000

C. Recoverable Amount (Being the higher of an Asset's Value in use and its Net Selling Price) = ₹ 94,750.

D. Carrying Value of a machine = ₹ 1,00,000 (recorded in the books)

E. Carrying amount is the amount at which an asset is recognized in the Balance Sheet after deducting any accumulated depreciation (amortization) and accumulated impairment losses thereon. In the given case, carrying amount of machine will be *lower of its recoverable amount* (i.e. ₹ 94,750) and its book value (i.e. ₹ 1,00,000). Therefore, the enterprise should carry its machine at Value of ₹ 94,750.

AS-29

PROBLEM 29.1

X Ltd. has its financial year ended 31.3.2011, fifteen law suits outstanding, none of which has been settled by the time the accounts are approved by the directors. The directors have estimated that the probable outcomes as below:

	Probability	*Amount of Loss ₹*
For first ten cases:		
Win	0.6	—
Loss-low damages	0.3	90,000
Loss-high damages	0.1	2,00,000
For remaining five cases:		
Win	0.5	—
Loss-low damages	0.3	60,000
Loss-high damages	0.2	1,00,000

The directors believe that the outcome of each case is independent of the outcome of all the others.

Estimate the amount of contingent loss and state the accounting treatment of such contingent loss. *[CA (PCC) May, 2010]*

Solution

As per AS 29 Contingent Liability should be disclosed in the financial statements if following conditions are satisfied:

1. There is a present obligation arising out of past events but not recognized as provision.
2. It is not probable that an outflow of resources emodying economic benefits will be required to settle the obligation.
3. The possibility of an outflow of resources embodying economic benefits is also remote.
4. The amount of the obligation cannot be measured with sufficient reliability to be recognized as provision.

   In this case, the probability of winning first 10 cases is 60% and for remaining five cases is 50%. In other words, probability of losing the cases is 40% and 50% respectively. According to AS 29, we make a provision if the loss is probable. As the loss does not appear to be probable and the probability or possibility of an outflow of resources embodying economic benefits is not remote rather there is reasonable possibility of loss, therefore, disclosure by way of note of contingent liability amount may be calculated as under:

Expected loss in first ten cases	= [₹ 90,000 × 0.3 + ₹ 2,00,000 × 0.1] × 10
	= [₹ 27,000 + ₹ 20,000] × 10
	= ₹ 47,000 × 10 = ₹ 4,70,000
Expected loss in remaining five cases	= [₹ 60,000 × 0.3 + ₹ 1,00,000 × 0.2] × 5
	= [₹ 18,000 + ₹ 20,000] × 5
	= ₹ 38,000 × 5 = ₹ 1,90,000
Total Contingent Liability	= ₹ 4,70,000 + ₹ 1,90,000 = ₹ 6,60,000.

PROBLEM 29.2

Sun Ltd. has entered into a sale contract of ₹ 5 crores with X Ltd. during 2010-11 financial year. The profit on this transaction is ₹ 1 crore. The delivery of goods is to take place during the first month of 2011-12 financial year. In case of failure of Sun Ltd. to deliver within the schedule, a comprensation of ₹ 1.5 crores is to be paid to X Ltd Sun Ltd. planned to manufacture the goods during the last month of 2010-11 financial year. As on balance sheet date (31.3.2011), the goods were not manufactured and it was unlikely that Sun Ltd. will be in a position to meet the contractual obligation.

(i) Should Sun Ltd. provide for contingency as per AS 29 ?

(ii) Should provision be measured as the excess of compensation to be paid over the profit? ***[CA (May 2010)]***

Solution

(i) AS 29 "Provisions" Contingent Liabilities and Contingent Assets" provides that when f an enterprise has a present obligation, as a result of past events, that probably requires an outflow of resources and a reliable estimate can be made of the amount of obligation, a provision should be recognised. Sun Ltd. has the obligation to deliver the goods within the scheduled time as per the contract. It is probable that Sun Ltd. will fail to deliver the goods within the schedule and it is also possible to estimate the amount of compensation. Therefore, Sun Ltd. should provide for the contingency amounting ₹ 1.5 crores as per AS 29.

(ii) Provision should not be measured as the excess of compensation to be paid over the profit. The goods were not manufactured before 31st March, 2011 'and no profit had accrued for the financial year 2010-2011. Therefore, provision should be made for the full amount of compensation amounting ₹.1.50 crores.

PROBLEM 29.3

An airline is required by law to overhaul its aircraft once in every three years. A company which operates aircrafts does not provide any provision as required by law in its final account. Discuss with reference to relevant Accounting Standard. ***[CA (Nov. 2010, May 2012)]***

Solution

AS	As per AS 29. A provision should be recognised only when an enterprise has a present obligation as a result of a past event.
Advice	In-the given case, there is no present obligation, therefore no provision is recognized as per AS 29. The cost of overhauling aircraft is not recognized as a provision because it is a future obligation and the incurring of the expenditure depends on the company's decision to continue operating the aircrafts. Even a legal requirement to overhaul does not require the company to make a provision for the cost of overhaul because there is no present obligation to overhaul the aircrafts. Further, the enterprises can avoid the future expenditure by its future action, for example by selling the aircraft. However, an obligation might arise to pay fines or penalties under the legislation after completion of three years. Assessment of probability of incurring fines and penalties depends upon the provisions of the legislation and the stringency of the enforcement regime. A provision should be recognized for the best estimate of any fines and penalties if airline continues to operate aircrafts for more than three years.

PROBLEM 29.4

A company had deferred research and development cost of ₹ 150 Lakhs. Sales expected in the subsequent years as under:

Years	Sales (₹ In Lakhs)
I	400
II	300
III	200
IV	100

(a) You are required to suggest how should Research and Development cost is to be charged to Profit and Loss account.

(b) If at the end of the IIIrd year, it is felt that no further benefit will accrue in the IVth year, how the unamortized expenditure would be dealt with in the accounts of the Company?

Solution

(a) Based on sales, research and development cost to be allocated as follows:

Years	Research and Development cost allocation (₹ In Lakhs)
I	$\frac{400}{1000} \times 150 = 60$
II	$\frac{300}{1000} \times 150 = 45$
III	$\frac{200}{1000} \times 150 = 30$
IV	$\frac{100}{1000} \times 150 = 15$

(b) If at the end of any year the circumstances do not justify further deferral as given in question at the end of IIIrd year, ₹ 45 Lakhs is to be charged as an expense immediately as per AS - 26.

PROBLEM 29.5

A company is in a dispute involving allegation of infringement of patents by a competitor company who is seeking damages of a huge sum of ₹ 900 lakhs. The directors are of the opinion that the claim can be successfully resisted by the company. How would you deal the same in the annual accounts of the company? ***[Nov. 2012]***

Solution

AS 29	As per para 14 of AS 29, 'Provision, Contingent Liabilities and Contingent Assets', a provision should be recognised when (a) an enterprise has a present obligation as a result of a past event; (b) It is probable that an outflow of resources embodying economic benefits will be required to settle the obligation; and (c) a reliable estimate can be made of the amount of the obligation. If these conditions are not met, no provision should be recognised. If these conditions are not met, no provision should be recognised.
Advice	Since the directors of the com pany are of the opinion that the claim can be successfully resisted by the com pany, therefore there will be no outflow of the resources. The company will disclose the same as contingent liability by way of the following note: "*Litigation is in process against the company relating to a dispute with a competitor who alleges that the company has infringed patents and is seeking damages of ₹ 900 lakhs. However, the directors are of the opinion that the claim can be successfully resisted by the company.*"

PROBLEM 29.6

An enterprise acquired patent right for ₹400 lakhs. The product life cycle has been estimated to be 5 years and the amortization was decided in the ratio of estimated future cash flows which are as under:

Years	1	2	3	4	5
Estimated Future Cash Flows (₹ in lakhs)	200	200	200	100	100

After 3rd year, it was ascertained that the patent would have an estimated balance future life of 3 years and the estimated cash flow after 5th year is expected to be ₹ 50 lakhs each year. Determine the amortization under Accounting Standard 26. ***[May 2013]***

Solution

AMORTIZATION OF COST AS PER AS 26

Year	*Net Cash Flows* ₹	*Amortization Ratio*	*Amortization Amount* ₹
1	200	.25	100
2	200	.25	100
3	200	.25	100
4	100	.40 (Revised)	40
5	100	.40 (Revised)	40
6	50	.20 (Revised)	20
			400

MISCELLENEOUS QUESTIONS

PROBLEM 1

A company acquired for its internal use a software on 28.01.2012 from the USA for US $ 1,00,000. The exchange rate on that date was ₹ 52 per USD. The seller allowed trade discount @ 5%. The other expenditure were:

(i) Import Duty: 20%

(ii) Purchase Tax: 10%

(iii) Entry Tax : 5% (Recoverable later from tax department)

(iv) Installation expenses : ₹ 25,000

(v) Profession fees for Clearance from Customs : ₹ 20,000

Compute the Cost of Software to be capitalized. **[Nov. 2012]**

Solution

Calculation of cost of software (intangible asset) acquired for internal use

Particulars	₹
Purchase cost of the software	$ 1,00,000
Less: Trade discount @ 5%	($ 5,000)
	$ 95,000
Cost in ₹ (US $ 95,000 × ₹ 52)	₹ 49,40,000
Add: Import duty on cost @ 20% (₹)	9,88,000
	59,28,000
Purchase tax @ 10% (₹)	5,92,800
Installation expenses (₹)	25,000
Profession free for clearance from customs (₹)	20,000
Cost of the software to be capitalised (₹)	65,65,800

Note: Entry Tax being a recoverable/refundable tax has not included as part of the cost of the asset.

PROBLEM 2

A new Plant X was acquired in exchange of old Plant B and on payment of ₹ 20,000. The carrying amount of the old Plant B was ₹ 1,75,000 (Historical cost less depreciation). The fair value of the Plant B on the date of exchange was ₹ 1,50,000.

Suggest the accounting entry in the books of the enterprise **[Nov. 2012]**

Solution

When a fixed asset is acquired in exchange for another asset, its cost is usually determined by reference to the fair market value of the consideration given. Accordingly, the value of Plant X will be

Particulars	₹
Exchange value of Plant B	1,50,000
Add: Additional cash paid	20,000
	1,70,000

Journal Entries to record the Acquisition of Plant X:

Date	Particulars	L.F.	Dr. (₹)	Cr. (₹)
1	Plant X A/c Dr.		1,70,000	
	To Plant B A/c			1,50,000
	To Bank A/c			20,000
	(Being new plant X acquired in exchange of Plant B on additional payment of ₹ 20,000)			
2	Profit and Loss A/c Dr.		25,000	
	To Plant B A/c			25,000
	(Being loss on exchange of old Plant B transferred to Profit and Loss Account)			

SECTION 2

PAPER 5: ADVANCED ACCOUNTING [GROUP-II]

REVISION ONE DAY BEFORE EXAMINATION

Important Short Answer Theory Questions for Revision

Important Short Answer Theory Questions for Revision

Paper 5: Advanced Accounting [Group II]

Standard Time : 1½ Hours

2.0 PARTNERSHIP – INSOLVENCY ETC.

Q. 2.1 Explain Garner v/s Murray rule applicable in the case of partnership firms. State, when is this rule not applicable. *[CA (PCC) May 2008]*

Answer

In the case of dissolution of a partnership firm due to insolvency, ***Garner vs Murray*** rule is applicable at the time of any partner becoming insolvent. It requires—

1. That the solvent partners should bear the loss arising due to insolvency of a partner in their capital ratio after making adjustments for past accumulated reserves, profits or losses, drawings, interest on drawings/capitals, remuneration to partners etc., to the date of dissolution but before making adjustment for profit or loss on realization in case of fluctuating capital. In case of fixed capital no such adjustments are required.
2. That the solvent partners should bring in cash equal to their respective shares of the loss on realization.

   Non-Applicability: This rule is not applicable when:

   1. When the solvent partner has a debit balance in the capital account.
   2. Only one partner is solvent.
   3. All partners are insolvent.
   4. The partnership deed provides for a specific method to be followed in case of insolvency of a partner, then the conditions given in the deed would prevail.

Q.2.2 A, B and C are partners; A became insolvent on 15.4.2010. The capital account balance of partner B is on the debit side. Partner B is solvent. Should partner B bear the loss arising on account of the insolvency of partner A? *[CA (PCC) May, 2007, 2010]*

Answer

According to ***Garner vs Murray*** Rule, if a solvent partner is having a debit balance in his capital account, then he cannot be called upon to bear the loss on account of the insolvency of the other partner. Hence, 'B' needs not bear the loss due to insolvency of partner 'A'.

Q.2.3 What is Piecemeal payment method under Partnership Dissolution? Briefly explain the two methods followed for determining the order in which the payments are made? *[CA (IPCC) May, 2010]*

Answer

Generally, the assets sold upon dissolution of partnership are realised only in small instalments over a period of time. In such circumstances the choice is either to distribute whatever is collected or to wait till whole amount is collected. Usually, the first cource is adopted. In order to ensure that the distributed cash amongst the partners is in proportion to their interest in the partnership concern either of the two methods described below may be followed for determining the order in which the payment should be made.

(i) Maximum Loss Method	Each instalment realised is considered to be the final payment i.e. outstanding assets and claims are considered worthless and partners' accounts are adjusted on that basis each time when a deposit is made following either Garner Vs. Murray rule or the profit sharing ratio rule.
(ii) Highest Relative Capital Method	According to this method, the partner who has the higher relative capital, that is, whose capital is greater in proportion to this profit sharing ration is first paid off. This method is also called as proportionate capital method.

Q.2.4 *W* paid a premium to other partners of the firm at the time of his admission to the firm, with a condition that the will not be dissolved before expiry of five years. The firm is dissolved after three years. W claims refund to premium.

(i) List the criteria for the calculation of the amount of refund.

(ii) Also list any two conditions when no claim in this respect will arise. ***[May 2014]***

Answer

If the firm is dissolved before the term expires, as is the case, *W* being a partner who has paid premium on admission will have to be repaid/refunded

The criteria for calculation of refund amount are:

(i) Terms upon which admission was made,

(ii) The time period for which it was agreed that the firm will not be dissolved.

(iii) The time period for which the firm has already been in existence.

No claim for refund will arise if:

(i) The firm is dissolved due to death of a partner,

(ii) If the dissolution of the firm is basically because of misconduct of W.

(iii) If the dissolution is through an agreement and such agreement does not have a stipulation for refund of premium.

3.0 ACCOUNTING FOR EMPLOYEE STOCK OPTION

Q.3.1 What is Employee Stock Option plan? Explain the importance of such plans in the modern time. ***[CA (IPCC) Nov. 2009]***

Answer

Meaning	It is a plan under which the enterprise grants employee stock options. Employee stock option is a contract that gives the employees of the enterprise the right, but not the obligation, for a specified period of time to purchase or subscribe the shares of the company at a fixed or determinable price.
Importance	1. Employee stock option plans encourage employees to have higher participation in the company. 2. Stock options provide an opportunity to employees to contribute in the growth of the company. 3. Stock option creates long term wealth in the hands of the employees. 4. They are important means to attract, retain and motivate the best available talent for the company. 5. It creates a common sense of ownership between the company and its employees.

4.0 ACCOUNTING FOR BUY-BACK OF SHARES

Q.4.1 Give four conditions to be fulfilled by a Joint Stock Company to buy back its equity Shrares. ***[May 2014]***

Answer

Procedural Conditions

1. **Authorised by Articles**—The buy-back must be authorized by the **Articles**
2. **Special Resolution/Board's Resolution**—The **special resolution** must be passed in the General Meeting of shareholders.

   OR

   The Board must pass a resolution at its meeting where the buy-back does not exceed 10% of the total equity paid up capital and free reserves of the company.
3. **Fully Paid Shares**—All the shares for buy-back must be fully paid-up.
4. **Time Limit**—The buy-back must be completed within **12 months** from the date of passing the Special Resolution/Board's Resolution.
5. **From Whom**— The buy-back can be :
   (a) from the existing shareholders or security holders on a proportionate basis;
   (b) from the open market;
   (c) by purchasing the securities issued to employees of the company pursuant to a scheme of stock option or sweat equity.
6. **Declaration of Solvency** —The company must file **Declaration of Solvency** with the Registrar and SEBI in the form of an affidavit signed by at least two directors of the company. The affidavit must state that the Board has made full inquiry into the affairs of the company as a result of which they have formed an option that the company is capable of meeting its liabilities and will not render insolvent within a period of one year from the date of declaration adopted by the Board.
7. **Destroy**— Company shall extinguish and physically destroy the shares or securities so bought back within 7 days of the last date of completion of buy-back.
8. **Restriction on further issue within 6 months**— Where a company completes a buy-back of its shares or other specified securities, it shall not make a further issue of the same king of shares or other secutiries including allotment of new shares or other specified securities within a period of 6 months except by way of:
   (a) a bonus issue or
   (b) in the discharge of subsisting obligations such as conversion of warrants, stock option schemes, sweat equaity or conversion of preference shares or debentures into equity shares.
9. **As per SEBI Guidelines**— In case of listed shares buy-back must be as per SEBI Guidelines and In case of unlisted shares buy-back must be as per Share Capital & Debentures Rules 2014.

   SEBI's Regulations for listed shares:
   (i) No offer of buy-back for at least 15% of the paid up capital and free reserves of the company shall be made from the open market.
   (ii) A company shall not make any offer of buy-back within a period 1 year reckoned from the date of closure of the preceding offer of buy-back, if any.
   (iii) The company shall ensure that at least 50% of the amount earmarked for buy-back is utilized for buying-back shares or other specified securities.

Accounting Treatment Condition [Sec 69(1)]

10. **Transfer of Certain Sums to Capital Redemption Reserve Account**—Where a company purchases its own shares out of free reserves or Secturities Premium, than a sum equal to the nominal value of the shares so purchased shall be transferred to the Capital Redemption Reserve (CRR) Account and details of such transfer must be disclosed in the balance sheet. The CRR can be utilized to issue to fully paid bonus shares to members.

Three Tests Conditions

11. **Maximum Limit of Amount of Equity Shares to be bought back**—The buy-back of the shares must **not exceed 25%** of **total paid-up capital and free reserves.**
12. **Maximum Limit of Number of Equity Shares to be bought back in any Financial Year**—The buy-back of equity shares in **any financial year** must not exceed **25% of its total paid up equity capital.**
13. **Maximum Debt-Equity Ratio**—The debt-equity ratio must **not be more than 2:1** after such buy-back. Here,

    Debt (after buy-back) = Secured + Unsecured Debt,

    Equity (after buy-back) = Capital + Free Reserves

    Note: For the purposes of Section 68, Free Reserves mean Free Reserves available for free distribution as dividend and include the Balance of Securities Premium A/c.

5.0 UNDERWRITTING OF SHARES & DEBENTURES

Q. 5.1 What do you mean by Firm Underwriting? ***[CA(PCC) Nov. 2007, May, 2010]***

Answer

'Firm underwriting' signifies a define commitment to take up a specified number of shares irrespective of the number of shares subscribed for by the public. In such a case, unless it has been otherwise agreed, the underwriter's liability is determined without taking into account the number of shares taken up 'firm' by him, i.e. the underwriter is obliged to take up:

1. the number of shares he has applied for 'firm'; and
2. the number of shares he is obliged to take up on the basis of the underwriting agreement.

9.0 LIQUIDATION OF COMPANIES

Q.9.1 What is Statement of Affairs of a liquidating company?

Answer

Statement of Affairs shows:

(a) **With regard to Assets:**

(i) Estimated Realisable Value of Assets not specifically pledged (as per list A).
(ii) Estimated Surplus from Assets specifically pledged (as per list B).
(iii) Estimated Total Assets available for creditors and contributories.

(b) **With regard to Liabilities:**

(i) Secured Creditors (as per List B).
(ii) Preferential Creditors (as per List C).
(iii) Debenture holders secured by floating charge (as per List D).
(iv) Unsecured Creditors (as per List E).

(c) **With regard to Share Capital:**

(i) Paid up Preference Share Capital (as per List F).

(ii) Paid up Equity Share Capital (as per List G).

(d) **Estimated deficiency/surplus as regards contributories (as per list H).**

Q. 9.2 What is Deficiency Account?

Answer

Meaning	Deficiency Account explains how the deficiency stated in the Statement of Affairs has taken place. It is divided into two parts: (a) Items Contributing to Deficiency which start with the deficit on a given date and contains every item that increases deficiency. (b) Items reducing Deficiency which start with the surplus on a given date and contain every item that reduces deficiency.
Balance	The excess of first part over the second part is deficiency and the excess of second part over the first part is surplus. The amount of such deficiency/surplus must be the same as shown by the Statement of Affairs.
Period	Deficiency Account must be prepared for such period being not less than 3 years as may be directed by the Official Liquidator (*in case of Compulsory Winding Up*) or Liquidator (*in case of Voluntary Winding up*).
Format	Deficiency Account is prepared in prescribed form(i.e., List H).

PROBLEM 9.3

What are Overriding Preferential Payments?

Solution

Accoding to Section 326 following are the over-riding preferential payments:

(a) Workmen's dues;

(b) So much of the debts due to the secured creditors as could not be realised by him because of pari-passu charge in favour of workmen, over the security held by him.

All such debts must be paid in full unless the assets are insufficient, in which case they shall abate in equal proportion.

Q. 9.4 What are Preferential Creditors?

Answer

Section 327 provides that subject to the provisions of Section 326, following preferential creditors shall be paid in priority to unsecured creditors or creditor having a floating charge:

(a) All revenues, taxes, cesses and rates, becoming due and payable by the company **within 12 months** next before the commencement of the winding up.

(b) All wages or salaries (including wages payable for time or piece work and salary earned wholly or in part by way of commission) of any employee due for the period not **exceeding 4 months within 12 months** next before commencement of winding up provided the amount payable to one claimant will not exceed such amount as may be notified.

(c) All accrued **holiday remuneration** becoming payable to any employee on termination of employment before winding up order or dissolution of the company.

(d) Unless the company is being wound up voluntarily for the purpose of reconstruction, all contributions payable during the 12 months next under the Employees' State Insurance Act, 1948, or any other law for the time being in force.

(e) All sums due as **compensation** to employees under the Workmen's Compensation Act, 1923.

(f) All sums due to any employee from a **provident fund, pension fund, gratuity fund** or any other fund, for the welfare of the employees maintained by the company.

(g) The expenses of any investigation held under Section 213 or 216 in so far as they are payable by the company.

All the preferential debts rank equally among themselves and are to be paid in full unless the assets are insufficient, in which case they will abate in equal proportion.

Q.9.5 Who is a Contributory?

Answer

According to Section 2 (26). "Contributory" means a person liable to Contribute to the assets of the Company in the event of its being wound up, and includes a holder of fully paid up shares. In some of the specific cases, the contributories will be as under:

Case	*Who is Contributory*
(a) In case of Death of a member	Legal Representatives
(b) In case of Insolvent member	Assignees subject to their power of disclaimer
(c) In case of winding up of a body corporate which was a member	Liquidator subject to his power ofdisclaimer

Q.9.6 When does the liability of List 'B' Contributories arise?

Answer

The liability of List 'B' Contributories arises only when the following 3 conditions are satisfied:

(a) if he had ceased to be a member during the 12 months preceding the date of Commencement of Winding up;

(b) if the debt/liability incurred upto the date of membership is still outstanding.

(c) if the present members are unable to pay the contribution required to be made by them.

Q.9.7 What is the Actual Amount of Liability of List 'B' Contributories?

Answer

The actual amount of liability of List 'B' Contributories is the least of the following 2 amounts:

(a) Creditors outstanding on date of ceasing to be member.

(b) Unpaid up amount on share (i.e., No. of shares held × Unpaid up amount per share).

Note: *If there are more than one List 'B' Contributories then such Contributories shall be liable to pay the concerned Creditors in proportion to their No. of shares held.*

Q.9.8 What is B list contributory? *[CA (PCE) Nov 2008]*

Answer

B list contributories are the shareholders who transferred partly paid shares (otherwise than by operation of law or by death) within one year, prior to the date of winding up. They may be called upon to pay an amount (not exceeding the amount not called up when the shares were transferred) to pay off such creditors, as existed on the date of transfer of shares and cannot be paid out of the funds otherwise available with the liquidator, provided also that the existing shareholders have failed to pay the amount due on the shares.

10.0 FINANCIAL STATEMENTS OF BANKING COMPANIES

Q.10.1 State the objectives of Capital Adequacy Norms. State the Minimum Capital Adequacy Ratio to be maintained.

Answer

Objectives of Capital Adequacy Norms	The fundamental objectives are: (a) to strengthen the soundness and stability of the banking system, (b) to achieve a high degree of consistency in its application to banks in different countries.
Minimum Capital Adequacy Ratio	All India Scheduled commercial Banks (excluding Regional Rural Banks) as well as foreign banks operating in India are required to achieve **such % of Capital Adequacy Ratio** (i.e., Ratio of Capital Fund to Risk Weighted Assets and off Balance Sheet Items) **as may be prescribed by RBI.**

Q.10.2 What are Non-Banking Assets? Also state the provision relating to the disclosure and disposition of these assets.

Answer

Meaning	Non-banking Assets are the immovable properties or tangible assets which are acquired in satisfaction of claims.
Disclosure	NBA are to be disclosed under the head 'Other Assets' on the Assets Side of Balance Sheet.
Disposition	NBA must be disposed off within 7 years from the date of acquisition or period extended by RBP [Sec 9]

Q.10.3 Mention the condition when a cash credit overdraft account is treated as 'out of order',

[CA (IPCC) May 2010]

Answer

A cash credit overdraft account is treated as NPA if it remains out of order for a period of more than 90 days. An account is treated as 'out of order' if any of the following conditions is satisfied:

(a) The outstanding balance remains continuously in excess of the sanctioned limit/drawing power.

(b) Though the outstanding balance is less than the sanctioned limit/drawing power –

- (i) there are no credits continuously for more than 90 days as on the date of balance sheet; or
- (ii) credits during the aforesaid period are not enough to cover the interest debited during the same period.

(c) Further any amount due to the bank under any credit facility is 'overdue' if it is not paid on the due date fixed by the bank.

Q.10.4 What is the percentage of NPA provision to be made by banks in respect of fully secured doubtful advances of more than 3 years old?

Answer

In case of Banking Companies, 100% NPA provision is made in respect of fully secured doubtful advances of more than 3 years. This provision is made irrespective of whether the advance is fully/partly secured or unsecured. However, in the case of government guaranteed advances this rate of provision does not apply.

Q.10.5 What are the restrictions imposed by the Banking Regulations Act, 1949 on payment of dividend in case of banking companies? ***[CA (PCC) May 2011]***

Answer

As per the Banking Regulations Act 1949, a banking company cannot pay dividend on its shares until all its capitalized expenses including preliminary expenses, organization expenses, share selling commission, brokerage, amount of losses incurred by tangible assets and any other item of expenditure not represented by tangible assets are completely written off.However, as per the Act, it is permissible for a banking company to pay dividend on its shares without writing off:

(i) The depreciation in the value of its investments in approved securities where such depreciation has not actually been capitalized or otherwise accounted for as a loss.

(ii) The depreciation in the value of its investments in shares, debentures or bonds (other than approved securities) where adequate provision for such deprecation has been made to the satisfaction of its auditors; and

(iii) The bad debts where adequate provision for such bad debts has been made to the satisfaction of its auditors.

11.0 FINANCIAL STATEMENTS OF LIFE INSURANCE COMPANIES

Q.11.1 What is Re insurance?

Answer

Re-insurance is an arrangement under which one insurance Company (called Re-insurer *or* Re-insurance Co.) insures the whole or a part of the subject matters already insured by another insurance Company (called Re-insured or Ceding Company). Thus, Ceding Company agrees to pass on whole or a part of risk to reinsurance company which agrees to accept the transferred risk.

Re-insurer receives the premium from the Re-insured and pays the commission and claim to the Re-insurer.

Q.11.2 What is Life Assurance Fund?

Answer

It refers to the fund which is retained to meet the aggregate liability on all outstanding policies. Until the liability on all outstanding policies is computed, the amount of profit of the life business cannot be ascertained. A life business is said to have earned profit only if its Life Assurance Fund exceeds its net liability on all outstanding policies.

The computation of the net liability on all outstanding policies is a complicated mathematical process which can be done only by experts in the field called 'Actuaries'. This Computation is carried out by LIC, every two years. As such, the life Insurance business cannot ascertain its profits every year.

Q.11.3 How is the Surplus of a Life Insurance Company distributed?

Answer

According to Section 28 of the Life Insurance Corporation Act 1956, **95%** of the surplus disclosed on a valuation must be allocated/reserved **for the policy holders** and the remaining (i.e., **5%**) must be utilised for such purposes as the Government may determine. The profit allocated to the **policy-holders** is distributed as bonus on with profit policies.

Statement showing the Distribution of Surplus

Particulars	₹
A. Total Surplus after Taxation	xxx
B. *Less*: Surplus to be carried forward	(xxx)
C. Surplus Available for distribution (A – B)	xxx

D. Share of Shareholders @ 5%	xxx
E. Share of Policy holders @ 95%	xxx
F. *Less*: Interim Bonus already paid	(xxx)
G. Amount Due to Policy holders (E – F)	xxx

Q.11.4 Explain in Brief the following principles and term of insurance business:

(i) Principle of Indemnity; (ii) Insurable interest; (iii) Principle of "UBERRIMAE FIDEI"; (iv) Catastrophic Loss

Answer

(i) **Principle of Indemnity:** Insurance is a contract of indemnity. The insurer is called idemnifier and the insured is the indemnified. In a contract of indemnity, only those who suffer loss are compensated to the extent of actual loss suffered by them. One cannot make profit by insuring his risks.

(ii) **Insurable interest:** All and sundry cannot enter into contracts of insurance. For example, A cannot insure the life of B who is a stranger. But if B, happens to be his wife or his debtor or business manager, A has insurable interest i.e. vested interest and therefore he can insure the life of B. For every type of policy insurable interest is insisted upon. In the absence of such interest the contract will amount to a wagering contract.

(iii) **Principle of UBERRIMAE FIDEI:** All contracts of insurance are contracts of uberrima fidei, i.e., contracts of utmost good faith. In a contract of insurance, however there is an implied condition that each party must disclose every material fact known to him. This is because the assessment of the risk and the determination of the premium by the insurer depend on the full and frank disclosure of all material facts is the proposal form.

(iv) **Catastrophic Loss:** A loss (or related losses) which is unbearable i.e. it causes severe consequences such as bankruptcy to a family, organization, or insurer.

12.0 FINANCIAL STATEMENTS OF GENERAL INSURANCE COMPANIES

Q.12.1 What is Average Clause under Insurance?

Answer

Average clause is introduced to discourage under insurance. Average clause is applicable in case of under insurance (i.e., where the sum insured of policy is less than the value of the subject matter of the insurance). In such a case the actual claim is proportionately reduced as under:

Average Clause Under Fire Insurance It may be noted that Fire Insurance Policies are always subject to **Average Clause**. Average clause is introduced to discourage under insurance. Average clause is applicable in case of under insurance (i.e., where the sum insured of policy is less than the value of the subject matter of the insurance). In such a case the actual claim is proportionately reduced as under:

Actual Claim accoding to Average Clause in case of Under Insurance

$$\text{Claim} = \text{Actual Loss} \times \frac{\text{Sum Insured}}{\text{Sum Insurable}}$$

Q.12.2 What is Double Insurance?

Answer

When more than one policy is taken to cover the same risk, it is called double insurance. Any person is free to insure her/his goods or property against fire or perils of the sea under more than one policy. But, in such cases, the insured cannot recover more than the insured value of peroperty from his insurers. All the insurers with whom she/he had insured will be liable to pay only a reteable proportion of the loss suffered by the insured.

Q.12.3 What is Provision for Unexpired Risks? *[May 2002, 2007]*

Answer

<table>
<tr><td>1. Meaning</td><td>Provision for Unexpired Risks is a provision created to meet the claims which may arise in respect of the policies which remain unexpired at the end of the year.</td></tr>
<tr><td>2. Minimum Reserve to be kept</td><td>Types of General Insurance Business — % of Net Premium
I. Marine Hull Insurance — 100%
II. Fire, Marine Cargo and Misc. Insurance — 40%
However, the income tax authorities allow 100% of the net premium in case of marine insurance and 50% of the net premium in case of other insurance.
Since there is no bar on creating such reserve at a percentage higher than those laid down by the Executive Committee, the Company may maintain such reserve at a higher percentage. The excess reserve over the minimum reserve is termed as 'Additional Reserve'.</td></tr>
<tr><td>3. Accounting Treatment</td><td>1. The difference between the aggregate amount of minimum provision and additional provision in the beginning and aggregate amount there of at the end is disclosed as 'Changes in Provision for Unexpired Risks' in Revenue Account.
2. Balance of Minimum provision and additional provision of unexpired risks is shown on the liabilities side of Balance Sheet.</td></tr>
</table>

13.0 FINANCIAL STATEMENTS OF ELECTRICITY COMPANIES

Q.13.1 State any four alternative Accounting Treatment of the Fund received by an Electricity Company from consumer towards Capital Expenditure/Service Line Contribution. [Nov. 2014]

Answer

Capital Service Line Contribution: Different SERCs prescribe Service Line cum Defvelopment (SLD) Charges Norms as per Sec. 47 of the Electricity Act. Accounting for and Reporting of this source of funds of Electricity Companies may be in any of the following ways:

1. Initial Recording as **Liability**, and subsequently recognized as **Income** over the life of the asset.
2. Recording as **Reserves** (as the amount is not refundable) and reported under the head Reserves and Surplus, **without** transferring any proportionate amount to the Income Statement over the life of asset,
3. Recording as **Reserves** (as the amount is not refundable) and **subsequent** transfer of proportionate amount to Income Statement during the expected life of the asset to match against Depreciation on total cost of such asset, or
4. Recording as reduction in the Cost of Non-Current Asset, and providing Depreciation on such reduced cost.

15.0 ACCOUNTING FOR BRANCHES

Q.15.1 Why goods are marked on invoice price by the head office while sending goods to the branch? ***[CA (IPCC) May 2011]***

Answer

Goods are marked on invoice price to achieve the following objectives:

1. To keep secret from the branch manager, the cost price of the goods and profit made, so that the branch manager may not start a rival and competitive business with the concern; and
2. To have effective control on stock i.e stock at any time must be equal to opening stock plus goods received from head office minus sales made at branch.
3. To dictate pricing policy to its branches, as well as save work at branch because prices have already been decided.

Q.15.2 What are the indicators of Non-Integral Foreign Operation (NFO)? ***[Nov. 2014]***

Answer

The indicators of a Non-Integral Foreign Operation are:

1. **Autonomy:** While the reporting enterprise may control the foreign operation, the activities of the foreign operation are carried out with a significant degree of autonomy from those of the reporting enterprise,
2. **Transaction Pattern:** Transactions with the reporting enterprise are not a high proportion of the foreign operation's activities,
3. **Financing:** The activities of the foreign operation are financed mainly from its own operations or local borrowings rather than from the reporting enterprise,
4. **Expenditure in Local Currency:** Cost of Labour, Material and other components of the foreign operation's products or services are primarily paid or settled in the local currency rather than in the reporting currency.
5. **Sales Pattern:** The foreign operation's sales are mainly in currencies other then the reporting currency.
6. **Effect of Cash Flows:** Cash Flows of the reporting enterprise are insulated from the day-to-day activities of the foreign operation rather than being directly affected by the activities of the foreing operation.
7. **Prices of products:** Sales Prices for the foreign operation's products are not primarily responsive on a short-term basis to changes in exchange rates but are dtermined more by local com petitiion or local government regulation, and
8. **Local Market:** There is an active local sales market for the foreign operation's products, although there might be significant amounts of exports.

The appropriate classification for each operation can be established from **factual information** and **proper judgment**, based on the indicators listed above.

16.0 SCHEDULE III TO THE COMPANIES ACT, 2013

Q.16.1 State under which head these accounts should be classified in Balance Sheet, as per Schedule III to The Companies Act 2013:

(i) Share application money received in excess of issued share capital.

(ii) Share option outstanding account.

(iii) Unpaid matured debenture and interest accrued thereon.

(iv) Uncalled liability on shares and other partly paid investments.

(v) **Calls unpaid.**

(vi) **Intangible Assets under development.**

(vii) **Money received against share warrant.**

(viii) **Long term maturity of finance lease obligation.** *[May 2014]*

Answer

Classification of following accounts for the presentation in Schedule III to the Companies Act, 2013

Sl. No.	*Accounts*	*Head*
(i)	Share application money received in excess of issue share capital	Other Current Liabilities
(ii)	Share option outstanding account	Reserve & Surplus
(iii)	Unpaid matured deb4enture and interest accrued thereon	Other Current Liabilities
(iv)	Uncalled liability on shares and other partly paid investments	Contingent Liabilities and commitments-commitments to the extent not provided for
(v)	Calls unpaid	Share Capital
(vi)	Intangible Assets under development	Fixed Assets
(vii)	Money received against share warrant	Shareholder's Funds
(viii)	Long term maturity of finance lease obligation	Long Term Borrowings

Q.16.2 Is non-disclosure of source from which Bonus shares have been issued, a violation of Schedule III to the Companies Act, 2013?

Answer

No since Schedule III does not require such disclosure. Schedule III merely requires the disclosure of aggregate number and class of shares allotted as fully paid up bonus shares for a period of 5 years immediately preceding the Balance Sheet date in the Notes to Accounts.

Q.16.3 Is non-disclosure of opening and closing WIP in the Statement of Profit & Loss, a violation of Schedule III to the Companies Act, 2013?

Answer

No since Schedule III does not require such disclosure unless difference between opening closing WIP is material.

17.0 ACCOUNTING STANDARDS

CONCEPTUAL FRAMEWORK FOR PREPARATION AND PRESENTATION OF FINANCIAL STATEMENTS

PROBLEM 1

Give the four qualitative characteristics which the financial statements should observe.

[CA (PCC) Nov 2008]

Solution

The financial statements should observe the following qualitative characteristics:

(*a*) Understandability

(*b*) Relevance

(*c*) Reliability

(*d*) Comparability.

PROBLEM 2

What are the qualitative characteristics of the financial statements which improve the usefulness of the information furnished therein? ***[CA (IPCC) Nov. 2011]***

Solution

The qualitative characteristics are attributes that improve the usefulness of information provided in financial statements. The framework suggests that the financial statements should observe and maintain the following qualitative characteristics as far as possible within limits of reasonable cost benefit.

1. Under-standability	The financial statements should present information in a manner as to be readily understandable by the users with reasonable knowledge of business and economic activities. It is not right to think that more disclosures are always better. A mass of irrelevant information creates confusion and can be even more harmful than non-disclosure. No relevant information can be however withheld on the grounds of complexity.
2. Relevance	The financial statements should contain relevant information only. Information, which is likely to influence the economic decisions by the users, is said to be relevant. Such information may help the users to evaluate past, present or future events or may help in confirming or correcting past evaluations. The relevance of a piece of information should be judged by its materiality. A piece of information is said to be material if its omission or misstatement can influence economic decisions of a user.
3. Reliability	To be useful, the information must be reliable; that is to say they must be free from material error and bias. The information provided are not likely to be reliable unless: (*a*) Transactions and events reported are faithfully represented. (*b*) Transactions and events are reported in terms of their substance and economic reality not merely on the basis of their legal form. This principle is called the principle of 'substance over form'.

	(*c*) The reporting of transactions and events are neutral, i.e. free from bias. (*d*) Prudence is exercised in reporting uncertain outcome of transactions or events.
4. Comparability	Comparison of financial statements is one of the most frequently used and most effective tools of financial analysis. The financial statements should permit both inter-firm and intra-firm comparison. One essential requirement of comparability is disclosure of financial effect of change in accounting policies.
5. True and Fair View	Financial statements are required to show a true and fair view of the performance, financial position and cash flows of an enterprises. The conceptual framework does not deal directly with this concept of true and fair view, yet the application of the principal qualitative characteristics and of appropriate accounting standards normally results in financial statements portraying true and fair view of information about an enterprise.

PROBLEM 3

"One of the characteristics of financial statements is neutrality"- Do you agree with this statement? ***[CA (PCC) May 2008]***

Solution

Yes, one of the characteristics of financial statements is neutrality. To be reliable, the information contained in financial statement must be neutral, that is free from bias. Financial Statements are not neutral if by the selection or presentation of information, they influence the making of a decision or judgement in order to achieve a predetermined result or outcome. Financial statements are said to depict the true and fair view of the business of the organization by virtue of neutrality.

PROBLEM 4

Discuss the concept of Cost v/s Fair value with reference to Indian Accounting Standards.

Solution

Cost Basis: The term Cost refers to cost of purchase, costs of conversion on other costs incurred in bringing the goods to its present condition and location. Assets are recorded at the amount of cash or cash equivalents paid or the fair value of the other consideration given to acquire them at the time of their acquisition. Liabilities are recorded at the amount of proceeds received in exchange for the obligation, or in some circumstances (*for example*, income taxes), at the amounts of cash or cash equivalents expected to be paid to satisfy the liability in the normal course of business.

Fair Value: Fair Value of an asset is the amount at which an enterprise expects to exchange an asset between knowledgeable and willing parties in an arm's length transaction.

Indian Accounting Standards are generally based on historical cost with a very few exceptions:

AS 2 "Valuation of Inventories"	Inventories are valued at net realizable value (NRV) if cost of inventories is more than NRV.
AS 10 "Accounting for Fixed Assets"	Items of fixed assets that have been retired from active use and are held for disposal are stated at net realizable value if their net book value is more than NRV.
AS 13 "Accounting for Investments"	Current investments are carried at lower of cost and fair value. The carrying amount of long term

	investments is reduced to recognise the permanent decline in value.
AS 15 "Employee Benefits"	The provision for defined benefits is made at fair value of the obligations.
AS 26 "Intangible Assets"	If an intangible asset is acquired in exchange for shares or other securities of the reporting enterprise, the asset is recorded at its fair value, or the fair value of the securities issued, whichever is more clearly evident.
AS 28 "Impairment of Assets"	Provision is made for impairment of assets.

On the other hand IFRS and US GAAPs are more towards fair value. Fair value concept requires a lot of estimation and to the extent, it is subjective in nature.

AS-5

PROBLEM 5.1

What is meant by Accounting Estimate? Give two examples for accounting estimate.

[CA (PCC) Nov. 2007]

Solution

As a result of the uncertainties in business activities, many financial statement items cannot be measured with precision but can only be estimated. This is called accounting estimates. On account of such uncertainties, management makes various estimates and assumptions of assets, liabilities, income and expenses as on the date of preparation of financial statements. This process of estimation involves judgments, which is based on the latest information available.

Examples of estimation in *some* fields are:

(i) Estimation of useful life of depreciable assets.

(ii) Estimation of provision to be made for bad and doubtful debts.

PROBLEM 5.2

When can an item qualify to be a prior period item as per AS 5? *[CA (PCC) May 2008]*

Solution

According to para 16 of AS 5 on 'Net Profit or Loss for the Period, Prior Period Items and Changes in Accounting Policies', prior period items refers to those income or expenses, which arise in the current period as a result of errors or omissions in the preparation of financial statements of one or more prior periods. The term does not include other adjustments necessitated by circumstances, which though related to prior periods, are determined in the current period e.g., arrears payable to workers in current period as a result of revision of wages with retrospective effect.

PROBLEM 5.3

Explain the provisions of AS -5 regarding accounting treatment of prior period items.

[CA (PCC JUNE 2009)]

Solution

As per AS 5, prior period items are income or expenses, which arise, in the current period as a result of errors or omission in the preparation of financial statements of one or more prior periods. The term does not include other adjustments necessitated by circumstances, which though related to prior periods, are determined in the current period. *Example*: arrears payable to workers in current period as a result of retrospective revision of wages.

The nature and amount of prior period items should be separately disclosed in the statement of profit and loss in manner that their impact on current profit or loss can be perceived.

As per para 19 of AS 5, prior period items are normally included in determination of net profit or loss for the current profit, they can be added (or deducted as the case may be) from the current profit. An alternative approach is to show such items in the statement of profit or loss after determination of current net profit or loss. In either case, the objective is to indicate the effect of such items on the current profit or loss.

PROBLEM 5.4

Give two examples on each of the following items:

(i) Change in Accounting Policy

(ii) Change in Accounting Estimate

(iii) Extra Ordinary Items

(iv) Prior Period Items. ***[Nov. 2012, 2014]***

Solution

(i) Examples of Changes in Accounting Policy:

a. Change of Depreciation method from WDV to SLM and vice-versa.

b. Change in Cost formula in measuring the cost of inventories.

(ii) Examples of Changes in Accounting Estimates:

a. Change in estimate of provision for doubtful debts on sundry debtors.

b. Change in estimate of useful life of fixed assets.

(iii) Examples of Extraordinary items:

a. Loss due to earthquakes/fire/strike

b. Attachment of property of the enterprise by government

(iv) Examples of Prior period items:

a. Applying incorrect Rate of Depreciation in one or more prior periods.

b. Omission to account for Income or Expenditure in one or more prior periods.

AS-11

PROBLEM 11.1

Explain "monetary item" as per Accounting Standard 11. How are foreign currency monetary items to be recognized at each Balance Sheet date? Classify the following as monetary or non-monetary item:

(i) Share Capital

(ii) Trade Receivables

(iii) Investments

(iv) Fixed Assets

[CA (PCC) May 2013]

Solution

1. As per AS 11 'The Effects of Changes in Foreign Exchange Rates', Monetary items are money held and assets and liabilities to be received or paid in fixed or determinable amounts of money.
2. Foreign currency monetary items should be reported using the closing rate at each balance sheet date. However, in certain circumstances, the closing rate may not reflect with reasonable accuracy the amount in reporting currency that is likely to be realised from, or required to disburse, a foreign currency monetary item at the balance sheet date. In such circumstances, the relevant monetary item should be reported in the reporting currency at the amount which is likely to be realised from or required to disburse, such item at the balance sheet date.

Share capital	Non-monetary
Trade receivables	Monetary
Investments	Non-monetary
Fixed assets	Non-monetary

AS-12

PROBLEM 12.1

Explain in brief the treatment of Refund of Government Grants in line with AS 12 in the following three situations:

(i) When Government Grant is related to revenue,

(ii) When Government Grant is related to specific fixed assets,

(iii) When Government Grant is in the nature of Promoter's contribution. ***[May 2014]***

Solution

As per AS 12, refund to Government Grant is treated in the following manner:

(a) When Government Grant is related to Revenue:

(i) The amount of refund is first adjusted against any unamortized deferred credit balance still remaining in respect of the Grant

(ii) Any excess refund over such deferred credit balance or where no deferred credit exists, is immediately charged to Profit & Loss Account.

(b) When Government Grant is related to specific Fixed Asset:

(i) The amount of refund will increase the Book Value of the Asset, if at the time of receipt of Grant, the cost of asset was reduced by the amount of Grand.

(ii) If at the time of receipt, the Grant amount was credited to Deferred Grant Account, then the amount of refund will first reduce the unamortized balance of Deferred Grant Account, any excess refund will reduce the Capital Reserve.

(c) When the Government Grant is in the nature of Promoter's Contribution:

Capital Reserve will be reduced by the amount of refund.

PROBLEM 12.2

How would you record a non-monetary grant received from the Government as per AS 12? ***[CA (PCC) May 2008]***

Solution

According to para 7.1 of AS 12 'Accounting for Government Grants', Government grants may take the form of non-monetary assets such as land or other resources, given at concessional rates. In these circumstances, it is usual to account for such assets at their acquisition cost. Non-monetary grants given free of cost are recorded at a nominal value.

PROBLEM 12.3

Explain the treatment of refund of Government Grants as per Accounting Standard 12.

[CA (IPCC) Nov. 2011]

Solution

HOW TO ACCOUNT FOR GRANT THAT BECOME REFUNDABLE

Case	Treatment
(i) The amount refundable in respect of a grant related to revenue.	Reduce the balance of unamortized deferred credit and charge excess refund to Profit and Loss Statement. **Journal Entry:** Grant A/c Dr. [with Unamortized Cr. Balance] P&L A.c Dr. [With Excess of Refund over Unamortized Cr. Balance] To Bank A/c [with Refund]
(ii) The amount refundable in respect of a grant related to a specific fixed asset.	Increase the book value of the asset & provide depreciation on the revised book value prospectively over the residual useful life of the asset. **Journal Entry:** Fixed Asset A/c Dr. To Grant A/c *or* Reduce the Capital Reserve or the deferred income balance, as appropriate, by the amount refundable. **Journal Entry:** Capital Reserve A/c Dr. To Grant A/c
(iii) The amount refundable in respect of a Government grants in the nature of promoters' contribution.	Reduce from the Capital Reserve. **Journal Entry:** Capital Reserve A/c Dr. To Grant A/c

AS-16

PROBLEM 16.1

Briefly indicate the items which are included in the expressions "Borrowing Cost" as per AS 16.

Solution

Borrowing costs are interest and other costs incurred by any enterprise in connection with the borrowing of funds. Borrowing cost may include:

(a) Interest and commitment charges on bank borrowings and other short term and long term borrowings.

(b) Amortisation of discounts or premiums relating to borrowings.

(c) Amortisation of ancillary costs incurred in connection with the arrangement of borrowings.
(d) Finance charges in respect of assets required under finance leases or under other similar arrangements; and
(e) Exchange differences arising from foreign currency borrowings to the extent that they are regarded as an adjustment to interest costs.

PROBLEM 16.2

Enumerate two points which the financial statements should disclose in respect of Borrowing Costs as per AS 16. ***[CA (PCC JUNE 2009)]***

Solution

As per AS 16, the Financial Statements should disclose the following:

(a) The accounting policy adopted for borrowing costs and
(b) The amount of borrowing costs capitalized during the period

AS-19

PROBLEM 19.1

Explain the types of leases as per AS 19. ***[CA (PCC) June, 2009]***

Solution

For the purpose of accounting AS 19 'Leases' classify the lease into two categories as follows:

Finance Lease	It is a lease, which transfers substantially all the risks and rewards incidental to ownership of an asset to the lessee by the lessor but not the legal ownership. As per para 8 of the standard, in following situations, the lease transactions are called Finance lease: 1. The lessee will get the ownership of leased asset at the end of the lease term. 2. The lessee has an option to buy the leased asset at the end of the lease term at price, which is lower than is its expected fair value at the date on which option will be exercised. 3. The lease term covers the major part of the life of asset even if title is not transferred. 4. At the beginning of lease term, present value of minimum lease rental covers the initial fair value. 5. The asset given on lease to lessee is of specialized nature and can only be used by the lessee without major modification.
Operating Lease	It is lease, which does not transfer all the risks and rewards incidental to ownership.

AS-20

PROBLEM 20.1

In the following list of Shares issued, for the purpose of calculation of Weighted Average Number of Shares, from whcih date weight is to be considered:

(i) Equity Shares issued in Exchange of cash,

(ii) Equity Shares issued as a result of Conversion of Debt Instrument,

(iii) Equity Shares issued in Exchange for the settlement of Liability of the Enterprise,

(iv) Equity Shares issued for rendering of Services to the Enterprise,

(v) Equity Shares issued in Lieu of Interest and/or Principal of an other Financial Instrument,

(vi) Equity Shares issued as consideration for the Acquisition of Asset other than in Cash.

[Nov. 2014]

Solution

When equity Shares are issued...	*Included with effect from the...*
(a) In exchange for Cash.	Date when cash is receivable.
(b) As a result of conversioni of a Debt Instrument to Equity.	Date of conversion.
(c) In lieu of Interest or Principal on other Financial Instruments.	Date when interest careases to accrue.
(d) In exchange for the settlement of a liability of the Enterprise.	Date when settlement becomes effective.
(e) As consideration for acquisition of an asset other than cash.	Date on which the acquisition is recognised.
(f) For the rendering of services to the enterprise.	Date on which the service are rendered.
(f) For the rendering of services to the enterprise.	Date on which the service are rendered.

Potential Equity Share: A Potential Equity Share is a Financial Instrument or other contract that entittles, or may entitle, its holder to Equity Shares. Some examples are:

(a) Debt Instruments or Preference Shares that are convertible into Equity Shares,

(b) Share Warrants,

(c) Options including Employee Stock Option Plans (ESOP) under which Employees of an Enterprise are entitled to receive Equity Shares as part of their remuneration, and other similar plans, and

(d) Shares which would be issued upon the satisfaction of certain conditions resulting from contractual arrangements **(Contingently Issuable Shares)**, such as the acquisition of a business or other assets, or shares issuable under a Loan Contract, upon default of payment of principal or interest, if the contract so provides

SECTION 3

PAPER 5: ADVANCED ACCOUNTING [GROUP-II]

TULSIAN'S MODEL TEST PAPERS

ATTENTION PLEASE

DEAR STUDENTS

Your Sincere and 100% Accurate Attempt of Tulsian's Model Test Papers under Examination conditions guarantees you 100% SURE SUCCESS in the Paper 5: Advanced Accounting of Group II

BEST OF LUCK!

Paper-5: Advanced Accounting
CA IPC (Group II)
Tulsian's Model Test Paper 1

Question No. 1 is compulsory.
Attempt any Five questions from the remaining Six questions
Wherever necessary suitable assumptions may be made by the candidates.
Working notes should form part of the answer.

Q.1 Answer the following questions: **[4 × 5 = 20]**

(a) A company has its share capital divided into shares of ₹ 10 each. On 1-4-2012, it granted 5,000 employees stock option at ₹ 50, when the market price was ₹ 140. The options were to be exercised between 1-12-2012 to 28-2-2013. The employees exercised their options for 4,800 shares only; remaining options lapsed. Pass the necessary journal entries for the year ended 31-3-2013, with regard to employees' stock option.

(b) M/s. ABC Limited has gone into liquidation on 25th June, 2013. Certain creditors could not receive payments out of realization of assets and contributions from A list contributories. The following are the details of certain transfers which took place in the year ended 31st March, 2013:

Shareholders	*No. of shares transferred*	*Date of ceasing to be a member*	*Creditors remaining unpaid and outstanding on the date of transfer (₹)*
P	4,000	10-5-2012	9,000
Q	3,000	22-7-2012	12,000
R	2,400	15-9-2012	13,500
S	1,600	14-12-2012	14,000
T	1,000	09-03-2013	14,200

All the shares are of ₹ 10 each, ₹ 8 per share paid up. Show the amount to be realized from the persons listed above. Ignore remuneration to liquidator and other expenses.

(c) The following particulars are extracted from the Books of the Commercial Bank Ltd. for the year ending 31st March, 2013.

(i) Interest and Discounts	1,98,64,800
(ii) Rebated on Bills Discounted (balance on 1.4.2012)	70,080
(iii) Bills discounted and purchased	77,46,400

It is ascertained that proportionate discount not yet earned on the Bills Discounted which will mature during 2013-14 amount to ₹ 96,860.

Pass the necessary Journal entries with narration adjusting the above and show:

(a) Rebate on Bills Discounted Account; and

(b) Interest and Discount Account in the ledger of the Commercial Bank Limited.

(d) The Life Fund of Well-life Assurance Co. was ₹.90,00,000 as on 31st March 2013. The interim bonus paid during the valuation period was ₹.1,50,000. The periodical actuarial valuation determined the net liability at ₹.75,00,000. Surplus brought forward from the previous valuation was ₹.9,00,000. The directors of the company proposed to carry forward ₹.10,00,000 and to divide the balance between the shareholders and the policy holders. You are required to show:

(i) The Valuation Balance Sheet.

(ii) The Net Profit for the valuation period.

(iii) The Distribution of the Surplus.

(e) Show adjustment Journal entry in the books of Head Office at the end of March, 2013 for incorporation of inter-branch transactions assuming that only Head Office maintains different branch accounts in its books.

A. Delhi Branch:

1. Received goods from Mumbai – ₹ 35,000 and 15,000 from Kolkata.

2. Sent goods to Chennai – ₹ 25,000, Kolkata – ₹ 20,000.

3. Bill Receivable received – ₹ 20,000 from Chennai.

4. Acceptances sent to Mumbai – ₹ 25,000, Kolkata – ₹ 10,000.

B. Mumbai Branch (apart from the above):

5. Received goods from Kolkata – ₹ 15,000 , Delhi – ₹ 20,000.

6. Cash sent too Delhi – ₹ 15,000, Kolkata – ₹ 7,000.

C. Chennai Branch (apart from the above):

7. Received goods from Kolkata – ₹ 30,000.

8. Acceptances and cash sent to Kolkata – ₹ 20,000 and ₹ 10,000 respectively.

D. Kolkata Branch (apart from the above):

9. Sent goods to Chennai – ₹ 35,000.

10. Paid cash to Chennai – ₹ 15,000.

11. Acceptances sent to Chennai – ₹ 15,000

All working should form part of the answer.

Q.2. *P* and *Q* are partners of *P & Co.* sharing Profit and losses in the ratio of 3 : 1 and *Q* and *R* are partners of *R & Co.*, sharing profits and losses in the ratio of 2 : 1. On 31st March, 2013, they decide to amalgamate and form a new firm *M/s PQR & Co.*, wherein *P, Q* and *R* would be partners sharing profits and losses in the ratio of 3 : 2 : 1. The Balance Sheets of two firms on the above date are as under:

Liabilities	*P & Co.* ₹	*R & Co.* ₹	*Assets*	*P & Co.* ₹	*R & Co.* ₹
Capitals:			*Fixed Assets:*		
P	2,40,000	----	Building	50,000	60,000
Q	1,60,000	2,00,000	Plant & machinery	1,50,000	1,60,000
R	—	1,00,000	Office Equipment	20,000	6,000
Reserves	50,000	1,50,000	*Current Assets:*		
Sundry Creditors	1,20,000	1,16,000	Stock-in-trade	1,20,000	140,000
Due to *P & Co.*	....	1,00,000	Sundry Debtors	1,60,000	2,00,000
Bank overdraft	80,000	----	Bank Balance	30,000	90,000
			Cash in hand	20,000	10,000
	—	—	Due from *R & Co.*	1,00,000	—
	6,50,000	6,66,000		6,50,000	6,66,000

The amalgamated firm took over the business on the following terms:

(a) Building of *P & Co.* was valued at ₹ 1, 00, 000.

(b) Plant and machinery of *P & Co.* was valued at ₹ 2,50,000 and that of *R & Co.* at ₹ 2,00,000.

(c) All stock in trade is to be appreciated by 20%.

(d) Goodwill valued of *P & Co.* at ₹ 1,20,000 and *R & Co.* at ₹ 60,000, but the same will not appear in the books of *PQR & Co.*

(e) Partners of new firm wiil bring the necessary cash to pay other partners to adjust their capitals according to the profit sharing ratio.

(f) Provisions for doubtful debts has to be carried forward at ₹ 12,000 in respect of debtors of *P & Co.* and ₹ 26,000 in respect of debtors of *R & Co.*

Required: Prepare the Balance Sheet of new firm and Capital Accounts of the partners in the books of old firms.

Q.3. Balance Sheet of Dee Limited on 31st March, 2013 was as follows:

Liabilities	₹	*Assets*	₹
Share Capital: Authorised Capital 50,000, Equity Shares of ₹ 10 each	5,00,000	Fixed Assets (at cost *less* depreciation) Debenture Redemption Fund Investment	8,00,000 2,00,000
Issued and Subscribed Capital 25,000 Equity shares of ₹ 10 each fully paid up	2,50,000	Cash balance Other Current Assets	2,50,000 10,00,000
Reserves and Surplus:			
General Reserve	2,75,000		
Profit and Loss A/c	1,00,000		
Debenture Redemption Reserve	2,50,000		
Secured Loans:			
12% Convertible Debentures (5,000 Debentures of ₹.100 each)	5,00,000		
Other Secured loans	2,50,000		
Current Liabilities and *Provisions:*	6,00,000		
Proposed Dividend	25,000		
	22,50,000		22,50,000

At the General Meeting it was resolved to:

1. Pay proposed dividend of 10% in cash.
2. Give existing shareholders the option to purchase one share of ₹.10 each at ₹.15 for every five shares held. This option was taken up by all the shareholders.
3. Redeem the debentures at a premium of 5% and also confer option to the debentureholders to convert 50% of their holding into equity shares at a predetermined price of ₹ 15 per share and balance payment to be made in cash.

Holders of 3,000 debentures opted to get their debentures redeemed in cash only while the rest opted for getting the same converted into equity shares as per the terms of issue. Debenture Redemption Fund Investments realized ₹ 1,80,000 on sales.

Required: Redraft the Balance Sheet after giving effects to the right issue and redemption of debentures. Also show the calculations in respect of number of equity shares issued and cash payment.

Q.4. X Ltd. and Y Ltd. were carrying on same business independently. The companies agreed to amalgamate on and from 1-4-2013 and formed a new company Z Ltd. to take over the assets and liabilities of the existing companies. The Balance Sheets of two companies as on 31-3-2013 are as follows:

Liabilities	*X Ltd.* ₹	*Y Ltd.* ₹	*Assets*	*X Ltd.* ₹	*Y Ltd.* ₹
Share capital: Equity shares of ₹ 10 each (fully paid up)	30,00,000	18,00,000	Land & building	27,00,000	13,50,000
			Plant & machinery	15,00,000	11,40,000
Securities premium	6,00,000	—	Investments (15,000 shares of Y Ltd.)	2,40,000	—
General reserve	9,00,000	7,50,000			
Profit & loss account	5,40,000	4,80,000	Stock	15,60,000	10,50,000
10% Debentures	15,00,000	—	Debtors	12,30,000	7,80,000
Secured loan	—	9,00,000	Cash at bank	90,000	1,20,000
Sundry creditors	7,80,000	5, 10,000			
	73,20,000	44,40,000		73,20,000	44,40,000

Following are the additional information:

(i) For the purpose of amalgamation, the shares of the existing companies are to be valued as under:

X Ltd. = ₹ 18 per share

Y Ltd. = ₹ 20 per share.

(ii) A contingent liability ofX Ltd. of ₹ 1,80,000 is to be treated as actual existing liability.

(iii) The shareholders ofX Ltd. and Y Ltd. are to be paid by issuing sufficient number of shares of Z Ltd. at a premium of ₹ 6 per share.

(iv) The face value of shares of Z Ltd. is to be of ₹ 10 each.

You are required to:

(i) Calculate the purchase consideration (i.e. the number of shares to be issued to X Ltd. and Y Ltd.)

(II) Prepare Realisation Account and Shareholders Account in the books of X Ltd. & Y Ltd.

(iii) Prepare the Balance Sheet of Z Ltd. after amalgamation.

Q.5. (a) A commercial Bank has the following capital funds and assets. Segregate the capital founds into Tier-1 and tire-II Capitals. Found out the Risk-Adjusted and Risk Weighted Assets and Capital Adequacy Ratio:

Capital Funds:	₹
Paid up Equity Share Capital	750
Statutory Reserve	150
Securities Premium	150
Capital Reserve (of which Capital Funds ₹ 40 Crore were due to revaluation of assets and balance due to sale)	
Assets:	
Cash balance with RBI	60
Claims on Banks	170
Other investments	2,300
Loss and Advances:	
Guaranteed by Government of India/State Government	400
Granted to Staff of bank fully covered by Supper Annuation	

Benefits and mortgage of Flat/house	50
Other Loans and Advances	6,170
Premises, Furniture and Fixtures, Other Assets	3,925
Intangible Assets	15
Off-Balance Sheet Items;	
Acceptance, Endorsements and Letter of Credit, Guarantees and Other obligations.	1,550

5.(b) From the following information Calculate

(a) Average Capital Cost, (b) Return on Equity, (c) Interest on Loans (d) Depreciation (e) Advance against Depreciation as per Regulation 21 of the Central Electricity Regulatory Commission (Terms and Conditons of Tariff) Regulations, 2004.

1. Date of Commercial Operation of COD = 1st April 2010
2. Approved Opening Capital cost as on 1st April 2010 = ₹ 1,50,000
3. Weighted Average Rate of Depreciation: 3.5%
4. Details of allowed Additional Capital Expenditure. Repayment of Loan and Weighted Average Rate of Interest on Loan is as Follows

	1st year	2nd year	3rd year	4th year
Additional Capital Expenditure (Allowed)	10,000	3,000	2,000	1,000
Repayment of Loan	8,000	10,000	10,000	11,000
Weighted Average Rate of Interest on Loan	7.4	7.5	7.6	7.5

Q.6. An Indian company Moon Star Limited has a branch at Verginia (USA). The Branch is a non-integral foreign operation of the Indian Company. The trial balance of the Branch as at 31st March, 2013 is as follows:

Particulars	*US $*	
	Dr.	*Cr.*
Office equipments	48,000	
Furniture and Furniture's	32,00	
Opening Stock	22,400	
Purchase	96,000	
Sales	—	1,66,400
Goods Sent from HO	32,000	
Salaries	3,200	
Carriage inward	400	
Rent, Rate & Taxes	800	
Insurance	400	
Trade Expenses	400	
Head Office Account	—	45,600
Sundry Debtors	9,600	
Sundry Creditors	—	6,800
Cash at Bank	2,000	
Cash in Hand	400	
	2,18,800	2,18,800

The following further information's are given:

(1) Salaries outstanding $400.

(2) Depreciate Office Equipment and Furniture & Fixtures @ 10% p.a. at written down value.

(3) The Head Office sent goods to Branch for ₹ 15,80,000
(4) The head Office shown an amount of ₹ 20,50,000 due from Branch.
(5) Closing Stock $21,500.
(6) There were no transit items either at the start or at the end of the year.
(7) On April 1,2011 when the fixed assets were purchased the rate of exchange was ₹ 43 to one $. On April, 1, 2012, the rate was ₹ 47 per $. On March 31, 2013 the rate was ₹ 50 per $. Average Rate during the year was ₹ 45 to one $.

Prepare:

(a) Trial Balance incorporating adjustment given converting dollars into rupees.
(b) Trading Profit and Loss Account for the year ended 31st March, 2013 and Balance Sheet as on date depicting the profitability and net position of the Branch as would appear in the books of Indian company for the purpose of incorporating in the main Balance Sheet.

Q.7 Answer any four of the following questions: [4 × 4 = 16]

(a) Mr. A bought a forward contract for three months of US $ 1,00,000 on 1st December at 1 US $ = ₹ 47.10 when exchange rate was US $ 1 = ₹ 47.02, On 31st December when he closed his books, exchange rate was US $ 1 = ₹ 47.15. On 31st January, he decided to sell the contract at ₹ 47.18 per dollar. Show how the profits from contract will be recognised in the books.

(b) A Ltd. purchased a machinery for ₹ 40 lakhs. (Useful life 4 years and residual value ₹ 8 lakhs) Government grant received is ₹ 16 lakhs.

Show the Journal Entry to be passed at the time of refund of grant in the begnning of 3rd year and the value of the fixed assets, if:

1. the grant is credited to fixed assets.
2. the grant is credited to Deffered Grant Account.

(c) Southern Tower Ltd. purchased a plant from M/s. Tatamaco Ltd. on 30.09.2012 with a quoted price ₹ 180 lakhs. Tatamaco offer 3 months credit with a condition that discount of 1.25% will be allowed if the payment were made within one month. VAT is 12.5% on the quoted price. Company incurred 2% on transportation costs and 3% on erection costs of the quoted price, Preoperative cost amount ₹ 1.50 lakhs. To Finance the purchase of the machinery, company took a term bank loan of ₹ 125 lakhs at an interest rate of 14.50% per annum. The machine was ready for use on 31.12.2012; however, it was put to use only on 01-04-2013:

(i) Find out the original cost.

(ii) Suggest the accounting treatment for the cost incurred during the period between the date the machine was ready for use and the actual date the machine was put to use.

(d) From the information financial you are required to compute the Basic and Diluted EPS (earning per share) for accounting year 01-04-2012 to 31-03-2013 and adjusted EPS for the year 01-04-2011 to 31-03-2012.

Net Profit for year ended 31-03-2012	₹ 75,50,000
Net Profit for year ended 31-03-2013	₹ 1,00,25,000
No. of Equity shares as on 01-04-2012	50,00,250
Bonus issue on 01-01-2013	1 share for every 2 held
No. of 12% convertible Debentures of ₹ 100 each	1,00,000
Interest of Debentures for the current year	3,00,000
Conversion Ratio of Debentures	10 shares per debenture
Tax Rate	30 percent

(e) NDA Corporation is engaged in research on a new process design for its product. It had incurred an expenditure of ₹ 530 lakhs on research upto 31st March, 2012.

The development of the process began on 1st April, 2012 and Development phase expendture was ₹ 360 lakhs upto 31st March, 2013 which meets assets recognition criteria.

From 1st April, 2013, the company will implement the new process design which will result in after tax saving of ₹ 80 lakhs per annum for the next five years.

The cost of capital of company is 10%

Explain:

(i) Accounting treatment for research expenses.

(ii) The cost of internally generated intangible asset as per AS 26.

(iii) The amout of amortization of the assets. (The present value of annuity factor of ₹ 1 for 5 years @ 10% = 3.7908)

ANSWERS TO TULSIAN'S MODEL TEST PAPER 1

Solution 1 (a).

JOURNAL

Date	Particulars		Dr. (₹)	Cr. (₹)
01.04.2012	Employees compensation expenses A/c [₹ 5,000 × (140 – 50)]	Dr.	4,50,000	
	To Employees Stock Option outstanding A/c			4,50,000
	(Being grant of 5,000 ESOPs to employees @ ₹ 50 when market price was ₹ 140)			
01.12.2012 to 28.02.2013	Bank A/c	Dr.	2,40,000	
	Employees Stock Option Outstanding A/c	Dr	4,32,000	
	To Equity share capital A/c			48,000
	To Securities premium A/c			6,24,000
	(Being allotment to employees 4,800 shares of ₹ 10 each at a premium of ₹ 130 at an exercise price of ₹ 50 each)			
31.03.2013	Employees Stock Option Outstanding A/c	Dr	18,000	
	To Employees compensation expenses A/c			18,000
	(Being reverse entry for lapse of 200 stock options)			
31.03.2013	Profit and Loss A/c	Dr.	4,32,000	
	To Employees compensation expenses A/c			4,32,000
	(Being transfer of employees compensation expenses)			

Solution 1. (b)

(A) STATEMENT OF LIABILITIES OF B LIST CONTRIBUTORIES

Shareholder	No. of shares transferred	Maximum liability upto ₹ 2 per share	Division of liability as on				Total
			22nd July	15th Sept.	14th Dec.	09th March	
Q	3,000	6,000	4,500	—	—	—	4,500
R	2,400	4,800	3,600	720	—	—	4,320
S	1,600	3,200	2,400	480	308	—	3,188
T	1,000	2,000	1,500	300	192	8	2,000
	8,000	1 6,000	1 2,000	1 ,500	500	8	1 4,008

Notes:

(i) 'P' transferred shares before one year preceding the date of winding up, therefore, he cannot be held liable for any liability on liquidation.

(ii) Liability of 'T' has been restricted to the maximum allowable limit of ₹ 2,000. Therefore, amount payable by T on 09 March is ₹ 8 only.

(iii) 'Q' will not be responsible for further debts incurred after 10th May (from the date when he ceases to be a member). Similarly, 'R' & 'S' will not be liable for the debts incurred after the date of their transfer of shares.

Working Note:

CALCULATION OF RATIO FOR DISCHARGE OF LIABILITIES

Date	*Cumulative liability (₹)*	*Increase in liabilities (₹)*	*Ratio of no. of shares held by Q, R, S&T*
22.07.2012	12,000	—	30 : 24 : 16 : 10
15.09.2012	13,500	1,500	24 : 16 : 10
14.12.2012	14,000	500	16 : 10
09.03.2013	14,200	200	Only T

Solution 1. (c)

(A) JOURNAL OF THE COMMERCIAL BANK LTD.

Date	*Particulars*		*Dr. (₹)*	*Cr. (₹)*
March 31	Rebate on Bills Discounted A/c	Dr.	70,080	
	To Interest and Discount A/c			70,080
	(Being the amount of provision for unexpired discount brought forward from the previous year credited to interest and Discount A/c)			
March 31	Interest and Discount A/c	Dr.	96,860	
	To Rebate on Bills Discounted A/c			96,860
	(Being provision for unexpired discount required at the end of the current year)			
March 31	Interest and Discount A/c	Dr.	1,98,38,020	
	To Profit & Loss A/c			1,98,38,020
	(Being transfer of balance to Profit and Loss A/c)			

Dr. **REBATE ON BILLS DISCOUNTED ACCOUNT** *Cr.*

Date	*Particulars*	*₹*	*Date*	*Particulars*	*₹*
March 31 2011	To Interest and Discount A/c	70,080	April 1	By Balance b/d	70,080
March 31 2011	To Balance c/d	9,860	March 31, 2011	By interest and Discount A/c (Rebate carried forward)	96,860
		1,66,940			1,66,940

(B) INTEREST AND DISCOUNT ACCOUNT

Date	*Particulars*	*₹*	*Date*	*Particulars*	*₹*
March 31,	To Profit & Loss A/c (transfer)	1,98,38,020	April 1	By Rebate on Bills Discounted A/c (opening balance)	70,080
March 31	To Rebate on Bills Discounted A/c	96,860	March 31	By Bills Discounted & purchased	1,98,64,800
		1,99,34,880			1,99,34,880

Solution 1. (d)

WELL LIFE ASSURANCE CO. LTD.
Valuation Balance Sheet as at March 31, 2013

Particulars	₹	*Particulars*	₹
Net Liability as per actuarial valuation	75,00,000	Life Fund as per Balance Sheet	90,00,000
Surplus (Bal. Fig.)	15,00,000		
	90,00,000		90,00,000

Net Profit for valuation period:

	₹
A. Surplus as per valuation balance sheet	15,00,000
B. *Add:* Interim Bonus distributed	1,50,000
C. *Less:* Surplus in the beginning	(9,00,000)
D. Net Profit for the valuation period	7,50,000

Distribution of Surplus

	₹
A. Total Surplus	16,50,000
B. *Less:* Surplus to be carried forward	10,00,000
	6,50,000
C. Shareholders (5% of ₹.6,50,000)	32,500
D. Policy holders (95% of ₹.6,50,000)	6,17,500
E. *Less:* Interim bonus already distributed	1,50,000
F. Bonus still due to Policy holders	4,67,500

Solution 1. (e)

JOURNAL ENTRY IN THE BOOKS OF HEAD OFFICE

Date	*Particulars*		*Dr.* (₹)	*Cr.* (₹)
31st Mar.	Mumbai Branch A/c	Dr.	3,000	
	Chennai Branch A/c	Dr.	70,000	
	To Delhi Branch A/c			15,000
	To Kolkata Branch A/c			58,000
	(Being adjustment entry passed by head office in respect of inter-branch transactions for the month of April, 2003.			

Working Note: **INTER-BRANCH TRANSACTIONS**

Particulars	*Delhi* ₹	*Mumbai* ₹	*Chennai* ₹	*Kolkata* ₹
A. Delhi Branch				
1. Received goods	50,000 (Dr.)	35,000 (Cr.)		15,000 (Cr.)
2. Sent goods	45,000 (Cr.)		25,000 (Dr.)	20,000 (Dr.)
3. Received B/R	20,000 (Dr.)		20,000 (Cr.)	
4. Sent acceptance	35,000 (Cr.)	25,000 (Dr.)		10,000 (Dr.)
B. Mumbai Branch				
5. Received goods	20,000 (Cr.)	35,000 (Dr.)		15,000 (Cr.)
6. Sent cash	15,000 (Dr.)	22,000 (Cr.)		7,000 (Dr.)

C. Chennai Branch				
7. Received goods			30,000 (Dr.)	30,000 (Cr.)
8. Sent cash and acceptances			30,000 (Cr.)	30,000 (Dr.)
D. Kolkata Branch				
9. Sent goods			35,000 (Dr.)	35,000 (Cr.)
10. Sent cash			15,000 (Dr.)	15,000 (Cr.)
11. Sent acceptances			15,000 (Dr.)	15,000 (Cr.)
	15,000 (Cr.)	3,000 (Dr.)	70,000 (Dr.)	58,000 (Cr.)

Solution 2

BALANCE SHEET OF M/S PQR & CO. AS AT 31ST MARCH, 2013

Liabilities	₹	*Assets*		₹
Capitals:		Building		
P	5,52,000	(₹.1, 00,000 + ₹.60,000)		1,60,000
Q	3,68,000	Plant & Machinery		
R	1,84,000	(₹ 2,50,000 + ₹ 2,00,000)		4,50,000
Sundry Creditors		Office Equipment		
(₹ 1,20,000 + 1,16,000)	2,36,000	(₹ 20,000 + ₹ 6,000)		26,000
Bank overdraft	80,000	Stock-in-trade		
		(₹.1, 44 ,000 + ₹.1, 68,000)		3,12,000
		Sundry Debtors	3,60,000	
		(₹ 1, 60,000 + ₹ .2,00,000)		
		Less: Provision	(38,000)	
		(₹ 12,000 + ₹ 26,000)		3,22,000
		Bank Balance		
		(₹ 30,000 + ₹ 90,000)		1,20,000
	—	Cash in hand		30,000*
	14,20,000			14,20,000

Dr. **PARTNERS' CAPITAL ACCOUNTS IN THE BOOKS OF P & CO.** *Cr.*

Particulars	P ₹	Q ₹	*Particulars*	P ₹	Q ₹
To Capital A/cs – M/s PQR & Co.	4,89,000	2,43,000	By Balance b/d	2,40,000	1,60,000
			By Reserve (3 : 1)	37,500	12,500
			By Profit on Realisation A/'c	2,11,500	70,500
	4,89,000	2,43,000		4,89,000	2,43,000

Dr. **PARTNERS' CAPITAL ACCOUNTS IN THE BOOKS OF R & CO.** *Cr.*

Particulars	P ₹	Q ₹	*Particulars*	P ₹	Q ₹
To Capital A/cs -M/s PQR & Co	3,68,000	1,84,000	By Balance b/d	2,00,000	1,00,000
			By Reserve (2 : 1)	1,00,000	50,000
			By Profit on Realisation	68,000	34,000
	3,68,000	1,84,000		3,68,000	1,84,000

Working Notes:

(i) Computation of Purchase Consideration

Particulars		*P & Co.* ₹	*R & Co.* ₹
Assets:			
Goodwill		1,20,000	60,000
Building		1,00,000	60,000
Plant & machinery		2,50,000	2,00,000
Office equipment		20,000	6,000
Stock-in-trade		1,44,000	1,68,000
Sundry Debtors		1,60,000	2,00,000
Bank balance		30,000	90,000
Cash in hand		20,000	10,000
Due from R & Co.		1,00,000	—
	(A)	9,44,000	7,94,000
Less: Liabilities:			
Creditors		1,20,000	1,16,000
Provision for doubtful debts		12,000	26,000
Due to P & Co.		—	1,00,000
Bank overdraft		80,000	—
	(B)	2,12,000	2,42,000
Purchase Consideration (A – B)		7,32,000	5,52,000

(ii) Computation of Proportionate Capital

M/s *PQR* & Co. (Purchase Consideration) (₹ 7,32,000 + ₹ 5,52,000)	12,84,000
Less: Goodwill Adjustment	(1,80,000)
Total Capital of new firm (Distributed in ratio 3 : 2 : 1)	11,04,000
P's Proportionate Capital	5,52,000
Q's Proportionate Capital	3,68,000
R's proportionate capital	1,84,000

(iii) Computation of Capital Adjustments

Particulars	*P* ₹	*Q* ₹	*R* ₹	*Total* ₹
Balance transferred from P & Co.	4,89,000	2,43,000		7,32,000
Balance transferred from R & Co.	—	3,68,000	1,84,000	5,52,000
	4,89,000	6,11,000	1,84,000	12,84,000
Less: Goodwill written off in the ratio of 3 : 2 : 1	(90,000)	(60,000)	(30,000)	(1,80,000)
Existing capital	3,99,000	5,51,000	1,54,000	11,04,000
Proportionate capital	5,52,000	3,68,000	1,84,000	11,04,000
Amount to be brought in (paid off)	1,53,000	(1,83,000)	30,000	

Dr. **REALISATION ACCOUNT IN THE BOOKS OF P & CO.** Cr.

Particulars		₹	Particulars	₹
To Building		50,000	By Creditors	1,20,000
To Plant & Machinery		1,50,000	By Bank overdraft	80,000
To Office Equipment		20,000	By M/s PQR & Co.	7,32,000
To Stock-in-trade		1,20,000	(purchase consideration)	
To Sundry debtors		1,60,000		
To Bank balance		30,000		
To Cash in hand		20,000		
To Due from R & Co.		1,00,000		
To Partners' Capital A/cs				
P	2,11,500			
Q	70,500	2,82,000		
		9,32,000		9,32,000

Dr. **REALISATION ACCOUNT IN THE BOOKS OF R & CO.** Cr.

Particulars		₹	Particulars	₹
To Building		60,000	By Creditors	1,16,000
To Plant & machinery		1,60,000	By Due to P & Co.	1,00,000
To Office equipment		6,000	By M/s PQR & Co.	5,52,000
To Stock-in-trade		1,40,000	(purchase consideration)	
To Sundry debtors		2,00,000		
To Bank balance		90,000		
To Cash in hand		10,000		
To Partners' Capital A/c:				
Q	68,000			
R	34,000	1,02,000		
		7,68,000		7,68,000

Solution 3

BALANCE SHEET OF DEE LTD. AS AT 31.3.2013

Particulars	Note No	₹ (lacs)
I. Equity and Liabilities		
(1) Shareholders' Funds		
(a) Share Capital (*₹ 10 each*)		3,70,000
(b) Reserves and Surplus	1	6,40,000
(2) Non-Current Liabilities [Secured Loans]		2,50,000
(3) Current Liabilities		6,00,000
Total		18,60,000
II. Assets		
(1) Non-Current Assets		
(a) Fixed Assets		
Tangible Assets		8,00,000
(2) Current Assets		
(a) Cash and Cash Equivalents		60,000
(b) Other Current Assets		10,00,000
Total		18,60,000

Notes To Accounts:

Particulars	₹ (lacs)
1. Reserves and Surplus	
General Reserve	4,80,000
Profit & Loss Account	1,00,000
Securities Premium	60,000
Total	6,40,000

CALCULATION OF NUMBER OF EQUITY SHARES ISSUED

I.	Number of equity shares issued as right issue (25,000 Shares/5)	5,000 shares
II.	Debentureholders who opted for the scheme of conversion into equity shares	
	2,000 debentureholders opted for the scheme	
	Total value (2,000 debentures × ₹.100)	₹ 2,00,000
	Premium on redemption @ 5%	₹ 10,000
		2,10,000
	50% of their holding converted into equity shares	₹ 1,05,000
	Number of equity shares to be issued to debentureholders = (₹ 1,05,000/₹ 15)	7,000 shares
	Total number of equity shares issued = (5,000 + 7,000) shares	12,000 shares

CASH PAYMENT TO DEBENTUREHOLDERS

	Particulars		₹
I.	3,000 Debentureholders preferred cash		
	Total cash paid to them	3,00,000	
	Premium on redemption @ 5%	15,000	3,15,000
II.	2,000 Debentureholders opted for the scheme		
	Total Value	2,00,000	
	Add: Premium on redemption @ 5%	10,000	
		2,10,000	
	50% of their value converted into equity shares	1,05,000	
	Balance paid to debentureholders in cash		1,05,000
	Total cash paid to debentureholders		4,20,000

Working Notes:

Dr. **(I) DEBENTURE REDEMPTION RESERVE ACCOUNT** Cr.

Particulars	₹	Particulars	₹
To Premium on redemption of debentures (15,000 + 10,000)	25,000	By Balance b/d	2,50,000
To Loss on sale of Debenture Redemption Reserve Investment	20,000		
To General Reserve	2,05,000		
	2,50,000		2,50,000

Dr. **(II) GENERAL RESERVE ACCOUNT** Cr.

Particulars	₹	Particulars	₹
To Balance c/d	4,80,000	By Balance b/d	2,75,000
		By Debenture Redemption Reserve	2,05,000
	4,80,000		4,80,000

(iii) Total of Securities Premium = 12000 shares × ₹ 5 = ₹ 60,000

Dr. **(IV) CASH ACCOUNT** Cr.

Particulars	₹	Particulars	₹
To Balance b/d	2,50,000	By Proposed Dividend	25,000
To Equity Shareholders (5,000 × 15)	75,000	By Debentureholders (₹ 1,05,000 + ₹ 3,15,000)	4,20,000
To Sale of Debenture Redemption Reserve Investment	1,80,000	By Balance c/d	60,000
	5,05,000		5,05,000

Solution 4

(I) CALCULATION OF PURCHASE CONSIDERATION *No. of shares*

Particulars	X Ltd.	Y Ltd.
Existing Number of shares	3,00,000	1,80,000
Less: Number of shares held bv X Ltd. in Y Ltd.	—	(15,000)
Net Number of Shares	3,00,000	1,65,000
Value per share	₹ 18	₹ 20
Purchase consideration	₹ 54,00,000	₹ 33,00,000
Number of shares of Z Ltd. @? 16 per share	3,37,500 shares	2,06,250 shares

DISCHARGE OF PURCHASE CONSIDERATION

Particulars	X Ltd.	Y Ltd.
Face Value of Share Capital		
X Ltd. = 3,37,500 shares × ₹ 10 each	33,75,000	
Y Ltd. = 2,06,250 shares × ₹ 10 each		20,62,500
Securities premium		
X Ltd. = 3,37,500 shares × ₹ 6 each	20,25,000	
Y Ltd. = 2,06,250 shares × ₹ 6 each		12,37,500
	54,00,000	33,00,000

(ii)

IN THE BOOKS OF X LTD.

REALIZATION ACCOUNT

Dr. *Cr.*

Particulars	₹	*Particulars*	₹
To Sundry Assets:		By 10%Debentures	15,00,000
Land and building	27,00,000	By Sundry creditors	
Plant and machinery	15,00,000	(7,80,000+1,80,000)	9,60,000
Investments	2,40,000	By Z Ltd.	
Stock	15,60,000	(Purchase consideration)	54,00,000
Debtors	12,30,000		
Bank	90,000		
To Equity Shareholders A/c (Profit)	5,40,000		
	78,60,000		78,60,000

EQUITY SHAREHOLDER'S ACCOUNT

Dr. *Cr.*

Particulars	₹	*Particulars*	₹
To Shares in Z Ltd. A/c	54,00,000	By Share capital	30,00,000
		By Securities premium	6,00,000
		By General reserve	9,00,000
		By Profit & loss A/c	3,60,000
		(5,40,000 – 1,80,000)	
		By Realization A/c	5,40,000
	54,00,000		54,00,000

(b)

IN THE BOOKS OF Y LTD.

REALIZATION ACCOUNT

Dr. *Cr.*

Particulars	₹	*Particulars*	₹
To Sundry Assets:		By Secured loan	9,00,000
Land and building	13,50,000	By Sundry creditors	5,10,000
Plant and machinery	11,40,000	By Z Ltd.	
Stock	10,50,000	(Purchase consideration)	33,00,000
Debtors	7,80,000		
Bank	1,20,000		
To Equity Shareholders A/c (Profit)	2,70,000		
	47,10,000		47,10,000

EQUITY SHAREHOLDERS ACCOUNT

Dr. *Cr.*

Particulars	₹	*Particulars*	₹
To Shares in Z Ltd. A/c	33,00,000	By Share capital	18,00,000
		By General reserve	7,50,000
		By Profit & loss A/c	4,80,000
		By Realization A/c	2,70,000
	33,00,000		33,00,000

BALANCE SHEET OF Z LTD. AS AT 31.3.2013

Particulars	Note No	₹
I. Equity and Liabilities		
(1) Shareholders' Funds		
(a) Share Capital (₹ 10 each)	1	54,37,500
(c) Reserves and Surplus [Securities Premium]		32,62,500
(2) Non-Current Liabilities [10% Debentures + Loan]		24,00,000
(3) Current Liabilities		
(a) Trade Payables [Creditors]		14,70,000
Total		125,70,000
II. Assets		
(1) Non-Current Assets		
(a) Fixed Assets		
Tangible Assets	2	66,90,000
Intangible Assets [Goodwill]		10,50,000
(2) Current Assets		
(a) Inventories		26,10,000
(b) Trade Receivables [Debtors]		20,10,000
(b) Cash and Cash Equivalents		2,10,000
Total		125,70,000

Notes To Accounts:

Particulars	₹
1. Share Capital	
5,43,750 Equity Shares of ₹ 10 each	54,37,500
(Of the above all Shares were issued for consideration otherwise than cash)	
2. Tangible Assets	
Land & Building	40,50,000
Plant & Machinery	26,40,000
Total	66,90,000

Working Note:

CALCULATION OF GOODWILL / (CAPITAL RESERVE)

Particulars		X Ltd. ₹	Y Ltd. ₹
Purchase consideration	(A)	54,00,000	33,00,000
Assets taken over of			
X (27,00,000 + 15,00,000 + 15,60,000 + 12,30,000 + 90,000)		70,80,000	
Y (13,50,000 + 11,40,000 + 10,50,000 + 7,80,000 + 1,20,000)		44,40,000	
Less: Liabilities taken over of X Ltd. (15,00,000 + 7,80,000 + 1,80,000)		(24,60,000)	
Liabilities taken over of Y Ltd. (9,00,000 + 5,10,000)			(14,10,000)
Net Assets	(B)	46,20,000	30,30,000
Goodwill (B – A)		7,80,000	2,70,000

Solution 5 (a)

CALCULATION OF CAPITAL FUNDS

Particulars	₹ in crores	₹ in crores
(i) Capital Funds – Tier I		
Equity Share Capital		750
Statutory Reserve		150
Securities Premium		150
Capital reserve (arising out of sale of assets) (90 – 40)		50
		1,100
Less: Intangible Assets		(15)
		1,085
Capital Funds – Tier II		
Capital reserve (arising out of revaluation of assets)	40	
Less: Discount to the extent of 55%	(22)	18
		1,103

CALCULATION OF RISK ADJUSTED ASSETS

Particulars	₹ in crores	% in risk weight	₹ in Crores
(ii) Risk Adjusted Assets			
Funded Risk Assets			
Cash balance with RBI	60	0	0
Claims on banks	170	20	34
Other investments	2,300	100	2,300
Loans and advances:			
(i) Guaranteed by the government	400	0	0
(ii) Granted to staff of bank, fully covered by super Annuation Benefits and mortgage of Flat/House	50	20	10
(iii) Other loans and advances	6,170	100	6,170
Other assets			
Premises, furniture and fixtures and other assets	3,925	100	3,925
			12,439
Off Balance Sheet Items:			
Acceptances, endorsements and Letters of credit, Guarantees and other obligations	1,550	100	1,550
			13,989

$$\text{Capital Adequacy Ratio} = \frac{\text{Capital fund}}{\text{Risk adjusted assets}} \times 100 = \frac{\text{Rs } 1{,}103 \text{ crores}}{\text{Rs } 13{,}989 \text{ crores}} \times 100 = 7.89\%$$

Solution 5 (b)

AVERAGE CAPITAL COST

Particulars	1st year	2nd year	3rd year	4th year
A. Opening Capital Cost	1,50,000	1,60,000	1,63,000	1,65,000
B. Additional Capital Cost	10,000	3,000	2,000	1,000
C. Closing Capital Cost (A + B)	1,60,000	1,63,000	1,65,000	1,66,000
D. Average Capital Cost [(A + C)/2]	1,55,000	1,61,500	1,64,000	1,65,500

RETURN ON EQUITY

Particulars	1st year	2nd year	3rd year	4th year
A. Opening Equity (30%)	45,000	48,000	48,900	49,500
B. Additional Equity (30%)	3,000	900	600	300
C. Closing Equity (A + B)	48,000	48,900	49,500	49,800
D. Average Equity [(A + C)/2]	46,500	48,450	49,200	49,650
E. Return on Equity (D × 14%)	6,510	6,783	6,888	6,951

COMPUTATION OF INTEREST ON LOANS

Particulars	1st year	2nd year	3rd year	4th year
A. Opening Loan (70%)	1,05,000	1,12,000	1,14,100	1,15,500
B. Additional Loan (70%)	7,000	2,100	1,400	700
C. *Less*: Repayment of Loan during the year	8,000	10,000	10,000	11,000
D. Net Closing Loan (A + B – C)	1,04,000	96,100	87,500	77,200
E. Average Loan [(A + D)/2]	1,04,500	1,00,050	91,800	82,350
F. Weighted Average Rate of Interest on Loan	7.4	7.5	7.6	7.5
G. Interest on Loan (E × F)	7,733	7,503.75	6,976.80	6,176.25

1. COMPUTATION OF DEPRECIATION

Particulars	1st year	2nd year	3rd year	4th year
A. Opening Capital Cost	1,50,000	1,60,000	1,63,000	1,65,000
B. Additional Capital Cost	10,000	3,000	2,000	1,000
C. Closing Capital Cost (A + B)	1,60,000	1,63,000	1,65,000	1,66,000
D. Average Capital Cost [(A + C)/2]	1,55,000	1,61,500	1,64,000	1,65,500
E. Weighted Average Rate of Dep.	3.5%	3.5%	3.5%	3.5%
F. Annualized Depreciation (D × E)	5,425	5,652.5	5,740	5,792.50
G. Advance Against Depreciation (AAD)	2,575	4,347.50	4,260	5,207.50
H. Total Depreciation (including AAD) for Tariff (F + G)	8,000	10,000	10,000	11,000

2. COMPUTATION OF ADVANCE AGAINST DEPRECIATION (AAD)

Particulars	1st year	2nd year	3rd year	4th year
A. Repayment of Loan (10% of Loan Amount)	8,000	10,000	10,000	11,000
B. Depreciation (Excluding AAD)	5,425	5,652.5	5,740	5,792.50
C. Difference between A & B (A – B)	2,575	4,347.50	4,260	5,207.50
D. Cumulative Repayment of Loan	8,000	18,000	28,000	39,000
E. Cumulative Depreciation (Excluding AAD) at the beg.	5,425	11,077.50	16,817.50	22,610
F. Difference between D & E (D – E)	2,575	6,922.50	11,182.50	16,390
G. Advance Against Depreciation (AAD) (Minimum of C & F)	2,575	4,347.50	4,260	5,207.50

Solution 6.

(A) IN THE BOOKS OF MOON STAR LTD. – AN INDIAN COMPANY TRIAL BALANCE (IN RUPEES) OF VERGINIA (USA) BRANCH AS ON 31ST MARCH, 2013

Dr. *Cr.*

Particulars	Dr. US $	Cr. US $	Conversion rate	Dr. US $	Cr. US $
Office Equipment	43,200		50	21,60,000	
Depreciation on Office Equipment	4,800		50	2,40,000	
Furniture and Fixtures	2,880		50	1,44,000	
Depreciation of furniture and fixtures	320		50	16,000	
Opening Stock	22,400		47	10,52,800	
Purchase	96,000		45	43,20,000	
Sales		1,66,400	45		74,88,000
Goods sent from H.O.	32,000			15,80,000	
Carriage inward	400		45	18,000	
Salaries (3,200 + 400)	3,600		45	1,62,000	
Outstanding salaries		400	50		20,000
Rent, rates and taxes	800		45	36,000	
Insurance	400		45	18,000	
Trade expenses	400		45	18,000	
Head Office A/c		45,600			20,50,000
Trade debtors	9,600		50	4,80,000	
Trade creditors		6,800	50		3,40,000
Cash at bank	2,000		50	1,00,000	
Cash in hand	400		50	20,000	
Exchange gain (bal. fig.)					4,66,800
	2,19,200	2,19,200		1,03,64,800	1,03,64,800

TRADING AND PROFIT AND LOSS ACCOUNT OF VERGINIA BRANCH

Dr. *for the year ended 31st March, 2013* Cr.

Particulars	₹	*Conversion*	₹
To Opening stock	10,52,800	By Sales	74,88,000
To Purchases	43,20,000	By Closing Stock	
To Goods from Head Office	15,80,000	(21,500 US $ × 50)	10,75,000
To Carriage inward	18,000		
To Gross profit c/d	15,92,200		
	85,63,000		85,63,000
To Salaries	1,62,000	By Gross profit b/d	15,92,200
To Rent, rates and taxes	36,000		
To Insurance	18,000		
To Trade expenses	18,000		
To Depreciation of office equipment	2,40,000		
To Depreciation of furniture and fixtures	16,000		
To Net Profit c/d	11,02,200		
	15,92,200		15,92,200

BALANCE SHEET OF VERGINIA BRANCH AS AT 31ST MARCH, 2013

Liabilities	₹	₹	*Particulars*	₹	₹
Head Office A/c	20,50,000		Office Equipment	24,00,000	
Add: Net Profit	11,02,200	31,52,000	*Less:* Depreciation	2,40,000	21,60,000
Foreign Currency			Furniture and fixtures	1,60,000	
Translation Reserve		4,66,800	*Less:* Depreciation	16,000	1,44,000
Trade creditors		3,40,000	Closing stock		10,75,000
Outstanding salaries		20,000	Trade debtors		4,80,000
			Cash in hand		20,000
			Cash at bank		1,00,000
		39,79,000			39,79,000

Solution 7(a)

AS 11	It is apparent from the facts given in the question that Mr. A entered into forward exchange contract for speculation purpose. Gain or loss on forward exchange contracts intended for trading or speculation purpose should be computed by multiplying the foreign currency amount of the forward exchange contract by the **difference between the forward rate available at the reporting date for the remaining maturity of the contract and the contracted forward rate** (or the forward rate last used to measure a gain or loss on that contract for an earlier period). The gain or loss so computed should be recognised in the Statement of Profit and Loss for the period and the premium or discount on the forward exchange contract is ignored and not recognised separately. In recording such contract, at each balance sheet date, the value of the contract is marked to its current market value and the gain or loss on the contract is recognised.

Advice	The premium on contract i.e., the difference between the contract rate and the spot rate amounting ₹ 8,000 [US$ 1,00,000 × (₹.47.10 – ₹.47.02)] will be ignored and not be recorded in the books. However, the profit on contract i.e. the difference between the sale rate and contract rate amounting ₹ 8,000 [US$ 1,00,000 × 0.08* (₹ 47.18 – ₹ 47.10)] will be recognized in the books of Mr. A on 31st January. **Note**: The answer has been given on the basis thai Mr. A is a small and mediumsized entity and AS 30 "Financial Instruments: Recognition and Measurement" is not applicable to him.

Solution 7(b)

Journal of A Ltd. (at the time of refund of grant)

If the grant is credited to fixed assets:

I Fixed Assets A/c Dr. ₹ 16 lakhs
To Bank A/c ₹ 16 lakhs

II The balance of fixed assets after two years depreciation will be ₹ 16 lakhs and now it will become (₹ 16 lakhs + ₹ 16 lakhs) = ₹ 32 lakhs on which depreciation will be charged for remaining two years. Depreciation = (32 – 8)/2 = ₹ 12 lakhs p.a. will be charged for next two years.

If the grant is credited to Deferred Grant Account:

As per para 14 of AS 12 income from Deffered Grant Account is allocated to Profit and Loss account usually over the periods and in the proportions in which depreciation on related assets is charged. Accordingly, in the first two years (₹ 16 lakhs/4 years) = ₹ 4 lakhs × 2 = ₹ 8 lakhs were credited to Profit and Loss Account and ₹ 8 lakhs was the balance of Deferred Grant Account after two years.

Therefore, on refund in the 3rd year, following entry will be passed:

I Deferred Grant A/c Dr. ₹ 8 lakhs
Profit & Loss A/c Dr. ₹ 8 lakhs
To Bank A/c ₹ 16 lakhs
(Being Government grant refunded)

II Deferred grant account will become Nil. The fixed assets will continue to be shown in the books at ₹ 24 lakhs and depreciation will continue to be charged at 8 lakhs per annum.

Working Notes:

(i) Balance of Fixed Assets after two years but before refund (under first alternative) = (₹ 40 lakhs – ₹ 16 lakhs) – (₹ 4 lakhs × 2) = ₹ 16 lakhs

(ii) Balance of Fixed Assets after two years but before refund (under second alternative) = ₹ 40 lakhs – (₹ 8 lakhs × 2) = ₹ 24 lakhs

Note: It is assumed that value of fixed assets is to be given after refund of government grant.

Solution 7(c)

(i) Original Cost of the Machine

Particulars	In lakhs	In lakhs
Quoted price	180.00	
Less: Discount @ 1.25%	2.25	177.75
Add: VAT @ 12.5%		22.50
Transportation @ 2%		3.60
Erection Cost @ 3%		5.40
Pre-operative Cost		1.50
Finance Cost (14.5% on ₹ 125 lakhs for the period 01.10.10 to 31.12.10)		4.53
Total		215.28

(ii) Cost incurred during the period between the date the machine was ready for use and the actual date the machine was put to use

Finance cost amounting to ₹ 4.53 lakhs (14.50% on ₹ 125 lakhs for the period 01.01.2013 to 31.03.2013) will be charged to Profit and Loss Account as per AS 16 "Borrowing Costs".

Solution 7(d)

1. Basic EPS for Financial Year 2012-2013

A.	Net Profit for the Year	1,00,25,000
B.	Weighted Average Shares Outstanding for FY 2012-2013 [50,00,250 + (50,00,250 × 1/2)]	75,00,375
C.	Basic EPS [A/B]	1,337

2. Diluted EPS for Financial Year 2012-2013

A.	Net Profits for the year	1,00,25,000
B.	After Tax Interest (1,00,000 Debentures × ₹ 100 Face Value × 12% × 3/12 × 0.70)	2,10,000
C.	Adjusted Equity Earnings for the year [A + B]	1,02,35,000
D.	Weighted Average Shares Outstanding for Basic EPS	75,00,375
E.	Add: Potential Equity Shares (to be computed only from the date of issue) (1,00,000 Debentures × Conversion Ratio 10 × 3/12)	2,50,000
F.	Adjusted Weighted Average Number of Equity Shares [D + E]	77,50,357
G.	Diluted EPS [C/F]	1.32

3. Adjusted EPS for Financial Year 2011-2012

A.	Net Profits for the year	75,50,000
B.	Adjusted Average Share Outstanding for FY 2011-2012	75,00,375
C.	Adjusted EPS for [A/B]	1.01

Note: Interest on debentures for full year amounts to ₹ 12,00,000 (i.e. 12% of ₹ 1,00,00,000). However, interest expense amounting ₹ 3,00,000 has been given in the question. It may be concluded that debentures have been issued during the year and interest has been provided for 3 months.

Solution 7. (e)

(i) **Reasearch Expenditure**—As per AS 26 the expenditure on research of new process design for its product 530 lakhs should be charged to Profit and Loss Account in the year in which it is incurred. It is presumed that the entire expenditure is incurred in the financial year 2011-12. Hence, it should be written off as an expense in that year itself.

(ii) **Cost of internally generated intangible asset**—The question states that the development phase expenditure amounting ₹ 360 lakhs incurred upto 31st March, 2011 meets asset recognization criteria. As per AS 26 for measurement of such internally generated intangible asset, fair value can be estimated by discounting estimated future net cash flows.

	₹
Savings (after tax) from implementation of new design for next 5 years	80 lakhs p.a
Company's cost of capital	10%
Annuity factor@ 10% for 5 years	3.7908
Present value of net cash flows (₹ 80 lakhs × 3.7908)	303.26 lakhs

The cost of an internally generated intangible asset would be lower of cost value 360 lakhs or present value of future net cash flows ₹ 303.26 lakhs.

Hence, cost of an internally generated intangible asset will be ₹ 303.26 lakhs.

The difference of ₹ 56.74 lakhs (i.e. ₹ 360 lakhs – ₹ 303.26 lakhs) will be amortized by the enterprise for the financial year 2011-12.

(iii) **Amortization**—The company can amortise ₹ 303.26 lakhs over a period of five years by charging ₹ 60.65 lakhs per annum from the financial year 2012-13 onwards.

Paper-5: Advanced Accounting
CA IPC (Group II)
Tulsian's Model Test Paper 2

Question No. 1 is compulsory.
Attempt any Five questions from the remaining Six questions
Wherever necessary suitable assumptions may be made by the candidates.
Working notes should form part of the answer.

Q.1 Answer the following questions: **[4 × 5 = 20]**

(a) On 1st April, 2011, a company offered 100 shares to each to its 400 employees ₹ 25 per share. The employees are given a month to accept the shares. The shares issued under the plan shall be subject to lock-in to transfer for three years from the grant data i.e., 30, April 2013. The market price of share of the company on the grant date is ₹ 30 per share. Due to post-vesting restrictions on transfer, the fair value of shares issued under the plan is estimated at ₹ 28 per share.
Up to 30th April, 2013, 50% of employees accepted the offer and paid ₹ 25 per share purchased. Normal value of each share is ₹ 10. Record the issue of shares in the books of the company under the aforesaid plan.

(b) A Liquidator is entitled to receive remuneration at 2% on the assets realized, 3% on the amount distributed to Preferential Creditors and 3% on the payment made to Unsecured Creditors. The assets were realized for ₹ 25,00,000 against which payment was made as follows:

Liquidation expenses	₹ 25,000
Secured Creditors	₹ 10,00,000
Preferential Creditors	₹ 75,000

The amount due to Unsecured Creditors was ₹ 15,00,000. You are asked to calculate the total Remuneration payable to Liquidator. Calculation shall be made to the nearest multiple of a rupee.

(c) From the following information, compute the amount of provisions to be made in the Profit and Loss Account of A commercial Bank:

Assets (Category of Advances)	*₹ in Lakhs*
Standard Advances	7,000
Sub-standard Advances (include secured exposures ₹ 1,000 lakhs and balances unsecured exposures ₹ 2,500 Lakhs includes ₹ 1,500 Lakhs in respect of infrastructure loan accounts where escrow accounts are available)	3,500
Doubtful advances-unsecured portion	1,500
Doubtful advances-secured portion	
For doubtful up to 1 year	500
For doubtful more than 1 year and up to 3 years	600
Four doubtful more than 3 years	300
Loss Advances	200

(d) Brahma Limited has three departments and submits the following information for the year ending on 31st March, 2013:

Particulars	*A*	*B*	*C*	*Total (₹)*
Purchases (units)	5,000	10,000	15,000	
Purchases (Amount)				8,40,000
Sales (units)	5,200	9,800	15,300	
Selling price (₹ per unit)	40	45	50	
Closing Stock (Units)	400	600	700	

Required: Prepare departmental trading account of Brahma Limited assuming that the rate of profit on sales is uniform in each case.

Q.2. XYZ Limited was incorporated for taking over the business of Y from 1st April, 2010. The following is the Balance Sheet of Y on 31st March, 2013:

Liabilities	*₹*	*Assets*	*₹*
Capital	10,08,000	Land and Building	16,00,000
Loans	12,00,000	Plant and Machinery	2,80,000
Creditors	7,12,000	Furniture	2,00,000
		Sundry Debtors	8,40,000
	29,20,000		29,20,000

The company takes over the business with fixed assets and loans on the following terms:

(a) The fixed assets should be depreciated @10%.

(b) The value of Goodwill is estimated at ₹ 8,00,000.

The company realized ₹ 8,00,000 from Sundry debtors as the agent of the vendor in full settlement and discharged all the trade creditors by paying ₹ 6,80,000 for a commission of 3% on the amount collected and 2% on the amount paid.

(Commission is treated as pre-incorporation profit)

The lenders accepted 10% preference shares of ₹ 100 each in discharge of their loan. After realization of debts and discharge of the liabilities, the total amount due to the vendor was settled by payment of ₹ 54,400 in cash and the balance in shares of fully paid equity shares of ₹ 10 each.

You are required to:

(i) Compute Purchase Consideration.

(ii) Pass Journal Entries in the books of XYZ Limited after taking over the business of Y.

(iii) Prepare the Balance Sheet of the company as on 1st April, 2013.

Q.3 (a). Extra Ltd. furnishes you with the following Balance Sheet as on 31st March, 2013:

[₹ in lakhs]

Liabilities	₹	*Assets*	₹
Share Capital		*Fixed Assets Less* depreciation	50
Equity shares of ₹ 10 each fully paid	100	Investments at cost	120
		Current Assets	142
9% Redeemable Preference Shares of ₹ 100 each fully paid	20		
Capital Reserves	8		
Revenue Reserves	50		
Securities Premium	60		
10% Debentures	4		
Current liabilities	70		
	312		312

(a) The company redeemed the preference shares at a premium of 10% on 1st April, 2013.

(b) It also bought back 3 lakhs equity shares of ₹ 10 each at ₹ 30 per share.

The payment for the above were made out of huge bank balances, which appeared as a part of the current assets.

(c) Included in its investment were "investments in own debentures" costing ₹ 2 lakhs (face value ₹ 2.20 lakhs). These debentures were cancelled on 1st April, 2013.

(d) The company had 1,00,000 equity stock options outstanding on the above mentioned date, to the employees at ₹ 20 when the market price was ₹ 30. (This was included under current liabilities). On 01.04.2013 employees exercised their options for 50,000 shares.

Pass the journal entries to record the above & Prepare Balance Sheet as at 01.04.2013.

Q.3 (b). The following balances appeared in the books of Paradise Ltd on 1-4-2012:

(i) 12% Debentures ₹ 7,50,000

(ii) Balance of Sinking Fund ₹ 6,00,000

(iii) Sinking Fund investment ₹ 6,00,000 represented by 10% ₹ 6,50,000 secured bonds of government of India.

Annual contribution to the Sinking funds was ₹ 1,20,000 made on 31st March each year. On 31-03-2013, balance at bank was ₹ 3,00,000 before receipt of interest. The company sold the investment at 90% for redemption of debentures at a premium of 10% on the above date.

You are required to prepare the following accounts for the year ended 31st March, 2013.

(1) Debentures Account

(2) Sinking Fund Account

(3) Sinking Fund Investment Account

(4) Bank Account

(5) Debenture Holders Account

Q.4 The Balance Sheet of X Limited as at 31st March 2013, was as follows:

Liabilities	₹	*Assets*	₹
Authorised and subscribed capital:	10,00,000	Fixed Assets:	
Equity shares of ₹ 100 each fully paid		Machineries	3,50,000
		Current Assets:	
Unsecured loans:		Stock	2,53,000
15% Debentures	3,00,000	Debtors	2,30,000
Accrued interest	45,000	Bank	20,000
Creditors	52,000	Profit & loss A/c	5,80,000
Provision for income tax	36,000		
	14,33,000		14,33,000

It was decided to reconstruct the company for which necessary resolution was passed and sanctions were obtained from the appropriate authorities. Accordingly, it was decided that:

(a) Each share be sub-divided into 10 fully paid up equity share of ₹ 10 each.

(b) After sub-division, each shareholder shall surrender to the company 50% of his holding for the purpose of reissue to debentureholders and creditors as necessary.

(c) Out of shares surrendered 10,000 shares of ₹ 10 each shall be converted into 10% Preference shares of ₹ 10 each fully paid up.

(d) The claims of the debentureholders shall be reduced by 50%. In consideration of the reduction, the debentureholder shall receive Preference Shares of ₹ 1,00,000 which are converted out of shares surrendered.

(e) Creditors claim shall be reduced by 25%. Remaining creditors are to be settled by the issue of equity shares of ₹ 10 each of out of shares surrendered.

(f) Balance of Profit and Loss account to be written off.

(g) The shares surrendered and not re-issued shall be cancelled.

Required: Pass Journal Entries giving effect to the above and the resultant Balance Sheet.

Q.5 (a) How will you disclose the following Ledger balances in the Final accounts of DVD bank:

₹ in lacs

Current accounts	700
Saving accounts	500
Fixed deposits	700

₹ in lacs

Cash credits	600
Term Loans	500
Bills discounted & purchased	800

Additional information:

(i) Included in the current accounts ledger are accounts overdrawn to the extent of ₹ 250 lacs.

(ii) One of the cash credit account of ₹ 10 lacs (including interest ₹ 1 lac) is doubtful.

(iii) 60% of term loans are secured by government guarantees, 20% of cash credits are unsecured, other portion is secured by tangible assets.

Q.5 (b) The trial balance of Tulsian Electric Supply Ltd. For the year ended 31st March,2013 is as below:

(₹ '000)

Particulars	Dr.	Cr.
Share Capital:		
Equity Shares of ₹.10 each		500,00
14% Preference Shares of ₹.100 each		150,00
Patents and trade mark	25,04	
15% Debentures		24,700
16% term loan		153,00
Land (additons during the year 20,50)	124,50	
Building (additions during the year 50,80)	351,34	
Plant & Machinery	570,58	
Mains	45,24	
Meters	31,50	
Electrical Instruments	15,30	
Office Rurniture	24,50	
Capital Reserve		40,20
Contingency Reserves		120,30
General Reserve		10,00
Transformers	164,40	
Opening Balance of Profit & Loss Account		350
Profit for the year 2012-13 subject to adjustments		5,000
Stock in hand	120,50	
Sundry Debtors	62,46	
Contingency Reserve Investments:		
SBI Bonds-2020	100,10	
Other Investments	20,00	
Cash & Bank	32,54	
Public lamps	30,40	
Depreciation Fund		258,16
Sundry Creditiors		65,24
Proposed dividend		121,00
	1718,40	1718,40

During 2012-13 1,00,000, 14% Preference Shares were redeemed at a premium of 10% out of proceeds of fresh issue of equity shares of necessary amounts at a premium of 10%

Required prepare for the above period general balance sheet as on 31st March,2013 as per the revised schedule VI:

Adjustments:

1. Transfer to Contingency Reserve ₹.1,70,000 & to General Reserve ₹.2,00,000
2. Loss on Contingency Reserve Investment ₹.10,000
3. Make a Provision for debts considered doubtful of ₹.1,014,000

Q.6 (a) A Limited has retail branch at Noida. Goods are sold to customers at cost plus 100%. The wholesale price is cost plus 80%. Goods are invoiced to Noida at wholesale price. From the following particulars, find out the profit made by the Head Office and Noida Branch for the year ended 31st March, 2013 using invoice method.

	Head Office ₹	Noida ₹
Opening Stock	50,000	—
Purchases	3,00,000	—
Goods sent to branch (at invoice value)	1,08,000	—
Sales	3,06,000	1,00,000
Expenses	90,000	4,000

Sales at Head Office are made only on wholesale basis and sales at branch are made only to customers. Stock at branch is valued at invoice price.

Q.6 (b) Mis. AM Enterprise had two departments, Cloth and Readymade Clothes. The readymade clothes were made by the firm itself out of the cloth supplied by the Cloth Department at its usual selling price. From the following figures, prepare Departmental Trading and Profit & Loss Account for the year ended 31st March, 2013:

	Cloth Department ₹	Readymade Clothes Department ₹
Opening Stock on 1st April, 2012	31,50,000	5,32,000
Purchases	2,10,00,000	1,68,000
Sales	2,31,00,000	47,25,000
Transfer to Readymade Clothes Department	31,50,000	—
Manufacturing expenses	—	6,30,000
Selling expenses	2, 10,000	73,500
Rent & warehousing	8,40,000	5,60,000
Stockon 31st March, 2013	21,00,000	6,72,000

In addition to the above, the following information is made available for necessary consideration:

The stock in the Readymade Clothes Department may be considered as consisting of 75% cloth and 25% other expenses. The Cloth Department earned a gross profit at the rate of 15% in 2011-12. General expenses of the business as a whole amount to ₹ 10,85,000.

Q.7 Answer any four of the following questions: **[4 × 4 = 16]**

(a) Cashier of A-One Limited embezzled cash amounting to ₹ 6,00,000 during March, 2012. However same comes to the notice of Company management during April, 2012 only. financial statements of the company are not approved by the Board of Directors of the company.

(i) With the help of provisions of AS 4 "contingencies and Event Occurring after the Balance Sheet Date" decide, whether the embezzlement of cash should be adjusted in the books of accounts for the ending March, 2012?

(ii) What will be your replay, if embezzlement of cash comes to the notice of company management only after approval of financial statements by the Board Directors of the company?

(b) M/s Dinesh & Company signed an agreement with workers tor increase in wages with retrospective effect. The out-flow on account of arrears was for 2007–08—₹ 10.00 lakhs, for 2008–09 ₹ 12.00 lakhs and for 2009-10 ₹ 12.00 lakhs. This amount is payable in September, 2010. The accountant wants to charge ₹ 22.00 lakhs as prior period charges in financial statement for 2010-11. Discuss.

(c) ABC Limited purchased a machinery for ₹ 25,00,000 which has estimated useful life of 10 years with the salvage value of ₹ 5,00,000. On purchase of the assets Central Government pays a grant for ₹ 5,00,000. Pass the journal entries with narration in the books of the company for the first year, treating Grant as deferred income.

(d) BHARAT & TUSHAR LTD. obtained a loan from a bank for ₹ 120 lakhs on 30-04-2011. It was utilized as follows:

Particulars	*Amount (₹ in lakhs)*
Construction of a shed	50
Purchase of a machinery	40
Working Capital	20
Advance for purchase of truck	10

Construction of shed was completed in March 2012. The machinery was installed on the same date. Delivery truck was not received. Total interest charged by the bank for the year ending 31-03-2012 was ₹ 18 lakhs. Calculate the Interest to be debited to Profit & Loss Account.

(e) X Ltd. sold JCB Machine having WDV of ₹ 50 Lakhs to Y Ltd. for ₹ 60 Lakhs and the same JCB was leased back of Y Ltd to X Ltd. The lease is operating lease.

Comment according to relevant Accounting Standard if

(i) Sale price of ₹ 60 Lakhs is equal to fair value

(ii) Fair Value is ₹ 50 Lakhs and sale price is ₹ 45 Lakhs.

(iii) Fair value is ₹ 55 Lakhs and sale price is ₹ 62 Lakhs

(iv) Fair value is ₹ 45 Lakhs and sale price is ₹ 48 Lakhs

(f) From the following information compute diluted earnings per share.

Net Profit for the year	₹ 12,00,000
Weighted average number of equity shares outstanding	5,00,000 shares
Average fair value of one equity share	₹ 20
Weighted average number of shares under option	1,00,000 shares
Exercise price per share under option	₹ 15

ANSWERS TO TULSIAN'S MODEL TEST PAPER 2

Solution 1 (a).

Fair Value of an option = ₹ 28 – ₹ 25 = ₹ 3

Number of employees accepting the offer = 400 employees × 50% = 200 employees

Number of shares issued = 200 employees × 100 shares/employee = 20,000 shares

Fair value of ESPP = 20,000 shares × ₹ 3 = ₹ 60,000

Expenses recognized in 2013-14 = ₹ 60,000

JOURNAL

Date	*Particulars*		*Dr. (₹)*	*Cr. (₹)*
30.04.2013	Bank (20,000 shares × ₹ 25)	Dr.	5,00,000	
	Employees Compensation Expense A/c	Dr.	60,000	
	To Share Capital A/c (20,000 shares × ₹ 10)			2,00,000
	To Securities Premium A/c (20,000 shares × ₹ 18)			3,60,000
	(Being the options accepted by 200 employees)			

Solution 1. (b)

CALCULATION OF TOTAL REMUNERATION PAYABLE TO LIQUIDATOR

Particulars		₹
2% on Assets realised	25,00,000 × 2%	50,000
3% on payment made to Preferential creditors	75,000 × 3%	2,250
3% on payment made to Unsecured creditors (Refer W.N.)		39,255
Total Remuneration payable to Liquidator		91,505

Notes:

Remuneration on payment to unsecured creditors

= Cash available for unsecured creditors × 3/103

= (₹ 25,00,000 – ₹ 25,000 – ₹ 10,00,000 – ₹ 75,000 – ₹ 50,000 – ₹ 2,250) × 3/103 = ₹ 39,225

Solution 1. (c)

CALCULATION OF THE AMOUNT OF PROVISIONS ON ASSETS *[₹ in lakhs]*

Assets	*Amount*	*% of Provision*	*Provision*
Standard	7,000	0.40	28
Sub-standard:			
Secured portion	1,000	15	150
Unsecured infrastructure loan account where escrow account is available	1,500	20	300
Other unsecured	1,000	25	250
Doubtful-Secured portion:			
Upto one year	500	25	125
More than 1 year but upto 3 years	600	40	240
For more than three years	300	100	300
Doubtful-unsecured portion	1,500	100	1,500
Loss	200	100	200
Required provision			**3,093**

Solution 1. (d)

Dr. **DEPARTMENTAL TRADING ACCOUNT FOR THE YEAR ENDED 31ST MARCH, 2013** *Cr.*

Particulars	A ₹	B ₹	C ₹	Particulars	A ₹	B ₹	C ₹
To Opening Stock	14,400	10,800	30,000	By Sales	2,08,000	4,41,000	7,65,000
To Purchases	1,20,000	2,70,000	4,50,000	By Closing stock	9,600		21,000
To Gross profit	83,200	1,76,400	3,06,000				
	2,17,600	4,57,200	7,86,000		2,17,600	4,57,200	7,86,000

Working Notes:

(I) GROSS PROFIT RATIO

Selling price of units purchased:		₹
Department A	(5,000 units × ₹ 40)	2,00,000
Department B	(10,000 units × ₹ 45)	4,50,000
Department C	(15,000 units × ₹ 50)	7,50,000
Total selling price of purchased units		14,00,000
Less: Purchases		(8,40,000)
Gross profit		5,60,000

$$\text{Gross Profit Ratio} = \frac{\text{Gross profit}}{\text{Selling price}} \times 100 = \frac{5,60,000}{14,00,000} \times 100 = 40\%$$

(II) STATEMENT SHOWING DEPARTMENT-WISE PER UNIT COST & PURCHASE COST

Particulars	A	B	C
Selling price per unit (₹)	40	45	50
Less: Profit margin @ 40% (₹)	(16)	(18)	(20)
Purchase price per unit (₹)	24	27	30
No. of units purchased	5,000	10,000	15,000
Purchases (purchase cost per unit × units purchased)	1,20,000	2,70,000	4,50,000

(III) STATEMENT SHOWING CALCULATION OF DEPARTMENT-WISE OPENING STOCK (IN UNITS)

Particulars	A	B	C
Sales (Units)	5,200	9,800	15,300
Add: Closing Stock (Units)	400	600	700
	5,600	10,400	16,000
Less: Purchases (Units)	(5,000)	(10,000)	(15,000)
Opening Stock (Units)	600	400	1,000

(VI) STATEMENT SHOWING DEPARTMENT-WISE COST OF OPENING AND CLOSING STOCK

Particulars	A	B	C
Cost of Opening Stock (₹)	600 × 24	400 × 27	1,000 × 30
	14,400	10,800	30,000
Cost of Closing Stock (₹)	400 × 24	600 × 27	700 × 30
	9,600	16,200	21,000

Solution 2.

(I) COMPUTATION OF PURCHASE CONSIDERATION

Particulars	*(₹)*
Assets taken over by Y	
Land and Building	16,00,000
Plant and Machinery	2,80,000
Furniture	2,00,000
	20,80,000
Less: Depreciation @ 10%	(2,08,000)
	18,72,000
Add: Goodwill	8,00,000
	26,72,000
Less: Loan	(12,00,000)
Purchase consideration	14,72,000

(II) JOURNAL OF XYZ LIMITED

Date	*Particulars*		*Dr. (₹)*	*Cr. (₹)*
1.4.13	Business Purchase A/c	Dr.	14,72,000	
	To Y			14,72,000
	(Being purchase consideration due for taking over the business of Y)			
	Land and Building A/c (16,00,000 – 1,60,000)	Dr.	14,40,000	
	Plant and Machinery A/c (2,80,000 – 28,000)	Dr.	2,52,000	
	Furniture A/c (2,00,000 – 20,000)	Dr.	1,80,000	
	Goodwill A/c	Dr.	8,00,000	
	To Loans A/c			12,00,000
	To Business Purchase A/c			14,72,000
	(Being assets and liabilities taken over)			
	Vendor's Debtors	Dr.	8,40,000	
	To Vendor's Suspense A/c			8,40,000
	(Being Vendor's debtors to be collected on behalf of Y)			
	Vendor's Suspense A/c	Dr.	7,12,000	
	To Vendor's Creditors			7,12,000
	(Being Vendor's creditors to be paid off on behalf of Y)			
	Bank A/c	Dr.	8,00,000	
	Vendor's Suspense A/c	Dr.	40,000	
	To Vendor's Debtors A/c			8,40,000
	(Being Vendor's debtors collected at loss)			
	Vendor's Creditors A/c	Dr.	7,12,000	
	To Bank A/c			6,80,000
	To Vendor's Suspense A/c			32,000
	(Being profit on payment to Vendor's creditors)			
	Vendor's Suspense A/c	Dr.	37,600	
	To Commission A/c			37,600
	(Being the commission @ 3% on Vendor's Debtors collected and 2% on payment to Vendor's Creditors)			

Vendor's Suspense A/c Dr.		82,400	
To Y			82,400
(Being transfer of the net balance of vendor's suspense account after realization of debtors and payment to creditors, to Y)			
Y Dr.		15,54,400	
To Equity share capital A/c			15,00,000
To Bank A/c			54,400
(Being allotment of 1,50,000 equity shares of ₹ 10 each as fully paid up and payment of cash as agreed in discharge of total amount due to Y)			
Loan A/c Dr.		12,00,000	
To 10% Preference share capital A/c			12,00,000
(Being issue of 12,000 10% preference shares for discharge of loan)			
Commission A/c Dr.		37,600	
To Capital Reserve A/c			37,600
(Being commission earned on settlement of vendor's debtors and creditors is treated as pre-incorporation profit which is transferred to capital reserve account)			

(III) BALANCE SHEET OF XYZ LIMITED AS AT 1ST APRIL, 2013

Particulars	*Note No*	₹
I. Equity and Liabilities		
(1) Shareholders' Funds		
(a) Share Capital	1	27,00,000
(c) Reserves and Surplus [Capital Reserve]		37,600
(2) Non-Current Liabilities		
(a) Long-term Borrowings		
(3) Current Liabilities		
Total		27,37,600
II. Assets		
(1) Non-Current Assets		
(a) Fixed Assets		
Tangible Assets		18,72,000
Intangible Assets [Goodwill]	2	8,00,000
(2) Current Assets		
(a) Cash and Cash Equivalents		65,600
Total		27,37,600

Notes To Accounts:

Particulars	₹
1. Share Capital	
1,50,000 Equity Shares of ₹ 10 each	15,00,000
12,000, 10% Pref. Shares of ₹ 100 each	12,00,000
(Of the above all Shares were issued for consideration otherwise than cash)	27,00,000

2. Tangible Assets	
Land & Building	14,40,000
Plant & Machinery	2,52,000
Furniture	1,80,000
	18,72,000

Working Note: *Calculation of Cash balance of XYZ Ltd.*

	₹
Cash collected from vendor's debtors	8,00,000
Less: Cash paid to vendor's creditors	(6,80,000)
Less: Cash paid to Y	(54,400)
	65,600

Solution 3. (a)

JOURNAL

(₹ in lakhs)

Date	Particulars		L.F	Dr. (₹)	Cr. (₹)
01.04.2013	9% Redeemable Preference Share Capital A/c	Dr.		20.00	
	Premium on redemption of Preference Shares A/c	Dr.		2.00	
	To Preference Sheraholders A/c				22.00
	(Being preference Share Capital Transferred to shareholders account)				
01.04.2013	Preference Shareholders A/c	Dr.		22.00	
	To Bank A/c				22.00
	(Being payment made to shareholders)				
01.04.2013	Equity Shares Buy Back A/c	Dr.		90.00	
	To Bank A/c				90.00
	(Being 3 lakhs equity shares of 10 each bought back @ 30 per share)				
01.04.2013	Equity Share Capital A/c	Dr.		30.00	
	Securities Premium A/c	Dr.		60.00	
	To Equity Shares buy back A/c				90.00
	(Being cancellation of shares bought back)				
01.04.2013	Revenue Reserve A/c (20 + 30)	Dr.		50.00	
	To Capital Redemption Reserve A/c				50.00
	(Being creation of capital redemption reserve account to the extent of the face value of preference shares redeemed and equity shares bought back as per the law)				
01.04.2013	10% Debentures A/c	Dr.		2.20	
	To Investments (Own Debentures) A/c				2.00
	To Capital Reserve A/c				0.20
	(Being cancellation of own debentures and the Profit on cancellation of debentures t/f to Capital Reserve)				
01.04.2013	Bank A/c	Dr.		10.00	
	Employees Stock Option Outstanding (Current liabilities) A/c	Dr.		5.00	
	To Equity Share Capital A/c				5.00
	To Securities Premium A/c				10.00
	(Being the allotment to employees, of 50,000 shares of ₹ 10 each at a premium of ₹ 20 per share in exercise of stock options by employees)				

01.04.2013	Securities Premium A/c Dr. To Premium on Redemption of Preference Shares A/c (Being premium on redemption of preference shares adjusted through securities premium)		2.00	2.00

BALANCE SHEET OF EXTRA LTD. AS AT 01.04.2013

Particulars	*Note No*	*₹ (lacs)*
I. Equity and Liabilities		
(1) Shareholders' Funds		
(a) Share Capital (*₹ 10 each)[100+5-30]*		75.00
(b) Reserves and Surplus	1	66.20
(2) Non-Current Liabilities [10% Debentures] [4.00 – 2.20]		1.80
(3) Current Liabilities [70 – 5]		65.00
Total		208.00
II. Assets		
(1) Non-Current Assets		
(a) Fixed Assets		
Tangible Assets		50.00
(b) Non-Current Investments [120 – 2]		118.00
(2) Current Assets [142 + 10 – 22 – 90]		40.00
Total		208.00

Notes To Accounts:

Particulars	*₹ (lacs)*
1. Reserves and Surplus	
Revenue Reserve [50 – 50]	0
Capital Reserve [8.00 + 0.20]	8.20
Capital Redemption Reserve	50.00
Securities Premium [60 + 10 – 60 – 2]	8.00
Total	66.20

Solution 3. (b)

Dr. **1. 12% DEBENTURES ACCOUNT** *Cr.*

Data	*Particulars*	*₹*	*Date*	*Particulars*	*₹*
31.3.13	To Debentures holders A/c	7,50,000	1.4.12	By Balance b/d	7,50,000
		7,50,000			7,50,000

Dr. **2. SINKING FUND ACCOUNT** Cr.

Data	Particulars	₹	Date	Particulars	₹
31.3.13	To 10% Sec. Bond A/c (loss)	15,000	1.4.12	By Balance b/d	6,00,000
			31.3.13	By Profit and loss A/c	1,20,000
31.3.13	To General reserve A/c (Bal. fig.)	7,70,000		By Interest on Sinking Fund A/c (interest on 10% Govt. bond (₹ 6,50,000 × 10%))	65,000
		7,85,000			7,85,000

Dr. **3. SINKING FUND INVESTMENT ACCOUNT (10% SECURED BONDS OF GOVT.)** Cr.

Data	Particulars	₹	Date	Particulars	₹
1.4.12	To Balance b/d	6,00,000	31.3.13	By Bank A/c (6,50,000 × 90% = 5,85,000)	5,85,000
			31.3.13	By Sinking Fund A/c	15,000
		6,00,000			6,00,000

Dr. **4. BANK ACCOUNT** Cr.

Data	Particulars	₹	Date	Particulars	₹
31.3.13	To Balance b/d	3,00,000	31.3.13	By 12% Debentures	8,25,000
	To Sinking Fund A/c Interest)	65,000		By Balance c/d	1,25,000
	To Sinking fund Investment A/c	5,85,000			
		9,50,000			9,50,000

Dr. **5. DEBENTURE HOLDERS ACCOUNT** Cr.

Data	Particulars	₹	Date	Particulars	₹
31.3.13	To Bank A/c	8,25,000	31.3.13	By 12% Debentures	7,50,000
			31.3.13	By Premium on redemption of debentures	75,000
		8,25,000			8,25,000

Solution 4.

JOURNAL OF X LIMITED

Date	Particulars		Dr. (₹)	Dr. (₹)
(i)	Equity Share Capital (₹ 100) A/c	Dr.	10,00,000	
	To Share Surrender A/c			5,00,000
	To Equity Share Capital (? 10) A/c			5,00,000
	(Sub-division of 10,000 equity shares of ₹ 100 each into 1,00,000 equity shares of ₹ 10 each and surrender of 50,000 of such sub-divided shares as per capital reduction scheme)			

(ii)	15% Debentures A/c	Dr.	1,50,000	
	Accrued Interest A/c	Dr.	22,500	
	To Reconstruction A/c			1,72,500
	(Transferred 50% of the claims of the debentureholders to Reconstruction A/c in consideration of which 10% Preference shares are being issued, out of share surrender A/c as per capital reduction scheme)			
(iii)	Creditors A/c	Dr.	52,000	
	To Reconstruction A/c			52,000
	(Transferred claims of the creditors to Reconstruction A/c, 25% of which is reduction and equity shares are issued in consideration of the balance amount)			
(iv)	Share Surrender A/c	Dr.	5,00,000	
	To 10% Preference Share Capital A/c			1,00,000
	To Equity Share Capital A/c			39,000
	To Reconstruction A/c			3,61,000
	(Issued preference and equity shares to discharge the claims of the debentureholders and the creditors respectively as per scheme and the balance in share surrender account is transferred to reconstruction account)			
(v)	Reconstruction A/c	Dr.	5,85,500	
	To Profit & Loss A/c			5,80,000
	To Capital Reserve A/c			5,500
	(Adjusted debit balance of profit and loss account against reconstruction account and the balance is transferred to Capital Reserve account)			

BALANCE SHEET OF X LTD. (AND REDUCED) AS AT 31.03.2013

Particulars	Note No	₹
I. Equity and Liabilities		
(1) Shareholders' Funds		
(a) Share Capital	1	6,39,000
(c) Reserves and Surplus (Capital Reserve)		5,500
(2) Non-Current Liabilities 15% (Debentures)		1,50,000
(a) Long-term Borrowings		
(3) Current Liabilities		
(a) Trade Payables		
(b) Short-term Provisions		36,000
(c) Other Current Liabilities [Accrued Interest]		22,500
Total		8,53,000
II. Assets		
(1) Non-Current Assets		
(a) Fixed Assets		
Tangible Assets (Machineries)		3,50,000
(2) Current Assets		
(a) Inventories		2,53,000
(b) Trade Receivables		2,30,000
(b) Cash and Cash Equivalents		20,000
Total		8,53,000

Notes To Accounts:

Particulars	₹
1. Share Capital	
53,900 Equity Shares of ₹ 10 each	5,39,000
10,000, 10% Pref. Shares of ₹ 10 each	1,00,000
(Of the above 10,000 Pref. Shares were issued for consideration otherwise than cash)	6,39,000

Solution 5. (a)

RELEVANT SCHEDULES (FORMING PART OF THE BALANCE SHEET) OF DVD BANK
SCHEDULE 3: DEPOSITS

₹ in lacs

A	Demand Deposits (700 + 250)	950
B	Saving Bank deposits	500
C	Term Deposits	700
		2,150

Schedule 9: Advances

₹ in lacs

A. (i)	Bills Discounted and Purchased	800
(ii)	Cash Credits and Overdrafts (600 + 250)	850
(iii)	Term Loans	500
		2.150
B. (i)	Secured by tangible assets (bal. fig.)	1,730
(ii)	Secured by Bank/Government Guarantees (500 × 60%)	300
(iii)	Unsecured (600 × 20%)	120
		2.150

Schedule 5: Other Liabilities & Provisions

₹ in lacs

Others (Provision for doubtful debts)	10

Profit and Loss Account (an extract)

₹ in lacs

Less: Provision for doubtful debts*	10

***Note:** It is assumed that the cash credit has been in 'doubtful' category for more than three years

Solution 5. (b)

Tulsian Electric Supply Ltd.
BALANCE SHEET as at 31st March, 2013

Particulars	Note No.	(₹ in '000)
I. EQUITY AND LIABILITIES		
(1) Shareholders' Funds		
(a) Share Capital	1	65,000
(b) Reserves and Surplus	2	21,376
(2) Non-Current Liabilities		
(a) Long-term Borrowings	3	40,000
(3) Current Liabilities		
(a) Trade Payables		6,524
(b) Short-Term Provisions	4	121,00
Total		145,000
II. ASSETS		
(1) Non-Current Assets		
(a) Fixed Assets		
(i) Tangible Assets	5	109,960
(ii) Intangible Assets		2504
(b) Non-Current Investments	6	12,000
(2) Current Assets		
(a) Inventories		12,050
(b) Trade Receivables	7	5232
(c) Cash and Cash Equivalents		3254
Total		145,000

Notes To Accounts:

1. Share Capital

Authorised Capital	
50,00,000 shares of ₹ 10 each	50,000
2,50,000 14% Pref. Shares of ₹ 100 each	25,000
	75,000
Issued & Subscribed Capital	
50,00,000 shares of ₹ 10 each	50,000
2,50,000 14% Pref. Shares of ₹ 100 each	25,000
Less: 1,00,000 14% Pref. Shares of ₹ 100 each	(10,000)
	65,000

2. Reserves and Surplus

Capital Reserve		4,020
Contingency Reserve (12,030 + 170 – 10)		12,190
Reserve (1000 + 200)		1,200
Profit & Loss Account		
Opening Balance	350	
Add: Profit for the period	5,000	
Less: Transfer to General Reserve	(200)	
Less: Transfer to Contingency Reserve	(170)	
Less: Provision for Doubtful Debts	(1,014)	3966
Total		**21,376**

3. Long-term Borrowings

15% Debentures	24,700
16% Term Loan	15,300
	40,000

4. Short-term Provisions

Proposed Dividend	12,100
	12,100

5. Tangible Assets

Land (10,400 + 20,50)	124,50
Building (30,054 + 50,80)	351,34
Plant & Machinery	570,58
Mains	45,24
Meters	31,50
Electrical Instruments	15,30
Office Rurniture	24,50
Transformers	164,40
Public lamps	30,40
Less: Depreciation Fund	(258,16)
Total	**109,960**

6. Non-Current Investments

SBI Bonds-2020 (100,10 – 10)	100,00
Other Investments	20,00
	120,00

7. Trade Receivables

Sundry Debtors	62,46
Less: Provision for Doubtful Debts	(10,14)
	52,32

Solution 6. (a)

Dr. **TRADING ACCOUNT FOR THE YEAR ENDED 31ST MARCH, 2013** *Cr.*

Particulars	*HO* ₹	*Branch* ₹	*Particulars*	*HO* ₹	*Branch* ₹
To Opening Stock	50,000	—	By Sales	3,06,000	1,00,000
To Purchases	3,00,000	—	By Goods sent to Branch	1,08,000	—
To Goods received from Head Office	—	1,08,000	By Closing Stock	1,20,000	18,000
To Gross Profit	1,84,000	10,000			
	5,34,000	1,18,000		5,34,000	1,18,000

Dr. **PROFIT AND LOSS A/C FOR THE YEAR ENDED 31ST MARCH, 2013** Cr.

Particulars	₹	₹	Particulars	₹	₹
To Expenses	90,000	4,000	By Gross Profit	1,84,000	10,000
To Stock Reserve against Branch $\left(18,000 \times \frac{80}{180}\right)$	8 000	—			
To Net Profit	86,000	6,000			
	184,000	10,000		184,000	10,000

Working Note: **Calculation of Closing Stock**

Particulars	Head Office ₹	Noida Branch ₹
Opening Stock	50,000	—
Goods purchased or Received from Head Office	3,00,000	1,08,000
Less: Cost of Goods sold or sent to Branch:		
Head Office [3,06,000 + 1,08,000) x 100/180]	(2,30,000)	
Branch 1,00,000 × 180/200]		(90,000)
Value of Closing Stock	1,20,000	18,000

Solution 6. (b)

(a) **DEPARTMENTAL TRADING AND PROFIT AND LOSS ACCOUNT**

for the year ended 31st March, 2013

Dr. Cr.

Particulars	Cloth (₹)	Ready-made Clothes (₹)	Total (₹)	Particulars	Cloth (₹)	Ready-made Clothes (₹)	Total (₹)
To Opening stock	31,50,000	5,32,000	36,82,000	By Sales	2,31,00,000	47,25,000	2,78,25,000
To Purchases	2,10,00,000	1,68,000	2,11,68,000	By Transferto Ready-made Clothes Deptt.	31,50,000	—	31,50,000
To Transfer from Cloth Department	—	31,50,000	31,50,000	By Closing from Cloth Stock	21,00,000	6,72,000	27,72,000
To Manufacturing expenses	—	6,30,000	6,30,000				
To Gross profit c/d	42,00,000	9,17,000	51,17,000				
	2,83,50,000	53,97,000	3,37,47,000		2.83.50.000	53.97.000	3.37.47.000
To Sellingexpenses	2,10,000	73,500	2,83,500	By Gross profit b/d	42,00,000	9,17,000	51,17,000
To Rent & warehousing	8,40,000	5,60,000	14,00,000				
To Net profit	31,50,000	2,83,500	34,33,500				
	42,00,000	9,17,000	51,17,000		42,00,000	9,17,000	51,17,000

Dr. **GENERAL PROFIT AND LOSS ACCOUNT** Cr.

Particulars	₹	Particulars	₹
To General Expenses	10,85,000	By Net Profit	34,33,500
To Stock Reserve on Closing Stock	80,640	By Stock Reserve on Opening Stock (No longer required)	59,850
To General Net Profit (Bal. fig.)	23,27,710		
	34,93,350		34,93,350

***Working Note:* Calculation of Stock Reserve**

$$\text{Gross Profit Ratio of Cloth Department} = \frac{\text{Gross Profit}}{\text{Total Sales}} \times 100$$

$$= \frac{\text{Rs } 42,00,000}{\text{Rs } (2,31,000 + 31,50,000)} \times 100 = 16\%$$

Stock Reserve on Closing Stock = ₹ 6,72,000 × 75% × 16% = ₹ 80,640

Stock reserve on opening stock = (₹ 5,32,000 × 75% × 15%) = ₹ 59,850

Solution 7. (a)

AS 4	As per AS 4, assets and Liabilities should be adjusted for events occurring after the balance sheet date that provide additional evidence to assist the estimation of amounts relating to conditions existing at the balance sheet date.
Advice	(a) Though the theft, by the cashier ₹ 6,00,000 was detected after the balance sheet date (before approval of financial statements) but it is an additional information materially affecting the determination of the cash amount relating to conditions existing at the balance sheet date. Therefore, it is necessary to make the necessary adjustments in the financial statements of the company for the ended 31st March, 2012 for recognition of the loss amounting ₹ 6,00,000. (b) If embezzlement of cash comes to the notice of company management only after approval of financial statements by board of directors of the company, then the treatment will be done as per the provisions of AS 5. This being extra ordinary item should be disclosed in the Statement of Profit and Loss as a part of loss for the year ending March, 2013. The nature and the amount of prior period item should be separately disclosed on the Statement of Profit and Loss in a manner that its impact on current profit on loss can be perceived.

Solution 7. (b)

AS 5	As per AS 5 the term prior period item refers only to income or expenses which arise in the current period as a result of errors or omission in the preparation of the financial statements of one or more prior periods. The term does not include other adjustments necessitated by circumstances, which though related to prior periods are determined in the current period.
Advice	1. The full amount of wage arrears paid to workers will be treated as an expense of current year and it will be charged to profit and loss account as current expenses and not as prior period expenses. 2. Additional wages is an expense arising from the ordinary activities of the company. Although abnormal in amount, such an expense does not qualify as an extraordinary item. However, as per Para 12 of AS 5 (Revised), when items of income and expense within profit or loss from ordinary activities are of such size, nature or incidence that their disclosure is relevant to explain the performance of the enterprise for the period, the nature and amount of such items should be disclosed separately.

Solution 7. (c)

JOURNAL OF ABC LTD.

Year	Particulars	Dr. (₹)	Cr. (₹)
1st	Machinery A/c Dr. To Bank A/c (Being machinery purchased)	25,00,000	25,00,000
	Bank A/c Dr. To Deferred Government Grant A/c (Being grant received from the government treated as deferred income)	5,00,000	5,00,000
	Depreciation A/c (25,00,000 – 5,00,000)/10 Dr. To Machinery A/c (Being depreciation charge on straight line method)	2,00,000	2,00,000
	Profit & Loss A/c Dr. To Depreciation A/c (Being depreciation transferred to P/L Account)	2,00,000	2,00,000
	Deferred Government Grant A/c (5,00,000)/10 Dr. To Profit & Loss A/c (Being proportionate government grant taken to P/L Account)	50,000	50,000

Solution 7. (d)

Qualifying Asset as per AS-16 = ₹ 50 lakhs (construction of a shed)
Borrowing cost to be capitalized = 18 × 50/120 = ₹ 7.5 lakhs
Interest to be debited to Profit or Loss account = ₹ (18 – 7.5) lakhs = ₹ 10.5 lakhs

Solution 7. (e)

According to AS 19, follows will be the treatment in the given situations:

(i) X Ltd. should immediately recognized the profit of ₹ 10 lakhs (i.e. 60 – 50) in its books.

(ii) The loss of ₹ 5 lakhs (50 – 45) to be immediately recognized by X Ltd. in its books provided loss is not compensated by future lease payments.

(iii) Profit of ₹ 5 lakhs (55 – 50) to be immediately recognized by X Ltd. in its books and balance profit of ₹ 7 lakhs (62-55) is to be amortised/deferred over lease period.

(iv) The loss of ₹ 5 lakhs (50 – 45) to be immediately recognized by X Ltd. in its books and profit of ₹ 3 lakhs (48 – 45) should be amortised/deferred over lease period.

Solution 7. (f)

COMPUTATION OF DILUTED EARNINGS PER SHARE

Particulars	Earnings (₹)	Shares	Earning per share (₹)
Net Profit for the year	12,00,000		
Weighted average number of equity shares outstanding		5,00,000	
Basic earnings per share (12,00,0000/5,00,000)			2.40

Weighted average number of shares under option		1,00,000	
Number of shares that would have been issued at fair value (1,00,000 xl5.00)/20.00)	——	(75,000)	——
Diluted earnings per share (12,00,0000/5,25,000)	*12,00,000	5,25,000	2.29

*The earnings have not been increased as the total number of shares has been increased only by the number of shares (25,000) deemed for the purpose of computation to have been issued for no consideration.

Paper-5: Advanced Accounting
CA IPC (Group II)
Tulsian's Model Test Paper 3

Question No. 1 is compulsory.
Attempt any Five questions from the remaining Six questions
Wherever necessary suitable assumptions may be made by the candidates.
Working notes should form part of the answer.

Q.1 Answer the following questions: **[4 × 5 = 20]**

(a) A Company has its share capital divided into shares of ₹ 10 each. On 1st April 2012, it granted 20,000 employees' stock options at ₹ 40, when the market price was ₹ 130. The options were to be exercised between 1st January 2013 to 15th March 2013. The employees exercised their options for 18,000 shares only; the remaining options lapsed. The company closes its books on 31st March every year. Pass Journal entries with regard to employees' stock options.

(b) Following is the Balance Sheet of M/S competent Limited as on 31st March, 2013:

Liabilities	₹	*Assets*	₹
Equity Shares of ₹ 10 Each)	12,50,000	Fixed Assets	76,50,000
Revenue reserve	15,00,000		
Securities Premium	2,50,000		
Profit & Loss Account	1,25,000		
Secured Loans:			
12% Debentures	18,75,000		
Unsecured Loans	10,00,000		
Current Liabilities	16,50,000		
	76,50,000		76,50,000

The company wants to buy back 25,000 equity shares of ₹ 10 each, on 1st April, 2013 at ₹ 20 per share. Buy back of shares is duly authorized by its articles and necessary resolution passed by the company towards this. The payment of buy back of shares will be made by the company out of sufficient back balance available as part of Current Assets.

Comment with your calculations, whether buy back of shares by company is within the provision of the companies Act, 1956. If you pass necessary journal entries towards buy back of shares and prepare of Balance Sheet after buy back of shares.

(c) Rising Sun Limited came up with an issue of 25,00,000 Equity shares of ₹ 10 each at par. 4,00,000 shares were issued to the promoters and balance offered to the public. Issue was underwritten by three underwriters A & Co., B & Co., and C & Co., equally, with firm underwriting of 1,00,000 shares each. Subscription totalled 17,26,000 shares, including the marked forms which were as under:

A&Co.	5,18,000 Shares
B&Co.	5,50,000 Shares
C&Co.	4,72,000 Shares

The underwriters had applied for the number of shares covered by firm underwriting. The amount payable on application and allotment were ₹ 3 & ₹ 2 respectively. The agreed commission is 3%.

You are required to calculate:

(i) The liability of each underwriter.

(ii) The amount payable and/or receivable by the underwriter.

(d) A company had 16,000, 12% debentures of 100 each outstanding as on 1st April, 2012, redeemable on 31st March, 2013. On that day, Sinking fund was ₹ 14,98,000 represented by 2,000 own debentures purchased at the average price of ₹ 99 and 9% stocks face value of ₹ 13,20,000. The annual instalment was ₹ 56,800.

On 31st March, 2013 the investments were realized at ₹ 98 and the debentures were redeemed. You are required to write up the following accounts for the year ending 31si March 2013:

(a) 12% Debentures Account

(b) Debenture Redemption Sinking Fund Account.

(e) The following particulars relate to a Limited Company which has gone into voluntary liquidation. You are required to prepare the Liquidator's Statement of Account allowing for his remuneration @2½% on all assets realized excluding call money received and 2% on the amount paid to unsecured creditors including preferential creditors.

Share capital issued:

10,000 Preference shares of ₹ 100 each fully paid up.

50,000 Equity shares of ₹ 10 each fully paid up.

30,000 Equity shares of ₹ 10 each, ₹ 8 paid up.

Assets realized ₹ 20,00,000 excluding the amount realized by sale of securities held by partly secured creditors.

	₹
Preferential creditors	50,000
Unsecured creditors	18,00,000
Partly secured creditors (Assets realized ₹ 3,20,000)	3,50,000
Debentureholders having floating charge on all assets of the company	6,00,000
Expenses of liquidation	10,000

A call of ₹ 2 per share on the partly paid equity shares was duly received except in case of one shareholder owning 1,000 shares.

Also calculate the percentage of amount paid to the unsecured creditors to the total unsecured creditors.

Q2. P and Q have been carrying on same business independently. Due to competition in the market, they decided to amalgamate and form a new company called PQ Ltd. Following is the Balance Sheet of P and Q as at 31.3.2013:

Liabilities	*P* ₹	*Q* ₹	*Assets*	*P* ₹	*Q* ₹
Capital	7,75,000	8,55,000	Plant & machinery	4,85,000	6,14,000
Current liabilities	6,23,500	5,57,600	Building	7,50,000	6,40,000
			Current Assets	1,63,500	1,58,600
	13,98,500	14,12,600		13,98,500	14,12,600

Following are the additional information:

(a) The authorised capital of the new company will be ₹.25,00,000 divided into 1,00,000 equity shares of ₹. 25 each.

(b) Liabilities of P includes ₹ 50 000 due to Q for the purchases made. Q made a profit of 20% on sale to P

(c) P has goods purchased from Q, cost to him ₹. 10, 000. This is included in the Current asset of P as at 31st March, 2013.

(d) The assets of P and Q are to be revalued as under:

	P	Q
Plant and Machinery	₹ 5,25,000	₹ 6,75,000
Building	₹ 7,75,000	₹ 6,48,000

(e) The purchase consideration is to be discharged as under:

(i) Issue 24,000 equity shares of ₹. 25 each fully paid up in the proportion of their profitability in the preceding 2 years. Profits for the preceding 2 years are given below:

	P ₹	Q ₹
Ist year	2,62,800	2,75,125
IInd Year	2,12,200	2,49,875
	4,75,000	5,25,000

(ii) Issue 12% preference shares of ₹. 10 each fully paid up at par to provide income equivalent to 8% return on capital employed in the business as on 31.3.2013 after revaluation of assets of P and Q respectively.

Required:

(i) Compute the amount of equity and preference shares issued to P and Q.

(ii) Prepare the Balance Sheet of P & 0 Ltd. immediately after amalgamation.

Q3 (a). Extra Ltd. furnishes you with the following Balance Sheet as on 31st March, 2013:

[₹ in lakhs]

Liabilities	₹	*Assets*	₹
Share Capital		*Fixed Assets Less* depreciation	50
Equity shares of ₹ 10 each fully paid	100	Investments at cost	120
		Current Assets	142
9% Redeemable Preference Shares of ₹ 100 each fully paid	20		
Capital Reserves	8		
Revenue Reserves	50		
Securities Premium	60		
10% Debentures	4		
Current liabilities	70		
	312		312

(a) The company redeemed the preference shares at a premium of 10% on 1st April, 2013.

(b) It also bought back 3 lakhs equity shares of ₹ 10 each at ₹ 30 per share. The payment for the above were made out of huge bank balances, which appeared as a part of the current assets.

(c) Included in its investment were "investments in own debentures" costing ₹ 2 lakhs (face value ₹ 2.20 lakhs). These debentures were cancelled on 1st April, 13.

(d) The company had 1,00,000 equity stock options outstanding on the above mentioned date, to the employees at ₹ 20 when the market price was ₹ 30. (This was included under current liabilities). On 01.04.2013 employees exercised their options for 50,000 shares. Pass the journal entries to record the above & Prepare Balance Sheet as at 01.04.13.

Q3 (b). Siva Ltd. has two departments *X* and *Y*. From the following particulars prepare departmental trading accounts and General Profit and Loss Account for the year ending 31st March. 2013:

	Department X ₹	*Department Y* ₹
Opening Stock (at cost)	80,000	48,000
Purchases	3,68,000	2,72,000
Carriage inward	8,000	8,000
Wages	48,000	32,000
Sales	5,60,000	4,48,000
Purchased good transferred		
By department *Y* to *X*	40,000	-
By department *X* to *Y*	–	32,000
Finished goods transferred		
By department *Y* to *X*	1,40,000	–
By department *X* to *Y*	–	1,60,000
Return of finished goods		
By department *Y* to *X*	40,000	–
By department *X* to *Y*	–	28,000
Closing stock		
Purchased goods	18,000	24,000
Finished goods	96,000	56,000

Purchased goods have been transferred mutually at their respective departmental purchase cost and finished goods at departmental market price and that 25% of the closing finished stock with each department represents finished goods received from the other department.

Q4 (a). Balance Sheet of *Y* Ltd. as at 31st March, 2013 was as follows:

	₹		₹
5,00,000 Equity Shares of ₹ 10 each fully paid	50,00,000	Goodwill	10,00,000
		Patent	5,00,000
9% 20,000 Preference Shares of ₹ 100 each fully paid	20,00,000	Land and Building	30,00,000
		Plant and Machinery	10,00,000
10% First Debentures	6,00,000	Furniture and Fixtures	2,00,000
10% Second Debentures	10,00,000	Computers	3,00,000
Debentures interest outstanding	1,60,000	Trade Investment	5,00,000
Trade Creditors	5,00,000	Debtors	5,00,000
Directors' Loan	1,00,000	Stock	10,00,000
Bank O/D	1,00,000	Discount on issue of Debentures	1,00,000
Outstanding Liabilities	40,000	Profit and Loss Account (Loss)	15,00,000
Provision for Tax	1,00,000		
	96,00,000		96,00,000

Note: *Preference Dividend is in arrears for last three years.*

A holds 10% first debentures for ₹ 4,00,000 and 10% second debentures for ₹ 6,00,000. He is also a creditor for ₹ 1,00,000. *B* holds 10% first debentures for ₹ 2,00,000 and 10% second debentures for ₹ 4,00,000 and is also a creditor for ₹ 50,000.

The following scheme of reconstruction has been agreed upon and duly approved by the court:

(a) All the equity shares be converted into fully paid equity shares of ₹ 5 each.

(b) The preference shares be reduced to ₹ 50 each and the preference shareholders agree to forego their arrears of preference dividends in consideration of which 9% preference shares are to be converted into 10% preference shares.

(c) Mr. '*A*' is to cancel ₹ 6,00,000 of his total debt including interest on debentures and to pay ₹ 1 lakh to the company and to receive new 12% debentures for the Balance Amount.

(d) Mr. '*B*' is to cancel ₹ 3,00,000 of his total debt including interest on debentures and to accept new 12% debentures for the balance amount.

(e) Trade creditors (other than *A* and *B*) agreed to forego 50% of their claim.

(f) Directors to accept settlement of their loans as to 60% thereof by allotment of equity shares and balance being waived.

(g) There were capital commitments totalling ₹ 3,00,000. These contracts are to be cancelled on payment of 5% of the contract price as a penalty.

(h) The Directors refund ₹ 1,10,000 of the fees previously received by them.

(i) Reconstruction expenses paid ₹ 10,000.

(j) The taxation liability of the company is settled at ₹ 80,000 and the same is paid immediately.

(k) The assets are revalued as under:

	₹
Land and Building	28,00,000
Plant and Machinery	4,00,000
Stock	7,00,000
Debtors	3,00,000
Computers	1,80,000
Furniture and Fixtures	1,00,000
Trade Investment	4,00,000

Required: Pass Journal entries for all the above mentioned transactions including amounts to be written off of Goodwill, Patents, Loss in Profit and Loss Account and Discount on issue of debentures. Prepare Bank Account and working of allocation of Interest on Debentures between *A* and *B*.

Q4 (b). The Life Fund of Well-life Assurance Co. was ₹.90,00,000 as on 31st March 2013. The interim bonus paid during the valuation period was ₹.1,50,000. The periodical actuarial valuation determined the net liability at ₹.75,00,000. Surplus brought forward from the previous valuation was ₹.9,00,000. The directors of the company proposed to carry forward ₹.10,00,000 and to divide the balance between the shareholders and the policy holders. You are required to show:

(i) The Valuation Balance Sheet.

(ii) The Net Profit for the valuation period.

(iii) The Distribution of the Surplus.

Q5 (a). From the following information prepare the Profit & Loss Account of Jawahar Bank Limited for the year ended 31st March, 2013. Also give necessary Schedules.

	Figures are in ₹ thousands
Interest earned on term loans	17.26
Interest earned on term loans classified as NPA	4.52
Interest received on term loans classified as NPA	2. 04
Interest on cash credits and overdrafts	38.54
Interest earned but not received on cash credit and overdraft treated as NPA	8.39
Interest on deposits	27.20
Commission	1.97
Profit on sale of investments	11.76
Profit on revaluation of investments	2. 76
Income from investments	15.53
Salaries, bonus and allowances	18. 75
Rent, taxes and lighting	1. 70
Printing and stationary	0. 75
Director's fees, allowances expenses	1.33
Law charges	0.22
Repairs and maintenance	0. 18
Insurance	0.30
Other information:	
Make necessary provision on risk assets:	
(i) Sub-standard	15.00
(ii) Doubtful for one year	7.00
(iii) Doubtful for two years	2.40
(iv) Loss assets	0.65
Investments	3700

Bank should not keep more than 25% of its investments as 'held-for-maturity' investment. The market value of its best 75% investments is ₹ 9,00,000 as on 31st March, 2013.

Q5 (b). Prepare Revenue Account in proper form for the year ended 31st March, 2013, from the following particulars related to Krishna General Insurance Co. for the year ended 2012 – 2013:

	Related to Direct business (₹)	*Related to Reinsurance (₹)*
Premiums:		
Amount received	30,00,000	2,40,000
Receivable at the beginning	1,80,000	24,000
Receivable at the end	2,40,000	36,000
Amount paid	–	3,60,000
Payable at the beginning	–	30,000
Payable at the end	–	42,000
Claims:		
Amount paid	18,00,000	1,80,000
Payable at the beginning	60,000	12,000
Payable at the end	1,20,000	18,000

Amount recovered	–	1,20,000
Receivable at the beginning	–	18,000
Receivable at the end	–	12,000
Commission:		
Amount paid	72,000	10,800
Amount received	–	14,400

Additional information:

(*i*) Interest, dividend and rent received 30,000

Income-tax in respect of above 6,000

(*ii*) Management expenses including ₹ 12,000 related to legal expenses regarding claims 1,32,000

(*iii*) Provision for income tax existing at the beginning of the year was ₹ 1,95,000, the income-tax actually paid during the year ₹ 1,68,000 and the provision necessary at the year end ₹ 2,07,000.

(*iv*) The net premium income of the company during the previous year was ₹ 24,00,000 on which reserve for unexpired risk @ 50% and additional reserve @ 7 ½% was created. This year, the balance to be carried forward is 50% of net premium on reserve for unexpired risk and 5% on additional reserve.

Q6. The Washington branch of XYZ Limited, Mumbai sent the following trial balance as on 31st December, 2013:

Particulars	$	$
Head Office A/c	—	22,800
Sales—	—	84,000
Debtors and Creditors	4,800	3,400
Machinery	24,000	—
Cash at Bank	1,200	—
Opening Stock	11,200	—
Goods from H.O.	64,000	—
Expenses	5,000	—
	1,10,200	1,10,200

In the books of head office, the Branch a/c stood as follows:

Dr. **WASHINGTON BRANCH ACCOUNT** *Cr.*

Particulars	₹	Particulars	₹
To Balance b/d	8,10,000	By Cash	28,76,000
To Goods sent to branch	29,26,000	By Balance c/d	8,60,000
	37,36,000		37,36,000

Goods are sent to the branch at cost *plus* 10% and the branch sells goods at Inovice price *plus* 25%. Machinery was acquired on 1st January, 2012, when $ 1.00 = ₹ 48.

Rates of Exchange were:

1st January, 2013	$ 1.00 = ₹ 46
31st December, 2013	$ 1.00 = ₹ 48
Average	$ 1.00 = ₹ 47

Machinery is depreciated @ 10% and the Branch Manager is entitled to a commission of 5% on the profit of the branch.

You are required to:

(i) Prepare the Branch Trading & Profit & Loss A/c in dollars.

(ii) Convert the Trial Balance of branch into Indian currency and prepare Branch Trading & Profit and Loss A/c and the Branch A/c in the books of head office.

Q.7 Answer any four of the following questions: [4 × 4 = 16]

(a) X Ltd. began construction of a new building on 1st April, 2012. It obtained Rs1 lakh special loan to finance the construction of the building on 1st 1st April, 2012 at an interest rate of 10%. The company's other outstanding two non-specific loans were:

Loans	*Rate of Interest*
₹ 5,00,000	11%
₹ 9,00,000	13%

The expenditure that were made on the building project were as follows:

	₹
1st April 2012	2,00,000
1st July 2012	2,50,000
1st Oct 2012	4,50,000
1st March 2012	1,20,000

Building was completed by 31st March, 2013 Following the principles prescribed in AS-16'Borrowing Cost,' calculate the amount of interest to be capitalized and pass one Journal Entry for capitalizing the cost and borrowing cost in respect of the building.

(b) Suraj Limited wishes to obtain a machine costing ₹ 30 lakhs by way of lease. The effective life of the machine is 14 years, but the company requires it only for the first 5 years. It enters into an agreement with Ashok Ltd., for a lease rental for ₹ 3 lakhs p.a. payable in arrears and the implicit rate of interest is 15%. The chief accountant of Suraj Limited is not sure about the treatment of these lease rentals and seeks your advise.

(c) Compute adjust earning per share and basic earning per share based on the following information:

Net Profit 2011-12	₹ 11,40,000
Net Profit 2012-13	₹ 22,50,000
No of Equity Shares outstanding	5,00,000

Unit 31st December, 2012

Bonus issue on 1st January, 2013: 1 Equity Share for each equity share outstanding as at 31st December, 2012

(d) Refiners and Projects Limited is a company in the oil and gas sector, it undertakes extensive research and development work as part of its operations. It has till the end of the financial year 31 March, 2011 spent ₹ 592,23 crores on research expenses.

The development of a new process was completed in the accounting year 2011-12 after incurring an expenditure of ₹ 322.26 crores. In the accounting year 2012-2013 the company implemented the new process resulting in a post tax saving of ₹ 100 crores in the first year of operation and savings of ₹ 80 crores per annum thereafter for the next four years.

The cost of capital to the company is 12 per cent

Kindly indicate how you will, in the background of accounting standards prescribed, proceed to record the transactions in the books of accounts of the company.

You are given to understand that the research expenses shown above do not include any general or selling and administrative expenses.

The present value discounted at 12 per cent of a Rupee can be adopted at .893, .797, .712, .636 and .567 for the purposes of calculation.

(e) X Ltd. has its financial year ended 31.3.2013, fifteen law suits outstanding, none of which has been settled by the time the accounts are approved by the directors. The directors have estimated that the probable outcomes as below:

	Probability	*Amount of Loss ₹*
For first ten cases:		
Win	0.6	—
Loss-low damages	0.3	90,000
Loss-high damages	0.1	2,00,000
For remaining five cases:		
Win	0.5	—
Loss-low damages	0.3	60,000
Loss-high damages	0.2	1,00,000

The directors believe that the outcome of each case is independent of the outcome of all the others.

Estimate the amount of contingent loss and state the accounting treatment of such contingent loss.

ANSWERS TO TULSIAN'S MODEL TEST PAPER 3

Solution 1 (a).

JOURNAL

Date	Particulars	Dr. (₹)	Cr. (₹)
01.04.2012	Employees compensation expense A/c Dr.	18,00,000	
	To Employees stock option outstanding A/c		18,00,000
	(Being grant of 20,000 stock option to employees at ₹ 40 when market price is ₹ 130)		
01.01.2013	Bank A/c Dr.	7,20,000	
15.03.2012	Employees stock option outstanding A/c Dr.	16,20,000	
	To Equity share capital A/c		1,80,000
	To Securities premium A/c		21,60,000
	(Being allotment to employees 18,000 equity shares of ₹ 10 each at a premium of ₹ 120 per share in exercise of their stock options)		
16.03.2013	Employees stock option outstanding A/c Dr.	1,80,000	
	To Employees compensation expense A/c		1,80,000
	(Being entry for lapse of stock options for 2,000 shares)		
31.03.2013	Profit & Loss A/c Dr.	16,20,000	
	To Employees compensation expense A/c		16,20,000
	(Being transfer of employees compensation expense to profit & loss account)		

Solution 1 (b).

(a) Determination of Buy back of maximum no. of shares as per the companies Act, 1956

1. Outstanding Shares Test = Max No. of shares that can be bought back
   25% of the outstanding Shares = 25% of 1,25,000 = 31,250
2. Resources Test = Max. No of shares that can be bought back
   = 25% of Shareholders' Fund/Buy back price per share
   = [25% (12.50 + 15 + 2.50 + 1.25)]/20 = 39,063
3. Debt Equity Ratio Test

Loan funds (₹) (18,75,000 + 10,00,000 + 16,50,000)	₹ 45,25,000
Minimum equity to be maintained after buy back [45,25,000/2]	₹ 22,62,500
Present Equity	₹ 31,25,000
Maximum permitted buy back of Equity (₹) [31,25,000 – 22,62,500]	8,62,500
Maximum number of shares that can be bough back [8,62,500/₹ 20]	43,125 shares

Hence, Company qualifies all test for buy-back of shares and come to the conclusion that it can buy maximum 31,250 shares (being the least in 3 Tests) as per Sec. 77A.

However, company wants to buy-back only 25,000 equity shares @₹ 20. Therefore buy-back of 25,000 shares, as desired by the company is within the provisions of the Companies Act, 1956.

JOURNAL

Date	Particulars	Dr. (₹)	Cr. (₹)
(a)	Equity Shares buy-back A/c Dr.	5,00,000	
	To Bank A/c		5,00,000
	(Being buy back of 25,000 equity shares of ₹ 10 each @ ₹ 20 per share)		

(b)	Equity Share Capital A/c Securities Premium A/c To Equity Shares buy-back A/c (Being cancellation of shares bought back)	Dr. Dr.	2,50,000 2,50,000	 5,00,000
(c)	Revenue Reserve A/c To Capital Redemption Reserve A/c (Being transfer of free reserves to capital redemption reserve to the extent of nominal value of capital bought back through free reserves)	Dr.	2,50,000	 2,50,000

BALANCE SHEET OF M/S COMPETENT LTD. AS AT 31.3.2013

Particulars	Note No	₹ (lacs)
I. Equity and Liabilities		
(1) Shareholders' Funds		
(a) Share Capital (₹ *10 each)*		10.00
(b) Reserves and Surplus	1	16.25
(2) Non-Current Liabilities		
(a) Long-term Borrowings	2	28.75
(3) Current Liabilities		16.50
Total		71.50
II. Assets		
(1) Non-Current Assets		
(a) Fixed Assets		46.50
(2) Current Assets [30 – 5]		25.00
Total		71.50

Notes To Accounts:

Particulars	₹
1. Reserves and Surplus	
Revenue Reserves	12.50
Capital Redemption Reserve	2.50
Profit & Loss Account	1.25
Total	16.25
2. Long-term Borrowings	
12% Debentures [Secured]	18.75
Unsecured Loan	10.00
	28.75

Note: Revaluation reserve account, Securities premium account and Profit and Loss account are considered as free reserves in total.

Solution 1 (c).

(I) CALCULATION OF LIABILITY OF UNDERWRITERS (IN SHARES)

	A&Co.	B&Co.	C& Co.	Total
Gross Liability	7,00,000	7,00,000	7,00,000	21,00,000
Less: Firm Underwriting	(1,00,000)	(1,00,000)	(1,00,000)	(3,00,000)
	6,00,000	6,00,000	6,00,000	18,00,000
Less: Marked applications	(5,18,000)	(5,50,000)	(4,72,000)	(15,40,000)
	82,000	50,000	1,28,000	2,60,000
Less: Unmarked applications 1/3 of (17,26,000 – 15,40,000)	(62,000)	(62,000)	(62,000)	(1,86,000)
	20,000	(12,000)	66,000	74,000
Adjustment of B & Co.'s Surplus in 1:1	(6,000)	12,000	(6,000)	—
Liability excluding the firm underwriting	14,000	—	60,000	74,000
Add: Firm Underwriting	1,00,000	1,00,000	1,00,000	3,00,000
Total liability	1,14,000	1,00,000	1,60,000	3,74,000

(II) CALCULATION OF AMOUNT PAYABLE/RECEIVABLE BY THE UNDERWRITERS

Total liability (No. of shares)	*1,14,000* ₹	*1,00,000* ₹	*1,60,000* ₹
Amount payable @ ₹ 5 (i.e. 3 + 2) per share	5,70,000	5,00,000	8,00,000
Less: Amount paid on firm application @ ₹ 3 per share	(3,00,000)	(3,00,000)	(3,00,000)
Balance payable	2,70,000	2,00,000	5,00,000
Underwriting Commission receivable (7,00,000x10x3%)	(2,10,000)	(2,10,000)	(2,10,000)
Amount payable/(receivable)	60,000	(10,000)	2,90,000

Solution 1 (d).

Dr. **(I) 12% DEBENTURES ACCOUNT** Cr.

Particulars	₹	*Particulars*	₹
To Own Debentures A/c	2,00,000	By Balance b/d	16,00,000
To Bank A/c	14,00,000		
	16,00,000		**16,00,000**

Dr. **(II) DEBENTURE REDEMPTION SINKING FUND ACCOUNT** Cr.

Particulars	₹	*Particulars*	₹
To 9% Stock A/c (loss)	6,400	By Balance b/d	14,98,000
To General Reserve A/c (b.f.)	16,93,200	By Profit and loss A/c	56,800
		By Interest on Sinking Fund A/c	1,42,800
		By Own Debentures A/c	2,000
	16,99,600		**16,99,600**

Working Notes:

(i) Amount of 9% Stock as on 1st April, 2012

Sinking Fund Balance as on 1st April, 2012	₹14,98,000
Less: Own debentures	₹(1,98,000)
	₹13,00,000

(ii) Sales Value of 9% Stock = (₹ 13,20,000/ ₹ 100) × ₹ 98 = ₹ 12, 93,600

(iii) Interest credited to Sinking Fund = (₹ 13,20,000 × 9%) + (₹ 2,00,000 × 12%)= ₹ 1,42,800

Dr. **(IV) OWN DEBENTURES ACCOUNT** Cr.

Particulars	₹	*Particulars*	₹
To Balance b/d	1,98,000	By 12% Debentures A/c	2,00,000
To Sinking Fund A/c	2,000		
	2,00,000		**2,00,000**

Dr. **(V) 9% STOCK ACCOUNT** Cr.

Particulars	₹	*Particulars*	₹
To Balance		By Bank A/c	12,93,600
(Face value 13,20,000)	13,00,000	By Sinking Fund A/c	
		(loss on sales)	6,400
	13,00,000		**13,00,000**

Solution 1 (e).

LIQUIDATOR'S FINAL STATEMENT OF ACCOUNT

Receipts	₹	*Payments*		₹
Assets Realised	20,00,000	Liquidator's remuneration		
Receipt of call money on 29,000 equity shares @2 per share	58,000	2.5% on 23,20,000*	58,000	
		2% on 50,000	1,000	
		2% on 13,12,745	26,255	85,255
		Liquidation Expenses		10,000
		Debenture holders having a floating charge on all assets		6,00,000
		Preferential creditors		50,000
		Unsecured creditors		13,12,745
	20,58,000			20,58,000

(ii) Percentage of amount paid to unsecured creditors to total unsecured creditors

$$= \frac{13,12,745}{18,30,000} \times 100 = 71.73\%$$

Working Notes:

(i) Total assets realised = ₹ 20,00,000 + ₹ 3,20,000 = ₹ 23,20,000

(ii) Unsecured portion in partly secured creditors = ₹ 3,50,000 – ₹ 3,20,000 = ₹ 30,000

(iii) Total unsecured creditors = ₹ 18,00,000 + ₹ 30,000 = ₹ 18,30,000

(iv) Liquidator's remuneration on payment to unsecured creditors

Cash available for unsecured creditors after all payments including payment to preferential creditors & liquidator's remuneration on it = ₹ 13,39,000

Liquidator's remuneration on unsecured creditors = $\frac{2}{102} \times 13,39,000$ = Rs. 26,255

Solution 2.

(i) Calculation of amount of equity shares issued to P and Q

Profit	*P* ₹	*Q* ₹
Ist year	2,62,800	2,75,125
IInd year	2,12,200	2,49,875
Total	4,75,000	5,25,000

No. of shares to be issued = 24,000 equity shares in the proportion of the preceding 2 years profitability

24000 × 475/1000	11,400 equity shares	
24000 × 525/1000		12,600 equity shares

Calculation of amount of 12% Preference shares issued to P and Q

	P	*Q*
Capital Employed	₹ 8,40,000	₹ 9,24,000
8% Return on Capital Employed	₹ 67,200	₹ 73,920
12% Preference shares to be issued $\left[67,200 \times \frac{100}{12}\right]$	₹. 5,60,000	
$\left[73,920 \times \frac{100}{12}\right]$		₹ 6,16,000

Total Purchase Consideration

	P	*Q*
Equity Shares	₹ 2,85,000	₹ 3,15,000
12% Preference Shares	₹ 5,60,000	₹ 6,16,000
Total	₹ 8,45,000	₹ 9,31,000

(II) BALANCE SHEET OF PQ LTD. AS AT 31.3.2013

Particulars	*Note No*	*₹ (lacs)*
I. Equity and Liabilities		
(1) Shareholders' Funds		
(a) Share Capital	1	17,76,000
(b) Reserves and Surplus		—
(2) Non-Current Liabilities		—
(3) Current Liabilities		11,31,100
Total		29,07,100
II. Assets		
(1) Non-Current Assets		
(a) Fixed Assets		
Tangible Assets	2	26,23,000
Intangible Assets [Goodwill]		14,000
(2) Current Assets		2,70,100
Total		29,07,100

Notes To Accounts:

Particulars	₹ (lacs)
1. Share Capital	
24,000 Equity Shares of ₹. 25 each	6,00,000
1,17,600, 12% Pref. Shares of ₹. 10 each	11,76,000
(Of the above all Shares were issued for consideration otherwise than cash)	17,76,000
2. Tangible Assets	
Land & Building	14,23,000
Plant & Machinery	26,23,000
Total	26,23,000

Working Notes:

(i) **Goodwill**

	P ₹	Q ₹
Plant and machinery	5,25,000	6,75,000
Building	7,75,000	6,48,000
Current assets	1,63,500	1,58,600
	14,63,500	14,81,600
Less: Current Liabilities	6,23,500	5,57,600
Net assets taken (capital employed)	8,40,000	9,24,000
Less: Purchase consideration	8,45,000	9,31,000
Goodwill	5,000	7,000
Total purchased goodwill		12,000
Add: Unrealised profitof ₹.10,000 @ 20% ₹. 2,000 is adjusted from current assets and from goodwill (since P & L A/c is not given)		2,000
Total Goodwill		14,000

(ii) Current Assets

	P ₹	Q ₹
Balances before amalgamation	1,63,500	1,58,600
Less: Liabilities of P due to Q	—	50,000
Less: Unrealised Profit on Stock (i.e. ₹ 10,000 × 20%)	2,000	—
Total	1,61,500	1,08,600
Grand Total		2,70,100

(iii) Current Liabilities

	P ₹	Q ₹
Balances before amalgamation	6,23,500	5,57,600
Less: Liabilities of P due to Q	50,000	—
Total	5,73,500	5,57,600
Grand Total		11,31,100

Solution 3 (a).

JOURNAL

(₹ in lakhs)

Date	Particulars		L.F	Dr. (₹)	Cr. (₹)
01.04.2013	9% Redeemable Preference Share Capital A/c Premium on redemption of Preference Shares A/c To Preference Sheraholders A/c (Being preference Share Capital Transferred to shareholders account)	Dr. Dr.		20.00 2.00	 22.00
01.04.2013	Preference Shareholders A/c To Bank A/c (Being payment made to shareholders)	Dr.		22.00	 22.00
01.04.2013	Equity Shares Buy Back A/c To Bank A/c (Being 3 lakhs equity shares of 10 each bought back @ 30 per share)	Dr.		90.00	 90.00
01.04.2013	Equity Share Capital A/c Securities Premium A/c To Equity Shares buy back A/c (Being cancellation of shares bought back)	Dr. Dr.		30.00 60.00	 90.00
01.04.2013	Revenue Reserve A/c (20 + 30) To Capital Redemption Reserve A/c (Being creation of capital redemption reserve account to the extent of the face value of preference shares redeemed and equity shares bought back as per the law)	Dr.		50.00	 50.00
01.04.2013	10% Debentures A/c To Investments (Own Debentures) A/c To Capital Reserve A/c (Being cancellation of own debentures and the Profit on cancellation of debentures t/f to Capital Reserve)	Dr.		2.20	 2.00 0.20
01.04.2013	Bank A/c Employees Stock Option Outstanding (Current liabilities) A/c To Equity Share Capital A/c To Securities Premium A/c (Being the allotment to employees, of 50,000 shares of ₹ 10 each at a premium of ₹ 20 per share in exercise of stock options by employees)	Dr. Dr.		10.00 5.00	 5.00 10.00
01.04.2013	Securities Premium A/c To Premium on Redemption of Preference Shares A/c (Being premium on redemption of preference shares adjusted through securities premium)	Dr.		2.00	 2.00

BALANCE SHEET OF EXTRA LTD. AS AT 01.04.2013

Particulars	Note No	₹ (lacs)
I. Equity and Liabilities		
(1) Shareholders' Funds		
(a) Share Capital (₹ *10 each)[100+5-30]*		75.00
(b) Reserves and Surplus	1	66.20
(2) Non-Current Liabilities [10% Debentures] [4.00 – 2.20]		1.80
(3) Current Liabilities [70 – 5]		65.00
Total		208.00
II. Assets		
(1) Non-Current Assets		
(a) Fixed Assets		
Tangible Assets		50.00
(b) Non-Current Investments [120 – 2]		118.00
(2) Current Assets [142 + 10 – 22 – 90]		40.00
Total		208.00

Notes To Accounts:

Particulars	₹ (lacs)
1. Reserves and Surplus	
Revenue Reserve [50 – 50]	0
Capital Reserve [8.00 + 0.20]	8.20
Capital Redemption Reserve	50.00
Securities Premium [60 + 10 – 60 – 2]	8.00
Total	66.20

Solution 3 (b).

DEPARTMENTAL TRADING ACCOUNT OF SIVA LTD.
for the year ended 31st March 2013

Dr. Cr.

Particulars	Department X ₹	Department Y ₹	Particulars	Department X ₹	Department Y ₹
To Opening Stock	80,000	48,000	By Sales	5,60,000	4,48,000
To Purchases	3,68,000	2,72,000	By Transfers:		
To Carriage inward	8,000	8,000	Purchased goods	32,000	40,000
To Wages	48,000	32,000	Finished goods	1,20,000*	1,12,000*
To Transfers:			By Closing Stock:		
Purchased goods	40,000	32,000	Purchased goods	18,000	24,000
Finished goods	1,12,000	1,20,000	Finished goods	96,000	56,000
To Gross Profit c/d	1,70,000	1,68,000			
	8,26,000	6,80,000		8,26,000	6,80,000

*Net transfers of finished goods by

Department *X* to *Y* = ₹.1,60,000 – ₹ 40,000 = ₹ 1,20,000

Department *Y* to *X* = ₹ 1,40,000 – ₹ 28,000 = ₹ 1,12,000

PROFIT AND LOSS ACCOUNT
for the year ended 31st March, 2013

Dr. | | | Cr.

Particulars	₹	Particulars	₹
To Provision for unrealized profit included in Closing Stock:		By Gross Profit b/d:	
Department X	1,70,000	Department X	7,200
Department Y	1,68,000	Department Y	3,500
To Net Profit	3,27,300		
	3,38,000		3,38,000

Working Notes:

(i) Calculation of Rates of Gross Profit Margin on Sales

	Department X ₹	Department Y ₹
Sales	5,60,000	4,48,000
Add: Transfer of finished goods	1,60,000	1,40,000
	7,20,000	5,88,000
Less: Return of finished goods	(40,000)	(28,000)
	6,80,000	5,60,000
Gross Profit	1,70,000	1,68,000
Gross Profit Margin =	$\frac{1,70,000}{6,80,000} \times 100 = 25\%$	$\frac{1,68,000}{5,60,000} \times 100 = 30\%$

(ii) Finished goods from other department included in the Closing Stock

	Department X ₹	Department Y ₹
Stock of Finished goods	96,000	56,000
Stock related to other department (25% of finished goods)	24,000	14,000

(iii) Unrealized profit included in the closing stock

Department X = 30% of ₹ 24,000 = ₹ 7,200

Department Y = 25% of ₹ 14,000 = ₹ 3,500

Solution 4 (a).

JOURNAL ENTRIES IN THE BOOKS OF *Y* LTD.

		(₹)	(₹)
(i) Equity Share Capital (₹ 10 each) A/c	Dr.	50,00,000	
To Equity Share Capital (₹ 5 each) A/c			25,00,000
To Reconstruction A/c			25,00,000
(Being conversion of 5,00,000 equity shares of ₹ 10 each fully paid into same number of fully paid equity shares of ₹ 5 each as per scheme of reconstruction)			
(ii) 9% Preference Share Capital (₹ 100 each) A/c	Dr.	20,00,000	
To 10% Preference Share Capital (₹ 100 each) A/c		10,00,000	
To Reconstruction A/c			10,00,000
(Being conversion of 9% preference shares of 100 each into same number of 10% preference share of ₹ 50 each and claims of preference dividends settled as per scheme of reconstruction)			
(iii) 10% First Debentures A/c	Dr.	4,00,000	
10% Second Debentures A/c	Dr.	6,00,000	
Trade Creditors A/c	Dr.	1,00,000	
Interest on Debentures Outstanding A/c	Dr.	1,00,000	
Bank A/c	Dr.	1,00,000	
To 12% New Debentures A/c			7,00,000
To Reconstruction A/c			6,00,000
(Being ₹ 6,00,000 due to *A* (Including creditors) cancelled and 12% new debentures allotted for balance amount as per scheme of reconstruction)			
(iv) 10% First Debentures A/c	Dr.	2,00,000	
10% Second Debentures A/c	Dr.	4,00,000	
Trade Creditors A/c	Dr.	50,000	
Interest on Debentures Outstanding A/c	Dr.	60,000	
To 12% New Debentures A/c	Dr.		4,10,000
To Reconstruction A/c			3,00,000
(Being ₹ 3,00,000 due to *B* (including creditors) cancelled and 12% new debentures allotted for balance amount as per scheme of reconstruction)			
(v) Trade Creditors A/c	Dr.	1,75,000	
To Reconstruction A/c			1,75,000
(Being remaining creditors sacrificed 50% of their claim)			
(vi) Directors' Loan A/c	Dr.	1,00,000	
To Equity Share Capital (₹ 5) A/c			60,000
To Reconstruction A/c			40,000
(Being Directors' loan claim settled by issuing 12,000 equity shares of ₹ 5 each as per scheme of reconstruction)			
(vii) Reconstruction A/c	Dr.	15,000	
To Bank A/c			15,000
(Being payment made for cancellation of capital commitments)			

(viii) Bank A/c	Dr.		1,10,000	
To Reconstruction A/c				1,10,000
(Being refund of fees by directors credited to reconstruction A/c				
(ix) Reconstruction A/c	Dr.		10,000	
To Bank A/c				10,000
(Being payment of reconstruction expenses)				
(x) Provision for Tax A/c	Dr.		1,00,000	
To Bank A/c				80,000
To Reconstruction A/c				20,000
(Being payment of tax for 80% of liability in full settlement)				
(xi) Reconstruction A/c	Dr.		47,20,000	
To Goodwill A/c				10,00,000
To Patent A/c				5,00,000
To Profit and Loss A/c				15,00,000
To Discount on issue of Debentures A/c				1,00,000
To Land and Building A/c				2,00,000
To Plant and Machinery A/c				6,00,000
To Furniture and Fixture A/c				1,00,000
To Computers Alc				1,20,000
To Trade Investment Alc				1,00,000
To Stock A/c				3,00,000
To Debtors A/c				2,00,000
(Being Writing off of losses and reduction in the value of assets as per scheme of reconstruction)				

Working Notes:

(i) *Outstanding interest on debentures have been allocated between A and B as follows:*

	A ₹	*B* ₹	Total
10% First Debentures	4,00,000	2,00,000	
10% Second Debentures	6,00,000	4,00,000	
	10,00,000	6,00,000	
Interest @ 10%	1,00,000	60,000	1,60,000

(II) BANK ACCOUNT

Dr. Cr.

	₹		₹
To A (reconstruction)	1,00,000	By Balance b/d	1,00,000
To Reconstruction A/c (paid by directors)	1,10,000	By Reconstruction A/c (Capital commitment penalty paid)	15,000
		By Reconstruction A/c (reconstruction expenses paid)	10,000
		By Provision for tax A/c (tax paid)	80,000
		By Balance c/d	5,000
	2,10,000		2,10,000

(iii) *Capital Reduction or Reorganisation Account can also be used in place of Reconstruction Account.*

Solution 4 (b).

WELL LIFE ASSURANCE CO. LTD.
Valuation Balance Sheet as at March 31, 2013

Particulars	₹	Particulars	₹
Net Liability as per actuarial valuation	75,00,000	Life Fund as per Balance Sheet	90,00,000
Surplus (Bal. Fig.)	15,00,000		
	90,00,000		90,00,000

Net Profit for valuation period:

	₹
A. Surplus as per valuation balance sheet	15,00,000
B. *Add:* Interim Bonus distributed	1,50,000
C. *Less:* Surplus in the beginning	(9,00,000)
D. Net Profit for the valuation period	7,50,000

Distribution of Surplus

A. Total Surplus	16,50,000
B. *Less:* Surplus to be carried forward	10,00,000
	6,50,000
C. Shareholders (5% of ₹.6,50,000)	32,500
D. Policy holders (95% of ₹.6,50,000)	6,17,500
E. *Less:* Interim bonus already distributed	1,50,000
F. Bonus still due to Policy holders	4,67,500

Solution 5 (a).

JAWAHAR BANK LIMITED
PROFIT & LOSS ACCOUNT FOR THE YEAR ENDED 31ST MARCH, 2013

Particulars	Schedule	₹ '000s
I. Income		
Interest earned	13	60.46
Other income	14	16.49
Total		76.95
II. Expenditure		
Interest expended	15	27.20
Operating expenses	16	23.23
Provisions & Contingencies (Refer W.N.)		1880.61
Total		1931.04
III. Profit/Loss		(1854.09)
IV. Appropriations		Nil

Schedule 13 - Interest Earned

	Rs'000s
Interest/discount on advances bills	
Interest on term loans [17.26 – (4.52 – 2.04)]	14.78
Interest on cash credits and overdrafts (38.54 – 8.39)	30.15
Income on investments	15.53
	60.46

Note: Interest on non-performing assets is recognized on receipt basis.

Schedule 14 - Other Income

	Rs'000s
Commission, exchange and brokerage	1.97
Profit on sale of investments	11.76
Profit on revaluation of investments	2.76
	16.49

Schedule 15 - Interest Expended

	Rs'000s
Interest on deposits	27.20

Schedule 16 - Operating Expenses

	Rs'000s
Payments to and provision for employees - salaries, bonus and allowances	18.75
Rent, taxes and lighting	1.70
Printing & stationery	0.75
Director's fee, allowances and expenses	1.33
Law charges	0.22
Repairs & maintenance	0.18
Insurance	0.30
	23.23

Working Note:

Provisions & Contingencies		₹ '000s
Provision for non-performing assets*		
Sub-standard (15 × 15%)		2.25
Doubtful for one year (7 × 25%)		1.75
Doubtful for two years (2. 40 x 40%)		0.96
Loss Assets (0.65 × 100%)		0.65
		5.61
Diminution in the value of current Investments:		
Cost 75% of ₹ 3,700 thousands**	27,75	
Less: Market value	(900)	1875.00
		1880.61

Note: It is assumed that all sub-standard and doubtful assets are fully secured.

**25% of investments classified as 'held for maturity' need not be marked to market as per RBI Guidelines. However, the remaining 75% investments have been marked to market according to RBI Guidelines.

Solution 5 (b).

FORM B – RA

NAME OF THE INSURER : KRISHNA GENERAL INSURANCE COMPANY

REGISTRATION NO. AND DATE OF REGISTRATION WITH IRDA : ....

Revenue Account for the year ended 31.3.2013

Particulars	*Schedule*	₹
1. Premium earned (Net)	1	27,03,000
2. Profit/Loss on sales/Redemption of investment	–	–
3. Other	–	–
4. Interest, dividend & rent (Gross)	–	30,000
Total (A)		27,33,000
1. Claims incurred (Net)	2	19,44,000
2. Commission	3	68,400
3. Operating expenses related to insurance business	4	1,20,000
Total (B)		21,32,400
Operating profit/Loss from insurance business (C) = (A – B)		6,00,600

Schedule – 1 **Premium Earned (Net)**

Particulars	₹
Premium received from direct business	30,60,000
Add: Premium on reinsurance accepted (2,40,000 + 36,000 – 24,000)	2,52,000
	33,12,000
Less: Premium on reinsurance ceded (3,60,000 + 42,000 – 30,000)	3,72,000
Net Premium	29,40,000
Adjustment for change in reserve for unexpired risk	2,37,000
Total premium earned (Net)	27,03,000

Schedule – 2 **Claims Incurred (Net)**

Particulars	₹
Claims paid (Direct)	18,00,000
Add: Legal expenses regarding claims	12,000
	18,12,000
Add: Reinsurance Accepted	1,80,000
	19,92,000
Less: Reinsurance ceded (1,20,000 + 12,000 –18,000)	1,14,000
	18,78,000
Add: Claims outstanding at the end (1,20,000 + 18,000)	1,38,000
	20,16,000
Less: Claims outstanding at the beginning (60,000 + 12,000)	72,000
Total Claim incurred	19,44,000

Schedule –3 Commission

Particulars	₹
Commission paid Direct	72,000
Add: Re-insurance accepted	10,800
	82,800
Less: Re-insurance ceded	14,400
Net Commission	68,400

Schedule – 4 Operating Expenses related to Insurance Business

Particulars	₹
Expenses of management (1,32,000 – 12,000)	1,20,000
	1,20,000

Working Notes :

(i) Calculation of premium received from direct business

	₹
Premium on direct business	30,00,000
Add: Premium outstanding at the end	2,40,000
Less: Premium outstanding at the beginning	1,80,000
	30,60,000

(ii) Computation of change in reserve for unexpired risk

Closing Reserve for unexpired risk (29,40,000 × 50%)	14,70,000
Add: Closing Additional reserve for unexpired risk (29,40,000 × 5%)	1,47,000
Less: Opening Reserve for unexpired risk (24,00,000 × 50%)	12,00,000
Opening Additional reserve for unexpired risk (24,00,000 × 7.5%)	1,80,000
	2,37,000

Solution 6.

Dr. **(i) TRADING AND PROFIT & LOSS A/C (IN DOLLARS)** *Cr.*

Particulars	₹	Particulars	₹
To Opening Stock	11,200	By Sales	84,000
To Goods from H.O.	64,000	By Closing Stock	8,000
To Gross Profit c/d	16,800		
	92,000		92,000
To Expenses	5,000	By Gross Profit b/d	16,800
To Depreciation	2,400		
To Manager's Commission	448		
To Net Profit c/d	8,952		
	16,800		16,800

(II) (A) CONVERTED TRIAL BALANCE

Particulars	Rate per Re.	Dr. (₹)	Cr. (₹)
Machinery	48	11,52,000	
Opening Stock	46	5,15,200	
Goods from H.O.	—	29,26,000	
Sales	47	—	39,48,000
Expenses	47	2,35,000	—
Debtors & Creditors	48	2,30,400	1,63,200
H.O. A/c	—	—	8,60,000
Cash at Bank	—	57,600	—
Difference of Exchange	—	—	1,45,000
	—	51,16,200	51,16,200
Closing Stock $ 8,000 (W.N.2)	48		₹ 3,84,000

(B) TRADING AND PROFIT & LOSS ACCOUNT

Dr. Cr.

Particulars	₹	Particulars	₹
To Opening Stock	5,15,200	By Sales	39,48,000
To Goods from H.O.	29,26,000	By Closing Stock	3,84,000
To Gross Profit c/d	8,90,800		
	43,32,000		43,32,000
To Expenses	2,35,000	By Gross Profit b/d	8,90,000
To Depreciation @ 10% on ₹ 11,52,000	1,15,200	By Exchange difference	1,45,000
To Manager's Commisson (W.N.1)	21,504		
To Net Profit c/d	6,63,296		
	10,35,000		10,35,000

Working Notes:

(i) Manager's Commission = 5/105 of [16,800 – (5,000 + 2,400] = $ 448 (approx)

Manager's commission in Rupees = $ 448 × 48 = ₹ 21,504

(ii) *Calculation of Closing Stock*

Opening Stock	11,200
Add: Goods from H.O.	64,000
Less: Cost of Goods Sold (at invoice price) [100/125 × 84,000]	(67,200)
Closing Stock	8,000

(iii) Alternatively, Manager's Commission may be calculated on Profit before charging Commission.

Solution 7 (a).

(i) Computation of Average Accumulated Expenses

	₹
₹ 2,00,000 × 12/12	= 2,00,000
₹ 2,50,000 × 9/12	= 1,87,500
₹ 4,50,000 × 6/12	= 2,25,000
₹ 1,20,000 × 1/12	= 10,000
	6,22,500

(ii) Calculation of Average Interest rate other than for Specific Borrowings

Amount of loan (in ₹)	*Rate of interest*		*Ampount of interest (in ₹)*
5,00,000	11%	=	55,000
9,00,000	13%	=	1,17,000
14,00,000			1,72,000
Weighted average rate of interest $\left(\frac{1,72,000}{1,40,000} \times 100\right)$		=	12.285% (approx)

(iii) Interest on Average Accumulated Expenses

Specific borrowings (₹ 1,00,000 × 10%)	= 10,000
Non-specific borrowings (₹ 5,22,500 × 12.285%)	= 64,189
Amount of interest to be capitalized	= 74,189

(iv) Total Expenses to be capitalized for building

	₹
Cost of building ₹(2,00,000 + 2,50,000 + 4,50,000 + 1,20,000)	10,20,000
Add: Amount of interest to be capitalised	74,189
	10,94,189

(v) Journal Entry

Date	Particulars	Dr. (₹)	Cr. (₹)
31.03.2012	Building account Dr. To Bank account (Being amount of cost of building and borrowing cost thereon capitalized)	10,94,189	 10,94,189

Solution 7 (b).

AS 19	As per AS 19, "Leases', a lease will be classified as finance lease if at the inception of the lease, the present value of minimum lease payments amounts to at least substantially equal to the fair value of leased asset.
Advice	1. The given lease agreement is an **operating lease** since: (a) the present value of minimum lease payment amounts [₹ 10.08 lakhs (i.e.₹ 3 lakhs × 3.36)] is substantially less than the fair value of leased asset(i.e ₹ 30 lakhs.) (b) the lease term (5 years) is substantially less than economic life of the asset (15 years) 2. Therefore, Lease payments under an **operating lease** should be recognized as an **expense** in the statement of profit and loss on a straight line basis over the lease term unless another systematic basis is more representative of the time pattern of the user's benefit.

Solution 7 (c).

Earning per share

Basic EPS 2011-12 = ₹ 11,40,000/5,00,000 shares = ₹ 2.28

Basic EPS 2012-13 = ₹ 22,50,000/10,00,000 shares = ₹ 2.25

Adjusted EPS 2011-12 = ₹ 11,40,000/10,00,000 shares = ₹ 1.14

Since the bonus issue is an issue without consideration, the issue is treated as if it has occurred prior to the beginning of the year 2011-12, the earliest period reported.

Solution 7 (d).

Accounting Treatment

Item	Provision of AS 26	Accounting Treatment
Reserach Expenses	As per AS 26 no intangible asset arising from research (or from the research phase of an internal project) should be recognised. Expenditure on research (or on the research phase of an internal project) should be recognised as an expense when it is incurred.	₹ 592.23 crores incurred on research till the end of financial year ended 31st March, 2011 cannot be capitalised and hence has to expensed in the year in which it is incrred. In case the same is still unexpensed it will have to be written off under 'Prior period Expenditure'.
Developement Expenditure	As per para 44 of the standard, an intangible asset arising from development (or from the development phase of an internal project) should be recognised if, and only if, an enterprise can demonstrate all of the conditions specified in the standard.	Development cost of ₹ 322.26 crores is eligible for capitalization assuming that the enterprise can demonstrate all the specified conditions.
Carrying Amount	As per AS 26, after initial recognition, an intangible asset should be carried at its cost less any accumulated amortization and any accumulated impairment losses.	Present value of future cash flows amounting ₹ 306.26 crores [(₹ 100 crores × 0.893) + (₹ 80 crores × 0.797) + (₹ 80 crores × 0.712) + (₹ 80 crores × 0.636) + (₹ 80 crores × 0.567)] is less than the cost incurred, it is prudent to carry the intangible asset at the discounted value of future cash flows (₹ 306.26 crores). The excess of cost incurred over present values amounting ₹ 16 crores (322.26 – 306.26) has to be recognised as an impairment loss in the year 2011-12.
Depreciation Amount	As per AS 26 depreciable amount of an intangible asset should be allocated on a systematic basis over the best estimate of its useful life. There is a rebuttable presumption that the useful life of an intangible asset will not exceed 10 years from the date when the asset is available for use. Amortization should commence when the asset is available for use.	The value of intangible asset should be amortized over a period of 5 years by following the straight line method. Therefore, an annual depreciatoon of ₹ 61.25 crores ₹ 306.26 (₹ 306.26 crores/5) should be charged for each year beginning with 2011-12.

Solution 7 (e).

As per AS 29 Contingent Liability should be disclosed in the financial statements if following conditions are satisfied:

1. There is a present obligation arising out of past events but not recognized as provision.
2. It is not probable that an outflow of resources emodying economic benefits will be required to settle the obligation.
3. The possibility of an outflow of resources embodying economic benefits is also remote.
4. The amount of the obligation cannot be measured with sufficient reliability to be recognized as provision.

In this case, the probability of winning first 10 cases is 60% and for remaining five cases is 50%. In other words, probability of losing the cases is 40% and 50% respectively. According to AS 29, we make a provision if the loss is probable. As the loss does not appear to be probable and the probability or possibility of an outflow of resources embodying economic benefits is not remote rather there is reasonable possibility of loss, therefore, disclosure by way of note of contingent liability amount may be calculated as under:

Expected loss in first ten cases	= [₹ 90,000 × 0.3 + ₹ 2,00,000 × 0.1] × 10
	= [₹ 27,000 + ₹ 20,000] × 10
	= ₹ 47,000 × 10 = ₹ 4,70,000
Expected loss in remaining five cases	= [₹ 60,000 × 0.3 + ₹ 1,00,000 × 0.2] × 5
	= [₹ 18,000 + ₹ 20,000] × 5
	= ₹ 38,000 × 5 = ₹ 1,90,000
Total Contingent Liability	= ₹ 4,70,000 + ₹ 1,90,000 = ₹ 6,60,000.

SECTION 4

PAPER 5: ADVANCED ACCOUNTING [GROUP-II]

IPC EXAMINATION PAPERS

Paper-5: Advanced Accounting
CA IPC (Group II)
Examination (November 2012)

Question No. 1 is compulsory.
Attempt any Five questions from the remaining Six questions
Wherever necessary suitable assumptions may be made by the candidates.
Working notes should form part of the answer.

Q.1 Answer the following questions: **[4 × 5 = 20]**

(a) A loan account remains out of order as on the date of Balance Sheet of a Bank. The account has been classified as doubtful assets (upto 1 year).

Details of the accounts are:

Outstanding	₹ 6,73,000
ECGC coverage	25% (Limited to ₹ 1,00,000)
Value of security held	₹ 1,50,000

Compute the necessary provision to be made by a bank as per applicable rates.

(b) ABC Ltd. came up with public issue of 3,00,000 Equity Shares of ₹ 10 each ₹ 15 per share. P, Q and R took underwriting of the issue in ratio of 3 : 2 : 1 with the provisions of firm underwriting of 20,000, 14,000 and 10,000 shares respectively.

Applications were received for 2,40,000 shares excluding firm underwriting. The marked applications from public were received as under:

P - 60,000; Q-50,000; R-60,000

Compute the liability of each underwriter as regards the number of shares to be taken up assuming that the benefit of firm underwriting is not given to individual underwriters.

(c) A company acquired for its internal use a software on 28.01.2012 from the USA for US $ 1,00,000. The exchange rate on that date was ₹ 52 per USD. The seller allowed trade discount @ 5%. The other expenditure were:

(i) Import Duty: 20%

(ii) Purchase Tax: 10%

(iii) Entry Tax : 5% (Recoverable later from tax department)

(iv) Installation expenses : ₹ 25,000

(v) Profession fees for Clearance from Customs : ₹ 20,000

Compute the Cost of Software to be capitalized.

(d) Give Journal entires in the books of Head Office to rectify or adjust the following:

(i) Goods set to Branch ₹ 12,000 stolen during transit. Branch manager refused to accept any liability.

(ii) Branch paid ₹ 15,000 as salary to the office of Head Office on his visit to the branch.

(iii) On 28th March, 2012, the H.O. dispatched goods to the Branch invoiced at ₹ 25,000 which was not received by Branch till 31st March, 2012.

(iv) A remittance of ₹ 10,000 set by the branch on 30th March, 2012, received by the Head Office on 1st April, 2012.

(v) Head Office made payment of ₹ 25,000 for purchase of goods by Branch and wrongly debited its own purchase account.

Q.2. P, Q and R are partners sharing profits and losses in the ratio 3 : 2 : 1 after allowing interest on capital @ 9% p.a. Their balance Sheet as at 31st March, 2012 are as follows:

Liabilities	*(₹)*	*Assets*	*(₹)*
Capital Accounts:		Plant & Machinery	1,08,000
P	50,000	Fixtures	20,000
Q	30,000	Stock	50,000
R	20,000	Sundry Debtors	30,000
Reserve Fund	60,000		
Creditors	48,000		
	2,08,000		2,08,000

The applied for conversion of the firm into a Private Limited Company named PQR Pvt. Ltd. and the certificate was received on 01-04-2012. They decided to maintain same profit sharing ratio and the preserve the priority in regard to repayment of capital as far as possible. For that purpose they decided to insert a clause of issuance of Preference shares in Memorandum of Association in addition to issuance of Equity Shares of ₹ 10 each.

On 01.04.2012, the value of goodwill is to be determined on the basis of 2 years' purchase of the average profit from the business of the last 5 years. The particulars of profits are as under:

		₹
Year ended 31.03.2008	Profit	10,000
Year ended 31.03.2009	Loss	5,000
Year ended 31.03.2010	Profit	18,000
Year ended 31.03.2011	Profit	27,000
Year ended 31.03.2012	Profit	30,000

The loss for the year ended 31-03-2009 was on account of loss by strike to the extent of ₹ 10,000.

It was agreed that rest of the assets are valued on the basis of the Balance Sheet as at 31-03-2012 except Plant & machinery which is valued at ₹ 1,02,000.

You are required to prepare (a) the Balance Sheet of the Company as at 01.04.2012, (b) Partners' Capital Accounts and (c) Statement showing the final settlement between the partners taking Q's capital as basis. **16**

Q.3 (a) M Ltd. furnishes the followinh summarized Balance Sheet as at 31st March, 2013:

Equity & Liabilities	*Rs' 000*	*Assets*	*Rs' 000*
Share Capital: Authorised *Issued and Subscribed* 3,00,000, Equity Shares of ₹ 10 each	3,000	Fixed Assets (at cost *less* depreciation) Non-Current Investments Current Assets	2,750 5,000 4,000

20,000, 9% Preference Shares of ₹ 100 each fully paid up Issued two months back for buy back purposes)	2,000	
Reserves and Surplus:		
Capital Reserve	10	
Revenue Reserve	4,000	
Securities Premium	500	
Profit and Loss A/c	1,800	
Non-Current Liabilities:		
10% Convertible Debentures	400	
Current Liabilities	40	
	11,750	11,750

(1) The company passed a resolution to buy back 20% of its equity capital @ ₹ 15 per share. For this purpose, it sold its investments of ₹ 30 lakhs for ₹ 25 lakhs.

(2) The company redeemed the preference shares at a premium of 10% on 1st April, 2013.

(3) Included in its investments were 'Investments in own debentures' costing ₹ 3 lakhs (face value ₹ 3.30 lakhs). These debentures were cancelled on 1st April, 2013.

You are required to pass necessary Journal entries and prepare the Balance Sheet on 01.04.2013. **12**

(b) Define the term Finance Lease. State any three situations when a lease would be classified as finance lease. **4**

Q.4. Following are the Balance Sheets as at March 31, 2013:

(₹ '000)

Liabilities	K Ltd.	W Ltd.	Assets	K Ltd.	W Ltd.
Share capital:			Goodwill	20	—
Equity Shares of			Other Fixed Assets	2,400	1,150
₹ 100 each	2,000	1,500	Debtors	625	615
9% Preference Shares of			Stock	412	680
₹ 100 each	700	400	Cash at bank	38	155
General Reserve	240	170	Own debentures		
Profit & Loss A/c	—	15	[Nominal value		
12% Debentures of			₹ 2,00,000]	192	—
₹ 100 each	600	200	Discount on issue of		
Sundry Creditors	560	315	debentures	2	—
			Profit & Loss A/c	411	—
	4,100	2,600		4,100	2,600

On 1.4.2013, K Ltd. adopted the following scheme of reconstruction:

(a) Each equity share shall be sub-divided into 10 equity shares of ₹ 10 each fully paid up. 50% of the equity share capital would be surrendered to the company.

(b) Preference dividends are in arrear for 3 years. Preference shareholders agreed to waive 80% of the dividend claim and accept payment for the balance.

(c) Own debentures of ₹ 80,000 were sold at ₹ 98 own-interest and remaining own debentures were cancelled.

(d) Debentureholders of ₹ 3,00,000 agreed to accept one machinery of book value of ₹ 3,20,000 in full settlement.

(e) Creditors, Debtors and Stocks were valued at ₹ 5,00,000 , ₹ 6,00,000 and ₹ 4,00,000 respectively. The goodwill, discount on issue of Debentures & Profit and Loss (Dr.) are to be written off.

(f) The Company paid ₹ 20,000 as penalty to avoid capital commitments of ₹ 4,00,000.

On 2.4.2013 a scheme of absorption was adopted. K Ltd. would take over W Ltd. The purchase consideration was fixed as below:

(i) Equity shareholders of W Ltd. will be given 50 equity shares of ₹ 10 each fully paid up, in exchange for every 5 shares held in W Ltd.

(ii) Issue of 10% Preference Shares of ₹ 100 each in the ratio of 4 Preference Shares of K Ltd. for every 5 Preference Shares held in W Ltd.

(iii) Issue of one 12% Debentures of ₹ 100 each of K Ltd. for every 12% Debentures in W Ltd.

Required: Give journal entries in the books of K Ltd. and draw the resultant Balance Sheet as at 2nd April, 2013. **16**

Q.5. (a) The following are the figures extracted from the books of KLM Bank Limited as on 31.3.2013:

	₹
Interest and discount received	38,00,160
Interest paid on deposits	22,95,360
Issued and Subscribed capital	10,00,000
Salaries and allowances	2,50,000
Directors fee and allowances	35,000
Rent and Taxes paid	1,00,000
Postage and Telegrams	65,340
Statutory Reserve Fund	8,00,000
Commission, Exchange and Brokerage	1,90,000
Rent received	72,000
Profit on sale of Investments	2,25,800
Depreciation on Bank's properties	40,000
Statutory Expenses	38,000
Preliminary Expenses	30,000
Auditor's Fees	12,000

The following further information is given:

(i) A customer to whom a sum of ₹ 10 lakhs has been advanced has become insolvent and it is expected only 55% can be recovered from his estate.

(ii) There were also other debts for which a provision of ₹ 2,00,000 was found necessary by the auditors.

(iii) Rebate on Bills discounted on 31.3.2012 was ₹ 15,000 and on 31.3.2013 was ₹ 20,000.

(iv) Provide ₹ 2,00,000 for Income-tax.

(v) The Directos desire to declare 5% dividend.

Required: Prepare the Profit and Loss account of KLM Bank Limited for the year ended 31.3.2013 and also show, how the Profit and Loss account will appear in the Balance Sheet, if the Profit and Loss account opening balance was Nil as on 31.3.2012. **8**

Q.5. (b) Prepare the Fire Insurance Revenue A/c as per IRDA regulations for the year ended 31st March, 2013 from the following details:

	₹
Claims paid	5,00,000
Legal expenses regarding claims	10,000
Premiums received	12,50,000
Re-insurance premium paid	50,000
Commission	3,00,000
Expenses of Management	2,00,000
Provision against unexpired risk on 1st April, 2012	5,75,000
Claims unpaid on 1st April, 2012	50,000
Claims unpaid on 31st March, 2013	80,000

Provision against unexpired risk @ 50% **less** Re-insurance **8**

Q.6. (a) Himalayas Ltd. had ₹ 10,00,000, 8% Debentures of ₹ 100 each as on 31st March, 2012. The company purchased in the open market following debentures for immediate cancellation:

On 01-07-2012-1,000 Debentures @ ₹ 97 (cum interest)

On 29-02-2013-1,800 Debentures @ ₹ 99 (ex interest)

Debenture interest due date is 30th September and 31st March.

Give Journal Entries in the books of the company for the year ended 31st March, 2013. **8**

Q.6. (b) Department *X* sells goods to Department *Y* at a profit of 20% on cost and to Department *Z* at 15% profit on cost. Department *Y* sells goods to *X* and *Z* at a profit of 10% and 20% on sales, respectively. Department *Z* charges 15% and 10% profit on cost to Department *X* and *Y*, respectively.

Department Managers are entitled to 10% commission on net profit after eliminating unrealised profit on departmental sales being eliminated. Departmental profits after charging Managers' commission, but before adjustment of unrealised profit are as under:

	₹
Department *X*	36,000
Department *Y*	27,000
Department *Z*	18,000

Stocks lying at different departments at the end of the year are as under:

	Dept. X ₹	*Dept. Y* ₹	*Dept. Z* ₹
Transfer from Department *X*	—	7,200	5,750
Transfer from Department *Y*	19,000	—	15,000
Transfer from Department *Z*	4,600	3,300	—

Required: Find out the correct departmental Profits after charging Managers' commission. **8**

Q.7. *Answer any* **four** *of the following:* **[4 × 4 = 16]**

(a) Annual lease rent = ₹ 40,000 at the end of each year

Lease period = 5 years

Guaranteed Residual Value = ₹ 14,000

Five value at the inception (beginning) of lease = ₹ 1,50,000

Interest rate implict on lease is 12.6%. The present value factors at 12.6% are 0.89, 0.79, 0.7, 0.622, 0.552 at the end of first, second, third, fourth and fifth year respectively.

Show the Journal entry to record the asset taken on finance lease in the books of the lessee.

(b) A new Plant X was acquired in exchange of old Plant B and on payment of ₹ 20,000. The carrying amount of the old Plant B was ₹ 1,75,000 (Historical cost less depreciation). The fair value of the Plant B on the date of exchange was ₹ 1,50,000.

Suggest the accounting entry in the books of the enterprise

(c) A company is in a dispute involving allegation of infringement of patents by a competitor company who is seeking damages of a huge sum of ₹ 900 lakhs. The directors are of the opinion that the claim can be successfully resisted by the company. How would you deal the same in the annual accounts of the company?

(d) State the conditions of issuance of Sweat Equity Shares by Joint Stock Companies.

(e) Give two examples of each of the following items:

(i) Change in Accounting Policy

(ii) Change in Accounting Estimate

(iii) Extra Ordinary Items

(iv) Prior Period Items.

Answers to IPC Examination Paper Nov. 2012

Solution 1.

(a) **Computation of Provision**

	₹
Doubtful Assets (upto 1 year)	6,73,000
Less: Value of security (excluding ECGC cover)	(1,50,000)
	5,23,000
Less: ECGC coverage (limited to ₹ 1,00,000)	(1,00,000)
Unsecured portion	4,23,000
Provision: for unsecured portion @100% on ₹ 2,23,000	4,23,000
for secured portion @ 25% on ₹ 1,50,000	37,000
Total provision to be made in the books of the bank	4,60,500

(b) Calculation of Liability of each Underwriter (in No. of Shares) assuming that the benefit of firm underwriting is not given to Individual Underwriters

Particulars	*P*	*Q*	*R*	*Total*
Gross Liability	1,50,000	1,00,000	50,000	3,00,000
Less: Marked Applications (excluding firm underwriting)	(60,000)	(50,000)	(60,000)	(1,70,000)
Balance	90,000	50,000	(10,000)	1,30,000
Less: Surplus of R allocated to P and Q in the ratio of 3.2	(6,000)	(4,000)	10,000	
Balance	84,000	46,000	–	1,30,000
Less: Unmarked applications including firm underwriting (Refer W.N.)	(57,000)	(38,000)	(19,000)	(1,14,000)
Net Liability	27,000	8,000	(19,000)	16,000
Less: Surplus of R allocated to P and Q in the ratio of 3 : 2	(11,400)	(7,600)	19,000	
	15,600	400	–	16,000
Add: Firm underwriting	20,000	14,000	10,000	44,000
Total Liability	35,600	14,400	10,000	60,000

Working Note:

A. Applications received from public	2,40,000
B. *Add:* Shares underwritten firm (20,000 + 14,000 + 10,000)	44,000
C. Total Applciations [A + B]	2,84,000
D. *Less:* Marked applications (60,000 + 50,000 + 60,000)	(1,70,000)
E. Unmarked applications including firm underwriting [C – D]	1,14,000

(c) Calculation of cost of software (intangible asset) acquired for internal use

	₹
Purchase cost of the software	$ 1,00,000
Less: Trade discount @ 5%	($ 5,000)
	$ 95,000

Cost in ₹ (US $ 95,000 × ₹ 52)	₹ 49,40,000
Add: Import duty on cost @ 20% (₹)	9,88,000
	59,28,000
Purchase tax @ 10% (₹)	5,92,800
Installation expenses (₹)	25,000
Profession free for clearance from customs (₹)	20,000
Cost of the software to be capitalised (₹)	65,65,800

Note: Entry Tax being a recoverable/refundable tax has not included as part of the cost of the asset.

(d) **Journal of Head Office**

Date	*Particulars*	*L.F*	*Dr. (₹)*	*Cr. (₹)*
(i)	Loss in transit A/c Dr.		12,000	
	To Purchases A/c			12,000
	(Being the Goods lost on account of theft during transit)			
(ii)	Salaries A/c Dr.		15,000	
	To Branch A/c			15,000
	(Being salary paid by the branch for H.P. employee)			
(iii)	No entry in the books of head office for goods sent to branch not received by branch till 31st March			
(iv)	Cash in transit A/c Dr.		10,000	
	To Branch A/c			10,000
	(Being remittance by branch not received by 31st March)			
(v)	Branch A/c Dr.		25,000	
	To Purchases A/c			25,000
	(Being rectification of entry for payment for goods purchased by branch wrongly debited to Purchase A/c)			

Note: In entry (i), it is assumed that refusal of branch manager (to accept liability of stolen goods) is accepted by the Head Office. Alternatively, Branch account will be credited on the basis of assumption that refusal of branch manager is not accepted by the Head Office.

Solution 2.

(a) **Balance Sheet of the PQR Pvt Ltd. as at 1.4.2012**

Particulars	Note No.	(₹)
I. EQUITY AND LIABILITIES		
(1) Shareholders' Funds		
(a) Share Capital	1	1,90,000
(2) Non-Current Liabilities		
(3) Current Liabilities		
(a) Trade Payables		48,000
Total		2,38,000

II. ASSETS		
(1) Non-Current Assets		
(a) Fixed Assets		
(i) Tangible Assets	2	1,22,000
(ii) Intangible Assets	3	36,000
(2) Current Assets		
(a) Inventories		50,000
(b) Trade Receivables		30,000
Total		2,38,000

Notes To Accounts:

1. Share Capital

Authorised Capital	
18,000 Equity Shares of ₹ 10 each	1,80,000
9% Pref. Shares of ₹ 100 each	10,000
	1,90,000
Issued & Subscribed Capital	
18,000 Equity Shares of ₹ 10 each	1,80,000
9% Pref. Shares of ₹ 100 each	10,000
(All the shares have been issued for consideration other than cash)	1,90,000
2. Tangible Assets	
Plant and Machinery	1,02,000
Fixtures	20,000
	1,22,000
3. Intangible Asset	
Goodwill	36,000

(b) *Dr.* **Capital Accounts of Partners** *Cr.*

Particulars	*P* ₹	*Q* ₹	*R* ₹	*Particulars*	*P* ₹	*Q* ₹	*R* ₹
To P & M A/c	3,000	2,000	1,000	By Balance b/d	50,000	30,000	20,000
To 9% Preference Shares	5,000	–	5,000	By Reserve fund	30,000	20,000	10,000
To Equity Shares	90,000	60,000	30,000	By Realization A/c (Profit on Sale of Business)	18,000	12,000	6,000
	98,000	62,000	36,000		98,000	62,000	36,000

The question of preference and equity shares to be issued to *P*, *Q* and *R* can be dealt with in the following manner:

Particulars	*P* ₹	*Q* ₹	*R* ₹
A. Total amount due as capital	95,000	60,000	35,000
B. Proportionate Capitals taking *Q*'s Capital as the Base Capital (for which Equity Shares should be issued)	90,000	60,000	30,000
C. Surplus Capital (A – B) (for which 9% Non-Cum Pref. Shares should be issued)	5,000	–	5,000

The above treatment is based on the principle that the function of interest in case of partnership is to compensate those partners who contribute capital in excess of what is required as per profit sharing ratio.

Working Notes: 1. Calculation of goodwill

Particulars	2007-08 ₹	2008-09 ₹	2009-10 ₹	2010-11 ₹	2011-12 ₹
Profits	10,000	(5,000)	18,000	27,000	30,000
Adjustment for abnormal loss in 2008-09	–	10,000	–	–	–
	10,000	5,000	18,000	27,000	30,000
					₹
Total Profit from 2007-08 to 2011-12					90,000
Average Profit (90,000/5)					18,000
Goodwill equal to 2 years' Purchase					36,000

2. Computation of Purchase consideration

	₹
Assets	
Goodwill	36,000
Plant and Machinery	1,02,000
Fixtures	20,000
Stock	50,000
Sundry Debtors	30,000
	2,38,000
Less: Liabilities	
Creditors	48,000
Purchase Consideration	1,90,000

Q3 (a) Solution:

Journal

(₹ in '000)

Date	Particulars		L.F	Dr. (₹)	Cr. (₹)
	Bank A/c	Dr.		2,500	
	Profit and Loss A/c	Dr.		500	
	To Investments A/c	Dr.			3,000
	(Being the investments sold for Buy back)				
	9% Redeemable Preference Share Capital A/c	Dr.		2,000	
	Premium on redemption of Preference Shares A/c	Dr.		200	
	To Preference Sheraholders A/c				2,200
	(Being the amount due to Preference Shareholders)				
	Preference Shareholders A/c	Dr.		2,200	
	To Bank A/c				2,200
	(Being the payment made to Preference Shareholders)				
	Revenue Reserve A/c	Dr.		2,000	
	To Capital Redemption Reserve A/c				2,000
	(Being the creation of Capital Redemption Reserve to the extent of the face value of preference shares redeemed and equity shares bought back as per the law)				
	Equity Share Capital A/c	Dr.		600	
	Securities Premium A/c	Dr.		300	
	To Equity Shares buy back A/c				900
	(Being cancellation of shares bought back)				

	Particulars		Dr. (₹)	Cr. (₹)
	Equity Shares Buy Back A/c Dr. To Bank A/c (Being the payment made for shares bought back)		90.00	90.00
	10% Debentures A/c Dr. To Investments (Own Debentures) A/c To Capital Reserve A/c (Being cancellation of own debentures and T/F of profit on cancellation of debentures)		330	300 30
	Securities Premium A/c Dr. To Premium on Redemption of Preference Shares A/c (Being premium on redemption of preference shares adjusted through securities premium)		200	200

Balance Sheet of M Ltd. as at 01.04.2013

Particulars	Note No	₹ ('000)
I. Equity and Liabilities		
(1) Shareholders' Funds		
(a) Share Capital	1	2,400
(b) Reserves and Surplus	2	5,340
(2) Non-Current Liabilities [10% Debentures] [400 – 330]		70
(3) Current Liabilities [70 – 5]		40
Total		7,850
II. Assets		
(1) Non-Current Assets		
(a) Fixed Assets		2,750
(b) Non-Current Investments [5,000 – 3,000 – 300]		1,700
(2) Current Assets [4,000 + 2,500 – 2,200 – 900]		3,400
Total		7,850

Notes To Accounts:

Particulars	₹ ('000)
1. Share Capital	
Authorised Capital	
2,40,000 Equity Shares of ₹ 10 each	2,400
Issued & Subscribed Capital	
2,40,000 Equity Shares of ₹ 10 each (60,000 Equity Shares bought back)	2,400
2. Reserves and Surplus	
Revenue Reserve [4,000 – 2,000]	2,000
Capital Reserve [10 + 30]	40
Capital Redemption Reserve	2,000
Securities Premium [500 – 200 – 300]	0
Surplus (P & L A/c) [1800 – 500]	1,300
Total	5,340

Q.3. (b) Refer to AS - 19 Leases on Page 16.51 of the Chapter 16 of the main textbook.

Q4 Solution:

Journal

Date	Particulars		L.F.	Dr. (₹)	Cr. (₹)
01.04.13	Equity Share Capital A/c	Dr.		20,00,000	
	To Equity Share Capital A/c				20,00,000
	(Being the sub-division of one share of ₹ 100 each into 10 shares of ₹ 10 each)				
	Equity Share Capital A/c	Dr.		10,00,000	
	To Reconstruction A/c				10,00,000
	(Being the reduction of capital by 50%)				
	Reconstruction A/c	Dr.		42,000	
	To Bank A/c				42,000
	(Being the payment in cash for 20% of arrears of preference dividend)				
	Bank A/c	Dr.		78,400	
	To Own Debentures A/c [(1,92,000/2,00,000) × 80,000]				76,800
	To Reconstruction A/c				1,600
	(Being the T/f of profit on sale of own Debentures)				
	12% Debentures A/c	Dr.		1,20,000	
	To Own debentures A/c [(1,92,000/2,00,000) × 1,20,000]				1,15,200
	To Reconstruction A/c				4,800
	(Being the T/f of profit on cancellation of own Debentures)				
	12.% Debentures A/c	Dr.		3,00,000	
	Reconstruction A/c	Dr.		20,000	
	To Machinery A/c				3,20,000
	(Being the machinery taken up by debentureholders)				
	Reconstruction A/c	Dr.		37,000	
	To Debtors A/c				25,000
	To Stock A/c				12,000
	(Being the Assets revalued)				
	Creditors A/c	Dr.		60,000	
	To Reconstruction A/c				60,000
	(Being the liabilities revalued)				
	Reconstruction A/c	Dr.		4,33,000	
	To Goodwill A/c				20,000
	To Discount on debentures A/c				2,000
	To Profit and Loss A/c				4,11,000
	(Being the losses w/o)				
	Reconstruction A/c	Dr.		20,000	
	To Bank A/c				20,000
	(Being the penalty paid for avoidance of capital commitments)				
	Reconstruction A/c	Dr.		5,14,400	
	To Capital Reserve A/c				5,14,400
	(Being the transfer of Balance to Capital Reserve)				
02.04.13	Business Purchase A/c	Dr.		18,20,000	
	To Liquidators of W Ltd.				18,20,000
	(Being the purchase of business)				

Fixed assets A/c	Dr.	11,50,000	
Stock A/c	Dr.	6,80,000	
Debtors A/c	Dr.	6,15,000	
Cash at bank A/c	Dr.	1,55,000	
To Sundry Ceditors A/c			3,15,000
To 12% Debentures A/c of W Ltd.			2,00,000
To Profit and loss A/c			15,000
To General Reserve A/c ₹ (1,70,000 + 80,000*)			2,50,000
To Business Purchase A/c			18,20,000
(Being the recording over of all assets and liabilities taken over)			
Liquidators of W Ltd. A/c	Dr.	18,20,000	
To Equity share capital A/c			15,00,000
To 10% Preference share capital A/c			3,20,000
(Being the purchase consideration discharged)			
12% Debentures of W Ltd. A/c	Dr.	2,00,000	
To 12% Debentures A/c			2,00,000
(Being the issue of 12% Debentures against Debentures of W Ltd.)			

**₹ 80,000 is the balancing figure adjusted to General Reserve Account as per AS 14 "Accounting for Amalgamation".

Balance Sheet of K Ltd. as at 02.04.2013

Particulars	Note No	₹
I. Equity and Liabilities		
(1) Shareholders' Funds		
(a) Share Capital	1	35,20,000
(b) Reserves and Surplus	2	10,19,400
(2) Non-Current Liabilities [12%Debentures]	3	3,80,000
(3) Current Liabilities		
(a) Trade Payables [Creditors]	4	8,15,000
Total		57,34,400
II. Assets		
(1) Non-Current Assets		
(a) Fixed Assets		
Tangible Assets	5	32,30,000
(2) Current Assets		
(a) Inventories	6	10,80,000
(b) Trade Receivables [Debtors]	7	12,15,000
(c) Cash and Cash Equivalents	8	2,09,400
Total		57,34,400

Notes To Accounts :

Particulars	₹
1. Share Capital	
2,50,000 Equity Shares of ₹ 10 each	25,00,000
10,200,9% Pref. Shares of ₹ 100 each	10,20,000
(Of the above 1,50,000 *Equity* Shares & 3200,*9% Pref. Shares* were issued for consideration otherwise than cash)	35,20,000

2. Reserves and Surplus	
General Reserve (2,40,000 + 2,50,000)	4,90,000
Profit & Loss Account	15,000
Capital Reserve	5,14,400
Total	10,19,400
3. Long-term Borrowings	
12% Debentures	6,00,000
Less: Settled in consideration of machinery	(3,00,000)
Less: Cancelled debentures	(1,20,000)
Add: 12% Debentures issue to W Ltd.	2,00,000
Total	3,80,000
4. Trade Payables	
of K Ltd.	5,60,000
Less: Reduction due to revaluation	(60,000)
Add: Trade Payables of W Ltd.	3,15,000
Total	8,15,000
5. Tangible assets	
Balance of Other Fixed Assets	24,00,000
Less: Machinery taken up by debenture holders	(3,20,000)
Add: Other Fixed Assets of W Ltd.	11,50,000
Total	32,30,000
6. Inventories	
of K Ltd.	4,12,000
Less: Reduction due to revaluation	(12,000)
Add: Inventories of W Ltd.	6,80,000
Total	10,80,000
7. Trade Receivables	
of K Ltd.	6,25,000
Less: Reduction due to revaluation	(25,000)
Add: Trade Receivables of W Ltd.	6,15,000
Total	12,15,000
8. Cash and Cash Equivalents	
of K Ltd.	38,000
Less: Payment of Arrear of Preference dividend	(42,000)
Add: Profit on Sale of own Debentures	78,400
Less: Penalty Paid	(20,000)
Add: Cash and Cash Equivalents of W Ltd.	1,55,000
Total	2,09,400

Working Notes:

(i) *Purchase Consideration:*

	₹
Equity share capital [(15,000 × 50/5) × ₹ 10]	= 15,00,000
9% Preference share capital [(4,000 × 4/5) × ₹ 100]	= 3,20,000
	18,20,000

(ii) *General Reserve:*

	₹
Share capital of W Ltd. (Equity + Preference)	19,00,000
Less: Share capital issued by K Ltd.	18,20,000
General reserve (resulted due to absorption)	80,000

Q5 (a) Solution:

KLM Bank Limited

Profit and Loss Account for the year ended 31st March, 2013

	Particulars	*Schedule*	*Year ended 31.03.2013*
I.	**Income:**		
	Interest earned	13	37,95,160
	Other income	14	4,87,800
	Total		42,82,960
II.	**Expenditure**		
	Interest expended	15	22,95,360
	Operating expenses	16	5,70,340
	Provisions and Contingencies (₹ 4,50,000 + 2,00,000 + 2,00,000)		8,50,000
	Total		37,15,700
III.	**Profits / Losses**		
	Net Profit for the year		5,67,260
	Profit brought forward		NIL
			5,67,260
IV.	**Appropriations**		
	Transfer to Statutory Reserve (25%)		1,41,815
	Proposed Dividend		50,000
	Balance carried over to Balance Sheet		3,75,445
			5,67,260

The Profit & Loss Account balance of ₹ 3,75,445 will appear in the Balance Sheet under the head 'Reserve and Surplus' in Schedule 2.

Schedule 13 – Interest Earned

		Year ended 31.03.2013 ₹
I.	**Income:**	
	Interest earned	37,95,160

Schedule 14 – Other Income

I.	Commission, exchange and brokerage	1,90,000
II.	Profit on sale of investments	2,25,800
III.	Rent received	72,000
		4,87,800

Schedule 15–Interest Expended

I.	Interests on Deposits	22,95,360

Schedule 16 – Operating Expenses

I.	Payment to and provisions for employees	2,50,000
II.	Rent, taxes and lighting	1,00,000
III.	Depreciation on Bank's property	40,000
IV.	Director's fees, allowances and expenses	35,000
V.	Auditor's fees	12,000
VI.	Law (statutory) charges	38,000
VII.	Postage and telegrams	65,340
VIII.	Preliminary expenses*	30,000
		5,70,340

*As per AS 26 Preliminary Expenses have been fully written off.

Working Note:

Interest/discount (net of rebate on bills discounted) (W.N. 1)	38,00,160
Add: Opening Rebate on bills discounted	15,000
Less: Closing Rebate on bills discounted	(20,000)
	37,95,160

Q5 (b) Solution:

FORM B - RA

Name of the Insurer :

Registration No. and Date of Registration with the IRDA

Fire Insurance Revenue Account
For the year ended 31st March, 2013

	Particulars	*Schedule*	*Amount*
1.	Premium earned	1	11,75,000
2.	Other income		—
3.	Interest, dividend and rent		—
	Total (A)		11,75,000
4.	Claims incurred	2	5,40,000
5.	Commission	3	3,00,000
6.	Operating expenses related to Insurance business	4	2,00,000
	Total (B)		10,40,000
	Operating Profit (A) – (B)		1,35,000

Schedule 1: Premium earned

	₹
Premium received	12,50,000
Less: Re-insurance Premium	(50,000)
	12,00,000
Less: Adjustment for Change in provision for un-expired risk (Refer W.N.)	25,000
	11,75,000

Schedule 2: Claims Incurred

Claims paid including legal expenses (5,10,000 + 10,000)	5,10,000
Add: Claims outstanding at the end of the year	80,000
Less: Claims outstanding at the beginnging of the year	(50,000)
Total claims incurred	5,40,000

Schedule 3: Commission

Commission paid	3,00,000

Schedule 4: Operating Expenses

Expenses of Management	2,00,000

Working Note:

Change in the Provision for Unexpired Risk

	₹
Closing Unexpired Risk Reserve [50% of ₹ 12,00,000]	6,00,000
Opening Unexpired Risk Reserve	(5,75,000)
	25,000

Q.6 (a) Solution: **Journal**

Date	*Particulars*		*L.F.*	*Dr.* (₹)	*Cr.* (₹)
01.07.12	Own Debentures A/c	Dr.		95,000	
	Debenture Interest A/c	Dr.		2,000	
	[1,000 × 100 × 8% × (3/12)]				
	To Bank A/c				97,000
	(Being 1,000 Debentures purchased @ ₹ 97 cum interest for immediate cancellation)				
01.07.12	8% Debentures A/c	Dr.		1,00,000	
	To Own Debentures A/c				95,000
	To Capital Reserve A/c				5,000
	(Being profit on cancellation of own Debentures t/f)				
30.09.12	Debenture Interest A/c	Dr.		36,000	
	[9,000 × 100 × 8% × (1/2)]				
	To Debenture holders A/c				36,000
	(Being interest accrued on 9,000 Debentures)				
	Debentureholders A/c	Dr.		36,000	
	To Bank A/c				36,000
	(Being interest amount paid)				
29.02.13	Own Debentures A/c	Dr.		1,78,200	
	Debenture Interest Account A/c	Dr.		6,000	
	[1,800 × 100 × 8% × (5/12)]				
	To Bank A/c				1,84,200
	(Being the Purchase of 1,800 Debentures @ ₹ 99 ex interest for immediate cancellation)				

29.02.13	8% Debentures A/c Dr. To Own Debentures A/c To Capital Reserve A/c (Being the Profit on cancellation of own Debentures t/f)		1,80,000	 1,78,200 1,800
31.03.13	Debentures Interest A/c Dr. [7,200 × 100 × 8% × (1/2)] To Debentureholders A/c (Being interest accrued on 7,200 Debentures)		28,800	 28,800
31.3.13	Profit and Loss A/c Dr. To Debentures Interest A/c (Being interest on debentures for the year transferred)		72,800	 72,800

Q6. (b) Solution:

Calculation of Correct Departmental Profits after charging Departmental Manager's Commission:

	Department X (₹)	Department Y (₹)	Department Z (₹)
Profit after charging managers' commission	36,000	27,000	18,000
Add: Managers' commission (1/9)	4,000	3,000	2,000
Profit before commission & unrealised profit	40,000	30,000	20,000
Less: Unrealised profit on stock	(1,950)	(4,900)	(900)
Profit before Manager's Commission	38,050	25,100	19,100
Less: Commission of Departmental Managers @10%	(3,805)	(2,510)	(1,910)
Correct Departmental Profits	34,245	22,590	17,190

Working Note:

Unrealised Profit on Stock

	Department X ₹	Department Y ₹	Department Z ₹	Total ₹
Unrealised Profit of Department X	—	1/6 of 7,200 = 1,200	15/115 of 5,750 = 750	1,950
Unrealised Profit of Department Y	10% of 19,000 = 1,900	—	20% of 15,000 = 3,000	4,900
Unrealised Profit of Department Z	15/115 of 4,600 = 600	1/11 of 3,300 = 300	—	900

Q7. Solution:

(a) **Journal of Lessee**

Date	Particulars	L.F.	Dr. (₹)	Cr. (₹)
	Asset A/c Dr. To Lessor (Being recognition of finance lease as an asset and a liability)		1,49,888	 1,49,888

Working Note:

Year	Lease Payments ₹	Discounting Factor (12.6%)	Present Value ₹
1	40,000	0.89	35,600
2	40,000	0.79	31,600
3	40,000	0.70	28,000
4	40,000	0.622	24,880
5	40,000	0.552	22,080
5	14,000 (GRV)	0.552	7,728
			1,49,888

(b) When a fixed asset is acquired in exchange for another asset, its cost is usually determined by reference to the fair market value of the consideration given. Accordingly, the value of Plant X will be

	₹
Exchange value of Plant B	1,50,000
Add: Additional cash paid	20,000
	1,70,000

Journal Entries to record the Acquisition of Plant X:

Date	Particulars	L.F.	Dr. (₹)	Cr. (₹)
1	Plant X A/c Dr.		1,70,000	
	To Plant B A/c			1,50,000
	To Bank A/c			20,000
	(Being new plant X acquired in exchange of Plant B on additional payment of ₹ 20,000)			
2	Profit and Loss A/c Dr.		25,000	
	To Plant B A/c			25,000
	(Being loss on exchange of old Plant B transferred to Profit and Loss Account)			

AS 29 As per para 14 of AS 29, 'Provision, Contingent Liabilities and Contingent Assets', a provision should be recognised when

(a) an enterprise has a present obligation as a result of a past event;

(b) It is probable that an outflow of resources embodying economic benefits will be required to settle the obligation; and

(c) a reliable estimate can be made of the amount of the obligation. If these conditions are not met, no provision should be recognised.

If these conditions are not met, no provision should be recognised.

Advice Since the directors of the com pany are of the opinion that the claim can be successfully resisted by the com pany, therefore there will be no outflow of the resources. The company will disclose the same as contingent liability by way of the following note: "*Litigation is in process against the company relating to a dispute with a competitor who alleges that the company has infringed patents and is seeking damages of ₹ 900 lakhs. However, the directors are of the opinion that the claim can be successfully resisted by the company.*"

(d) A company may issue sweat equity shares of a class of shares already issued, if the following conditions are fulfilled.

(i) the issue of sweat equity shares is authorised by a special resolution passed by the company in the general meeting.

(ii) the Resolution specified the number of shares, current market price, the consideration if any, and the class or classes of directors or employees to whom such equity shares are to be issued.

(iii) not less than one year has, at the time of the issue, elapsed since the date on whcih the company was entitled to commence business.

(iv) the sweat equity shares of company, whose equity shares are listed on a recognised stock exchange, are issued in accordance with the regulations made by the Securities and Exchange Board of India (SEBI) in this behalf. But in the case of company whose equity shares are not listed on any recognised stock exchange, the sweat equity shares are issued in accordance with the guidelines as may be prescribed.

(e) **(i) Examples of Changes in Accounting Policy:**

a. Change of Depreciation method from WDV to SLM and vice-versa.

b. Change in Cost formula in measuring the cost of inventories.

(ii) Examples of Changes in Accounting Estimates:

a. Change in estimate of provision for doubtful debts on sundry debtors.

b. Change in estimate of useful life of fixed assets.

(iii) Examples of Extraordinary items:

a. Loss due to earthquakes/fire/strike

b. Attachment of property of the enterprise by government

(iv) Examples of Prior period items:

a. Applying incorrect Rate of Depreciation in one or more prior periods.

b. Omission to account for Income or Expenditure in one or more prior periods.

Paper-5: Advanced Accounting CA IPC (Group II) Examination (May 2013)

Question No. 1 is compulsory.
Attempt any Five questions from the remaining Six questions
Wherever necessary suitable assumptions may be made by the candidates.
Working notes should form part of the answer.

Q.1 Answer the following questions: [4 × 5 = 20]

(a) From the following information compute basic and diluted earnings per share.

Net Profit for the year	₹ 24,00,000
Weighted average number of equity shares outstanding	10,00,000 shares
Average fair value of one equity share	₹ 25
Weighted average number of shares under option	2,00,000 shares
Exercise price per share under option	₹ 20

(b) Closing stock for the year ending on 31.3.2013 is ₹ 1, 50,000 which includes stock damaged in a fire in 2011-12. On 31.3.2012, the estimated net realisable value of the damaged stock was ₹ 12,000. The revised estimate of net realisable value of damaged goods included in closing stock at 2012-2013 is ₹ 4,000. Find the value of closing stock to be shown in Profit and Loss account for the year 2012-13.

(c) An engineering goods compnay provides after sales warranty for 2 years to its customers. Based on past experience, the company has the following policy for making provision for warranties on the invoice amount, on the remaining balnce warranty period:

Less than 1 year: 2% provision

More than 1 year: 3% provision

The company has raised invoices as under:

Invoice Date	Amount ₹
19th January, 2011	40,000
29th January, 2012	25,000
15th October, 2012	90,000

Calculate the provision to be made for warranty under Accounting Standard 29 as at 31st March, 2012 and 31st March, 2013. Also compute amount to be debited to Profit and Loss Account for the year ended 31st March, 2013.

(d) An enterprise acquired patent right for ₹400 lakhs. The product life cycle has been estimated to be 5 years and the amortization was decided in the ratio of estimated future cash flows which are as under:

Years	1	2	3	4	5
Estimated Future Cash Flows (₹ in lakhs)	200	200	200	100	100

After 3rd year, it was ascertained that the patent would have an estimated balance future life of 3 years and the estimated cash flow after 5th year is expected to be ₹ 50 lakhs each year. Determine the amortization under Accounting Standard 26.

Q2. The following is the Balance Sheet of M/s *P* and *Q* as on 31st March, 2012:

Liabilities	₹	*Assets*	₹
P's Capital	50,000	Machinery	54,000
Q's Capital	30,000	Furniture	5,000
Q's Loan	15,000	Investments	50,000
General Reserve	20,000	Stock	20,000
Creditors	40,000	Debtors	21,000
		Cash	5,000
	1,55,000		1,55,000

It was agreed that Mr. *R* is to be admitted for a fourth share in the future profits from 1st April, 2012. He is required to contribute cash towards goodwill and ₹ 15,000 towards capital. The following further information is furnished:

(a) *P* and *Q* share the profits in the ratio of 3 : 2.

(b) Mr *P* was receiving a salary of ₹ 750 p.m from the very inception of the firm in 2005 in addition to share of profit.

(c) The future profit sharing ratio between *P*, *Q* and *R* will be 2 : 1 : 1. Mr *P* will not get any salary after the admission of Mr *R*.

(d) The goodwill of the firm shall be determined on the basis of 3 years' purchase of the average profits from business of the last 5 years. The particulars of the profits are as under:
2007-2008 Profit ₹ 25,000, 2008-2009 Profit ₹ 12,500, 2009-2010 Loss ₹ 2,500, 2010-2011 Profit ₹ 35,000, 2011-2012 Profit ₹ 30,000.
The above profits and losses are after charging the salary of Mr *P*. The profit for the year ended. 31st March 2008 included an extraneous profits of ₹ 40,000 and the loss of the year ended 31st March 2010 was on account of loss by strike to the extent of ₹ 20,000. It was agreed that the value of the goodwill of the firm shall appear in the book of the firm.

(e) The cash trading profit for the year ended 31st March, 2013 was ₹ 50,000 before depreciation.

(f) Each partner withdrew ₹ 1,000 p.m. as drawings.

(g) The value of the other assets and liabilities as on 31st March, 2013 were Machinery (before depreciation) ₹ 60,000, Furniture (before depreciation) ₹ 10,000, Investments ₹ 50,000, Stock ₹ 15,000, Debtors ₹ 30,000, Creditors ₹ 20,000.

(h) Provide depreciation @ 10% on Machinery and @ 5% on furnitures on the closing balance and interest @ 6% on *Q*'s loan. The loan along with interest would be repaid within next 12 months.

(i) Investments are held from inception of the firm and interest is received @ 10% p.a.

(j) The partners applied for conversion of the firm into a Private Limited Company. Certificate was received on 1st April, 2013. They decided to convert Capital A/cs of the partners into share capital in the ratio of 2 : 1 : 1 on the basis of total Capital as on 31st March, 2013. If necessary, partners have to subscribe to fresh capital or withdraw.

Required: Prepare the Profit and Loss Account for the year ended 31st March, 2013 and the Balance Sheet as at 1st April 2013.

Q3. (a) A company issued 1,50,000 shares of ₹ 10 each at a premium of ₹ 10. The entire issue was underwritten as follows:

X – 90,000 shares (Firm underwriting 12,000 shares)

Y – 37,500 shares (Firm underwriting 4,500 shares)

Z – 22,500 shares (Firm underwriting 15,000 shares)

Total applications received by the company (excluding firm underwriting and marked applications) were 22,500 shares.

The marked applications (excluding firm underwriting) were as follows:

X- 15,000 shares; Y- 30,000 shares: Z- 7,500 shares.

Commission payable to underwriters is at 5% of the issue price. The underwriting contract provides that credit for unmarked applications be given to the underwriters in proportion to the shares underwritten and benefit of firm underwiriting is to be given to individual underwriters.

(i) Determine the liability of each underwriter (number of shares)

(ii) Compute the amount payable or due to underwriters; and

(iii) Pass necessary journal entries in the books of co. relating to underwriting.

(b) Arihant Limited has its share capital divided into equity shares of ₹ 10 each, On 1.10.2012 it granted 20,000 employees' stock option at ₹ 50 per share, when the market price was ₹ 120 per share. The options were to be exercised between 10th December, 2012 and 31st March, 2013. The employees exercised their options for 16,000 shares only and the remaining options lapsed. The company closes its books on 31st March every year. Show Journal entries (with narration) as would appear in the books of the company upto 31th March, 2013.

Q4. The summarized Balance Sheet of Bad Luck Ltd. as on 31st March, 2013 was as follows:

Particulars	Note No	₹ (lacs)
I. Equity and Liabilities		
(1) Shareholders' Funds		
(a) Share Capital	1	7.50
(b) Reserves and Surplus	2	(10.00)
(2) Non-Current Liabilities (Long-term Borrowings)	3	5.00
(3) Current Liabilities		
(a) Short-term Borrowings	4	5.00
(b) Trade Payables [Creditors]		2.50
Total		10.00
II. Assets		
(1) Non-Current Assets		
(a) Fixed Assets		
Tangible Assets	5	5.50
Intangible Assets	6	1.50
(2) Current Assets		
(a) Inventories		1.50
(b) Trade Receivables		1.25
(c) Deferred revenue expenditure		0.25
Total		10.00

Notes To Accounts:

Particulars		*₹ (lacs)*
1. Share Capital		
5000 Equity Shares of ₹ 100 each		5.00
2500, 8% Pref. Shares of ₹ 100 each		2.50
		7.50
2. Reserves and Surplus (Profit and Loss A/c)		(10.00)
3. Long-term Borrowings (8% Debentures)		5.00
4. Short-term Borrowings		
Loan from Directors		3.00
Bank Overdraft		2.00
		5.00
5. Tangible Assets		
Freehold Property		4.00
Plant & Machinery		1.50
Total		5.50
6. Intangible Assets		
Goodwill		1.00
Trademark		0.50
		1.50

The followig scheme of internal reconstruction was framed, approved by the Court, all the concerned parties and implemented:

(i) The preference shares to be written down to ₹ 25 each and the equity shares to ₹ 20 each. Each class of shares then to be conveted into shares of ₹ 100 each.

(ii) The debenture holders to take over freehold property (book value ₹ 2,00,000) at a valuation of ₹ 2,50,000 in part repayment of their holdings. Remaining freehold property to be revalued at ₹ 6,00,000.

(iii) Loan from directors to be waived off in full.

(iv) Stock of ₹ 50,000 to be written off, ₹ 12,500 to be provided for bad debts.

(v) Profit and Loss account balance, Trademark, Goodwill and Deferred Revenue Expenditure to be written off.

Pass Journal Entries for all the above mentioned transactions. Also, Prepare Capital Reducation account and company's Balance Sheet immediately after reconstruction.

Q5. (a) From the following information of M/s. Bachao Insurance Co. Ltd., engaged in fire insurance business, prepare the Revenue Account reserving 40% of the net premiums for unexpired risks and an additional reserve of ₹ 3,50,000:

Particulars	*Amount (₹)*
Reserve for unexpired risk (opening)	7,50,000
Additional Reserve (opening)	1,50,000
Premium received	16,80,000
Re-insurance premium	1,12,500
Re-insurance recoveries	30,000
Claims paid	9,60,000

Estimated liability in respect of outstanding claims:	On April 1,2012	97,500
	On March 31,2013	1,35,000
Expenses of management (includes ₹ 45, 000 in connection with claims)		4,20,000
Interest and dividend		75,000
Profit on sale of investments		15,000
Commission		1,75,000

(b) The following information is available in the books of X Bank Limited as on 31st March, 2013:

	₹
Bill discounted	1,37,05,000
Rebate on Bills discounted (as on 1.4.2012)	2,21,600
Discount received	10,56,650

Details of bills discounted are as follows:

Value of bill (₹)	*Due date*	*Rate of Discount*
18,25,000	5.6.2013	12%
50,00,000	12.6.2013	12%
28,20,000	25.6.2013	14%
40,60,000	6.7.2013	16%

Required: Calculate the rebate on bills discounted as on 31.3.2013 and give necessary journal entries.

Q6. ABCD Ltd., Delhi, has a branch in New York, USA which is an integral foreign operation of the Company. At the end of 31st March, 2013, the following ledger balances have been extracted from the books of the Delhi Office and the New York office.

Particulars	*Delhi (₹ thousands)*		*New York ($ thousands)*	
	Debit	*Credit*	*Debit*	*Credit*
Share Capital	—	1,250	—	—
Reserve & Surplus	—	940	—	—
Land	475	—	—	—
Buildings (Cost)	1,000	—	—	—
Buildings Depreciation Reserve	—	200	—	—
Plant & Machinery (Cost)	2,000	—	100	—
Plant & Machinery Depreciation Reserve	—	500	—	20
Trade Receivables/ Payables	500	270	60	20
Opening Stock	250	—	25	—
Branch Stock Reserve	—	65	—	—
Cash & Bank Balances	125	—	4	—
Purchases/Sales	275	600	25	125
Goods sent to Branch	—	1500	30	—
Managing Director's salary	50	—	—	—
Wages & Salaries	100	—	18	—
Rent	—	—	6	—
Office Expenses	25	—	12	—
Commission Receipts	—	275	—	100
Branch/H.O. Current A/c	800	—	—	15
	5,600	5,600	280	280

Additional Information

(i) Closing Stock: Delhi ₹ 2,00,000, New York $ 10 (ii) Head Office always sent goods to the Branch at cost *plus* 25%, (iii) Provision is to be made for doubtful debts at 5%, (iv) Depreciation is to be provided on buildings at 10% and on plant and machinery at 20% on written down values,

You are required:

(a) to convert the Branch Trial balance into rupees; (use the following rates of exchange) Opening rate 1 $ = ₹ 50, Closing rate 1 $ = ₹ 55, Average rate 1 $ = ₹ 52, For Fixed Assets 1 $ = ₹ 45

(b) to prepare the Trading and Profit & Loss Account for the year ending on 31st March, 2013, showing to the extent possible, H.O. results and Branch results separately.

Q.7 Answer any four of the following: **[4 × 4 = 16]**

(a) Neel Limited has its corporate office in Mumbai and sells its products to stockists all over India. On 31st March, 2013, the company wants to recognize receipt of cheques bearing date 31st March, 2013 or before, as "Cheques in Hand" by reducing "Trade Receivables". The "Cheques in Hand" is shown in the Balance Sheet as an item of cash and cash equivalents. All cheques are presented to the bank in the month of April 2013 and are also realized in the same month in normal course after deposit in the bank. State with reasons, whether each of the following is an adjusting event and how this fact is to be disclosed by the company, with reference to the relevant accounting standard.

(i) Cheques collected by the marketing personnel of the company from the stockists on or before 31st March, 2013.

(ii) Cheques sent by the stockists through courier on or before 31st March, 2013.

(b) Explain "monetary item" as per Accounting Standard 11. How are foreign currency monetary items to be recognized at each Balance Sheet date? Classify the following as monetary or non-monetary item:

(i) Share Capital

(ii) Trade Receivables

(iii) Investments

(iv) Fixed Assets

(c) Department *A* sells goods to Department *B* at a profit of 50% on cost and to Department *C* at 20% profit on cost. Department *B* sells goods to *A* and *C* at a profit of 25% and 15% on sales, respectively. Department *C* charges 30% and 40% profit on cost to Department *A* and *B*, respectively.

Stocks lying at different departments at the end of the year are as under:

	Dept. A ₹	*Dept. B* ₹	*Dept. C* ₹
Transfer from Department *A*	—	45,000	42,000
Transfer from Department *B*	40,000	—	72,000
Transfer from Department *C*	39,000	42,000	—

Required: Calculate the unrealized profit of each department and also total unrealized profit.

(d) Explain Garner v/s Murrary rule applicable in the case of partnership firms. State, when is this rule not applicable.

(e) What are the qualitative characteristics of the finanical statements which improve the usefulness of the information furnished therein?

Answers to IPC Examination Paper May 2013

Solution 1(a).

COMPUTATION OF DILUTED EARNINGS PER SHARE

Particulars	*Earnings* (₹)	*Shares*	*Earning per share* (₹)
Net Profit for the year	24,00,000		
Weighted average number of equity shares outstanding		10,00,000	
Basic earnings per share (24,00,0000/10,00,000)			2.40
Weighted average number of shares under option		2,00,000	
Number of shares that would have been issued at fair value (2,00,000 × 20.00)/25.00)	—	(1,60,000)	—
Diluted earnings per share (24,00,0000/10,40,000)	24,00,000	10,40,000	2.31

*The earnings have not been increased as the total number of shares has been increased only by the number of shares (40,000) deemed for the purpose of computation to have been issued for no consideration.

Solution 1(b).

AS-5	As per AS 5 the effect of a change in accounting estimate should be classified using the same classification in the statement of profit and loss as was used previously for the estimate.
Advice	The fall in estimated net realisable value of damaged stock ₹ 8,000 is the effect of change in accounting estimate. Thus, the value of closing stock for the year 2012-13 will be as follows:

	₹
Closing Stock (including damaged goods)	1,50,000
Less: Revised value of damaged goods	(4,000)
Closing stock (excluding damaged goods)	1,46,000

Solution 1(c).

A. Provision as at 31-3-2013 = ₹ 25,000 × 0.2 + ₹ 90,000 × .03 = ₹ 3,200

B. *Less:* Provision as at 31-3-2012 = ₹ 40,000 × 0.2 + ₹ 25,000 × .03 = ₹ 1,550

C. Amount debited to Profit and Loss Account (A – B) = ₹ 1,650

Note: *No provision is to be made on 31-3-2013 in respect of sales amounting to ₹ 40,000 made on 19-01-2011 because the warranty period of 2 years has already expired.*

Solution 1(d).

AMORTIZATION OF COST AS PER AS 26

Year	Net Cash Flows ₹	Amortization Ratio	Amortization Amount ₹
1	200	.25	100
2	200	.25	100
3	200	.25	100
4	100	.40 (Revised)	40
5	100	.40 (Revised)	40
6	50	.20 (Revised)	20
			400

It may be seen from above that from third year onwards, the balance of carrying amount i.e., ₹ 100,00,000 has been amortized in the ratio of revised net cash flows.

Solution 2.

PROFIT AND LOSS ACCOUNT

Dr. *for the year ending on 31st March, 2013* Cr.

Particulars		₹	Particulars	₹
To Depreciation on Machinery		6,000	By Trading Profit	50,000
To Depreciation on furniture		500	By Interest on Investment	5,000
To Interest on Q's loan		900		
To Net Profit to:				
P's Capital A/c	23,800			
Q's Capital A/c	11,900			
R's Capital A/c	11,900	47,600		
		55,000		55,000

BALANCE SHEET OF THE PQR PVT LTD. AS AT 1.4.2013

Particulars	Note No.	(₹)
I. EQUITY AND LIABILITIES		
(1) Shareholders' Funds		
(a) Share Capital		1,41,600
(2) Current Liabilities		
(a) Short Term borrowings	1	15,900
(b) Trade Payables		20,000
Total		1,77,500
II. ASSETS		
(1) Non-Current Assets		
(a) Fixed Assets		
(i) Tangible Assets	2	63,500
(ii) Non-current investments		50,000
(2) Current Assets		
(a) Inventories		15,000
(b) Trade Receivables		30,000
(c) Cash and cash equivalents		19,000
Total		2,38,000

Notes To Accounts:

		₹
1. **Short term borrowings**		
Loan from Q		15,900
2. **Tangible assets**		
Machinery	54,000	
Furniture	9,500	63,500

Working Notes: 1. Calculation of goodwill

Particulars	*2007-08* ₹	*2008-09* ₹	*2009-10* ₹	*2010-11* ₹	*2011-12* ₹
Profits/(Loss)	25,000	12,500	(2,500)	35,000	30,000
Adjustment for Abnormal Profit & Loss	(40,000)	—	20,000	—	—
Add: Salary of partner (750 × 12)	9,000	9,000	9,000	9,000	9,000
Less: Interest on Non-Trading Investments	(5,000)	(5,000)	(5,000)	(5,000)	(5,000)
	(11,000)	16,500	21,500	39,000	34,000
					₹
Total Profit for five years					1,00,000
Average Profit (` 1,00,000/5)					20,000
Goodwill equal to 3 years' Purchase					60,000
New partner's share of goodwill for 1/4 share					15,000

2. Sacrificing Ratio: P's sacrifice = 3/5 – 1/2 = 1/10, Q's sacrifice = 2/5 – 1/4 = 3/20
3. As per AS 26 "Intangible Assets", only purchased goodwill should appear in the books. Therefore, goodwill though required to be shown in the books as per the requirement of the question, has been adjusted through capital accounts of the partenrs in line with the provisions of AS 26.

4. *Dr.* **CAPITAL ACCOUNTS OF PARTNERS** *Cr.*

Particulars	*P* ₹	*Q* ₹	*R* ₹	*Particulars*	*P* ₹	*Q* ₹	*R* ₹
To Drawings A/c	12,000	12,000	12,000	By Balance b/d	50,000	30,000	—
To P	—	—	6,000	By General Reserve	12,000	8,000	—
To Q	—	—	9,000	By R	6,000	9,000	—
To Balance c/d	79,800	46,900	14,900	By Bank A/c	—	—	30,000
				By P & L A/c	23,800	11,900	11,900
	91,800	58,900	41,900		91,800	58,900	41,900

5. **BALANCE SHEET OF M/S XYZ & CO. AS AT 31ST MARCH, 2013**

Liabilities		₹	*Assets*		₹
P's Capital	79,800		Machinery	60,000	
Q's Capital	46,900		*Less* : Depreciation	(6,000)	54,000
R's Capital	14,900	1,41,600	Furniture	10,000	
			Less : Depreciation	(500)	9,500
Q's Loan	15,000		Investments		50,000
Add : Interest due	900	15,900	Stock-in-trade		15,000
Creditors		20,000	Debtors		30,000
			Cash		19,000
		1,77,500			1,77,500

6. **CALCULATION OF CLOSING CASH BALANCE**

Particulars	₹
Opening cash balance	5,000
Add: Cash brought in by R	30,000
Less: Drawings (12,000 + 12,000 + 12,000)	36,000
Less: Additions to Machine (60,000 – 54,000)	6,000
Less: Addition to Furniture (10,000 – 5,000)	5,000
Cash Trading Profit	50,000
Add: Investment Interest	5,000
Add: Decrease in Stock Balance	5,000
Less: Increase in Debtors	9,000
Less: Decrease in Creditors	20,000
Closing Cash Balance	19,000

7. **ADJUSTMENT OF CAPITALS**

Particulars	*P*	*Q*	*R*
A. Adjusted Capitals	79,800	46,900	14,900
B. Distribution of Shares in the ratio of 2:1:1	70,800	35,400	35,400
C. Surplus to be withdrawn (Shortage to be brought in)	9,000	11,500	(20,500)

Solution 3(a).

COMPUTATION OF UNDERWRITERS' LIABILITY (NUMBER OF SHARES)

Particulars	*X*	*Y*	*Z*
A Gross Liability	90,000	37,500	22,500
B *Less:* Marked applications	(15,000)	(30,000)	(7,500)
C *Less:* Unmarked applications in ratio of 12:5:3	(13,500)	(5,625)	3,375
D *Less:* Firm Underwriting	(12,000)	(4,500)	(15,000)
E Balance	49,500	(2,625)	(3,375)
F *Less:* Surplus of Y & Z distributed to X	(6,000)	2,625	3,375
G Net Liability (excluding firm underwriting)	43,500	Nil	Nil
H *Add:* Firm Underwriting	12,000	4,500	15,000
I Total Liability (number of shares)	55,500	4,500	15,000

(b) COMPUTATION OF AMOUNTS PAYABLE BY UNDERWRITERS

Particulars	₹	₹	₹
Liability towards shares to be subscribed @ 20 per share	11,10,000	90,000	3,00,000
Less: Commission @ 5% on 1,50,000 shares @ ₹ 20	(90,000)	(37,500)	(22,500)
Net Amount to be paid by Underwriters	10,20,000	52,500	2,77,500

(c) JOURNAL OF THE COMPANY

Date	Particulars	L.F.	Dr. (₹)	Cr. (₹)
	X Dr.		11,10,000	
	Y Dr.		90,000	
	Z Dr.		3,00,000	
	To Share Capital A/c			7,50,000
	To Securities Premium A/c			7,50,000
	(Being shares including firm underwritten shares allotted to underwriters)			
	Underwriting Commission A/c Dr.		1,50,000	
	To X			90,000
	To Y			37,500
	To Z			22,500
	(Being underwriting commission on the shares underwritten)			
	Bank A/c Dr.		13,50,000	
	To X			10,20,000
	To Y			52,500
	To Z			2,77,500
	(Being the amount received towards shares allotted to underwrittens less underwriting commission due to them)			

Solution 3(b).

JOURNAL

Date	Particulars	Dr. (₹)	Cr. (₹)
10.12.12 to 31.3.13	Bank A/c Dr.	8,00,000	
	Employee Stock Option Outstanding A/c Dr.	11,20,000	
	To Equity Share Capital A/c		1,60,000
	To Securities Premium A/c		17,60,000
	(Being shares issued to the employees against the options vested to them in pursuance of Employee Stock Option Plan)		
31.3.13	Profit and Loss A/c Dr.	11,20,000	
	To Employee Compensation Expense A/c		11,20,000
	(Being transfer of employee compensation transferred to Profit and Loss Account)		

Solution 4.

JOURNAL OF BAD LUCK LTD.

Date	Particulars		Dr. (₹)	Cr. (₹)
(i)	8% Preference Share Capital A/c (₹ 100)	Dr.	2,50,000	
	To 8% Preference Share Capital A/c (₹ 25)			62,500
	To Capital Reduction A/c			1,87,500
	(Being preference shares of ₹100 each reduced to ₹ 25 each as per the scheme)			
(ii)	Equity Share Capital A/c (₹ 100)	Dr.	5,00,000	
	To Equity Share Capital A/c (₹ 20)			1,00,000
	To Capital Reduction A/c			4,00,000
	(Being equity shares of ₹ 100 each reduced to ₹ 20 each as per the scheme)			
(iii)	8% Preference Share Capital A/c (₹ 25)	Dr.	62,500	
	To 8% Preference Share Capital A/c (₹ 100)			62,500
	(Being the conversion of 2,500 shares of ₹ 25 each into 625 shares of ₹ 100 each as per the scheme)			
(iv)	Equity Share Capital A/c (₹ 20)	Dr.	1,00,000	
	To Equity Share Capital A/c (₹ 100)			1,00,000
	(Being the conversion of 5,000 shares of ₹ 20 each in to 1,000 shares of ₹ 100 each as per the scheme)			
(v)	Freehold Property A/c	Dr.	50,000	
	To Capital Reduction A/c			50,000
	(Being appreciation in the value of property)			
(vi)	8% Debentures A/c	Dr.	2,50,000	
	To Freehold Property A/c			2,50,000
	(Being claim of debentureholders settled in part by transfer of freehold property as per the scheme)			
(vii)	Freehold Property A/c	Dr.	4,00,000	
	To Capital Reduction A/c			4,00,000
	(Being appreciation in the value of remaining property)			
(viii)	Director's Loan A/c	Dr.	3,00,000	
	To Capital Reduction A/c			3,00,000
	(Being Director's loan waived in full)			
(ix)	Capital Reduction A/c	Dr.	13,37,500	
	To Profit and Loss A/c			10,00,000
	To Deferred Revenue Expenditure A/c			25,000
	To Inventories A/c			50,000
	To Provision for Doubtful Debts A/c			12,500
	To Goodwill A/c			1,00,000
	To Trademark			50,000
	To Capital Reserve A/c			1,00,000
	(Being the various assets written off as per the scheme)			

Dr. **CAPITAL REDUCTION ACCOUNT** Cr.

Particulars	₹	Particulars	₹
To Provision for Doubtful Debts A/c	12,500	By Preference Share Capital A/c	1,87,500
To Inventories A/c	50,000	By Freehold Property A/c	4,50,000
To Trademark A/c	50,000	By Equity Share Capital A/c	4,00,000
To Deferred Revenue Exp. A/c	60,000	By Director's loan A/c	3,00,000
To Goodwill A/c	1,00,000		
To Profit and loss A/c	10,00,000		
To Capital reserve A/c	1,00,000		
	13,37,500		**13,37,500**

BALANCE SHEET OF BAD LUCK LTD. (AND REDUCED) AS AT 31.03.2013

Particulars	Note No	₹
I. Equity and Liabilities		
(1) Shareholders' Funds		
(a) Share Capital	1	1,62,500
(b) Reserves and Surplus[Capital Reserve]		1,00,000
(2) Non-Current Liabilities		
Long-term Borrowings [8% Debentures]		2,50,000
(3) Current Liabilities		
(a) Short-term Borrowings [Bank Overdraft]		2,00,000
(b) Trade Payables [Creditors]		2,50,000
Total		9,62,500
II. Assets		
(1) Non-Current Assets		
(a) Fixed Assets		
Tangible Assets	2	7,50,000
(2) Current Assets		
(a) Inventories		1,00,000
(b) Trade Receivables [1,50,000 – 12,500]		1,12,500
Total		9,62,500

Notes To Accounts:

Particulars	₹
1. Share Capital	
1,000 Equity Shares of ₹ 100 each	1,00,000
625,8% Pref. Shares of ₹ 100 each	62,500
	1,62,500
2. Tangible Assets	
Frehold Property	6,00,000
Plant & Machinery	1,50,000
Total	7,50,000

Solution 5(a).

FORM B-RA NAME OF THE INSURER: M/S BACHAO INSURANCE CO. LTD.
REVENUE ACCOUNT FOR THE YEAR ENDED 31ST MARCH, 2013

Particulars	*Schedule*	₹
Premium earned (Net)	1	14,90,500
Profit on sale of investment		15,000
Interest, dividend and rent (Gross)		75,000
Total (A)		15,80,500
Claims incurred (Net)	2	10,12,500
Commission	3	1,75,000
Operatinq expenses related to insurance business	4	3,75,000
Total (B)		15,62,500
Operating Profit for Fire Insurance Business (A-B)		18,000

SCHEDULE -1

Premium Earned (Net)	₹
Premium received	16,80,000
Less: Premium on reinsurance ceded	(1,12,500)
Less: Adjustment for change in reserve for Unexpired Risk	(77,000)
Net premium earned	14,90,500

SCHEDULE-2

Claim Incurred (Net)	₹
Claim paid	9,60,000
Add: Surveyor's fee & legal expenses paid for settlement of claim	45,000
Add: Outstanding claims at the end	1,35,000
Less: Outstanding claims in the beg.	(97,500)
Claim incurred (Net)	10,12,500

SCHEDULE-3

Commission	₹
Commission paid	1,75,000

SCHEDULE-4

Operating expenses related to insurance business	₹
Expenses of Management	4,20,000
Less: Surveyor's fee & legal expenses	(45,000)
	3,75,000

Working Note:

CALCULATION FOR CHANGE IN RESERVE FOR UNEXPIRED RISK

		₹
Unexpired risk reserve at the beginning (including additional reserve)		9,00,000
Less: Reserve for unexpired risk as at the end (40% of ₹ 15,67,500)	6,27,000	
Additional reserve at the end	3,50,000	(9,77,000)
Change in Provision for Unexpired Risk		77,000

Solution 5(b).

STATEMENT SHOWING REBATE ON BILLS DISCOUNTED

Value of bill (₹)	*Due Date*	*Days after 31 March*	*Rate of discount*	*Discount Amount*
18,25,000	5 June	(30+31+5) = 66	12%	39,600
50,00,000	12 June	(30+31+12) = 73	12%	1,20,000
28,20,000	25 June	(30+31+25) = 86	14%	93,021
40,60,000	6. July	(30+31+30+6) = 97	16%	1,72,633
1,37,05,000		Rebate on bills discounted on 31.3.2008		4,25,254

JOURNAL

Particulars		*Dr. (₹)*	*Cr. (₹)*
Rebate on Bills Discounted A/c	Dr.	2,21,600	
To Discount on Bills A/c			2,21,600
(Being the opening balance of rebate on bills discounted account transferred to discount on bills account)			
Discount on Bills A/c	Dr.	4,25,254	
To Rebate on Bills Discounted A/c			4,25,254
(Being the provision made on 31st March 2008)			
Discount on Bills A/c	Dr.	8,52,996*	
To Profit and Loss A/c			8,52,966
(Being the transfer of discount on bills, of the year, to Profit and Loss Account)			

Note: * Credit to Profit and Loss A/c = ₹ 10,56,650 + ₹ 2,21,600 – ₹ 4,25,254 = ₹ 8,52,996

Solution 6.

ABCD LTD.

(a) NEW YORK BRANCH TRIAL BALANCE (IN RUPEES) AS ON 31ST MARCH, 2013

Particulars	*Conversion rate per A $*	*(₹ '000) Dr.*	*(₹ '000) Cr.*
Plant & Machinery (cost)	₹ 45	45,00	
Plant & Machinery Depreciation Reserve	₹ 45		9,00
Trade Receivables/Trade Payables	₹ 55	33,00	11,00
Opening Stock	₹ 50	12,50	
Cash & Bank Balances	₹ 55	2,20	
Purchases/Sales	₹ 52	13,00	65,00
Goods received from H.O.	Actual	15,00	
Wages & Salaries	₹ 52	9,36	
Rent	₹ 52	3,12	
Office expenses	₹ 52	6,24	
Commission Receipts	₹ 52		52,00
H.O. Current Account	Actual		8,00
		139,42	145,00
Exchange loss (*balancing figure*)		5,58	—
		145,00	145,00

(b) TRADING AND PROFIT & LOSS ACCOUNT

Dr. *for the year ending on 31st March, 2013* Cr.

(₹ '000)

Particulars	*H.O.* ₹	*Branch* ₹	*Total* ₹	*Particulars* ₹	*H.O.* ₹	*Branch* ₹	*Total*
To Opening Stock	250	1250	1500	By Sales	600	6500	7100
To Purchases	275	1300	1575	By Goods sent to Branch	1500	—	1500
To Goods received	—	1500	1500				
To Wages & Salaries	100	936	1036				
To Gross Profit	1675	1514.55	3189.55	By Closing Stock	200	0.55	200.55
	2300	6500.55	8800.55		2300	6500.55	8800.55
				By Gross Profit b/d	1675	1514.55	3189.55
To Rent	—	312	312	By Commission receipts	275	5200	5475
To Office expenses	25	624	649				
To Provision for doubtful debts @ 5%	25	165	190				
To Depreciation	380	720	1100				
To Balance c/d	1520	4893.55	6413.55				
	1950	6714.55	8664.55		1950	6714.55	8664.55
To Exchange loss			558	By Balance b/d			6413.55
To MD Salary			50	By Branch Stock Reserve			64.89
To Balance c/d			5870.44				
			6478.44				6478.44

Working Notes:

(i) *Calculation of Depreciation* (₹ '000)

		H.O.	*Branch*
A	Building-Cost	1000	—
B	*Less* : Depreciation Reserve	200	—
C	Building at WDV	800	
D	Depreciation on Building @ 10%	80	
E	Plant & Machinery Cost	2000	4500
F	*Less*: Depreciation Reserve	(500)	(900)
G	Plant & Machinery at WDV	1500	3600
H	Depreciation on Plant & Machinery @ 20%	300	720
I	Total Depreciation (D + H)	380	720

(ii) *Calculation of Branch Stock Reserve* (₹ *'000*)

A	Reserve on closing stock (0.55 × 1/5)	0.11
B	*Less* : Opening Branch Stock Reserve	(65)
C	Reversal of Reserve required	(64.89)

Solution 7(a).

(i) **1.** Collection of cheques by the marketing personnel is an adjusting event as per AS 4 'Contingencies and Events Occurring after the Balance Sheet Date'.

2. Reason: Handing over of cheques by the stockist to the marketing employees discharges the liability of the stockist. Therefore, cheques collected by the marketing personnel of the company on or before 31-3-2013 require adjustment from the Stockists' Accounts i.e. from 'Trade Receivables A/c' even though these cheques (dated on or before 31-3-2013) are presented in the bank in the month of April, 2013 in the normal course.

3. Disclosure: Such 'cheques in hand' will be shown in the Balance Sheet as 'Cash and Cash equivalents' with a disclosure in the Notes to accounts about the accounting policy followed by the company from such cheques.

(ii) **1.** The collection of cheques after balance sheet date is not an adjusting event since Collection of cheques after 31-3-2013 does not represent any condition existing on the Balance Sheet date i.e. 31st March.

2. Cheques that are received after the balance sheet date should be accounted for in the period in which they are received even though the same may be dated 31st March or before as per AS 4.

3. The collection of cheques after Balance Sheet date does not represent any material change affecting financial position of the enterprise, hence no disclosure in the Director's Report is necessary.

Solution 7(b).

1. As per AS 11 'The Effects of Changes in Foreign Exchange Rates', Monetary items are money held and assets and liabilities to be received or paid in fixed or determinable amounts of money.
2. Foreign currency monetary items should be reported using the closing rate at each balance sheet date. However, in certain circumstances, the closing rate may not reflect with reasonable accuracy the amount in reporting currency that is likely to be

realised from, or required to disburse, a foreign currency monetary item at the balance sheet date. In such circumstances, the relevant monetary item should be reported in the reporting currency at the amount which is likely to be realised from or required to disburse, such item at the balance sheet date.

Share capital	Non-monetary
Trade receivables	Monetary
Investments	Non-monetary
Fixed assets	Non-monetary

Solution 7(c).

UNREALISED PROFIT ON STOCK

Particulars	*Department A* ₹	*Department B* ₹	*Department C* ₹	*Total* ₹
Unrealised Profit of Department *A*	—	45,000 × 50/150 = 15,000	42,000 × 20/120 = 7,000	22,000
Unrealised Profit of Department *B*	40,000 × .25 = 10,000	—	72,000 × .15 = 10,800	20,800
Unrealised Profit of Department *C*	39,000 × 30/130 = 9,000	42,000 × 40/140 = 12,000	—	21,000
				63,800

Solution 7(d).

In the case of dissolution of a partnership firm due to insolvency, **Garner vs Murray** rule is applicable at the time of any partner becoming insolvent. It requires—

1. That the solvent partners should bear the loss arising due to insolvency of a partner in their capital ratio after making adjustments for past accumulated reserves, profits or losses, drawings, interest on drawings/capitals, remuneration to partners etc., to the date of dissolution but before making adjustment for profit or loss on realization in case of fluctuating capital. In case of fixed capital no such adjustments are required.
2. That the solvent partners should bring in cash equal to their respective shares of the loss on realization.

   Non-Applicability: This rule is not applicable when:

   1. When the solvent partner has a debit balance in the capital account.
   2. Only one partner is solvent.
   3. All partners are insolvent.
   4. The partnership deed provides for a specific method to be followed in case of insolvency of a partner, then the conditions given in the deed would prevail.

Solution 7(e).

The qualitative characteristics are attributes that improve the usefulness of information provided in financial statements. The framework suggests that the financial statements should observe and maintain the following qualitative characteristics as far as possible within limits of reasonable cost benefit.

1. Under-standability	The financial statements should present information in a manner as to be readily understandable by the users with reasonable knowledge of business and economic activities. It is not right to think that more disclosures are always better. A mass of irrelevant information creates confusion and can be even more harmful than non-disclosure. No relevant information can be however withheld on the grounds of complexity.
2. Relevance	The financial statements should contain relevant information only. Information, which is likely to influence the economic decisions by the users, is said to be relevant. Such information may help the users to evaluate past, present or future events or may help in confirming or correcting past evaluations. The relevance of a piece of information should be judged by its materiality. A piece of information is said to be material if its omission or misstatement can influence economic decisions of a user.
3. Reliability	To be useful, the information must be reliable; that is to say they must be free from material error and bias. The information provided are not likely to be reliable unless: (*a*) Transactions and events reported are faithfully represented. (*b*) Transactions and events are reported in terms of their substance and economic reality not merely on the basis of their legal form. This principle is called the principle of substance over form'. (*c*) The reporting of transactions and events are neutral, i.e. free from bias. (*d*) Prudence is exercised in reporting uncertain outcome of transactions or events.
4. Comparability	Comparison of financial statements is one of the most frequently used and most effective tools of financial analysis. The financial statements should permit both inter-firm and intra-firm comparison. One essential requirement of comparability is disclosure of financial effect of change in accounting policies.
5. True and Fair View	Financial statements are required to show a true and fair view of the performance, financial position and cash flows of an enterprises. The conceptual framework does not deal directly with this concept of true and fair view, yet the application of the principal qualitative characteristics and of appropriate accounting standards normally results in financial statements portraying true and fair view of information about an enterprise.

Paper-5: Advanced Accounting
CA IPC (Group II) Examination (Nov. 2013)

Question No. 1 is compulsory.
Attempt any Five questions from the remaining Six questions
Wherever necessary suitable assumptions may be made by the candidates.
Working notes should form part of the answer.

Q.1 Answer the following questions: [4 × 5 = 20]

(a) State with reasons, how the following events would be dealt with in the financial statements of Pradeep Ltd. for the year ended 31st March, 2013:

(i) An agreement to sell a land for ₹30 lakh to another company was entered into on 1st March, 2013. The value of land is shown at ₹20 lakh in the Balance Sheet as on 31st March, 2012. However, the Sale Deed was registered on 15th April, 2013.

(ii) The negotiation with another company for acquisition of its business was started on 2nd February, 2013. Pradeep Ltd. invested ₹40 lakh on 12th April, 2013.

(b) Cost of a machine acquired on 01.04.2009 was ₹5,00,000. The machine is expected to realize ₹50,000 at the end of its working life of 10 years. Straight-line depreciation of ₹45,000 per year has been charged upto 2011–2012. For and from 2012–13, the company switched over to 15% p.a. reducing balance method of depreciation in respect of the machine. The new rate of depreciation is based on revised useful life of 15 years. The new rate shall apply with retrospective effect from 01.04.2009. State how would you deal with the above in the annual accounts of the Company for the year ended 31st March, 2013 in the light of AS 5.

(c) Beekay Ltd. purchased fixed assets costing ₹5,000 lakh on 01.04.2012 payable in foreign currency (US$) on 05.04.2013. Exchange rate of 1 US$ = ₹50.00 and ₹54.98 as on 01.04.2012 and 31.03.2013 respectively.

The company also obtained a soft loan of US$ 1 lakh on 01.04.2012 payable in three annual equal instalments. First instalment was due on 01.05.2013.

You are required to state, how these transactions would be accounted for in the books of accounts ending 31st March, 2013.

(d) (i) Vasudha Ltd. provides following information:

Raw Material stock holding period	:	3.5 months
Work-in-progress holding period	:	1 month
Finished goods holding period	:	4.5 months
Debtors collection period	:	6 months

You are required to compute the operating cycle of Vasudha Ltd. What would happen if the trade payables of the company are paid in 14 months-whether these should be classified as current or non-current liability?

(ii) The Management of Kshitij Ltd. contends that the work in progress is not valued since it is difficult to ascertain the same in view of the multiple processes involved. They opine that the value of opening and closing work in progress would be more or less the same. Accordingly, the management had not separately disclosed the work in progress in its financial statements. Comment in line with Revised Schedule VI.

Q2. Avi and Bishnu are partners of Abhay & Co. sharing profit and losses in the ratio 3 : 1 and Bishnu and Joe are partners of Bijoy & Co. sharing profit and losses in the ratio 2 : 1. On 31st March, 2013, they decided to amalgamate and form a new firm M/s Abeejay & Co., wherein Avi, Bishnu and Joe would be partners sharing profit and losses in the ratio 3 : 2 : 1. The Balance Sheets of the two firms on 31st March, 2013 were as under:

Liabilities	*Abhay & Co. (₹)*	*Bijoy & Co. (₹)*	*Assets*	*Abhay & Co. (₹)*	*Bijoy & Co. (₹)*
Capitals:			Building	3,50,000	2,80,000
Avi	5,31,000		Plant & Machinery	2,00,000	1,50,000
Bishnu	2,00,000	3,97,000	Vechicles	–	90,000
Joe		2,00,000	Furniture	–	10,000
Reserves	12,000	9,000	Office Equipments	38,000	45,000
Sundry Creditors	1,20,000	89,000	Stock in trade	65,000	70,000
Bank O/D	90,000		Sundry Debtors	1,00,000	90,000
Due to R & Co.		1,00,000	Bank Balances	80,000	60,000
			Cash in hand	20,000	–
			Due from R & Co.	1,00,000	–
	9,53,000	7,95,000		9,53,000	7,95,000

The amalgamated firm M/s Abeejay & Co. took over the business on the following terms:

(a) Goodwill of Abhay & Co. was worth ₹42,000 and that of Bijoy & Co. ₹30,000. Goodwill account was not to be opened in the books of the new firm, the adjustments being recorded through capital accounts of the partners.

(b) The following assets were valued as below:

	Abhay & Co. (₹)	*Bijoy & Co. (₹)*
Building	4,00,000	3,00,000
Plant & Machinery	2,50,000	2,00,000
Vehicles	–	98,000
Furniture	–	11,000
Office Equipments	39,000	50,000
Stock in trade	70,000	80,000

(c) Provision for doubtful debt was carried forward at ₹ 4,000 in respect of Debtors of Abhay & Co. and ₹3,000 in respect of Debtors of Bijoy & Co.

(d) Partners of new firm brought necessary cash to pay other partners to adjust their capitals according to the profit sharing ratio.

You are required to:

(i) Prepare the Balance Sheet of the new firm as on 31st March, 2013.

(ii) Prepare Capital Accounts of the partners in the books of old firms. **[16 Marks]**

Q3. (a) M Limited recently made a public issue of debentures. The following information is available in respect of the issue:

(i) 3,00,000 partly convertible debentures of face value and issue price of ₹100 per debenture were issued;

(ii) Conversion of 50% of each debenture is to be done on expiry of 6 months from date of close of issue;

(iii) Date of closure of subscription list is 1st June, 2012. Date of allotment is 1st July, 2012;

(iv) Interest on debenture at the rate of 12% is payable from date of allotment;

(v) Equity share of ₹ 10 each are issued at ₹50 per share for the purpose of conversion;

(vi) Underwriting commission is 2%;

(vii) 2,25,000 debentures were applied for;

(viii) Interest on debentures is payable half yearly on 30th September and 31st March.

Give Journal entries for all transactions relating to the above, including cash and bank entries for the year ended 31st March, 2013. **[8 Marks]**

(b) The summarized Balance Sheet of Entyce Ltd. as on 31st March, 2013 read as under:

Liabilities	₹
Share Capital: 4,00,000 equity shares of ₹ 10 each fully paid up	40,00,000
General Reserve	50,00,000
Debenture Redemption Reserve	35,00,000
12% Convertible Debentures: 80,000 Debentures of ₹ 100 each	80,00,000
Other Loans	45,00,000
Current Liabilities and Provisions	90,00,000
	3,40,00,000
Assets:	
Fixed Assets (at cost less depreciation)	1,50,00,000
Debenture Redemption Reserve Investments	30,00,000
Cash and Bank Balances	40,00,000
Other Current Assets	1,20,00,000
	3,40,00,000

The debentures are due for redemption on 1st April, 2013. The terms of issue of debentures provided that they were redeemable at a premium 5% and also conferred option to the debentureholders to convert 25% of their holding into equity shares at a predetermined price of ₹11.90 per share and the balance payment in cash.

Assuming that:

(i) Except for debentureholders holding 12,000 debentures in aggregate, rest of them exercised the option for maximum conversion,

(ii) The investments realized ₹32,00,000 on sale,

(iii) All the transactions were taken place on 1st April, 2013 without any lag, and

(iv) Premium on redemption of debentures is to be adjusted against General Reserve.

Redraft the Balance Sheet of Entyce Ltd. as on 01.04.2013 after giving effect to the redemption. Show your calculations in respect of the number of equity shares to be allotted and the cash payment necessary. **[8 Marks]**

Q4. The summarized Balance Sheet of Vasant Ltd. as on 31st March, 2013, being the date of voluntary winding up is as under:

Liabilities	*Amount* ₹	*Assets*	*Amount* ₹
Share Capital:		Land & Building	1,30,000
Issued: 10% Pref. Shares of ₹10 each	1,50,000	Sundry Current Assets	4,36,000
10,000 Equity Shares of ₹10 each, fully paid up	1,00,000	Profit and Loss Account	35,000
5,000 Equity Shares of ₹ 10 each, ₹8 per share paid up	40,000	Debenture issue expenses not written off	2,000
13% Debentures	1,50,000		
Mortgage Loan	70,000		
Bank overdraft	30,000		
Trade Creditors	38,000		
Income Tax Arrears (assessment concluded in February, 2013)	25,000		
	6,03,000		6,03,000

Mortgage loan was secured against Land & Building. Debentures were secured by a floating charge on all assets. The company was unable to meet the payments and therefore the debentureholders apointed a Receiver for the debentureholders. He brought the Land & Buildings to auction and realized ₹1,60,000. He also took charge of Sundry Assets of value of ₹2,36,000 and realized ₹2,00,000. The Bank overdraft was secured by personal guarantee of the directors of the company and on the Bank raising a demand, the Directors paid off the due from their personal resources. Costs incurred by the Receiver were ₹1,950 and by the Liquidator ₹3,000. The receiver was not entitled to any remuneration but the Liquidator was to receive 2% fee on the value of assets realized by him. Preference Shareholders have not been paid dividend for period after 31st March, 2011 and interest for the last half year was due to the Debentureholders. Rest of the assets were realized at ₹1,50,000.

Prepare the accounts to be submitted by the receiver and Liquidator. **[16 Marks]**

Q5. Following information has been provided in respect of Watson Power Generation Project:

1. Date of commercial operation/work completed date : 1st April, 1995
2. Capital Cost at the beginning of the year 2010–11 : ₹135.39 Crore
3. Useful life : 35 years
4. Details of allowed capital expenditure, details of actual repayment of loan and weighted average rate of interest on loan is as follows:

	2010–11 (₹ in Crore)	*2011–12 (₹ in Crore)*	*2012–13 (₹ in Crore)*
Additional Capital Expenditure (allowed above)	1.63	0.98	0.52
Repayment of Loan during the year (net)	0.96	0.87	0.68
Weighted Average Rate of Interest on Loan	7.35%	7.48%	7.50%
Value of Land	0.00	0.00	0.00

5. Depreciation recovered upto 2008–09 = ₹49.05 Crore
6. Depreciation recovered in 2009–10 = ₹3.26 Crore
7. Cumulative Repayment of Loan upto 2009–10 = ₹14,00 Crore

From the above information, calculate the following as per the Central Electricity Commission (Terms and Conditions of Tariff) Regulations, 2009;

(a) Average Capital Cost;
(b) Return on Equity;
(c) Interest on Loans;
(d) Depreciation.

[16 Marks]

Q6. Martis Ltd. has several departments. Goods supplied to each department are debited to a Memorandom Departmental Stock Account at cost, plus a fixed percentage (mark-up) to given the normal selling price. The mark-up is credited to a memorandom departmental 'Mark-up account', any reduction in selling prices (mark-down) will require adjustment in the stock account and in mark-up account. The mark up for Department *A* for the last three years has been 25%. Figures relevant to Department *A* for the year ended 31st March, 2013 were as follows:

Opening stock as on 1st April, 2012, at cost	₹ 65,000
Purchase at cost	₹ 2,00,000
Sales	₹ 3,00,000

It is further assertained that:

(1) Shortage of stock found in the year ending 31.03.2013, costing ₹ 1,000 were written off.
(2) Opening stock on 01.04.12 including goods costing ₹ 6,000 had been sold during the year and bad been marked down in the selling price by ₹ 600. The remaining stock had been sold during the year.
(3) Goods purchased during the year were marked down by ₹ 1,200 from a cost of ₹ 15,000. Marked-down stock costing ₹ 5,000 remained unsold on 31.03.13.
(4) The departmental closing stock is to be valued at cost subject to adjustment for mark-up and mark-down.

You are required to prepare:

(i) A Departmental Trading Account for Department *A* for the year ended 31st March, 2013 in the books of Head Office.
(ii) A Memorandom Stock Account for the year.
(iii) A Memorandom Mark-up Account for the year. **[12 Marks]**

(b) From the following information of STP Bank Ltd. pertaining to the financial year 2012–13, compute the provisions to be made in the Profit and Loss Account:

	₹ in lakh
Assets	
Standard	30,000
Sub-standard	20,000
Doubtful:	
For one year (secured)	8,000
For two years and three years (secured)	2,500
For more than three years (secured by mortgage of Plant & Machinery ₹ 500 lakh)	2,000
Loss Assets	1,700

[4 Mark]

Q.7 Answer any four of the following: **[4 × 4 = 16]**

(a) Classify the following into either operating or finance lease:

(i) Lessee has option to purchase the asset at lower than fair value, at the end of lease term;

(ii) Economic life of the asset is 7 years, lease term is 6 years, but asset is not acquired at the end of the lease term;

(iii) Economic life of the asset is 6 years, lease term is 2 years, but the asset is of special nature and has been procured only for use of the lessee;

(iv) Present value (PV) of Minimum lease payment (MLP) = "X". Fair value of the asset is "Y".

(b) Plymouth Ltd. is engaged in research on a new process design for its product. It had incurred ₹ 10 lakh on research during first 5 months of the financial year 2012–13. The development of the process began on 1st September, 2012 and upto 31st March, 2013, a sum of ₹ 8 lakh was incurred as Development Phase Expenditure, which meets assets recognition criteria.

From 1st April, 2013, the Company has implemented the new process design and it is likely that this will result in after tax saving of ₹ 2 lakh per annum for next five years.

The cost of capital is 10%. The present value of annuity factor of ₹ 1 for 5 years @ 10% is 3.7908.

Decide the treatment of Research and Development Cost of the project as per AS 26.

(c) State the basis on which the following common expenses, the benefit of which is shared by all the departments is distributed among the departments;

(i) Rent, rates and taxes, insurance of building;

(ii) Selling expenses such as discount, bad debts, selling commission and other such selling expenses;

(iii) Carriage Inward;

(iv) Depreciation;

(v) Interest on loan;

(vi) Profit or loss on sale of investment;

(vii) Wages;

(viii) Lighting and Heating Expenses;

(d) Raj & Co. has taken a loan of US$ 20,000 at the beginning of the financial year for a specific project at an interest rate of 6% per annum, payable annually. On the day of taking loan, the exchange rate between currencies was ₹ 48 per 1 US$. The exchange rate at the closing of the financial year was ₹50 per 1 US$. The corresponding amount could have been borrowed by the company in Indian Rupee at an interest rate of 11% per annum. Determine the treatment of borrowing cost in the books of accounts.

(e) Explain in short, the following principles and term of insurance business:

(i) Principle of Indemnity;

(ii) Insurable interest;

(iii) Principle of "UBERRIMAE FIDEI".

(iv) Catastrophic Loss.

Answers to IPC Examination Paper Nov. 2013

Solution 1(a). (i)

AS 4	Asper AS 4 "Contingencies and Events Occuring after the Balance Sheet Date", assets and liabilities should be adjusted for events occurring after the balance sheet date that provide additional evidence to assist the estimation of amounts relating to conditions existing at the balance sheet date.
Advice	Sale of immovable property before the closure of the books of accounts is clearly an event occurring after the balance sheet date but agreement to sell was effected on 1st March, 2013 i.e. before the balance sheet date. Registration of the sale deed on 15th April, 2013, simply provides additional information relating to the conditions existing at the balance sheet date. Therefore, adjustment to assets for sale of land is necessary in the financial statements of Pradeep Ltd. for the year ended 31st March, 2013.

Solution 1(a). (ii)

AS 4	As per AS 4 (Revised) defines "Events occurring after the balance sheet date" as those significant events, both favorable and unfavorable, that occur between the balance sheet date and the date on which the financial statements are approved by the Board of Directors in the case of a company.
Advice	The acquisition of another company is an event occurring after the balance sheet date. However, no adjustment to assets and liabilities is required as the event does not affect the determination and the condition of the amounts stated in the financial statements for the year ended 31st March, 2013. Disclosure should be made in the report of the approving authority of those events occurring after the balance sheet date that represent material changes and commitments affecting the financial position of the enterprise, the investment of ₹40 lakhs in April, 2013 in the acquisition of another company should be disclosed in the report of the Board of Directors to enable users of financial statements to make proper evaluations and decisions.

Solution 1(b).

WDV of asset at the end of year 2011–12 = ₹ 5,00,000 – ₹ 45,000 × 3 = ₹ 3,65,000

WDV of asset at the end of year 2011–12 (by reducing balance method)

$= ₹\ 5,00,000\ (1 - 0.15)^3 = ₹\ 3,07,062.50$

Depreciation to be charged in year 2012–13

= (₹ 3,65,000 – ₹ 3,07,062.50) + 15% of ₹ 3,07,062.50

₹ 57,937.50 + 46,059.38 = ₹ 1,03,997 (approx.)

AS 4	As per AS 5 'Net profit or loss for the period, Prior Period Items and Changes in Accounting Policies' the revision of remaining useful life is change in accounting estimate, and adoption of reducing balance method of depreciation instead of the straight-line method is change in accounting policy.
Advice	Since it is difficult to segregate impact of these two changes, the entire amount of difference between depreciation at old rate and depreciation charged in 2012–13 (₹ 1,03,997 – ₹ 45,000 = ₹ 58,997) is regarded as an effect of change in accounting estimate as per provisions of the standard. The effect of this change in accounting estimate should be properly disclosed in the financial statements of the company for the year ended 31st March, 2013.

Solution 1(c).

AS 4	As per AS 11 (Revised) 'The Effects of Changes in Foreign Exchange Rates', exchange differences arising on the settlement of monetary items or on reporting an enterprise's monetary items at rates different from those at which they were initially recorded during the period, or reported in previous financial statements, should be recognised as income or as an expense in the period in which they arise.
Advice	Since MCA has given an option for the enterprises to capitalize the exchange differences arising on reporting of long term foreign currency monetary items till 31st March, 2020, the company can capitalize the exchange differences arising due to long term loans linked with the acquisition of fixed assets.

Transaction 1: Calculation of exchange difference on fixed assets

Foreign Exchange Liability = 5,000/50 = US$ 100 lakhs

Exchange Difference = US$ 100 lakhs × (₹ 54.98 – ₹ 50) = ₹ 498 lakhs.

Loss due to exchange difference amounting ₹ 498 lakhs will be capitalised and added in the carrying value of fixed assets. Depreciation on the unamortised amount will be provided in the remaining years.

Transaction 2: Soft loan exchange difference (US $ 1 lakh i.e. ₹ 50 lakhs)

Value of loan 31.3.2013 → US $ 1 lakh × 54.98 = ₹ 54,98,000

AS 11 also provides that in case of liability designated as long-term foreign currency monetary item*, the exchange difference is to be accumulated in the Foreign Currency Monetary Item Translation Difference (FCMITD) and should be written off over the useful life of such long-term liability, by recognition as income or expenses in each of such periods. Exchange difference between reporting currency (INR) and foreign currency (USD) as on 31.03.2013 = US $ 1 lakh × ₹ (54.98 – 50) = ₹ 4.98 lakh.

Loan account is to be increased to 54.98 lakh and FCMITD account is to be debited by 4.98 lakh. Since loan is repayable in 3 equal annual instalments, ₹ 4.98 lakh/3 = ₹ 1.66 lakh is to be charged in Profit and Loss Account for the year ended 31st March, 2013 and balance in FCMITD A/c ₹ (4.98 lakh – 1.66 lakh) = ₹ 3.32 lakh is to be shown on the

'Equity & Liabilities' side of the Balance Sheet as a negative figure under the head 'Reserve and Surplus' as a separate line item.

Note: The above answer is given on the basis that the company has availed the option under para 46A of AS 11.

Solution 1(d).

(i) According to Schedule VI "An operating cycle is the time between the acquisition of assets for processing and their realization in cash or cash equivalents".

Therefore, operating cycle of Vasudha Ltd. will be computed as:

= 3.5 + 1 + 4.5 + 6 = 15 months

A Liability shall be classified as current when it is expected to be settled in the Company's normal operating cycle.

Since the operating cycle of Vasudha Ltd. is 15 months, trade payables expected to be paid in 14 months should be treated as a current liability.

(ii) Revised schedule VI does not require WIP to be disclosed in the Statement of Profit and Loss, thus amounts for which WIP have been completed at the beginning and at the end of the accounting period may not be disclosed. Therefore, the non-disclosure in the financial statements by the company may not amount to violation of Revised Schedule VI if the differences between opening and closing WIP are not material.

Solution 2.

BALANCE SHEET OF M/S ABEEJAY & CO. AS AT 31ST MARCH, 2013

Liabilities		₹	*Assets*		₹
Capitals:			Building		7,00,000
Avi	7,71,000		(₹ 4,00,000 + ₹ 3,00,000)		
Bishnu	5,14,000		Plant & machinery		
Joe	2,57,000	15,42,000	(₹ 2,50,000 + ₹ 2,00,000)		4,50,000
Sundry creditors			Office equipment		
(1,20,000 + 89,000)		2,09,000	(₹ 39,000 + ₹ 50,000)		89,000
Bank overdraft		90,000	Vehicle		98,000
			Furniture		11,000
			Stock-in-trade		
			(₹ 70,000 + ₹ 80,000)		1,50,000
			Sundry debtors		
			(₹ 1,00,000 + ₹ 90,000)	1,90,000	
			Less: Provision for doubtful		
			debts (₹ 4,000 + ₹ 3,000)	(7,000)	1,83,000
			Bank balance		
			(₹ 80,000 + ₹ 60,000)		1,40,000
			Cash in hand		20,000*
		18,41,000			18,41,000

PARTNERS' CAPITAL ACCOUNTS IN THE BOOKS OF ABHAY & CO.

Particulars	*Avi (₹)*	*Bishnu (₹)*	*Particulars*	*Avi (₹)*	*Bishnu (₹)*
To Capital A/cs— M/s Abeejay & Co.	6,48,000	2,39,000	By Balance b/d	5,31,000	2,00,000
			By Reserve	9,000	3,000
			By Realisation A/c	1,08,000	36,000
	6,48,000	2,39,000		6,48,000	2,39,000

PARTNERS' CAPITAL ACCOUNTS IN THE BOOKS OF BIJOY & CO.

Particulars	*Bishnu (₹)*	*Joe (₹)*	*Particulars*	*Bishnu (₹)*	*Joe (₹)*
To Capital A/cs— M/s Abjeey & Co.	4,83,667	2,43,333	By Balance b/d	3,97,000	2,00,000
			By Reserve	6,000	3,000
			By Realisation A/c	80,667	40,333
	4,83,667	2,43,333		4,83,667	2,43,333

Working Notes:

1. Computation of purchase considerations

		Abhay & Co. ₹	*Bijoy & Co.* ₹
Assets:			
Goodwill		42,000	30,000
Building		4,00,000	3,00,000
Vehicle		–	98,000
Furniture		–	11,000
Plant & machinery		2,50,000	2,00,000
Office equipment		39,000	50,000
Stock-in-trade		70,000	80,000
Sundry debtors		1,00,000	90,000
Bank balance		80,000	60,000
Cash in hand		20,000	–
Due from R & Co.		1,00,000	–
	(A)	11,01,000	9,19,000
Liabilities:			
Creditors		1,20,000	89,000
Provision for doubtful debts		4,000	3,000
Due to R & Co.		–	1,00,000
Bank overdraft		90,000	–
	(B)	2,14,000	1,92,000
Purchase consideration (A – B)		8,87,000	7,27,000

2. Computation of proportionate capitals

	₹
M/s Abeejay & Co. (Purchase Consideration) (₹ 8,87,000 + ₹ 7,27,000)	16,14,000
Less: Goodwill adjustment	(72,000)
Total capital of new firm (Distributed in ratio 3 : 2 : 1)	15,42,000
Avi's proportionate capital	7,71,000
Bishnu's proportionate capital	5,14,000
Joe's proportionate capital	2,57,000

3. Computation of Capital Adjustments

	Avi ₹	Bishnu ₹	Joe ₹	Total ₹
Balance transferred from Abhay & Co.	6,48,000	2,39,000		8,87,000
Balance transferred from Bijoy & Co.		4,83,667	2,43,333	7,27,000
	6,48,000	7,22,667	2,43,333	16,14,000
Less: Goodwill written off in the ratio of 3 : 2 : 1	(36,000)	(24,000)	(12,000)	(72,000)
Existing capital	6,12,000	6,98,667	2,31,333	15,42,000
Proportionate capital	7,71,000	5,14,000	2,57,000	15,42,000
Amount to be brought in (paid off)	1,59,000	(1,84,667)	25,667	

4. Realisation Account in the books of Abhay & Co.

		₹		₹
To Building		3,50,000	By Creditors	1,20,000
To Plant & machinery		2,00,000	By Bank overdraft	90,000
To Office equipment		38,000	By M/s Abeejay & Co.	8,87,000
To Stock-in-trade		65,000	(purchase consideration)	
To Sundry debtors		1,00,000	(W.N.1)	
To Bank balance		80,000		
To Cash in hand		20,000		
To Due from R & Co.		1,00,000		
To Partners' capital A/cs:				
Avi	1,08,000			
Bishnu	36,000	1,44,000		
		10,97,000		10,97,000

5. Realisation Account in the books of Bijoy & Co.

		₹		₹
To Building		2,80,000	By Creditors	89,000
To Plant & machinery		1,50,000	By Due to R & Co.	1,00,000
To Office equipment		45,000	By M/s Abjeejay & Co.	7,27,000
To Vehicle		90,000	(purchase consideration)	
To Furniture		10,000		
To Stock-in-trade		70,000		
To Sundry debtors		90,000		
To Bank balance		60,000		
To Partners' capital A/cs :				
Bishnu	80,667			
Joe	40,333	1,21,000		
		9,16,000		9,16,000

Note: The above answer has been given on the basis that Realization account is prepared while closing the books of Old firms and New firm takes over the business of both old firms.

Solution 3.

JOURNAL

Date	Particulars		Dr. (₹)	Cr. (₹)
1.6.2012	Bank A/c	Dr.	2,25,00,000	
	To Debenture Application and Allotment A/c			2,25,00,000
	(Application money received on 2,25,000 debentures @ ₹ 100 each)			
1.7.2012	Debenture Application and Allotment A/c	Dr.	2,25,00,000	
	Underwriters A/c	Dr.	75,00,000	
	To 12% Debentures A/c			3,00,00,000
	(Allotment of 2,25,000 debentures to applicants and 75,000 debentures to underwriters)			
	Underwriting Commission	Dr.	6,00,000	
	To Underwriters A/c			6,00,000
	(Commission payable to underwriters @ 2% on ₹ 3,00,00,000)			
	Bank A/c	Dr.	69,00,000	
	To Underwriters A/c			69,00,000
	(Amount received from underwriters in settlement of account)			
30.9.2012	Debenture Interest A/c	Dr.	9,00,000	
	To Bank A/c			9,00,000
	(Interest paid on debentures for 3 months @ 12% on ₹ 3,00,00,000)			
1.12.2012	12% Debentures A/c	Dr.	1,50,00,000	
	To Equity Share Capital A/c			30,00,000
	To Securities Premium A/c			1,20,00,000
	(Conversion of 50% of debentures into shares of ₹ 50 each with a face value of ₹ 10)			
31.3.2012	Debenture Interest A/c	Dr.	12,00,000	
	To Bank A/c			12,00,000
	(Interest paid on debentures for the half year)			
31.3.2013	Profit & loss A/c	Dr.	6,00,000	
	To Underwriting commission			6,00,000
	(Being underwriting commission charged to Profit & Loss A/c at the year end)			
31.3.2013	Profit & Loss A/c	Dr.	21,00,000	
	To Debenture Interest			21,00,000
	(Being interest on debenture 12,00,000 + 9,00,000 charged to Profit & lss A/c at the year end)			

Working Notes:

Calculation of Debenture Interest for the half year ended 31st March, 2013

Interest on ₹ 1,50,00,000 for 6 months @ 12%	=	₹ 9,00,000
Interest on ₹ 1,50,00,000 for 2 months @ 12%	=	₹ 3,00,000
		₹ 12,00,000

Solution 3(b).

BALANCE SHEET OF ENTYCE LIMITED AS AT 01.04.2013

Particulars	Note No	Figures as the end of current reporting period
I. Equity and Liabilities		
(1) Shareholders' Funds		
(a) Share Capital	1	55,00,000
(b) Reserves and Surplus	2	85,85,000
(2) Non-Current Liabilities		
(a) Long-term borrowings-Unsecured Loans		45,00,000
(3) Current Liabilities		
(a) Short-term provisions		90,00,000
Total		2,75,85,000
II. Assets		
(1) Non-Current Assets		
(a) Fixed Assets		
Tangible Assets		1,50,00,000
(2) Current Assets		
(a) Cash and cash equivalents		5,85,000
(b) Other current assets		1,20,00,000
Total		2,75,85,000

Notes To Accounts:

		₹
1. Share Capital		
5,50,000 Equity Shares of ₹ 10 each		55,00,000
2. Reserve and Surplus		
General Reserve	50,00,000	
Add: Debenture Redemption Reserve transfer	35,00,000	
	85,00,000	
Add: Profit on sale of investments	2,00,000	
	87,00,000	
Less: Premium on redemption of debentures (80,000 × ₹ 5)	(4,00,000)	83,00,000
Securities Premium Account (1,50,000 × ₹ 1.9)		2,85,000
		85,85,000

Working Notes:

1. Redemption Value of debentures opting for conversion = [25% (80,000 – 12,000)] × ₹ 105 = ₹ 17,85,000
2. Number of Equity Shares to be allotted = 17,85,000/₹ 11.90 = 1,50,000 shares of ₹ 10 each.

(ii) Calculation of cash to be paid

Number of debentures	80,000
Less: Number of debentures to be converted into equity shares	17,000
	63,000
Redemption value of 63,000 debentures (63,000 × ₹ 105)	₹ 66,15,000

(iii) Cash and Bank Balance

Balance before redemption	40,00,000
Add: Proceeds of investments sold	32,00,000
	72,00,000
Less: Cash paid to debenture holders	(66,15,000)
	5,85,000

Solution 4.

RECEIVER'S RECEIPTS AND PAYMENTS ACCOUNT

Receipts	(₹)	(₹)	*Payments*	(₹)	(₹)
Sundry Assets realised		2,00,000	Cost of the Receiver		1,950
Surplus received from Mortgage loan:			Preferential payments:		
Sale Proceeds of land and building	1,60,000		Income Taxes (raised within 12 months)	–	25,000
Less: Applied to discharge of mortgage loan	(70,000)	90,000	Debentures holders:		
			Principal amount	1,50,000	
			Interest for half year	9,750	1,59,750
			Surplus transferred to the Liquidator		1,03,300
		2,90,000			2,90,000

LIQUIDATOR'S FINAL STATEMENT OF ACCOUNT

Receipts	₹	*Payments*		₹
Surplus received from Receiver	1,03,300	Cost of Liquidation		3,000
Assets Realised	1,50,000	Remuneration to Liquidator (1,50,000 × 2%)		3,000
Calls on Contributies:		Unsecured Creditors:		
On holder of 5,000 Equity Shares at the rate of ₹ 1.38 per share	6,900	Trade	38,000	
		Directors for Bank O/D cleared	30,000	68,000
		Preferential Shareholders:		
		Capital	1,50,000	
		Arrears of Dividends	30,000	1,80,000
		Equity shareholders: Return of money to holders of 10,000 equity share at 62 paise each		6,200
	2,60,200			2,60,200

Working Notes:

Call from partly paid shares

Deficit before call from Equity Shares = ₹ (1,03,300 + 1,50,000) – ₹(3,000 + 3,000 + 68,000 + 1,80,000)	=	₹ 700
Notional call on 5,000 shares @ ₹ 2 each		10,000
Net balance after notional call	(a)	9,300
No. of shares deemed fully paid	(b)	15,000

Refund on fully paid shares $\frac{9,300}{15,000}$ = ₹ 0.62

Calls on partly paid share (₹ 2 – ₹ 0.62) = ₹ 1.38

Solution 5(a).

AVERAGE CAPITAL COST

(₹ in crores)

Particulars	2010–11 ₹	2011–12 ₹	2012–13 ₹
Opening Capital Cost (A)	135.39	137.02	138
Additional capital expenditure (allowed above) (B)	1.63	0.98	0.52
Closing Capital Cost (A) + (B)	137.02	138	138.52
Average Capital cost	136.21	137.51	138.26

Solution 5(b).

RETURN ON EQUITY

	Particulars	2010–11 ₹	2011–12 ₹	2012–13 ₹
A	Opening Capital Cost	135.39	137.02	138
B	Equity-Opening considered now [(A) × 0.30]	40.617	41.106	41.4
C	Additional allowable capital expenditure	1.63	0.98	0.52
D	Addition of Equity due to admitted additional capital expenditure [(C) × 0.30]	0.489	0.294	0.156
E	Equity-Closing [(B) + (D)]	41.106	41.4	41.556
F	Average equity [(B) + (E)]/2	40.861	41.253	41.478
G	Return on Equity (F × 14%)	5.720	5.775	5.807

Solution 5(c).

INTEREST ON LOAN

	Particulars	2010–11 ₹	2011–12 ₹	2012–13 ₹
A	Opening Capital Cost	135.39	137.02	138
B	Gross Opening loan-considered at 70% of	94.773	95.914	96.6
C	Cumulative Repayment of Loan upto previous year	14	14.96	15.83
D	Net Loan Opening [(B) – (C)]	80.773	80.954	80.77
E	Additional capital expenditure (allowed above)	1.63	0.98	0.52
F	Addition of loan due to approved additional capital expenditure-considered at 70% of (E)	1.141	0.686	0.364
G	Repayment of loan during the year (net)	0.96	0.87	0.68
H	Net Loan Closing [(D) + (F) – (G)]	80.954	80.77	80.454
I	Average Loan {(D) + (H)/2}	80.864	80.862	80.612
J	Weighted Average Rate of Interest on Loan	7.35%	7.48%	7.50%
K	Interest on Loan [(I) × (J)]	5.944	6.048	6.046

Solution 5(d).

Depreciation

Name of the Power Station: Wastan Power Generation Project	
Date of commercial operation/Work Completed Date	1/4/95
Beginning of Current year	1/4/10
Useful life	35 Years
Remaining Useful Life	20 Years

(Figures in ₹ crores)

S.N.		2010–11 ₹	2011–12 ₹	2012–13 ₹
	Capital cost at beginning of the year	135.39	137.02	138
	Additional capitalisation during the year	1.63	0.98	0.52
	Closing capital cost	137.02	138	138.52
1.	Average capital cost	136.205	137.51	138.26
2.	*Less*: Value of Land	0.000	0.000	0.000
3.	Capital cost for depreciation (1–2)	136.205	137.51	138.26
4.	Depreciable value (90% of 3)	122.585	123.759	124.434
5.	Depreciation recovered upto 2008–09	49.05		
6.	Depreication recovered in 2009–10	3.26		
7.	Depreciation recovered upto previous year	52.31	55.824	59.400
8.	Balance depreciation to be recovered (4–7)	70.27	67.936	65.035
9.	Balance useful life of 35 years	20	19	18
10.	Yearly depreciation from 2010–11 (8/9)	3.514	3.576	3.613
11.	Depreciation recovered upto the year (7+10)	55.824	59.400	63.013

Solution 6.

(i) DEPARTMENT TRADING ACCOUNT IN THE BOOKS OF HEAD OFFICE

For the year ending on 31.03.2013

Dr. *Cr.*

Particulars	₹	*Particulars*	₹
To Opening Stock	65,000	By Sales	3,00,000
To Purchases	2,00,000	By Shortage	1,000
To Gross Profit c/d	58,880	By Closing Stock	22,880
	3,23,880		3,23,880

(ii) MEMORANDOM STOCK ACCOUNT (FOR DEPARTMENT A) (AT SELLING PRICE)

Dr. *Cr.*

Particulars	₹	*Particulars*	₹
To Balance b/d (₹ 65,000 + 25% of ₹ 65,000)	81,250	By Profit & Loss A/c (Cost of Shortage)	1,000
To Purchases (₹ 2,00,000 + 25% of ₹ 2,00,000)	2,50,000	By Memorandom Department Mark up A/c (Loan on Shortage) (₹ 1,000 × 25%)	250
		By Memorandom Departmental Mark-up A/c (Mark-down on Current Purchases)	1,200
		By Debtors A/c (Sales)	3,00,000
		By Memorandom Departmental Mark-up A/c (Mark Down on Opening Stock)	600
		By Balance c/d	28,200
	3,31,250		3,31,250

(iii) MEMORANDUM DEPARTMENTAL MARK-UP ACCOUNT

Dr. Cr.

Particulars	₹	Particulars	₹
To Memorandum Departmental Stock A/c (₹ 1,000 × 25/100)	250	By Balance b/d (₹ 81,250 × 25/125)	16,250
To Memorandum Departmental Stock A/c	1200	By Memorandum Departmental Stock A/c (2,50,000 × 25/125)	50,000
To Memorandum Departmental Stock A/c	600		
To Gross Profit transferred to Profit & Loss A/c	58,880		
To Balance c/d [(₹ 28,200 + 400*) × 25/125 – 400]	5,320		
	66,250		66,250

*[₹ 1,200 × 5,000/15,000] = 400

Working Notes:

(i) Calculation of Cost of Sales

	Particulars	₹
A	Sales as per Books	3,00,000
B	*Add*: Mark-down in opening stock (given)	600
C	*Add*: Mark-down in sales out of current Purchases (₹ 1,200 × 10,000/15,000)	800
D	Value of sales if there was no mark-down (A + B + C)	3,01,400
E	*Less*: Gross Profit (25/125 of ₹ 3,01,400) subject to Mark Down (₹ 600 + ₹ 800)	(60,280)
F	Cost of Sales (D – E)	2,41,120

(ii) Calculation of Closing Stock

	Particulars	₹
A	Opening Stock	65,000
B	*Add*: Purchases	2,00,000
C	*Less*: Cost of Sales	(2,41,120)
D	*Less*: Shortage	(1,000)
E	Closing Stock (A + B + C + D)	22,880

Solution 6(b).

CALCULATION OF AMOUNT OF PROVISION TO BE MADE IN THE PROFIT AND LOSS ACCOUNT

Classification of Assets	*Amount of Advances (₹ in lakhs)*	*% age of provision (₹ in lakhs)*	*Amount of provision (₹ in lakhs)*
Standard assets	30,000	0.40	120
Sub-standard assets*	20,000	15	3,000
Doubtful assets:			
For one year (secured)	8,000	25	2,000
For two to three years (secured)	2,500	40	1,000
For more than three years: unsecured	1,500	100	1,500
secured	500	100	500
Loss Assets	1,700	100	1,700
Total provision required			9,820

* Considered as fully secured

Solution 7(a).

(i) If it becomes certain at the inception of lease itself that the option will be exercised by the lessee, it is a Finance Lease*.

(ii) The lease will be classified as a finance lease, since a substantial portion of the life of the asset is covered by the lease term.

(iii) Since the asset is procured only for the use lessee, it is a finance lease.

(iv) The lease is a finance lease if X = Y, or where X substantially equals Y.

Solution 7(b).

Research Expenditure: According to AS 26 'Intangible Assets', the expenditure on research of new process design for its product ₹ 10 lakhs should be charged to Profit and Loss Account in the year in which it is incurred. It is presumed that the entire expenditure is incurred in the financial year 2012–13. Hence, it should be written off as an expense in that year itself.

Cost of internally generated intangible asset: It is given that development phase expenditure amounting ₹ 8 lakhs incurred upto 31st March, 2013 meets asset recognition criteria. As per AS 26, for measurement of such internally generated intangible asset, fair value can be estimated by discounting estimated future net cash flows.

Savings (after tax) from implementation of new design for next 5 years	₹ 2 lakhs p.a.
Company's cost of capital	10%
Annuity factor @ 10% for 5 years	3.7908
Present value of net cash flows (₹ 2 lakhs × 3.7908)	₹ 7.582 lakhs

The cost of an internally generated intangible asset would be lower of cost value ₹ 8 lakhs or present value of future net cash flows ₹ 7.582 lakhs.

Hence, cost of an internally generated intangible asset will be ₹ 7.582 lakhs.

The difference of ₹ 0.418 lakhs (i.e. ₹ 8 lakhs – ₹ 7.582 lakhs) will be amortized by Plymouth for the financial year 2012–13.

Amortisation: The company can amortise ₹ 7.582 lakhs over a period of five years by charging ₹ 1.5164 lakhs per annum from the financial year 2013–2014 onwards.

Solution 7(c).

ALLOCATION OF EXPENSES

S.No.	Expenses	Basis
1.	Rent, rates and taxes, repairs, insurance of building	Floor area occupied by each department (if given) otherwise on time basis
2.	Selling expenses, e.g., discount, bad debts, selling commission, and other such selling expenses	Sales of each department
3.	Carriage inward	Purchases of each department
4.	Depreciation	Value of assets of each department otherwise on time basis
5.	Interest on loan	Utilisation of loan amount in each department (if can be identified), otherwise in combined P&L A/c
6.	Profit & loss on sale of investment	Value of investments sold in each department (if value can be identified), otherwise in combined P&L A/c
7.	Wages	Time devoted to each department
8.	Lighting and Heating expenses (eg. energy expenses)	Consumption of energy by each department

Solution 7(d).

The following computations would be made to determine that amount of borrowing costs for the purpose of AS 16 'Borrowing Costs':

Interest for the period = US $ 20,000 × ₹ 50 per US $ × 6% = ₹ 60,000.

Increase in the liability towards the principal amount = US $ 20,000 × ₹ (50–48) = ₹ 40,000. (A)

Interest that would have resulted if the loan was taken in Indian Currency
= US $ 20,000 × 48 × 11% = ₹ 1,05,600

Difference between interest on local currency borrowing and foreign currency borrowing
= ₹ 1,05,600 – ₹ 60,000 = ₹ 45,600 (B)

In the above case, ₹ 40,000 (A) is less than ₹ 45,600 (B), therefore the entire exchange difference of ₹ 40,000 would be considered as borrowing costs. The total borrowing cost would be ₹ 1,00,000 (₹ 60,000 + ₹ 40,000)

Solution 7(e).

(i) Principle of Indemnity: Insurance is a contract of indemnity. The insurer is called indemnifier and the insured is the indemnified. In a contract of indemnity, only those who suffer loss are compensated to the extent of actual loss suffered by them. One cannot make profit by insuring his risks.

(ii) Insurable Interest: All and sundry cannot enter into contracts of insurance. For example, A cannot insure the life of B who is a total stranger. But if B, happens to be his wife or his debtor or business manager, A has insurable interest i.e. vested interest and therefore he can insure the life of B. For every type of policy insurable interest is insisted upon. In the absence of such interest the contract will amount to a wagering contract.

(iii) Principle of UBERRIMAE FIDEI: Under ordinary law of contract there is no positive duty to tell the whole truth in relation to the subject-matter of the contract. There is only the negative obligation to tell nothing but the truth. In a contract of insurance, however there is an implied condition that each party must disclose every material fact known to him. All contracts of insurance are contracts of uberrima fidei, i.e., contracts of utmost good faith. This is because the assessment of the risk and the determination of the premium by the insurer depend on the full and frank disclosure of all material facts in the proposal form.

(iv) Catastrophic Loss: A loss (or related losses) which is unbearable i.e. it causes severe consequences such as bankruptcy to a family, organization, or insurer.

Paper-5: Advanced Accounting CA IPC (Group II) Examination (May 2014)

Question No. 1 is compulsory.
Attempt any Five questions from the remaining Six questions
Wherever necessary suitable assumptions may be made by the candidates.
Working notes should form part of the answer.

Q.1 Answer the following questions: **[4 × 5 = 20]**

(a) In its Final Accounts for the year ended 31st March, 2014, Z Ltd. made a provision of 3% of its total debtors. On 10th March, 2014, a debtor of ₹ 5 lakhs suffered a heavy loss and became insolvent in April 2014. The loss was not insured.

State giving reasons, if the company may provide for the full loss in its accounts for the year ended 31st March, 2014.

(b) Suhana Ltd. issued 12% secured debentures of ₹ 100 Lakhs on 01.05.2013, to be utilized as under:

Particulars	*Amount (₹ in lakhs)*
Construction of factory building	40
Purchase of Machinery	35
Working Capital	25

In March 2014, construction of the factory building was completed and machinery was installed and ready for it's intended use. Total interest on debentures for the financial year ended 31.03.2014 was ₹ 11,00,000. During the year 2013-14, the company had invested idle fund out of money raised from debentures in banks' fixed deposit and had earned an interest of ₹ 2,00,000.

Show the treatment of interest under Accounting Standard 16 and also explain nature of assets.

(c) What do you uinderstand by the term "Interest rate implicit on lease"?

Calculate the interest rate implicit on lease from the following details:

Annual Lease Rent	₹ 80,000 at the end of each yea
Lease Period	5 Years
Guaranteed Residual Value	₹ 40,000
Unguaranteed Residual Value	₹ 24,000
Fair Value at the inception of the lease	₹ 3,20,000

Discounted rates for the first 5 years are as below:

At 10% 0.909, 0.826, 0.751, 0.683, 0621

At 14% 0.877, 0.769, 0.675, 0.592, 0.519

(d) The following informatiion is available for AB Ltd. for the accounting year 2012-13 and 2013-14:

Net profit for	
Year 2012-13	22,00,000
Year 2013-14	30,00,000

No of shares outstanding prior to right issue 10,00,000 shares.

Right issue: One new share for each five shares outstanding i.e. 2,00,000 *shares.*

: Right Issue price ₹ 25

: Last date to exercise right 31st July, 2013

Fair value of one equity share immediately prior to exercise of rights on 31.07.2013 is ₹ 32.

You are required to compute:

(i) Basic earnings per share for the year 2012-13.

(ii) Restated basic earnings per share for the year 2012-13 for right issue.

(iii) Basic earnings per share for the year 2013-14.

Q.2. The partners P, Q & R have called you to assist them in winding up the affairs of their partnership on 31.12.2013. Their balance sheet as on that date is given below:

Liabilities	₹	*Assets*	₹
Capital Accounts:		Land & Building	50,000
P	65,000	Plant & Machinery	46,000
Q	50,500	Furniture & Fixture	10,000
R	32,000	Stock	14,500
Sundry Creditors	16,000	Debtors	14,000
		Cash at Bank	9,000
		Loan P	13,000
		Loan Q	7,000
	1,63,500		1,63,500

(a) The partners share profit and losses in the ratio of 4:3:2.

(b) Cash is distributed to the partners at the end of each month.

(c) A summary of liquidatioin transactions are as follows:

January 2014

- ₹ 9,000 - collected from debtors; balance is uncollectable.
- ₹ 8,000 - received from the sale of entire furniture
- ₹ 1,000 - Liquidation expenses paid.
- ₹ 6,000 - Cash retained in the business at the end of montjh

February 2014

- ₹ 1,000 - Liquidation expenses paid.
- As part payment of his capital, R accepted a machinery for ₹ 9,000 (book value ₹ 3,500)
- ₹ 2,000 - Cash retained in the business at the end of month

March 2014

- ₹ 38,000 - received on the sale of remaining plant and machinery.
- ₹ 10,000 - received from the sale of entire stock.
- ₹ 1,700 - Liquidation expenses paid.
- ₹ 41,000 - Received on sale of land & building.
- No Cash is retained in the business.

You are required to prepare a schedule of cash payments amongst the partners by "Higher Relative Capital Method".

Q.3.(a) ZED Ltd. had 25,000, 10% Debentures of ₹ 100 each outstanding as on 1st April, 2013. redeemable on 31st March, 2014. On 1st April, 2013, Sinking Fund was ₹ 24 lakhs represented bty 3,000 own Debentures purchased at the average price of ₹ 98 and 8% Stocks of face value of ₹ 22 lakhs. The annual installment towards Sinking. Fund was ₹ 90,000.

On 31st March, 2014, the investments were realized at ₹ 97 and the Debentures were redeemed.

Draw the following Accounts for the year ended 31st March, 2014:

(i) 10% Debenture Account,

(ii) Debenture Redemption Sinking Fund Account,

(iii) Show the necessary working notes.

Q.3.(b) A company made a public issue of 2,00,000 equity shares of ₹ 10 each at a premium of ₹ 2 per share. The entire issue was underwritten by the underwriters L, M, N and O in the ratio of 4:3:2:1 respectively with the provision of firm underwriting of 5,000, 4,000, 2,000 and 2,000 shares respectively.

The company received application for 1,50,000 shares (excluding firm underwriting) from public, out of which applications for 55,000, 40,000, 42,000 and 8,000 shares were marked in favour of L, M, N and O respectively.

Calculate the liability of each underwriter as regards the number of shares to be taken up assuming that the benefit of underwriting is not given to the individual underwriter.

Q.4. P Ltd. and Q Ltd. were carrying on the business of manufacturing of auto components. both the companies decided to amalgamare and a new company PQ Ltd. is to be formed with an Authorized Capital of ₹ 10,00,000 divided into 1,00,000 equity shares of ₹ 10 each. The Balance Sheet of the companies as on 31.03.2014 were as under:

Balance Sheet of P Limited as at 31.03.2014

Particulars	Amount (₹)
I. Equity and Liabilities	
1. Shareholder's Fund	
(a) Share Capital	1,40,00
(b) Reserves & Surplus (Profit & Loss A/c)	30,000
2. Non Current Liabilities (8 % Secured Debentures)	1,10,000
3. Current Liabilities (Trade Payables)	54,000
Total	3,34,000
II. Assets	
1. Non-current Assets	
(a) Fixed Assets	
Bulding at cost less Depreciation	1,00,000
Plant & Machinery at cost *less* Depreciation	25,000
2. Current Assets	
(a) Inventories	1,35,000
(b) Trade Receivables	44,000
(c) Cash at bank	30,000
Total	3,34,000

Balance Sheet of Q Limited as at 31.03.2014

Particulars	Amount (₹)
I. Equity and Liabilities	
1. Shareholder's Fund	
(a) Share Capital	2,50,000
(b) Reserves & Surplus	
General Reserve	1,20,000
Profit & Loss A/c	35,000
2. Current Liabilities (Trade Payables)	1,40,000
Total	5,45,000
II. Assets	
1. Non-current assets	
(a) Fixed Assets	
Building at cost less depreciation	1,90,000
Plant & Machinery at cost less depreciation	80,000
Furniture & Fixture at cost less depreciation	25,000
2. Current Assets	
(a) Inventories	50,000
(b) Trade Receivables	1,42,000
(c) Cash at bank	58,000
Total	5,45,000

The assets and liabilities of the existing companies are to be transferred at book value with the exception of some items detailed below:

(i) Goodwill of P Ltd. was worth ₹ 50,000 and of Q Ltd. was worth ₹ 1,50,000,.

(ii) Furniture & Fixture of Q Ltd. was valued at ₹ 35,000.

(iii) The debtors of P Ltd. are realized fully and bank balance of P Ltd. are to be retained by the liquidator and the sundry creditors are to be paid of the proceeds thereof.

(iv) The debentures of P Ltd. are to be dischareged by issue of 8% debentures of PQ Ltd. at a premium of 10%.

You are required to:

(i) Compute the basis on which shares in PQ Ltd. will be issued at par to the shareholders of the existing companies.

(ii) Draw up a Balance Sheet of PQ Ltd. as at 1st April, 2014, the date of completiion of amalgamatiion.

(iii) Write up Journal entires including bank entries for closing the books of P Ltd.

Q.5.(a) Jay Electyricity Company keeps accounts under the Double Accounts System. It decides to replace its old Plant with a new Plant. The Plant when installed in 2004 cost the company ₹ 75 lakhs, the components of materials, labour and overheads being in the ratio of 4 : 4 : 2. It is ascertained that the cost of materials has gone up by 250% and the cost of the labour has gone up by 200%. The proportion of material, labour and overheads has changed to 5 : 4 : 4.

The cost of the new plantm is ₹ 250 lakhs. In addition, goods worth ₹ 38 lakhs have been used in the construction of the new Plant. The old Plant was sold as scrap for ₹ 15 lakhs.

You are required to calculate:

(i) The amount to be capitalized.

(ii) The amount of be charged to Revenue.

Necessary Ledger Accounts are to be drawn as working notes.

(b) From the following informationi of XYZ Marine Insurance Ltd. for the year ending 31st March, 2014, find out the

(i) Ne Premium earned (ii) Net claims Incurred

Particulars	*Direct Business (₹)*	*Re-insurance (₹)*
Premium Received	92,00,000	7,86,000
Premium Receivable as on 01.04.2013	4,59,000	37,000
Premium Receivable as on 31.03.2014	3,94,000	33,000
Premium Paid		6,36,000
Premium Payable as on 01.04.2013		28,000
Premium payable as on 31.03.2014		20,000
Claims Paid	73,00,000	5,80,000
Claims payable as on 01.04.2013	94,000	16,000
Claims payable as on 31.03.2014	1,01,000	12,000
Claims received		2,10,000
Claims receivable as on 01.04.2013		42,000
Claims receivable as on 31.03.2014		39,000

Q.6.(a) Pass necessary Journal entries in the books of an independent Brach of a Company, wherever required, to rectify or adjust the following:

(i) Income of ₹ 2,800 allocated to the Branch by Head Office but not recorded in the Branch books.

(ii) Provision for doubtful debts, whose accounts are kept by the Head Office, not provided earlier for ₹ 1,000.

(iii) Branch paid ₹ 3,000 as salary to a Head Office Manager, but the amount paid has been debited by the Branch to Salaries Account.

(iv) Branch incurred travelling expenses of ₹ 5,000 on behalf of other Branches, but not recorded in the books of Branch.

(v) A remittance of ₹ 1,50,000 sent by the Branch has not received by Head Office on the date of reconcillation of Accounts.

(vi) Head Office allocates ₹ 75,000 to the Branch as Head Office expenses, which has not yet been recorded by the Branch.

(vii) Head Office collected ₹ 30,000 directly from a branch Customer. The intimation of the fact has been received by the Branch only now.

(viii) Goods dispatched by the Head office amounting to ₹ 10,000, but not received by the Branch till date of reconcillation. The Goods have been received subsequently.

Q.6.(b) Department P sells goods to Department S at a profit of 25% on cost and to Department Q at a profit of 15% on cost. Department S sells goods to P and Q at a profit of 20% and 30% on sales respectively. Department Q sells goods to P and S at 20% and 10% profit on cost respectively.

Departmental Managers are entitled to 10% commission on net profit subject to unrealized profit on departmental sales bei8ng eliminated. Departmental profits after charging Manager's commission, but before adjustement of unrealized profits are as below:

	₹
Department P	90,000
Department S	60,000
Department Q	45,000

Stock tying at different Departments at the end of the year are as below:

Figures in ₹

	Departments		
	P	*S*	*Q*
Transfer from P	-	18,000	14,000
Transfer from S	48,000	-	38,000
Transfer from Q	12,000	8,000	

Find out correct Departmental Profits after charging Managers'm Commission.

Q.7. Answer any four of the following: **[4 × 4 = 16]**

(a) A loan account remains out of order as on the date of Balance Sheet of a Bank. The account has been classified as doubtful assets (up to 3 years). Detail of the account is:

Outstanding	₹ 7,24,000
ECGC Cover	30% of outstanding (Subject to maximum of ₹ 1,50,000)
Value of security	
As per valuation on the date of grant of loan	2,25,000
As per realizable value as on date of Balance Sheet	1,75,000

Compute the necessary provision to be made by bank as per applicable rate.

(b) State under which head these accounts should be classified in Balance Sheet, as per Schedule III to The Companies Act 2013:

(i) Share application money received in excess of issued share capital.

(ii) Share option outstanding account.

(iii) Unpaid matured debenture and interest accrued thereon.

(iv) Uncalled liability on shares and other partly paid investments.

(v) Calls unpaid.

(vi) Intangible Assets under development.

(vii) Money received against share warrant.

(viii) Long term maturity of finance lease obligation.

(c) Explain in brief the treatment of Refund of Government Grants in line with AS 12 in the following three situations:

(i) When Government Grant is related to revenue,

(ii) When Government Grant is related to specific fixed assets,

(iii) When Government Grant is in the nature of Promoter's contribution.

(d) *W* paid a premium to other partners of the firm at the time of his admission to the firm, with a condition that the will not be dissolved before expiry of five years. The firm is dissolved after three years. W claims refund to premium.

(i) List the criteria for the calculation of the amount of refund.

(ii) Also list any two conditions when no claim in this respect will arise.

(e) Give four conditions to be fulfilled by a Joint Stock Company to buy back its equity Shares.

Answers to IPC Examination Paper May 2014

Solution 1(a)

AS 4: According to para 8.2 of Accounting Standard 4 "Contingencies and Events Occurring after the Balance Sheet Date", adjustments to assets and liabilities are required for events occurring after the balance sheet date that provide additional informationi materially affecting the determination of the amounts relating to conditions existing at the balance sheet date.

Decision: Though the debtor became insolvent after balance sheet date, yet he had suffered heavy loss (not convered by the insurance), before the balance sheet date and this loss was the cause of the insolvency of the debtor.

Therefore the company must make full provision for bad debts amounting ₹ 5 lakhs i its final accounts for the year ended 31st March, 2014.

Solution 1(b)

AS 16: According to para 6 of AS 16 "Borrowing Costs", borrowing costs that are directly attributable to the acquisition, construction or proiduction of a qualifying asset should be capitalised as part of the cost of that asset. The amount of borrowing costs eligible for capitalisation should be determined in accordance with this Standard. Other borrowing costs should be recognised as an expense in the period in which they are incurred.

Also para 10 of AS 16 "Borrowing Costs" states that to the extent that funds are borrowed specifically for the purpose of obtaining a qualifying asset, the amoubnt of borrowing costs eligible for capiotalisation on that asset should be determined as the actual borrowing costs incurred on that borrowing during the period less any income on the temporary investment of those borrowings.

Decision: Eligible borrowing cost = ₹ 11,00,000 – ₹ 2,00,000 = ₹ 9,00,000

Sr. No.	Particulars	Nature of assets	Interest to be Capitalized (₹)	Interest to be charged to Profit & Loss Account (₹)
i.	Construction of factory building	Qualifying Asset	9,00,000 × 40/100 = ₹ 3,60,000	NIL
ii.	Purchase of Machinery	Not a Qualitfying Asset	NIL	9,00,000 × 35/100 = ₹ 3,15,000
iii.	Working Capital	Not a Qualifying Asset	NIL	9,00,000 × 25/100 = ₹ 2,25,000
	Total		₹ 3,60,000	₹ 5,40,000

Solution 1(c)

AS 19: As per para 3 of AS 19 'Leases' the interest rate implicit in the lease is the discount rate that, at the inception of the lease, causes the aggregate present value of

(a) the minimum lease payments under a finance lease from the standpoint of the lessor; and

(b) any unguaranteed residual value accruing to the lessor, to be equal to the fair value of the leased asset.

Calculation of Interest rate Implicit on Lease

Present value at discount rate of 10%

Year	Liease Payments (₹)	Disc. Factor (10%)	Present Value (₹)
1	80,000	0.909	72,720
2	80,000	0.826	66,080
3	80,000	0.751	60,080
4	80,000	0.683	54,640
5	80,000	0.621	49,680
5	40,000	0.621	24,840
5	24,000	0.621	14,904
	Total		3,42,944

Present value at a discount rate of 14%

Year	Liease Payments (₹)	Disc. Factor (10%)	Present Value (₹)
1	80,000	0.877	70,160
2	80,000	0.769	61,520
3	80,000	0.675	54,000
4	80,000	0.592	47,360
5	80,000	0.519	41,520
5	40,000	0.519	20,760
5	24,000	0.519	12,456
	Total		3,07,776

$$\text{Interest Rate Implicit on Lease} = 10\% + \frac{14\% - 10\%}{3,42,944 - 3,07,776} \times (3,42,944 - 3,20,000)$$

$$= 10\% + 2.609\% = 12.609\% \text{ or say } 12.61\%$$

Solution 1(d)

Computation of Basic Earnings per Share

	Particulars	Previous (₹)	Current (₹)
(i)	EPS for the previous year as originally reported = Net profit for the year attributable to equity share holder/weighted average number of equity shares outstanding during the year [₹ 22,00,000/10,00,000]	2.20	
(ii)	EPS for previous year restated for the right issue [₹ 22,00,000/10,00,000 shares × 1.04]	2.12	
(iii)	EPS for the current year (including effect of right issue) $\frac{₹\ 30,00,000}{(10,00,000 \times 1.04 \times 4/) + (12,00,000 \times 8/12)}$		2.62

Working Notes: 1. Computation of theoretical ex-rights fair value per share =

$$\frac{\text{Fair value of all oustanding shares immediately prior to exercise of rights+total amount received from exercise}}{\text{Number of shares outstanding prior to exercise + number of shares issued in the exercise}}$$

$$\frac{(₹\ 32 \times 10,00,000) + (₹\ 25 \times 2,00,000)}{10,00,000 + 2,00,000} = ₹\ 30.83$$

2. Computation of adjustment factor =

$$\frac{\text{Fair value per share prior to exercise of rights}}{\text{Theoretical ex-rights value per share}} = ₹\ 32/₹\ 30.83 = 1.04 \text{ (approx.)}$$

Solution 2

Particulars	*Cash* ₹	*Creditors* ₹	*Capitals* *P* (₹)	*Q* (₹)	*R* (₹)
Balance due after loan		16,000	52,000	43,500	32,000
January					
Balance available	9,000				
Realization less expenses and cash retained	10,000				
Amount available and paid	19,000	(16,000)	–	–	3,000
Balance due	–	–	52,000	43,500	29,000
February					
Opening Balance	6,000				
Expenses paid and cash carried forward	3,000				
Available for distribution	3,000				
Cash paid to Q and Machinery given to R			–	3,000	9,000
Balance due	–		52,000	40,500	20,000
March					
Opening Balance	2,000				
Amount realized less expenses	87,300				
Amount paid to partners	89,300		41,689	32,767	14,844
Loss			10,311	7,733	5,156

Working Note:

(i) Highest Relative Capital Basis

Particulars	*P* (₹)	*Q* (₹)	*R* (₹)
Scheme of payment for January			
Balance of Capital Accounts	65,000	50,500	32,000
Less: Loans	(13,000)	(7,000)	
A. Net Actual Capital	52,000	43,5000	32,000
B. Profit Sharing Ratio	4	3	2
C. Capital/Profit sharing Ratio [A/B]	13,000	14,500	16,000
D. Capital in profit sharing ratio, taking P's capital as base capital	52,000	39,000	26,000
E. Surplus Capital [A – D]		4,500	6,000
F. Profit Sharing Ratio		3	2
G. Surplus Capital/Profit sharing Ratio [E/F]		1,500	3,000
H. Capital in profit sharing ratio, taking Q's capital as base capital		4,500	3,000
I. Revised Surplus Capital [E – G]			3,000

(ii) Scheme of distributiion of available cash for March:

Particulars	P (₹)	Q (₹)	R (₹)
A. Balance of Capital Accounts end of February	52,000	40,5000	20,000
B. Profit Sharing Ratio	4	3	2
C. Capital/Profit sharing Ratio [A/B]	13,000	13,500	10,000
D. Capital in profit sharing ratio, taking R's capital as base capital	40,000	30,000	20,000
E. Surplus Capital [A – D]	12,000	10,500	
F. Profit Sharing Ratio	4	3	
G. Surplus Capital/Profit sharing Ratio [E/F]	3,000	3,500	
H. Capital in profit sharing ratio taking P's capital as base	12,000	9,000	
I. Surplus Capital [E – H]	-	1,500	
J. Payment ₹ 1500		(1,500)	
K. Balance of Surplus Capital [H – J]	12,000	9,000	
L. Payment ₹ 21000	(12,000)	(9,000)	
M. Balance due [A – J – L]	40,000	30,000	20,000
N. Balance Cash Payment [₹ 89,300 – ₹ 22,500]	(29,689)	(22,267)	(14,844)
O. Total Cash Payment (₹ 89,000)	41,689	32,767	14,844
P. Loss [A – O]	10,311	7,733	5,156

Solution 3 (a)

Dr. **10% Debentures Account** Cr.

Date	Particulars	₹	Date	Particulars	₹
31.03.14	To Own Debentures	3,00,000	01.04.13	By Balance b/d	25,00,000
	To Bank	22,00,000			
		25,00,000			25,00,000

Dr. **Debenture Redemption Sinking Fund Account** Cr.

Date	Particulars	₹	Date	Particulars	₹
31.03.14	To General Reserve	27,30,000	01.04.13	By Balance b/d	24,00,000
			31.03.14	By Profit & Loss a/c	90,000
			31.03.14	By Interest on Sinking Fund	2,06,000
			31.03.14	By Own Debentures	6,000
			31.03.14	By 8% Stock (Profit)	28,000
		27,30,000			27,30,000

Working Notes:

1. Opening 8% Stock = ₹ 24,00,000 – ₹ 2,94,000 = ₹ 21,06,000
2. Sale value of 8% Stock

   Number = ₹ 22 lakhs/₹ 100 = 22,000 no.

   Sale Value = 22,000 × ₹ 897 = ₹ 21,34,000

3. **Interest credited to Sinking Fund Account**

	₹
Interest on 8% Stock (₹ 22 Lakh × 8/100)	1,76,000
Interest on own Debentures (3,000 × ₹ 100 × 10/100)	30,000
	2,06,000

4. Dr. **Own Debentures Account** Cr.

Date	*Particulars*	₹	*Date*	*Particulars*	₹
01.04.13	To Balance b/d	2,94,000	31.03.14	By 10% Debentures	3,00,000
31.03.14	To Sinking Fund A/c	6,000			
		3,00,000			3,00,000

5. Dr. **8% Stock Account** Cr.

Date	*Particulars*	₹	*Date*	*Particulars*	₹
01.04.13	To Balance b/d	21,06,000	31.03.14	By Bank A/c	21,34,000
31.03.14	To Sinking Fund A/c (Profit)	28,000			
		21,34,000			21,34,000

Note: Since the balance of Debenture Redemption Sinking Fund Account is more than the nominal value of debentures redeemed, the amount equal to the amount of debentures redeemed may be transferred to General Reserve Account i.e. ₹ 25,00,000 and excess of fund i.e. ₹ 2,30,000 may be transferred to Capital Reserve Account on the assumption that it is a capital profit received on the appreciation in the value of investment or settlement of liability for a lesser amount that was usually payable.

Solution 3 (b)

Calculation of liability of each underwriter assuming that the benefit of firm underwriting is not given to individual underwriter

Particulars	*No. of shares*				
	L	*M*	*N*	*O*	*Total*
Gross underwriting	80,000	60,000	40,000	20,000	2,00,000
Less: Marked Application (excluding firm underwriting)	(55,000)	(40,000)	(42,000)	(8,000)	(1,45,000)
Balance	25,000	20,000	(2,000)	12,000	55,000
Less: Surplus of N allotted to L., M & O in the ratio of 4:3:1	(1,000)	(750)	2,000	(250)	
Balance	24,000	19,250	–	11,750	55,000
Less: Unmarked applications including firm underwriting	(7,200)	(5,400)	(3,600)	(1,800)	(18,000)
Net Liability	16,800	13,850	(3,600)	9,950	37,000
Less: Surplus of N allotted to L, M & O in the ratio of 4:3:1		(1,800)	(1,350)	3,600	(450)
Balance	15,000	12,500	–	9,500	37,000
Add: Firm Underwriting	5,000	4,000	2,000	2,000	13,000
Net Liability	20,000	16,500	2,000	11,500	50,000

Working Note:

Particulars	*No. of shares*
Application received from public	1,50,000
Add: Firm underwriting	13,000
Total Applications	1,63,000
Less: Marked applications	(1,45,000)
Unmarked application including firm underwriting	18,000

Solution 4

Calculation of Purchase Consideration

	P Ltd. (₹)	*Q Ltd. (₹)*
Assets taken over:		
Goodwill	50,000	1,50,000
Building	1,00,000	1,90,000
Plant & Machinery	25,000	80,000
Furniture & Fixtures	–	35,000
Inventories	1,35,000	50,000
Trade Receivables	–	1,42,000
Cash at Bank	–	58,000
	3,10,000	7,05,000
Less: Liabilities taken over:		
8% Debentures	(1,21,000)	–
Trade Payables	–	(1,40,000)
Net Assets taken over	1,89,000	5,65,000
To be satisfied by issue of shares of PQ Ltd. of ₹ 10 each at par	18,900	56,500

Balance Sheet of PQ Limited as at 1st April, 2014

Particulars	*Note No.*	*Amount (₹)*
I. Equity and Liabilities		
(1) Shareholder's Funds		
(a) Share Capital	1	7,54,000
(b) Reserve & Surplus	2	11,000
(2) Non-Current Liabilities		
(a) Long term borrowings	3	1,10,000
(3) Current Liabilities		
(a) Trade Payables		1,40,000
Total		10,15,000
II. Assets		
(1) Non-Current assets		
(a) Fixed Assets		
Tangible 4		4,30,000
Intangible 5		2,00,000

(2) Current Assets		
(a) Inventories	1,85,000	
(b) Trade Receivables		1,42,000
(c) Cash at Bank		58,000
Total		10,15,000

Notes to Accounts:

		₹
1. Share Capital		
Authorized		
1,00,000 shares of ₹ 10 eac		10,00,000
Issued, Subscribed and Paid up		
75,400 shares of ₹ 10 each		7,54,000
(All the above shares are allotted as fully paid up pursuant to scheme of amalgamation withut payments being received in cash)		
2. **Reserve & Surplus**		
Securities Premium Account [₹ 1,10,000 × 10%]		11,000
3. **Long term borrowings**		
8% Debentures		1,10,000
4. **Tangible Fixed Assets**		
Building		
P Ltd.	1,00,000	
Q Ltd.	1,90,000	2,90,000
Plant & Machinery		
P Ltd.	25,000	
Q Ltd.	80,000	1,05,000
Furniture & Fixture		
Q Ltd.		35,000
		4,30,000
5. **Intangible Asset**		
Goodwill		
P Ltd.	50,000	
Q. Ltd.	1,50,000	2,00,000

Journal of P Ltd.

Date	Particulars		Dr. (₹)	Cr. (₹)
1	Realization A/c	Dr.	3,04,000	
	To Building			1,00,000
	To Plant & Machinery			25,000
	To Inventories			1,35,000
	To Trade Receivables			44,000
	(Being all assets except cash transferred to Realization Account)			

Date	Particulars		Dr. (₹)	Cr. (₹)
2	8% Debentures A/c	Dr.	1,10,000	
	Trade Payables	Dr.	54,000	
	To Realization A/c			1,64,000
	(Being all liabilities transferred to Realization Account)			
3	Equity Share Capital A/c	Dr.	1,40,000	
	Profit & Loss A/c	Dr.	30,000	
	To Equity Shareholder's A/c			1,70,000
	(Being Equity transferred to Equity Shareholder's Account)			
4	PQ Ltd	Dr.	1,89,000	
	To Realization A/c			1,89,000
	(Being Purchase consideration due)			
5	Bank A/c	Dr.	44,000	
	To Realization A/c			44,000
	(Being cash received from trade receivables in full)			
6	Realization A/c	Dr.	54,000	
	To Bank A/c			54,000
	(Being payment made to Trade Payables)			
7	Share in PQ Ltd.	Dr.	1,89,000	
	To PQ Ltd.			1,89,000
	(Being purchase consideration received in the form of Equity Shares of PQ Ltd.)			
8	Realization A/c (balancing figure)	Dr.	39,000	
	To Equity Shareholder's A/c			39,000
	(Being profit on realization transferred to Equity Shareholder's A/c)			
9	Equity Shareholder's A/c	Dr.	2,09,000	
	To Shares in PQ Ltd.			1,89,000
	To Bank A/c			20,000
	(Being final payment made to shareholders)			

Solution 5 (a)

Jay Electricity Company

	Old Ratio	Cost of Old Plant (₹ in lakhs)	% increase	Current Cost (₹ in lakhs)	New Ratio
Materials	4	30	250%	75	5
Labour	4	30	200%	60	4
Overheads	2	15		60	4
		75		195	

Amount to be Capitalized

	₹ in lakhs
Cost of New Plant	250
Add: Cost of Materials used	38
	288
Less: Estimated Current Cost of Replacing the Plant	(195)
Amount to be Capitalized	93

Amount to be charged to Revenue

	₹ in lakhs
Estimated Current Cost of Replacement	195
Less: Cash Sales of Scrap	(15)
Less: Materials used*	(38)
Amount to be charged to Revenue	142

Working Notes:

Dr. **Plant Account** (₹ in lakhs)

Particulars	*(₹ in lakhs)*	*Particulars*	*(₹ in lakhs)*
To balance b/d	75	By Balance c/d	168
To Bank A/c (250-195)	55		
To Replacement A/c	38		
	168		168

Dr. **Replacement Account** (₹ in lakhs)

Particulars	*(₹ in lakhs)*	*Particulars*	*(₹ in lakhs)*
To Bank A/c	195	By Bank A/c	15
		By Plant A/c	38
		By Revenue A/c	142
	195		195

Note: It is pertinent to note that the Electricity Act, 2003 does not deal with replacement Accounting based on 'Double Accounting System'.

Q.5.(b) **Books of XYZ Marine Insurance Ltd.**

Particulars	₹ *in lakhs*
(I) Net Premium earned	
Premium from Direct Business received	92,00,000
Add: Receivable at the end	3,94,000
Less: Receivable at the beg.	(4,59,000)
Sub Total (A)	91,35,000
Premium on reinsurance accepted	7,86,000
Add: Receivable at the end	33,000
Less: Receivable at the beg.	(37,000)
Sub Total (B)	7,82,000

Premium on reinsurance Ceded	6,36,000
Add: Payable at the end	20,000
Less: Payable at the beg.	(28,000)
Sub Total (C)	6,28,000
Premium Earned (A+B+C)	92,89,000
(II) Net Claims Incurred	
Claims paid on direct business	73,00,000
Add: Outstanding at the end	1,01,000
Less: Outstanding at the beg.	(94,000)
Sub Total (A)	73,07,000
Reinsurance claims	5,80,000
Add: Outstanding at the end	12,000
Less: Outstanding at the beg.	(16,000)
Sub Total (B)	5,76,000
Claims received from reinsurance	2,10,000
Add: Outstanding at the end	39,000
Less: Outstanding at the beg.	(42,000)
Sub Total (C)	2,07,000
Net Claim Incurred (A+B+C)	76,76,000

Solution 6 (a)

Journal of Branch

Date	*Particulars*	*Dr. (₹)*	*Cr. (₹)*
(i)	Head Office A/c Dr. To Income A/c (Being the income allocated by the Head office not recorded earlier, now recorded)	2,800	2,800
(ii)	Provision for Doubtful Debts A/c Dr. To Head Office A/c (Being the provision for doubtful debts not provided earlier, now provided for)	1,000	1,000
(iii)	Head Office A/c Dr. To Salaries A/c (Being rectification of salary paid on behalf of Head Office)	3,000	3,000
(iv)	Head Office A/c Dr. To Cash A/c (Being expenditure incurred on account of other branch, now recorded in books)	5,000	5,000
(v)	No entry in Branch Books is required.		
(vi)	Expenses A/c Dr. To Head Office A/c (Being allocated expenses of Head Office recorded)	75,000	75,000

Date	Particulars		Dr. (₹)	Cr. (₹)
(vii)	Head Office A/c	Dr.	30,000	
	To Debtors A/c			30,000
	(Being adjustment entry for collection from Branch Debtrors directly by Head Office)			
(viii)	Good-in-transit A/c	Dr.	10,000	
	To Head Office Account			10,000
	(Being goods sent by Head Office still in-transit)			

Solution 6 (b)

Calculation of Correct Department Profits

Particulars	*Department P (₹)*	*Department S (₹)*	*Department Q (₹)*
Profit after charging Manager's Commission	90,000	60,000	45,000
Add: Manager's Commission (1/9)	10,000	6,667	5,000
	1,00,000	66,667	50,000
Less: Unrealised profit on Stock (WN0	(5,426)	(21,000)	(2,727)
Profit Before Manager's Commission	94,574	45,667	47,273
Less: Manager's Commission 10%	(9,457)	(4,567)	(4,727)
Correct Profit after Manager's Commission	85,117	41,100	42,546

Working Notes:

	Department P (₹)	*Department S (₹)*	*Department Q (₹)*	*Total (₹)*
Unrealized Profit of:				
Department P	–	25/125 × 18,000 = 3,600	15/115 × 14,000 = 1,826	5,426
Department S	20/100 × 48,000 = 9,600	–	30/10 × 38,000 = 11,400	21,000
Department Q	20/120 × 12,000 = 2,000	10/100 × 8,000 = 727		2,727

Solution 7 (a)

Computation of provision to be made by a Bank

	₹
Outstanding Value of Doubtful Asset (up to 3 years)	7,24,000
Less: Value of security (excluding ECGC cover)	(₹ 1,75,000)
Sub Total	₹ 5,49,000
Less: ECGC Cover (subject to ₹ 1,50,000 maximum)	(₹ 1,50,000)
Unsecured Portion	₹ 3,99,000
Provision:	
For unsecured portion @ 100% of ₹ 3,99,000	₹ 3,99,000
₹For secured portion @ 40% of ₹ 1,75,000	₹ 70,000
Total Provision	₹ 4,69,000

Solution 7 (b)

Classification of following accounts for the presentation in Schedule III to the Companies Act, 2013

Sl. No.	Accounts	Head
(i)	Share application money received in excess of issue share capital	Other Current Liabilities
(ii)	Share option outstanding account	Reserve & Surplus
(iii)	Unpaid matured deb4enture and interest accrued thereon	Other Current Liabilities
(iv)	Uncalled liability on shares and other partly paid investments	Contingent Liabilities and commitments-commitments to the extent not provided for
(v)	Calls unpaid	Share Capital
(vi)	Intangible Assets under development	Fixed Assets
(vii)	Money received against share warrant	Shareholder's Funds
(viii)	Long term maturity of finance lease obligation	Long Term Borrowings

Solution 7 (c) As per AS 12, refund to Government Grant is treated in the following manner:

(a) When Government Grant is related to Revenue:

(i) The amount of refund is first adjusted against any unamortized deferred credit balance still remaining in respect of the Grant

(ii) Any excess refund over such deferred credit balance or where no deferred credit exists, is immediately charged to Profit & Loss Account.

(b) When Government Grant is related to specific Fixed Asset:

(i) The amount of refund will increase the Book Value of the Asset, if at the time of receipt of Grant, the cost of asset was reduced by the amount of Grand.

(ii) If at the time of receipt, the Grant amount was credited to Deferred Grant Account, then the amount of refund will first reduce the unamortized balance of Deferred Grant Account, any excess refund will reduce the Capital Reserve.

(c) When the Government Grant is in the nature of Promoter's Contribution: Capital Reserve will be reduced by the amount of refund.

Solution 7 (d) If the firm is dissolved before the term expires, as is the case, *W* being a partner who has paid premium on admission will have to be repaid/refunded

The criteria for calculation of refund amount are:

(i) Terms upon which admission was made,

(ii) The time period for which it was agreed that the firm will not be dissolved.

(iii) The time period for which the firm has already been in existence.

No claim for refund will arise if:

(i) The firm is dissolved due to death of a partner,

(ii) If the dissolution of the firm is basically because of misconduct of W.

(iii) If the dissolution is through an agreement and such agreement does not have a stipulation for refund of premium.

Solution 7 (e)

Refer to Page 4.1 & 4.2 of Ch. 4 of Text Book.

Paper-5: Advanced Accounting CA IPC (Group II) Examination (Nov 2014)

Question No. 1 is compulsory.
Attempt any Five questions from the remaining Six questions
Wherever necessary suitable assumptions may be made by the candidates.
Working notes should form part of the answer.

Q.1(a) A Machine having expected useful life of 6 years, is leased for 4 years. Both the Cost and the Fair Value of the Machinery are ₹ 7,00,000. The amount will be paid in 4 equal instalments and at the termination of lease, Lessor will get back the Machinery. The unguaranteed Residual Value at the end of the 4th year is ₹ 70,000. The IRR of the investment is 10%. The Present Value of Annuity Factor of ₹ 1 due at the end of 4th year at 10% IRR is 3.169. The Present Value of ₹ 1 due at the end of 4th year at 10% Rate Interest is 0.683.

State with reasons whether the Lease Constitutes FInance Lease and also compute the Unread Finance Income.

Q.1(b) A Company is showing an intangible Asset at ₹ 88 Lakhs as on 01.04.2013. This Asset was acquired for ₹ 120 Lakhs on 01.04.2009 and the same was available for use from that date. The Company has been following the policy of amortization of the Intangible Assets over a period of 15 years on Straight line basis. Commeent on the accounting treatment of the above with references to the relevant Accounting Standard.

Q.1(c) Stem Ltd purchased a Plant for US$ 30,000 on 30th November 2013, payable after 6 months. The Company entered into a forward contract for 6 months @ ₹ 62.15 9 per Dollar. On 30th November 2013, the Exchange Rate was ₹ 60.75 per Dollar. How will you recognize the Profit or Loss on Forward Contract in the books of Stem Ltd, for the year ended 31st March 2014?

Q.1(d) WZW Ltd, Is in dispute involvingm allegation of infringement of patents by a Competitor Company who is seeking damages of a huge sum of ₹ 1000 Lakhs. The directors are of the opinion that the claim can be successfully resisted by the Company. How would you deal the same in the Annual Accounts of the company?

Q.2. P and Q were carrying on business sharing profits and losses equally. The Firm's Balance Sheet as at 31.12.2013 was:

Liabilities	₹	*Assets*	₹
Capital Accounts:		Plant	1,60,000
P – 1,50,000		Bulding	48,000
Q – 1,30,000	2,80,000	Debtors	75,000
Sundry Creditors	80,000	Stock	70,000
Bank Overdraft	45,000	Joint Life Policy	6,000
		Profit & Loss A/c	30,000
		Drawings Account: P – 9,000	
		Q – 7,000	16,000
	4,05,000		4,05,000

The operations of the business were carried on till 30.06.2014, P & Q both withdrew in equal amount of profit made during the current period of six months after charging depreciation at 10% per annum on Plant and after writing off 5% on Building.

During the current period of six months, Creditors were reduced by ₹ 20,000 and Bank Overdraft by ₹ 5,000.

The Joint Life Policy was surrendered for ₹ 6,000 before 30th June 2014. Stock was valued at ₹ 84,000 and Debtors at ₹ 68,000 on 30th June 2014. The other items remainedm the same as at 31.12.2013.

On 30.06.2014, the Firm sold its business to PQ Ltd. The value of Goodwill was estimated at ₹ 1,30,000 and the remaining assets were valued on the basis of the Balance Sheet as on 30.06.2014.

PQ Ltd paid the purchase consideration in Equity Shares of ₹ 10 each.

You are required to prepare:

(a) Balance Sheet of the Firm as at 30.06.2014.

(b) Realisation Account.

(c) Partner's Capital Accounts showing the final settlement between them.

Q.3.(a) X Ltd granted 500 Stock Options to its employees on 01.04.2011 at ₹ 50 per Share. The vesting period is 2½ years and the maximum exercise period is one year. Market Price on that date is ₹ 140 per Share. All the options were exercised on 30.06.2014. Pass Journal Entries giving suitable narrations, if the Face Value of Equity Share is ₹ 10 per Share.

Q.3.(b) Venus Limited recently made a public issue in respect of which the following information is available:

(i) No. of Partly Convertible Debentures issued 4,00,000, Face Value and Issue Price of ₹ 100 per Debenture.

(ii) Convertible Portion per Debenture –80%, Date of Conversion – on expiry of 7 months from the date of closing of issue.

(iii) Date of Closure of Subscription List – 01.06.2013, Date of Allotment – 01.07.2013, Rate of Interest on Debentures – 10% p.a. payable from the date of allotment. Value of Equity Share for the purpose of conversion – ₹ 40 (Face Value ₹ 10)

(iv) Underwriting Commission –3%.

(v) No. of Debentures applied for 3,00,000.

(vi) Interest Payable on Debentures – half yearly on 30th September and 31st March.

Write relevant Journal entries for all transactions arising out of the above during the year ended on 31st March 2014 (including Cash and bank entries).

Q.4. The Balance Sheet of X Ltd, as at 31st March 2014, was as follows:

Particulars		₹
Equity and Liabilities		
1. Share Holder's Funds		
Share Capital:	(a) 40,000 Equity Shares of ₹ 100 each fully paid	40,00,000
	(b) 20,000, 10% Preference Shares of ₹ 100 each fully paid	20,00,000
Reserves & Surplus:	(a) Securities Premium Account	1,50,000
	(b) Profit & Loss Account	(23,00,000)

2. Non-Current Liabilities: Long Term borrowings –7% Debentures of ₹ 100 each			4,00,000
3. Current Liabilities: Other Current Liabilities – Creditors			10,00,000
– Loan from Director			2,00,000
Total Liabilities			**54,50,000**
Assets			
1. Non-Current Assets			
Fixed Assets	(a) Land & Building	20,00,000	
	(b) Plant and Machinery	12,00,000	32,00,000
Intangible Assets: Goodwill			4,00,000
2. Current Assets			
	(a) Debtors	12,00,000	
	(b) Stock	5,00,000	
	(c) Cash at Bank	1,50,000	18,50,000
Total Assets			**54,50,000**

No Dividend on Prefernce Shares has been paid for last 5 years.

The following scheme of reorganization was duly approved by the Court:

(a) Each Equity Share be reduced to ₹ 25.

(b) Each existing Preference Share to be reduced to ₹ 75, and then exchanged for one new 13% Preference Share of ₹ 50 each and one Equity Share of ₹ 25 each.

(c) Preference Shareholders have forgone their right for Dividend for four years. One year's Dividend at the old rate is however, payable to them in fully paid Equity Shares of ₹ 25.

(d) The Debenture Holders be given the option to either acdept 90% of their claims in cash or to convert their claims in full into new 13% Preference Shares of ₹ 50 each issued at par. One-fourth (in value) of the Debentrue Holders accepted Preference Shares for their claims. The rest were paid in cash.

(e) Contingent Liability of ₹ 2,00,000 is payable which has been created by wrong ac tion of one Director. He has agreed to compensate this loss out of the Loan given by the Director to the Company

(f) Goodwill does not have any value in the present. Decrease the value of Plant & Machinery, Stock and Debtors by ₹ 3,00,000, ₹ 1,00,000 and ₹ 2,00,000 respectively. Increase the value of Land & Building to ₹ 25,00,000.

(g) 50,000 new Equity Shares of ₹ 25 each are to be issued at par payable in full on application. The issue was underwritten for a Commission of 4%. Shares were fully taken up.

(h) Total Expenses incurred by the Company in connection with the Scheme excluding Underwriting Commission amounted to ₹ 20,000.

Pass necessary Journal Entries to record the above transactions.

Q.5.(a) Metro General Insurance Company submits the following information for the year ended 31st march 2014:

Particulars		*Direct Business (₹)*	*Reinsurance (₹)*
Premium received		75,25,000	8,25,000
Premium paid		–	4,90,000
claims Paid during the Year		49,70,000	5,10,000
claims Payable:	1st April 2013	6,85,000	95,000
	31st March 2014	7,38,000	70,000
Claims Received		–	3,95,000
Claims Receivable:	1st April 2013	–	75,000
	31st March 2014	–	1,25,000
Expenses of Management		2,90,000	–
Commission:	On Insurance Accepted	1,60,000	15,000
	On Insurance Ceded	–	18,000

The aollowing additional information are also available:

(i) Expenses of Management include ₹ 45,000 Surveyor's Fees and ₹ 55,000. Legal Expenses for settlement of claims.

(ii) Reserve for Unexpired Risk is to be maintained @ 40%. The balance of Reserve for Unexpired Risk as on 01.04.2013 was ₹ 28,40,000.

You are required to make the Revenue Account for the year ended 31st March 2014.

Q.5.(b) A Commercial Bank has the following Capital Funds and Assets. Segregate the Capital Funds into Tier I and Tier II capitals. Find out the Risk Adjusted Asset and Risk Weighted Asset Ratio. State your observation on the Risk Weighted Asset Ratio.

Particulars	*₹ Crores*
Equity Share Capital	400.00
Statutory Reserve	250.00
Capital Reserve (of which ₹ 18 Crores were deu to Revaluation of Assets & balance due to Sale of Capital Assets)	86.00
Assets:	
Cash Balance with RBI	12.00
Balance with other Banks	20.00
Other Investments	40.000
Loans & Advances	
(a) Guaranteed by Government	14.50
(b) Others	5,465.00
Premises, Furniture & Fixtures	74.00
Off Balance Sheet Items	
(a) Guarantees and Other Obligations	700.00
(b) Acceptance, Endorsements and Letter of Credit	4,900.00

Q.6.(a) LMN is having branch at Mumbai. Goods are invoiced to the Branch at 25% Profit on Sale. Branch has been instructed to send all cash daily to Head Office. All expenses are paid by Head Office except Petty Expenses, which are met by the Branch. From the following particulars, prepare Branch Account in the Books of Head Office:

Particulars	₹	Particulars	₹
Opening Stock (Invoice Price)	40,000	Credit Sales	70,000
Opening Sundry Debtors	25,000	Discount Allowed to Debetors	300
Opening Cash in Hand	1,000	Expenses Paid by Head Office:	
Opening Office Furntirue	4,000	Salary	4,000
Goods Invoiced from Head Office (Invoice Price)	1,80,000	Staff Welfare	750
Goods Return to Head Office	6,000	Telephone Expense	1,200
Goods Return by Debtors	1,250	Other Misc. Expenses paid by Branch	700
Cash Received from Debtors	65,000	Closing Stock (at Invoice Price)	35,000
Cash Sales	1,20,000	Depreciation to be provided on Branch Furniture	10%

Q.6.(b) Mega Ltd, has two departments, A and B. From the following particulars, prepare Departmental Trading A/c and general Profit & Loss Account for the year ended 31st March 2014.

Particulars	Department A	Department B
Opening Stock as on 01.04.2013 (at Cost)	70,000	54,000
Purchases	3,92,000	2,98,000
Carriage Inward	6,000	9,000
Wages	54,000	36,000
Sales	5,72,000	4,60,000
Purchase Goods Transferred:		
By Department B to A	50,000	
By Department A to B		36,000
Finished Goods Transferred:		
By Department B to A	1,50,000	
By Department A to B		1,75,000
Return of Finished Goods:		
By Department B to A	45,000	
By Department A to B		32,000
Closing Stock		
Purchase Goods	24,000	30,000
Finished Goods	1,02,000	62,000

Purchased Goods have been transferred mutually at their respective Departmental Purchase Cost and Finished Goods at Departmental Market Price and that 30% of the Closing Finished Stock with each Department represents Finished Goods received from the other Department.

Q.7.(a) Give two examples of each of the following items:

(i) Change in Accounting olicy

(ii) Change in Accounting Estimate

(iii) Extra Ordinary Items

(iv) Prior Period Items.

Q.7.(b) What are the indicators of Non-Integral Foreign Operation (NFO)?

Q.7.(c) In the following list of Shares issued, for the purpose of calculation of Weighted Average Number of Shares, from whcih date weight is to be considered:

(i) Equity Shares issued in Exchange of cash,

(ii) Equity Shares issued as a result of Conversion of Debt Instrument,

(iii) Equity Shares issued in Exchange for the settlement of Liability of the Enterprise,

(iv) Equity Shares issued for rendering of Services to the Enterprise,

(v) Equity Shares issued in Lieu of Interest and/or Principal of an other Financial Instrument,

(vi) Equity Shares issued as consideration for the Acquisition of Asset other than in Cash.

Also Define Potential Equity Share.

Q.7.(d) Find out the Income to be recognized by ABC Bank Ltd, for the year ended 31st March 2014, in respect of Interest on Advance [₹ in Lakhs] as detailed below:

	Performing Assets		*Non-performing Assets*	
	Interest earned	*Interest received*	*Interest earned*	*Interest received*
Term Loans	280	180	170	20
Cash Credits and Overdrafts	1,700	1,630	310	48
Bills Purchased and Discounted	400	400	180	70

Q.7.(e) State any four alternative Accounting Treatment of the Fund received by an Electricity Company from consumer towards Capital Expenditure/Service Line Contribution.

Answers to IPC Examination Paper 5 [Nov 2014]

Solution 1(a)

1. Finance vs Operating Lease

Particulars		₹
(a) PV of Unguaranteed Residual Value	[₹ 70,000 × 0.683]	47,810
(b) PV of Lease Payments	[₹ 7,00,000 – ₹ 47,810]	6,52,190
(c) % of PV of MLP to Fair Value	[₹ 6,52,190/₹ 7,00,000	**93.17%**

Conclusion: The Lease is a **Finance Lease** since the Lease Term is 67%, 4/6th of the Asset's Useful Life. Also, the Present Value of Lease Payments is approximate 93% of the Fair Value, Constituting substantial portion of the Fair Value.

2. Computation of Unearned Finance Income

	Particulars	₹
	Annual Lease Payment = $\frac{\text{PV of Lease Payments}}{\text{Annuity Factor for 3 years at 10\%}} = \frac{₹\ 6,52,190}{3.169}$	2,05,803
	Total Lease Rentals for the Lease = Period = ₹ 2,05,803 p.a × 4 years = MLP	8,23,212
Add:	Residual Value	70,000
	Gross Investment in the Lease	**8,93,212**
Less:	Present Value of MLP & URV = (6,52,190 + 47,810) **(See Note)**	(7,00,000)
	Unearned Finance Income	**1,93,212**

Note: PV of MLP & URV equals the Fair Value/Cost of Equipment at the inception of the lease = **₹ 7,00,000.**

Solution 1(b)

1. **Rebuttable Presumption:** AS – 26 assumes that the useful life of an Intangible Asset will not exceed a period of 10 years, but this presumption is rebuttable.
2. **Amotisation Amount as per Company Policy:**
   (a) Amotisation Amount (₹ 120 Lakhs/15 years) = ₹ 8 Lakhs p.a.
   (b) Accumulated Amortisation upto 31.3.2014 = ₹ 8 Lakhs × = ₹ 32 Lakhs.
   (c) Carrying Amount = ₹ 120 Lakhs – ₹ 32 Lakhs = ₹ 88 Lakhs = as per Books
3. **Future Amortisation:** The balance carrying Amount of ₹ 88 Lakhs should be amortised over the balance Useful Life of 11 years at ₹ 8 Lakhs p.a.

Solution 1(c)

Treatment as per AS – 11

Particulars	₹
A. Value at the rate prevailing at the inception of Forward Contract (30,000$ × 60.75)	18,22,500
B. Value at the forward rate (30,000$ × 62.15)	18,64,500
C. Total Loss on entering into forward contract [A – B]	42,000
D. Loss to be recognized for the year ended 31.3.2014 (42,000 × 4/6)	28,000

Interest Payments should be charged to Profit and Loss Acount of each year at the Transaction Value on payment dates.

Solution 1(d) Conditions as to recognition of Provision are **not satisfied.** Only a Disclosure Note of Contingent Liability is required.

Solution 2

Dr. **1. Realisation Account** Cr.

Particulars ₹	Particulars	₹	
To Sundry Assets A/c		By Creditors A/c	60,000
– Stock	84,000	By Bank Overdraft A/c	40,000
– Debetors	68,000	By PQ Ltd (Purchase Consideration)	3,79,600
– Plant	1,52,000		
– Building	45,600		
To Profit t/f to:			
– P's Capital A/c 65,000			
– Q's Capital A/c 65,000	1,30,000		
	4,79,600		4,79,6000

Dr. **2. Partner's capital Accounts** Cr.

Particulars	P	Q	Particulars	P	Q
To Drawings A/c	9,000	7,000	By balance b/d	1,50,000	1,30,000
To P&L A/c	15,000	15,000	By Profit	15,600	15,600
To Drawings A/c	7,800	7,800			
To balance c/d	1,33,800	1,15,800			
	1,65,600	**1,45,600**		**1,65,600**	**1,45,600**
To Shares in PQ Ltd	1,98,800	1,80,800	By balance b/d	1,33,800	1,15,800
			By Realisation A/c	65,000	65,000
	1,98,800	**1,80,800**	**Total**	**1,98,800**	**1,80,800**

Working Notes:

1: Balance Sheet as on 30th September 2014

Liabilities	₹	Assets	₹
		Non-Current Assets:	
Sundry Creditors (80,000 – 20,000)	60,000	Building (48,000 – 5%)	45,6000
Bank Overdraft (45,000 – 5,000)	40,000	Plant (16,000 – 10% × 6 months)	1,52,000
Total Capital (Bal. fig)	**2,49,600**	**Current Assets:** Stock	84,000
		Debtors	68,000
	3,49,600		**3,49,600**

2: Profit earned during six months to 30th June 2014

Particulars	₹
A. Total Capital on 30th June 2014	2,49,600
B. Net Capital on 31.12.2013 (capital 2,80,000 – P & L Dr. 30,000 – Drawings 16,000)	2,34,000
C. **Net Increase (after Drawings)**	15,600
D. *Add:* Drawings (1/2 of Total Profit), hence equal to the Net Increase after Drawings	15,600
E. **Total Profit for the period**	**31,200**

3. Purchase Consideration = ₹ 2 49,600 + ₹ 1,30,000 = ₹ 3,79,600

Solution 3(a)

1. Computation of Expenses to be recognised

Particulars	Result
(A) **Fair Value of Option per Share** (₹ 140 – ₹ 50)	**₹ 90**
(B) No. of Shares vesting under the Scheme	500 Shares
(C) Total Fair Value of Options [A × B]	₹ 45,000

(D) Amount (in ratio of 1:1:1/2) for 2011-2012 ₹ 18,000, 2012–2013, ₹ 18,000, 2013–2014 ₹ 9,000

2. Journal

Date	Particulars		Dr. (₹)	Cr. (₹)
31.3.2012	Employees Compensation Expense A/c	Dr.	18,000	
	To Employees Stock Option Outstanding A/c			18,000
	(Being Employeee Compensation Expense recognised)			
31.3.2012	Profit and Loss A/c	Dr.	18,000	
	To Employees Compensation Expense A/c			18,000
	(Being t/f of Employees Compensation Expense)			
31.3.2013	Employees Compensation Expense A/c	Dr.	18,000	
	To Employees Stack Option Outstanding A/c			18,000
	(Being Employee Compensation Expense recognised)			
31.3.2013	Profit and Loss A/c	Dr.	18,000	
	To Employees Compensation Expense A/c			9,000
	To Employees Stock Option Outstanding A/c			9,000
	(Being balance of Employee Compensation Expense amortised ` 45,000 – ` 36,000)			
30.6.2013	Bank A/c (500 Shares × ₹ 50)	Dr.	25,000	
	Employees Stock Option Outstanding A/c (500 Shares × ₹ 90)	Dr.	45,000	
	To Equity Share Capital A/c (500 Shares × ₹ 10)			5,000
	To Securities Premium A/c (500 Shares × ₹ 130)		65,000	
	(Being 500 Shares allotted to Employees under ESOP at a Premium of ₹ 1350 per Share, ₹ 50 per Share received in Cash, balance being ESOP Entitlement)			
31.3.2014	Profit and Loss A/c	Dr.	9,000	
	To Employees Compensation Expense A/c			9,000
	(Being t/f of Employees Compensation Expense of the year)			

Solution 3

Journal of Venus Ltd.

Date	Particulars		Dr. (₹)	Cr. (₹)
01.6.2013	Bank A/c [3,00,000 Debentures × ₹ 100]	Dr.	3,00,00,000	
	To Debenture Application & Allotment A/c			3,00,00,000
	(Being application money received for 3,00,000 Debentures at ₹ 100 each)			

Date	Particulars		Dr. (₹)	Cr. (₹)
01.7.2013	Debenture Application & Allotment A/c	Dr.	3,00,00,000	
	Underwriters A/c	Dr.	1,00,00,000	
	To Debentures A/c			4,00,00,00
	(Being allotment of 3,00,000 Debentures to Applicants, balance to Underwriters.)			
01.7.2013	Underwriting Commission A/c [4,00,00,000 × 3%]	Dr.	12,00,000	
	To Underwriters A/c			12,00,000
	(Being Commission Payable to Underwriters at 3%)			
01.7.2013	Bank A/c	Dr.	88,00,000	
	To Underwriters A/c			88,00,000
	(Being balance amount receivable from Underwriters, received)			
30.9.2013	Debenture Interest A/c	Dr.	10,00,000	
	To Bank A/c			10,00,000
	(Being Debenture Interest paid at 10% p.a. for 3 months)			
01.9.2014	10% Debentures A/c	Dr.	3,20,00,000	
	To Equity Share Capital A/c (at ₹ 10)			80,00,000
	To Secutiries Premium A/c (at ₹ 30)			2,40,00,000
	(Being 8,00,000 Shares issued on Conversion of 4,00,000 × 80% = 3,20,000 Debentures)			
31.3.2014	Debenture Interest A/c	Dr.	12,00,000	
	To Cash/Bank			12,00,000
	(Being Interest paid on Debentures for 2nd half-year, computed as under (4,00,000 × 10% × 3/12 + 80,00,000 × 10% × 3/2)			
31.3.2014	Profit & Loss A/c		22,00,000	
	To Debenture Interest			22,00,000
	(Being Total Interest for the year Transferred to P&L)			

Solution 4

Journal

Date	Particulars		Dr. (₹)	Cr. (₹)
1.	Equity Share Capital (₹ 100) A/c	Dr.	40,00,000	
	To Equity Share Capital (₹ 25) A/c			10,00,000
	To Reconstruction A/c			30,00,000
	(Being Equity Shares of ₹ 100 each reduced to 25 each, and balance transferred to Reconstruction A/c, as per approved Scheme of Reconstruction dated....)			
2.	10% Preference Share Capital (₹ 100) A/c	Dr.	20,00,000	
	To 13% Preference Share Capital (₹ 50) A/c			10,00,000
	To Equity Share Capital (₹ 25) A/c			5,00,000
	To Reconstruction A/c			5,00,000

Date	Particulars		Dr. (₹)	Cr. (₹)
	(Being 20,000 Preference Shares of ₹ 100 each are converted into 20,000 13% Preference Shares of ₹ 50 each & 20,000 Equity Shares of ₹ 25 each)			
3.	Reconstruction A/c	Dr.	2,00,000	
	To Equity Share capital (₹ 25) A/c			2,00,000
	(Being Equity Shares issued for arrears of Pref. Share Dividend)			
4.	7% Debentures A/c	Dr.	4,00,000	
	To 13% Preference Share Capital (₹ 50) A/c			1,00,000
	To Bank A/c			2,70,000
	To Reconstruction A/c			30,000
	(Being 3/4 of Debentureholders opting to take 13% Preference Shares at par, and remaining Debentureholders taking 90% cash payment for their Claims.)			
5.	Director's Loan A/c	Dr.	2,00,000	
	To Provision for Expenses/Contingent Liability			2,00,000
	(Being Contingent Liability provided & adjusted Interest of Loan payable to Director)			
6.	Bank A/c	Dr.	12,50,000	
	To Equity Share Application & Allotment A/c			12,50,000
	(Being application money received on the 50,000 Equity Shares at ₹ 25 each)			
7.	Equity Share Application & Allotment A/c	Dr.	12,50,000	
	To Equity Share Capital (₹ 25) A/c			12,50,000
	(Being Application Money transferred to Equity Capital A/c, on allotment)			
8.	Reconstruction A/c	Dr.	50,000	
	To Bank A/c			50,000
	(Being Underwriting Commission paid, 4% on ₹ 12,50,000)			
9.	Land and Buildings A/c	Dr.	5,00,000	
	To Reconstruction A/c			5,00,000
	(Being value of Land and Buildings appreciated as per Reconstruction Scheme)			
10.	Reconstruction A/c	Dr.	20,000	
	To Bank A/c			20,000
	(Being payment of expenses on reconstruction)			
11.	Reconstruction A/c	Dr.	23,00,000	
	To Profit and Loss A/c			23,00,000
	Being Profit and Loss A/c Debit balance written off using Reconstruction A/c)			
12.	Reconstruction A/c	Dr.	10,00,000	
	To Goodwill A/c			4,00,000
	To Plant and Machinery A/c			3,00,000

Date	Particulars	Dr. (₹)	Cr. (₹)
	To Stock A/c To Debetors A/c (Being various losses/intangible items written off using Reconstruction A/c, as per approvied Scheme of Reconstruction dated....)		1,00,000 2,00,000
13.	Reconstruction A/c Dr. To Capital Reserve A/c (Being balance in Reconstruction A/c t/f to Capital Reserve)	4,60,000	4,60,000

Working Note:

Dr. **Reconstruction Account** Cr.

Particulars	₹	Particulars	₹
To Bank A/c (Preference Dividend)	2,00,000	By Equity Share Capital (₹ 100) A/c	30,00,000
To Bank, (Expenses)	20,000	By 10% Preference Share Capital (₹ 100) A/c	5,00,000
To Goodwill A./c	4,00,000	By Debentureholders A/c	30,000
To Plant and Machinery A/c	3,00,000	By Land and Buildings A/c	5,00,000
To Stock A/c	1,00,000		
To Debtores A/c	2,00,000		
To Profit & Loss A/c	23,00,000		
To Bank A/c (Underwriting Comm.)	50,000		
To Capital Reserve A/c **(b.f)**	**4,60,000**		
	40,30,000		40,30,000

Solution 5(a)

From–B–RA–Revenue Account of Metro General Insurance Co. Ltd for the year ending 31st March 2014

Particulars	Sch.	This Yr	Last Yr
Premium Earned (Net)	1	75,56,000	
Total (A)		**75,56,000**	
1. Claims Incurred (Net)	2	51,63,000	
2. Commission	3	1,57,000	
3. Operating Expenses related to Insurance Business (2,90,000 – Legal Exps 55,000 – Surveyor Fees 45,000)	4	1,90,000	
Total (B)		**55,10,000**	
Operating Profit/(Loss) from Marine Insurance Business (A – B)		**20,46,000**	
Appropriations		**NIL**	
Total (C)		**20,46,000**	

Schedule 1 – Premum Earned (Net)

Particulars	This Yr
Premiums from Direct Business Written	75,25,000
Add: Premium on Re-Insurance accepted	8,25,000
Less: Premium on Re-Insurance ceded	(4,90,000)
Total Premium Earned (Net)	78,60,000
Less: Adjustment for change in Unexpired Risk Reserve **(Note)**	(3,04,000)
Total Premium Earned (Net)	75,56,000

Note: Adjustment for Changes in Reserve for Unexpired Risks is computed as under:

Particulars	Reserve
Closing balance required (40% of 78,60,000)	31,44,000
Less: Opening Balance available	28,40,000
Amt to be transferred to Reserve for the year	**3,04,000**

Schedule 2 – Claims Paid (Net)

Particulars	This Yr
Claims Paid – Direct (49,70,000 + 7,38,000 – 6,85,000)	50,23,000
Add: Claims on Re-Insurance accepted (5,10,000 + 70,000 – 95,000)	4,85,000
Less: Claims on Re-Insurance Ceded (3,95,000 + 1,25,000 – 75,000)	(4,45,000)
Add: Surveyor's Fees	45,000
Add: Legal Expenses	55,000
Total claims Incurred	**51,63,000**

Schedule 3 – Commission

Particulars	This Yr
Commision paid: Direct	1,60,000
Add: Commission on Re-Insurance accepted	15,000
Less: Commission on Re-Insurance ceded	(18,000)
Net Commission	**1,57,000**

Solution 5(b)

1. Computation of Tier I and Tier II Capital

Particulars			₹ *Crores*
Tier I – Capital:	Equity Share Capital		400.00
	Statutory Reserve		250.00
	Capital Reserve arising out of Surplus on Sale of Assets = Total 86 – Revaluation of Assets 18		68.000
	Total	**(A)**	**718.00**
Tier II – Capital:	Revaluation Reserve		18.00
	Less: Discount at 55%		(9.90)
	Total	**(B)**	**8.10**
	Grand Total	**(A + B)**	**726.10**

2. Computation of Risk Weighted Assets

Particulars	(%) Weight	₹ Crores	₹ Crores
Cash Balance with RBI	0	12.00	0
Balance with Other Banks	20	20.00	4.00
Other Investments (assumed Other than Equity Shares)	100	40.00	40.00
Loans and Advances:			
(i) Guaranteed by the Government	0	14.50	0
(ii) Others	100	5,465.00	5,465.00
Premises, Furniture and FIxtures	100	74.00	74.00
Off-Balance Sheet Items:			
(i) Guarantees and other Obligations	100	700.00	700.00
(ii) Acceptance, Endorsements and Letter of Credit	100	4,900.00	4,900.00
Total			**11,183.00**

3. Capital to Risk-Weighted Assets Ratio (CRAR)

$$= \frac{\text{Capital Funds}}{\text{Risk Adjusted Assets}} \times 100 = \frac{726.00}{11183.00} \times 100 = 6.49\%.$$

Inference: Benchmark CRAR is 9% whereas the Bank's CRAR is only **6.49%.** Higher the CRAR – better stability – less risky, and lower the CRAR – lower stability – more risky.

Solution 6(a)

Dr. **Branch Account in the books of Head Office** Cr.

Particulars		₹	Particulars		₹
To Balance b/d:			By Stock Reserve on Op Stock (₹ 40,000 × 25%)		10,000
– Stock	40,000		By Stock Reserve (₹ 1,80,000 × 25%)		45,000
– Debtors	25,000				
– Furniture	4,000		By Goods Sent to Branch A/c (Returns)		6,000
– Cash	1,000	70,000	By H.O Cash (65,000 + 1,20,000)		1,85,000
To Goods sent to Branch A/c		1,80,000			
To Stock Reserve (₹ 6,000 × 25%)		1,500	By balance c/d:		
To Bank A/c:			– Stock	35,000	
– Staff Welfare	750		– Debetors	28,450	
– Salary	4,000		– Cash (1,000 – 700)	300	
– Telephone	1,200	5,950	– Furniture (4,000 – 10%)	3,600	67,350
To Stock Reserve on Cl Stock (35,000 × 25%)		8,750			
To P & L A/c –		47,150			
		3,13,350			**3,13,350**

Working Notes:

1. Branch Debetors Account (To ascertain Closing Debtors)

Particulars	₹	Particulars	₹
To balance b/d	25,000	By Cash (Collections)	65,000
To Credit Sales	70,000	By Sales Returns	1,250
		By Discount Allowed	300
		By balance c/d **(balancing figure)**	**28,450**
	95,000		**95,000**

2. Depreciation on Furniture is not debited as a separate item in the Branch Account since the Furniture (Closing Balance) at the end is shown at the Depreciated Value.
3. Sales Returns and Discount are accounted for automatically since opening and Closing baliances of Debetors are state in the Branch Account.

Solution 6(b)

Department Tranding and Profit and Loss A/c for the year ending 31st March (₹)

Particulars	*Dept A*	*Dept B*	*Total*	*Particulars*	*Dept A*	*Dept B*	*Total*
To Opening Stock	70,000	54,000	1,24,000	By Sales	5,72,000	4,60,000	10,32,000
To Purchases	3,92,000	2,98,000	6,90,000	By Tfr – Pur. Goods	36,000	50,000	86,000
To Carriage Inward	6,000	9,000	15,000	By Tfr – FG	1,75,000	1,50,000	3,25,000
To Wages	54,000	36,000	90,000	By Tfr – FG Return	32,000	45,000	77,000
To Purc. Goods t/f	50,000	36,000	86,000	By Closing Stock			
To FG t/f	1,50,000	1,75,000	3,25,000	– Purc. Goods	24,000	30,000	54,000
To Return of FG t/f	45,000	32,000	77,000	– FG	1,02,000	62,000	1,64,000
To Gross Profit	**1,74,000**	**1,57,000**	**3,31,000**				
Total	**9,41,000**	**7,97,000**	**17,38,000**	**Total**	**9,41,000**	**7,97,000**	**17,38,000**
To Stock Reserve	8,311	4,609	12,920	By Gross Profit b/d	1,74,000	1,57,000	3,31,000
To Net Profit	**1,65,689**	**1,52,391**	**3,18,080**				
Total	**1,74,000**	**1,57,000**	**3,31,000**	**Total**	**1,74,000**	**1,57,000**	**3,31,000**

Working Note:

1. GP ratio

Particulars	*A*	*B*
Sales	5,72,000	4,60,000
Add: Transfer of Finished Goods	1,75,000	1,50,000
Less: Return of Finished Goods	(45,000)	(32,000)
Net Sales	**7,02,000**	**5,78,000**
Gross Profit as computed above	1,74,000	1,57,000
Gross Profit Ratio	24.78%	27.16%

2. Stock Reserve to be provided

Particulars	*A*	*B*
Closing stock of Finished Goods	₹ 1,02,000	₹ 62,000
Element of Finished Goods from other Department 30%	30,600	18,600
Gross Profit Ratio of Other Department	27.16%	24.78%
Stock Reserve required to be maintained	**8,311**	**4,609**

Solution 7(a)

Examples of Changes in Accounting Policy:

a. Change of Depreciation method from WDV to SLM and vice-versa.

b. Change in Cost formula in measuring the cost of inventories.

(ii) Examples of Changes in Accounting Estimates:

a. Change in estimate of provision for doubtful debts on sundry debtors.

b. Change in estimate of useful life of fixed assets.

(iii) Examples of Extraordinary items:

a. Loss due to earthquakes/fire/strike

b. Attachment of property of the enterprise by government

(iv) Examples of Prior period items:

a. Applying incorrect Rate of Depreciation in one or more prior periods.

b. Omission to account for Income or Expenditure in one or more prior periods.

Solution 7(b)

The indicators of a Non-Integral Foreign Operation are:

1. **Autonomy:** While the reporting enterprise may control the foreign operation, the activities of the foreign operation are carried out with a significant degree of autonomy from those of the reporting enterprise,
2. **Transaction Pattern:** Transactions with the reporting enterprise are not a high proportion of the foreign operation's activities,
3. **Financing:** The activities of the foreign operation are financed mainly from its own operations or local borrowings rather than from the reporting enterprise,
4. **Expenditure in Local Currency:** Cost of Labour, Material and other components of the foreign operation's products or services are primarily paid or settled in the local currency rather than in the reporting currency.
5. **Sales Pattern:** The foreign operation's sales are mainly in currencies other then the reporting currency.
6. **Effect of Cash Flows:** Cash Flows of the reporting enterprise are insulated from the day-to-day activities of the foreign operation rather than being directly affected by the activities of the foreing operation.
7. **Prices of products:** Sales Prices for the foreign operation's products are not primarily responsive on a short-term basis to changes in exchange rates but are dtermined morc by looal oom potitiion or local government regulation, and
8. **Local Market:** There is an active local sales market for the foreign operation's products, although there might be significant amounts of exports.

The appropriate classification for each operation can be established from **factual information** and **proper judgment,** based on the indicators listed above.

Solution 7(c)

When equity Shares are issued...	*Included with effect from the...*
(a) In exchange for Cash.	Date when cash is receivable.
(b) As a result of conversioni of a Debt Instrument to Equity.	Date of conversion.
(c) In lieu of Interest or Principal on other Financial Instruments.	Date when interest careases to accrue.

(d) In exchange for the settlement of a liability of the Enterprise.	Date when settlement becomes effective.
(e) As consideration for acquisition of an asset other than cash.	Date on which the acquisition is recognised.
(f) For the rendering of services to the enterprise.	Date on which the service are rendered.
(f) For the rendering of services to the enterprise.	Date on which the service are rendered.

Potential Equity Share: A Potential Equity Share is a Financial Instrument or other contract that entittles, or may entitle, its holder to Equity Shares. Some examples are:

(a) Debt Instruments or Preference Shares that are convertible into Equity Shares,

(b) Share Warrants,

(c) Options including Employee Stock Option Plans (ESOP) under which Employees of an Enterprise are entitled to receive Equity Shares as part of their remuneration, and other similar plans, and

(d) Shares which would be issued upon the satisfaction of certain conditions resulting from contractual arrangements **(Contingently Issuable Shares)**, such as the acquisition of a business or other assets, or shares issuable under a Loan Contract, upon default of payment of principal or interest, if the contract so provides.

Solution 7(d)

Particulars	*Performing Asset (On Accrual basis)*	*Non-Performing Asset (On Receipt Basis)*	*Total Interest (in ₹ Crores)*
Interest on Term Loan	280	20	300
Interest on Cash Credit and Overdrafts	1,700	48	1,748
Interest on Bills Purchased and Discounted	40	70	470
Total Income to be recognised	**2380**	**138**	**2,518**

Solution 7(e)

Capital Service Line Contribution: Different SERCs prescribe Service Line cum Defvelopment (SLD) Charges Norms as per Sec. 47 of the Electricity Act. Accounting for and Reporting of this source of funds of Electricity Companies may be in any of the following ways:

1. Initial Recording as **Liability**, and subsequently recognized as **Income** over the life of the asset.
2. Recording as **Reserves** (as the amount is not refundable) and reported under the head Reserves and Surplus, **without** transferring any p8roportionate amount to the Income Statement over the life of asset,
3. Recording as **Reserves** (as the amount is not refundable) and **subsequent** transfer of proportionate amount to Income Statement during the expected life of the asset to match against Depreciation on total cost of such asset, or
4. Recording as reduction in the Cost of Non-Current Asset, and providing Depreciation on such reduced cost.